ADVANCED TORT LAW: A PROBLEM APPROACH
Second Edition

ADVANCED TORT LAW: A PROBLEM APPROACH

Second Edition

Vincent R. Johnson
Professor of Law
St. Mary's University

ISBN: 978-1-6304-4783-0 (casebook)
ISBN: 978-1-6304-4784-7 (looseleaf)
ISBN: 978-1-6304-4785-4 (eBook)

Library of Congress Cataloging-in-Publication Data

Johnson, Vincent R., author.
    Advanced tort law : a problem approach / Vincent R. Johnson, Professor of Law, St. Mary's University. — Second Edition.
        pages cm
    Includes index.
    ISBN 978-1-6304-4783-0
    1. Torts—United States. I. Title.
    KF1250.J638 2014
    346.7303—dc23
                                                                                    2014026724

This publication is designed to provide authoritative information in regard to the subject matter covered. It is sold with the understanding that the publisher is not engaged in rendering legal, accounting, or other professional services. If legal advice or other expert assistance is required, the services of a competent professional should be sought.

LexisNexis and the Knowledge Burst logo are registered trademarks of Reed Elsevier Properties Inc., used under license. Matthew Bender and the Matthew Bender Flame Design are registered trademarks of Matthew Bender Properties Inc.

No copyright is claimed by LexisNexis or Matthew Bender & Company, Inc., in the text of statutes, regulations, and excerpts from court opinions quoted within this work. Permission to copy material may be licensed for a fee from the Copyright Clearance Center, 222 Rosewood Drive, Danvers, Mass. 01923, telephone (978) 750-8400.

NOTE TO USERS
To ensure that you are using the latest materials available in this area, please be sure to periodically check the LexisNexis Law School web site for downloadable updates and supplements at www.lexisnexis.com/lawschool.

Editorial Offices
121 Chanlon Rd., New Providence, NJ 07974 (908) 464-6800
201 Mission St., San Francisco, CA 94105-1831 (415) 908-3200
www.lexisnexis.com

MATTHEW◊BENDER

Dedications

To
Tom and Nancy Shaffer
at Notre Dame,
good friends for more than thirty years

Preface

Advanced Tort Law: A Problem Approach is designed for use in upper-level law school courses. This book reflects the belief that the most effective teaching materials for students beyond the first year of law school are centered on problems of the kind that lawyers face in practice.

Clear Narrative Text. The chapters in *Advanced Tort Law* focus on five intriguing subjects which normally receive little attention in basic torts courses: misrepresentation, defamation, invasion of privacy, tortious interference, and injurious falsehood. In each chapter, the law is laid out in a clear narrative format, which quotes liberally from pertinent court opinions, statutes, and other sources. Because upper-level law students are already well acquainted with the American litigation process, each topic focuses primarily on operative rules and policies, and their application to particular fact situations. The text minimizes the procedural complexities of cases that have already been decided.

Fifty-Eight Discussion Problems. The main instructional feature of *Advanced Tort Law* is the fifty-eight discussion problems. Roughly every eight to ten pages, there is a problem for students to prepare in advance of class. A good answer requires a confident grasp of the rules, concepts, and principles addressed in the text or in basic law school courses. The problems, which test whether students have learned the assigned material, are designed to form the basis for classroom discussions. If a class meets twice a week over the course of a typical law school semester, each reading assignment is likely to include about fifteen to twenty pages of reading material and two discussion problems.

Preparation for Practicing Law in the 21st Century. Many of the problems in *Advanced Tort Law* are based on actual cases or stories in the news. With rare exceptions, the names have been changed. The facts in the problems often diverge from those which gave rise to the underlying disputes in order to raise questions important to the course.

The problems challenge students to explore how the law applies to the kinds of facts they will encounter in twenty-first century law practice. The hypothetical scenarios are designed to help users of the book develop the problem-solving skills that effective lawyers need.

Cutting-Edge Legal Issues. Although the torts discussed in this book are ancient in origin, they are often on the front lines of litigation in the Digital Age. There are abundant references to issues raised by recent communications technology developments, including blogging, texting, and social networking. The text addresses numerous practical questions that Americans confront in contemporary life, such as the liability issues that arise from anonymous postings on the Internet or from corporate press releases designed to mislead investors.

Advanced Tort Law: A Problem Approach is accompanied by a comprehensive teacher's manual. I will be happy to share with professors adopting this book a set of PowerPoint slides corresponding to the various chapters. Please contact me at: vjohnson@stmarytx.edu.

Preface

I hope that you enjoy using *Advanced Tort Law: A Problem Approach.*

Vincent R. Johnson
London, United Kingdom
March 31, 2014

Acknowledgments

My work on this book benefitted significantly from the editorial efforts of several research assistants at St. Mary's University School of Law in San Antonio, Texas. Foremost among that group were Amy Bresnen, Melinda Uriegas, and Karen Oster. Each made a major contribution to the book, regularly demonstrating the skills and habits that distinguish the best lawyers.

I am grateful to Dean Charles E. Cantu and St. Mary's University School of Law for supporting this project. My St. Mary's University colleague Chenglin Liu regularly raises issues that enrich my understanding of tort law.

My largest debt of gratitude is to my wife, Jill Torbert, a very able lawyer and community leader. Jill is a wonderful source of insight, perspective, and good companionship.

Some of the language and ideas in *Advanced Tort Law: A Problem Approach* and the related Teacher's Manual borrow from my earlier writings, including: Vincent R. Johnson, *Studies in American Tort Law* (Carolina Academic Press, 5th ed. 2013); Vincent R. Johnson, *Mastering Torts: A Student's Guide to the Law of Torts* (Carolina Academic Press, 5th ed. 2013); Vincent R. Johnson, "The Boundary-Line Function of the Economic Loss Rule," 66 *Washington & Lee Law Review* 523–85 (2009); Vincent R. Johnson, "The Unlawful Conduct Defense in Legal Malpractice Law," 77 *UMKC Law Review* 43–83 (2008); Vincent R. Johnson, "Standardized Tests, Erroneous Scores, and Tort Liability," 38 *Rutgers Law Journal* 655-717 (2007); Vincent R. Johnson, "Cybersecurity, Identity Theft, and the Limits of Tort Liability," 57 *South Carolina Law Review* 255–311 (2005); and Vincent R. Johnson and Shawn Lovorn, "Misrepresentation by Lawyers about Credentials or Experience," 57 *Oklahoma Law Review* 529–77 (2004). In this book, substantial excerpts from these works are indicated by a specific citation, but brief passages have not been cited. Footnotes generally have been omitted from quoted material. The original sources contain citations to supporting authorities.

With regard to the editing in this book: An ellipsis at the end of a paragraph indicates the omission of words at the end of the paragraph and, in some cases, the omission of one or more following paragraphs. Similarly, an ellipsis at the beginning of a paragraph denotes the omission of words at the beginning of the paragraph and, in some cases, the omission of one or more preceding paragraphs.

Excerpts from the various *Restatements of the Law* quoted in the book are reproduced with the permission of the American Law Institute, which holds the copyrights to those works. All rights reserved by the American Law Institute. Those works include: *Restatement (Second) of Torts*, copyright © 1965 and 1977; *Restatement (Third) of Torts: Products Liability*, copyright © 1998; *Restatement (Third) of Torts: Liability for Physical Harm*, copyright © 2010 and 2012; *Restatement (Third) of Torts: Liability for Economic Harm* (Tentative Draft No. 1, April 4, 2012), copyright © 2012; *Restatement (Second) of Agency*, copyright © 1958; *Restatement (Third) of Agency*, copyright © 2006; *Restatement (Third) of Restitution & Unjust Enrichment*, copyright © 2001; *Restatement (Third) of Unfair Competition*, copyright © 1995; and *Restatement (Third) of the Law Governing Lawyers*, copyright © 2000.

Table of Contents

Table of Contents

Table of Contents

Table of Contents

Table of Contents

Table of Contents

Table of Contents

Table of Contents

Table of Contents

Table of Contents

Chapter 1

BEYOND PHYSICAL HARM

A. THE SUBJECT MATTER OF "ADVANCED" TORT LAW

The "advanced" tort causes of action that are the focus of this book are intellectually challenging, passionately litigated, colorfully reported by the press, and fundamentally important to the conduct of business and the operation of government. Just why this is so can be understood only by viewing the law of torts from a broad perspective.

The first issue is a simple but difficult one: namely, where does a basic torts course end and an advanced torts course begin? It is not easy to answer this question because law schools differ in what they require during the first-year of law studies. There are many different torts casebooks. Those texts vary in how they organize the law of torts, and professors are free to decide what to assign and what to skip. More importantly, some law schools limit the basic coverage of torts to four credit hours, while other schools require five or six credit hours of study.

Basic Torts Courses Focus on Personal Injury and Property Damage. Most knowledgeable persons would agree that first-year torts courses focus primarily on compensation for personal injuries (including emotional distress) and harm to tangible property. Basic courses address these issues by teaching the law related to simple intentional torts (*e.g.*, battery, assault, false imprisonment, and trespass), negligence (*e.g.*, auto accidents, medical malpractice, and premises liability), and strict liability (*e.g.*, manufacturing defects, abnormally dangerous activities, and *respondeat superior*).

All basic torts courses deal with the compensability of economic losses resulting from physical harm, such as an accident victim's lost wages or medical expenses. However, little time is typically spent in a first-year torts class on compensation for *purely economic injuries* arising in cases not involving personal injuries or property damages.

This Text Focuses on Purely Economic Losses. This text organizes the subject of "advanced" tort law by focusing mainly on liability for *purely economic losses*. The book includes five principal areas of tort law:

- Misrepresentation (fraud, negligent misrepresentation, and strict liability for misrepresentation);

- Defamation (libel and slander);

- Invasion of privacy (appropriation of name or likeness, public disclosure of private facts, intrusion upon seclusion, and false light);

- Tortious interference with contract or prospective advantage; and

- Injurious falsehood (trade libel, slander of title, and related claims).

Typically, these actions do not involve physical injury to a person or harm to tangible property, although there are exceptions. For example, if the safety of an apartment complex is misrepresented, the plaintiff may be attacked, or if the predatory tendencies of an adult are fraudulently concealed, a child may be molested. Nevertheless, these five torts usually do not involve physical harm.

Related Losses. The tort actions that are the focus of this book sometimes award relief for harm that is not "economic" in any ordinary sense of the term. For example, a victim whose character is defamed may suffer not only economic losses, such as the loss of a job or a business opportunity, but also emotional distress and harm to reputation. If adequately established by the evidence, all such losses may be compensable in a suit for libel or slander, even though some of the losses are more properly thought of as personal or relational, rather than economic. Naturally, the defamation chapter of this text will consider all of the kinds of damages that may be recovered in a suit for libel or slander. Similarly, while some tort claims for invasion of privacy are concerned with recovery of economic losses, others are not. The text will deal with the full range of potential liability for invasion of privacy.

The unifying theme that runs throughout this book is compensation for *purely economic losses*. As explained below, the five areas of tort law that are the focus of this book are also closely related to one another in several ways.

1.   Unifying Themes

a.   Doctrinal Relationship

State of Mind. First, these five areas of tort law (misrepresentation, defamation, invasion of privacy, tortious interference, and injurious falsehood) share certain doctrinal similarities. In a number of instances (but not always), the issue of liability turns on the actor's state of mind. For example, the "*scienter*" requirement of a misrepresentation action for fraud is similar to the "actual malice" standard that plays an important role in defamation, false-light invasion of privacy, and injurious falsehood. In each case, liability sometimes depends upon proving that the defendant acted with knowledge of the falsity of the offending statement or with reckless disregard for whether it was true or false.

Fact Versus Opinion. Similarly, there is an important distinction between statements of fact and statements of opinion. This distinction plays a role not only in the law of misrepresentation, but also in actions for defamation, false-light invasion of privacy, and injurious falsehood. In each case, a defendant will not be held liable unless there has been a provably false assertion of fact.

Privilege. Likewise, the absolute and qualified privileges that will defeat a defamation action will also typically bar liability for invasion of privacy, tortious interference, or injurious falsehood. Consequently, if a witness testifying at trial enjoys the absolute protection of the judicial proceedings privilege, the privilege will likely defeat any of the tort actions discussed in this text.

b.   Practical Considerations

Viewed in practical terms, the five areas of tort liability covered in this book (misrepresentation, defamation, invasion of privacy, tortious interference, and injurious falsehood) are related in several ways. At least four connections come to mind.

Minimal Tort Reform. First, these five theories of liability have generally escaped the waves of tort reform that have reshaped much of tort law in recent decades. Thus, in each area, the relevant principles of law are still largely defined by common law (and constitutional) principles, rather than by statutes. At a time when many areas of tort law are becoming increasingly unprofitable for the plaintiffs' bar due to statutory limitations enacted by tort reformers, some of these advanced tort causes of action remain viable and vibrant. Savvy students planning on entering law practice may want to keep this in mind.

Importance to Businesses. Second, all of these advanced torts are of particular interest to business entities. Thus, some corporations, such as publishers, broadcasters, or sellers of products or investments, are often sued for defamation or misrepresentation, and they often assert tortious interference claims against competitors. It would be fair to refer to these five areas of tort liability as "business torts."

Treatment in the Restatement. Third, the conceptual coherence of these five areas of tort law is evidenced by the fact that they appeared in close proximity to one another in volumes three and four of the *Restatement (Second) of Torts*. Moreover, the "advanced" nature of these causes of action is suggested by the American Law Institute's ongoing work on the *Restatement (Third) of Torts*. That work has been underway for more than fifteen years, and there are now final versions of the material on products liability,[1] apportionment of liability,[2] and for most purposes physical and emotional harm.[3] Yet, the five areas of tort law addressed in this book have yet to be "restated." That project is now underway.[4]

Litigation Alternatives. Finally, a lawyer faced with a problem that implicates one of these five theories of tort liability must often think through all of these tort actions. The various causes of action are sometimes closely related alternatives for imposing liability. For example, a false statement about a person that is not actionable under the law of defamation may form the basis of a claim for false-light invasion of privacy. In addition, a single course of events may warrant several different advanced tort claims. For example, false statements about a corporation and its products may, on appropriate facts, support claims for defamation (of the entity or perhaps its agents), injurious falsehood ("trade libel" of the corporation's products), and tortious interference (with the corporation's business relationships).

---

[1] *See* RESTATEMENT (THIRD) OF TORTS: PRODUCTS LIABILITY (1998).

[2] *See* RESTATEMENT (THIRD) OF TORTS: APPORTIONMENT OF LIABILITY (2000).

[3] *See* RESTATEMENT (THIRD) OF TORTS: LIABILITY FOR PHYSICAL AND EMOTIONAL HARM (volume 1, 2010; volume 2, 2012).

[4] *See* RESTATEMENT (THIRD) OF TORTS: LIABILITY FOR ECONOMIC HARM (Tentative Draft No. 1, 2012); RESTATEMENT (THIRD) OF TORTS: LIABILITY FOR ECONOMIC HARM (Preliminary Draft No. 2, 2013).

c.   First Amendment Issues

Communication Torts. The five areas of advanced tort law that are the focus of this text (misrepresentation, defamation, invasion of privacy, tortious interference, and injurious falsehood) are related by the fact that they frequently involve harm caused not by overtly tortious means, such as physical violence, but by language. They are, in that sense, "communication torts," often involving a "publication," "publicity," or "reliance" requirement. Consequently, First Amendment principles governing speech and press play a large role in determining whether and to what extent tort liability may be imposed. This is particularly true with respect to libel, slander, false-light invasion of privacy, tortious interference, and injurious falsehood.

B.   LIABILITY FOR ECONOMIC LOSSES

Because the advanced torts discussed in this book play a major role in compensating purely economic losses, it is essential for readers to be aware of the debate currently swirling around what is often called the "economic loss rule." Today there are multiple versions of the rule. As explained below, a consensus is beginning to reject the idea that there is a unified economic loss rule broadly applicable throughout the law of torts. Instead, the consensus holds that narrower formulations of the rule apply in selected areas of the law, such as cases involving defective products or the performance of contractual duties.[5]

The following sections suggest why the economic loss rule has emerged as an issue of great importance in contemporary tort litigation. They also explain how narrow versions of the rule reflect the role that the economic loss rule plays in defining the boundary line between contract law and torts.[6]

1.   The Broad Formulation of Economic Loss Rule

The nature of the common law sometimes produces surprises. Scholars or judges looking back on court decisions occasionally conclude that, even though certain cases did not seem to be related, they are actually proof of a broader rule that is potentially applicable to a wide range of disputes. This is precisely what happened in the late 1990s and early 2000s.

The Broad Formulation of the Rule. Proponents of what could be called the "broad" formulation of the American economic loss rule argued that there is a common law rule which holds that purely economic losses (*i.e.,* monetary losses

---

[5] *See Lesiak v. Cent. Valley Ag Co-op., Inc.*, 808 N.W.2d 67, 81 (Neb. 2012) ("the economic loss doctrine precludes tort remedies only where . . . either (1) a defective product caused the damage or (2) the duty which was allegedly breached arose solely from the contractual relationship between the parties").

[6] *See* Vincent R. Johnson, *The Boundary-Line Function of the Economic Loss Rule*, 66 WASH. & LEE L. REV. 523, 523–38 (2009). This article has been quoted or cited by 20 state and federal courts. Some of the material in this chapter was drawn from the article. *See also Lesiak v. Cent. Valley Ag Co-op., Inc.*, 808 N.W.2d 67, 81 (Neb. 2012) ("Multiple rationales have been given to support the doctrine's existence. But the primary rationale, and the one that we find most compelling, is to maintain the line of demarcation between tort law and contract law").

where there is no personal injury or property damage) cannot be recovered in a tort action for negligence or strict liability (the latter being simply a theory of recovery that sometimes substitutes for negligence). Purely economic losses, the proponents said, are compensable only under contract law principles. Some scholars and courts agreed with these contentions, at least in certain contexts. Many scholars and jurists did not.[7] The issue of whether there is a unified economic loss rule was raised in scores of cases across the country. The resulting decisions were often confused and inconsistent.

The BP Oil Spill ("Deepwater Horizon"). In thinking about whether, under American tort law, there is a broadly applicable economic loss rule, it is important to remember that the potential stakes are huge. Many losses today are purely economic. Consider, for example, the 2010 BP oil spill in the Gulf of Mexico.[8] That oil spill, which was probably caused by negligence (or by activities that would result in strict liability), caused billions of dollars of damages. Most of those losses were purely economic. Of course, some persons suffered personal injuries (*e.g.*, the 11 men killed in an explosion) and others suffered harm to property (*e.g.*, the operators of boats that were damaged when they came into contact with the oil, or the property owners along the coast whose beaches were polluted). However, most of the oil spill claims were for purely economic losses related to the profitability of businesses.

For example, some persons were afraid that seafood from the Gulf had been contaminated, and therefore they did not buy those products. As a result, purely economic losses were suffered by the companies that sell seafood, by the businesses that would have transported or stored those products, and by the workers who were laid off or worked fewer hours because of the diminished demand for seafood.

Similarly, some persons feared that the water along the Gulf coast was contaminated and too dangerous for swimming. They therefore took their vacations elsewhere. As a result, the hotels, restaurants, and stores along the coast had fewer customers and therefore suffered purely economic losses.

In the end, there was no landmark court ruling on the economic loss rule related to the BP oil spill. Under pressure from the Obama Administration and extremely bad publicity, BP voluntarily agreed to pay more than $20 billion in losses. Lawsuits were filed and a global settlement was reached, but disputes emerged over which claims should be paid.[9]

If the tort claims of persons who suffered purely economic losses as a result of the BP oil spill had been decided in court, those plaintiffs might have been barred from recovery by a broad formulation of the economic loss rule. Moreover, if claimants were relegated to contract law remedies, they might have recovered nothing under that theory either. The hotels and restaurants along the coast, for

---

[7] *See, e.g., Tiara Condo. Ass'n, Inc. v. Marsh & McLennan Companies, Inc.*, 110 So. 3d 399, 407 (Fla. 2013) (limiting the "economic loss rule to cases involving products liability").

[8] *See* Vincent R. Johnson, *Tort Laws Would Make It Hard to Win Relief from BP*, Hous. Chron., June 19, 2010.

[9] *See* Neil Webb, *How BP Decided to Fight the Deepwater Settlement*, Am. Lawyer, Mar. 6, 2014.

example, presumably had no contracts with BP which would have protected them from economic losses caused by drilling far off shore. It is unlikely that they could have sued BP for breach of contract.

Why Did Proponents Think There Was a Rule? Virtually no tort law scholars talked about an "economic loss rule" a quarter of a century ago. Indeed, few persons thought that such a rule existed. So why did some courts and scholars begin to believe that such a rule was part of American common law tort principles? It seems that they were influenced by decisions that courts had made in at least three kinds of cases.

Defective Products. First, in cases involving defective products, courts have long refused to permit recovery under tort principles if the defective product merely harms itself.[10] Only if the product defect causes personal injuries or damages "other property"[11] can a victim bring an action for negligence (or strict liability).

For example, if, as the result of defect, a new smart phone catches fire and scorches the plaintiff's skin or burns down the plaintiff's house, the plaintiff can sue in tort to recover compensation for those losses. In contrast, if the defective smart phone simply short circuits and does not work anymore, the plaintiff can recover compensation for economic losses only in a contract action for breach of warranty, not in a tort action for negligence or strict liability.

Similarly:

> [I]f a person buys a can of paint and applies the paint to a door, the person has a potential tort claim . . . if toxic odors from the paint make the plaintiff sick or if the paint eats away at the door and damages that 'other' property. However, if the paint simply fails to adhere to the door effectively and flakes off, or quickly discolors, causing no other damage but making the paint's purchase a waste of money, the buyer's sole avenue for recovery is rooted in contract principles.[12]

The idea behind these types of rulings is that when a plaintiff buys a product, the plaintiff has a chance to decide how much to spend and what features and guarantees should be part of the bargain. Denying a disappointed product purchaser a tort action for negligence in cases involving purely economic losses creates an incentive for consumers to exercise diligence to protect their own interests. They have an incentive to strike a good bargain with sellers and are held to the terms of the bargain they strike. The rulings in cases involving defective products were one bit of evidence that negligence that causes purely economic losses is not actionable under tort principles.[13]

---

[10] *See Lincoln Gen. Ins. Co. v. Detroit Diesel Corp.*, 293 S.W.3d 487, 493 (Tenn. 2009) (citing RESTATEMENT (THIRD) OF TORTS: PRODUCTS LIABILITY § 21).

[11] *See Fed. Ins. Co. v. J.K. Mfg. Co.*, 933 F. Supp. 2d 1065, 1078 (N.D. Ill. 2013).

[12] *Chevron USA, Inc. v. Aker Mar., Inc.*, 604 F.3d 888, 900 n.11 (5th Cir. 2010).

[13] *See Rinehart v. Morton Bldgs., Inc.*, 305 P.3d 622, 629 (Kan. 2013).

Traffic Jams. Second, when a driver negligently causes a traffic accident, the individuals who suffer personal injuries or property damages are allowed to commence tort actions to recover damages for physical harm caused by negligence. In contrast, suppose that a traffic accident results in a traffic jam, and that persons do not arrive at work on time and therefore earn less money. Those persons are not allowed to sue the negligent driver to recover their purely economic losses.[14]

A similar point is illustrated by the famous *Kinsman* cases which involved two ships that crashed into a bridge on the Buffalo River. In *Kinsman No. 1*,[15] the owners of properties that were flooded when ice formed a dam at the point of the wreckage were allowed to recover compensation under negligence principles for the resulting property damage. In contrast, in *Kinsman No. 2*,[16] the businesses that incurred additional transportation expenses because the wreckage made the river unnavigable were denied compensation. The Second Circuit expressed its decision in *Kinsman No. 2* in opaque language, stating that the losses were too "tenuous and remote."[17] A better, clearer explanation might be to say that recovery was denied in *Kinsman No. 2* because the alleged negligence caused purely economic losses, not personal injuries or property damages. The traffic jam cases and the *Kinsman* decisions were more evidence that seemed to support the idea that there is a broadly applicable economic loss rule.

Key Employees and the Law of Tortious Interference. Third, American cases have generally agreed that interference with the performance of a contract is actionable as a tort only if the interference is intentional. Negligent interference with a contract is ordinarily not actionable.[18]

Suppose that Person A *intentionally* induces Person B, who is a key employee of Person C, to breach B's contract with C. Cases like this routinely hold that A is liable to C for purely economic harm caused by B's breach.[19]

In contrast, suppose that Person A *negligently* injures Person B, a key employee of Person C, by causing an auto accident. On these facts, a court is likely to hold that C cannot sue A for the economic losses that it suffered as a result of A's *negligent* injury of B.[20] Only *intentional* interference with contractual rights is actionable as a tort. The decisions in these kinds of cases was more evidence that American tort law does not provide a remedy for negligence that causes purely economic losses.

The Search for a Unified Theory. Relying on these and other bits of scattered precedent, some scholars and jurists argued that there is a unified rule, broadly applicable in American tort law, which means that negligence that causes purely

---

[14] *See Petition of Kinsman Transit Co.*, 388 F.2d 821, 825 n.8 (2d Cir. 1968) (dicta).

[15] *See Petition of Kinsman Transit Co.*, 338 F.2d 708 (2d Cir. 1964).

[16] *See Petition of Kinsman Transit Co.*, 388 F.2d 821, 825 (2d Cir. 1968).

[17] *Id.* at 825.

[18] RESTATEMENT (SECOND) OF TORTS § 766C (1979).

[19] *Cf. A. & M. Wholesale Hardware Co. v. Circor Instrumentation Techs., Inc.*, 2014 U.S. Dist. LEXIS 23032, at *25 (D.N.J. Feb. 24, 2014) ("attempting to illicitly acquire . . . [a] key employee").

[20] *See, e.g., Gosch v. Juelfs*, 701 N.W.2d 90, 91 (Iowa 2005) (an employer who was "unable to hire a replacement driver . . . and sustained a substantial loss of income" could not recover from a motorist whose negligence fatally injured a key employee).

economic losses is never actionable under negligence or strict liability principles. That rule, they said, explains the result in all of these cases. Proponents of a broad rule also insisted that the only avenue of recourse for victims of accidentally caused pure economic loss is under contract principles. This argument was favorably received by critics of American tort law who believed that mid- and late-twentieth century jurists had gone too far in favoring plaintiffs at the expense of businesses.

2.   Narrow Formulations of the Economic Loss Rule

Many Exceptions. It soon became clear that if there is a single, broad economic loss rule, it is a rule with many exceptions. For example, lawyers who commit malpractice can be sued for negligently causing purely economic losses (*e.g.,* the failure of a business transaction or a loss of a claim or defense in litigation).[21] Similarly, businesses are routinely held liable for purely economic losses caused by the tort of negligent misrepresentation[22] (*e.g.,* the inability of a lender to collect on a loan made to a company whose financial position was negligently misrepresented). Other exceptions relate to actions for defamation, breach of fiduciary duty, nuisance, loss of consortium, wrongful death, spoliation of evidence, and unreasonable failure to settle a claim within insurance policy limits, all of which may, on appropriate facts, afford recovery for negligence causing purely economic losses. So too, statutory causes of action, even when based on negligence or strict liability principles, usually trump the judicially designed economic loss rule.[23]

Courts sometimes explain the exceptions to the economic loss rule by saying that negligence causing purely economic harm is actionable where there is a "special relationship" between the plaintiff and defendant. However, this line of reasoning cannot justify all of the exceptions, such as the principles allowing recovery of purely economic losses in wrongful death actions or claims against strangers for economic losses caused by spoliation of evidence.

At Odds with Public Policy. Scholars and courts not only identified a long list of exceptions to the supposedly broad economic loss rule, they also argued that an expansive formulation of the rule undercuts the important public policy considerations that shape American tort law. Those policies include the ideas that liability should be based on fault, that tort rules should impose liability to deter conduct that caused unnecessary losses, and that enterprises that benefit from dangerous activities should be forced to internalize the costs of harm arising from those activities.

---

[21] *See Annett Holdings, Inc. v. Kum & Go, L.C.,* 801 N.W.2d 499, 504 (Iowa 2011) ("purely economic losses are recoverable in actions asserting claims of professional negligence against attorneys and accountants"); *see also Sharon Acad. v. Wieczorek Ins.,* 2013 Vt. Super. LEXIS 34, at *16 (Nov. 13, 2013) ("because Vermont has recognized a broker's duty to obtain the insurance requested by an insured, claims by an insured for breach of that duty are not barred by the economic loss rule"); *but see Maeda Pac. Corp. v. GMP Haw., Inc.,* 2011 Guam LEXIS 20, at *40 (July 6, 2011) ("contract law is better suited to resolve professional negligence claims against engineers and architects than tort law, at least in cases where no personal injury or other property damage is present" and "[t]his appears to be the majority trend").

[22] *See Annett Holdings, Inc. v. Kum & Go, L.C.,* 801 N.W.2d 499, 504 (Iowa 2011).

[23] *See SCS Builders, Inc. v. Searcy,* 390 S.W.3d 534, 541 (Tex. App. 2012) (deceptive trade practices act claim).

One Rule or Several. The truth may be that there is not one economic loss rule broadly applicable throughout the field of torts, but rather several more limited rules that govern recovery of economic losses in selected areas of the law. For example, the rules that limit the liability of accountants to third parties for harm caused by negligence, or that save careless drivers from liability to the employer of a person injured in an auto accident, may be fundamentally distinct from the ones that bar compensation in tort for purely economic losses resulting from defective products or misperformance of obligations arising only under contract.

Breach of Purely Contractual Duties. Of course, American jurists have always recognized that there are limits to the negligence theory of tort liability. It is widely agreed, for example, that a breach of a purely contractual duty cannot be the basis of a tort action for negligence.[24] For example, suppose that a newspaper agrees to publish an advertisement, but negligently fails to do so. As a result, the business that paid to have the ad published suffers economic losses. The business can sue the newspaper for breach of contract (subject to the rules that limit recovery of consequential damages), but cannot bring a tort cause of action for negligence.[25]

The Emerging Consensus. Recently, a jurisprudential consensus about the economic loss rule has begun to emerge. The consensus holds that there is no unified broadly applicable economic loss rule, but only a narrow economic loss rule that relegates potential plaintiffs to contract remedies when that avenue for redress makes sense. Thus, if there was a contract between the plaintiff and the defendant, and the claim relates to a breach of the contractual obligations, rather than to duties imposed by tort law, the plaintiff can only sue for breach of contract, not under tort law for negligence or strict liability.[26] Similarly, if there was no contract between the plaintiff and defendant, the narrow formulation of the economic loss rule does not bar a tort action.[27]

The Sharyland Decision. Consider the case of *Sharyland Water Supply Corp. v. City of Alton*.[28] That case was decided by the Texas Supreme Court, the highest court of America's second largest and second most populous state. These are the essential facts: A city hired Company A to install and operate a clean water system for the city. Years later, the city hired Company B to install and operate a waste water system for the city. Because Company B negligently installed the waste

---

[24] *See U.S. Fire Ins. Co. v. Sonitrol Mgmt. Corp.*, 192 P.3d 543, 547 (Colo. Ct. App. 2008) (contractual duty to monitor an alarm system).

[25] *Cf. Sw. Bell Tel. Co. v. DeLanney*, 809 S.W.2d 493 (Tex. 1991).

[26] *See, e.g., Maeda Pac. Corp. v. GMP Haw., Inc.*, 2011 Guam LEXIS 20, at *46 (July 6, 2011) ("where a party in privity of contract with a design professional is seeking to recover [pure] economic loss damages . . . such a party is limited to contractual remedies"); *Fish v. Tex. Legislative Serv., P'ship*, 2012 Tex. App. LEXIS 749, at *46 (Jan. 27, 2012) (the economic loss rule barred recovery because the alleged damages arose only from the nonperformance of duties governed by a partnership agreement); *Exela Pharmsci, Inc. v. Teva Pharmaceuticals USA, Inc.*, 2012 Va. Cir. LEXIS 65 (Aug. 31, 2012) ("purely economic losses suffered as a result of the breach of a duty assumed by a contract cannot be recovered in a tort action").

[27] *See Sullivan v. Pulte Home Corp.*, 306 P.3d 1, 3 (Ariz. 2013) ("[w]e decline to extend the doctrine to non-contracting parties").

[28] 354 S.W.3d 407 (Tex. 2011).

water lines above and in close proximity to the clean water lines, there was a risk that the clean water supply would become contaminated. The clean water lines also no longer complied with the requirements of state law. Money would have to be spent by Company A to move the clean water lines or otherwise protect them from contamination.

The *Sharyland* dispute concerned purely economic losses because the negligent installation of the waste water lines did not cause personal injury or property damage. As of the time of the lawsuit, the waste water lines had not corroded the clean water lines, and the clean water supply had not been contaminated. The question was simply whether Company A could sue under the law of negligence to make Company B pay for the costs of bringing the clean water into compliance with state law. Company A would not have to have needed to incur those costs if Company B had not been negligent.

The Texas Supreme Court held that Company A could sue Company B for negligently causing pure economic losses. There was no contract between Company A and Company B, so the dispute did not involve the performance of contractual duties owed by Company B to Company A. Moreover, Company A was not even an intended third-party beneficiary of the city's contract with Company B. It made no sense, the court concluded, to say that Company A's only remedy against Company B was under contract principles. The court thus endorsed a narrow version of the economic loss rule, which holds that the rule does not bar a negligence claim between parties not even remotely in privity.

Note that the result might well have been different if Company A had not existed and the city had sued Company B for purely economic losses relating to clean water lines that the city had previously installed and operated for itself. In the case, the claim arising from the negligent installation of the waste water lines would have been a claim between the parties to the waste water contract (the city and Company B). It, therefore, could be argued that if the city wanted protection from purely economic consequential damages that might be caused by Company B's negligent performance of purely contractual duties, it should have bargained for that protection.[29]

The Restatement Draft. Current draft of the *Restatement (Third) of Torts: Liability for Economic Loss* endorses a narrow version of the economic loss rule. Section 3 is entitled "Preclusion of Tort Liability Arising from Contract (Economic Loss Rule)." That section states that "[e]xcept as provided elsewhere in this *Restatement*, there is no liability in tort for economic loss caused by negligence in the performance or negotiation of a contract between the parties."[30]

---

[29] *Cf. Flagstaff Affordable Hous. Ltd. P'ship v. Design Alliance, Inc.*, 223 P.3d 664, 670 (Ariz. 2010) ("[w]e . . . apply the economic loss doctrine and hold that a contracting party is limited to its contractual remedies for purely economic loss from construction defects").

[30] *See* RESTATEMENT (THIRD) OF TORTS: LIABILITY FOR ECONOMIC HARM § 3 (Tentative Draft No. 1, 2012).

3.   The Economic Loss Rule Today

Less Confusion, But Confusion Nonetheless. While a consensus in favor of a narrow version of the economic loss rule has started to take hold, there is still much confusion about whether American tort law provides remedies for negligently caused purely economic losses.[31] The jurisprudential ferment is great. Chief Justice Shirley S. Abrahamson of the Supreme Court of Wisconsin noted that the economic loss doctrine was an issue before her state high court or intermediate court forty-seven times in one five-year period. She lamented that at "the current pace, the economic loss doctrine may consume much of tort law if left unchecked."[32]

With more than 50 different American jurisdictions, it will take years for the law to evolve to the point where it is reasonably uniform in dealing with this subject. However, a few points seem clear.

The Economic Loss Rule and Advanced Torts. The torts with which this text is concerned — misrepresentation, defamation, invasion of privacy, tortious interference, and injurious falsehood — are generally treated as exceptions to the economic loss rule or beyond the reach of the rule's provisions.[33] In many instances, the advanced tort causes of action are intentional torts (rather than based on lack of care or strict liability). Most courts hold that the economic loss rule does not protect a defendant from liability for intentional torts.[34] "In cases where economic losses are deliberately and tortiously inflicted there is little reason to save the defendant from liability, whether under the economic loss rule or otherwise."[35] Moreover, even when an advanced tort cause of action — such as negligent misrepresentation — is based on negligence rather than intentionally tortious conduct, it is often treated as an exception to the economic loss rule.[36]

Nevertheless, there is so much confusion and litigation relating to the economic loss rule that a defendant might argue, against the great weight of authority, that one of these advanced tort causes of action should fail because recovery would violate the rule. Thus, plaintiffs must have a sufficiently clear understanding of the economic loss rule to be able to refute these kinds of arguments. It can certainly be argued that when "established tort principles entitle a third party to protection

---

[31] *See In re Chinese Manufactured Drywall Products Liab. Litig.*, 680 F. Supp. 2d 780, 788 (E.D. La. 2010) ("[t]he difficulty in determining whether to apply the doctrine has been recognized by courts and scholars alike"); *David v. Hett*, 270 P.3d 1102, 1109 (Kan. 2011) ("the economic loss . . . is viewed differently in various jurisdictions. Some apply it more restrictedly to commercial settings, while others extend it more broadly as an effort to preserve distinctions between contract law and torts. More recently, some have limited the doctrine's reach when an independent duty can serve as the basis for a tort claim").

[32] *See Grams v. Milk Products, Inc.*, 699 N.W.2d 167, 181 (Wis. 2005) (Abrahamson, C.J., dissenting).

[33] *See Sharyland Water Supply Corp. v. City of Alton*, 354 S.W.3d 407, 418–19 (Tex. 2011) (compensation for pure economic loss is commonly available in actions for fraud, fraudulent inducement, tortious interference with contract, and business disparagement).

[34] *See Lick Branch Unit, LLC v. Reed*, 2014 U.S. Dist. LEXIS 16259, at *51 (E.D. Tenn. Feb. 10, 2014) ("the position that the doctrine applies to intentional torts is 'extreme' ").

[35] *Id.*

[36] *See Rinehart v. Morton Bldgs., Inc.*, 305 P.3d 622, 632 (Kan. 2013).

under tort law for economic loss, an agreement [entered into by other persons] to which the third party never assented should not be permitted to vitiate his or her right to tort remedies."[37]

It Is Difficult to Recover Purely Economic Losses. The terms and scope of the economic loss rule are the subject of disagreement. However, there is no dispute as to the underlying reality. Recovery in tort actions today for purely economic losses is often difficult to obtain.

On the one hand, the economic loss rule may be a barrier to liability. On the other hand, the requirements of the advanced tort causes of action discussed in this book are exceptionally demanding. As the following chapters illustrate, their requirements are complex. It is often difficult to prove a *prima facie* case. Thus, in order to be effective, lawyers representing plaintiffs must navigate between opposing hazards — disqualifying barriers and essential requirements — just as ancient Mediterranean mariners needed to thread a perilous course between Scylla and Charybdis.

Particular aspects of the debate about the economic loss rule will be discussed in the subsequent chapters. Some of the discussion problems in the book raise issues about whether economic losses resulting from negligence are properly compensable under tort law.

PROBLEM 1-1: INADEQUATE INSURANCE

Temple Condominium Association (Temple) retained Mathy & McLaren (Mathy) as its insurance broker to secure condominium insurance coverage. Mathy arranged windstorm coverage for Temple through Citifund Insurance (Citifund), which issued a policy that contained a loss limit of $55 million.

Temple's condominium sustained significant damage caused by two hurricanes. After being assured by Mathy that the loss limits coverage was "per occurrence" (meaning that Temple would be entitled to up to $110 million), Temple proceeded with a more expensive option for remediation efforts, rather than cheaper alternative.

When Temple sought payment from Citifund, Citifund claimed that the loss limit was $55 million "in aggregate," not "per occurrence," and that Temple was not entitled more than $55 million. Temple sued Citifund. Eventually, Citifund agreed to pay $88 million. That amount was far less than the $100 million spent by Temple.

Temple then sued Mathy for (1) negligence, (2) professional malpractice, and (3) intentional fraud, seeking to recover the unreimbursed $12 million it had spent on repairs. Are Temple's claims barred by the economic loss rule?

---

[37] *Joseph Painting Co. v. Larson Eng'g, Inc.*, 2010 Ariz. App. Unpub. LEXIS 2, at *9 (Mar. 4, 2010).

Chapter 2

MISREPRESENTATION

A. FRAUD

Widespread Applicability. Fraud is an ancient tort that is recognized in every American jurisdiction.[1] It is a particularly useful cause of action because there is no shortage of deception in human affairs. Not surprisingly, a great body of precedent tracks the contours of the rules which determine whether particular statements, alleged to be fraudulent, are or are not actionable. The rules are the result of centuries of hard-fought litigation, and they do a fair job in defining the terms for liability. Today, claims of fraudulent conduct are alleged in a tremendous number of lawsuits.

Economic Harm and Physical Harm. The objective of suing in tort for fraud is usually recovery of compensation for purely economic losses (losses not involving personal injuries or property damage). This is normally the case, for example, when one business entity accuses another of committing fraud in a commercial transaction. However, on appropriate facts, proof of fraud may support an award of damages for physical harm. This is true if the plaintiff:

- is assaulted after being deceived about the safety of an apartment complex;[2]

- is deformed by improperly performed liposuction after relying on a Yellow Pages ad that misrepresented a doctor's qualifications;[3] or

- suffers life threatening health problems after using a mislabeled prescription acne medication.[4]

Fraud Versus Deceit. The action for fraud is sometimes called the tort of deceit. To a large extent, the terms "fraud" and "deceit" are interchangeable. Each refers to liability for harm caused by misrepresentation of a highly culpable variety (*i.e.*, intentionally or recklessly false). However, American cases speak more frequently of liability for "fraud," than for "deceit."

Fraud and Other Tort Actions for Misrepresentation. Fraud is one of three tort actions for misrepresentation. The other two deal with misrepresentations that are

---

[1] *See* W. PAGE KEETON ET AL., PROSSER AND KEETON ON TORTS 727 (5th ed. 1984) (tracing the writ of deceit to 1201).

[2] *See O'Hara v. Western Seven Trees Corp.*, 75 Cal. App. 3d 798 (1977).

[3] *See Knepper v. Brown*, 195 P.3d 383 (Or. 2008) (imposing liability for fraud on the publisher of the ad after the doctor settled with the plaintiff).

[4] *See Freeman v. Hoffman-La Roche, Inc.*, 618 N.W.2d 827, 844–45 (Neb. 2000) (finding that a cause of action was stated).

negligently false or innocently made.

The tort of negligent misrepresentation differs substantially from fraud. While it shares many of the same doctrinal requirements, the scope of liability is limited in important ways that are discussed in detail below (*see* part B-3 of this chapter). Moreover, the *Restatement* and other authorities hold that only persons acting in the course of a business, trade, or profession, or in a matter in which they have a pecuniary interest, are subject to liability for negligent misrepresentation causing purely economic harm. Fraud, in contrast, as applied in most states, has a potentially broader reach. Negligent misrepresentation is therefore not an all-purpose substitute for fraud in cases where it might be proved that the defendant acted carelessly, but not that the defendant intentionally or recklessly made a material misstatement. The tort of negligent misrepresentation, which is nevertheless an important cause of action, is discussed in part B of this chapter. Many cases allege both fraud and negligent misrepresentation when the level of the defendant's culpability is unclear.

In a few narrow areas of the law, misrepresentations can give rise to strict liability. However, there is no broadly applicable tort theory of strict liability for misrepresentation. Tort liability for innocent misrepresentation is far more rare than liability for fraud or negligent misrepresentation. Innocent misrepresentation is discussed in part C of this chapter.

Restitution and Contract Remedies for Misrepresentation. In many situations, tort remedies are not an aggrieved individual's only avenues of recourse for harm caused by misrepresentation. Other remedies may be available under the law of restitution or under contract principles.

According to the *Restatement (Third) of Restitution and Unjust Enrichment*, "[a] transfer induced by fraud or material misrepresentation is subject to rescission and restitution."[5] If the deal is rescinded, there must be a return of whatever benefits were conferred. Of course, even if rescission is possible, a tort action for damages may be the preferable remedy if the plaintiff wants to keep, rather than return, or cannot return in the same condition, whatever was acquired in the fraudulent transaction (*e.g.*, a house or a car that the plaintiff purchased).

In cases involving the sale of goods, a similar restitutionary remedy is available under the law of warranty.[6] A claim for such relief is subject to contract defenses, including, notably, the parol evidence rule.[7]

Elements of Fraud. A common law action for fraud is generally agreed to have five elements. Although courts vary in articulating the requirements,[8] the plaintiff normally must show that there was (1) a material misrepresentation, (2) which was made with "*scienter*" (usually meaning knowledge of falsity or reckless disregard for the truth), (3) which was intended or expected to cause reliance, which was (4)

---

[5] *See* RESTATEMENT (THIRD) OF RESTITUTION & UNJUST ENRICHMENT § 13(1) (2011).

[6] RESTATEMENT (SECOND) OF TORTS § 552C cmt. b (1977).

[7] *Cf.* UNIFORM COMMERCIAL CODE 2-202 (LEXIS 2014).

[8] *See, e.g., Smidt v. Porter*, 695 N.W.2d 9, 22 (Iowa 2005) (requiring "(1) representation; (2) falsity; (3) materiality; (4) scienter; (5) intent; (6) justifiable reliance; and (7) resulting injury").

justifiably relied upon by the plaintiff, who as a result (5) suffered damage.[9]

Materiality. Only "material" misrepresentations are actionable. "Materiality" simply means that the matter is such that it would be given weight in the plaintiff's decision-making process. This may be true either because a reasonable person would attach importance to the facts or because the defendant knows that the matter is important to the plaintiff.[10] To be material, a matter need not be the sole or predominant factor in the plaintiff's choice of a course of action. Note, however, that while the threshold for "materiality" is low, a plaintiff may recover only if it is shown that the material misrepresentation factually and proximately caused damages.

Heightened Pleading Requirements for Fraud. "Accusations of fraud can do serious damage to the goodwill of a business firm or a professional person."[11] Perhaps for this reason, Rule 9(b) of the Federal Rules of Civil Procedure requires a complaint alleging fraud to state "the circumstances constituting fraud . . . with particularity." Most states have a similar requirement.

As the California Supreme Court has recognized, the particularity requirement necessitates pleading facts which "show how, when, where, to whom, and by what means the representations were tendered."[12] The First Circuit has been even more specific, stating that a complaint must "specify the time, place, speaker, and content of the alleged misrepresentations," as well as "explain how the misrepresentations were fraudulent and plead those events which give rise to a strong inference that the defendant had an intent to defraud, knowledge of the falsity, or a reckless disregard for the truth."[13]

Sometimes, the allegations in a case fall far short of this type of demanding standard. In one recent case, a claim that attorneys committed fraud by submitting documents to a state court was dismissed because the plaintiff did not even allege that the attorneys knew the statements were false[14] or otherwise acted with *scienter*.

Clear and Convincing Evidence of Fraud. Many jurisdictions say that the burden of proof regarding allegations of fraud is higher than the ordinary "preponderance of the evidence" standard. Fraud often must be established by "clear and convincing evidence" or by a "clear preponderance of the evidence."[15] However, in some states, the higher standard of persuasion does not apply to the

---

[9] The sections of the third RESTATEMENT OF TORTS that will deal with fraud are now being formulated. *See* RESTATEMENT (THIRD) OF TORTS: LIAB. FOR ECON. HARM §§ 9–15 (Council Draft No. 2, 2013).

[10] *See* RESTATEMENT (SECOND) OF TORTS § 538 (1977); *see also Robbins v. Capozzi*, 100 S.W.3d 18, 24 (Tex. App. 2002).

[11] *Banker's Trust Co. v. Old Republic Ins. Co.*, 959 F.2d 677 (7th Cir. 1992) (Posner, J.).

[12] *Lazar v. Superior Court*, 909 P.2d 981, 989 (Cal. 1996).

[13] *Cohen v. S.A.C. Trading Corp.*, 711 F.3d 353, 359 (2d Cir. 2013).

[14] *O'Neill v. Hernandez*, 2009 U.S. Dist. LEXIS 27448, at *29 (S.D.N.Y. Mar. 31, 2009).

[15] *See, e.g., Tapestry Vill. Place Indep. Living, L.L.C. v. Vill. Place at Marion, L.P.*, 2009 Iowa App. LEXIS 331, at *7–*8 (May 6, 2009).

damage element of a fraud action.[16] Other states reject the higher standard altogether.[17]

Common Law Fraud and DTPA Laws. It is important to understand the relationship of the common law tort action for fraud to state statutes that protect consumers from certain forms of fraudulent conduct. All states have adopted a Deceptive Trade Practices Act (DTPA) which affords redress to consumers who have been harmed by misrepresentations and other forms of abusive conduct relating to sales of products and services. These statutes typically have some advantages over a common law fraud action, such as, perhaps, a reduced culpability requirement. DTPA laws also often allow recovery of compensation for attorney's fees incurred in asserting the DTPA claim. In contrast, such attorney's fees are almost never recoverable in a common law fraud action. Many DTPA laws, at least under some circumstances (such as cases involving deliberate deception), also entitle the plaintiff to receive treble damages (or some other multiple of compensatory damages) in order to punish the defendant.

On the other hand, the usefulness of state deceptive trade practices laws may be limited by various statutory requirements. For example, transactions over a certain dollar value may be excluded from the coverage of the act. Also, DTPA statutes generally protect only those who qualify as "consumers," as that term has been defined by the state's statute or interpreted by case law. Consequently, a common law action for fraud sometimes allows recovery on facts that will not support a DTPA claim.

Many law schools offer an upper-level course on Deceptive Trade Practices, which focuses on the state's DTPA law. Such legislation is also studied in courses on Consumer Protection Law.

It is not uncommon to see a complaint asserting alternative causes of action: Count I, common law fraud; Count II, violation of the DTPA; Count III, breach of warranty. In these types of cases, the availability of relief under the state deceptive trade practices law does not preclude a claim for relief under common law tort, contract, or restitutionary principles. Of course, if a plaintiff is successful on a number of different theories, issues will arise as to whether the plaintiff needs to make an election of remedies to prevent over-compensation. These issues are explored in courses on Remedies.

Securities Fraud. State and federal securities laws address fraudulent conduct related to the sale of securities. Such laws typically create private rights of action. Securities fraud is a specialized field of law that in important respects departs from common law principles. Such legislation is discussed in detail in courses on Business Associations or Securities Regulation. Suits alleging securities fraud under applicable statutory provisions sometimes also include common law fraud claims.[18]

---

[16] *See Kilduff v. Adams, Inc.*, 593 A.2d 478 (Conn. 1991).

[17] *See State v. Alpine Air Prods.*, 500 N.W.2d 788, 791 (Minn. 1993).

[18] *See In re Enron Corp. Securities, Derivative & "ERISA" Litigation*, 490 F. Supp. 2d 784 (S.D. Tex. 2007) (involving Texas statutory claims and common law fraud).

Cross-References to Common Law Fraud. One of the reasons that it is so important to have a confident grasp of the common law principles governing fraud is that so many other areas of the law refer to fraud. For example, it is professional misconduct for a lawyer to engage in actions involving "dishonesty, fraud, deceit or misrepresentation."[19] In many states, fraudulent concealment will toll the running of the statute of limitations[20] or destroy a person's consent to conduct that otherwise is tortious.[21] Similarly, a deed or other document obtained by fraud may be declared invalid. In addressing the issues that arise in connection with these kinds of provisions, it is often useful to argue whether certain conduct does or does not trigger the rule by pointing to the requirements of a common law fraud action and the distinctions that courts have drawn in determining whether statements are actionable as fraud. In other words, the tort principles governing liability for fraud can be, and frequently are, used as aids in determining what the law means in other contexts when it speaks of "fraud," particularly if other definitions are absent.

PROBLEM 2-1: THE WIDOW'S FARM

After her husband died in 1992, Gerta Tirol sold her 163-acre farm to her third son, Barry, and his wife, Nancy, on a Contract for Deed. The contract carried 7.5% interest and was payable in 30 annual installments due on July 1 of each year. Gerta retained a life estate in her house, which was located on the farm, and continued to live there until her death.

Barry and Nancy failed to make timely payments under the Contract for Deed, which resulted in a total delinquency of about $75,000 by December 2014. In early January 2015, Barry and Nancy approached Gerta about the interest arrearage.

Barry told Gerta that he did not believe the farm would produce enough income to pay off the delinquent interest obligation plus the principal balance remaining on the contract. Nancy told her about the hard times she and Barry had encountered while trying to make ends meet on the farm. According to Barry and Nancy, a loan officer at the bank advised them to obtain a waiver-of-interest document from Gerta indicating her agreement to forgive all of the back interest.

Thereafter, Gerta signed a document prepared by Nancy stating:

> I, Gerta Tirol, on January 24, 2015, voluntarily waive the back interest due to me on the land known as the farm of Barry and Nancy Tirol under the Contract for Deed dated July 2, 1992. The back interest accrued between January 1, 1996 and January 24, 2015.

After Gerta died on September 1, 2015, Barry and Nancy commenced a legal action seeking a declaratory judgment stating that the waiver of interest document was valid. The administrator of Gerta's estate opposed the request on the ground that the waiver had been procured by fraud.

---

[19] MODEL RULES OF PROF'L CONDUCT R. 8.4 (2014).

[20] *See Delanno, Inc. v. Peace*, 237 S.W.3d 81, 84 (Ark. 2006).

[21] *See* FOWLER V. HARPER, FLEMING JAMES, JR., & OSCAR S. GRAY, LAW OF TORTS § 3.10 (3d ed. 2006).

The evidence presented to the court shows that Barry and Nancy's financial statements reflected a net worth of $466,137.00 on January 18, 2013, with a projected income in the amount of $186,155.00; a net worth of $252,738.00 on January 30, 2014, with a projected income of $227,306.00; a net worth of $326,367.00 on February 1, 2015, with a projected income of $228,343.00; and a net worth of $308,295.00 on January 30, 2016, with a projected income of $190,198.00. In addition, a real estate broker testified that the agricultural value of the farm was in excess of $600,000.00. The value of the land for subdivision development was considerably higher.

In addition, Barry testified on cross-examination that prior to having Gerta sign the waiver document, he had met with his bankers and was told that he could borrow enough money at 5% interest to pay off the Contract for Deed, rather than continue paying 7.5% interest to Gerta.

You are a law clerk for the judge who will rule on the request for declaratory relief. The judge has explained that if Barry and Nancy committed fraud, as defined by common law principles, the waiver of interest document will be declared invalid. Please provide an analysis of the fraud issue.

1.   The *Scienter* Requirement

Intentional and Reckless Falsity. The plaintiff in a fraud action must prove *scienter*, a particularly culpable state of mind. In general, *scienter* is established by evidence showing that the defendant acted with knowledge of falsity or reckless disregard for the truth. Section 526 of the *Restatement (Second) of Torts* is even more precise. The *Restatement* provides that a misrepresentation is "fraudulent" — that is to say, made with *scienter* — if the speaker:

(a) knows or believes that the matter is not as he represents it to be,

(b) does not have the confidence in the accuracy of his representation that he states or implies, or

(c) knows that he does not have the basis for his representation that he states or implies.[22]

Expressions of Definiteness in the Face of Uncertainty. There is no difficulty in proving *scienter* if the evidence shows that the defendant deliberately falsified the facts. However, in the eyes of the law, recklessly creating a misimpression is just as bad as lying. Suppose that the defendant lacks knowledge about a particular matter — such as whether a business has signed a large contract with an important customer. If the defendant makes that assertion with definiteness and conviction, despite harboring doubts about its truth, the defendant lacks the confidence in the statement that is implied, and thus has acted with *scienter*. Put differently, if the defendant does not know something for certain, but gives the impression that he or she knows for certain, and turns out to be wrong, the defendant may be liable for having fraudulently asserted the matter in question.

---

[22] Restatement (Second) of Torts § 526 (1977).

In a famous old case, *Sovereign Pocohontas Co. v. Bond*,[23] the defendant unequivocally asserted that the company was making money. The statement was made for the purpose of inducing the plaintiff to refrain from collecting a debt. In fact, the company was losing money and the representations constituted glaringly false statements. The court held that if knowledge is possible, one who represents a mere belief as knowledge recklessly misrepresents a fact upon which an action for deceit may be based. Similarly, in *IKON Office Solutions, Inc. v. Eifert*,[24] the Texas Court of Appeals wrote that in order to prove common law fraud, it was necessary to show that when the defendant made the misrepresentation, the defendant "knew it was false or made it recklessly without any knowledge of the truth and as a positive assertion."

Lack of Belief in Truth. In *Hedin v. Minneapolis Medical & Surgical Institute*,[25] the Minnesota Supreme Court explained:

> The doctor, with his skill and ability, should be able to approximate to the truth when giving his opinion. . . . If he . . . does not believe the statement true, . . . but represents it as true, . . . it is to be inferred that he intended to deceive . . . [and an] action for deceit will lie.[26]

A Narrower Definition of Scienter. While the general rule is that *scienter* is established by knowledge of falsity *or* reckless disregard for the truth, some decisions appear to define *scienter* more narrowly. In those states, a plaintiff must show that the defendant knew that the representation was false.

2.   What Constitutes an Actionable Misrepresentation?

a.   Words and Actions

Oral and Written Misrepresentation. A misrepresentation may consist of only words, whether written or oral. A false entry about grade point average or class rank on a job applicant's resume,[27] or a false statement on a law firm's website about its success in prior cases, is just as much a misrepresentation as if those falsities had been shouted from the roof tops. Of course, in many instances, the issue is not what constitutes a misrepresentation, but whether a particular statement was ever made. In that respect, a fraud claim based on written statements, such as those contained in a letter or newspaper advertisement, may have advantages in terms of proof over a suit based on oral misrepresentations.

Misrepresentation by Conduct. In many cases, the defendant's actions, rather than oral or written words, are alleged to have misrepresented the facts. If a serious defect in hardwood flooring is hidden from a buyer by the seller's strategic

---

[23] 120 F.2d 39 (D.C. Cir. 1941).

[24] 125 S.W.3d 113, 124 (Tex. App. 2003).

[25] 64 N.W. 158 (Minn. 1895).

[26] *Id.* at 159–60.

[27] *See Baker v. Dorfman*, 239 F.3d 415, 423 (2d Cir. 2000) (affirming a finding that an attorney committed fraud where representations in the attorney's resume were "either false or grossly misleading, and created the false impression [that the attorney was] an experienced litigator").

placement of a rug, there has been a misrepresentation of the facts just as surely as if the seller had said that the hardwood was in good condition. In *Cadek v. Great Lakes Dragway, Inc.*,[28] the Seventh Circuit found that a race track misrepresented its fire-fighting capability by parking an inoperable fire truck near the place where drivers signed releases.

Objectively Misleading. Whether a statement is misleading is ordinarily judged by an objective standard. For example, in *Austin v. Albany Law School of Union University*,[29] three recent law school graduates commenced an action against their alma mater alleging statutory deceptive trade practices, common law fraud, and negligent misrepresentation. According to a New York trial court considering the claims:

> The Complaint focuses on graduate employment data published by ALS on its Internet website and in its marketing materials. . . .

> The Complaint . . . alleges that the employment data reported and marketed by ALS is "grossly inflated" due to the inclusion of the following types of employment within the aggregate percentage figure published by the law school: (a) positions for which a JD is not required or preferred; (b) part-time or temporary positions; (c) research assistants and fellows funded by the law school; (d) graduates who were employed within nine months of graduation, but who were not employed on the reporting date of the survey; and (e) graduates who have been "forced" to start solo practices due to their inability to find other employment. . . .

> . . . [T]he alleged deceptive acts or practices are directed principally at college graduates deciding whether to pursue a legal education at ALS. . . . Thus, in considering a reasonable consumer acting reasonably under the circumstances, the Court is mindful that it is dealing with a reasonably well-educated (though not necessarily sophisticated) group of consumers. . . .

> . . . [P]laintiffs do not (and cannot) seriously contend that ALS's published employment rates literally are false. . . .

> Rather, plaintiffs argue principally that the employment data . . . creates the false impression "that the overwhelming majority of [the school's] graduates are gainfully employed" through the inclusion of "temporary and part-time employment and/or employment for which a JD was not required or preferred". . . . In other words, plaintiffs take issue with ALS's publication of statistics that "count as employed" those who have secured employment in any capacity in any kind of job. . . .

> However, the challenged representations merely are unadorned percentages of recent ALS graduates who are "employ[ed]". . . . Nowhere is it stated or implied that these figures represent anything other than the percentage of recent graduates who obtained "employment," as such term

[handwritten margin notes: "law school grossly inflated employment stats" and "school never claimed that the # was anything more than employed"]

---

[28] 58 F.3d 1209 (7th Cir. 1995).

[29] 38 Misc. 3d 988 (N.Y. Sup. Ct. 2013).

commonly and ordinarily is understood. . . . There simply is nothing in the challenged representations that would lead reasonable consumers acting reasonably to believe that ALS's published "employment" rate carved out compensated positions for which a JD is not required or preferred, part-time employment, temporary employment, contract employment, post-graduate fellowships, research assistantships and/or certain types of solo legal practices. . . .

The Court is not persuaded that GBL § 349 [the deceptive trade practices law] requires an institution such as ALS to ascertain these types of individualized needs and guarantee that its published employment statistics suit each prospective or current student. Nor would it be reasonable for students to read all of their hopes and aspirations concerning the practice of law into the unadorned employment rate published by ALS. Rather, insofar as plaintiffs' decision to attend ALS turned on an employment rate limited to positions for which a JD is required or preferred, it was incumbent upon plaintiffs to ascertain whether ALS's published data fit their particular assumptions and met their specific needs.

. . . .

Accordingly, even viewing the allegations of the complaint in a light most favorable to plaintiffs . . . ALS's publication of aggregated "employment rates" cannot be considered deceptive or misleading to a reasonable consumer acting reasonably under the circumstances. . . .[30]

The *Austin* court dismissed the statutory deceptive trade practices claims. It also concluded that "[f]or the reasons stated above, plaintiffs cannot establish that ALS's representations regarding its published employment rates were false (or materially misleading),"[31] and therefore dismissed the fraud and negligent misrepresentation claims.

b.   Silence and the Duty to Speak

General Rule: No Duty to Speak. It has long been urged, as a matter of etiquette, that "silence is golden." The same rule applies in the legal arena, too. In general, there is no duty to disclose information merely because another person would find that information useful, interesting, or beneficial. The no-duty-to-speak rule finds wide application in the field of torts, particularly in connection with actions for fraud. For example, courts have held that:

- a reporter had no duty to disclose that he intended to disobey a judge's instruction to the media not to disclose the identity of the plaintiff, a sexual assault victim, who testified following the judge's instruction;[32]

---

[30] *Id.* at 837–42.

[31] *Id.* at 843.

[32] *Doe v. Associated Press*, 331 F.3d 417 (4th Cir. 2003).

- a builder selling a new home had no duty to disclose that there was a hostile neighbor;[33] and

- a bank selling a condominium had no duty to disclose that a nearby toxic waste problem, which had recently been cleaned up, had caused difficulty selling the unit.[34]

However, the general rule on silence is subject to several important exceptions which impose a duty to speak. Those exceptions are discussed below.

Unknown Facts. Under the law of fraud, if there is a duty to speak, that is only because facts are known to the defendant. In *Tapestry Village Place Independent Living, L.L.C. v. Village Place at Marion, L.P.*,[35] the Iowa Court of Appeals wrote:

> Here, the district court found

> [t]he cause of the defective windows on which [Tapestry's fraud] claims are based was insufficient structural support to hold the windows in place. This condition was concealed by the siding and was only discovered when siding was removed for a remodeling project that occurred after the sale. The evidence does not support a finding that the sellers . . . were aware of the insufficient support or the concealed deterioration underlying the windows at the time of the sale. . . . The Court finds that their representations were not knowingly false or made with an intent to deceive.[36]

The court affirmed the dismissal of Tapestry's fraud claims.

(1) Half-Truths

The Rule Against Incompleteness. Although there may be no duty to speak, one who elects to address a subject must be mindful of the rule on half-truths.[37] A story cannot be told in such a way that it is so incomplete as to pose a serious risk of misleading the listener. As the Fifth Circuit explained: "one who voluntarily elects to make a partial disclosure is deemed to have assumed a duty to tell the whole truth . . . even though the speaker was under no duty to make the partial disclosure in the first place."[38] Thus, according to the *Restatement*, the seller of property cannot say his title has been upheld by a particular court unless he also discloses his knowledge that an appeal from the decision is pending.[39]

Under the rule on half-truths, a cause of action will lie where:

---

[33] *Levine v. The Kramer Group*, 807 A.2d 264 (N.J. Super. Ct. App. Div. 2002).

[34] *Urman v. S. Boston Sav. Bk.*, 674 N.E.2d 1078, 1080 (Mass. 1997).

[35] 2009 Iowa App. LEXIS 331 (May 6, 2009).

[36] *Id.* at *9–*11.

[37] *See* RESTATEMENT (SECOND) OF TORTS §§ 529 & 551(2)(b) (1977); *see also Meade v. Cedarapids, Inc.*, 164 F.3d 1218, 1222 (9th Cir. 1999) (quoting *Gregory v. Novak*, 855 P.2d 1142, 1144 (Or. Ct. App. 1993)).

[38] *Union Pac. Res. Group, Inc. v. Rhone-Poulenc, Inc.*, 247 F.3d 574, 584 (5th Cir. 2001).

[39] *See* RESTATEMENT (SECOND) OF TORTS § 529 cmt. a (1977).

- a bank fails to disclose that it lacks the capacity to fund a loan that it has committed to make;[40]

- letters of recommendation cast an administrator in a positive light without mentioning prior complaints of his sexual impropriety with students;[41]

- a vendor of houses that are advertised as multifamily investment properties fails to reveal that multifamily use would violate the zoning laws;[42] or

- the owner of Playboy magazine discloses general concerns to the publisher of a Spanish version of the magazine in Mexico, but fails to disclose that the magazine's founder strongly opposes distribution of the Spanish version in the United States.[43]

In re Conduct of Hiller[44] was a case where an attorney stated that property had been sold, but failed to disclose the *pro forma* character of the transfer. He did so in order to trigger an opponent's repayment obligations under a promissory note. The court held that the knowingly deceptive conduct violated the attorney disciplinary rule prohibiting misrepresentation.

Long Line of Cases. The rule against half-truths has been part of American law for scores of years. In one old New York case, with an opinion by Benjamin N. Cardozo, the New York Court of Appeals held that while a vendor of property was under no duty to mention planned streets, having disclosed two of them, he was obliged to reveal a third street which, if opened, would divide the plot in half.[45]

The same principle continues to be applied today. Thus, in *Columbia/HCA Healthcare Corp. v. Cottey*,[46] the Texas Court of Appeals ruled that partial disclosures about a retirement plan were fraudulent because they failed to indicate that the plan could be rescinded at any time.

Half-Truth Versus Other Negative Information. Something is not a half-truth merely because negative information of another sort could be revealed, but has not yet been disclosed. Rather, a half-truth exists, and additional disclosure is required, only when the undisclosed facts are so directly related to the initial statement, or so pertinent to an understanding of that subject, that the recipient of the initial statement would feel misled about that particular assertion of fact. This nexus requirement is important; otherwise, the half-truth rule might be read so broadly as to devour both the general rule that countenances silence and the exceptions that impose duties to speak. The comments of the Supreme Judicial Court of Massachusetts in *Kannavos v. Annino*, are illuminating:

---

[40] *See Fid. Mortgage Co. v. Cook*, 821 S.W.2d 39, 43 (Ark. 1991) (imposing liability).

[41] *See Randi W. v. Muroc Joint Unified Sch. Dist.*, 929 P.2d 582, 591–592 (Cal. 1997).

[42] *See Kannavos v. Annino*, 247 N.E.2d 708, 711 (Mass. 1969).

[43] *See Playboy Enterprises, Inc. v. Editorial Caballero, S.A. de C.V.*, 202 S.W.3d 250, 263 (Tex. App. 2006).

[44] 694 P.2d 540, 544 (Or. 1985).

[45] 178 N.E. 672, 674 (N.Y. 1931).

[46] 72 S.W.3d 735, 744 (Tex. App. 2002).

Although there may be no duty imposed upon one party to a transaction to speak for the information of the other if he does speak *with reference to a given point* of information, voluntarily or at the other's request, he is bound to speak honestly and to divulge all the material facts *bearing upon the point* that lie within his knowledge.[47]

(2)   Duty to Correct Prior Statements

Statements Originally Believed to Be True. There is a duty to correct previous statements which, though true Bwhen made, have become false or misleading as a result of subsequent developments.[48] The duty extends until the recipient of the information is no longer able to protect personal interests by foregoing reliance on the now-erroneous representation of fact.[49]

The duty-to-correct exception is illustrated by *McGrath v. Zenith Radio Corporation.*[50] In that case, the defendants had told the plaintiff, an executive, that he was the "heir apparent" to the presidency of a soon-to-be-acquired subsidiary. However, before the executive released his shares of stock and options to facilitate the acquisition, the defendants learned that there were serious doubts as to whether the plaintiff would ever become president. They did not disclose those developments. In an opinion by Chief Judge Thomas E. Fairchild, the Seventh Circuit upheld a judgment in favor of the executive. In releasing his options and selling his shares, the executive had relied on the assurances that the defendants had made indicating that the relevant decision makers believed that he would become the new corporate head. "The making of the original statements, the discovery of their falsehood, and the failure to correct them before plaintiff relied on them were 'elements in a continuing course of conduct' capable of establishing fraud."[51]

Statements Originally Known to Be False. A related rule deals with statements that were originally known to be false, but never expected to induce reliance. If events develop so that reliance is foreseeable, there is a duty to correct the earlier statements.[52] Suppose, for example, that a person brags about the size of a ranch when no one is interested in buying or selling the ranch. That's just bragging, not fraud. However, if someone who heard the statement becomes interested in acquiring the ranch and foreseeably might rely on the facts previously asserted, the person who made the statement has a duty to correct the original assertion.

---

[47] 247 N.E.2d 708, 711 (Mass. 1969) (emphasis added).

[48] *See Sharff v. Pioneer Financial Services, Inc.*, 1993 U.S. Dist. LEXIS 3802, at *17–*19 (N.D. Ill. Mar. 22, 1993); *Mahan v. Greenwood*, 108 S.W.3d 467, 494 (Tex. App. 2003); 2 FOWLER V. HARPER ET AL., THE LAW OF TORTS § 7.14 (3d ed. 2006).

[49] *Cf.* RESTATEMENT (SECOND) OF TORTS § 551 cmt. h (1977).

[50] 651 F.2d 458 (7th Cir. 1981).

[51] *Id.* at 468.

[52] *See* RESTATEMENT (SECOND) OF TORTS § 551(2)(d) (1977).

(3)   Fiduciary and Confidential Relationships

A fiduciary has a duty to disclose information because a fiduciary relationship entails trust and confidence which imposes a duty to speak.[53] For example, in *Michel v. Palos Verdes Network Group, Inc.*,[54] the California Court of Appeal found that a real estate broker owed fiduciary obligations to the purchasers he was representing. Therefore, the broker had a duty to disclose to the broker's clients all material information, regardless of how the information was obtained.[55]

Matter of Law or Fact. Fiduciary relationships arise either as a matter of law or as a matter of fact. All lawyer-client relations are fiduciary. Therefore, all lawyers owe their clients special disclosure obligations as a matter of law. In contrast, a fiduciary relationship arises as a matter of fact only where there is a special relationship between persons that is so close and trusting that it is fair to impose higher duties than the law normally demands.

Persons Known to Represent Adverse Interests. Courts are reluctant to say that relationships are fiduciary as a matter of fact and therefore subject to demanding fiduciary standards. For example, in *La Ventana Ranch Owners' Association, Inc. v. Davis*,[56] the Texas Court of Appeals declined to find that there was a fiduciary relationship between homeowners and members of a homeowners' association architectural committee.

In *Swenson v. Bender*,[57] a case involving claims for breach of fiduciary duty and conversion rather than misrepresentation, the Minnesota Court of Appeals found that there was no fiduciary relationship between a doctoral candidate and the online university academic advisor who reported her suspected plagiarism and allegedly stole her ideas. As the court explained:

> . . . A "fiduciary" is "[a] person who is required to act for the benefit of another person on all matters within the scope of their relationship." . . . The duty imposed on fiduciaries is "the highest standard of duty implied by law." . . .

> No *per se* relationship existed here. *Per se* fiduciary relationships include trustee-beneficiary, attorney-client, business partnerships, director-corporation, officer-corporation, and husband-wife. . . . [N]o Minnesota appellate court has held the advisor-student relationship to be of a fiduciary nature as a matter of law. . . .

> The trial testimony . . . also does not demonstrate that Bender undertook a fiduciary obligation regarding Swenson. The supreme court has concluded that a fiduciary relationship cannot arise even out of a long, close, and trusting relationship when the purportedly trusting party "should have known the [other party] was representing adverse interests." Given Bend-

---

[53] *See id.* § 551(2)(a).

[54] 156 Cal. App. 4th 756 (2007).

[55] *Id.* at 802–03.

[56] 363 S.W.3d 632 (Tex. App. 2011).

[57] 764 N.W.2d 596 (Minn. Ct. App. 2009).

er's roles as adjunct instructor at Capella and as member of the committee assigned to assess Swenson's academic paper, Swenson should have known that Bender had an independent obligation to Capella that at least paralleled, if not superseded, her obligation to Swenson as it regards the dissertation's subject matter. Bender's role prevented her from being bound to act only for Swenson's benefit on all matters.

. . . It is undisputed that Capella faculty are obligated to report plagiarism. Separately, as an independent reviewer of Swenson's dissertation, Bender testified without contradiction that she also had a duty to evaluate the quality of Swenson's academic performance as reflected in her dissertation. The scope and character of Bender and Swenson's relationship cannot be defined without incorporating Bender's independent and competing obligations to the university. So considered, the advisor-student relationship between Bender and Swenson is neither unique nor one in which Swenson, as student, could have reasonably assumed confidentiality in her discussions of her dissertation concepts with Bender.

. . . Having concluded that Bender and Swenson were not in a fiduciary relationship, there could be no breach of fiduciary duty. . . .

. . . [T]he district court expressly determined that Bender had not "converted" Swenson's ideas, finding both that Swenson failed to prove that any of her allegedly stolen ideas were new and that "Swenson has not established the value of her ideas at any point." . . . It is therefore impossible to conclude that Bender breached any duty by stealing Swenson's ideas.[58]

Fiduciary Versus "Arm's-Length" Relationships. Fiduciary relationships may be contrasted with ordinary "arm's-length" commercial relationships, such as the typical relationship between a store and its customers. In arm's-length relationships each party is expected to look after its own interests. In such circumstances, there are no special duties to reveal information, even if that information is material to a transaction between the parties.

Occasionally, statutes provide that particular kinds of relationships are *not* fiduciary. For example, in *Harrouk v. Fierman*,[59] the Georgia Court of Appeals was faced with a statute which said that a real estate "broker shall not be deemed to have a fiduciary relationship with any party . . . but shall only be responsible for exercising reasonable care in the discharge of its specified duties as provided in this chapter and, in the case of a client, as specified in the brokerage engagement."[60] In *Harrouk*, the defendants, a real estate broker and a real estate agent, failed to inform the plaintiff that a property, which the plaintiff had previously asked the defendants to inquire about, had become available for purchase. The plaintiff subsequently sued for the losses that he sustained when, without his knowledge, the defendant agent purchased the property for himself after the agency was asked to

---

[58] *Id.* at 601–03.

[59] 662 S.E.2d 892 (Ga. Ct. App. 2008).

[60] *Id.* at 894.

list it. The court held that in the absence of a fiduciary relationship between the plaintiff and the defendants, or an agreement to inform the plaintiff when the property came onto the market, there was no duty to disclose the property's availability. Therefore the plaintiff's action for common law fraud failed.

Reasons for Allowing Trust. In fiduciary relationships, there are special reasons that allow one party to trust another and that oblige the other to act in the best interests of the one who relies. For example, because laypersons must depend upon the expertise of professionals, such as lawyers, and are typically not able to protect themselves adequately, professionals are sometimes subject to fiduciary obligations. Similarly, if a person, by words or acts, has induced the trust of another, and the circumstances are such that trust is reasonable, the trusted person may be treated as a fiduciary.

In *Pellegrini v. Cliffwood-Blue Moon Joint Venture, Inc.*,[61] the court found that the relationship between a geophysicist contractor and a joint venture was a mere arm's-length transaction. The joint venture was therefore under no duty to disclose that a particular oil well was not part of the contract and that the geophysicist would earn no royalties therefrom.

Non-Professional Relationships. As a general rule, courts are reluctant to characterize a non-professional relationship as fiduciary. Consequently, it is not surprising that there is no fiduciary relationship as a matter of law between a college and its alumni donors, or even between a professor and a student. In *Brzica v. Trustees of Dartmouth College*,[62] the New Hampshire Supreme Court held that a college had no duty to disclose its intent to use alumni donations to eliminate single-sex fraternities and sororities. And in *Ho v. University of Texas at Arlington*,[63] the Texas Court of Appeals held that a professor did not have an affirmative duty to tell a student that she would not obtain her doctoral degree if she failed part of the oral dissertation.

In *Gomez-Jimenez v. New York Law School*,[64] a New York appellate court considered "the propriety of the disclosures of post-graduate employment and salary data by defendant New York Law School to prospective students" between 2005 and 2012. In rejecting claims for fraud and negligent misrepresentation, the court wrote:

> [T]he employment and salary data disclosed by defendant was not actually false (even if it was incomplete). Thus, the fraud claim fails insofar as it is based on fraudulent misrepresentations. . . . Furthermore, because plaintiffs have not alleged any special relationship or fiduciary obligation requiring a duty of full and complete disclosure from defendants to its prospective students, we dismiss plaintiff's claim to the extent that it is based on fraudulent concealment . . . .[65]

---

[61] 115 S.W.3d 577 (Tex. App. 2003).

[62] 791 A.2d 990 (N.H. 2002).

[63] 984 S.W.2d 672 (Tex. App. 1998).

[64] 103 A.D.3d 13 (N.Y. App. Div. 2012).

[65] *Id.* at 59–60.

In contrast, in *Curl v. Key*,[66] the defendant, who was referred to as "uncle" by the plaintiffs and who was the best friend of their deceased father, was held to be a fiduciary. He had secured the plaintiffs' signatures on a document which was purportedly a "peace paper" that would prevent other relatives from harassing them. Instead, the paper deceptively deeded certain property to the defendant. The North Carolina Supreme Court held that a confidential relationship existed and that the deed could be set aside on grounds of fraud.

Scope of Relationship. Presumably, the duties of a fiduciary extend only as far as the scope of the relationship. Thus, it is fair to require a lawyer to disclose material information pertinent to the client's case, but not to require the lawyer to provide useful investment information unrelated to the legal representation.

Fraud Versus Breach of Fiduciary Duty. In many cases, a person harmed by a fiduciary's breach of disclosure obligations has the option of framing the claim in different ways. As discussed above, the claim may be litigated as a cause of action for fraud. However, it is also possible to bring a common law tort action against a fiduciary for intentional, reckless, or negligent breach of fiduciary duty.[67] How the claim is framed will have important consequences. For example, a claim for fraud may be subject to a longer statute of limitations than a claim for negligent breach of fiduciary duty. Conversely, a claim for negligent breach of fiduciary duty may be covered by liability insurance, even though fraud is routinely excluded from insurance coverage.[68] Consequently, it is important for a lawyer to carefully consider the consequences of particular allegations.

(4)   Facts "Basic to the Transaction"

Traps and Swindling. According to the *Restatement (Second) of Torts*, there is a duty to disclose facts "basic to the transaction,"[69] the nondisclosure of which would be tantamount to deliberate victimization. "Thus a seller who knows that his cattle are infected with tick fever . . . is not free to unload them on the buyer and take his money, when he knows that the buyer is unaware of the fact [and] could not easily discover it."[70] "In general, the cases in which the rule . . . has been applied have been those in which the advantage taken of the plaintiff's ignorance is so shocking to the ethical sense of the community, and is so extreme and unfair, as to amount to a form of swindling, in which the plaintiff is led by appearances into a bargain that is a trap, of whose essence and substance he is unaware."[71]

Undisclosed facts have been found to be "basic to the transaction," and therefore actionable, where:

---

[66] 316 S.E.2d 272 (N.C. 1984).

[67] *See* RESTATEMENT (SECOND) OF TORTS § 874 (1979); *see also* RESTATEMENT (THIRD) OF THE LAW GOVERNING LAWYERS § 49 (2000).

[68] *Cf.* SUSAN SAAB FORTNEY & VINCENT R. JOHNSON, LEGAL MALPRACTICE LAW: PROBLEMS AND PREVENTION 411 (2008).

[69] RESTATEMENT (SECOND) OF TORTS § 551 (1977).

[70] *Id.* § 551 cmt. l.

[71] *Id.*

- the seller of a new house failed to disclose that the saline content of the soil would not support vegetation;[72]

- a trademark licensor did not disclose that it had hired the person representing a licensee in negotiations to act as a "double agent";[73]

- an employer failed to reveal that the project for which an employee was being hired was likely to be discontinued in the near future;[74]

- the purchaser of property and others neglected to make known that they intended to employ a scheme to deprive the vendors of their security interest in land;[75] and

- a seller failed to disclose that cattle had not been vaccinated and therefore could not enter the state.[76]

Reasonable Reliance on Disclosure. In discussing the "facts basic to the transaction" exception, the *Restatement* commentary explains:

> There are situations in which the defendant not only knows that his bargaining adversary is acting under a mistake basic to the transaction, but also knows that the adversary, by reason of the relation between them, the customs of the trade or other objective circumstances, is reasonably relying upon a disclosure of the unrevealed fact if it exists. In this type of case good faith and fair dealing may require a disclosure.[77]

In *Schaler Tel. Co. v. Golden Sky Systems, Inc.*,[78] the Eighth Circuit held that the seller of satellite television services had no reason to expect the buyer to disclose its alleged inability to obtain financing for the transaction.

The facts-basic-to-the-transaction exception is narrow, and therefore will often not apply. For example, in *Lithuanian Commerce Corp. v. Sara Lee Hosiery*,[79] the court held that a manufacturer's failure to disclose to a distributor negative opinions from a marketing survey was not so shocking as to support an action for fraud.

(5)   Facts "Not Reasonably Discoverable"

Many tort cases hold that persons have a duty to disclose material facts that are not reasonably discoverable.[80] This is true even if the facts are not so important as to qualify as "basic to the transaction." The facts need only be material and not

---

[72] *See Griffith v. Byers Constr. Co.*, 510 P.2d 198 (Kan. 1973).

[73] *See Television Events & Marketing, Inc. v. Amcon Distributing Co.*, 488 F. Supp. 2d 1071, 1082 (D. Haw. 2006).

[74] *See Berger v. Security Pacific Info. Sys.*, 795 P.2d 1380 (Colo. Ct. App. 1990); *see also Pearson v. Simmonds Precision Prod., Inc.*, 624 A.2d 1134 (Vt. 1993).

[75] *See Dewey v. Lutz*, 462 N.W.2d 435 (N.D. 1990).

[76] *See Ducheneaux v. Miller*, 488 N.W.2d 902 (S.D. 1992).

[77] RESTATEMENT (SECOND) OF TORTS § 551 cmt. l (1977).

[78] 298 F.3d 736 (8th Cir. 2002).

[79] 179 F.R.D. 450, 478 (D. N.J. 1998).

[80] *See, e.g., Busch Oil Co. v. Amoco Oil Co.*, 1996 U.S. Dist. LEXIS 4705 (W.D. Mich. Feb. 20, 1996);

discoverable through the exercise of reasonable care.

Policy Basis. This exception to the general rule of nondisclosure may be justified on public policy grounds. Ordinarily there is no duty to speak because a rule countenancing nondisclosure creates incentives for persons to actively protect their own interests. Individuals cannot stand idly by waiting for others to inform them of everything they need to know. Rather, under the general rule, the individual bears the risk of loss: one who fails to gather and properly evaluate relevant facts before making a decision risks the consequences of making a bad choice. A person who neglects to act diligently loses. Thus, the general rule permitting nondisclosure furthers the law's interest in discouraging the waste of talent and resources.

The exception concerning facts not reasonably discoverable recognizes the limits of the general rule. If facts are not discoverable, it is futile to place the burden of discovery on the plaintiff. The plaintiff will simply be relegated to making a potentially bad decision without access to material information. Recognizing the need for a legal remedy, the New York Appellate Division, in *Stambovsky v. Ackley*,[81] explained:

> Where a condition which has been created by the seller materially impairs the value of the contract and is peculiarly within the knowledge of the seller or unlikely to be discovered by a prudent purchaser exercising due care with respect to the subject transaction, nondisclosure constitutes a basis for rescission as a matter of equity. Any other outcome places upon the buyer not merely the obligation to exercise care in his purchase but rather to be omniscient with respect to any fact which may affect the bargain. No practical purpose is served by imposing such a burden upon a purchaser. To the contrary, it encourages predatory business practice. . . .[82]

"Discoverable" Versus "Reasonably Discoverable." This exception creating duty to speak extends to cases where facts, though discoverable through great efforts, are not *reasonably* discoverable. Any other decision would force laypersons to hire numerous experts to assist them in their decisions.[83] The exception was articulated by the Supreme Court of Kansas in *Wolf v. Brungardt*[84] in the following terms:

> Where one party to a contract has . . . knowledge which is not within the fair and reasonable reach of the other party and which he could not discover by the exercise of reasonable diligence . . . he is under a real obligation to speak, and his silence constitutes fraud.[85]

Timm v. Clement, 574 N.W.2d 368 (Iowa Ct. App. 1997); *Holcomb v. Zinke*, 365 N.W.2d 507 (N.D. 1985); *Mitchell v. Christensen*, 31 P.3d 572 (Utah 2001); *Quashnock v. Frost*, 445 A.2d 121 (Pa. 1982).

[81] 169 A.D.2d 254 (N.Y. App. Div. 1991).

[82] *Id.* at 676.

[83] *See, e.g., Mitchell v. Christensen*, 31 P.3d 572, 575 (Utah 2001).

[84] 524 P.2d 726 (Kan. 1974).

[85] *Id.* at 734.

Many of the cases relating to this exception have involved the sale or lease of real property. There is no apparent reason, however, why courts should limit the rule to real estate.

For example, in *Sullivan's Stone Factory v. State Compensation Insurance Fund*,[86] the issue was whether the defendants had an obligation to disclose the existence of certain insurance regulations. The court held that there was such a duty because the defendants had "knowledge of material facts which are not accessible to the plaintiff."[87] In response to the defendants' argument that the regulations were in fact accessible, the court noted that:

> [T]he duty arises from a disparity in knowledge. For there to be a duty, it is not necessary that the undisclosed information be literally inaccessible to the plaintiff; it is only necessary that the defendant's access to it be superior to the plaintiff's access.[88]

Not Apparent to an Ordinary Person. When is a fact not reasonably discoverable? In the real estate context, one court determined that "the proper standard is whether the defect would be apparent to ordinary prudent persons with like experience, not to persons with specialized knowledge."[89] Consider how the exception for facts not reasonably discoverable might be applied to the context of lawyers and clients.

> Presumably, if an undisclosed matter relating to an attorney's credentials or experience obviously is connected to the subject matter of the representation, that matter should qualify as reasonably discoverable through inquiry, and disclosure should not be required. For example, a client can always ask, "Have you ever handled this kind of case before?" This type of logical question involves information that is reasonably discoverable. There will, of course, be difficult cases relating to whether information about credentials or experience should be disclosed. For example, has professional malpractice become such a part of public consciousness that a client is obliged to ask a lawyer "have you been sued for malpractice?" Or is malpractice still so uncommon that the reasonable prudent client would not think or have the courage to inquire? There is no easy answer to these questions.
>
> Most clients do not ask — and, indeed, do not think to ask — whether an attorney has ever been disbarred, reprimanded, or suspended from practice. Yet, such information about a lawyer's disciplinary history is often easily discoverable. In Texas, for example, anyone can go to the State Bar website for information about any of the more than 70,000 Texas attorneys, including public disciplinary sanctions in Texas and other states. Similarly, the Internet provides an increasing amount of information about persons who commit criminal conduct. It can be argued that such information, if it

---

[86] 2009 Cal. App. Unpub. LEXIS 3976 (May 20, 2009).

[87] *Sullivan's Stone Factory*, 2009 Cal. App. Unpub. LEXIS 3976, at *12 (May 20, 2009).

[88] *Id.* at *13.

[89] *See Mitchell v. Christensen*, 31 P.3d 572, 575 (Utah 2001).

is free or available at a nominal cost, is reasonably discoverable, and therefore the exception for facts not reasonably discoverable should not impose a duty to speak.

Other types of information are harder to obtain. For example, it may be difficult for a client to determine whether an attorney has been subject to court-imposed sanctions that are not readily discoverable through computer-based technology, such as sanctions imposed by a trial court that did not result in a reported decision. The law should not require clients to take burdensome steps to learn unusual information about an attorney that materially bears upon the representation. There is, however, value to reading narrowly the exception for facts not reasonably discoverable. Clients should be encouraged to ask good questions of their attorneys and gather information to protect their own interests. . . .[90]

Nonprofessionals. There is reason to think that the disclosure obligations of professionals are greater than those of nonprofessionals. Not surprisingly, in *Queen v. Lambert*,[91] the Georgia Court of Appeals opined that existence of "a confidential relationship imposes a greater duty on the parties to reveal what should be revealed and a lessened duty to discover independently what could have been discovered through the exercise of ordinary care."[92]

Obvious Matters. Of course, some things are so obvious that they should be discovered by a careful person. Thus, in *Robbins v. Capozzi*,[93] the Texas Court of Appeals held that the vendor of a condominium did not have a duty to disclose the problems that the vendor's daughter had encountered when attempting to park her car in the condominium garage. The purchaser could easily have discovered, by attempting to park there herself, that her vehicle was too large for the allotted space.

(6) Disclosures Required by Reasonable Care

According to some courts, disclosure of material information may be required by the principles that obligate a person to exercise reasonable care to prevent foreseeable *physical* harm. For example, in *B.N. v. K.K.*,[94] a doctor, who knew he had genital herpes, had sexual relations with a nurse without disclosing that information. After the nurse contracted the disease, she commenced a tort action alleging various claims, including negligence and fraud. In finding that the nurse stated a cause of action for negligence, the Maryland Court of Appeals wrote:

> One who knows he or she has a highly infectious disease can readily foresee the danger that the disease may be communicated to others with whom the infected person comes into contact. As a consequence, the infected person

---

[90] *See* Vincent R. Johnson and Shawn M. Lovorn, *Misrepresentation by Lawyers About Credentials or Experience*, 57 Okla. L. Rev. 529, 542–43 (2004).

[91] 577 S.E.2d 72 (Ga. Ct. App. 2003).

[92] *Id.* at 74.

[93] 100 S.W.3d 18, 24 (Tex. App. 2002).

[94] 538 A.2d 1175 (Md. 1988).

has a duty to take reasonable precautions — whether by warning others or by avoiding contact with them — to avoid transmitting the disease. . . .[95]

Then, in finding that the claim for fraud was also viable, the court explained:

> We have recognized that if the likelihood of physical harm is present, certain tort duties may arise under circumstances in which they otherwise would not. . . .
>
> . . . [T]he existence of a confidential relationship is not essential to Ms. N.'s cause of action for fraud because, as we hold . . . , Dr. K. had a general tort duty, at the least, to disclose his condition before engaging in intercourse with her. . . . That duty he breached, according to the allegations of the complaint. . . .

PROBLEM 2-2: THE CHURCH OF THE TRUE TOMORROW

The Church of the True Tomorrow is a fundamentalist Christian sect with settlements on nine ranches spread throughout west and central Texas. The chief ecclesiastical officer of the Church is the Deacon, who is the ultimate authority on religious issues and all other matters relating to the settlements.

The settlements are self-contained living units which provide church members with employment, medical care, entertainment, and residences. Each settlement is headed by a Rector, who is assisted by Assistant Rectors. The Rector and Assistant Rectors are responsible for the formal education of the children in each settlement.

The settlements are insular communities. Outsiders are not admitted and Church members rarely leave the settlements, except with the permission of the Deacon. As the needs at the various settlements change, the Deacon reassigns Rectors, Assistant Rectors, and other Church members.

Persons can join the Church of the True Tomorrow and move into a settlement only after going through an extensive process of religious education and character formation. Residents of the settlements are strongly discouraged from leaving the settlements. They are told that abandoning a settlement without the permission of the Deacon is a sin which carries with it serious spiritual consequences.

Four persons, ages 18 to 22, who left the settlements without permission, have filed suits against the Church of the True Tomorrow. These persons (John Smiths 1 to 4) allege that they were sexually abused by Rectors or Assistant Rectors. Presumably in an effort to reach church assets, the plaintiffs have sued the Church for fraud.

The allegations are of four types. First, the plaintiffs allege that the Deacon reassigned Rectors and Assistant Rectors when allegations of sexual impropriety surfaced. This was done, they allege, to keep parents and children in the settlements from becoming aware of the allegations of sexual impropriety.

Second, the plaintiffs allege that the secretary to the Deacon misleadingly responded to a letter from a Church member. They allege that Rector Charles

---

[95] *Id.* at 1179.

Warton had a history of molesting children which was unknown to Church members. In a letter to the Deacon, member Alice Avila had written: "The children in our school literally follow him (Warton) around, he is so kind and shows so much interest in them." The secretary to the Deacon then responded: "We are most happy to hear that you are so pleased with Rector Warton. We are happy to hear that he is doing well and shows so much interest in the children." Allegedly the Deacon knew that Rector Warton had previously been convicted of sexual perversion.

Third, the complaints allege that the Church's act of placing Rectors and Assistant Rectors in the settlements with unsupervised access to children constituted affirmative representations that the Church did not know that certain Rectors and Assistant Rectors had histories of sexually molesting children and that the Church did not know that they were a danger to children.

Fourth, the plaintiffs allege that aside from any conduct on the part of the Church, the Church had a duty to disclose to Church members that allegations of sexual misconduct had been made against several Rectors and Assistant Rectors.

The Church of the True Tomorrow denied that it had any knowledge of sexual misconduct by Rectors or Assistant Rectors. Further, the Church argued that it had made no misrepresentations of fact and had no duty to disclose information to the plaintiffs.

The state district court, without opinion, dismissed the complaints for failure to state a claim upon which relief could be granted. You are a third-year law student interning for a judge on the state court of appeals. Please advise the judge on whether the order of the district court should be reversed or affirmed, keeping in mind the rules governing actions for fraud. If you believe that the order should be reversed, be prepared to discuss with the judge what the plaintiffs will need to prove at trial.

c.   Limits on Disclosure Obligations

(1)   General Principles[96]

It is just as important to know what principles limit disclosure obligations as it is to understand what circumstances trigger a duty to speak. Two important limits (relating to the scope of fiduciary duties and materiality) have already been mentioned. These and other limiting principles are discussed below:

Scope of Fiduciary Relationships. The disclosure obligations of fiduciaries are limited to the scope of the fiduciary relationship. In the case of lawyers, for example, duties to clients generally extend no further than the scope of the legal representation. Within that scope, a lawyer owes a client a panoply of demanding duties, including, among others, loyalty, confidentiality, diligence, competence, and candor. However, lawyers have no obligation to advance the interests of clients falling outside the scope of the representation. They have not been hired to

---

[96] Some of the material and language in this section is drawn from Vincent R. Johnson, *"Absolute and Perfect Candor" to Clients*, 34 St. Mary's L.J. 737, 778–92 (2003).

perform those tasks, and it would be unfair to impose such obligations on them in the absence of either a well-established customary practice or an agreement with the client accompanied, in the usual case, by compensation. As to information falling outside the scope of the representation, the lawyer has discretion as to how those facts should be handled. The attorney may elect to communicate those facts or may choose not to do so. There is no legally enforceable duty to disclose to the client information outside the scope of representation. Similarly, with only limited exceptions, when the representation terminates, the special duties that commence with the inception of the attorney-client relationship come to an end. "A lawyer has no general continuing obligation to pass on to a former client information relating to the former representation."[97] Similar principles limit the duties of other fiduciaries.

Modification by Agreement of the Parties. Within a broad range, fiduciary obligations, including the duty of candor, are subject to modification by the parties to the relationship. For example, in *National Plan Administrators, Inc. v. National Health Insurance Co.*,[98] the Texas Supreme Court wrote:

> NPA asserts that any fiduciary duties were limited by the parties' agreement and urges us to adopt section 376 of the *Restatement (Second) of Agency* which states that the "existence and extent of the duties of the agent to the principal are determined by the terms of the agreement between the parties." . . . After NPA filed its brief, the *Second Restatement* was superseded by the *Third Restatement*. Section 376 of the *Second Restatement* does not appear verbatim in the *Third Restatement*, but the *Third Restatement* carries forward the principle that the parameters of an agency relationship are to be established by the agreement of the parties. According to the *Third Restatement*, "[a]n agent has a duty to act in accordance with the express and implied terms of any contract between the agent and the principal." *Restatement (Third) of Agency* § 8.07 (2006). "This section makes the basic point that an agent's duties of performance to the principal are subject to the terms of any contract between them." *Id.* cmt. a. The *Restatement's* position and our prior cases are consistent in respecting the right of persons to define the terms of their business relationships, . . . particularly sophisticated parties. . . . We have also noted that common-law agency principles may be limited contractually, . . . that a contractual obligation does not generally give rise to a fiduciary duty, . . . and that fiduciary duties are equitable in nature and generally not subject to hard and fast rules. . . . We agree with NPA that the extent of its duties to National Health should be considered in light of the parties' written contract.[99]

Consequently, one way to defeat a fraud claim based on alleged nondisclosure is to prove that there was an agreement between the parties that expressly or implicitly provided that such information need not be disclosed.

---

[97] RESTATEMENT (THIRD) OF THE LAW GOVERNING LAWYERS § 33 cmt. h (2000).

[98] 235 S.W.3d 695 (Tex. 2007).

[99] *Id.* at 702.

Materiality. There is never a duty to convey "immaterial" information. Unverified information of dubious authenticity or reliability is one type of information which, depending on the facts, may be found to lack materiality.

Insight into this principle can be drawn from *STAR Centers, Inc. v. Faegre & Benson, L.L.P.*[100] The suit alleged legal malpractice and breach of fiduciary duty, rather than fraud, but the Minnesota Supreme Court decided the case based on principles of materiality. The plaintiff in *STAR Centers* (STAR) asserted that its law firm (Faegre) knew that it sought information about the viability of a lender known as Consortium. Through certain dealings, the firm learned that Consortium had denied a loan to another entity, but did not communicate that information to the plaintiff. In holding that the nondisclosure would not support an action for breach of fiduciary duty, the court wrote:

> [T]hat a lender refused to fund a loan, without more, reveals nothing material about the lender. To a prospective borrower, the reasons for the lender's refusal are what matters. . . . There is no evidence in the record that Faegre learned why Consortium refused to fund the loan. . . . Finally, there is no evidence in the record that Faegre knew about Consortium's lending practices. . . . Therefore, reasonable minds can reach only one conclusion: that the information Faegre obtained about Consortium from Cemara's inquiry did not constitute a material matter bearing on its representation of STAR.[101]

In *STAR Centers*, the law firm had defended Consortium in a previous law suit. As part of its analysis, the Minnesota Supreme Court reprinted a portion of an affidavit by the plaintiff's attorney in the prior case attesting to the law firm's knowledge of Consortium's financial strength. The affidavit stated:

> Shortly after Faegre made its first appearance on behalf of Consortium in the case, Denver Golf's attorney told Faegre that he "thought Consortium may have engaged in fraud." He also told Faegre that he did not believe that Consortium had sufficient capital to fund all of its commitments. He sought information that might substantiate his belief that there was a misrepresentation in Consortium's brochure, and did not assert that he had such proof.[102]

In the subsequent malpractice suit, one issue was whether it was a breach of fiduciary duty for the law firm not to disclose that information to STAR, since STAR was interested in Consortium's viability as a lender. Focusing on the unreliable nature of the information, the court concluded that the law firm had not breached its fiduciary duties. It wrote:

> To determine whether the oral allegations of fraud constituted information that was material to Faegre's representation of STAR, we must analyze them within their context. First, Denver Golf and Consortium were litigating a claim that Consortium breached a contract by refusing to fund

---

[100] 644 N.W.2d 72 (Minn. 2002).

[101] *Id.* at 77–78.

[102] *Id.* at 78.

a loan. Denver Golf's complaint did not allege fraud. Second, there is no evidence in the record that Denver Golf offered evidence to support its allegations of fraud. The attorney mentioned fraud in the context of a request for information to support his belief that Consortium engaged in fraud. . . . Without some evidence to support the oral allegations, Faegre had no reason to think that they were anything but litigation tactics, and reasonable minds can conclude only that the unsubstantiated allegations of fraud were not material to Faegre's representation of STAR. Therefore, we hold as a matter of law that Faegre did not learn information that was material to its representation of STAR from the oral allegations of fraud.[103]

In other contexts, courts have similarly recognized that unreliable information need not be disclosed. Thus, courts have held that securities laws requiring revelation of material facts do not require dissemination of speculative information.[104]

Information Already Known. Generally, there is no compelling reason to tell someone what they already know. This is why, under the law of informed consent, a doctor is not required to warn a patient of risks that the patient already understands.[105] It is also why a possessor of land ordinarily is not obliged to disclose dangers that are "known or obvious." The same principle applies to the law of misrepresentation. There is ordinarily no duty to disclose what is already known.[106]

Competing Obligations to Others. Disclosure obligations to one person are sometimes limited by competing obligations to others. For example, lawyers normally serve many clients, simultaneously and sequentially. Sometimes the duties of confidentiality to one client conflict with disclosure obligations to another. In the most extreme case, ethics rules require the lawyer to decline or withdraw from proposed or existing representation, rather than breach confidentiality. However, there is never a duty to disclose to one client what must be held confidential to protect another.

There are, of course, cases where courts conclude that the balance tips in favor of candor, notwithstanding the competing interests of others. For example, in *Dahlgren v. First National Bank of Holdrege*,[107] the Eighth Circuit wrote:

> When a third party asks a bank about its customer's financial affairs or condition, the bank's general duty of confidentiality to its customers is at issue. Nonetheless, though the issue has not been squarely addressed, we agree with the district court that the Supreme Court of Nebraska would

---

[103] *Id.*

[104] *See Garcia v. Cordova*, 930 F.2d 826, 830 (10th Cir. 1991); *cf. Arnold v. Soc'y for Sav. Bancorp, Inc.*, 650 A.2d 1270, 1280–81 (Del. 1994).

[105] *See, e.g., Yeates v. Harms*, 393 P.2d 982, 991 (Kan. 1964); *Scott v. Bradford*, 606 P.2d 554, 558 (Okla. 1980).

[106] *See* RESTATEMENT (SECOND) OF TORTS § 343A(1) & cmt. e (1965); *see also Brownsville Navigation Dist. v. Izaguirre*, 829 S.W.2d 159, 160 (Tex. 1992).

[107] 533 F.3d 681 (8th Cir. 2008).

apply . . . [standard] tort principles to claims that a bank deceived or misled the third party in responding to the inquiry.[108]

Harm to the Plaintiff or Others. Ordinary disclosure obligations sometimes give way to special circumstances. Thus, nonrevelation of information may be excused if its dissemination poses unreasonable risks.

Consider the words of the American Law Institute addressing the duties of attorneys:

> Under conditions of extreme necessity, a lawyer may properly refuse for a client's own benefit to disclose documents to the client unless a tribunal has required disclosure. Thus, a lawyer who reasonably concludes that showing a psychiatric report to a mentally ill client is likely to cause serious harm may deny the client access to the report. Ordinarily, however, what will be useful to the client is for the client to decide.[109]

The same principles apply when disclosure threatens harm to third persons.[110]

In some cases, the threat that justifies nondisclosure is economic, rather than physical, harm, or the risk of legal liability. For example, in *North American Catholic Educational Programming Foundation, Inc. v. Cardinale*,[111] the plaintiff alleged that the defendants fraudulently caused it to forego purchasing preferred shares in a certain entity (Clearwire) in which the plaintiff was a minor owner by failing to disclose that Clearwire was well along in negotiating a sale of assets to a party named McCaw. In evaluating this claim, the court wrote:

> [I]f Clearwire were on the edge of completing a deal with McCaw, then one might argue that there was a duty to disclose. . . .
>
> . . . [However,] both case law and common sense cabin a company's obligation to disclose ongoing negotiations that have not yet led to an agreement and might easily fail. . . . Apart from the risks of prejudicing negotiations, disclosure could itself be the basis for securities-law claims by stock purchasers if the trumpeted negotiations eventually failed; some cases even purport to establish *per se* rules against such disclosure claims based merely on negotiations.[112]

Personal or Privacy Interests. Privacy interests may also occasionally trump rules that would otherwise require disclosure of information to a client. Consider, again, the case of lawyers:

> [A] lawyer presumably does not have to disclose to a client a disciplinary sanction in the nature of a private reprimand. In that situation, there has already been a judicial or quasi-judicial determination that the public interest is best served by the reprimand being private, rather than public.

---

[108] *Id.* at 693.

[109] RESTATEMENT (THIRD) OF THE LAW GOVERNING LAWYERS § 46 cmt. c (2000).

[110] *Id.* § 20 cmt. c.

[111] 567 F.3d 8 (1st Cir. 2009).

[112] 2009 U.S. App. LEXIS 10481, at *15–*16 (1st Cir. May 19, 2009).

As a second example, consider the domestic privacy interests of lawyers. Those interests ordinarily mean an attorney has no duty to disclose to a client marital difficulties that may affect the lawyer's performance.[113]

Privacy interests may also limit the duty to disclose.[114]

Of course, a lawyer who is having marital difficulties has a duty to act reasonably. In an extreme case, where the difficulties pose a serious threat to the representation, the lawyer may have a duty to disclose the risks or withdraw.

(2)   Fraud Versus Professional Malpractice

In suits against professionals, courts sometimes go to great lengths to characterize what might be viewed as fraudulent conduct as professional malpractice (*i.e.*, lack of care, negligence) rather than as fraud. For example, in *Kelly v. VinZant*,[115] an initial surgery had unexpected adverse consequences. After the patient asked the doctor whether he had done something wrong, the doctor responded, "All my surgeries are good; I do not do bad surgeries."[116] In reliance on that allegedly false assurance, the patient consented to a second surgery, which was also unsuccessful. The Supreme Court of Kansas allowed the possibility that "when alleged fraud occurs separately from and subsequent to . . . malpractice and gives rise to damages separate and distinct from those flowing from the malpractice, a plaintiff is entitled to allege and prove such a cause of action."[117] As the court explained, "[t]ypically, these actions arise from fraudulent statements intended to conceal malpractice."[118] However, the court held that "when fraud is a part of the informed consent process, the claim is for malpractice, not fraud."[119] Because the plaintiff's claim in *Kelly* was essentially that the defendant physician had misrepresented the skill that he possessed, the plaintiff could not allege fraud, but only professional malpractice. Nevertheless, the court appeared to conclude that the elements of fraud and medical malpractice were intertwined. Quoting an earlier case, *Bonin v. Vannaman*,[120] the *Kelly* court elaborated:

> [Even though] malpractice covers every way in which a patient is injured through the dereliction of a doctor in his professional capacity, the approach, depending on the facts, can be through any of several familiar forms of action. But no matter what the approach, it remains an action for malpractice, not one for deceit, contract or anything else. A well recognized ground for recovery is where a physician represents that he has the skill to

---

[113] *Cf. Albany Urology Clinic, P.C. v. Cleveland*, 528 S.E.2d 777, 782 n.19 (Ga. 2000) (suggesting that there is no duty to disclose where a doctor, "the night before receiving patients, is served with divorce papers").

[114] Vincent R. Johnson and Shawn M. Lovorn, *Misrepresentation by Lawyers About Credentials or Experience*, 57 Okla. L. Rev. 529, 532–33 (2004).

[115] 197 P.3d 803 (Kan. 2008).

[116] *Id.* at 806.

[117] *Id.* at 810.

[118] *Id.*

[119] *Id.*

[120] 929 P.2d 754, 764–766 (Kan. 1996).

perform a certain operation when in fact he does not. This form of action requires the same elements of proof that an action in fraud requires, yet it could not be successfully disputed that as between the two it is an action for malpractice.[121]

The Consequences of Labeling Deceptive Conduct as Fraud. What are the consequences of saying that conduct that otherwise would constitute fraud is actionable only as professional malpractice? One possibility is that the characterization may trigger the types of restrictions that have been enacted in recent decades to protect doctors from malpractice liability, such as caps on the amount of damages that may be recovered, limits on permissible contingent fees, stricter statutes of limitations or statutes of repose, or requirements that the filing of a claim be supported by an affidavit of merit. It is also possible that characterizing fraudulent conduct as malpractice may have some advantages for plaintiffs. It might be easier to impute conduct to an employer or partners on a vicarious liability basis or to collect a judgment from malpractice insurance proceeds, if the misconduct is "malpractice" rather than "fraud." It is typically difficult, although not necessarily impossible, to establish that fraud occurred within the scope of the actor's employment or partnership affairs. Moreover, malpractice insurance normally provides no coverage for losses arising from fraudulent conduct. The analysis in a particular case depends on applicable law and the specific terms of the defendant's insurance policy.

Misrepresentation as a Failure to Obtain Informed Consent. A significant case involving fraudulent conduct by a professional is *Howard v. University of Medicine & Dentistry of New Jersey*.[122] In *Howard*, the Supreme Court of New Jersey considered "what causes of action will lie when a plaintiff contends that a physician misrepresented his credentials and experience at the time he obtained the plaintiff's consent to surgery."[123] In *Howard*, the plaintiffs, a husband and wife, alleged that the defendant neurosurgeon had falsely represented that he was board certified and had "performed approximately sixty corpectomies in each of the eleven years he had been performing such surgical procedures."[124] The wife "was opposed to the surgery and it was only after [the doctor's] specific claims of skill and experience that she and her husband decided to go ahead with the procedure."[125]

The court held that misrepresentations about a physician's credentials and experience supported a claim for negligence based on lack of informed consent, but not "a separate and distinct claim based on fraud."[126] The court failed to explain why a claim for fraud was unavailable. It merely noted:

---

[121]   197 P.3d at 809 (Kan. 2008) (quotation marks omitted).

[122]   800 A.2d 73 (N.J. 2002). The discussion of *Howard* in this section is based extensively on views expressed in Vincent R. Johnson and Shawn M. Lovorn, *Misrepresentation by Lawyers About Credentials or Experience*, 57 OKLA. L. REV. 529, 568–76 (2004).

[123]   *Id.* at 75.

[124]   *Id.* at 76.

[125]   *Id.*

[126]   *Id.* at 77.

Few jurisdictions have confronted the question of what cause of action should lie when a doctor allegedly misrepresents his credentials or experience. . . . Although some suggest that a claim based in fraud may be appropriate if a doctor actively misrepresents his or her background or credentials, we are aware of no court that has so held.[127]

The court concluded that it was "not convinced that . . . a novel fraud or deceit-based cause of action" was necessary where such claim "would admit of the possibility of punitive damages, and . . . circumvent the requirements for proof of both causation and damages imposed in a traditional informed consent setting."[128] The court was "especially reluctant" to extend the law because "plaintiff's damages from this alleged 'fraud' [arose] exclusively from the doctor-patient relationship. . . ."[129]

The alleged fault in *Howard* was outright lying by the defendant, not simply nondisclosure. Why the court was concerned that punitive damages would be imposed if outright lying was proved is unclear. In addition, it is far from apparent why an action for fraud "would circumvent the requirements for proof of both causation and damages imposed in a traditional informed consent setting."[130] Causation and damages *are* elements of an action for fraud. The court's reluctance to entertain a fraud claim arising exclusively from a doctor-patient relationship is puzzling. *Howard* involved alleged *lying* in the course of a *fiduciary* relationship. The one case cited by the court, *Spinosa v. Weinstein*,[131] sheds little light on *Howard's* reluctance to permit a claim for fraud. The court invoked *Spinosa* for the proposition that

> concealment or failure to disclose [a] doctor's own malpractice does not give rise to a claim of fraud or deceit independent of medical malpractice, and . . . [the] intentional tort of fraud [is] actionable only when the alleged fraud occurs separately from and subsequent to the malpractice . . . and then only where the fraud claim gives rise to damages separate and distinct from those flowing from the malpractice.[132]

One would have expected the *Howard* court to announce that deceit actively practiced on a patient by a physician is intolerable, and that outright lying about credentials or experience is actionable fraud. Perhaps the court was only trying to ensure that a judgment in favor of the plaintiff would be covered by the defendant's malpractice insurance, which would cover negligence but not fraudulent conduct.

On the subject of informed consent, the *Howard* court held that "significant misrepresentations concerning a physician's qualifications can affect the validity of consent obtained."[133] The court further stated that "a serious misrepresentation

---

[127] *Id.* at 81–82.

[128] *Id.* at 82.

[129] *Id.*

[130] *See id.*

[131] 168 A.D.2d 32, 41 (N.Y. App. Div. 1991).

[132] *Howard*, 800 A.2d at 82.

[133] *Id.* at 83.

concerning the quality or extent of a physician's professional experience . . . can be material to the grant of intelligent and informed consent to the procedure."[134]

Proving that Misrepresentation Increased the Risk. The plaintiff husband in *Howard* alleged that "defendant's misrepresentations induced [him] to consent to a surgical procedure . . . that he would not have undergone had he known the truth about defendant's qualifications."[135] Ultimately, the court held that plaintiff's claim was founded on "lack of informed consent."[136] The *Howard* court concluded that "if an objectively reasonable person could find that physician experience was material in determining the medical risk of the corpectomy procedure to which plaintiff consented, . . . and if a reasonably prudent person in plaintiff's position . . . informed of the [doctor's] misrepresentations about his experience would not have consented, then a claim . . . may be maintained."[137]

The court opined that it would be inherently difficult for plaintiffs to meet the materiality standard because that would require proof that the defendant's true level of experience increased the risk of injury from the procedures the defendant performed. The court clearly intended to set a high bar for recovery based on misrepresentation of credentials or experience, for the court explained the "stringent test" as imposing "a significant gatekeeper function on the trial court to prevent insubstantial claims concerning alleged misrepresentations about a physician's experience from proceeding to a jury."[138] The court created a two-prong test for establishing proximate cause when doctors misrepresent their experience: (1) "whether the more limited experience or credentials possessed by [the doctor] could have substantially increased [the patient's] risk" and (2) "whether that substantially increased risk would cause a reasonably prudent person not to consent to undergo the procedure."[139]

If the plaintiff is able to surmount the high bar for proving proximate causation of harm under *Howard*, recovery for professional negligence is permitted even if the physician otherwise exercised care in performing professional services.[140] The misrepresentation of credentials or experience is all that is needed to establish that a duty was breached.

Howard offers guidance to courts dealing with the issue of misrepresentation of professional credentials or experience. However, it is important to consider carefully what *Howard* did not decide, what it decided incorrectly, and what advantages an informed-consent theory has over alternative causes of action.

First, *Howard* did not address whether there is a professional duty to disclose information about credentials or experience. Rather, the court limited itself to an analysis of theories of recovery applicable in a case where a misrepresentation

---

[134] *Id.*

[135] *Id.* at 84.

[136] *Id.*

[137] *Id.*

[138] *Id.* at 85.

[139] *Id.*

[140] *Id.*

allegedly has been made by an affirmative misstatement. There is, however, no reason why informed consent principles could not be applied to cases involving nondisclosure rather than affirmative misrepresentation. Doctors have been held liable for not disclosing, rather than actively misrepresenting, material facts.[141]

Split of Authority on Disclosure of Adverse Information About Credentials or Experience. There is a clear split of authority about whether disclosure of adverse information relating to a professional's credentials and experience is legally required. On the one hand, there are those authorities that favor disclosure. Professor Dan B. Dobbs has written that the "[e]xperience and success rate of the physician or surgeon are relevant, not to the decision to accept treatment, but to the decision to accept it at the hands of the defendant. . . ."[142] Decisions by courts in Wisconsin, Maryland, Delaware, and Connecticut have held that there is a duty on doctors, enforceable in an informed-consent action, to disclose information about their past experience to patients. In *Johnson by Adler v. Kokemoor*,[143] the Supreme Court of Wisconsin held that when different physicians have substantially different success rates with the same procedure, and a reasonable person in the patient's position would consider such information material, such statistical evidence may be admitted in an informed-consent case in which the plaintiff contends that the defendant surgeon failed to disclose his own inexperience. In *Dingle v. Belin*,[144] the high court of Maryland stated that, to obtain informed consent, it may be necessary to disclose precisely who will be conducting or superintending the procedure or therapy. In *Barriocanal v. Gibbs*,[145] the Superior Court of Delaware held that a trial court improperly excluded expert testimony that a surgeon had breached the standard of care for informed consent by failing to inform a patient of his lack of recent experience performing aneurysm surgery. In addition, in *Hidding v. Williams*,[146] the Louisiana Court of Appeals held that a physician's failure to disclose his chronic alcohol abuse to a patient and his wife vitiated their consent to surgery. In *DeGennaro v. Tandon*,[147] the Appellate Court of Connecticut affirmed a malpractice judgment based, in part, on a dentist's failure to disclose that she was using equipment with which she was unfamiliar.

However, there is also authority to the contrary. A number of courts have held that nondisclosure of information about medical credentials or experience will not support an action based on lack of informed consent. In *Duttry v. Patterson*,[148] the Supreme Court of Pennsylvania held that a surgeon's personal characteristics and experience are irrelevant to an informed consent claim. In *Kaskie v. Wright*,[149] the Pennsylvania Superior Court found that parents could not state a cause of action for

---

[141] *See, e.g., Haley v. United States*, 739 F.2d 1502 (10th Cir. 1984).

[142] Dan B. Dobbs, The Law of Torts 660–61 (2000); *see also Hales v. Pittman*, 576 P.2d 493, 500 (Ariz. 1978).

[143] 545 N.W.2d 495, 507 (Wis. 1996).

[144] 749 A.2d 157, 165–66 (Md. 2000).

[145] 697 A.2d 1169 (Del. Super. Ct. 1997).

[146] 578 So. 2d 1192, 1198 (La. Ct. App. 1991).

[147] 873 A.2d 191, 197 (Conn. App. Ct. 2005).

[148] 771 A.2d 1255, 1259 (Pa. 2001).

[149] 589 A.2d 213, 216 (Pa. Super. Ct. 1991).

lack of informed consent where they were not informed before their son's operation that the surgeon was an alcoholic and unlicensed to practice medicine. In *Whiteside v. Lukson*,[150] the Washington Court of Appeals held that "a surgeon's lack of experience in performing a particular surgical procedure is not a material fact for purposes . . . of failure to secure an informed consent." And in *Abram by Abram v. Children's Hospital*,[151] the New York Appellate Division held that, under state statutes, a patient could not state a claim for lack of informed consent based on the defendant's failure to disclose the providers' qualifications.

Second, *Howard's* conclusion that an action for fraud is not available against a professional for an outright lie relating to credentials or experience cannot be justified. A misstatement of fact, made with knowledge of falsity or reckless disregard for the truth, is actionable fraud. The rule is ubiquitously applicable to a broad range of contexts. Surely, a fraud claim against a professional is no different from a fraud claim against anyone else.[152] If the patient or client prefers to sue for fraud, rather than lack of informed consent (perhaps to benefit from a longer statute of limitations or to avoid caps on damages), that should be his or her option.

Precedent Treating Misrepresentation of Credentials as Fraud. There is no good reason why a false statement of material fact about a doctor's or lawyer's credentials or past experience cannot support an action for fraud, provided that each of the requirements of the tort is met. In 1881, the Supreme Court of Michigan decided *De May v. Roberts*,[153] a case involving a physician who brought a young man without medical qualifications to the plaintiff's home to assist him in attending to a woman while she gave birth. Because the assistant's lack of training was not disclosed, the court held that the woman's consent to his presence and touching did "not preclude her from maintaining an action and recovering substantial damages upon afterwards ascertaining his true character."[154] The court found that both the doctor and his alleged assistant were "guilty of deceit" for "obtaining admission at such a time and under such circumstances without fully disclosing [the assistant's] true character," and thus, the plaintiff could recover damages.[155]

However, if a patient or client opts to sue for lack of informed consent, rather than fraud, the informed-consent theory offers courts a useful structure for dealing with the difficult question of whether liability should be imposed. Using the informed-consent rationale articulated in *Howard*, recovery would be permitted only where the defendant's deficiency in credentials or experience increased the risk of the harm that the plaintiff suffered and a reasonable person would not have consented to the representation because of the increased risk.

Related Precedent Favoring an Informed-Consent Rationale. The New Jersey Supreme Court's decision in *Howard* to treat fraud by a professional as a

---

[150] 947 P.2d 1263, 1265 (Wash. Ct. App. 1997).

[151] 151 A.D.2d 972 (N.Y. App. Div. 1989).

[152] *Cf. Vega v. Jones, Day, Reavis & Pogue*, 121 Cal. App. 4th 282, 289 (2004) (stating the point with respect to lawyers).

[153] 9 N.W. 146 (Mich. 1881).

[154] *Id.* at 149.

[155] *Id.*

negligent departure from the standard of care is not unique. In the medical context, some courts have held the availability of an adequate informed-consent remedy obviates the need for an additional action based on breach of trust.[156] For example, in *Neade v. Portes*,[157] the Illinois Supreme Court held that a cause of action for breach of fiduciary duty, based on a physician's failure to disclose his alleged financial interest in a medical incentive fund, could not be maintained because it was duplicative of a medical negligence claim. There is similar precedent in the legal field. In *Aiken v. Hancock*,[158] the Texas Court of Appeals held that a former client's allegations that his attorney falsely represented that he was prepared to try the case and that an expert witness was prepared to testify were actionable under a theory of legal malpractice, but did not constitute a claim for breach of fiduciary duty.

Problem 2-3: The Addicted Doctor

Karolyn Plata had suffered from a variety of medical problems for several years. Her friends eventually recommended that she see a new doctor in town, Robert Donovan. Donovan was a general practitioner with an outgoing personality. He quickly made a good impression on a number of his patients.

Donovan saw Plata at his office approximately ten times over an eight-month period. He had an excellent professional demeanor, but never succeeded in diagnosing Plata's basic medical problems. He also never referred her to specialists who could have ordered the tests which would have revealed that she was the victim of continuing exposure to toxic chemicals at the plant where she worked. Had Plata's problems been properly diagnosed, she could have ended her exposure to toxic substances by being reassigned to another position, taking other steps to enforce her right to a safe workplace, or leaving her job.

Plata's relationship with Dr. Donovan ended when she learned that he was indicted for illegal distribution of prescription medications. The articles in the newspaper said that, unknown to his patients, Donovan was addicted to controlled substances, apparently during the entire period when he treated Plata.

Plata says that she would never have consented to be treated by a doctor with a drug addiction. She is furious that Donovan hid his addiction from her and other patients, and distraught over the time and money she wasted on medical services from Donovan and the opportunity she lost for effective medical treatment.

Please prepare an analysis of whether Plata can sue Donovan for fraud and, if so, whether an action for fraud would be preferable or inferior to suing Donovan for professional negligence.

---

[156] *See Hales v. Pittman*, 576 P.2d 493, 497 (Ariz. 1978).

[157] 739 N.E.2d 496, 503 (Ill. 2000).

[158] 115 S.W.3d 26, 28–29 (Tex. App. 2003).

d.   Statements of Opinion

Fact Versus Opinion. Some authorities assert that an action for fraud must be based on a misrepresentation of fact and not a mere assertion of opinion. This is an overstatement because, in some instances, a misleading statement of opinion will suffice as the predicate for a fraud action. These matters were discussed by the Minnesota Supreme Court more than a century ago:

> Generally speaking, the representations must be as to a material fact, susceptible of knowledge; and, if they appear to be mere matters of opinion or conjecture, they are not actionable. There are many cases, however, in which even a false assertion of an opinion will amount to a fraud, the reason being that, under the circumstances, the other party has a right to rely upon what is stated or represented. Thus, the liability may arise where one has or assumes to have knowledge upon a subject of which the other is ignorant, and knowingly makes false statements, on which the other relies.[159]

Professional Opinions. Not surprisingly, many of the cases in which reliance on opinion is permissible involve statements by professionals. If a doctor, lawyer, or other professional knows of the misleading nature of a statement of opinion, or acts with reckless indifference thereto, a layperson who detrimentally relies may be entitled to sue for damages.

Special Rules. In sorting out which statements of opinion are actionable, and which are not, several distinct rules have evolved. These rules concern (1) "puffing," (2) misrepresentation of state of mind, (3) implicit statements of fact, and (4) opinions intended to induce reliance.

(1)   Puffing

"Puffing" is sales talk, language that casts a rosy glow over a transaction, but says nothing specific about the facts.[160] Words like "fine," "first-class," and "best" are typical examples of puffing. Under a longstanding rule of tort law, puffing is permissible. According to the Illinois Appellate Court "[p]uffing is defined as a bare and naked statement as to value of a product and is considered a nonactionable assertion of opinion."[161]

Vague Positive Statements. In *Prudential Insurance Co. of America v. Jefferson Associates, Ltd.*,[162] the Texas Supreme Court found that representations by a vendor that a building was "superb," "super fine," and "one of the finest little properties in the City of Austin" were merely puffing and could not constitute fraud. This makes good sense. The law of fraud is concerned with statements that threaten to distort decision making processes. Misrepresentations of concrete fact

[159] *Hedin v. Minneapolis Med. & Surgical Inst.*, 64 N.W. 158, 159 (Minn. 1895).

[160] *See generally* W. PAGE KEETON ET AL., PROSSER AND KEETON ON TORTS 757 (5th ed. 1984).

[161] *See Miller v. William Chevrolet/GEO, Inc.*, 762 N.E.2d 1, 7 (Ill. App. Ct. 2001) (internal quotation marks omitted).

[162] 896 S.W.2d 156, 163 (Tex. 1995).

have that potential. Vague statements which assert nothing specific generally do not.

In *In re Toyota Motor Corp. Unintended Acceleration Marketing, Sales Practices and Products Liability Litigation*,[163] a federal court in California dealt with tort claims arising from the alleged sudden, unintended acceleration of automobiles. The court held that some asserted misrepresentations were actionable and others were not:

> The Court agrees that some of Toyota's alleged statements may fairly be characterized as generalized opinions (*e.g.*, . . . "high quality, reliable, and dependable," "outstanding quality, dependability, and peace of mind"). . . . These statements constitute "puffing" and are not analogous to the type of opinion that may be construed as actionable under limited circumstances. *See 625 3rd St. Associates, L.P. v. Alliant Credit Union*, 633 F. Supp. 2d 1040, 1051–52 (N.D. Cal. 2009) (construing CEO's opinion regarding the financial health and prospects of his company, when made in the context of a significant corporate transaction, as factual misstatements).
>
> *[handwritten margin note: Puffing examples]*
>
> However, other statements cited by Plaintiffs have a factual basis and may be proven true or false during discovery. *See, e.g.*, . . . (stating to NHTSA [the National Highway Traffic Safety Administration] there was "no evidence of a system or component failure" and "vehicles operated as designed"); . . . (stating to NHTSA that no defect trend had emerged . . .); . . . (telling customer "[i]t is virtually impossible for this type of . . . incident to happen."). The foregoing allegations demonstrate Plaintiffs have sufficiently alleged actionable statements. . . .[164]
>
> *[handwritten margin note: Statements that go beyond puffing]*

Greasing the Wheels of Commerce. "Puffing" by sellers often renders difficult, burdensome, or annoying transactions a bit more pleasant or tolerable, and it also greases the wheels of the economy by increasing the frequency of commercial exchange. To that extent it is not merely harmless, but in some sense beneficial. However, the rule on puffing applies not only to those involved in business or the professions, but to ordinary persons involved in the humdrum affairs of daily life.

Puffing by Professionals. Professionals regularly engage in puffing because it is important to impress clients and potential clients. Like everyone else, professionals may contend that the glass is half full, rather than half empty. As the Second Circuit stated, "[i]t can be expected that any professional will convey to potential clients a healthy self-estimation."[165] However, statements that extend beyond expressing a favorable opinion, and instead assert false facts, are actionable. There is an important difference between a flattering characterization and a gross exaggeration. In *Baker v. Dorfman*,[166] the Second Circuit found that statements in an attorney's resume went beyond puffing and "were either false or grossly

---

[163] 754 F. Supp. 2d 1145 (C.D. Cal. 2010).

[164] *Id.* at 1229.

[165] *Baker v. Dorfman*, 239 F.3d 415, 423 (2d Cir. 2000).

[166] *Id.*

misleading, and created the false impression [of his being] . . . an experienced litigator."[167]

(2)   State of Mind

As Lord Bowen famously remarked in *Edgington v. Fitzmaurice*, "The state of a man's mind . . . is as much a fact as the state of his digestion."[168] If a plaintiff can prove that the defendant misrepresented his state of mind when uttering an opinion, the defendant may be liable for fraud.

Misrepresenting One's State of Mind. In *Graubard Mollen Dannett & Horowitz v. Moskovitz*,[169] the New York Court of Appeals held that a law firm stated a claim by alleging that the defendant attorney, a former partner in the firm, represented orally to the partnership that he "would act to ensure the future of the firm . . . when he never intended to do so. . . ."[170] Consistently, in *Bogle v. Bragg*,[171] the Georgia Court of Appeals stated that an action for "fraud may be predicated on a promise made with a present intention not to perform."[172]

In *Tessier v. Rockefeller*,[173] the New Hampshire Supreme Court held that there was evidence to support the plaintiff's fraud claim based on misrepresentation of state of mind. At the time that the defendant lawyer said he would not report the plaintiff's husband (also a lawyer) to disciplinary authorities if the couple relinquished certain property interests, the lawyer knew that she had a mandatory ethical obligation to report such misconduct.

Of course, it may be hard to prove that the defendant's state of mind was not as represented. However, in the current digital age, electronic records of phone calls, e-mails, and text messages can sometimes supply precisely the proof that the plaintiff needs. Moreover, disgruntled present or former employees are often only too pleased to reveal information showing that an executive's statements misrepresented the executive's state of mind.

Nonperformance or Partial Performance of Obligations. Nonperformance of an agreement, by itself, does not establish that there was never an intent to perform. However, failure to perform is circumstantial evidence which, when taken together with other facts, may allow a jury to conclude that the nonperforming party misrepresented its state of mind at the time the agreement was entered into. Conversely, partial performance of an agreement tends to show that there was an honest intent to perform obligations contractually. In many instances, when the partial performance ceases, the plaintiff's action is for breach of contract, not fraud.

---

[167] *Id.* at 423.

[168] L.R. 29 Ch. Div. 459, 483 (1885).

[169] 653 N.E.2d 1179, 1184 (N.Y. 1995). *Cf. Martin v. Ohio State Univ. Found.*, 742 N.E.2d 1198, 1205 (Ohio Ct. App. 2000).

[170] 653 N.E.2d 1179, 1184 (N.Y. 1995).

[171] 548 S.E.2d 396, 400 (Ga. Ct. App. 2001).

[172] *Id.*

[173] 33 A.3d 1118 (N.H. 2011).

Quick Changes of Mind. A quick change of mind may be circumstantial evidence that the defendant did not believe what the defendant previously asserted. For example, in *Adams v. Gillig,*[174] the defendant induced the plaintiff to sell a lot by falsely stating that he would build only single-family dwellings, yet the very next day he engaged an architect to design a public garage. The court held that while there would have been no liability if the buyer had merely changed his mind as to use of the property after the transaction had been completed, the circumstantial evidence showed that he in fact never intended to use the property for residences and had intentionally deceived the plaintiff by misrepresenting his state of mind.

Part of a Scheme to Defraud. Evidence that the defendant's statements were part of a larger scheme to defraud can sometimes show that the defendant's statements misrepresented the defendant's state of mind. In *Petrakopoulou v. DHR Intern., Inc.,*[175] a federal court in Illinois found that the plaintiff (Petrakopoulou) adequately alleged a cause of action for fraud. As the court explained:

> [T]he amended complaint identifies who made the alleged fraudulent claims (David Hoffman and Geoff Hoffman); what the fraudulent claims were (that DHR would provide Petrakopoulou with a salary of $250,000; a signing bonus of $50,000; an administrative assistant; three months' notice of termination with compensation; and legal fees of up to £9,000.00); and it alleges when, where, and how the claims were made (by email communications as well as face-to-face meetings during the period from May 2006 to May 2007).
>
> DHR . . . complains, however, that Petrakopoulou has failed to identify any misrepresentations beyond the statements or terms of the parties' employment agreement. As a result, DHR maintains that Petrakopoulou's fraudulent misrepresentation claim is simply a "repackaging" of her breach-of-contract claim, and is therefore "duplicative and inappropriate."
>
> In response, Petrakopoulou cites to cases in which courts have allowed "promissory fraud" claims of the kind she asserts here — *i.e.,* claims alleging fraud based on a false representation of intent regarding future conduct — to be asserted in tandem with breach of contract claims. . . . It is true, as DHR points out, that Illinois generally does not recognize promissory fraud claims. *See, e.g., General Elec. Credit,* 126 Ill. Dec. 676, 532 N.E.2d at 364 ("As a general rule, promissory fraud, based on future acts, is not actionable in Illinois."); *see also Bradley Real Estate Trust v. Dolan Associates Ltd.,* 266 Ill. App. 3d 709, 203 Ill. Dec. 582, 640 N.E.2d 9, 12–13, 203 Ill. Dec. 582 (1994) (explaining that under Illinois law, "a statement of future intention cannot generally be the basis of a claim of fraud because alleged misrepresentations must be statements of present or preexisting facts, and not statements of future intent or conduct"). It is also true, however, that Illinois recognizes an exception to this general rule:

---

[174] 92 N.E. 670 (N.Y. 1910).

[175] 660 F. Supp. 2d 935 (N.D. Ill. 2009).

Exception to the general rule against promissory fraud [handwritten margin note]

such claims are permitted where "the fraud is one element of a pattern of fraudulent acts, and the scheme is intended to induce the promisee to act for the promisor's benefit at the time of the promise." . . .

Courts and commentators alike have remarked upon the difficulty of determining when Illinois' so-called "scheme-to-defraud" exception applies. . . . Nevertheless, the Seventh Circuit has offered the following gloss: "Our best interpretation is that promissory fraud is actionable only if it either is particularly egregious or, what may amount to the same thing, it is embedded in a larger pattern of deceptions or enticements that reasonably induces reliance and against which the law ought to provide a remedy." . . .

Petrakopoulou's fraudulent misrepresentation claim clearly falls within the scheme-to-defraud exception. In unmistakable terms, Petrakopoulou's complaint claims that DHR's alleged misrepresentations are part of a larger scheme to lure executive recruiters such as herself away from competing firms by means of sham employment agreements. . . . DHR goes on to argue that the scheme alleged by Petrakopoulou is not credible in light of other allegations in her complaint. For example, DHR argues:

> Plaintiff's claim that Petrakopoulou's claims that "DHR had no intention of performing under her Employment Agreement is undermined by her own allegations suggesting that DHR indeed did take steps to abide by its contractual obligations." For example, DHR incorporated a French office and named Ms. Petrakopoulou its director or "gérant." DHR signed a lease for office space in Paris. Furthermore, Plaintiff does not dispute that DHR paid her the agreed upon monthly salary from October 2007 through March 2008. The fact that DHR performed under the Agreement undermines Plaintiff's conclusory allegation that DHR had no intention of honoring her contract at the time it was executed.

. . . These contentions, however, plainly raise questions of a factual nature and are not appropriately addressed at the motion-to-dismiss stage. Consequently, I conclude that Petrakopoulou has properly alleged a claim for fraudulent misrepresentation.[176]

Predictions. Unfulfilled predictions of what will occur in the future are generally not actionable. In *McElrath v. Electric Investment Co.*,[177] the Minnesota Supreme Court held that the assertion that a particular hotel "would become an important summer resort" could not serve as the basis for a lawsuit. The prediction rested wholly on conjecture and speculation. However, the defendant's representation that a local traction company intended to extend its line past the property was held to be actionable.

The line between predictions and misrepresentations of existing fact is sometimes not clear, but courts must nevertheless decide the suits that come before them. In *Arkoma Basin Exploration Co., Inc. v. FMF Associates 1990-A, Ltd.*,[178]

---

[176] *Id.* at 938–39.

[177] 131 N.W. 380 (Minn. 1911).

[178] 249 S.W.3d 380 (Tex. 2008).

a case involving a natural gas field, the Texas Supreme Court, applying Virginia law, arrived at something of a split decision. It held that reserve estimates for a mature field constituted actionable misrepresentations of fact, but that reserve estimates for a new field constituted expressions of opinion that were not actionable.

Predictions Intended as Facts. In *Rose v. Whittier College*,[179] a law school facing financial problems offered its twenty tenured law professors a buyout. Law school administrators told the professors that "if they did not accept the buyout offer, they would face a 50 to 100 percent increase in workload, teaching five or six courses a year instead of the standard three or four" and that "their salaries would be frozen for the indefinite future if they did not accept the buyout offer."[180] Soon after the plaintiff accepted the buyout, the law school's bar results improved. Then, "tenured professors who had not accepted Whittier's buyout offer . . . were given a three percent raise" and "[n]o tenured professor who rejected the buyout offer experienced an increased course load." In a subsequent action by the plaintiff, which included a claim for fraud, the court entered a judgment against Whittier. On appeal, Whittier argued that the statements at issue were nonactionable statements of opinion and prediction. In affirming the compensatory damage award, a California appellate court wrote:

> Expressions of opinion are not generally treated as representations of fact, and therefore are not usually grounds for a misrepresentation cause of action. . . . "[W]here there is a reasonable doubt as to whether a particular statement is an expression of opinion or the affirmation of a fact, the determination rests with the trier of the facts." . . .

> Whittier's statements to the tenured professors concerning salaries and workloads were made under circumstances indicating they were intended as expressions of fact, not opinion. Both Rose and David Treiman, another tenured professor who accepted the buyout offer, testified at the trial that Whittier's administrators said there would be no raises for the indefinite future and that workloads would increase if they remained on the Law School faculty. Rose further testified that he understood the administrators' representations to be statements of fact. The trial court's factual determination that Whittier's statements concerning workloads and salaries were actionable representations of fact is supported by substantial evidence. . . .

> Whittier next argues that its statements regarding workloads and salaries were not actionable because they were mere predictions of future events. It is true as a general rule that "an actionable misrepresentation must be made about past or existing facts [and that] statements regarding future events are merely deemed opinions. . . ." There are, however, recognized exceptions to this general rule. . . . One such exception is when one party has special or superior knowledge such that the other may rely upon the former's opinion. . . . The trial court found that exception to be applicable here.

---

[179] 2011 Cal. App. Unpub. LEXIS 8416 (Nov. 3, 2011).

[180] *Id.* at *4.

The trial court found that Rose's reliance on Whittier's misrepresentations was justified because Whittier's administrators not only had information not available to a professor, but were also responsible for making decisions on the very issues at stake, including salaries and work load. That information included the opinions and conclusions of its outside consultant Huron, who "repeatedly advised [Whittier] it was unrealistic to expect that salaries could be frozen." Whittier's nondisclosure of this information precludes it from characterizing its misrepresentations as mere opinions or predictions of future events. . . .[181]

PROBLEM 2-4: THE DISAPPOINTED ASSOCIATE

Alvin Avis, a law school graduate, passed the bar and was employed as an associate with Fortney & Hazard, a malpractice defense law firm. After seeing an ad placed by the Solomon Law Firm, which sought an associate to handle criminal defense matters, Avis submitted a resume because he really wanted to work in that area of the law. Alice Solomon, the principal in the two-lawyer Solomon Law Firm, needed to replace her current associate, Gail Bright, who was leaving the firm for a government position in the city attorney's office.

Solomon interviewed Avis on two occasions. She was not sure that he was the right fit for the position (but of course she did not tell him that). However, Solomon had received only a few resumes, and she was even less enthusiastic about the other candidates. Faced with Bright's impending departure, she offered Avis the job at an agreed monthly salary for "as long as they both thought it was a good arrangement." Avis cheerfully accepted.

The day that Avis accepted the new job, he informed Fortney & Hazard that he was tendering his resignation and would be joining the Solomon Law Firm in two weeks. The partners at Fortney & Hazard accepted the resignation and wished Avis well in his new position.

The following day, Solomon concluded that she had made the wrong decision. After reviewing the files pending in her office and her trial schedule, she realized that she had no time to closely supervise Avis, who had never practiced criminal law. Solomon knew that what she needed was an experienced associate. Solomon called Avis and withdrew the job offer.

A day later, Solomon received a resume from Robert Deux, a lawyer with considerable experience in criminal defense work. Solomon promptly interviewed and hired Duex, who began work a few days later.

Avis believes that he may have a viable tort claim for fraud against the Soloman Law Firm. Please analyze the merits of suing the firm for fraud.

---

[181] *Id.* at *7–*10.

(3)   Implicit Statements of Fact

Some Basis, Not Entirely Inconsistent. Every statement of opinion carries with it at least two implicit statements of fact: first, that the speaker has some factual basis for uttering the view expressed, and second, that the facts known to the speaker are not wholly inconsistent with the espoused opinion.[182] A lawyer cannot say that he is "good at oil and gas law," if he knows nothing about the subject, nor can he make that claim if he has recently been held liable for malpractice based on incompetence in the oil and gas field.

In *Crown Cork & Seal Co. v. Hires Bottling of Chicago*,[183] the seller of bottling equipment told the buyer that the machinery was "first class equipment" and that buying it would be a "very fine move." The Seventh Circuit, in an opinion by Judge Thomas E. Fairchild, found that fraud was a plausible defense to an action to enforce a promissory note and that summary judgment for the defendant was inappropriate:

> It is true that the expressions attributed to Stern were in the phraseology characteristic of opinion: "fine move," "first-class," "better equipment." If the deficiency complained of were merely performance which compared unfavorably with other machines with respect to efficiency, economy, or quality of product, the rule that statements of opinion are not actionable would clearly apply. But the alleged defect here is that the equipment is incapable of producing Hires' wares in a condition fit to be marketed [because of sediment, bad taste, and high bacterial count]. When Stern, who was allegedly familiar with Hires' business, made such statements in response to Holland's question, they implied, at least, an assertion of fact that the equipment was capable of producing Hires' goods in marketable condition.[184]

Opinions Implying That Facts Exist. Another example of an expression of opinion giving rise to an implicit statement of fact can be drawn from the medical context. Predictions of success, as mere opinions about the future, typically are not actionable.[185] However, in an early case,[186] the Minnesota Supreme Court stated:

> The plaintiff, an illiterate man, badly injured in an accident . . . consulted with the physician . . . as to his condition and the probability of a recovery. After an examination by the surgeons, he was positively assured . . . that he could be cured, and by treatment at that institute could and would be made sound and well. . . . [T]here was something more in defendants' statements than the mere expression of his opinion upon a matter of

---

[182] *See* RESTATEMENT (SECOND) OF TORTS § 539 (1977).

[183] 371 F.2d 256 (7th Cir. 1967).

[184] *Id.* at 258.

[185] *See Maness v. Reese*, 489 S.W.2d 660, 663 (Tex. App. 1972); W. PAGE KEETON ET AL., PROSSER AND KEETON ON TORTS 762 (5th ed. 1984).

[186] *Hedin v. Minneapolis Med. & Surgical Inst.*, 64 N.W. 158 (Minn. 1895).

conjecture and uncertainty. It amounted to a representation that plaintiff's physical condition was such as to insure a complete recovery.[187]

The court indicated that if the implicit assertion of fact about the plaintiff's physical condition was knowingly false, an action for deceit would lie.

Another example of an opinion falsely implying facts involves a young lawyer who was employed as a law clerk to a justice on the Kansas Court of Appeals. The clerk exercised extremely bad judgment in sending out tweets about a case that was being argued at the court. That suit involved a lawyer [K] who had allegedly committed misconduct. In a subsequent disciplinary action against the clerk, the court stated:

> "It is professional misconduct for a lawyer to . . . engage in conduct involving dishonesty, fraud, deceit or misrepresentation." KRPC 8.4(c). Respondent misrepresented the law and facts in her prediction . . . [that K would be disbarred] for seven years. She had no legal or factual basis on which to base such a prediction. ***.[188]

The court found that the law clerk's tweets, which were disrespectful of a litigant appearing before the court, also amounted to "conduct prejudicial to the administration of justice" and improperly implied that the clerk could influence a government official. Noting that the law clerk had already lost her job at the court and had been unemployed for several months as a result of the bad publicity surrounding the event, the court imposed only a light disciplinary sanction in the form of an informal admonition.

(4)   Statements of Law

Sometimes Nonactionable. Some decisions hold that statements of law are not actionable under the law of misrepresentation. Potentially falling within the sweep of this broad rule are assertions about what the law is, what effect a particular law has, or what varieties of conduct are, or are not, legal. Thus, in *In re Backer*,[189] the Sixth Circuit wrote:

> Generally, Kentucky law does not recognize misrepresentations of law, only misrepresentations of fact, unless a confidential or trust relationship exists between the parties. . . . [See] *Fields v. Life & Cas. Ins. Co. of Tenn.*, 349 F. Supp. 612 (E.D. Ky. 1972) (holding that misrepresentation of insurance agent to plaintiff that continuing to pay premiums on ex-husband's policy would entitle her to continued beneficiary rights is a mere misrepresentation of law and not actionable). Extrapolating from the general rule, "it has been held that, as a rule, fraud cannot be predicated on misrepresentations as to the legal effect of a written instrument. . . ." 37 Am. Jur. 2d Fraud and Deceit § 99 (citing *Mut. Life Ins. Co. of N.Y. v. Phinney*, 178 U.S. 327 (1900)).

---

[187] 64 N.W. at 159.

[188] *In re Kansas Attorney*, In the Supreme Court of Kansas Before a Hearing Panel Appointed Under Supreme Court Order 2012 SC 94 (Jan. 13, 2014).

[189] 2002 U.S. App. LEXIS 22172 (6th Cir. Oct. 22, 2002).

Plaintiff alleges that the misrepresentations consist of Manning's attorney's statement to Plaintiff [a nonclient] that, as to him, there was no difference between forbearance and settlement, and Manning's statement, "it's over." These statements can, at best, be construed as statements regarding the legal effect of the document as to Plaintiff, or perhaps a prediction as to the long-run practical effect for Plaintiff, *i.e.*, that Plaintiff would never have sufficient funds or assets in the future to make it worthwhile for Defendants to proceed against such additional assets. No misrepresentations of fact are apparent from these statements, and therefore the statements are not actionable as fraud.[190]

Presumed to Know the Law. The proposition that statements of law cannot serve as the basis for a fraud claim seems to reflect two somewhat contradictory ideas. The first is that everyone is presumed to know the law and that therefore no one could justifiably rely upon an incorrect assertion of the law. The second idea is that the law is so complex and uncertain that a statement of law is an unreliable (and nonactionable) expression of opinion. Neither of these suppositions withstand analysis. As Judge Charles D. Breitel observed for the New York Court of Appeals in *National Conversion Corp. v. Cedar Building Corp.*,[191] "[i]f ignorance of the law did not in fact exist, we would not have lawyers to advise and courts to decide what the law is." Moreover, if the law were incomprehensible, the study of law would be not only a hopeless endeavor, but one that is useless.

No Bright-Line Rule. As Professor Alan Gunn has explained, in most states there is no bright-line rule that immunizes statements of law from liability. Whether a statement of law is actionable depends upon the facts.

> The real distinction between "fact" and "law" cannot be a distinction between statements that make representations about legal matters and statements that do not. Many ordinary "factual" statements necessarily carry with them representations about law. Consider, for instance, "John and Helen are married," or "that blue car over there is mine." Under most circumstances, these statements would be taken as factual, yet neither of them can be true unless certain legal relationships — marriage and ownership, respectively — exist. What makes these statements "legal" or "factual" is not their content, but rather the circumstances under which they are made. If, for instance, John approaches a lawyer for advice about his legal relationship with Helen, which is uncertain because one of them obtained a possibly shaky Caribbean divorce before their wedding, the lawyer's opinion that John and Helen are married is a statement of law, which is actionable [perhaps under the law of legal malpractice]. . . . If, instead of asking a lawyer, John asks his cousin Charlie for legal advice, Charlie's conclusion is still a statement of law, but not one John can properly rely on, as he should not seek legal advice from a dolt like Charlie. But now suppose that someone interested in asking Helen for a date asks Charlie whether she is single. If Charlie answers, "No, she and John are

---

[190] *Id.* at 531.

[191] 246 N.E. 2d 351, 355 (N.Y. 1969) (quoting *Municipal Metallic Bed Mfg. Corp. v. Dobbs*, 171 N.E. 75, 76 (1930)).

married," the answer would be taken as stating a fact, so if Charlie knew that John and Helen had never gone through a marriage ceremony or that they had, but John's prior divorce was not valid, Charlie would have lied. Even lawyers may make "statements of fact" about legal relationships in this way. . . . Ultimately, the distinction is to be found not by asking whether the statement is "about" law or fact, but by asking whether the misrepresentation is one that the law of deceit should protect people against.[192]

Among the cases in which statements of law are actionable are at least four particular situations:

Law of Other Jurisdictions. First, statements about the law of another jurisdiction are often actionable. Even if one could be presumed to know local law, it would be unreasonable for the legal system to expect acquaintance with the law of places where one does not reside or regularly do business.[193]

Statements of Law Which Imply Facts. Second, if a statement of law implies facts which are inaccurate, the statement may be actionable. For example, an assertion that the plumbing and wiring in a house meet applicable building code requirements may be interpreted as a representation that fixtures of a certain type exist within the walls of the structure. If those representations are not true, an action will lie.[194]

Law Stated as a Fact. Third, if the speaker intends for a statement of law to be treated as a fact, it is actionable. For example, in *National Conversion Corp. v. Cedar Building Corp.*,[195] a lease contained a false representation that the leased premises were not subject to restrictions imposed by the zoning laws. Further, the lessor dissuaded the lessee from adjourning the negotiations to verify that fact by stating unequivocally, "[we] own the property, . . . we know the area[,] . . . we guarantee it." The court held that it would be unfair not to allow reliance on that assurance.[196]

Statements of Law by Lawyers. Fourth, statements of law by lawyers or other fiduciaries are often actionable, for it is reasonable for laypersons to rely on such assertions.

PROBLEM 2-5: THE UNEXPECTED PREMIUM

Taller Co. was in the business of selling, fabricating, and installing plastic materials. Because Taller encountered financial difficulties, ProMax, Inc. acquired all of Taller's assets at a tax lien sale.

---

[192] VINCENT R. JOHNSON, TEACHING TORTS: A TEACHER'S GUIDE TO STUDIES IN AMERICAN TORT LAW 376 (Carolina Academic Press, 5th ed. 2013).

[193] *See* RESTATEMENT (SECOND) OF TORTS § 545 cmt. e (1977).

[194] *Sorenson v. Gardner*, 334 P.2d 471 (Or. 1959).

[195] 246 N.E.2d 351 (N.Y. 1969).

[196] *Id.* at 354.

ProMax then obtained worker's compensation insurance through a broker, Bill Bosco, from the state Worker's Compensation Insurance Fund (WCIF). Bosco had previously assisted Taller with obtaining worker's compensation insurance and was familiar with Taller's claims history.

Bosco told ProMax, Inc. that WCIF had quoted an estimated annual premium of about $50,000, but that the amount due was subject to adjustment based on a review of the applicable claims history later in the year. After the policy had been in effect for almost eleven months, WCIF charged ProMax a revised premium that was more than 150% greater than the premium that had been originally quoted. The revised premium was arrived at based on a review of both ProMax's claims history and Taller Co.'s previous claims history.

Lucy Parker, the president of ProMax, has sought advice from your law firm about suing Bosco for fraud. Parker alleges that Bosco knew that under the applicable administrative regulations, Taller's claims history would be used in setting ProMax, Inc.'s premium unless ProMax established a material change in ownership and employees. Parker and others at ProMax were unaware that state insurance regulations permitted a predecessor firm's claims history to be used in calculating the premium of a successor firm. Parker believes that Bosco did not disclose this information to ProMax, Inc. because his commission would be higher if ProMax's insurance premium was ultimately higher.

A partner at your firm believes that it is impossible to successfully litigate a claim for fraud against Bosco because the administrative regulations permitting the premium rating practices in question are established by state law and, of course, were a matter of public record. Please prepare to discuss with the partner whether it is likely that a cause of action for fraud can be stated.

3.   Intent to Induce Reliance or Expectation of Reliance

Purpose and Knowledge. Cases frequently say that to be liable for fraud the defendant must intend to induce reliance by the plaintiff. For example, in *Jean v. Tyson-Jean*,[197] the Texas Court of Appeals found that "[b]ecause appellant testified there was no 'intention' on the part of [others] to defraud her, actual fraud could not have been proved." Of course, under basic tort principles, intent includes both purpose and knowledge.[198] "[A] defendant who acts with knowledge that a result will follow is considered to intend the result."[199] Purpose means that the defendant desired to produce the result. Knowledge means that the result was substantially certain to follow, which is to say, certain for all practical purposes.

Expectation of Reliance. However, in some cases expectation of reliance will suffice as a basis for liability, even if the defendant does not intend to induce reliance. Thus, according to the *Restatement*, liability for fraud extends to persons whom the defendant "intends or has reason to expect to act or to refrain from

---

[197] 118 S.W.3d 1, 9 n.9 (Tex. App. 2003).

[198] *See* Restatement (Third) of Torts: Liability for Physical and Emotional Harm § 1 (2010).

[199] *Ernst & Young, L.L.P. v. Pacific Mutual Life Ins. Co.*, 51 S.W.3d 573, 578–80 (Tex. 2001).

action in reliance upon the misrepresentation."[200]

a.   Direct Recipients

If there are direct dealings between the plaintiff and defendant, foreseeability of reliance typically poses few problems. The conduct of the parties tends to establish that reliance was highly foreseeable to, if not plainly desired by, the defendant.

b.   Unintended Recipients

If the defendant knows that the recipient intends to convey information to a third person, there will often be little difficulty showing that reliance by the third person was intended or expected.[201] Illustratively, when a misrepresentation is made to an agent, reliance by the principal is quite foreseeable, since agents have a duty to convey material information to their principals.

Difficult questions arise in cases where there are no direct dealings between the parties and no reason for the defendant to expect that false or misleading statements will reach the plaintiff in particular.

(1)   Commercial Documents

The *Restatement (Second) of Torts* contains a provision addressing written misrepresentations incorporated into commercial documents. Section 532 provides:

> One who embodies a fraudulent misrepresentation in an article of commerce, a muniment of title, a negotiable instrument or a similar commercial document, is subject to liability for pecuniary loss caused to another who deals with him or with a third person regarding the article or document in justifiable reliance upon the truth of the representation.[202]

The *Restatement* gives as examples false recitals in deeds, bonds, and promissory notes, and mislabeled merchandise containers. According to the commentary, "the maker of a fraudulent misrepresentation incorporated in a document has reason to expect that it will reach and influence any person whom the document reaches."[203]

The *Restatement* rule was applied by the Maryland Court of Appeals in *Diamond Point Plaza Ltd. Partnership v. Wells Fargo Bank, N.A.*,[204] an action for fraud by the assignee of a mortgage for misrepresentations contained in loan documents. The court wrote:

> Diamond Point . . . made a fraudulent misrepresentation in a commercial document, for the purpose of inducing Pinnacle and PaineWebber to extend a loan, aware that PaineWebber likely would sell that loan in the secondary

---

[200] RESTATEMENT (SECOND) OF TORTS § 531 (1977).

[201] *See id.* § 533.

[202] *See id.* § 532.

[203] *Id.* § 532 cmt. b.

[204] 929 A.2d 932 (Md. 2007).

market. Diamond Point would thus have reason to expect that the loan documents, including its borrower's certificates, would be presented to, would be considered by, and would influence the decision of prospective buyers in the secondary market. . . . Liability is not defeated by the fact that Diamond Point's representations were not made directly to Wells Fargo.[205]

In an effort to restrict the commercial document rule, the *Restatement* commentary explains that it is:

> limited to those documents or chattels that are in themselves articles of commerce.[206] It does not apply to an ordinary letter misrepresenting the title to land or to a report furnished by an accountant to a corporation concerning its finances, because these documents are not to be expected to have commercial circulation.[207]

Expected Commercial Circulation. However, questions can be raised about the reach of the underlying principle. If a business misrepresents its assets, products, or other business characteristics in a promotional brochure, may any person reached by the brochure sue for damages caused by reliance on the false statements? Presumably the company intended the brochure to have "commercial circulation" and, in many cases, intended the statements to induce reliance. In such instances, would it be fair to say that "the intent to induce reliance follows the brochure"? Moreover, misrepresentations on a website are the equivalent of misrepresentations in a brochure. Websites are merely the electronic equivalent of documents that are intended to have circulation. Businesses tout their products and services on websites for the purpose of inducing reliance. Should they be held liable for losses suffered by another who reads the website and relies? Would there be a risk of unlimited liability? If so, and if the defendant intended to deceive readers, would unlimited liability be a concern?

Misleading Advertisements. There are certainly cases that support the idea that written misstatements intended for commercial circulation may, at least in some cases, be relied upon by anyone whom the statement reaches who is harmed by entering into a foreseeable transaction. For example, in *Knepper v. Brown*,[208] the Oregon Supreme Court held that the publisher of a misleading Yellow Pages ad was liable to an unknown person who relied on the ad's misrepresentation of a doctor's credentials and as a result suffered physical harm from a botched liposuction procedure. Similarly, in *Pleasant v. Bradford*,[209] decided by the Texas Court of Appeals, a realtor was held liable for misstatements about a residence in

---

[205] *Id.* at 946.

[206] According to BALLENTINE'S LAW DICTIONARY (3d. ed., LEXIS 2009), *articles of commerce* means "Articles which are the subject of trade and barter, offered in the market as something having an existence and value independent of the parties to them; commodities to be shipped or forwarded from one state to another and then put up for sale." Dictionary.com (last visited Jan. 30, 2014) says that an *article of commerce* is "an article that is offered for sale."

[207] *See* RESTATEMENT (SECOND) OF TORTS § 532 (1977).

[208] 195 P.3d 383 (Or. 2008).

[209] 260 S.W.3d 546 (Tex. App. 2008).

a Multiple Listing Service entry. Although there was a dispute over how the plaintiffs received a copy of the erroneous listing, a judgment for the plaintiffs was affirmed.

Do cases like these stand for a general rule that fraudulent advertisements will readily give rise to liability, or is something more required? In *Pleasant*, there was no specter of unlimited liability. Only one person could buy the misrepresented house. And, in *Knepper*, the plaintiff suffered personal injury, not purely economic loss. Liability for physical injury typically requires foreseeability of harm, nothing more. Thus, it was not surprising that the publisher was held liable. Cases involving purely economic loss are sometimes subject to special requirements because the scope of liability is potentially broader. Discussed below is the question of whether liability in such cases depends on whether there is special reason to expect reliance (something more than foreseeability).

(2)   Public Filings

In many situations, an action for fraud may be based on false statements in public filings. Some legislative enactments require filings to protect a particular class of persons. Persons making such filings therefore have reason to expect that the information they submit will be relied upon by members of that class in transactions of the kind in which the enactment is intended to afford protection.[210] For example, filings made pursuant to a statute requiring corporations to report their financial positions generally may be relied upon not only by persons making deposits or investments, but also by those lending money to the entities in question.[211] In addition, filers who direct the attention of others to what they said in a public filing have reason to expect reliance by the others on the statements contained in the filing.[212]

(3)   Special Reason to Expect Reliance

The commentary to the *Restatement's* basic rule on "expectation of influencing conduct"[213] states that a general risk of reliance — the type of risk that is inherent in virtually every misrepresentation — is an insufficient predicate for liability.[214] Rather, according to the American Law Institute:

> The maker of the misrepresentation must have information that would lead a reasonable man to conclude that there is an especial likelihood that it will reach those persons and will influence their conduct. . . .[215]

Always a Requirement? Some courts have gone to great lengths to indicate that merely foreseeable reliance is insufficient to allow a third party to sue for fraud. They appear to hold that a special reason to expect reliance is necessary even in

---

[210] *See* RESTATEMENT (SECOND) OF TORTS § 536 (1977).

[211] *See id.* § 536 cmt. e.

[212] *See id.* § 532 cmt. g.

[213] *Id.* § 531.

[214] *Id.* § 531 cmt. d.

[215] *Id.*

cases involving misrepresentations in documents intended for commercial circulation or publicly filed.

Nonactionable Deception of the Enron Investors. In *In re Enron Corporation Securities, Derivative & "ERISA" Litigation*,[216] a federal district court in Texas wrote:

> Plaintiffs allege that Defendants helped Enron conceal its deteriorating financial condition from the investing public and conspired with Enron to "cook its books" through deceptive transactions. . . . Merrill Lynch and others purportedly devised or executed these transactions to hide Enron's fraudulent accounting from rating agencies and investors, as well as issued through its analysts, even as Enron was descending into bankruptcy in late 2001, "buy" or "strong buy" recommendations for Enron securities, which Merrill Lynch knew would be "widely disseminated in the financial news media" and would be "available to Plaintiffs and other investors." . . . The conspiracy "amounted to a giant Ponzi scheme. . . ."[217]

The plaintiffs in *Enron* were the purchasers or holders of Enron and Enron-related securities between 1997 and 2001, the period of the alleged wrongdoing. In addressing the plaintiffs' common law fraud claim, the court noted:

> The complaint . . . asserts that . . . Merrill Lynch intended that the misrepresentations on Enron's balance sheets, which it helped to create, would be targeted at Enron investors with the goal of inducing Plaintiffs and other investors to purchase Enron securities. Merrill Lynch's enthusiastic analyst reports, even up to the filing of Enron's bankruptcy, were also intended to induce investors to purchase. . . .
>
> Plaintiffs claim they relied on Merrill Lynch's representations, especially the persistent "buy" recommendations repeated by financial information services, in deciding to purchase or hold their Enron securities rather than to sell them, as well as on the SEC-filed financial statements which Defendants knew were used by investors to make investment decisions. . . . Moreover, they argue that Merrill Lynch had a duty to disclose where it voluntarily disclosed some information but not the whole truth, where it made a representation and failed to disclose new information that made the earlier representation misleading or untrue, or where it made a partial disclosure and conveyed a false impression. . . . They claim justifiable reliance on the SEC-filed statements and the analyst commentary, reported in general-circulation financial publications, as well as the fact that Defendants helped Enron deceive the ratings agencies upon which Plaintiffs also relied.[218]

Analyzing the fraud claim, Judge Melinda Harmon wrote:

---

[216] 490 F. Supp. 2d 784 (S.D. Tex. 2007).

[217] *Id.* at 787.

[218] *Id.* at 793 n.10.

Texas . . . recognizes a common law fraud cause of action where the false representation was made with the intent of reaching and deceiving a third person and thereby causing that third party injury; privity is not required between the fraudfeasor and the person he is trying to influence. Section 531 of the *Restatement (Second) of Torts* (1977) requires more than probability of reliance and more than an obvious risk that a misrepresentation might be repeated to the third party; the fraudfeasor must "have information that would lead a reasonable man to conclude there is *an especial likelihood* that it will reach those persons *and will influence their conduct.*" . . .

. . . [T]his Court agrees with Merrill Lynch that under Texas law Plaintiffs cannot establish intent to induce reliance based on the argument that Defendants had a reason to expect that Plaintiffs and other investors would review and rely on Enron's financial reports, SEC-filed documents, analyst reports and analyst recommendations simply because these materials are standardly disseminated into the marketplace and available to the investing community. . . .[219]

The court then discussed an earlier decision of the Texas Supreme Court:

The facts in [*Ernst & Young, L.L.P. v. Pacific Mutual Life Ins. Co.*, 51 S.W.3d 573, 575–77 (Tex. 2001)], relevant to this action, are as follows. Interfirst Bank, in 1982, issued a series of notes scheduled to mature in 1989. After Interfirst began having financial troubles, it merged in 1986 with RepublicBank Corporation. Ernst & Young audited RepublicBank's financial statements for the year ending December 31, 1986, confirming RepublicBank's financial stability, and issued an unqualified opinion that the statements in the report fairly represented RepublicBank's financial state; that report and financial statement were incorporated by RepublicBank into its annual report to its shareholders and the Form 10-K filed with the SEC. Moreover, after the merger[,] RepublicBank offered a number of securities and prospectuses that incorporated the 1986 Form 10-K and Form S-3 registrations statements, with Ernst & Young's audit opinion and financial information.

Pacific purchased some of the original Interfirst notes in 1987, one month after the merger. Subsequently RepublicBank filed for bankruptcy and the Interfirst notes lost their value. Pacific sued Ernst & Young and claimed that in deciding to buy the notes, Pacific had relied on the report of the auditor and on documents that incorporated it and that were filed with the SEC. . . . Pacific contended that the audit opinion misrepresented that the audit report complied with GAAP [Generally Accepted Accounting Principles], that the financial statements misrepresented RepublicBank's financial position, and that Ernst & Young had violated GAAS [Generally Accepted Auditing Standards].

Ernst & Young moved for summary judgment, arguing that as a matter of law it did not specifically intend for Pacific to rely on representations in its

---

[219] *Id.* at 794–822.

1986 audit report of RepublicBank when Pacific decided to purchase the Interfirst Notes. The trial court granted the summary judgment. The court of appeals reversed, concluding there were fact issues on each element of Pacific's common-law fraud cause of action, including intent ("reason to expect"), to which it applied the *Restatement (Second) of Torts* § 531 (1977):

> One who makes a fraudulent misrepresentation is subject to liability to the persons or class of persons whom he intends or has reason to expect to act or to refrain from action in reliance upon the misrepresentation for pecuniary loss suffered by them through their justifiable reliance in the type of transaction in which he intends or has reason to expect their conduct to be influenced.

Rest §531

The Texas Supreme Court found that while not employing the "reason to expect" language, Texas courts examining intent to defraud have concluded that "a defendant who acts with knowledge that a result will follow is considered to intend the result," consistent with § 531, which "requires a degree of certainty that goes beyond mere foreseeability.". . . . Nevertheless the high court determined that the appellate court had not properly applied the "reason-to-expect" standard in § 531 and emphasized that comments to § 531 "illustrate the narrow scope of the reason-to-expect standard and foreclose the potential for 'unlimited liability. . . .' " . . . In sum, "[T]he claimant's reliance must be 'especially likely' and justifiable, and the transaction sued upon must be the type the defendant contemplated." . . .

Pacific presented affidavit evidence, based on generalized industry practice or understanding that prospectuses and proxy materials are widely distributed throughout the investment community and that public accounting firms like Ernst & Young expected that investors would rely on them and on SEC-filed documents in evaluating securities for investment. It further argued that § 536 of the *Restatement (Second) of Torts* supported a presumption that Ernst & Young had reason to expect Pacific's reliance on publicly available information, especially documents filed with the SEC pursuant to statutes designed to protect investors:

> If a statute requires information to be . . . filed . . . for the protection of a particular class of persons, one who makes a fraudulent misrepresentation in so doing is subject to liability to the persons for pecuniary loss suffered through their justifiable reliance upon the misrepresentation in a transaction of the kind in which the statute is intended to protect them.

. . . Comment e of the *Restatement* indicated that "the general purpose behind a statute requiring a corporation to publicly report its financial condition is to make the information available to all who consider it important in determining their course of action 'in any type of transaction with the corporation in question.' " . . .

The Texas Supreme Court first concluded that § 536 did not apply to Pacific because it had purchased securities of a different entity (InterFirst) than the one (RepublicBank) for which Ernst & Young had filed the SEC documents. Furthermore it emphatically concluded that § 536's reach does not "extend to open-market purchases of unrelated securities." . . . The high court further noted that unlike § 531, § 536 had no counterpart in Texas common law fraud jurisprudence, that other courts rarely applied it, and that because it "effectively alleviates a claimant's burden to show intent to induce reliance in fraud actions, it should be applied narrowly if at all." . . . The court pointed out that investors had other remedies for securities violations under federal and state securities laws, and stated that it was "reluctant to apply section 536's presumption and subject market participants to liability for fraud damages to an almost limitless class of potential plaintiffs." . . . Thus the Texas Supreme Court did not embrace the argument of a presumption of reliance based on a securities issuer's SEC filed documents nor apply section 536's presumption for policy reasons, specifically because doing so would create "an almost limitless class of potential plaintiffs." . . . [220]

Returning to the facts of the case before it, the *Enron* court wrote:

Therefore to establish fraudulent intent, Plaintiffs must allege and show more than that information was available in the investment community, pursuant to industry custom, and that it was foreseeable that it would reach them; Plaintiffs must show that Plaintiffs' "reliance must be 'especially likely' and justifiable, and that the transaction sued upon must be the type the defendant contemplated." . . . *See also Great Plains Trust Co. v. Morgan Stanley Dean Witter & Co.*, 313 F.3d 305, 323–24 (5th Cir. 2002) (construing and applying *Pacific Mutual*) ("It is therefore insufficient for a plaintiff to allege what is commonly 'known' or 'expected,' because 'even an obvious risk that a third person will rely on a representation is not enough to impose liability' "). . . . Plaintiffs have failed to do so here.[221]

Nevertheless, the court allowed the *Enron* plaintiffs to supplement their complaint to attempt to cure its deficiencies.

PROBLEM 2-6: THE RENOVATED MANSION

Bob and Carol East bought and renovated an old Mediterranean mansion in a recently designated city historic district. They called the house "Fernwood" because it was set on a shady lot with many ferns and trees. Through "sweat equity" and substantial capital investment, the Easts not only saved Fernwood, but did such an excellent job that the house was featured on the cover of the brochure for the historic district's first annual Autumn Home Tour. The event was intended to raise funds for the historic district's neighborhood association and to increase public consciousness about the importance of historic preservation.

In conjunction with the home tour, an article appeared in *The Tribune*, a local newspaper. Fernwood was featured in the article and Bob and Carol were

---

[220] 490 F. Supp. 2d at 823–24.

[221] *Id.* at 824–25.

extensively quoted. According to the article, Carol said, "We fell in love with the house at first sight and knew we could save it from demolition. It took four long years to restore the house. It was not until the end of the renovation process that we learned that the house was actually designed by Atlee Wright, the famous architect. That was a wonderful surprise."

Actually, Carol was not sure about whether Wright designed the house. She thought that must be true because Fernwood's floor plan and style were very similar to another mansion in a different city historic district which Wright had in fact designed and built. However, Carol had no documentation for her claim that Wright had designed her home. Of course, the claim made the article more interesting because Wright was an architect of national reputation and the most famous builder in the history of the city.

Six months after the home tour, Bob and Carol sold Fernwood to Charles Friar. Friar "flipped" the house four months later in a heated real estate market, selling Fernwood to Emile Segovia, an eager buyer. Segovia told Friar that he had gone through Fernwood on the home tour and had read the article in *The Tribune*. The Easts never met Segovia but they knew he was going to buy the house from Friar before the sale closed, because they had remained friends with Friar.

Soon after moving into Fernwood, Segovia learned through research in the archives at the local library that the house was designed by an architect of no particular acclaim, rather than by Wright. That meant that the house was worth a lot less than it would have been worth if Wright had been the architect, and even less than he had paid for it.

Segovia has consulted you about whether he can successfully sue the Easts, *The Tribune*, or Friar for fraud. Please prepare a detailed analysis.

4.   Justifiable Reliance

Decisions routinely state that "justifiable reliance" is an essential element of an action for fraud, and many plaintiffs are denied recovery due to failure to prove justifiable reliance. In understanding this element of tort liability, it is useful to separate two related issues: actual reliance (cause in fact) and fault on the part of the plaintiff (which, depending on the regime[222] means contributory negligence,[223] comparative negligence,[224] or comparative fault[225]). These issues are explored below.

---

[222] Contributory negligence, comparative negligence, and comparative fault are explored in detail in first-year law school courses on Torts. Four states (Alabama, Maryland, North Carolina, and Virginia) and the District of Columbia continue to adhere to the common law rule of contributory negligence. The remaining 46 states have adopted comparative negligence or comparative fault.

[223] Under contributory negligence, any carelessness on the part of the plaintiff is a total defense to an action for negligence. Classic contributory negligence is not a defense to an intentional tort, strict liability, or, in some states, recklessness.

[224] In states with comparative negligence, negligence on the part of the plaintiff is compared to negligence on the part of the defendant. If the state has "pure" comparative negligence, the plaintiff's recovery is diminished in proportion to the plaintiff's share of the negligence. If the state has "modified" comparative negligence, a plaintiff less negligent than the defendant is allowed reduced recovery, and a plaintiff more negligent than the defendant is barred from receiving compensation. If the plaintiff and

a.   Actual Reliance (Cause in Fact)

Factual causation is an essential element in every tort action. This normally means that the plaintiff must show that "but for" the defendant's tortious conduct, harm would not have occurred. In a suit for fraud, the plaintiff must demonstrate that, had the misrepresentation not been made, damages would not have been suffered. This inevitably requires the plaintiff to prove that the plaintiff relied on the misrepresentation.

To put the point somewhat differently, a cause of action for fraud protects the plaintiff's decision-making process from being distorted by false, misleading, or incomplete information. No serious harm is caused by a misrepresentation unless the plaintiff relies.

The reliance element of a fraud action sometimes limits the tort's usefulness as a vehicle for suing sellers of products to protect consumers from harm. For example, in *Buckland v. Threshold Enterprises, Ltd.*,[226] the California Court of Appeal wrote:

> Buckland concedes she suspected respondents' packaging and marketing was false or misleading, and she bought respondents' products solely to pursue litigation upon the vindication of her suspicions. She therefore lacked the requisite confidence in the truth and material completeness of their representations, and cannot establish actual reliance for the purpose of her fraud claims.[227]

Representation Must Reach the Plaintiff. Among other things, the reliance requirement means that the plaintiff must prove that the defendant's allegedly fraudulent statements reached the plaintiff. *Serchion v. Capstone Partners, Inc.*[228] was a real estate dispute where the seller sued to cancel an allegedly fraudulent deed. The Georgia Court of Appeals affirmed summary judgment for the defendant buyer. After reviewing the five elements of an action for fraud, the court wrote:

> Serchion [the plaintiff seller] testified in his deposition that he had never spoken with or had any communications from any representatives of either of the defendants prior to or at the closing of the transaction; rather, his

---

defendant are equally negligent, whether the plaintiff is allowed reduced recovery in a "modified" state depends upon the language of the controlling statute or court decision. If a plaintiff is responsible for 55% of the negligence which caused the plaintiff's harm, the plaintiff can recover 45% of the plaintiff's losses in a pure comparative negligence state and nothing in a modified comparative negligence state. Recklessness is like negligence in the sense that it involves lack of care (however, the deficiency is extreme rather than ordinary). Mindful of this fact, states with comparative negligence regimes generally allow negligence on the part of the plaintiff to be a defense to an action based on recklessness. However, comparative negligence is not a defense to an intentional tort.

[225] In the many states that have adopted comparative fault, "fault" on the part of the plaintiff is offset against "fault" on the part of the defendant on a "pure" or "modified" basis. The analysis is the same as with comparative negligence, except that "fault" is normally defined to include not only negligence and recklessness, but conduct giving rise to strict liability and post-accident failure to mitigate damages, although not intentionally tortious conduct.

[226] 155 Cal. App. 4th 798 (2007).

[227] *Id.* at 550.

[228] 679 S.E.2d 40 (Ga. Ct. App. 2009).

exclusive source of information on the deal was his own real estate agent. He did not overhear or observe any communications between his real estate agent and any agents of the defendants. Because he presented no affidavits or other testimony from his own agent (or from others) as to what communications or representations his agent may have received from agents of the defendants, he presented no admissible evidence as to what those communications or representations were.[229]

Reliance on Nondisclosed Facts. In cases based on failure to disclose material information, a question arises as to how the plaintiff establishes justifiable reliance. According to the California Court of Appeal, "actual reliance for the purpose of fraud by omission occurs only when the plaintiff reposes confidence in the material completeness of the defendant's representations, and acts upon this confidence."[230] "The plaintiff must establish that 'had the omitted information been disclosed, he or she would have been aware of it and behaved differently.' "[231]

Evaluating the Plaintiff's Claims of Reliance. Presumably, in every fraud action, the plaintiff will testify that he or she relied upon the defendant's misrepresentation. However, in evaluating that self-serving declaration, the jury may take other facts into account.

If the evidence demonstrates that the plaintiff knew the defendant's statement was false,[232] or was aware of the existence of the allegedly undisclosed fact, it will be impossible for the plaintiff to persuade the jury that the plaintiff was in fact misled. For example, in *Miller v. Kennedy & Minshew, P.C.*,[233] the client had discovered the information that was allegedly withheld by his attorney, yet continued the representation. The Texas Court of Appeals found that on those facts the law firm had committed no actionable deception that would prevent it from collecting its fee.

Reliance on Persons with Expertise. Similarly, it may be hard to establish reliance on a misrepresentation in cases where the plaintiff has a sophisticated understanding about the matters in question (perhaps even a better understanding than the defendant) or has access to expert advice that could readily establish that the defendant's statement is undependable. Thus, in *Coastal Bank SSB v. Chase Bank, N.A.*,[234] a dispute involving communications between banks, the Texas Court of Appeals noted:

> This was an arm's length transaction between two sophisticated financial institutions who were both represented by counsel. While such a relationship is not, standing alone, dispositive of the issue of reliance, it is a factor to be considered.[235]

---

[229] *Id.* at *8.

[230] *Buckland v. Threshold Enterprises, Ltd.*, 155 Cal. App. 4th 798, 808–809 (2007).

[231] 155 Cal. App. 4th 798 at 807 (citing *Mirkin v. Wasserman*, 858 P.2d 568 (Cal. 1993)).

[232] *See Richter v. Wagner Oil Co.*, 90 S.W.3d 890, 896 (Tex. App. 2002).

[233] 142 S.W.3d 325, 343–44 (Tex. App. 2003).

[234] 135 S.W.3d 840 (Tex. App. 2004).

[235] *Id.* at 842–43.

Relatedly, in *Williams Ford, Inc. v. Hartford Courant Co.*,[236] the Supreme Court of Connecticut held that reliance is not assumed in communications between sophisticated commercial parties, but is a question of fact.

Reliance After Inspection. Reliance is also difficult to prove if the plaintiff has made an exhaustive investigation of the facts.[237] Of course, in these kinds of cases, the significance of the plaintiff's inspection turns upon what an inspection would likely have revealed. The mere fact that the plaintiff has made an investigation does not mean that claims of reliance must be rejected as a matter of law. If the investigation failed to disclose the falsity of the defendant's representations, the plaintiff may still be able to persuade the jury that the representations were relied upon.[238]

Red Flags and Actual Reliance. If there are danger signals that would have placed a reasonable person on notice that the defendant's representations were unreliable, it will be difficult for the plaintiff to prove actual reliance. For example, in *In re AHT Corporation*,[239] a business represented by both general and outside counsel could not establish that it relied on another company's representations that all of its shareholders supported a merger. The plaintiff knew that the other company's co-founder and 21% shareholder was leaving corporate management due to a disagreement over the direction that the company was taking and had not participated in the negotiations. The plaintiff was also aware that the co-founder's status as a board member was unclear.

b. Reasonableness of Reliance (Comparative Negligence)

It is easy to see how the question of actual reliance shades into the question of whether reliance was justifiable or, as some say, reasonable. If the plaintiff's alleged reliance was unreasonable, it is more likely that reliance in fact did not occur. Unfortunately, as the law of fraud developed in thousands of decisions over hundreds of years, courts were often not careful to separate the question of actual reliance from the issue of what consequences should flow from unreasonable conduct on the part of the plaintiff.

Reasonable Versus Justifiable. In thinking about these matters, the first thing to note is that "justifiable reliance" is not necessarily "reasonable reliance." A gullible customer of low intelligence may justifiably rely on a store manager's deceptive statements, even though the customer has not acted as a reasonable prudent person would have acted under similar circumstances. Courts have allowed recovery in these kinds of cases despite the absence of reasonable reliance.

Courts are sometimes reluctant to allow a fraudfeasor to escape liability on the ground that the plaintiff's reliance was unreasonable. For example, in *Behr v.*

---

[236] 657 A.2d 212, 222 (Conn. 1995).

[237] *See* RESTATEMENT (SECOND) OF TORTS § 547 (1977).

[238] *See Shahram v. Re/Max P.V. Realty*, 2009 Cal. App. Unpub. LEXIS 2781, at *13 (Apr. 8, 2009).

[239] 2005 U.S. App. LEXIS 1813 (2d Cir. 2005).

Redmond,[240] the defendant was found to have fraudulently concealed from his girlfriend the risk of contracting herpes by implying that it was okay to have sex if he was not experiencing an active outbreak. The defendant argued that his girlfriend's reliance on his statements was "unreasonable." Rejecting that argument, the California Court of Appeal concluded that "[i]n light of the relationship of intimacy and trust between the parties, . . . [the defendant's] long experience with the disease, and his apparent knowledge about its contagiousness, the jury could reasonably conclude that Behr justifiably relied on Redmond's assurance that it was okay to have sex with him."[241]

Some decisions say that what is required in a fraud action is "reasonable reliance."[242] For example, in *MacDonald v. Thomas M. Cooley Law School*,[243] the United States Court of Appeals rejected a fraud claim by recent graduates related to a law school's alleged misrepresentation of the employment statistics pertaining to earlier classes. As the court explained:

> . . . [T]he graduates [cannot] establish a claim for fraudulent misrepresentation based on the statistic for "average starting salary for all graduates" because their reliance on it was unreasonable. . . .

> Here, the statement "average starting salary for all graduates" expressly contradicted other statements in the very same report showing that the report itself was based not on data for the entire class, but on data from those who completed the surveys. The Cooley graduates' reliance on the statement that the "[a]verage starting salary for all graduates" was "$54,796" was unreasonable in light of both the statement that the "[n]umber of graduates with employment status known" was less than the total number of graduates and the very title of the report (a "Salary Survey").[244]

Two Kinds of Culpability. Second, it is important to remember that an action for fraud is not inevitably based on intentional misconduct. In most states, *scienter* may be established based on knowledge of falsity (intent) or by reckless disregard for the truth (recklessness). Thus, there are really two questions about whether the plaintiff's conduct is an affirmative defense to liability. The first is whether unreasonable conduct is a defense to fraud in a case involving intentional misrepresentation and the second is whether the same conduct is a defense to fraud based on reckless misrepresentation.

Negligence as a Defense to Intentionally False Deception. Even in the many states that have enacted comparative fault regimes, negligence on the part of the plaintiff does not reduce or preclude recovery in an action based on intentional wrongdoing. Thus, it is fair to conclude that courts *should* hold that if the plaintiff

---

[240] 193 Cal. App. 4th 517 (2011).

[241] *Id.* at 106–07.

[242] *See, e.g., Short v. Haywood Printing Co., Inc.*, 667 N.E.2d 209, 213 (Ind. Ct. App. 1996) ("the plaintiff cannot recover for fraud unless he reasonably relied").

[243] 724 F.3d 654 (6th Cir. 2013).

[244] *Id.* at 664–65.

proves that the defendant acted with knowledge of the misstatement's falsity, it should be irrelevant that the plaintiff acted unreasonably in relying on the misstatement, provided that reliance in fact occurred. From a practical standpoint, this makes sense. A defendant who deliberately victimizes a person by uttering a deliberate lie should not be able to escape liability by arguing that the victim was careless in being deceived. Various decisions have reached this result. For example, in *Tratchel v. Essex Group, Inc.*,[245] the manufacturer of a gas control unit fraudulently concealed a product defect, which led to an explosion when the purchaser tried to light a furnace. Noting that the jury had been instructed that fraud required knowledge that the representation was false and intent to deceive, the Iowa Supreme Court held that the trial court properly declined to allow the assertion of a comparative fault defense to the fraud claim.[246]

Negligence as a Defense to Recklessly False Deception. In contrast, it may logically be urged in comparative fault states (and in comparative negligence states where negligence is a defense to recklessness) that the unreasonableness of the plaintiff's reliance *should* be an affirmative defense to a fraud action based on reckless disregard for the truth. However, if the plaintiff in fact relied on the defendant's misstatement, the unreasonableness of the plaintiff's conduct should not be treated as a total bar to liability under the rubric of lack of "justifiable reliance." Rather, if *scienter* is based on recklessness, the unreasonableness of the plaintiff's conduct *should* be treated as comparative fault or comparative negligence. That would normally mean that the plaintiff's unreasonableness would be only a partial bar to recovery. This proposed course of action is nothing more than a straight-forward application of established principles. In most states, a lack of ordinary care (negligence) is normally a partial defense to an extreme lack of care (recklessness). Some scholars would go even further and hold that comparative fault should be a defense to any fraud action.[247] Occasional decisions appear to endorse that position. Thus, in *In re Wallace's Bookstores, Inc.*,[248] a bankruptcy court in Kentucky held that a defrauded creditor's claim could be reduced by a partial defense of comparative fault.

Confusing Reliance with Affirmative Defenses. Unfortunately, courts have not yet reached the point of dependably differentiating actual reliance (cause in fact) from unreasonable reliance (contributory negligence, comparative negligence, or comparative fault). While some courts make such distinctions, others do not. Thus, one must expect that for years to come it will be possible to defeat an action for fraud in some courts by proving that the plaintiff's reliance was unreasonable. For

---

[245] 452 N.W.2d 171 (Iowa 1990).

[246] *Id.* at 180–81.

[247] *See* Andrew R. Klein, *Comparative Fault and Fraud*, 48 Ariz. L. Rev. 983, 985 (2006) (arguing "that comparative fault jurisdictions should not bar plaintiffs from recovering in fraud when they fail to establish justifiable reliance on a misrepresentation," even if fraud is intentionally perpetrated). *See also Loughridge v. Goodyear Tire and Rubber Co.*, 207 F. Supp. 2d 1187 (D. Colo. 2002) (holding that, under applicable state statutory provisions, comparative fault is a defense to fraud in the context of products liability).

[248] 317 B.R. 709 (Bankr. E.D. Ky. 2004).

example, in *Arp v. United Community Bank*,[249] the Georgia Court of Appeals held that the plaintiff could not rely on a bank's allegedly fraudulent statements that it had obtained an insurance policy on the plaintiff's wife's life because the plaintiff could have reviewed the documents that would have demonstrated that there was no such insurance. The court appears to have conflated the two very different issues of actual reliance and fault on the part of the plaintiff.

c.   Duty to Investigate

Against this backdrop of imprecision relating to the issues of actual reliance and unreasonable reliance, certain rules have developed dealing with whether there is a duty on the plaintiff to investigate the facts. Two particular rules relate to whether there is an obligation to question or verify an affirmative statement and what action is required when there are danger signals.

(1)   Questioning Affirmative Statements

As a general rule, if the defendant makes an affirmative representation, the plaintiff may rely upon its truth and need not investigate, so long as the statement is not obviously false and there are no danger signals calling for inquiry. For example, in an early case which is still good law, *Judd v. Walker*,[250] the Missouri Supreme Court held that the plaintiff could rely upon the defendant's definite statement as to the acreage of land and was not required to measure the property himself. The court noted that one need not deal "with [one's] fellow man as if he was a thief or a robber."[251] The same principle still applies. As the Connecticut Superior Court recently explained, "the victim of a misrepresentation has no duty to investigate the truthfulness of the deceit. . . ."[252]

No Duty to Investigate Affirmative Representations. A lawyer or doctor who lies to a client or patient about the professional's credentials or experience will not be permitted to argue that a client or patient should not have trusted those representations. These sentiments are consistent with the view of the American Law Institute. According to the *Restatement (Second) of Torts*, the rule that there is no duty to question affirmative statements applies "not only when an investigation would involve an expenditure of effort and money out of proportion to the magnitude of the transaction, but also when it could be made without any considerable trouble or expense."[253]

(a)   Reliance by Sophisticated Persons

Many courts hold that the rule that a person may rely upon express assurances applies to sophisticated entities, as well as to those less able to protect their own

---

[249] 612 S.E.2d 534 (Ga. Ct. App. 2005).

[250] 114 S.W. 979 (Mo. 1908).

[251] *Id.* at 981.

[252] *Chapman Lumber, Inc. v. Tager*, 2003 Conn. Super. LEXIS 2350, at *11 (Aug. 21, 2003).

[253] Restatement (Second) of Torts § 540 cmt. a (1977).

interests.[254] For example, in *Fire Insurance Exchange v. Bell*,[255] the Indiana Supreme Court held that an attorney was allowed to rely upon opposing counsel's representations during settlement negotiations about the amount of insurance coverage that was available. However, other courts are to the contrary. For example, in *Lazard Freres & Co. v. Protective Life Ins. Co.*,[256] Judge Guido Calabresi, explaining the facts of the case, wrote for the Second Circuit:

> According to Protective[,] . . . Lazard set the whole deal up in such a way that Protective had to rely on Lazard's representations and had to commit itself to purchase the MCC bank debt before it had the opportunity to examine the Scheme Report. It would therefore appear that Protective might have been justified in relying on Lazard's alleged misrepresentations when it orally committed itself to purchase the MCC bank debt. . . .

> This conclusion, nevertheless, seems to us to be too simple. As a substantial and sophisticated player in the bank debt market, Protective was under a further duty to protect itself from misrepresentation. It could easily have done so by insisting on an examination of the Scheme Report as a condition of closing. . . .

> [W]here . . . a party has been put on notice of the existence of material facts which have not been documented and he nevertheless proceeds with a transaction without securing the available documentation or inserting appropriate language in the agreement for his protection, he may truly be said to have willingly assumed the business risk that the facts may not be as represented. Succinctly put, a party will not be heard to complain that he has been defrauded when it is his own evident lack of due care which is responsible for his predicament.

> . . . .We believe that the failure to insert such language into the contract — by itself — renders reliance on the misrepresentation unreasonable as a matter of law.[257]

Truth Not Discoverable by Due Diligence. Of course, even if the plaintiff is a sophisticated party, the fact that the plaintiff could have conducted an investigation will not bar a claim for fraud if the nature of the fraud is such that the truth was peculiarly within the knowledge of the defendants and could not have been discovered by due diligence. For example, in *Bank of America Corp. v. Lemgruber*,[258] a federal district court in New York found that a cause of action was stated where the plaintiff alleged that sham transactions and fictitious assets were used to conceal the falsity of the defendant's statements.

---

[254] *See Vmark Software, Inc. v. EMC Corp.*, 642 N.E.2d 587, 595 n.11 (Mass. Ct. App. 1994) (computer software licensor and licensee). *See also Williams Ford, Inc. v. Hartford Courant Co.*, 657 A.2d 212 (Conn. 1995) (holding that a claim for negligent misrepresentation can exist between two sophisticated commercial parties with full access to information concerning a business transaction).

[255] 643 N.E.2d 310 (Ind. 1994).

[256] 108 F.3d 1531 (2d Cir. 1997).

[257] *Id.* at 1543.

[258] 385 F. Supp. 2d 200, 231 (S.D.N.Y. 2005).

PROBLEM 2-7: THE "ABSOLUTELY BEAUTIFUL" JAGUAR

Lisa Raber advertised her 2004 Jaguar XKR convertible for sale on eBay. The advertisement described the car as "absolutely beautiful," with three minor blemishes in the form of a missing remote control to unlock the doors, an erratic CD changer, and a missing cover for the extra tire. The ad said that the car was being sold "as is" and that the seller's disclosures were made "to the best of my knowledge." Andrea Sajo, who lived on the east coast, purchased the Jaguar on eBay for $17,000, and it was delivered to her from Oregon.

Soon after the car arrived, Sajo began experiencing difficulties with the Jaguar. An inspection of the car revealed that the car had been damaged in a major accident sometime earlier and had been repaired and repainted. Also, the car still needed extensive electrical repairs and a new catalytic converter costing a total of roughly $8,500. When Sajo demanded a return of her money, Raber refused. Sajo then sued for fraud. Please analyze whether the claim should succeed or fail.

(2)   Danger Signals

If there are "danger signals" that would cause a reasonable person to inquire, and the plaintiff fails to do so, the plaintiff may be precluded from claiming that the defendant misrepresented the facts. For example, if there are water marks on the living room ceiling in a house for sale, and the buyer knowingly fails to investigate, it may be impossible for the buyer to successfully complain that the seller failed to disclose the defective condition of the roof. Of course, if an inquiry is made and the seller repeatedly assures the buyer that the marks antedated successful repairs to the roof, an action for fraud may lie. This would be true, for example, if the seller knows that the statements are false or lacks confidence in their truth, since the plaintiff has no easy way of discovering the actual state of affairs.[259]

In *Greycas, Inc. v. Proud*,[260] the defendant required a loan applicant to supply an attorney's opinion letter containing assurances that there were no prior liens on the equipment that was to serve as security. The court held that the defendant finance company could rely upon the attorney's assurances, even though it would not have been hard for it to conduct its own UCC lien search. If, however, the opinion letter had disclosed that the attorney was the loan applicant's brother-in-law (which he was), the analysis could be different. As Judge Richard Posner explained for the Seventh Circuit, that "might have been a warning signal that [the finance company] could ignore only at its peril"; "[t]o go forward in the face of a known danger is to assume the risk."[261]

Schlaifer Nance & Co. v. Estate of Warhol,[262] contains expansive language about a sophisticated entity's duty to investigate, but is best viewed simply as a "danger signal" case. In *Estate of Warhol*, the plaintiff (SNC) alleged that the estate of the

---

[259] *See Sippy v. Cristich*, 609 P.2d 204 (Kan. Ct. App. 1980).

[260] 826 F.2d 1560 (7th Cir. 1987).

[261] *Id.* at 1566 (affirming a liability for negligent misrepresentation because there was no danger signal).

[262] 119 F.3d 91 (2d Cir. 1997).

artist Andy Warhol had represented that it controlled the rights to Warhol's works, and that SNC relied on those representations in entering into a licensing agreement. In fact, many of Warhol's works were in the public domain and the artist himself had transferred some rights to particular persons. Addressing these facts, the court wrote:

> Circumstances may be so suspicious as to suggest to a reasonably prudent plaintiff that the defendants' representations may be false, and that the plaintiff cannot reasonably rely on those representations, but rather must "make additional inquiry to determine their accuracy." . . . Put another way, if the plaintiff "has the means of knowing, by the exercise of ordinary intelligence, the truth, or the real quality of the subject of the representation, he must make use of those means, or he will not be heard to complain that he was induced to enter into the transaction by misrepresentations."
> . . .

> The parties involved in this litigation are not widows or orphans. "Where sophisticated businessmen engaged in major transactions enjoy access to critical information but fail to take advantage of that access, New York courts are particularly disinclined to entertain claims of justifiable reliance." . . .

> . . . [W]e will accept SNC's assertion that the Estate failed to reveal copyright problems in order to deceive SNC. Nevertheless, it was unreasonable for SNC, a sophisticated licensing concern, to rely on these misrepresentations or material omissions. The Estate's actions, the Agreement, and other circumstances should have raised more than one eyebrow, compelling SNC's officers or employees to investigate the extent of the Estate's control over Warhol's works.

> Throughout the trial, SNC maintained that it did not know that many of Warhol's works lacked copyright protection. The testimony and documentary evidence, however, paint a different tableau.

> In December 1985, well before Warhol died, Hughes informed SNC that the artist "owns copyrights on most of his images," but not all. Indeed, when SNC negotiated an agreement with Warhol in 1986, the draft provided that the final agreement would contain a list of Warhol's artworks to which he did not own the copyright. From the outset, SNC had notice that Warhol did not control all the rights to his known works of art.

> These red flags continued to fly after Warhol's death. For example, Ricarda Heising, one of SNC's attorneys, admitted in her deposition that, when she was drafting the Agreement between the Estate and SNC in 1987, she "expected" that Warhol did not own the copyrights to all of his art because of the "sheer magnitude of . . . the body of his works." The implication was that Warhol was so prolific, it would have been difficult to imagine that all of his works remained out of the public domain. She also testified that it would have been unlikely that Warhol owned the copyrights to many of his works because he spent a significant portion of his career as a commercial artist. As a commercial artist, Heising explained, Warhol often sold to his

clients the rights to a commissioned work, thereby surrendering the copyright. And it is well established that commercial artists' work is often made for hire, the rights to which rest in the employer or other person for whom the work is prepared. . . .

. . . . Not only the SNC lawyers, but the Schlaifers themselves, were aware of the copyright problems. During a telephone call with counsel on October 16, 1987, Susanne Nance Schlaifer jotted a note that there were "potentially lots of problems if [Andy Warhol] didn't © or at least put © notice on works." Despite her concerns, neither she nor any employee of SNC asked to see the Estate's files regarding Warhol's artworks.

Her husband, Roger Schlaifer, acknowledged at trial that he had testified in another lawsuit. . . . In that testimony, he explained that before he signed the Agreement, he read Exhibit D of the Agreement and "noticed that a number [of the artworks] were not copyrighted." Even a cursory review of Exhibit D illustrates that while many of Warhol's works bore copyright notices such as "© Andy Warhol" and "© Andy Warhol Enterprises, Inc.," other works had copyright notices showing ownership by others, and many contained no copyright notices at all.

. . . [In addition, the] Agreement itself provided notice of copyright problems. . . .

The Agreement set forth rather broad assurances that the Estate held the rights to all of Warhol's "Existing Artworks," and defined that term to mean all works known to exist when the Agreement was signed. The Estate did not guarantee control over all artworks, but simply those known to "[e]xist" at the inception of the Agreement. Hence, the Agreement makes clear that there was a spectrum of artworks about which the Estate and SNC had no information — artworks that could easily lack copyright protection.

. . . .

The testimony of SNC lawyers, the documentary evidence, the Agreement, and the notes of the attorneys negotiating the Agreement raise numerous questions regarding the ownership of Warhol copyrights. All these questions, as a matter of law, illustrate that it was unreasonable for SNC to rely on the Estate's representations that it owned all rights to every Warhol work. . . .[263]

Similarly, in *Doe v. Dilling*,[264] the Illinois Supreme Court held that a woman could not prove that she justifiably relied on statements by her fiancé's parents which denied that he was HIV-positive. The court based its analysis in part on the danger-signal rule. The court wrote:

Doe was a college-educated woman who . . . ran her own business. . . . Doe testified that she was "very aware" of sexually transmitted diseases (STDs) and that HIV was such a disease. . . . After meeting Albert through a

---

[263] *Id.* at 98–101.

[264] 888 N.E.2d 24 (Ill. 2008).

personal ad and beginning a steady dating relationship, Doe initiated a conversation with Albert about STDs, expressed her concerns about remaining free of STDs, asked him if he had anything to tell her in this regard, and believed what he told her. However, when she first saw Albert naked, she noticed what she acknowledged was "unusual" pigmentation on his genitalia. She asked him about it, and believed his explanation, despite the fact that, as Dr. Cornfield testified, such warts are generally known to be spread through sexual contact and considered a form of STD. This fact should have placed Doe on notice at that point in time that something could be amiss with respect to Albert's sexual health and that she ran a risk of potentially contracting an STD by engaging in sexual conduct with him.[265]

(3)   Assumption of the Risk

As some of the cases in the prior section suggest, courts sometimes allude to the idea of assumption of the risk in concluding that the plaintiff is unable to establish justifiable reliance. Other cases, without using the term, seem to embrace the concept of assumption of the risk. *Lehman v. Keller*[266] was a suit where the buyers of a house had signed a purchase and sale agreement which stated that they had "ten days from the date of signing to submit an inspection report and an amendment setting forth defects in the property" and that if "the buyers fail to do so, then they accept the property 'as is . . . with all faults including but not limited to . . . damage from termites and other wood destroying organisms.' "[267] Despite the fact that the seller's property disclosure statement had revealed knowledge of prior termite damage under the house that had allegedly been repaired, the buyers did not conduct an inspection prior to closing. The Georgia Court of Appeals held that the buyer's fraud claim for concealed termite damage was barred as a matter of law because they did not exercise due diligence.

If assumption of the risk in the fraud context means simply that there was no reliance, the concept plays an unobjectionable (and relatively clear) role in this field of law. Assumption of the risk merely negates an essential element of the plaintiff's *prima facie* case and creates a total obstacle to liability. However, assumption of the risk should ordinarily not be thought of as an affirmative defense to fraud. Today, in a wide range of circumstances, assumption of the risk implied from the plaintiff's conduct is only a partial defense under comparative negligence and comparative fault principles.[268] This is probably not what courts mean when they say that a plaintiff suing for fraud assumed the risk.

(4)   Statute of Limitations

Whether the plaintiff was obliged to investigate the facts bears not only on whether the plaintiff justifiably relied upon a misrepresentation, but sometimes on the running of the statute of limitations. For example, the New York statute of

---

[265] *Id.* at 40.

[266] 677 S.E.2d 415 (Ga. Ct. App. 2009).

[267] *Id.* at *2–*3.

[268] *See, e.g., Coleman v. Ramada Hotel Operating Co.*, 933 F.2d 470 (7th Cir. 1991).

limitations for common law fraud is "the greater of six years from the date the cause of action accrued or two years from the time the plaintiff or the person under whom the plaintiff claims discovered the fraud, or could with reasonable diligence have discovered it."[269] Thus, an assessment of the timeliness of an action often depends on when the plaintiff had actual notice or "inquiry notice" of the fraud. In *Cohen v. S.A.C. Trading Corp.*,[270] the United States Court of Appeals for the Second Circuit found that a fraud claim arising from misrepresentations about a settlement that were made roughly two decades earlier was not necessarily time-barred:

> The facts in the present record do not support a conclusion that reasonable diligence would have uncovered Steven's lawsuit against Lurie, as the information available to Patricia in 1991 did not suggest in any way that Steven had sued Lurie, much less that he received a concealed payment in settlement of the suit. . . .
>
> Nor did the fact that Patricia had and expressed suspicions in 1991 that Steven was lying in telling her that the Lurie Investment was worthless put her on inquiry notice of the concealed fact that he had sued Lurie and received a $5.5 million settlement payment. . . . So far as the record revealed, Patricia's suspicions that Steven had concealed payments due him and that the Lurie Investment was more valuable than Steven claimed were based on nothing but intuition or wishful thinking. The record includes no fact known to Patricia in 1991 that gave rise to any duty to investigate the Lurie matter. The fact that she distrusted her former husband and thought he might be lying is not an objective fact that supports a duty to investigate.[271]

Works of Art. Claims for fraud related to works of art often raise the issue of whether the action has been timely filed and the related question of whether the plaintiff should have discovered the fraud earlier. In *De Sole v. Knoedler Gallery, LLC*,[272] a federal court in New York found that an action for fraud related to a "Rothko" painting was timely under the New York statute of limitations quoted above:

> [W]hile it is true that the De Soles could have arranged for a forensic examination at the time of purchase, they had "no reason to suspect the authenticity of their painting" at that time. . . . The De Soles purchased the purported Rothko from Knoedler — at that time, the oldest and most venerable art gallery in New York City. . . . Freedman, Knoedler's president, "unequivocally, repeatedly, and consistently" represented to the De Soles that the work was an authentic Rothko. . . . Knoedler also represented that the anonymous seller was Knoedler's client, that he and his father were personally known to Knoedler, and that the father had obtained the work directly from Rothko, on the advice of David Herbert.

---

[269] N.Y. C.P.L.R. § 213(8) (LEXIS 2014).

[270] 711 F.3d 353 (2d Cir. 2013).

[271] *Id.* at 363.

[272] 2013 U.S. Dist. LEXIS 142111 (Sept. 30, 2013).

. . . Moreover, Freedman told the De Soles that Mark Rothko's son, Christopher Rothko, and other Rothko experts, including the individual responsible for the Rothko catalogue raisonné, had examined the work and had attested to its authenticity. . . . Freedman also told the De Soles that the purported work would be included in a forthcoming supplement to the Rothko catalogue raisonné, then being prepared by the National Gallery of Art. . . .

In addition to these oral representations, Defendants provided written assurances concerning the origin and authenticity of the work prior to the purchase. . . .

In sum, the fact that forensic testing was available to the De Soles at the time of purchase does not trigger the running of the two-year discovery period, because the De Soles "had no reason to suspect the authenticity of their painting [at the time of purchase]."[273]

d.   Written Disclaimers of Reliance

Business documents, such as agreements of sale, sometimes contain contractual disclaimers of reliance. The question is whether these provisions mean what they say.

In *IKON Office Solutions, Inc. v. Eifert*,[274] the Texas Court of Appeals addressed this issue.

[A] party's specific disclaimer of reliance on extra contractual representations may, under certain circumstances, preclude a fraudulent inducement claim. *See, e.g., Schlumberger Tech. Corp. v. Swanson*, 959 S.W.2d 171, 180–81 (Tex. 1997). In *Schlumberger*, the supreme court held "that a release that clearly expresses the parties' intent to waive fraudulent inducement claims, or one that disclaims reliance on representations about specific matters in dispute, can preclude a claim of fraudulent inducement." . . . The *Schlumberger* court emphasized "that a disclaimer of reliance or merger clause will not always bar a fraudulent inducement claim." . . . [T]he court explained:

The contract and the circumstances surrounding its formation determine whether the disclaimer of reliance is binding. . . . Because the parties were attempting to put an end to their deal, and had become embroiled in a dispute over the feasibility and value of the project, we conclude that the disclaimer of reliance the Swansons gave conclusively negates the element of reliance.

. . . The surrounding circumstances noted by the supreme court included the following: the parties (1) were attempting to end their relationship, (2) were "embroiled in a dispute," (3) were dealing at arm's length, (4) were represented by highly competent and able legal counsel during the

[273] *Id.* at *38–*40.
[274] 125 S.W.3d 113, 124 (Tex. App. 2003).

negotiations over the terms of the release itself, (5) were knowledgeable and sophisticated business players, and (6) the terms of the release "in clear language . . . unequivocally disclaimed reliance" on the specific representations of the value of the project, which representations were the basis for the Swansons' lawsuit. . . .

With these principles in mind, we turn now to the contract and the alleged misrepresentations in the present case. . . .

The Agreements in the present case contain merger clauses.[275] The Acquisition Agreement includes a statement that it "constitutes the entire agreement concerning the subject matter hereof. No modification or waiver hereof shall be binding upon any party unless in writing and signed by or on behalf of the party against which the modification or waiver is asserted." The Employment Agreement is referenced in, and attached to, the Acquisition Agreement. The Employment Agreement, to which Eifert's job description was attached, contains clauses stating it contains the entire agreement between the parties; supersedes prior employee and compensation agreements; and can be changed, modified or extended only in writing. It also contains a provision stating, "[N]o commitments have been made relative to bonuses, guarantees or any other special provisions, except as specifically identified herein."

Eifert's job description was the subject of lengthy and intense dispute and negotiation, with Eifert being given the opportunity to review and revise the description on at least two occasions. Eifert was assisted by an attorney and an accountant. Almost all of the *Schlumberger* factors are present: Eifert's sophistication (he had bought out four other dealerships); advice from an attorney and an accountant; a contract attempting to put an end to the dispute at issue (*i.e.*, the scope of Eifert's responsibilities); an arm's length transaction; and a lawsuit based on the very terms that were in dispute. . . . *Cf. Fletcher v. Edwards*, [26 S.W.3d 66, 76–77 (Tex. App. 2000)] (distinguishing case from *Schlumberger* because when Fletchers signed real estate contracts at issue containing "as is" clause, they were not attempting to resolve present dispute about availability of water, were not represented by counsel, and were not "sophisticated business players" as were the Swansons in *Schlumberger*).

. . . The merger clauses were not boiler-plate. A merger clause freely negotiated by similarly sophisticated parties as part of the bargain in an arm's-length transaction has a different effect than a provision in a standard form contract which cannot be negotiated and cannot serve as the basis of the parties' bargain. . . .

The only question in this case is whether the merger clauses in the agreements at issue are sufficiently broad and specific to conclusively negate the reliance element of Eifert's common law fraud claim considering

---

[275] [n.6] A "merger clause" is "[a] provision in a contract to the effect that the written terms may not be varied by prior or oral agreements because all such agreements have been merged into the written document." . . .

the Employment Agreement's detailed provisions regarding Eifert's job position, titles, responsibilities and duties. . . . [I]n a very recent decision with facts similar to this case, the United States Court of Appeals for the Fifth Circuit discussed *Schlumberger* and concluded that the merger clauses in the employment contracts before it were clear and unequivocal disclaimers of reliance, and thus summary judgment was proper for the defendant on the plaintiffs' common law fraud claim. *See Armstrong v. Am. Home Shield Corp.*, 333 F.3d 566, 571 (5th Cir. 2003).

. . . .

Other Texas courts of appeals have held that merger clauses less specific than that in *Schlumberger* conclusively negated the reliance element of a fraud claim. . . .

We conclude . . . [that] to the extent Eifert relies on representations outside the Acquisition and Employment Agreements (including the job description) to establish his fraud claim, the evidence is legally insufficient to support that claim. . . .[276]

In *Italian Cowboy Partners, Ltd. v. Prudential Insurance Co.*,[277] the Texas Supreme Court held that language in a lease agreement, stating that the lessor did not make any representations outside the agreement, was not a clear and unequivocal disclaimer of reliance, and was insufficient to bar a fraud claim related to persistent sewer gas odors at a restaurant.

PROBLEM 2-8: THE OVERSTATED SQUARE FOOTAGE

Javier and Ashley Binford purchased a house after receiving from the seller's realtor, Domain, Inc., an information sheet which overstated the square footage of the house. The residence was represented as having 1,825 square feet of living space. After the deal had closed, the Binfords learned that the actual square footage of the house was only 1,575 square feet.

The Binfords sued Domain, Inc., for fraud. At trial, Javier and Ashley said that they had relied on Domain's representation of square footage. Javier testified that in his search for "a great deal," he depended on a house's price per square foot and that factor was his "biggest concern." Ashley likewise testified that the low price per square foot, as calculated based on what the information sheet said, was "important" to her. She indicated that price per square foot was "the overriding factor" in her decision to purchase the house. The jury found that Domain, Inc. had committed fraud and awarded damages to the Binfords in the amount of several thousand dollars.

On appeal, Domain, Inc. now argues that the evidence of reliance by the Binfords on its erroneous statement of square footage was legally and factually insufficient. First, Domain points to the evidence at trial which showed that, before purchasing the house, the Binfords had visited the website of the Adams County

---

[276] 125 S.W.3d at 124–28 (Tex. App. 2003).

[277] 341 S.W.3d 323 (Tex. 2011).

[handwritten margin note, top: If Domain knew ACAD was often wrong, more likely center]

Appraisal District (ACAD) to confirm the amount of property taxes on the house. They saw on the ACAD website that the square footage of the house was the same as Domain had listed in its information sheet for the residence. Moreover, the Binfords had been told by their own realtor, Cooper Realty, that local realtors get a lot of their information from ACAD and that they could check the ACAD website themselves.

[handwritten margin note: Buyers could've looked online to get the right info]

Second, Domain argues that the Binfords could not have relied upon anything that the information sheet said about square footage because they moved into the house under a lease arrangement prior to the closing of the sale. During that period of more than 30 days, the Binfords had the opportunity to inspect any aspect of the house they wanted to inspect. Nothing was hidden from them.

[handwritten margin note: They could've inspected the house]

Third, Domain points out that the Binfords signed a form printed on Cooper Realty stationery provided by an agent of their own realtor in which they disclaimed any reliance on misrepresentations. The form said:

> The Buyer is advised to verify all information important to him/her and to ask the appropriate questions of the appropriate authorities himself/herself or through an attorney with respect to important issues such as . . . size of structure. . . . Any statements with respect to problems or with respect to the availability or existence of any of these items which were made by the Realtor and his/her associates were made based on information given to the Realtor by the Seller/Owner and/or government agencies, and/or others, and there is no intention that the Buyer rely on the statements of the Realtor and his/her associates. . . .

> Having read the foregoing disclaimer, I/we, the prospective Buyer(s), by my/our signature(s) below, state that I/we have not relied upon any statement given to me/us by the Realtor and/or his/her associates with regard to the property, and my/our decision to make an offer on the property and to subsequently purchase the property is based on my/our independent decision with or without legal counsel.

The Binfords signed the form on the signature lines marked "Buyer(s)," the sellers of the house signed the same form on the signature lines marked "Seller(s)."

You are a third-year law student interning for a judge on the court that will decide the appeal. Based on the materials in this chapter, please provide the judge with a pre-argument assessment of the reliance issue.

5. Damages

It is essential to prove that a fraudulent misrepresentation caused damage. Absent such proof, recovery will be denied. For example, in *Byington v. Mize*,[278] the plaintiff alleged that the defendant-physician had fraudulently induced him to consent to surgery by telling him that he had performed arthroscopy on football star Troy Aikman when, in actuality, he had never performed arthroscopy on

---

[278] 2002 Tex. App. LEXIS 5008 (July 15, 2002) (involving claims for fraudulent inducement, constructive fraud, and negligent misrepresentation).

anyone.[279] The appellate court held that even if the trial court erred in dismissing the plaintiff's claim for fraud, the error was harmless because the plaintiff failed to show that the physician was negligent in performing the patient's surgery or in caring for him thereafter, and thus, the alleged misrepresentation did not injure the plaintiff.[280]

a.   Proximate Causation

The usual principles of proximate causation apply to a fraud action. For example, in *Knepper v. Brown*,[281] the defendant published a misleading advertisement which induced the plaintiff to submit to liposuction at the hands of a doctor whose credentials were misrepresented in the ad. As a result, the plaintiff suffered continuing pain and "misshapenness," which the plaintiff's expert described as an "uncorrectable disaster."[282] In challenging a jury finding of fraud, the defendant argued that the plaintiff had failed to prove proximate causation of damages. Affirming the $1.58 million judgment for the plaintiff, the Oregon Supreme Court wrote:

> We begin our analysis by noting that this is a fraud case, *i.e.*, a case involving an intentional tort. Our past cases have referred to proximate cause (or "proximate injury") as one of nine elements of a claim for tortious fraud. Although our more recent cases have employed a more abbreviated list of the elements of fraud . . . (listing five elements), we agree that some notion of proximate cause is subsumed under the last element in that abbreviated list: "Damage to the plaintiff, resulting from [the plaintiff's] reliance [on defendant's representation]." . . .

> The question, then, is whether that notion of proximate cause or proximate injury is equivalent to the concept of "reasonable foreseeability," as we have used that phrase in [negligence] cases. . . . We are persuaded that it is.

> Courts have noted that, when an intentional tort is involved, the range of legal causation can be quite broad. . . . Still, the historical references to "proximate injury" as an element of fraud indicates that courts also recognize that there is some limitation on the consequences for which a perpetrator of an intentional fraud may be held liable. A requirement that any claimed damages be foreseeable appropriately recognizes that the scope of liability for an intentional, fraudulent misrepresentation depends on the nature of the misrepresentation, the audience to whom the misrepresentation was directed, and the nature of the action or forbearance, intended or negligent, that the misrepresentation justifiably induced. *Restatement (Second) of Torts* § 548A (1977) incorporates that requirement:

---

[279] *Id.* at *3–*4.

[280] *Id.* at *4.

[281] 195 P.3d 383 (Or. 2008).

[282] *Id.* at 385.

"A fraudulent misrepresentation is a legal cause of a pecuniary loss resulting from action or inaction in reliance upon it if, but only if, the loss might reasonably be expected to result from the reliance."

. . . .

When we apply that foreseeability principle in the present case, it is clear that plaintiffs' damages reasonably might be expected to result from their reliance on Dex's misrepresentation. An advertisement that misrepresents a medical provider's qualifications self-evidently creates a risk that a consumer who seeks treatment from the provider in reliance on that misrepresentation will suffer an adverse result that would not have occurred if the provider's qualifications had been as represented. The testimony at trial showed that Knepper's injuries fell precisely within the foreseeable risk of harm that the misrepresentation created: Knepper testified that she wanted to have a board-certified plastic surgeon perform the liposuction, and a juror could infer from that testimony that Knepper believed that she was more likely to suffer an adverse result from being treated by a medical provider who was not board certified in plastic surgery. Further, plaintiffs' medical expert testified that he had *never* seen adverse results like the ones that Knepper experienced from a medical provider who was certified in plastic surgery. A juror could infer from that testimony that plaintiffs' injuries probably would not have occurred if Knepper had received treatment from a board-certified plastic surgeon (as she believed Brown to be). Stated in terms of the applicable legal standard, Dex had reason to expect that Knepper would act in justifiable reliance on Dex's misrepresentation by retaining Brown for the surgery, and that an adverse result was more likely if Brown, rather than a board-certified plastic surgeon, performed liposuction surgery. There is no additional requirement that plaintiffs also prove that Dex in fact did foresee that Knepper would suffer the *particular* adverse results of the medical services that Brown performed. It follows that plaintiffs' injuries were foreseeable as a result of Dex's intentional misrepresentation, and that is all that plaintiffs had to show. Dex must respond in damages accordingly.[283]

The court further held that evidence of malice was not required:

This is not a case of the unwitting publication of an advertisement that turns out to be false. It is, instead, a case in which the publisher took a knowing and active part in the perpetration of the fraud. Punishing fraud has no impermissible "chilling" effect on the right to express views on "any subject whatever." *See* Article I, section 8, of the Oregon Constitution (protecting such a right of expression). Fraud is excepted from that constitutional protection. . . .[284]

---

[283] *Id.* at 387–88.

[284] *Id.* at 389.

PROBLEM 2-9: THE FACEBOOK SUICIDE

Sarah Garza, 14, was delighted when a cute teenage boy named Matthew Tilden contacted her on Facebook and began sending her flirtatious messages. Sarah, who suffered from depression and various physical impairments, corresponded with Matthew for more than a month. During that month, Matthew's electronic messages were the center of her life, the only thing that gave her joy. Then, without warning, Matthew said that he was ending their cyberfriendship because he had learned that other students thought she was fat and dumb. Sarah pleaded with Matthew not to break off the relationship. She told him that she would kill herself if he abandoned her, but Matthew was unmoved.

The next day Sarah committed suicide by taking an overdose of her mother's pills. Between the overdose and her death, Sarah was in a coma for 18 hours. Her family later discovered that Matthew never existed. He was a fiction created by a woman, Hazel Adams, who lived down the street. Adams pretended to be a teenage boy on Facebook. What she did to Sarah, she did just for fun.

Sarah's parents, Alex and Toni Garza, are emotionally destroyed. They have sought your legal advice as to whether they can commence a tort action against Adams. Please prepare an analysis of whether the Garzas, as representatives of Sarah's estate or as Sarah's closest survivors, can maintain either a survival action[285] or a wrongful death action[286] against Adams based on fraud. Take into account what you have learned in this chapter and basic principles of tort law.

b.   "Benefit of the Bargain" and "Out of Pocket" Damages

Economic losses for fraud (and other forms of tortious misrepresentation) are generally measured one of two ways. Under the "contract rule," "benefit of the bargain" damages are an amount equivalent to the difference between what the plaintiff was promised and what the plaintiff received. For example, suppose that a misrepresentation is made relating to a computer. If the computer would have been

---

[285] At common law, the death of either party ended most kinds of tort litigation. B's claim against A vanished if either A or B died. Statutes in every jurisdiction now prevent a lawsuit from terminating when one of the parties dies. These laws are called "survival statutes." With certain exceptions (*e.g.*, perhaps defamation), the statutes allow the estate of the decedent to maintain the tort action the decedent could have litigated if the decedent had lived. Thus, the losses that accrued between the occurrence of the tort and the death of the decedent are normally compensable. Damages may include compensation for costs of medical care and an amount for the pain and suffering that the decedent experienced prior to death. Amounts recovered in a "survival" action are distributed to the beneficiaries of the decedent's estate, regardless of whether those persons are family members.

[286] The common law gave no right of recovery to the survivors of someone whom the defendant had killed. Today, "wrongful-death statutes" in every state create a cause of action for the benefit of a defined class of persons left behind when the defendant has tortiously killed someone. In some states, recovery in a wrongful-death action is limited to pecuniary losses, such as income or benefits the survivor has lost as a result of the death. However, most states, either by way of express statutory language or by judicial construction of terms like "pecuniary," now permit recovery in a wrongful-death action of the value of lost companionship, society, advice, and guidance. Some states also allow damages for grief or other forms of emotional distress. Amounts recovered in a wrongful-death action go to persons in the statutorily defined class (typically close family members), not to the estate of the decedent.

worth $1000 if it had been as represented, but is only worth $820, the plaintiff may recover $180, the amount necessary to ensure that the plaintiff enjoys the benefit of the bargain that was entered into with the defendant.

Alternatively, the "tort rule" focuses on what the plaintiff lost and awards compensation for "out of pocket" losses. Thus, suppose that the plaintiff pays $900 for a computer which, because of a misrepresentation, is worth only $820. The plaintiff may recover "out of pocket" damages in the amount of $80, an amount equivalent to the difference between what the plaintiff paid and what the plaintiff received.

Whether damages are calculated under a "benefit of the bargain" rule or an "out of pocket" rule often depends on the facts. In some cases, the victim of a misrepresentation never entered into a contract, so it makes little sense to talk about "benefit of the bargain." In other cases, the plaintiff may have been the party to a contract, but may fail to prove with reasonable certainty what the bargain was worth, in which case "out of pocket" losses may be a more reliable measure of damages.

Plaintiff Must Prove the Value of What Was Received. Under either the "benefit of the bargain" rule or the "out of pocket" rule, the plaintiff must prove with reasonable certainty the value of what was received. Otherwise, it will be impossible to compute the amount of the plaintiff's damages.

For example, in *Highland Capital Management, L.P. v. Ryder Scott Co.*,[287] the holders of a bankrupt oil and gas company's (Seven Seas Petroleum's) unsecured subordinated notes asserted claims based on fraud, negligent misrepresentation, and other theories against a consulting firm that had issued erroneous reports about the company's proven reserves. A Texas appellate court affirmed summary judgment for the defendants because the plaintiffs failed to introduce evidence regarding the value of what they received when they purchased the notes. The plaintiffs had introduced affidavits from their portfolio managers, but the court found that evidence lacking. As the court explained:

> Appellants do not explain how the affiants' testimony regarding the interest that was paid on the bonds after their purchase is probative of the fair market value of the bonds at the time of their purchase. The connection is not obvious. No reasonable inference can be drawn regarding the fair market value of the Unsecured Bonds at the time of purchase from the testimony regarding the interest payments received by Appellants.

> We also disagree with Appellants that Plumer's and Funsten's testimony indicating that the Unsecured Bonds were later considered "essentially worthless" is, without more, competent evidence sufficient to raise a genuine issue of material fact regarding the fair market value of the securities at the varying times Appellants purchased the bonds. *See* [*Woodyard v. Hunt*, 695 S.W.2d 730, 733 (Tex. App. 1985)] (explaining in fraud case "damages are measured by comparing values represented and received at the time of sale, not at some future time"). Affiants' imprecise

---

[287] 402 S.W.3d 719 (Tex. App. 2012).

testimony stating that the securities were later considered "essentially worthless" does not permit an inference that the securities had no greater value at the time of Appellants' purchases.

Appellants' petition states that the Unsecured Bonds were purchased over a three-year period, some more than three years before the adjusted valuation of the oil reserves in mid-2002. The affiants' testimony and undisputed portions of the record indicate that events affecting Seven Seas' assets transpired during that time frame. For example, as discussed by the affiants, Seven Seas incurred secured debt during that period. Seven Seas also conducted exploration activities in the Guaduas Field during that time leading to more information about the field's oil reserves. The potential effect of these and other events on the value of the securities issued by Seven Seas highlights that the affiants' statements regarding the subsequent worthlessness of the securities is not evidence from which a fact finder could calculate the fair market value of the securities at the various times of Appellants' purchases.[288]

Complexity in Application. While the "benefit of the bargain" and "out of pocket" rules are simple in theory, their application to a case involving competing versions of the facts can be complex. For example, in *Pleasant v. Bradford*,[289] the plaintiffs paid $119,200 for a house (the "Vasquez house") which they were told had 1,824 square feet of living space, but in fact had only 1,571 square feet. "This measurement was 253 square feet less than that represented by the MLS listing, resulting in a price per square foot of $76.07 rather than $65.52."[290] In affirming a judgment for the purchasers in a suit alleging fraud, negligent misrepresentation, and violation of the state Deceptive Trade Practices Act, the Texas Court of Appeals wrote:

> Appellants assert that the Bradfords failed to introduce any evidence of the value of the house as represented. The jury awarded the Bradfords $2,621.08 in "benefit-of-the-bargain" damages. Benefit-of-the-bargain damages are the difference, at the time of the sale, between the value as represented (the value of the house if it had contained 1,824 square feet) and the value as received (the value of the house given its actual square footage). . . . Appellants do not dispute that evidence of the value as received was introduced: the Bradfords' expert appraised the home at $111,000 (after two earlier appraisals of $114,500 and $117,000), the appraisal that alerted the Bradfords to the square footage misrepresentation gave the home a value of $119,500, and appellants' expert appraised the home at $122,500. However, the Bradfords never introduced a specific appraised value of the house that assumed it did in fact contain 1,824 square feet.
>
> . . . [We conclude, however, that] the purchase price agreed to by the Bradfords and appellants, at a time when both parties believed the house

---

[288] *Id.* at 729–30.

[289] 260 S.W.3d 546 (Tex. App. 2008).

[290] *Id.* at 552.

contained 1,824 square feet, is evidence of the house's value as represented.
. . .

Appellants' real problem with the damage evidence is . . . that the jury did not adhere to that evidence and, thus, that the damages award is not supported by the evidence. In addition to the jury question on benefit-of-the-bargain damages, the court submitted a jury question on "out-of-pocket" damages, which are the difference at the time of the sale between the value the buyer paid and the value as received. . . . Because the jury's answer of $5,000 is not identical to its benefit-of-the-bargain award of $2,621.08, it is apparent that the jury did not, in fact, conclude that the value as represented equaled the purchase price. Given this fact, and the specificity of the damages figure with no readily apparent source from the record, appellants assert that the jury's award of damages under the benefit-of-the-bargain measure of damages was arbitrary.

. . . We have previously held that "evidence corresponding to the precise amount found by the jury is not essential" in order to withstand a legal-sufficiency challenge. . . .

So long as a rational basis for the calculation of damages exists, a jury's finding will not be disregarded merely because its reasoning in arriving at its figure may be unclear. . . . Conversely, a jury cannot arbitrarily award an amount neither authorized nor supported by the evidence presented at trial. . . .

. . . [W]hile appellants are correct that a jury award is not *per se* rational simply because it falls in between the figures presented by expert testimony, neither is a damages award *per se* arbitrary because it does not match up precisely with figures presented in expert testimony. . . .

This was not a case in which there were only certain figures that the jury could select in making the damages award. The jury heard five different appraisals for the value of the home as received: $111,000, $114,500, $117,000, $119,500, and $122,500. The jury also heard two different purchase prices, which were evidence of the value of the home as represented: the accepted offer of $118,000 and the final contract price of $119,200 [which included an amount for repairs]. In addition, the jury may have determined or adjusted its award based on square footage valuations. The jury was presented with different amounts of the square footage of the home as received: 1,567 square feet according to the Bradfords' expert witness's appraisal, 1,571 square feet according to the lender bank's pre-closing appraisal, and 1,597 square feet according to appellants' expert witness's appraisal. This enabled three different starting points for a comparison between the house as received and the house with its represented 1,824 square feet. The jury was also presented with two separate dollar-per-square-foot adjustment amounts used by the expert witnesses in appraising the Vasquez home based on sales of homes with higher or lower square footage amounts. The Bradfords' expert witness testified to an adjustment of $46.67 per square foot, whereas appellants' expert witness used an adjustment of only $20 per square foot. Finally, we note that the jury may have taken into consideration the price-per-square-foot amounts of the Vasquez home and comparable houses sold in the area. The MLS listing offered the Vasquez house at a price per square foot of $65.52. The Bradfords testified that the other houses they had looked at had prices per square foot in the $75 to $80 range. Altogether, the five appraisals of the Vasquez home entered into evidence used ten comparable home sales, each with separate prices per square foot ranging from $69.48 to $82.45.

Based on all of the above evidence, we find that this was not a case in which the jury only had distinct damages figures to choose from or in which there were no variables involved in applying a predetermined formula. . . . The evidence presented the jury with a range of possible reasonable values. $2,621.08 was within the range of damage amounts supported by the evidence. . . . The evidence was legally and factually sufficient to support the jury's finding of $2,621.08 for benefit-of-the-bargain damages.[291]

Interestingly, the *Pleasant* opinion does not explain why, after the jury had calculated "benefit of the bargain damages" at $2621.08 and "out of pocket" losses at $5,000, the district court opted for the "benefit of the bargain" measure and "awarded the Bradfords $2,621.08 in damages, plus attorneys' fees, interest, and costs."[292] (The award of prejudgment interests and costs was permitted by Texas law, and presumably the award of attorneys' fees was based on provisions of the Texas Deceptive Trade Practices Act, which the defendants allegedly violated.)

Diminished Value of Mass-Marketed Products. Issues of immense importance arise relating to whether "benefit of the bargain" damages can be recovered when misrepresentations are made relating to mass-marketed products. Courts have often been reluctant to permit recovery of compensation for diminished product value. However, as discussed below, the rationales adopted by the courts vary.

"Not What Was Bargained for" Versus "No-Injury Products Liability." In *Wallis v. Ford Motor Co.*,[293] a sport utility vehicle owner brought a class action against the vehicle's manufacturer, alleging in part common law fraud based on the manufacturer's knowing concealment of the fact that the SUV had a design defect that caused it to roll over under normal operations. The action did not seek compensation for personal injuries or property damages that had occurred, but for the diminished value of the SUV resulting from the concealed defect. The Supreme Court of Arkansas wrote:

[T]his court has applied two measures of damages for common-law fraud: (1) the benefit-of-the-bargain measure . . . and (2) the out-of-pocket measure. . . .

Our application of benefit-of-the-bargain damages in common-law fraud cases has . . . been limited to instances where the actual product received by the purchaser manifests that it is different from that which was promised. For instance, in *Currier v. Spencer*, 299 Ark. 182, 772 S.W.2d 309

---

[291] *Id.* at 558–61.

[292] *Id.* at 552.

[293] 208 S.W.3d 153 (Ark. 2005).

(1989), Currier, a car dealer, placed an advertisement to sell a one-owner 1984 Datsun 300 ZX. Spencer responded to the advertisement and purchased the car for $8,250, with $5,000 paid in cash and the other $3,250 paid by check. Before the check cleared, Spencer experienced problems with his car and discovered the car had been wrecked and consisted of two cars welded together. He stopped payment on the check, whereupon Currier filed a lawsuit in contract to recover the unpaid balance due under the purchase agreement. Spencer responded by filing a counterclaim that included claims for misrepresentation, and breach of express and implied warranties. The trial court dismissed Currier's contract claim but awarded damages of $1,500 on Spencer's breach of warranty and misrepresentation claims. That amount represented the difference between the purchase price of the car, $8,250, and its actual value, $6,750. On appeal, we affirmed the award and said, "the standard measure of damages for either breach of warranty or misrepresentation is the difference in value between the product as warranted and its actual value." Likewise, in *Moore Ford Co. v. Smith*, 270 Ark. 340, 604 S.W.2d 943 (1980), another misrepresentation action, the appellee brought suit when she discovered that her "new car" had prior body work done on the hood and fender. The jury awarded her $1,250 in compensatory damages, and we affirmed.

. . . [T]he principle undergirding our case law is that benefit-of-the-bargain damages are only awarded in fraud cases where a party proves that the product received is not what was bargained for; that is, the product received in fact manifests that it is different from that which was promised.

[handwritten margin note: principle undergirding benefit of the bargain damages]

Several other jurisdictions have addressed what type of damages must be alleged in order for a plaintiff to successfully bring a common-law fraud claim for allegedly defective products. In *Briehl v. General Motors Corp.*, 172 F.3d 623 (8th Cir. 1999), the plaintiffs brought a class-action fraud lawsuit based on an allegedly defective anti-lock brake system (ABS) in vehicles manufactured by General Motors. As in this case, the plaintiffs did not allege that the brake system had ever malfunctioned or failed. The Eighth Circuit Court of Appeals held that "[t]he Plaintiff's conclusory assertions that they, as a class, have experienced damages . . . are simply too speculative to allow this case to go forward. The Plaintiffs' assertions that their ABS-equipped vehicles are defective and that they have suffered a loss in resale value as a result of the defect is insufficient as a matter of law to plead a claim under any theory the Plaintiffs have advanced." . . .

More recently, the Wisconsin Supreme Court has held that the mere "propensity" for premature product failure is not enough to constitute cognizable damages. *Tietsworth v. Harley-Davidson, Inc.*, 270 Wis.2d 146, 677 N.W.2d 233 (2004). In *Tietsworth*, a class-action lawsuit was filed on behalf of certain Harley-Davidson motorcycle owners seeking damages for an alleged defect in the motorcycles' engines. In the original complaint, the plaintiffs pleaded claims based on negligence, strict products liability, fraud, and deceptive trade practices. Once again, as in this case, the plaintiffs did not allege any personal injury or property damage arising out of the engine defect; nor did they allege that the motorcycle engines had actually failed or malfunctioned in any way. . . . The . . . Wisconsin Supreme Court . . . [concluded] "an allegation that a product is diminished in value because the product line has demonstrated a propensity for premature failure such that the product might or will at some point in the future fail prematurely is too uncertain and speculative to constitute a legally cognizable tort injury and is therefore insufficient to state damages in a tort claim for fraud." . . .

Notwithstanding the above-cited authority to the contrary, Wallis suggests that the decision by the Fifth Circuit Court of Appeals in *Coghlan v. Wellcraft Marine Corp.*, 240 F.3d 449 (5th Cir. 2001), supports his position that damages are cognizable where there is a propensity for a product to fail prematurely as a result of an alleged defect. In the *Coghlan* case, the Coghlans bought a fishing boat that they believed to be "all-fiberglass." A few months after purchase, they discovered that the boat was not in fact "all fiberglass" as represented; instead, it was composed of 1.5 inches of plywood. The Coghlans filed a class-action lawsuit. . . . On appeal, the Fifth Circuit ruled that as to several of the claims, including the fraud claim, the Coghlans had asserted a cognizable injury in the complaint even though the only damage sought was the "benefit of their bargain with Wellcraft, or the difference in value between what they were promised, an all fiberglass boat, and what they received, a hybrid wood-fiberglass boat." . . . [T]he Fifth Circuit . . . explained . . . :

> The key distinction between this case and a "no-injury" product liability suit is that the Coghlans' claims are rooted in basic contract law rather than the law of product liability: the Coghlans assert they were promised one thing but were given a different, less valuable thing. The core allegation in a no-injury product liability class action is essentially the same as in a traditional products liability case: the defendant produced or sold a defective product and/or failed to warn of the product's dangers. The wrongful act in a no-injury products suit is thus the placing of a dangerous/defective product in the stream of commerce. In contrast, the wrongful act alleged by the Coghlans is Wellcraft's failure to uphold its end of their bargain and to deliver what was promised. The striking feature of a typical no-injury class is that the plaintiffs have either not yet experienced a malfunction because of the alleged defect or have experienced a malfunction but not been harmed by it. Therefore, the plaintiffs in a no-injury products liability case have not suffered any physical harm or out-of-pocket economic loss. Here, the damages sought by the Coghlans are not rooted in the alleged defect of the product as such, but in the fact that they did not receive the benefit of their bargain.
> . . .

In view of the above-quoted analysis by the Fifth Circuit, it is clear that the *Coghlan* case ultimately supports our conclusion. In a no-injury products liability case, it is the wrongful act of placing a dangerous or defective product in the stream of commerce that creates the cause of action; whereas, in a misrepresentation or a fraud case, such as *Coghlan*, the cause of action rests solely on the premise that a party did not receive the benefit of his or her bargain. In order to prove the later claim, a party must show that the product delivered was not in fact what was promised. For example, the Coghlans bargained for an "all fiberglass" boat; instead, they received a boat with 1.5 inches of plywood. In this respect, Wallis attempts to merge two separate causes of action: he seeks to recover benefit-of-the-bargain damages for the wrongful act of placing an allegedly defective product in the stream of commerce. Yet, the *Coghlan* case clearly states that such damages are not rooted in the alleged defect of the product, but in the fact that the purchaser has not received the benefit of his or her bargain; that is, the product delivered in fact manifests that it is different from that which was promised. Here, there is no allegation in the complaint that the Ford Explorer has not, to date, been exactly what Wallis bargained for; that is, he does not allege that the vehicle has actually malfunctioned or that the defect has manifested itself.

Moreover, numerous other jurisdictions have refused to award benefit-of-the-bargain damages when there is no allegation that the product received was not the bargained-for product. . . .

Despite the fact that some jurisdictions have concluded that the "diminution in value" of a product alone is enough to succeed on a common-law fraud claim, *Miller v. William Chevrolet/GEO, Inc.*, 326 Ill. App. 3d 642, 762 N.E.2d 1, 260 Ill. Dec. 735 (2001); *Khan v. Shiley Incorporated*, 217 Cal. App. 3d 848, 266 Cal. Rptr. 106 (1990), we decline to adopt this principle. According to our well-settled case law, common-law fraud claims not resulting in injury are not actionable. . . . Accordingly, we hold that Wallis's common-law fraud claim for an allegedly defective vehicle is insufficient to survive a Rule 12(b)(6) motion to dismiss where the only injury alleged is a diminution in value of the vehicle.[294]

Speculation on Loss of Resale Value or the Risk of Product Failure. The *Briehl* and *Tietsworth* cases cited in the above excerpt based their decisions on the fact that damages for diminished resale value or the propensity for premature product failure were too speculative to be legally cognizable. In so ruling, those courts rooted their decisions in the well-established principle that damages must always be proved with reasonable certainty. If recovery of diminished value damages are to be denied in cases involving misrepresentations relating to mass-marketed products, is the speculative-damages rationale preferable to the "no-injury product defect" rationale?

c.   The Economic Loss Rule and Fraud Relating to a Contract

Cases like those discussed in the preceding section, relating to whether damages may be recovered for harm caused by misrepresentation relating to mass-marketed products, raise the issue of whether contract law (as opposed to tort law) provides a better or more appropriate channel for legal relief. Recall the "economic loss rule" discussed in Chapter 1. One of the functions of this so-called

---

[294] *Id.* at 319–25.

rule, which sometimes bars actions in tort, is to define the boundary line between contract law and tort law. What this means is that in disputes where fraud (or negligent or innocent misrepresentation) relates to a contract, the tort claim is sometimes not actionable. However, this is certainly not always the case. Consider the following excerpt from a law review article:[295]

> ***The Boundary Line Between Torts and Contracts***. If there is a convincing rationale for the economic loss rule, it is that the rule performs a critical boundary-line function, separating the law of torts from the law of contracts. . . .

> ***Private Ordering***. Purely economic losses, authorities urge, are more properly subject to resolution under contract principles, which defer to private ordering, than by reference to tort standards. Under the logic of private ordering, "individuals are the best judges of their own interests; individuals maximize those interests through contracts; the expectation and reliance interests created by contracts deserve protection; promoting private contracting produces a social benefit; contract law provides the framework through which the individual and social benefits are realized in practice."[296]

> ***Incentive to Bargain***. If a person wishes to be protected from economic harm, it is argued, he or she must bargain for protection and pay the price of securing those benefits. One who fails to do so has no right to complain that another has neglected to exercise care to save him or her from non-physical harm. Put differently, the economic loss rule performs critical bargain-forcing functions. On one hand, the economic loss rule forces (or at least encourages) the parties to a contract to think about and bargain over the economic losses that may arise from the contract. . . . On the other hand, the economic loss rule ensures respect for decisions made by the parties with respect to loss allocation. . . .

> ***Drowning in a Sea of Tort***. . . . [W]hile there are certainly cases where tort law and contract law can and should offer overlapping, alternative remedies, there must be a point at which tort law leaves off and only contract law governs. Otherwise "contract law would drown in a sea of tort,"[297] since tort law frequently offers potential plaintiffs more generous terms of recovery. . . .

> ***Product-Related Economic Losses***. The boundary-line function of the economic loss rule is most clearly established in the field of products liability. If a defective product causes <u>physical harm</u> to a person or to property other than the product itself, <u>a tort action</u> may be brought. In contrast, if the loss is <u>solely of an economic nature</u>, such as where a product

---

[295] The excerpt is taken from Vincent R. Johnson, *The Boundary-Line Function of the Economic Loss Rule*, 66 Wash. & Lee L. Rev. 523, 566–74 (2009) (citations omitted). Subheadings have been inserted.

[296] [n.108] Jay M. Feinman, *The Economic Loss Rule and Private Ordering*, 48 Ariz. L. Rev. 813, 814 (2006).

[297] [n.117] *E. River S.S. Corp. v. Transamerica Delaval, Inc.*, 476 U.S. 858, 866 (1986).

defect injures the product itself or impairs the product's value, the plaintiff ordinarily is relegated to compensation under contract principles. Illustratively, if a person buys a can of paint and applies the paint to a door, the person has a potential tort claim (and perhaps a contract claim as well based on breach of warranty) if toxic odors from the paint make the plaintiff sick or if the paint eats away at the door and damages that "other" property. However, if the paint simply fails to adhere to the door effectively and flakes off, or quickly discolors, causing no other damage but making the paint's purchase a waste of money, the buyer's sole avenue for recovery is rooted in contract principles.

UCC Remedies. The economic loss rule operates sensibly in the products liability field because the commercial nature of the underlying transaction means that a contract-law remedy is not only feasible, but routinely available. The sale that produces the distribution of the defective product allows the parties to determine how economic risks relating to the quality of the product should be allocated and supplies default rules relating to warranties that resolve disputes if the parties do not specify particular terms of recovery. In addition, the ubiquitous adoption of the Uniform Commercial Code (UCC) means that there is a carefully crafted statutory mechanism available for resolving economic loss claims. . . .

Bargaining for What You Want. The abundance of products available in the American market theoretically makes it possible for buyers to bargain for the level of economic loss protection they desire. Referring again to the previous example, a consumer can elect to purchase cheap paint or expensive paint or something in between. It is neither surprising nor unfair if "you get what you pay for." . . .

Claims by Persons Not in Privity. A number of courts have rejected arguments that contract principles define the extent of the duty where the economic injurer and victim were not in privity. . . .

Recognizing third-party rights under tort law in these types of cases does not undermine the public policy in favor of private ordering. Rather, it merely recognizes that private ordering takes place not in a vacuum, but within a context of other obligations. When the issue of whether economic losses are compensable relates to third-party protection, the intent of the parties is not the only relevant consideration. . . .

With respect to the boundary-line function of the economic loss rule, decisions holding that third-party claims are not foreclosed by the rule make sense. If there is no agreement between the parties to a lawsuit, there is no risk that recognizing tort obligations will violate the parties' freedom to contract, because there never was an effort to exercise such freedom. . . . The purpose of the economic loss rule is not to leave injured persons remediless for economic losses, but to ensure respect for private ordering by relegating a plaintiff to contract remedies in cases where there is an agreement between the parties allocating economic risks. . . .

Suits by Purchasers. Occasionally, courts have held that the economic loss rule bars a tort claim related to a contract even where the parties to the lawsuit are not in privity. These decisions can sometimes be explained as a natural application of the economic loss rule in the context of a sale of goods, as where a disappointed purchaser of a product sues the manufacturer or wholesaler of the goods (rather than the retailer). A purchaser seeking purely economic losses should not be permitted to complain, under tort principles, against anyone in the chain of distribution that the product the plaintiff bought was not better (*i.e.*, more effective, more valuable, or more "reasonable") than what the plaintiff bargained for under the law of contract. Absent fraud or some other breach of an independent duty, contract principles normally are the buyer's sole remedy for purely economic loss related to purchased goods, regardless of whether the suit is against the retailer, with whom the purchaser was in privity, or against a wholesaler or manufacturer up the chain of distribution. . . .

Independent Duties Under Tort Law. In their efforts to articulate the limits of the economic loss rule, courts have focused on the source of the duty allegedly violated for the purpose of drawing a distinction. Often, they have articulated a bright-line test.[298] Thus, the Supreme Court of Colorado wrote broadly:

Where there exists a duty of care independent of any contractual obligations, the economic loss rule has no application and does not bar a plaintiff's tort claim because the claim is based on a recognized independent duty of care and thus falls outside the scope of the economic loss rule.[299]

Elaborating on this theme, the Supreme Court of Pennsylvania quoted a decision of the Supreme Court of South Carolina with approval:

The question . . . is not whether the damages are physical or economic. Rather, the question of whether the plaintiff may maintain an action in tort for purely economic loss turns on the determination of the source of the duty plaintiff claims the defendant owed. A breach of a duty which arises under the provisions of a contract between the parties must be redressed under contract, and a tort action will not lie. A breach of duty arising independently of any contract duties between the parties, however, may support a tort action.[300]

. . . .

Fraud Relating to a Contract. Courts have struggled with the issue of whether recovery in tort is barred by the economic loss rule when the plaintiff alleges that fraud was committed in the context of a contractual

---

[298] [n.200] *See Indem. Ins. Co. of N. Am. v. Am. Aviation, Inc.*, 891 So. 2d 532, 537 (Fla. 2004). . . .

[299] [n.201] *A.C. Excavating, Inc. v. Yacht Club II Homeowners Ass'n*, 114 P.3d 862, 866 (Colo. 2005).

. . .

[300] [n.202] *Bilt-Rite Contractors, Inc. v. Architectural Studio*, 866 A.2d 270, 288 (Pa. 2005) (quoting *Tommy L. Griffin Plumbing & Heating Co. v. Jordan, Jones & Goulding, Inc.*, 463 S.E.2d 85, 88 (S.C. 1995)).

relation. Fraud in the inducement is generally actionable because pre-contractual misrepresentation violates obligations arising from tort principles that are independent of the terms of the agreement the parties ultimately reach. In contrast, claims for fraud in the performance of a contract are sometimes barred, presumably on the theory that they relate to purely contractual duties. For example, the United States District Court for the Middle District of Florida held that where the "alleged fraud [was] nothing more than a refusal to divulge an intent to breach the contract," such fraud was "not separate from the alleged breach," and, therefore, the fraud claim was barred by the economic loss rule.[301]

Some claims of fraud simply restate in different terms that obligations arising under the contract were breached. Thus, the economic loss rule should normally bar recovery in tort if a fraud claim alleges simply that there was misrepresentation about . . . the characteristics or quantity of the goods sold under a contract[302] or the number of hours worked under a consulting agreement.[303] A "mere contract claim cloaked in the language of tort," should be decided under contract principles. Thus, courts have stated that, in the usual case, "a claim arising out of the provisions of a contract must find remedy under contract law,"[304] and that "[t]he economic loss doctrine stands for the general rule that 'ordinarily, a breach of contract does not give rise to a tort action by the promisee against the promisor.' "[305]

Still, it is incorrect to state that claims for fraud in the performance of a contract are never actionable. Entry into a contract creates no license to commit fraud. In *Robinson Helicopter Co., Inc. v. Dana Corp.*,[306] the Supreme Court of California held that a helicopter manufacturer's fraud and intentional misrepresentation claims against a supplier of clutch parts was not barred by the economic loss rule where the supplier provided false certificates of conformance with manufacturing specifications. Under the parties' contract and applicable principles of aviation law, it was essential that the clutch parts be produced in conformance with the terms of a design certificate. The defendant changed the production process without notice by grinding the clutch parts differently, thus affecting their hardness and increasing their failure rate. The defendant nevertheless "continued to provide written certificates to Robinson with each delivery of clutches [which stated] that the clutches had been manufactured in conformance with Robinson's written specifications." In explaining its decision holding that the economic loss rule did not bar the tort claims, the court wrote:

---

[301] [n.214] *Welnia, LLC v. Bodymedia, Inc.*, 2008 U.S. Dist. LEXIS 59269 (M.D. Fla. Aug. 4, 2008).

[302] [n.215] *Cf. Giles v. Gen. Motors Acceptance Corp.*, 494 F.3d 865, 880 (9th Cir. 2007) (finding that a fraud claim not barred by the economic loss rule, involved "extraneous" matters and did not "duplicate" a contract suit).

[303] [n.216] *See Pratham Design Innovation Pvt. Ltd. v. Infovision 21, Inc.*, 2007 U.S. Dist. LEXIS 93691 (E.D. Mich. Dec. 21, 2007). . . .

[304] [n.218] *White v. Holiday Kamper & Boats*, 2008 U.S. Dist. LEXIS 68700 (D.S.C. Sept. 9, 2008).

[305] *Carolina Ports Auth. v. Lloyd A. Fry Roofing, Co.*, 240 S.E.2d 345, 350 (N.C. 1978).

[306] 102 P.3d 268, 272 (Cal. 2004).

Dana's tortious conduct was separate from the breach itself, which involved Dana's provision of the nonconforming clutches. In addition, Dana's provision of faulty clutches exposed Robinson to liability for personal damages if a helicopter crashed and to disciplinary action by the FAA. Thus, Dana's fraud is a tort independent of the breach. . . .

Waiver of Rights Under Tort Law. If tort law recognizes an independent source of duty that affords protection to the plaintiff . . . , the plaintiff should be entitled to relief for a breach of that duty unless, by entering into a contract with the defendant, the plaintiff effectively waived that protection. A useful approach to ascertaining whether contract law should displace tort principles in a case when there is an independent tort duty is to think in terms of established notions of preemption because that is what is actually taking place: Contract law is preempting tort law. Put differently, the boundary line between what is actionable in tort and what is actionable in contract is being moved.

There are at least three useful points of reference. The first concerns preemption of state law by federal law, the second concerns displacement of common law by statutes, and the third relates to written releases from tort liability. Each of these sources of guidance suggests that preemption of established tort principles should be recognized only in limited circumstances.

Federal law does not preempt state tort law unless that is the "clear and manifest" purpose of Congress.[307] Absent such a showing, a plaintiff is not deprived of state tort claims. The text of a law can expressly indicate Congress's intent to preempt or, in limited cases, that intent can be implied from the language and structure of a statute. However, there is generally a presumption against preemption by federal law. Recognizing that state law serves a useful purpose as the primary source of tort remedies, courts are reluctant to hold that federal preemption alters the balance between freedom of action and liability that has been carefully crafted by the matrix of state statutes and common law decisions that define tort obligations.

Likewise, statutory law replaces common law principles only when that is the necessary implication of the actions of the legislature. As one contemporary authority on New York state law explains:

Where a change in the common law is to be effectuated the legislative intent to do so must be clearly and plainly expressed. When . . . a statute is intended to abrogate a common law right or to confer a right not vested by the common law, it will be so construed as not to go beyond the letter; and not even to that extent unless it appears to be according to the spirit and intention of the act.[308]

---

[307] [n.232] *Rice v. Santa Fe Elevator Corp.*, 331 U.S. 218, 230 (1947) (citing *Napier v. Atl. Coast Line R.R. Co.*, 272 U.S. 605, 611 (1926)). . . .

[308] [n.236] *Cf.* N.Y. STAT. LAW § 301 cmt. (2008) (noting that the legislature is presumed to be acquainted with the common law and that "statutes in derogation or in contravention" of the common law

Similarly, contractual releases from tort liability are strictly construed because they threaten to undermine the important public policies relating to fault, proportionality, deterrence, individual responsibility, and compensation that form the intellectual foundations of tort law. A release from liability for physical harm is not valid unless it is clear, specific, and consistent with the public interest. A release is not expansively construed to abrogate the plaintiff's rights under tort law merely because the release is a form of contract. Rather, the plaintiff's rights under tort law are waived only to the extent that the release contract so provides, and only if the waiver is consistent with public policy and fair to the plaintiff. . . .

Contractual Preemption of Tort Remedies. . . . [I]t makes sense to hold that . . . the terms of a contract between the parties abrogates otherwise applicable tort principles only if the agreement clearly evidences an intent to do so or if such displacement is a necessary consequence of the validity of the agreement. Further, even if these conditions are met, relinquishment of rights under tort law should be recognized only when depriving the plaintiff of those rights is consistent with public policy. Boilerplate provisions in standard-form contracts should be subject to careful scrutiny. There is no reason for the law to presume that the parties to a contract have bargained to relinquish rights that arise under tort law.[309]

There is no wholesale exception that immunizes commercial transactions, or even sales of mass-marketed products, from the law of fraud. Indeed, a tort action for fraud routinely provides compensation for purely economic losses arising from commercial sales. However, as courts struggle with the interpretation of the unsettled economic loss rule, it is necessary for lawyers to grapple with the rationale underlying the rule and question how it relates to the law of contracts. Many decisions have found that claims for fraud were not barred by the economic loss rule, but other decisions have sometimes reached a contrary result.

Draft for the Third Restatement. The draft for the relevant section of the *Restatement (Third) of Torts* now provides that "Except as provided elsewhere in this *Restatement*, there is no liability in tort for economic loss caused by negligence in the performance or negotiation of a contract between the parties."[310] Elaborating on that blackletter rule, the comment states:

A contract precludes common-law tort claims for financial loss based on negligent conduct that the contract regulates. . . . It does not foreclose tort claims based on conduct outside the contract's scope. . . . Close cases can arise when an act of negligence occurs at the fringe of a contract's coverage. The important question then is whether allowing the tort claim creates a risk of interference with an allocation of risk made by the parties. A contract can allocate a risk without mentioning it explicitly; silence may itself serve as an allocation if the risk falls within the scope of activity the

---

are to be strictly construed, so as to change the common law only to the extent "required by the words of the act"). . . .

[309] 102 P.3d at 274.

[310] Restatement (Third) of Torts: Liab. for Econ. Harm § 3 (Tent. Draft No. 1, 2012).

contract governs. On the other hand, the purpose of this Section is to protect the bargain the parties made, not to penalize the plaintiff for failing to make a broader one. Navigating between these points may require study of the transaction and its logic. . . . The extent to which a contract precludes liability in tort for economic loss is a question for the court.[311]

PROBLEM 2-10: THE DEFECTIVE CELL PHONE

Alex Chang purchased a new Vision-3 cell phone from GlobalC, Inc., at one of their local retail outlets soon after the new phone hit the market. The cell phone was "state of the art," with Internet access, GPS, and every other feature imaginable.

Although the "apps" on the phone worked very well, Chang had trouble with his phone calls breaking up. Soon thereafter, national newspapers reported that a class action had been filed against GlobalC on behalf of unhappy consumers for concealing test results which showed that phone calls on the Vision-3 broke up at a much higher rate than was usual for the current generation of cell phones. The news articles said that efforts by GlobalC to correct the problem had repeatedly failed before retail sales of the phone commenced, and that there had been an intense effort by GlobalC management to conceal adverse test results in order to stay on schedule for the initial "rollout" date for the Vision-3. An ad for the Vision-3 had claimed that it had the "Best Phone Reception Available."

In response to the bad publicity about calls breaking up, GlobalC sent a text message to buyers assuring them of its 110% commitment to customer satisfaction. Press releases from GlobalC panned the news reports merely as being a mouthpiece for GlobalC's competitors, and denied that GlobalC had any information when it launched retail sales of the Vision-3 indicating that the phone had a bad record of dropping calls.

Chang paid $695 for his phone, but sold it a month later for only $100 because the bad publicity surrounding the Vision-3 was so intense that no one wanted to buy a second-hand Vision-3. The product booklet that Chang received when he bought his Vision-3 said that the exclusive remedy for breach of express or implied warranties was a free replacement of the Vision-3 cell phone.

If evidence establishes that GlobalC concealed from buyers information about the propensity of the Vision-3 to drop phone calls, can Chang state a claim for fraud against GlobalC? If so, what damages can be recovered?

d.   Noneconomic Losses

Although many fraud actions are concerned with compensation for purely economic losses, other cases involve claims for physical harm resulting from personal injury or property damages. In these cases, damages are computed under the same rules that apply to any case concerned with physical harm. Damages in fraud cases giving rise to personal injuries typically include such things as compensation for the costs of medical care, lost wages, and emotional distress. In

---

[311] *Id.* § 3 cmt. c.

cases involving fraud resulting in property damages, compensation may include amounts for the cost of replacement or repairs, rental of substitute property, and, in some cases, lost profits.

e.   Punitive Damages

Fraudulent conduct is the type of wrongdoing that may justify an award of punitive damages beyond whatever compensatory damages are awarded. For example, in *Rogers v. Alexander*,[312] the evidence showed that a purported "investor" and his accountant committed fraud by making misrepresentations to owners of a home health care business. The scheme involved numerous acts of deception, including false statements that the investor was a certified public accountant and had personal contacts with 50 to 100 doctors. The investor also provided the plaintiffs with a misleading balance sheet and improperly transferred business funds to a separate bank account. The Texas Court of Appeals affirmed a judgment awarding the plaintiffs more than $2 million in compensatory damages. It also approved awards of punitive damages in the amount of $750,000 against the investor and $100,000 against the accountant.

Occasionally, statutory language relating to punitive damages may be especially receptive to such an award in an action for fraud. Illustratively, a Colorado statute states, with certain exceptions,[313] that:

> In all civil actions in which damages are assessed by a jury for a wrong done to the person or to personal or real property, and the injury complained of is *attended by circumstances of fraud*, malice, or willful and wanton conduct, the jury, in addition to the actual damages sustained by such party, may award him reasonable exemplary damages.[314]

In *Berger v. Security Pacific Information Systems, Inc.*,[315] a case involving an employer's fraudulent failure to disclose that the position for which the plaintiff was being hired would be discontinued, the Colorado Court of Appeals held that under the quoted statutory language, "because plaintiff was awarded actual damages on her fraudulent concealment claim, an award of punitive damages was authorized." Or as stated by a federal district court in Colorado in a later case, *Level 3 Communications, LLC v. Liebert Corp.*,[316] "the jury's finding that the elements of fraud existed in this case also established the 'circumstances of fraud' required for exemplary damages."

Note, however, that the availability of punitive damages has been greatly limited in recent years by the adoption of numerous statutory restrictions at the state level and by constitutional principles recognized by the United States Supreme Court.

---

[312] 244 S.W.3d 370 (Tex. App. 2007).

[313] *See* Colo. Rev. Stat. Ann. § 13-21-102(1) (LEXIS 2014) (permitting disallowance of punitive damages).

[314] *Id.* § 13-21-102(1)(a) (emphasis added).

[315] 795 P.2d 1380 (Colo. Ct. App. 1990).

[316] 2006 U.S. Dist. LEXIS 27163 (D. Colo. May 8, 2006), *rev'd on other grounds*, 535 F.3d 1146, 1165 (10th Cir. 2008).

(1)   State-Law Restrictions

Certain jurisdictions limit awards of punitive damages to cases of intentional or malicious conduct. For example, in Wisconsin, "[t]he plaintiff may receive punitive damages if evidence is submitted showing that the defendant acted maliciously toward the plaintiff or in an intentional disregard of the rights of the plaintiff."[317] It seems likely that some forms of fraudulent conduct, such as operation of an investment scheme intended to bilk investors, would satisfy this type of standard. However, other forms of fraud might not. Perhaps that would be the case where an officer or director states to a creditor with unwarranted confidence, but without a sufficient factual basis, that a corporation is making money.

"A growing majority of states requires clear and convincing evidence before punitive damages can be considered."[318] In Colorado, a punitive damages award requires proof beyond a reasonable doubt.[319] (This, of course, seriously restricts the imposition of punitive damages in Colorado under the provision quoted earlier in this section.)

Many jurisdictions limit the amount of punitive damages. Such limitations vary greatly. For example, Alaska generally restricts a punitive award to the greater of three times compensatory damages or $500,000.[320] However, it seems likely that cases alleging fraud will often trigger an exception to that rule, which provides that, if the defendant's action is motivated by financial gain, punitive damages are limited to the greater of four times compensatory damages, four times aggregate amount of financial gain, or $7,000,000.[321] In Colorado, punitive damages may not exceed actual damages or, if there are aggravating circumstances, three times actual damages.[322] In Kansas, an amount awarded to punish the defendant, with certain exceptions, may be no more than $5 million or the gross income of the defendant, whichever is less.[323] In Texas, except when conduct violates certain provisions of the penal code, "Exemplary damages awarded against a defendant may not exceed an amount equal to the greater of: (1) (A) two times the amount of economic damages; plus (B) an amount equal to any noneconomic damages found by the jury, not to exceed $750,000; or (2) $200,000."[324]

Many states have passed laws requiring part of any punitive damages award to be forfeited to the state.[325] However, a claim for fraud might escape the terms of the capping statute. For example, an Iowa statute requires forfeiture of at least 75% of a punitive award, unless the defendant's conduct was directed specifically at

---

[317] Wis. Stat. Ann. § 895.043(3) (LEXIS 2014).

[318] *Rodriguez v. Suzuki Motor Corp.*, 936 S.W.2d 104, 110 (Mo. 1996).

[319] *See* Colo. Rev. Stat. Ann. § 13-25-127(1) (LEXIS 2014) (emphasis added).

[320] *See* Alaska Stat. § 09.17.020(f) (LEXIS 2014).

[321] *See id.* § 09.17.020(g).

[322] Colo. Rev. Stat. Ann. § 13-21-102 (LEXIS 2014).

[323] Kan. Stat. Ann. § 60-3701(1)(e)-(f) (LEXIS 2014).

[324] Tex. Civ. Prac. & Rem. Code § 41.008 (LEXIS 2014).

[325] *See, e.g.*, 735 Ill. Comp. Stat. Ann. 5/2-1207 (LEXIS 2014) (providing for discretionary forfeiture amount).

the claimant.[326] The defendant in many fraud actions will be shown to have specifically intended to induce the plaintiff's reliance, and in such cases it could be argued that the Iowa cap would not apply.

A Nebraska constitutional provision precludes an award of punitive damages.[327] In Washington State, a similar rule applies by reason of judicial decision.[328] Punitive damages are not available in New Hampshire, except if expressly provided for by statute.[329] In Connecticut, damages awarded to punish may not exceed litigation expenses less taxable costs.[330] In Kansas, the amount of punitive damages is to be determined by judges, not juries.[331]

(2)   Constitutional Limitations

State Farm Mutual Automobile Ins. Co. v. Campbell[332] is a landmark decision dealing with constitutional restrictions on punitive damages. The decision arose out of an insurance company's fraudulent practices and now imposes limits on punitive damages in all types of tort litigation.

In *State Farm*, the question was "whether . . . an award of $145 million in punitive damages, where full compensatory damages are $1 million, . . . [was] excessive and in violation of the Due Process Clause of the Fourteenth Amendment to the Constitution of the United States."[333] State Farm had refused to settle an auto accident case that clearly should have been settled. When the case was taken to trial, the judgment greatly exceeded what could have been paid to settle the case. State Farm then refused to be responsible for the amount of the judgment in excess of insurance coverage despite the fact that the Campbells had earlier been assured by counsel that their assets were not at risk. During the pendency of an appeal, the Campbells, represented by their own lawyer, settled the case by agreeing to pursue a bad faith action against State Farm and give the auto-accident plaintiff 90% percent of any verdict against State Farm. During the trial of the bad faith action:

> [T]he Campbells introduced evidence that State Farm's decision to take the case to trial was a result of a national scheme to meet corporate fiscal goals by capping payouts on claims company wide regardless of the merits of those claims. This scheme was referred to as State Farm's "Performance, Planning and Review," or PP & R, policy. To prove the existence of this scheme, the trial court allowed the Campbells to introduce extensive expert

---

[326] Iowa Code Ann. § 668A.1(2)(b) (LEXIS 2014).

[327] *See* Neb. Const. art. VII, § 5 (LEXIS 2014). *See also Distinctive Printing and Packaging Co. v. Cox*, 443 N.W.2d 566, 574 (Neb. 1989).

[328] *See Spokane Truck & Dray Co. v. Hoefer*, 25 P. 1072, 1074–75 (Wash. 1891).

[329] *See* N.H. Rev. Stat. Ann. § 507:16 (LEXIS 2014).

[330] *See Triangle Sheet Metal Works, Inc. v. Silver*, 222 A.2d 220, 225 (Conn. 1966).

[331] *See* Kan. Stat. Ann. § 60-3702(b) (LEXIS 2014).

[332] 538 U.S. 408 (2003).

[333] *Id.* at 412.

testimony regarding fraudulent practices by State Farm in its nation-wide operations. . . .

Evidence pertaining to the PP & R policy concerned State Farm's business practices for over 20 years in numerous States. Most of these practices bore no relation to third-party automobile insurance claims, the type of claim underlying the Campbells' complaint against the company.[334]

After considerable litigation, the Utah Supreme Court ultimately approved an award of $1 million in compensatory damages and $145 million in punitive damages. Addressing these facts, Justice Anthony Kennedy wrote for the U.S. Supreme Court:

The Due Process Clause of the Fourteenth Amendment prohibits the imposition of grossly excessive or arbitrary punishments on a tortfeasor. . . . The reason is that "[e]lementary notions of fairness enshrined in our constitutional jurisprudence dictate that a person receive fair notice not only of the conduct that will subject him to punishment, but also of the severity of the penalty that a State may impose." . . .

. . . [In *BMW of North America, Inc. v. Gore*, 517 U.S. 559 (1996),] we instructed courts reviewing punitive damages to consider three guideposts: (1) the degree of reprehensibility of the defendant's misconduct; (2) the disparity between the actual or potential harm suffered by the plaintiff and the punitive damages award; and (3) the difference between the punitive damages awarded by the jury and the civil penalties authorized or imposed in comparable cases. . . .

Under the principles outlined in . . . [*Gore*], this case is neither close nor difficult. It was error to reinstate the jury's $145 million punitive damages award. . . .

"[T]he most important indicium of the reasonableness of a punitive damages award is the degree of reprehensibility of the defendant's conduct." . . . We have instructed courts to determine the reprehensibility of a defendant by considering whether: the harm caused was physical as opposed to economic; the tortious conduct evinced an indifference to or a reckless disregard of the health or safety of others; the target of the conduct had financial vulnerability; the conduct involved repeated actions or was an isolated incident; and the harm was the result of intentional malice, trickery, or deceit, or mere accident. . . . The existence of any one of these factors weighing in favor of a plaintiff may not be sufficient to sustain a punitive damages award; and the absence of all of them renders any award suspect. It should be presumed a plaintiff has been made whole for his injuries by compensatory damages, so punitive damages should only be awarded if the defendant's culpability, after having paid compensatory damages, is so reprehensible as to warrant the imposition of further sanctions to achieve punishment or deterrence. . . .

---

[334] *Id.* at 415.

. . . State Farm's handling of the claims against the Campbells merits no praise. The trial court found that State Farm's employees altered the company's records to make Campbell appear less culpable. State Farm disregarded the overwhelming likelihood of liability and the near-certain probability that, by taking the case to trial, a judgment in excess of the policy limits would be awarded. State Farm amplified the harm by at first assuring the Campbells their assets would be safe from any verdict and by later telling them, postjudgment, to put a for-sale sign on their house. While we do not suggest there was error in awarding punitive damages . . . , a more modest punishment for this reprehensible conduct could have satisfied the State's legitimate objectives. . . .

This case, instead, was used as a platform to expose, and punish, the perceived deficiencies of State Farm's operations throughout the country. . . .

A State cannot punish a defendant for conduct that may have been lawful where it occurred. . . . Nor, as a general rule, does a State have a legitimate concern in imposing punitive damages to punish a defendant for unlawful acts committed outside of the State's jurisdiction. . . .

Here, . . . much of the out-of-state conduct was lawful where it occurred. . . . Lawful out-of-state conduct may be probative when it demonstrates the deliberateness and culpability of the defendant's action in the State where it is tortious, but that conduct must have a nexus to the specific harm suffered by the plaintiff. . . .

. . . [T]he Utah courts erred. . . . The courts awarded punitive damages to punish and deter conduct that bore no relation to the Campbells' harm. A defendant's dissimilar acts, independent from the acts upon which liability was premised, may not serve as the basis for punitive damages. A defendant should be punished for the conduct that harmed the plaintiff, not for being an unsavory individual or business. Due process does not permit courts, in the calculation of punitive damages, to adjudicate the merits of other parties' hypothetical claims against a defendant under the guise of the reprehensibility analysis. . . . Punishment on these bases creates the possibility of multiple punitive damages awards for the same conduct; for in the usual case nonparties are not bound by the judgment some other plaintiff obtains. . . .

. . . Although "[o]ur holdings that a recidivist may be punished more severely than a first offender recognize that repeated misconduct is more reprehensible than an individual instance of malfeasance," . . . in the context of civil actions courts must ensure the conduct in question replicates the prior transgressions. . . .

. . . Although evidence of other acts need not be identical to have relevance in the calculation of punitive damages, the Utah court erred here because evidence pertaining to claims that had nothing to do with a third-party lawsuit was introduced at length. . . .

Turning to the second *Gore* guidepost, we have been reluctant to identify concrete constitutional limits on the ratio between harm, or potential harm, to the plaintiff and the punitive damages award. . . . We decline again to impose a bright-line ratio which a punitive damages award cannot exceed. . . . [H]owever, . . . in practice, few awards exceeding a single-digit ratio between punitive and compensatory damages, to a significant degree, will satisfy due process. . . . While these ratios are not binding, they are instructive. They demonstrate what should be obvious: Single-digit multipliers are more likely to comport with due process, while still achieving the State's goals of deterrence and retribution, than awards with ratios in range of . . . 145 to 1.

Nonetheless, because there are no rigid benchmarks that a punitive damages award may not surpass, ratios greater than those we have previously upheld may comport with due process where "a particularly egregious act has resulted in only a small amount of economic damages." . . . The converse is also true, however. When compensatory damages are substantial, then a lesser ratio, perhaps only equal to compensatory damages, can reach the outermost limit of the due process guarantee. . . .

. . . The compensatory award in this case was substantial; the Campbells were awarded $1 million for a year and a half of emotional distress. This was complete compensation. The harm arose from a transaction in the economic realm, not from some physical assault or trauma; there were no physical injuries; and State Farm paid the excess verdict before the complaint was filed, so the Campbells suffered only minor economic injuries for the 18-month period in which State Farm refused to resolve the claim against them. . . .

The Utah Supreme Court sought to justify the massive award by pointing to . . . the fact that State Farm's policies have affected numerous Utah consumers; the fact that State Farm will only be punished in one out of every 50,000 cases as a matter of statistical probability; and State Farm's enormous wealth. . . .

. . . [T]he argument that State Farm will be punished in only the rare case, coupled with reference to its assets (which, of course, are what other insured parties in Utah and other States must rely upon for payment of claims) had little to do with the actual harm sustained by the Campbells. The wealth of a defendant cannot justify an otherwise unconstitutional punitive damages award. . . .

The third guidepost in *Gore* is the disparity between the punitive damages award and the "civil penalties authorized or imposed in comparable cases." . . . The existence of a criminal penalty does have bearing on the seriousness with which a State views the wrongful action. When used to determine the dollar amount of the award, however, the criminal penalty has less utility. . . .

Here, we need not dwell long on this guidepost. The most relevant civil sanction under Utah state law for the wrong done to the Campbells appears to be a $10,000 fine for an act of fraud . . . an amount dwarfed by the $145 million punitive damages award. . . .

An application of the *Gore* guideposts to the facts of this case, especially in light of the substantial compensatory damages awarded (a portion of which contained a punitive element), likely would justify a punitive damages award at or near the amount of compensatory damages. . . .[335]

The judgment of the Utah Supreme Court in *State Farm* was reversed, and the case was remanded for further proceedings.

Subsequent to *State Farm*, the Supreme Court emphasized that an award of punitive damages may not be based, even in part, on a jury's desire to punish a defendant for harming nonparties. In *Philip Morris USA v. Williams*,[336] the jury, in response to the plaintiff's argument that many other smokers had been killed by the defendant's cigarettes, made a large punitive damages award to the estate of a heavy smoker. In remanding the case for further proceedings, Justice Stephen Breyer's opinion for the court explained:

> [T]he Due Process Clause prohibits a State from punishing an individual without first providing that individual with "an opportunity to present every available defense." . . . Yet a defendant threatened with punishment for injuring a nonparty victim has no opportunity to defend against the charge, by showing, for example in a case such as this, that the other victim was not entitled to damages because he or she knew that smoking was dangerous or did not rely upon the defendant's statements to the contrary.
>
> . . . [T]o permit punishment for injuring a nonparty victim would add a near standardless dimension to the punitive damages equation. How many such victims are there? How seriously were they injured? Under what circumstances did injury occur? The trial will not likely answer such questions as to nonparty victims. The jury will be left to speculate. . . .
>
> . . . [W]e can find no authority supporting the use of punitive damages awards for the purpose of punishing a defendant for harming others. . . .
>
> Respondent argues that she is free to show harm to other victims because it is relevant to a different part of the punitive damages constitutional equation, namely, reprehensibility. That is to say, harm to others shows more reprehensible conduct. Philip Morris, in turn, does not deny that a plaintiff may show harm to others in order to demonstrate reprehensibility. Nor do we. . . . Yet for the reasons given above, a jury may not go further than this and use a punitive damages verdict to punish a defendant directly on account of harms it is alleged to have visited on nonparties.
>
> . . . We . . . conclude that the Due Process Clause requires States to provide assurance that juries are not asking the wrong question, i.e.,

---

[335] *Id.* at 416–29.

[336] 549 U.S. 346 (2007).

seeking, not simply to determine reprehensibility, but also to punish for harm caused strangers.[337]

The teachings of *State Farm* continue to shape the rulings of the United States Supreme Court in the field of punitive damages. In *Exxon Shipping Co. v. Baker*,[338] a case arising from an Alaskan oil spill, the Court held that, under federal maritime law, an award of punitive damages could not exceed the jury's substantial compensatory damages award of $507.5 million.

Liability for punitive damages may be imposed on an employer vicariously under a *respondeat superior* theory without violating due process. In *Pacific Mutual Life Ins. Co. v. Haslip*,[339] the court wrote:

> Imposing exemplary damages on the corporation when its agent commits intentional fraud creates a strong incentive for vigilance by those in a position "to guard substantially against the evil to be prevented." . . . If an insurer were liable for such damages only upon proof that it was at fault independently, it would have an incentive to minimize oversight of its agents. Imposing liability without independent fault deters fraud more than a less stringent rule. It therefore rationally advances the State's goal.[340]

Some states have limited employer vicarious liability for punitive damages by statute.[341]

PROBLEM 2-11: THE PONZI SCHEME

Green Future, Inc., was organized as a corporation, with Dave Donnelly as the CEO. The board of directors consisted mainly of business executives who are (or at least were) close friends of Donnelly, as well as a few persons who are regarded as "pillars" of the community, including a law school dean.

Shares in Green Future, Inc. were publicly sold to investors on a continuing basis for about twenty years and the resulting capital was then invested (everyone

---

[337] *Id.* at 353–55.

[338] 554 U.S. 471 (2008).

[339] 499 U.S. 1 (1991).

[340] *Id.* at 14.

[341] *See, e.g.*, ALASKA STAT. § 09.17.020(k) (LEXIS 2014). This section provides:

> In a civil action in which an employer is determined to be vicariously liable for the act or omission of an employee, punitive damages may not be awarded against the employer under principles of vicarious liability unless
>
>> (1) the employer or the employer's managerial agent (A) authorized the act or omission and the manner in which the act was performed or omission occurred; or (B) ratified or approved the act or omission after the act or omission occurred; or
>>
>> (2) the employee (A) was unfit to perform the act or avoid the omission and the employer or the employer's managerial agent acted recklessly in employing or retaining the employee; or (B) was employed in a managerial capacity and was acting within the scope of employment.
>
> In this subsection, "managerial agent" means a management level employee with the stature and authority to exercise control, discretion, and independent judgment over a certain area of the employer's business and with some power to set policy for the employer.

thought) in a variety of "green" technologies. When Green Future was started by Donnelly in the early 1990s, it was far ahead of its time. Virtually no one was then promoting investments in environmentally friendly energy sources and products.

For almost twenty years, Green Future paid near record dividends, regularly outperforming the Dow Jones Industrial Average and virtually all mutual funds. The profits reaped by investors were as regular as an atomic clock. Donnelly said that this was because he was "always ahead of the curve." There was never a bad quarter, not even during the economic woes that followed the dot-com collapse at the end of the 1990s, the terrorist attacks on September 11, 2001, or the Wall Street "meltdown" in 2008.

Donnelly ran the corporation with an iron fist. No one — not even members of the board of directors — ever questioned his investment strategies, his numbers, or his judgment. Donnelly, Green Future, and the investors all profited handsomely.

It came as a great shock to Donnelly's loyal investors when a major newspaper reported that Donnelly was the target of a criminal investigation and likely to be indicted for running a Ponzi scheme.[342] In the wake of the report, it "all made sense." How else was Green Future able to pay such fabulous returns for such a long period of time?

Donnelly and Green Future had defrauded 832 investors in 13 states. One of those investors was Catherine Iverson, who lived in State A. Iverson had invested $400,000 in Green Future, which was essentially all of her retirement savings. She had relied upon Donnelly's repeated assurances that her money would be safe. Iverson was one of about 200 investors in State A who lost a total of $85 million in the Ponzi scheme.

In State A, investment fraud causing actual losses in excess of $10,000 is a Class C felony, punishable by a fine not exceeding $20,000 plus not more than fifteen years in jail.

Donnelly has fled the country. However, he might be located and extradited to the United States to face trial on criminal charges. Green Future has ceased doing business, but still has some assets. Iverson wants to sue both Donnelly and Green Future for fraud and hopes to recover not only the money she lost, but punitive damages to make an example of Donnelly and his nefarious enterprise. Please advise Iverson about the obstacles she will face in her quest for compensatory and punitive awards based on fraud.

---

[342] A *Ponzi scheme* is "a fraudulent investment operation that pays returns to its investors from existing capital or new capital paid by new investors, rather than from profit earned by the individual or organization running the operation. Operators of Ponzi schemes usually entice new investors by offering higher returns than other investments, in the form of short-term returns that are either abnormally high or unusually consistent. The perpetuation of the high returns requires an ever-increasing flow of money from new investors to sustain the scheme." http://en.wikipedia.org/wiki/Ponzi_scheme (last visited Jan. 30, 2014).

6.   Defenses and Other Obstacles to Recovery

Defenses to fraud based on contributory negligence, comparative negligence, and comparative fault are discussed in Part A-4 of this chapter, and the economic loss rule is discussed in Part A-5. Several other important defenses or potential obstacles to recovery are considered in the following sections.

a.   Federal and State Preemption of Fraud Claims

Federal Preemption. In some instances, statutory provisions supplant a common law action for fraud. To begin with, a state tort action may be preempted by federal law.[343] For example, the federal Securities Litigation Uniform Standards Act of 1998 (SLUSA) "preempts state-law class actions that allege an untrue statement or omission of a material fact . . . 'in connection with the purchase or sale of a covered security.' "[344]

State Preemption. Courts sometimes also hold that certain forms of state legislation eclipse common law relief. For example, many states have adopted property disclosure laws, which require certain sellers of real estate to make disclosures with regard to a wide range of matters related to the property (*e.g.*, the presence of asbestos, radon gas, flooding problems, nuisance neighbors, nearby munitions, or tree diseases, and the prior occurrence of deaths on the property).[345] While such laws generally expand the common law disclosure obligations of property sellers and do not preclude relief under the law of fraud,[346] occasional decisions have held certain property disclosure laws define the full extent of a seller's disclosure obligations in a particular context.[347]

b.   Statutory Obligations That Are Not Privately Enforceable

In some cases, statutory disclosure obligations are not enforceable by an aggrieved individual in a civil cause of action. In New York, for example, the Martin Act imposes voluminous disclosure requirements related to newly constructed condominiums. In *Kerusa Co. LLC v. W10Z/515 Real Estate Ltd. Partnership*,[348] the New York Court of Appeals held that the disappointed purchaser of a luxury condominium on Park Avenue in New York City could not maintain a common law fraud action based on disclosure obligations arising under the Martin Act. This was true because the state attorney general was the only person with standing to enforce the Act, which provided purchasers with no private right of action.

---

[343] *See generally Wyeth v. Levine*, 555 U.S. 555 (2009) (discussing preemption principles).

[344] *Kutten v. Bank of Am., N.A.*, 530 F.3d 669, 670 (8th Cir. Mo. 2008) (citing 15 U.S.C. § 77p(b)).

[345] *See, e.g.*, CAL. CIV. CODE § 1102.1 et seq. (LEXIS 2014).

[346] *See, e.g., id.* § 1102.8.

[347] *See, e.g., Nobrega v. Edison Glen Assoc.*, 772 A.2d 368, 374 (N.J. 2001).

[348] 906 N.E.2d 1049 (N.Y. 2009).

c.   Inactionability of Fraud in Non-Business Settings

Allowing Recovery for Fraud Relating to Personal Decisions. The great majority of cases involving allegations of fraud arise from business settings and involve purely economic losses. However, many cases have applied the same rules to disputes involving personal injuries, even if the claim arises from a personal, rather than business, context. For example, a person who deceives another into engaging in sexual relations by failing to disclose or misrepresenting a serious disease may be held liable for fraud in an action where compensation for personal injuries is the chief objective of the lawsuit.[349] Other decisions have also involved facts far removed from a buy-and-sell sort of business relationship. For example, in *Burr v. Board of County Commissioners*,[350] the plaintiffs were fraudulently induced to adopt a child who was at risk for serious physical and emotional problems. Because misrepresentations to the plaintiffs about the origins of the child had been made by representatives of the defendant with knowledge of their falsity and with intent to induce reliance, the court held that an action for fraud would lie and that damages could be recovered.

Denying Recovery for Fraud in Noncommercial Contexts. However, occasional decisions have held that fraud arising in purely private settings is not actionable. In *Doe v. Dilling*,[351] the plaintiff alleged that the parents of her deceased fiancé (Albert) had deceived her by telling her that their son was suffering from heavy-metal poisoning and Lyme disease, when he was actually HIV-positive and had been diagnosed with AIDS. As a result, the plaintiff allegedly suffered physical harm by reason of her own delayed testing and treatment for HIV. The Illinois Supreme Court might have denied recovery because under the state "Confidentiality Act, the parents had a statutory legal duty to maintain confidentiality if they knew anything about Albert's HIV status."[352] Instead, the court chose to reject the plaintiff's fraud claim on broader grounds. The court found that prior Illinois decisions had not recognized the tort of fraudulent misrepresentation in purely private settings. It also distinguished cases from other jurisdictions which had imposed liability for fraudulent transmission of serious diseases on the ground that in those cases the plaintiffs had sued the person who actually communicated the disease. The court concluded that the plaintiff's fraud claim failed because it was inappropriate to extend the tort "beyond its general historical application to cases arising in the commercial context."[353] The court further concluded that its rejection of the fraud claim dictated rejection of the plaintiff's action for negligent misrepresentation because "the elements of these two torts are essentially the same."[354]

If the *Doe* court had merely held that the plaintiff's misrepresentation claims failed because the parents had no duty to disclose information about their son to

---

[349] *See, e.g., Behr v. Redmond*, 193 Cal. App. 4th 517 (2011).

[350] 491 N.E.2d 1101 (Ohio 1986).

[351] 888 N.E.2d 24 (Ill. 2008).

[352] *Id.* at 37.

[353] *Id.* at 40.

[354] *Id.* at 45.

protect the plaintiff from harm, the decision would have been unremarkable. Courts often find that there is no duty to act, rescue, or disclose information, even when it is foreseeable that, absent such efforts, harm will befall another. However, *Doe* was a case that allegedly involved an affirmative misrepresentation (lying), rather than nondisclosure. Tort law routinely holds that even if one has no duty to act, a person who chooses to act is subject to liability for failure to exercise care. *Doe* is a questionable decision which should not be followed by other courts.

Fraudulent Online Relationships. In *Bonhomme v. St. James*,[355] the Supreme Court of Illinois considered the viability of a fraud claim arising from an Internet-based relationship that lasted almost two years. The defendant posed as a man named "Jesse" and "created a universe of approximately 20 fictional online characters either related to or involved with Jesse."[356] According to the court:

> These characters communicated with plaintiff from separate and distinct email accounts and even sent photos, handwritten mail, and packages from different states and foreign countries. For her part, plaintiff sent gifts totaling more than $10,000 to defendant, Jesse, and various other characters.[357]

As the online prank played out, the plaintiff was told that Jesse attempted suicide and later died of a disease. The plaintiff suffered great emotional distress and spent more than $5,000 on a therapist. In rejecting the viability of an action for fraud, the Supreme Court of Illinois wrote:

> [T]he crucial question in this case is whether the facts at issue are purely personal in nature, or whether there exists some commercial, transactional, or regulatory component that moves them beyond the purely personal. This is not a difficult question to answer. When all is said and done, what lies beneath this case is two private persons engaged in a long-distance personal relationship. To be sure, it was a personal relationship built wholly on one party's relentless deceit, but it was a purely personal relationship nonetheless. Indeed, all of the hallmarks of ordinary human relationship are present: correspondence, conversation, intimacy, trust, mutual benefi-cence, emotional support, affection, disappointment, and even grief. And just as importantly, there is absolutely nothing of the commercial, trans-actional, or regulatory at work. Plaintiff and defendant were not engaged in any kind of business dealings or bargaining, and the veracity of represen-tations made in the context of purely private personal relationships is simply not something the state regulates or in which the state possesses any kind of valid public policy interest. Consequently, as regrettable as the alleged facts are, we hold that they are not the types of facts upon which a claim for fraudulent misrepresentation may be pled.[358]

One can understand the reluctance of the Illinois courts to undertake the

---

[355] 970 N.E.2d 1 (Ill. 2012).

[356] *Id.* at 3.

[357] *Id.*

[358] *Id.* at 10–12.

daunting task of offering judicial remedies for harm caused by every deceptive statement disseminated via the Internet. Yet, the decision in *Bonhomme* seems at odds with cases allowing claims for fraud related to clergy sexual abuse and perhaps other cases discussed earlier in this chapter. More pointedly, why should fraud provide a remedy only for deception in business and financial transactions? Is it less important to deter fraudulent practices that cause physical or emotional harm to individuals?

The Illinois Supreme Court noted in *Bonhomme* that a victim of fraudulent misrepresentations of a purely personal nature may have other remedies. But why should the aggrieved plaintiff be deprived of the doctrinal clarity that has emerged from the well-developed law of fraud concerning important distinctions such as silence versus affirmative misstatement, fact versus opinion, prediction versus state of mind, and failure to investigate versus justifiable reliance. As of this writing, *Bonhomme* has not been cited by a court outside of Illinois.

d.   Ratification of a Fraudulent Transaction

Full Knowledge and Intent to Abide by the Contract and Waive Rights. The right to sue for fraud in a business transaction can be waived by knowing ratification of the transaction. In *Wells v. Dotson*,[359] a friend (Claude Dotson) induced an elderly widow (Mildred Snow) to lease certain property to him on favorable terms with an option to purchase. After Mildred died in 2005, her estate became involved in a dispute in which Dotson sought to enforce his right to purchase the land. Certain interested parties (Wells, Stewart, Phillips, and Sterling; collectively "Appellants") alleged that Dotson had defrauded Mildred. In addressing the dispute, Justice Sam Griffith wrote for the Texas Court of Appeals:

> Appellants . . . argue that the trial court erred in granting summary judgment in Appellees' favor because Appellees failed to demonstrate as a matter of law that Appellants' counterclaims were barred by the affirmative defense of ratification. Acts done in affirmance of a contract can amount to a waiver of fraudulent inducement only where they are done with full knowledge of the fraud and of all material facts and with the intention, clearly manifested, of abiding by the contract and waiving all right to recover for the deception. . . . Acts which, although in affirmance of the contract, do not indicate any intention to waive the fraud, cannot be held to operate as a waiver. . . . Express ratification of a fraudulently induced contract is not necessary, but any act based on a recognition of the contract as subsisting or any conduct inconsistent with avoidance of the contract has the effect of waiving the right to rescind the contract on the basis of fraud. . . . As a result of ratification, the defrauded party waives the defense of fraud and is bound by the terms of the contract. . . .

> The question is largely one of intent. . . . That is, there must be evidence of an intent to relinquish or conduct that warrants an inference of relinquishment. . . . Moreover, there can be no waiver of fraud without full knowledge of all the circumstances. . . .

---

[359] 261 S.W.3d 275 (Tex. App. 2008).

Appellants argue that Appellees presented no evidence that Mildred (1) received benefits under the contract, (2) conducted herself in a manner indicating that she "recognized the [contract] as subsisting and binding [,]" (3) affirmed the contract, (4) continued to comply with the contract after she became aware of the alleged fraud, or (5) intended to give validity to the acts of Appellees. Having reviewed the summary judgment record, we disagree.

In his deposition, Wells testified that in late 1993 or early 1994, he and his mother, Phillips, consulted a lawyer as to the meaning of the contract Mildred had entered into with Dotson. They later expressed to Mildred their concern that the contract was not in her best interest and informed her of what the lawyer had told them. Wells further testified that Mildred knew as early as 1994 that there was something wrong with the contract and that Dotson had taken advantage of her. However, according to Wells, even with such knowledge, Mildred declined to take any action to have the contract set aside.

Likewise, Stewart testified in her deposition that, in 1995, she explained to Mildred that Mildred had no rights under the contract. Stewart further testified that Mildred understood her and, after telling Stewart she would pray about it, later stated, "I gave my word, and I can't go back on my word." . . .

Phillips testified . . . that she was present when Mildred signed the contract with Dotson. Phillips further testified that, at that time, she told Dotson's lawyer in Mildred's presence that she thought Dotson was taking Mildred "to the cleaners" because Dotson was trying to make a false friendship with Mildred to induce her to sign the contract and, as a result, Mildred loved Dotson like a son. Phillips stated that she and her son, Wells, later attempted to explain to Mildred the effect of the contract. . . . Mildred told her, "If he takes me to the cleaners, he'll just have to take me . . . I've prayed about it[.] I've studied on it . . . I can't go back on my word[.] I can't welch on a deal." In summary, Phillips testified that she had clearly warned Mildred, Mildred carefully considered and understood the warning, and determined that she would not do anything to undo what she felt was her obligation. Phillips confirmed that in 2003, Mildred signed documents conveying property to Dotson pursuant to the contract. Phillips further confirmed that Mildred received money from Dotson annually pursuant to their agreement and deposited that money in the bank.

Sterling testified at her deposition that she spoke with Mildred in 1995. . . . Sterling stated that Mildred tearfully said to her, "I just can't believe Buddy took advantage of me like that." . . . Sterling testified that Mildred did nothing to disturb her agreement with Dotson from 1995 until the date of her death in 2005. Sterling further testified that Mildred told her that, after she entered into the contract, Phillips and Wells had met with a lawyer who looked at the contract. Sterling stated that Mildred told her that Phillips and Wells then met with her and showed her a letter from the lawyer in an attempt to try to convince her how unfair her agreement with

Dotson was to her. Sterling again confirmed that Mildred chose to not attempt to have the agreement set aside.

In our review of the summary judgment record, we have not encountered any evidence that contradicts the aforementioned deposition testimony given by Wells, Stewart, Phillips, and Sterling respectively. The testimony each offered is largely consistent and demonstrates that Mildred acted in affirmance of her contract with Dotson with full knowledge that he had taken advantage of her and treated her unfairly. Mildred continued to accept lease payments from Dotson, expressed to Appellees that in spite of Dotson's acts, she, bound by her word, intended to abide by the contract, and, in fact, transferred one of the tracts of land to Dotson in accordance with the contract. Therefore, we hold that the trial court did not err in granting summary judgment on Appellees' affirmative defense of ratification as it pertains to Appellants' fraud in the inducement claim. . . .[360]

Problem 2-12: The Professional Football Team

The Ramblers had played professional football in San Gabriel for twenty-five years when they broke the news that they were moving to Wimmer City, a larger, wealthier metropolitan area with a new stadium. Elected officials and civic leaders in San Gabriel tried to stop the move, by enticing the Ramblers to stay and suing to prevent the change of cities. The efforts were to no avail. The Ramblers left San Gabriel and played football in Wimmer City for the next ten years.

A nonprofit organization, the Downtown Athletic League (DAL), was formed in San Gabriel to win back the Ramblers. DAL arranged the financing and construction of a new stadium (the "San Gabriel Arena"). DAL also mounted an aggressive public relations campaign to sign the Ramblers to a long-term contract to play in the San Gabriel Arena.

As part of its promotional efforts, DAL launched a marketing effort to sell personal seat licenses (PSLs) and luxury box seats to fans. By purchasing a PSL or luxury box seat, a fan acquired the right and obligation to buy season tickets in designated seats for the Ramblers' games for the next 10 seasons. Because of strong demand, an accounting firm, AccuNumber, Ltd., was retained to conduct a lottery for PSL and luxury box seating assignments. To be included in the lottery, a fan had to submit a PSL or luxury box seat application and a 25% deposit for the first year, and, if accepted, had to pay an additional 25% within 15 days of the invoice date and the remaining 50% within six months. A schedule was set for payments relating to the following nine seasons.

On July 20, 2014, DAL issued a press release entitled "2014 Games Sell Out in First Phase of the Ramblers' Ticket Drive." The release declared that there were more applications for PSLs and luxury box seats in the first round of marketing which closed on July 17th than there were seats available, and that a lottery would be held to determine who gets seats. According to the release, "46,980 seats were sold, including 44,700 PSLs and 2,280 luxury box seats." The release further said

---

[360] *Id.* at 282–83.

that, "Along with seats already committed to the NFL and the Ramblers, this represents a sellout for 2014 and 80% of the seats for an expanded stadium in 2015."

The press release quoted marketing director Ted Gannett as saying that luxury boxes were completely sold out for 2014 and that some applicants would be asked to share boxes for that season. Said Gannett, "The response is so strong and the enthusiasm so real that, not only did we sell out for 2014, we expect to be fully sold out for the 2015 season by Thanksgiving."

No copy of the press release was ever provided to representatives of the Ramblers, but they were aware of the contents of the release from press reports.

In fact, roughly 45,000 PSL applications had been received, but AccuNumber ultimately excluded about 10 percent of them from the lottery due to credit card problems. Additional applicants were disqualified from the lottery due to bounced checks and for other reasons. In the end, a total of only 37,000 PSL and luxury box seats were sold and assigned as a result of the first phase of marketing.

On August 7, 2014, the Ramblers executed a binding contract (the "Contract") with DAL, the City of San Gabriel, and other entities. The Ramblers committed to play at the new San Gabriel Arena for ten consecutive football seasons. At the end of the first year, the parties executed an addendum to the Contract (the "Supplementary Agreement"). The Supplementary Agreement made changes with regard to advertising revenue, construction dates for the stadium expansion, and other issues. Otherwise, the terms of the Contract remained in effect.

Although all PSL and luxury box seats had not been sold at the time the 2014 Contract was executed, the Ramblers ultimately sold out the Arena for the 2014 football season. However, the Ramblers' performance faltered at the end of 2014 and their won-lost record fell below .500 in 2015. While gross ticket sales in 2015 were about the same as the previous year, the Ramblers did not sell out, due to the expansion of the stadium. Attendance slipped further in 2016, when the Ramblers won only four of sixteen games.

The Ramblers have now sued the DAL, the City of San Gabriel, and AccuNumber, Ltd. for fraud. The management of the Ramblers alleges that it relied on the "sellout" representations that were disseminated in DAL's press release and would not have signed the Contract or moved back to San Gabriel from Wimmer City if the truth had been disclosed. The Ramblers' theory of damages is that a sellout of PSLs and luxury box seats in 2014 would have created an "excess demand" for tickets that would have resulted in season sellouts for the next nine years. The Ramblers have expert witnesses who will testify that, by contracting with DAL and the City of San Gabriel, the Ramblers lost the opportunity to move to San Antonio, where the team would have realized greater profits and enhanced franchise value.

You are an assistant city attorney for the City of San Gabriel. The City has never been involved in this kind of lawsuit. You need to prepare to brief the mayor and city manager (both of whom are nonlawyers) about the legal viability of the Ramblers' fraud claim so that they can decide whether to incur the considerable expense of hiring an outside firm to defend the City. They also want to know whether expenses could be saved by striking a deal to have one law firm represent all of the defendants in the case. Discovery in the Ramblers' suit has not yet taken place, and the complaint reveals few facts other than those discussed above.

e.   Unlawful Conduct Defense

Unlawful conduct on the part of the plaintiff may constitute a total bar to liability for fraud, as well as other tort claims. For example, in *Sharpe v. Turley*,[361] the Texas Court of Appeals held that because an individual had no legal right to remove documents placed in a trash dumpster, the unlawful acts rule precluded the individual from bringing an action for fraud against a third party's attorney. The individual had alleged that the attorney had defrauded him into turning over the documents.

The contours of what is sometimes called the "unlawful conduct defense" are very much in flux. Nevertheless, the defense appears to play an increasingly important role in modern tort litigation. Consider the following explanation of the unlawful conduct defense.[362]

Traditional Rejection of an "Outlaw" Doctrine. Not long ago, American tort law clearly rejected an "outlaw" doctrine: a plaintiff engaged in tortious or criminal acts was not treated as an outlaw who could be injured with impunity. As this principle was expressed in the *Restatement (Second) of Torts*: "One is not barred from recovery for an interference with his legally protected interests merely because at the time of the interference he was committing a tort or a crime."[363]

This was true regardless of whether the plaintiff's claim was based on intent, recklessness, negligence, or strict liability. The plaintiff's unlawful conduct might give rise to a defense such as contributory or comparative negligence under ordinary tort principles, or might trigger a privilege assertable against the plaintiff, such as one to prevent crime or to conduct a citizen's arrest. However, unlawful conduct, by itself, did not inevitably bar the courthouse doors.

Various cases allowed plaintiffs to sue for harm that they suffered while engaged in illegal gambling, fornication, doing unlicensed business, or while unlawfully present in the United States. Other suits permitted recovery by persons injured while trespassing on another's property, or while traveling unlawfully on Sunday or in an unregistered vehicle.

The second *Restatement*'s rejection of a rule making tortious or criminal conduct an absolute obstacle to recovery in tort was not surprising. The same position had been embraced four decades earlier by the first *Restatement*, and the most respected legal commentators had renounced the contrary view.

The Rise of a Defense. Much has changed in American tort law during the past thirty years, including the rules relating to unlawful conduct. Today, in an

---

[361] 191 S.W.3d 362, 369 (Tex. App. 2006).

[362] The discussion below is based on, and language is borrowed from, Vincent R. Johnson, *The Unlawful Conduct Defense in Legal Malpractice Law*, 77 UMKC L. Rev. 43–83 (2008). Additional supporting citations can be found in the article.

[363] Restatement (Second) of Torts § 889 (1979).

important range of cases, statutes and court decisions in many states now provide that injuries arising from the plaintiff's serious unlawful conduct are not compensable under tort law. For example, in *Barker v. Kallash*,[364] the New York Court of Appeals ruled that:

> [W]hen the plaintiff has engaged in activities prohibited, as opposed to merely regulated, by law, the courts will not entertain the suit if the plaintiff's conduct constituted a serious violation of the law and the injuries for which he seeks recovery were the direct result of that violation.[365]

In *Barker*, the court held that a fifteen-year-old boy who was injured while constructing a "pipe bomb" was precluded from recovering from the nine-year-old boy who supplied the gunpowder.

Statutory Unlawful Conduct Defenses. A number of states have enacted statutes which foreclose lawsuits seeking damages for injuries resulting from serious unlawful conduct. These laws hearken back to harsh common law rules, which, at various times in Anglo-American history, have denied legal protection to an "outlaw."[366] Some of the new laws are short and elegant. One California statute, enacted by a voter initiative, provides simply that:

> In any action for damages based on negligence, a person may not recover any damages if the plaintiff's injuries were in any way proximately caused by the plaintiff's commission of any felony, or immediate flight therefrom, and the plaintiff has been duly convicted of that felony.[367]

Similarly, an Ohio statute provides in part that:

> Recovery on a claim for relief in a tort action is barred to any person or the person's legal representative if . . . [t]he person has been convicted of or has pleaded guilty to a felony, or to a misdemeanor that is an offense of violence, arising out of criminal conduct that was a proximate cause of the injury or loss for which relief is claimed in the tort action.[368]

Some state laws are detailed. For example, an Alaska statute addresses with great specificity the types of criminal activity that give rise to an unlawful conduct defense, the significance of pleas of guilty or *nolo contendere*, and how the rule operates in cases where there has been no prior conviction.[369]

---

[364] 468 N.E.2d 39 (N.Y. 1984).

[365] *Id.* at 41.

[366] *See* Joseph H. King, Jr., *Outlaws and Outlier Doctrines: The Serious Misconduct Bar in Tort Law*, 43 Wm. & Mary L. Rev. 1011, 1014–18 (2002).

[367] Cal. Civ. Code § 3333.3 (LEXIS 2014).

[368] Ohio Rev. Code Ann. § 2307.60(B)(2)(a) (LEXIS 2014).

[369] Alaska Stat. § 09.65.210 (LEXIS 2014). Section 09.65.210 provides:

> A person who suffers personal injury or death or the person's personal representative . . . may not recover damages for the personal injury or death if the injury or death occurred while the person was
>
> (1) engaged in the commission of a felony, the person has been convicted of the felony, including conviction based on a guilty plea or plea of nolo contendere, and the party defending

Statutes creating an unlawful conduct defense are animated by a common theme. They seek to punish persons who have engaged in serious wrongdoing by curtailing their rights to sue for damages and preventing them from shifting responsibility for their anti-social conduct. The text of the Proposition that led to the enactment of the California law quoted above included a blunt statement of findings and purpose, which obviously the voters found appealing. That statement read:

> Insurance costs have skyrocketed for those Californians who have taken responsibility for their actions. . . . [C]riminal felons are law breakers, and should not be rewarded for their irresponsibility. . . . However, under current laws, . . . criminals have been able to recover damages from law-abiding citizens for injuries suffered during the commission of their crimes. . . . Californians must change the system that rewards individuals who fail to take essential personal responsibility to prevent them from seeking unreasonable damages or from suing law-abiding citizens.[370]

One might conclude that the Proposition was intended to protect only "law-abiding citizens," persons who were blameless, innocent of fault. However, a subsequent case addressing the quoted language made clear that the initiative had a broader reach: "[l]aw abiding cannot and does not mean free of all blame."[371] "In expressly barring negligence claims, the initiative presupposes that the defendants, in fact, may have been negligent."[372]

At least one state, more than a quarter century ago, passed legislation rejecting an outlaw doctrine with language paralleling the rule of the *Restatement (Second) of Torts*, quoted above in the text. That Massachusetts statute provides:

> The violation of a criminal statute, ordinance or regulation by a plaintiff which contributed to said injury, death or damage, shall be considered as evidence of negligence of that plaintiff, but the violation of said statute,

---

against the claim proves by clear and convincing evidence that the felony substantially contributed to the personal injury or death;

(2) engaged in conduct that would constitute the commission of an unclassified felony, a class A felony, or a class B felony for which the person was not convicted and the party defending against the claim proves by clear and convincing evidence

(A) the felonious conduct; and

(B) that the felonious conduct substantially contributed to the personal injury or death;

. . .

(4) operating a vehicle, aircraft, or watercraft while under the influence of intoxicating liquor or any controlled substance in violation of AS 28.35.030, was convicted, including conviction based on a guilty plea or plea of nolo contendere, and the party defending against the claim proves by clear and convincing evidence that the conduct substantially contributed to the personal injury or death; or

(5) engaged in conduct that would constitute a violation of AS 28.35.030 for which the person was not convicted if the party defending against the claim proves by clear and convincing evidence

(A) the violation of AS 28.35.030; and

(B) that the conduct substantially contributed to the personal injury or death.

[370] 1996 Cal. Legis. Serv. Prop. 213.

[371] *Gage v. Network Appliance, Inc.*, 2005 Cal. App. Unpub. LEXIS 11046 (Nov. 30, 2005).

[372] *Id.* at *13.

ordinance or regulation shall not as a matter of law and for that reason alone, serve to bar a plaintiff from recovery.[373]

However, the recent trend is to the contrary.

Statutory Variables. In general, state statutes that bar a civil action for damages based on the plaintiff's own unlawful conduct vary in five important respects. Those variations concern: (1) the nature of the unlawful conduct that triggers the rule; (2) the theories of recovery that are barred; (3) types of damages that may not be recovered; (4) how closely the unlawful conduct must be related to the injuries for which recovery is sought; and (5) whether there must have been a prior adjudication of criminal responsibility.

(1) Conduct That Triggers a Statutory Ban. Statutory versions of the unlawful conduct defense require proof of a serious criminal act. Typically, the act must be a felony, or a particular type of felony. However, in some cases, certain misdemeanors, such as operating a vehicle while under the influence of intoxicating liquor, may suffice to foreclose relief in a civil cause of action.

(2) Types of Claims Barred. One California statute establishing an unlawful conduct defense refers only to *negligence* claims arising from felonious conduct. Quite logically, that provision has been interpreted as not precluding *intentional* tort actions. The statute is therefore unlikely to have any impact on a suit for fraud.

(3) Damages That May Not Be Recovered. Statutory unlawful conduct defenses sometimes specify what types of damages may not be recovered by a plaintiff, rather than what theories of liability (*e.g.*, negligence) are foreclosed. For example, an Alaska law provides that if the person has engaged in certain forms of criminal conduct (such as "a felony . . . [of which] the person has been convicted"[374]), that person, or the person's personal representative, "may not recover damages for the [resulting] personal injury or death."[375] While fraud often gives rise to purely economic losses, sometimes a fraud claim seeks compensation for personal injury, and, in rare cases, for death.

(4) Close Connection. Statutes barring a plaintiff's action based on unlawful conduct do so only if that conduct is sufficiently linked to the damages the plaintiff seeks to recover. Yet, how strong that link must be varies with the language of the statute. Some statutes say that the plaintiff's injuries must have been "proximately cause[d]" or "*in any way* proximately caused" by the criminal conduct of the plaintiff. Other statutes use language which might be found to be less demanding, requiring simply that the plaintiff's conduct must have "substantially contributed" to the injuries for which recovery is sought. As any law student knows, the principles of proximate causation cover broad territory. However, a nexus requirement framed in terms of whether the plaintiff's conduct "substantially contributed" to the plaintiff's harm might deny judicial relief in an even wider range of cases. To the extent that the unlawful conduct defense forecloses all civil redress, it is reasonable to ask whether "proximate causation" or "substantial contribution" are

---

[373] Mass. Gen. Laws Ann. ch. 231, § 85 (LEXIS 2014).

[374] Alaska Stat. § 09.65.210(1) (LEXIS 2014).

[375] *Id.* § 09.65.210.

sufficiently demanding standards for ascertaining whether the plaintiff's unlawful conduct and injuries are so closely related that recovery should be denied.

Interestingly, court decisions embracing an unlawful conduct defense as a matter of common law sometimes impose what seems to be a more demanding causation requirement than found in many statutes. According to the New York Court of Appeals, "a serious violation of the law" bars recovery only for those injuries which are "the *direct* result" of that violation.[376] Although what "direct" means has not been definitively charted by New York courts, the language suggests a connection closer than mere proximate causation is required.

(5) Necessity of Prior Adjudication. Some statutes creating an unlawful conduct defense only bar a civil action for damages if the injured party was previously found guilty of a criminal offense. This obviously poses difficulties to an assertion of the defense in a wrongful death or survival action arising from fatal injuries which caused death too soon for prosecution to be commenced and completed.

Other statutes allow the injured person's criminal responsibility for a crime of which the person was not convicted to be established in the civil action itself. To the extent that the standard of proof applicable in the civil suit is less demanding than the "beyond a reasonable doubt" standard applicable in a criminal prosecution, there is less certainty that the plaintiff in fact engaged in unlawful conduct inimical to the interests of society.

Common Law Unlawful Conduct Defenses. Even in the absence of a statute specifying that serious criminal conduct forecloses a civil action for damages, courts have denied redress as a matter of common law to persons whose claims were based on their own illegal acts. In *Chapman v. Superior Court*,[377] the California Court of Appeal concluded that public policy barred a former public official, who pleaded guilty to wilful commission of a crime, from maintaining a legal malpractice action against an attorney based on the attorney's alleged misinterpretation of a statute. And in *Saks v. Sawtelle, Goode, Davidson & Troilo*,[378] the Texas Court of Appeals determined that public policy precluded judicial consideration of a legal malpractice suit for damages by clients who were convicted of knowingly committing bank fraud after they had allegedly received negligent advice relating to a bank loan transaction. According to the Alabama Supreme Court in *Oden v. Pepsi Cola Bottling Co. of Decatur, Inc.*:

> This rule promotes the desirable public policy objective of preventing those who knowingly and intentionally engage in an illegal or immoral act involving moral turpitude from imposing liability on others for the consequences of their own behavior. Even so, such a rule derives principally not from consideration for the defendant, "but from a desire to see that those

---

[376] *Barker v. Kallash*, 468 N.E.2d 39, 41 (N.Y. 1984).

[377] 130 Cal. App. 4th 261, 275 (2005).

[378] 880 S.W.2d 466 (Tex. App. 1994).

who transgress the moral or criminal code shall not receive aid from the judicial branch of government."[379]

Or, as explained by the Michigan Supreme Court in *Orzel by Orzel v. Scott Drug Co.*, if a common law unlawful conduct defense were not recognized by the judiciary, several unacceptable consequences would result:

First, by making relief potentially available for wrongdoers, courts in effect would condone and encourage illegal conduct. . . . Second, some wrongdoers would be able to receive a profit or compensation as a result of their illegal acts. Third, . . . the public would view the legal system as a mockery of justice. Fourth, . . . wrongdoers would be able to shift much of the responsibility for their illegal acts to other parties.[380]

Widespread Application. An unlawful conduct defense has been applied as a matter of common law in a wide range of cases. Decisions have held, for example:

- that a suspect shot during a robbery could not sue the police for failing to arrest him prior to the robbery;[381]

- that the owner and manufacturer of a vending machine were not liable to the estate of a minor who was killed when the machine fell on him during his attempt to steal drinks;[382]

- that a guide who was convicted of transporting hunters without a license could not sue the state for damages in the form of lost business that were allegedly attributable to the state's negligence in responding to the guide's request for a license;[383]

- that the perpetrator of manslaughter had no claim against the manufacturer and seller of the shotgun for direct personal losses alleged to have resulted from the shooting;[384]

- that a customer could not recover from a bar that had served him liquor in violation of a dramshop law;[385] and

- that a passenger could not impose responsibility on a driver for injuries resulting from the operation of a stolen vehicle.[386]

Vague Formulations of Prohibited Conduct. Like statutory versions of the unlawful conduct outlaw doctrine, which often require proof of a felony, some common law versions of the defense also require clear proof of criminal conduct.

---

[379] 621 So. 2d 953, 954–55 (Ala. 1993).

[380] 537 N.W.2d 208, 213 (Mich. 1995).

[381] *See Amato v. United States*, 549 F. Supp. 863, 867 (D.N.J. 1982), *aff'd without op.*, 729 F.2d 1445 (3d Cir. 1984).

[382] *See Oden v. Pepsi Cola Bottling Co. of Decatur, Inc.*, 621 So. 2d 953, 954–55 (Ala. 1993).

[383] *See Beligard v. State*, 896 P.2d 230, 233–34 n.6 (Alaska 1995).

[384] *See Adkinson v. Rossi Arms Co.*, 659 P.2d 1236 (Alaska 1983).

[385] *See Lord v. Fogcutter Bar*, 813 P.2d 660 (Alaska 1991); *see also Vandenburg v. Brosnan*, 129 A.D.2d 793 (N.Y. App. Div. 1987), *aff'd*, 519 N.E.2d 618 (N.Y. 1988).

[386] *See Lee v. Nationwide Mut. Ins. Co.*, 497 S.E.2d 328 (Va. 1998).

However, other common law formulations of the defense are broadly worded and may encompass conduct that does not amount to a felony or even a serious misdemeanor. For example, as stated by the Supreme Court of Iowa in *Cole v. Taylor*, the general rule is that:

> a person cannot maintain an action if, in order to establish his cause of action, he must rely, in whole or in part, on an illegal or immoral act or transaction to which he is a party, or to maintain a claim for damages based on his own wrong or caused by his own neglect, . . . or where he must base his cause of action, in whole or in part, on a violation by himself of the criminal or penal laws. . . .[387]

Moreover, while many statutes bar a civil action for damages only where the defendant has been previously convicted of a specified criminal offense, cases have held that a common law defense predicated on unlawful conduct bars tort claims even in the absence of prior prosecution and conviction. Thus, the rule has been found applicable where unlawful conduct resulted in the death of an intoxicated driver during a high-speed race.[388] Broad application of the common law defense based on unlawful conduct has even been held to bar claims by persons who did not engage in unlawful conduct, such as a surviving spouse's claim for loss of consortium.[389]

Common Law Requirements. The Michigan Court of Appeals, in *Poch v. Anderson*, offered a detailed outline for the common law defense:

> [W]hen a plaintiff's action is based on his own illegal conduct, the claim is generally barred. . . . This maxim, known as the wrongful-conduct rule, has its exceptions. The mere fact that a plaintiff engaged in illegal conduct at the time of his injury does not mean that his claim is automatically barred. . . . To fall under the bar of the rule, the plaintiff's conduct must be prohibited or almost entirely prohibited under a penal or criminal statute. . . . There must also be a sufficient causal nexus between the plaintiff's illegal conduct and the plaintiff's asserted damages. . . . Another possible exception to the wrongful conduct rule is where both the plaintiff and the defendant have engaged in illegal conduct, but the defendant's culpability for the damages is greater than the plaintiff's culpability. . . . Finally, a plaintiff's claim is not barred by his wrongful conduct if a statute violated by the defendant explicitly authorizes recovery by a person similarly situated as the plaintiff. . . .[390]

As the quotation suggests, common-law versions of an unlawful conduct defense are not necessarily simple. In *Rico v. Flores*, the Fifth Circuit recently reversed a judgment for the defendants, finding that, under Texas law, "there are multiple versions of the unlawful acts rule, versions which emphasize different links between a plaintiff's illegal acts and injuries suffered . . . [and that] the contours of the

---

[387] 301 N.W.2d 766, 768 (Iowa 1981) (quoting 1 C.J.S. Actions § 13 pp. 996–97).

[388] *See La Page v. Smith*, 166 A.D.2d 831 (N.Y. App. Div. 1990).

[389] *See Cole v. Taylor*, 301 N.W.2d 766, 768 (Iowa 1981).

[390] 580 N.W.2d 456, 458 (Mich. Ct. App. 1998).

unlawful acts rule are simply too unclear to say that because of this rule, Plaintiffs have no possibility of recovery."[391] *Rico* involved claims related to the deaths of ten illegal aliens who stowed away in a grain hopper railroad car in an attempt to pass undetected through the Border Patrol checkpoint.

Application of the Common Law Defense. A number of decisions in the medical malpractice field have applied a common law unlawful conduct defense to bar civil actions for damages. Thus, courts have held that allegedly negligent psychologists, psychiatrists, pharmacists, physicians, and other mental health care professionals or their employers were not liable for damages suffered by patients as a result of crimes committed by those patients.

In the legal malpractice field, the unlawful conduct defense finds its clearest endorsement in the decisions that have required persons alleging defective criminal representation to first overturn their convictions and, in some states, prove their innocence of the crimes for which they were prosecuted. Although these cases do not use the term "unlawful conduct defense," they clearly seize upon the defendant's unlawful conduct to insulate attorneys from liability.

In Pari Delicto. Another variation of the unlawful conduct defense includes the cases holding that an action for damages is barred by the affirmative defense of *in pari delicto*. Parties stand *"in pari delicto"* when they are equally at fault. According to the Latin maxim *in pari delicto potior est conditio defendentis*, "in a case of equal or mutual fault . . . the position of the [defending] party . . . is the better one." Put differently, "[i]n the familiar economic language of the Chicago School, among wrongdoers equally at fault the law ought not to redistribute losses caused by the wrong itself, but rather should leave the parties where it finds them."[392] Under the rule of *in pari delicto*, the "[s]uit is barred not because the defendant is right, but rather because the plaintiff, being equally wrong, has forfeited any claim to the aid of the court."[393]

The *in pari delicto* defense "is grounded on two premises: first, that courts should not lend their good offices to mediating disputes among wrongdoers; and second, that denying judicial relief to an admitted wrongdoer is an effective means of deterring illegality."[394] The effect of the *in pari delicto* doctrine is that generally "there is no recourse between wrongdoers."[395]

Numerous legal malpractice claims have been barred by the *in pari delicto* doctrine. Generally, those cases have involved clients who lied to courts on their attorneys' advice. A client who has engaged in such knowingly wrongful conduct is typically barred from recovering damages in a malpractice action for losses that arise from the perjury.

The doctrine of *in pari delicto* covers some of the same ground as the general

---

[391] 481 F.3d 234, 243–44 (5th Cir. 2007).

[392] *Pantely v. Garris, Garris & Garris, P.C.*, 447 N.W.2d 864, 867 (Mich. Ct. App. 1989).

[393] *Id.* at 867.

[394] *Bateman Eichler, Hill Richards, Inc. v. Berner*, 472 U.S. 299, 306 (1985).

[395] *Patten v. Raddatz*, 895 P.2d 633 (Mont. 1995) (barring a tort action arising from a long-term relationship involving drug use and prostitution).

wrongful conduct defense discussed above. Thus, one court wrote simply, without reference to the defendant's degree of fault, that "[t]he doctrine of *in pari delicto* is the 'principle that a plaintiff who has participated in wrongdoing may not recover damages resulting from the wrongdoing.' "[396]

Clarity and Focus. As an aid to legal analysis, a carefully conceptualized wrongful conduct defense has two advantages over the doctrine of *in pari delicto*. The first is clarity and the second is focus. Courts recognizing a wrongful conduct defense often endeavor to be clear about what type of conduct gives rise to the defense and how closely that conduct must be related to the injuries for which the plaintiff seeks recovery. The same has not always been true of courts applying the *in pari delicto* doctrine. Courts sometimes say that the doctrine is applicable to any case involving "an immoral or illegal transaction . . . [entailing] moral turpitude."[397] By referring to "immorality," those courts greatly and imprecisely expand the range of offending conduct that might trigger the defense and, by requiring "moral turpitude," they raise all of the issues and disagreements that have surrounded that phrase in other areas of the law. Moreover, the Latin name of the *in pari delicto* doctrine, as well as the equitable maxim quoted above, does little to enhance clarity in analysis or certainty in application.

Misorienting the Analysis. By focusing on whether the parties are "equally at fault," the *in pari delicto* doctrine misorients the analysis. The question is not whether the plaintiff is *equally* at fault with the defendant. Indeed, any rule framed in terms of an equality requirement would be both rarely useful and the subject of frequent dispute. In only one in a hundred cases — the 50-50 case — will the plaintiff and defendant be *equally* at fault. If recovery were barred only in such instances, there would be endless litigation over whether the plaintiff and defendant were to blame to precisely the same extent. Yet this is generally not what modern courts are looking for when they speak of *in pari delicto*. In some cases, what the courts mean is that the plaintiff's knowing participation in unlawful conduct was so serious and so closely connected to the damages for which recovery is sought that it is fair to foreclose recovery. If that is so, it is far preferable to address those considerations (the seriousness of the plaintiff's conduct and its relationship to the plaintiff's harm) under an unlawful conduct defense that expressly incorporates those factors than by invoking the imprecise language of *in pari delicto*.

In other cases, what the courts mean when they invoke the phrase *in pari delicto* is that the plaintiff was *more at fault* than the defendant. Thus, in one recent legal malpractice case, the court held that a claim against an attorney for negligence was barred by *in pari delicto* because the plaintiff had engaged in fraudulent conduct.[398] As the court explained, the claim was foreclosed from judicial consideration because "[t]he actual fraud of Mr. Gosman [the client] is *more objectionable* than the alleged negligence of Peabody [the attorney]."[399] Cases like this illustrate two points. First,

---

[396] *Reed v. Cedar County*, 2007 U.S. Dist. LEXIS 9915 (N.D. Iowa. Feb. 12, 2007).

[397] *Tillman v. Shofner*, 90 P.3d 582, 584 (Okla. Civ. App. 2004) (quoting *Bowlan v. Lunsford*, 54 P.2d 666, 668 (Okla. 1936)).

[398] *See In re Gosman*, 382 B.R. 826, 838 (Bankr. S.D. Fla. 2007).

[399] *Id.* at 838 (emphasis added).

it makes little sense to talk about the relevant defense in the language of "*in pari delicto*" if the question is not whether the plaintiff was equally at fault, but rather more at fault. Second, if a comparison between the fault of the parties is to be made, that inquiry may be better framed in the language of comparative negligence or comparative fault, than in terms of whether a total defense precludes recovery (regardless of whether that defense is called *in pari delicto*, unlawful conduct, or something else).

Courts recognizing the *in pari delicto* doctrine sometimes do not apply it because *the defendant* was more at fault than the plaintiff. In those cases, the parties, in fact, are not *in pari delicto*, so it is not surprising that a defense so named is inapplicable.

Unclean Hands. A number of cases have held that a legal claim may be barred by the doctrine of unclean hands. In one case, a lender who had previously been found liable for a violation of the state's Interest Act in a suit commenced against him by a borrower was precluded from litigating a claim that his violation resulted from incorrect advice provided to him by his attorney.[400] The court found it irrelevant that the earlier case did not involve fraud because the relevant principle was that "courts do not aid parties whose causes of action are founded on any illegal or immoral acts, including the violation of a statute, to assert rights growing out of such acts or to relieve themselves of the consequences of those acts."[401] This formulation of an unlawful conduct bar to liability is exceptionally broad and creates an unreasonable and unnecessary risk that relief will be foreclosed in a range of cases far wider than is appropriate.

Throughout the law of torts, a statutory violation by the plaintiff, even if proximately causing the plaintiff's injuries, is normally not a total bar to relief, but only an obstacle to recovery to the extent provided by applicable principles of comparative negligence or comparative fault. "Immoral" conduct that is not a violation of legislative or common-law rules is not a defense at all. And whether recovery is permitted or foreclosed is determined by reference to well-developed principles of proximate causation, not whether the rights asserted "grow out of" particular acts.

Applying the doctrine of unclean hands to many cases is not a useful path of analysis for at least two reasons. First, unclean hands is an equitable defense that properly has no application when legal relief, such as a request for damages, is at issue. Second, the rubric of "unclean hands" obfuscates the issue of just what type of conduct gives rise to the defense or how closely that conduct must be connected to the relief being sought in order for the action to be barred. The better path is to forego the opaque language of "unclean hands" and engage in a careful analysis of the facts in light of a clearly articulated unlawful conduct defense.

Lack of Proximate Causation. It is possible to speak of the plaintiff's unlawful conduct not as an affirmative defense to be pleaded and proved by the defendant, but as an obstacle to the plaintiff's proof of a *prima facie* case of liability. For

---

[400] *See Buttitta v. Newell*, 531 N.E.2d 957, 960–61 (Ill. App. Ct. 1988).

[401] *Id.* at 961.

example, *Shahbaz v. Horwitz*[402] held that a client who was found guilty of fraud in a civil suit could not successfully maintain a negligence action against the law firm that had assisted him in the fraudulent transaction, because the proximate causation element of a malpractice claim includes "determining cause in fact and considering various policy factors that may preclude imposition of liability."[403] The court reasoned that just as an intentional tortfeasor cannot obtain contribution from a negligent joint tortfeasor and a party cannot obtain indemnity or insurance for intentional wrongdoing, so too public policy forbids intentional tortfeasors . . . from shifting their liability for intentional wrongdoing to their negligent attorneys. Although the court acknowledged that "[o]ther states have barred intentional wrongdoers from bringing malpractice actions against negligent attorneys under the doctrine, *in pari delicto*,"[404] it found that the defendants' "contentions reduce[d] to an attack on proximate causation."[405]

In framing the issue in causation terms, the *Shahbaz* court followed essentially the same path that states have taken in holding that plaintiffs must prove exoneration or innocence when alleging negligence in the context of criminal representation. It viewed the critical issue as one of causation.

Restoring an Earlier Balance. The recent emergence of an unlawful conduct defense in American tort law is, in a sense, a restoration of the balance struck, on other grounds, during much of the twentieth century regarding the availability of compensation for negligence. Even as the first and second *Restatements* rejected an outlaw doctrine, they held that a plaintiff's unlawfully tortious or criminal conduct could give rise to the defense of contributory negligence. Until roughly the early 1970s, contributory negligence was a total defense to a negligence claim in most jurisdictions. Thus, recognition of an unlawful conduct defense today in negligence cases dictates the same result that was often reached under the contributory negligence doctrine in the age of pre-comparative principles. In either case, a plaintiff suing in negligence to recover for injuries to which the plaintiff's own serious unlawful conduct contributed is barred from receiving compensation.

Comparative Principles and the Unlawful Conduct Defense. Nevertheless, the widespread endorsement of comparative negligence and comparative fault in 46 states cannot be ignored. The substitution of proportionality principles for the earlier all-or-nothing rule of contributory negligence ranks as the most important development in the field of tort law in the last hundred years. Today, in a wide range of situations, the law favors the view that liability should not only be based on fault, but limited in proportion to fault. In that respect, the emergence of an unlawful conduct defense that is a total bar to recovery is out of step with the strongest trend in modern American tort law because it ignores fault on the part of the defendant and focuses wholly on the fault of the plaintiff. Such an approach to issues of liability is infirm because the law should embrace rules that create an incentive for both the defendant and the plaintiff to exercise care to avoid losses that could be minimized

---

[402] 2008 Cal. App. Unpub. LEXIS 2601 (Mar. 27, 2008).

[403] *Id.* at *19 (quoting *Viner v. Sweet*, 70 P.3d 1046, 1048 n.1 (Cal. 2003)).

[404] 2008 Cal. App. Unpub. LEXIS 2601, at *30 n.9 (Mar. 27, 2008).

[405] *Id.* at *27.

through lawful and otherwise appropriate conduct. Courts should be reluctant to expansively create doctrines, such as some versions of the modern unlawful conduct defense, which abrogate state comparative negligence and comparative fault schemes.

Mindful of these concerns, in *Dugger v. Arredondo*,[406] the Texas Supreme Court held that a common law unlawful acts doctrine was not available as an affirmative defense in personal injury and wrongful death cases because "[l]ike other common law assumption-of-the-risk defenses, it was abrogated by . . . [the state's adoption of a statutory] proportionate responsibility scheme."[407] Clarifying that point, Justice Paul Green explained, "Unless the requirements of the affirmative defense in section 93.001 [a statutory unlawful conduct rule with a limited scope[408]] are satisfied, a plaintiff's share of responsibility for his or her injuries should be compared against the defendant's."[409]

The Path of Future Development. In deciding whether and to what extent an unlawful conduct defense should foreclose otherwise viable theories of compensation, courts must balance a number of important considerations. The path chosen by the courts must encourage lawful conduct and personal responsibility; prevent persons from profiting from wrongful conduct; create appropriate incentives for the exercise of care; protect innocent persons from wrongdoing; and embrace rules that are sufficiently clear and administratively convenient that they can be applied fairly by courts and can encourage the voluntary resolution of disputes.

The most desirable course is one that steers clear of extremes. Unlawful conduct by plaintiffs should not be overlooked, nor should it be too readily disqualifying from judicial recourse. The courthouse doors should be closed only if the plaintiff's unlawful conduct is so serious, so well established, and so closely connected to the injuries for which the plaintiff seeks compensation that the petition for relief should wholly be rejected because sound public policy demands it.

f.   Other Public Policy Issues

The unlawful conduct defense is essentially a rule of public policy. However, other types of public policy issues arise in suits for fraud.

Considerations Related to the Right of Privacy. In *Kathleen K. v. Robert B.*,[410] the plaintiff's complaint alleged that the defendant, knowing he had genital herpes, assured the plaintiff that he was free from venereal disease. Relying on

---

[406]   408 S.W.3d 825 (Tex. 2013).

[407]   *Id.* at 836.

[408]   Section 93.001 provides in relevant part:

   (a) It is an affirmative defense to a civil action for damages for personal injury or death that the plaintiff, at the time the cause of action arose, was: (1) committing a felony, for which the plaintiff has been finally convicted, that was the sole cause of the damages sustained by the plaintiff; or (2) committing or attempting to commit suicide, and the plaintiff's conduct in committing or attempting to commit suicide was the sole cause of the damages sustained. . . .

Tex. Civ. Prac. & Rem. Code § 93.001 (LEXIS 2014).

[409]   *Id.* at 836.

[410]   150 Cal. App. 3d 992 (1984).

that falsehood, the plaintiff had sexual relations with the defendant and, as a result, contracted herpes. In an action alleging, in part, that the defendant had committed fraud, the defendant argued that it was "not the business" of courts to "supervise the promises made between two consenting adults as to the circumstances of their private sexual conduct." The California Court of Appeal disagreed. In reversing a judgment dismissing the complaint, the court found that although a constitutional "right of privacy" limits the law's inquiry into matters involving private sexual conduct of consenting adults, that right is subordinate to the state's right to enact laws which promote health, welfare, and safety. Several other cases have also recognized the viability of fraud claims related to herpes.[411]

Problem 2-13: The Defrauded Nightclub

The Century Club (the "Club") was served by the Liquor Control Board (the "LCB") with an Order to Show Cause why its liquor license should not be revoked after a raid on the club established that it had admitted and sold alcohol to 27 underage customers (the "Minors") on a particular evening. The Minors had gained entry to the club after each presenting two pieces of false identification. Although the Club, on the night in question, had denied admission to several other persons who it determined had presented counterfeit identification, it had been unable to detect the inauthentic nature of the driver's licenses and other documents the Minors used to deceive Club security.

Because the Order to Show Cause posed a major threat to the financial viability of the nightclub, the Club hired a large law firm to mount a full scale defense of the Club's license.

Aside from possible revocation of the Club's liquor license, the law firm considered the risk that criminal charges would be brought against either the Club or its principals. State law makes it a Class C misdemeanor to recklessly furnish alcohol to a minor. However, under § 723 of the Alcoholic Beverage Code:

> A licensee in a criminal prosecution or in a proceeding before the Liquor Control Board based upon a charge of unlawfully furnishing an alcoholic beverage to a minor may offer either or both of the following proofs as a defense or defenses to the prosecution or proceeding:
>
> (1) That:
>
> > (A) the purchaser: (i) falsely represented the purchaser's age by presenting two (2) forms of identification showing the purchaser to be at least twenty-one (21) years of age; (ii) produced a driver's license bearing the purchaser's photograph; or (iii) produced a photographic identification card or a similar card, issued under the laws of another state or the federal government, showing that the purchaser was of legal age to make the purchase;
> >
> > (B) the appearance of the purchaser was such that an ordinary

---

[411] *See Behr v. Redmond*, 193 Cal. App. 4th 517 (2011); *B.N. v. K.K.*, 538 A.2d 1175 (Md. 1988); *R.A.P. v. B.J.P.*, 428 N.W.2d 103, 109 (Minn. Ct. App. 1988).

prudent person would believe the purchaser to be of legal age to make the purchase; and

(C)   the sale was made in good faith based upon the reasonable belief that the purchaser was actually of legal age to make the purchase.

(2)   That the permittee or its agent had taken all reasonable precautions in instructing employees, in hiring employees, and in supervising them as to sale of alcoholic beverages to minors.

No criminal prosecution has been commenced yet against the Club or persons associated with it. However, such action is anticipated if the Club is not entirely successful in answering the Order to Show Cause. The hearing on the Order to Show Cause before the LCB has been delayed for an undetermined period of time due to a state financial crisis caused by a shortfall in tax revenue. It is impossible to determine when the hearing will be held because the LCB has continually extended the date for the hearing as it works through a backlog of pending matters.

Each of the Minors has been charged with a Class C misdemeanor based on presentation of false identification for the purpose of purchasing alcohol. Some of the Minors have pled guilty. Others are awaiting trial of their charges.

As part of its aggressive defense of the Club, the law firm has sued the 27 Minors for common law fraud. The action seeks to recover the attorney's fees incurred by the Club in fighting the Order to Show Cause, damages for harm to business reputation, compensation for losses, and punitive damages.

The Minors have moved to dismiss the complaint based on *in pari delicto*, unclean hands, and the defendant's involvement in unlawful conduct. You are a law clerk for the trial judge who must decide the motion. Please prepare a memo briefing the judge on relevant legal issues. There is no statute or case on point in your state. You are therefore to consider the law of other jurisdictions.

B.   NEGLIGENT MISREPRESENTATION

Actions for negligent misrepresentation share some of the same requirements that are applicable in actions for fraud. Among other things, the plaintiff must establish reliance on the misrepresentation which caused damages.

Where fraud and negligent misrepresentation differ relates mainly to culpability, scope of liability, and defenses. In a suit for negligent misrepresentation, rather than fraud, the requirement of *scienter* is replaced by the necessity of proving that the defendant was merely negligent as to the falsity of the statement. The scope of liability for purely economic losses caused by negligent misrepresentation typically extends less far than liability for fraud because reduced culpability on the part of the defendant justifies less exposure to liability. Finally, unreasonable conduct on the part of the plaintiff is more likely to constitute a total or partial defense to negligent misrepresentation than to fraud. Throughout the law, negligence by a plaintiff routinely offsets negligence by a defendant, but it is rarely a barrier to recovery for an intentional tort.

The central landmark in the law of negligent misrepresentation is § 552 of the *Restatement (Second) of Torts*, which has been widely adopted by the courts.[412] That section provides:

> One who, in the course of his business, profession or employment, or in any other transaction in which he has a pecuniary interest, supplies false information for the guidance of others in their business transactions, is subject to liability for pecuniary loss caused to them by their justifiable reliance upon the information, if he fails to exercise reasonable care or competence in obtaining or communicating the information.[413]

Law on Neg. Misrep.

In *Liberty Surplus Ins. Corp., Inc. v. First Indemnity Insurance Services, Inc.*,[414] the Florida District Court of Appeal held that misstatements in an insurance application about an applicant's prior claims record, which was submitted by an insurance broker to a legal malpractice insurer, met the requirements of § 552.

In *Dahlgren v. First Nat. Bank of Holdrege*,[415] cattle investors and corn producers sued a bank. They alleged in part that the bank had committed fraud and negligent misrepresentation in statements relating to a feedlot (DCC, which was operated by Dennis Damrow and affiliated with DFF). The feedlot was a long-time customer of the bank. Essentially, the plaintiffs argued that the bank misled them into continuing to do business with the feedlot. The *Dahlgren* opinion offers a useful illustration of how courts apply § 552, and of how important principles that have evolved in the law of fraud find application in negligent misrepresentation claims. In *Dahlgren*, the Eighth Circuit quoted § 552, then addressed the Erickson claims:

> Lloyd Erickson and the corporation he owned with his son began feeding cattle and delivering corn to DCC in the late 1980s. Both were also long-standing customers of the Bank. In early 2000, the Ericksons heard negative rumors about Damrow from the Carter Feeders shareholders. [Carter Feeders was a second feedlot that Damrow managed.] Erickson testified that, at a meeting in May, his father asked Bank president Riley and former DCC loan officer Eric Titus whether DCC is "an okay place to [be] feeding?" Titus responded, "as far as we know, everything is fine." Based on that assurance, the Ericksons continued to do business with DCC, delivering corn to DCC in September and purchasing two lots of cattle. Erickson and Erickson Land and Cattle lost $66,393.58 in cattle, $69,743.66 in corn and incurred $26,476.62 in attorneys' fees after DCC was placed in receivership.

> There is ample evidence in the record that Titus was aware of significant financial problems with DCC when he made this affirmative misrepresentation. Titus had tracked past due DCC notes and overdrafts for years,

loan officer knew there were significant financial problems

---

[412] *See also* RESTATEMENT (THIRD) OF TORTS: LIAB. FOR ECON. HARM § 5 (Tent. Draft No. 1, 2012) ("Negligent Misrepresentation").

[413] RESTATEMENT (SECOND) OF TORTS § 552(1) (1977).

[414] 31 So. 3d 852, 857 (Fla. Dist. Ct. App. 2010).

[415] 533 F.3d 681 (8th Cir. 2008).

reported to the Bank's board of directors about the deteriorating Carter Feeders situation on January 3, 2000, and was present for the discussion of the Damrow lines of credit at that meeting, which led to the board's decision to end its relationship with Damrow and DCC. Titus repeatedly stated, "I do not recall," when asked about his knowledge of the financial condition of DCC, testimony the jury likely considered evasive. At a minimum, Titus was negligent in telling Bank customer Erickson that "everything is fine" at DCC without disclosing that the Bank had ended its relationships with Damrow. In these circumstances a reasonable jury could find that Titus made this false and misleading statement intending to influence or guide the Ericksons into continuing to do business with DCC, or at least knowing that his statement would have that influence. . . . The verdict in favor of Erickson and Erickson Land and Cattle on their tort claims is affirmed.[416]

The court later turned to the Wells claims. It wrote:

Gary and Bob Wells own and operate Wells AG Enterprises, BJW Farms, and EWW Farms, Inc. Dwayne Kudlacek is Gary Wells's brother-in-law. . . .

Gary and Bob testified that they annually asked their loan officers at the Bank if it was safe to do business with DCC and were repeatedly assured that it was. In August 2000, Gary asked Eric Titus if it would be safe to take corn to DCC. Titus replied that he was planning on delivering some of his own corn to DCC. Wells inferred it was safe to do so himself and told Bob and Kudlacek that Titus would deliver corn to DCC in August 2000. All three testified they relied on this statement in delivering corn to DCC that fall. Wells AG Enterprises, BJW Farms, EWW Farms, Inc., and Dwayne Kudlacek lost a total of $171,702.19 in corn in DCC's bankruptcy.

Titus's August 2000 statement to Gary Wells cannot be the basis for these plaintiffs' tort claims because it was a statement of present intent, and there is no evidence that Titus, who personally fed bison at DCC that year, misrepresented his intention. Nor did that statement require the disclosure of what Titus knew as DCC's former loan officer in order to make it not misleading. None of the Wells plaintiffs relied on any other representations by the Bank when they did business with DCC in late 2000. Accordingly, they failed to prove that they would not have entered into the loss-causing transactions in the absence of a false representation or non-disclosure by the Bank. . . .[417]

The court next turned to the Dixon Grandstra claims, writing:

Granstra and DG Farms, Inc., rest their tort claims on what loan officer Sterr told banker Adams in 1999. Plaintiffs contend there was ample evidence that Sterr knew of negative financial and credit issues at DCC. Therefore, he was guilty of at least negligent misrepresentation when he gave false or incomplete information to Adams. However, the Granstra

---

[416] *Id.* at 694.

[417] *Id.* at 695–96.

plaintiffs cannot recover because no reasonable person would expect Sterr's statements in mid-1999 to influence cattle investors the following year.

Plaintiffs' expert, Dr. Jones, testified to the volatility of this market, where prices fluctuate significantly within a matter of months. Jones testified that financial information about a cattle feeding operation can become unreliable even during a single four-five month cattle feeding cycle. Thus, in this investment market, there is a rather short limit on the period of time in which a banker making a general statement that a feedlot customer is a "safe place to do business" or is "sound" or is an "excellent credit" would intend or expect that statement to influence an inquiring third-party contemplating cattle or corn transactions with the feedlot. Whether or not the banker expects that the bank will participate in the third party's transactions, his misrepresentation or non-disclosure, whether fraudulent or merely negligent, does not have the requisite relationship to the third party's much later, loss-causing transaction to be tortious, particularly a transaction occurring after the bank is no longer financing the customer. *See Restatement (Second) of Torts*, §§ 531, 551(2)(e), 552(2)(b). Although the relevant time period will often be a question of fact for the jury, no reasonable jury could find that Sterr's statement in mid-1999 was intended to influence or could be expected to influence the Granstra plaintiffs' cattle purchases in late 2000. Accordingly, the district court erred when it denied the Bank's motion for judgment as a matter of law on the tort claims of Granstra and DG Farms, Inc.[418]

The court thereafter addressed Theodore Collin's claims:

Collin was employed by the Bank as a loan officer and vice president from 1983 until January 2000, when he left to work at another bank in Holdrege. Collin began delivering corn and feeding cattle at DCC in 1993. In the fall of 2000, Collin delivered corn and bought cattle at DCC. He lost $22,501.59 in cattle, $27,766.16 in corn and spent $1,216.00 in attorney's fees as a result of these transactions in DCC's bankruptcy.

Collin's claims fail as a matter of law. As a member of the Bank's loan committee from 1990 through early 1998, Collin was aware of DCC overdrafts and past-due DFF notes. . . . Collin testified that he expected Sterr to advise if there were any financial concerns with DCC. But neither Collin nor any other witness testified that the Bank ever supplied Collin false information for the purpose of influencing his DCC investments. Instead, he claimed that Slominski and Sterr misled him during loan committee meetings. The Bank's knowledge that Collin was also a DCC investor does not transform information shared during loan committee meetings into business guidance for purposes of a fraudulent or negligent misrepresentation claim.

Without evidence the Bank supplied information to guide or influence Collin's personal transactions, he cannot maintain an action for negligent misrepresentation. *See Farr v. Designer Phosphate & Premix Int'l, Inc.,*

---

[418] *Id.* at 696–97.

253 Neb. 201, 570 N.W.2d 320, 326 (1997) (§ 552 requires "that one supplying the misrepresentation must *intend* to supply the information and that such person must intend that the information will induce reliance and influence the transaction") (emphasis in original). Nor did Collin present evidence giving rise to a duty to disclose under § 551(2) [dealing with exceptions to the "no duty to speak" rule] after he began working for a competing bank and the Bank terminated its relationship with DCC.

. . . [T]he independent information available and known to Collin compels the conclusion that he could not have reasonably relied on the loan committee statements when he did business with DCC in the fall of 2000. After leaving the Bank in early 2000, Collin did a comprehensive analysis of DCC and DFF for his new employer and personally inspected cattle at the feedlot. With this information in hand, no reasonable jury could find that Collin instead relied on statements made in loan committee meetings from years earlier when he decided to do business with DCC in the fall of 2000. . . . The district court erred when it denied the Bank's motion for judgment as a matter of law on Collin's tort claims.[419]

Finally, the court addressed the Dave Dahlgren claims:

Every February from 1995 through 1999, during a review conducted by Dahlgren's loan officer, Ted Collin, Dahlgren would ask if it was a good idea to continue doing business with DCC. Collin replied to each inquiry, in substance, "Well, you know, I wouldn't be doing business there if I didn't think it was okay also." Dahlgren testified that he relied on Collin's statements when he delivered corn to DCC in the fall of 2000, and purchased cattle on November 9, 2000. . . .

. . . The fraudulent concealment and negligent misrepresentation claims falter on the specific nature of Collin's annual reassurance, "I wouldn't be doing business there if I didn't think it was okay also." These were statements of personal opinion and present intent that did not, without a more specific inquiry from Dahlgren related to particular transactions he was contemplating, impose a duty to disclose the details of a customer's financial affairs known to Collin as a loan officer of the Bank. . . . [T]he district court erred when it denied the Bank's motion for judgment as a matter of law on the Dahlgren plaintiffs' tort claims.[420]

1.   Negligence Rather than *Scienter*

Whether the plaintiff acted negligently in making a statement often requires detailed consideration of the facts. In this respect, negligent misrepresentation is no different from many negligence actions involving personal injury or property damage where whether the defendant acted unreasonably is determined from the totality of the circumstances.

---

[419] *Id.* at 697–98.

[420] *Id.* at 698–99.

In *Goldstein v. Williams*,[421] the California Court of Appeal held that the evidence was sufficient to support a jury finding that the seller of a condominium was liable for negligently misrepresenting plumbing problems in the unit. The court explained:

> There is substantial evidence to support the finding that, when Williams represented she was unaware of any "significant defects/malfunctions" in the "plumbing/Sewers/Septics," it was unreasonable for her to believe her statement to be true. The plumbing problem in the unit's bathroom had created significant damages in 2003, requiring repairs taking nearly six months to complete. . . . Moreover, a trier of fact could infer, from the fact the same bathroom plumbing remained a source of problems requiring Williams to have a plumber repair the problems (on average) every six or seven months even though the unit was a new condominium conversion, Williams lacked reasonable grounds to believe the unit had no plumbing problems. The fact Williams specifically asked her real estate agent whether the plumbing problems should be revealed could permit a trier of fact to infer Williams was cognizant her problems appeared abnormal. Finally, the fact the same bathroom again flooded within days of Goldstein moving into the unit provided additional grounds from which the trier of fact could infer Williams lacked reasonable grounds to believe her statement was true.[422]

2.   Recovery for Negligent Nondisclosure

There is an important question, not definitively resolved, about whether silence can form the basis for a negligent-misrepresentation action or whether there must be some type of affirmative misstatement. Suppose, for example, that the defendant fails to disclose material information, which other principles of law, such as the rules about facts basic to the transaction or facts not reasonably discoverable (*see* Part A-2-b), create a duty to reveal. Can the defendant be sued for negligent misrepresentation? Or are the rules of negligent misrepresentation applicable only if there has been some type of false or misleading statement, as opposed to mere silence?

Negligent Nondisclosure Claims Barred. When the *Restatement* speaks of liability for negligently "supply[ing] false information,"[423] it seems to suggest that there must be an affirmative misstatement. Thus, in *Eberts v. Goderstad*,[424] an action where a home seller argued that the purchaser's claim for negligent misrepresentation triggered an insurer's duty to defend, the Seventh Circuit recently wrote:

> The problem with this argument is that negligent misrepresentation by nondisclosure has not been recognized as a tort in Wisconsin. . . . The

---

[421] 2009 Cal. App. Unpub. LEXIS 4683 (June 4, 2009).

[422] *Id.* at *5–*6.

[423] RESTATEMENT (SECOND) OF TORTS § 552(1) (1977).

[424] 569 F.3d 757 (7th Cir. 2009).

foundational and oft-cited case of *Ollerman v. O'Rourke Co.* specifically declined to adopt a negligent misrepresentation-by-nondisclosure claim, 94 Wis. 2d 17, 288 N.W.2d 95, 112 (1980); *Ollerman's* endorsement of a limited species of liability for nondisclosure pertained to the tort of intentional misrepresentation. . . . Negligent misrepresentation by nondisclosure is a claim of questionable heritage and has been soundly rejected in some jurisdictions. *See, e.g., Martin v. Ohio State Univ. Found.*, 139 Ohio App. 3d 89, 742 N.E.2d 1198, 1209 (2000) ("A negligent misrepresentation claim does not lie for omissions: there must be an affirmative false statement."); *Binette v. Dyer Library Ass'n*, 688 A.2d 898, 903 (Me. 1996); *Richey v. Patrick*, 904 P.2d 798, 802 (Wyo. 1995); *Matthews v. Kincaid*, 746 P.2d 470, 471 (Alaska 1987).[425]

Negligent Nondisclosure Claims Actionable. Other cases have expressly held that for purposes of liability for negligent misrepresentation, there is no difference between misleading silence and a false or misleading utterance. Thus, in *In re Agrobiotech, Inc.*,[426] a federal district court in Nevada wrote that "silence about material facts basic to the transaction, when combined with a duty to speak, is the functional equivalent of a misrepresentation or 'supplying false information' under *Restatement* § 552." Similarly, in *Roberts v. Ball, Hunt, Hart, Brown & Baerwitz*,[427] the California Court of Appeal held that attorneys could be liable for negligent misrepresentation based on failure to disclose doubts about a partnership's status as a general partnership.

3.   Scope of Liability

Logically, one would not expect the scope of liability for negligent misrepresentation to extend as far as in an action for fraud, for the conduct of the defendant is less culpable. Because that is true, imposing equally broad liability would risk running afoul of the proportionality principle, which holds that liability should be proportional to fault.[428]

A restricted scope of liability for negligent misrepresentation means that, in some cases, the plaintiff may be unable to show a sufficiently close connection to the defendant to state a cause of action. Thus, a plaintiff who directly receives negligently false information from a defendant usually stands in a far better position to sue than one who receives the same information indirectly. Yet many potential plaintiffs fall within the latter class. For example, statements about the financial integrity of a business enterprise often circulate widely in the community. In some cases, those representations intentionally, or at least foreseeably, are transmitted indirectly to potential plaintiffs by intermediaries.

Economic Harm Versus Physical Harm. It is not surprising that intricate rules have emerged for the purpose of defining whether an indirect recipient of

---

[425] *Id.* at 765–66.

[426] 291 F. Supp. 2d 1186, 1192 (D. Nev. 2003).

[427] 57 Cal. App. 3d 104, 110 (1976).

[428] *See generally* VINCENT R. JOHNSON, STUDIES IN AMERICAN TORT LAW 7 (Carolina Academic Press, 5th ed. 2013).

negligently false statements may sue for economic losses resulting from reliance on such information. The three principal views, which are discussed below, have been shaped mainly in cases involving auditors and financial statements. It must be emphasized, however, that these special rules set the applicable legal standard only for cases involving purely economic losses (*e.g.*, damages resulting from bad investments or failed loans). In cases involving physical harm (*i.e.*, personal injury or property damage), the extent of liability is defined by the usual rules of factual and proximate causation. That generally means that any loosely foreseeable physical harm resulting from negligent misrepresentation is compensable, provided that the other elements of the tort are met.

Ordinary Causation Principles Apply. Of course, the usual principles of factual and proximate causation also apply to cases involving purely economic loss, as well as to cases seeking compensation of physical harm. For example, in *Travelers Casualty & Surety Company of America v. Ernst & Young LLP*,[429] an insurance company sued an accounting firm to recover millions of dollars in losses that it suffered under a surety bond it wrote for a construction project. The insurer allegedly issued the bond in reliance on a negligently audited financial statement. The insurer argued that the accounting firm had been careless in failing to conduct the necessary inquiries and perform the proper audit tests to confirm the amount of losses that the bonded party ("FGH") was expected to incur on another project (Petrodrill). (The greater those losses, the more likely it was that FGH would not perform on the bonded project, and the greater the chances that the insurer would have to pay to complete the bonded project (the "Pasha project").) In upholding a jury verdict that the accounting firm was liable for negligent misrepresentation, Judge Emilio M. Garza's opinion for the Fifth Circuit applied basic principles of factual and proximate causation relating to whether the negligently audited financial statements were a "substantial factor" in producing the losses incurred under the surety bond and whether liability was prevented by principles of superseding causation. One of the key facts was that the insurer had initially declined to issue the bond after considering the financial statements in question, but later agreed to bond the construction project after FGH lobbied heavily and made certain changes to increase the company's liquidity to get the bond issued. Judge Garza wrote:

> E&Y's argument that the evidence was insufficient for a rational jury to find that its negligent audit proximately caused Travelers financial harm . . . fails. "In order for an act of negligence to proximately cause the [plaintiff's] damage, the fact finder must find that the negligence was both the cause in fact and legal cause of the damage." . . . To be held liable, a defendant's negligence "need not be the sole cause of an injury," . . . but the defendant's negligence must be a "substantial factor in producing the injury." . . . Still, a negligent defendant may be shielded from liability if a superseding cause is found — "[a] superseding cause is an act of a third person or other force which by its intervention prevents the [defendant] from being liable for harm to another which his antecedent negligence is a substantial factor in bringing about." . . .

---

[429] 542 F.3d 475 (5th Cir. 2008).

. . . First, E&Y argues that Travelers initially declined to issue any bonds to FGH based on the 1999 financials. According to E&Y, the only decision by Travelers "based on" the 1999 financials was to deny coverage in May. E&Y insists that it was Travelers' independent judgment in response to FGH's representations that led to Travelers' later decision to bond the Pasha project in September. According to E&Y, Travelers' decision to decline bonds in May, and its later reliance on FGH's representations both served to break the chain of causation between E&Y's negligence and the bond decision.

E&Y's claim that the only decision "based on" the negligently audited financials was the May declination ignores the trial testimony of Pete and Schwait indicating that Travelers continued to rely on the audited financials up until it issued the Pasha bond. And even if Travelers also relied upon representations from FGH management, this would not necessarily prevent E&Y's negligent audit from being a cause in fact of Travelers' harm. . . . Travelers' underwriters testified that had they known that no reasonable loss estimate could be generated for Petrodrill (*i.e.*, absent E&Y's negligence), they would not have issued the Pasha bond, even taking into account the positive developments from FGH's liquidity campaign. The jury was free to believe this testimony and thus reasonably conclude that E&Y's negligent audit was a cause in fact of Travelers' decision to issue the bond.

Next, E&Y argues that FGH's lobbying campaign and later misrepresentations made by FGH management were a superseding cause of Travelers' decision to issue the Pasha bonds. In describing the superseding cause doctrine, the Mississippi Supreme Court has stated, "an original actor's negligence may be superceded by a subsequent actor's negligence, if the subsequent negligence was unforeseeable." . . . However, "if an antecedent negligent act puts in motion an agency which continues in operation until an injury occurs it would appear to be more like a second proximate cause than a remote and unactionable cause." *Eckman v. Moore*, 876 So. 2d 975, 981 (Miss. 2004). Put another way, "[t]he question is, did the facts constitute a succession of events so linked together as to make a natural whole, or was there some new and independent cause intervening between the alleged wrong and the injury?" . . .

E&Y also argues that Travelers' decision to reverse course and issue the Pasha bond in September 2000 was "unforeseeable." While this argument is placed under the heading "proximate cause," the argument simply attacks the wisdom of Travelers' decision to issue the Pasha bond. . . . In the proximate cause context, the proper foreseeability inquiry is whether "the plaintiff's injuries and damages fall within a particular kind or class of injury or harm which reasonably could be expected to flow from the defendant's negligence." . . .

. . . [B]ased on the evidence at trial, the jury could have reasonably concluded that E&Y's negligence played a role in enabling some of FGH's intervening representations. . . . For example, one reason FGH was able to claim that its liquidity campaign was sufficient to cover its estimated losses was because it could point back to E&Y's negligent audit that attested to the accuracy of the Petrodrill loss figure. As Schwait and Pete testified, when FGH continued to tell them that the Petrodrill loss estimate was $60 million, the underwriters relied on the fact that the figure had been tested and found by E&Y to have a reasonable accounting basis in the 1999 financials.

At this stage, the only question we ask is whether there is evidence sufficient such that a reasonable jury could have reached the conclusion reached by this jury as to the lack of a superseding cause. While the FGH liquidity campaign and the representations of FGH management came after the audit, and played an undeniable role in causing Travelers to issue the Pasha bond, the jury could have reasonably concluded that the intervening acts of FGH's management did not sever the causal chain between Travelers' harm and E&Y's negligent audit. Accordingly, the evidence does not justify our reversing the jury's conclusion on this issue. . . .[430]

Because the insured (FGH) was 75% responsible and the accounting firm (E&Y) was 25% responsible for the losses suffered by Travelers under the terms of the performance bond, the accounting firm was held liable for $14,443,210.87, which was 25% of the losses.

Although ordinary causation principles apply to all negligent misrepresentation cases, the additional rules discussed below sometimes further restrict the scope of liability in cases involving only economic loss.

a.   Three Views: Foreseeability, Privity, and Intended Reliance

Jurisdictions generally subscribe to one of three views for defining the scope of liability in negligent misrepresentation cases based on purely economic loss.

The Foreseeability View. At one end of the spectrum, some courts impose a test which is not far different from the standard applicable to fraud claims. Nothing more is required than foreseeability of reliance, or perhaps something roughly equivalent to special reason to expect reliance. Thus, in *Touche Ross & Co. v. Commercial Union Insurance Co.*,[431] the Mississippi Supreme Court explained:

[A]n independent auditor is liable to reasonably foreseeable users of the audit, who request and receive a financial statement from the audited entity for a proper business purpose, and who then detrimentally rely on the financial statement, suffering a loss, proximately caused by the auditor's negligence. Such a rule protects third parties, who request, receive and rely on a financial statement, while it also protects the auditor from an unlimited number of potential users, who may otherwise read the financial statement,

---

[430] *Id.* at 485–89.

[431] 514 So. 2d 315 (Miss. 1987).

once published. Of course, the auditor remains free to limit the dissemination of his opinion through a separate agreement with the audited entity.[432]

The Privity or Near-Privity View. Other courts, standing at the opposite end of the spectrum, hold that not only is mere foreseeability an insufficient basis for liability, but there must be proof of privity between the parties, or something approaching privity,[433] before liability will attach. New York adheres to this type of near-privity rule in defining the scope of liability to third parties for negligent misrepresentation causing purely economic loss. To understand the New York view, it is useful to consider four cases:

The first case, *Glanzer v. Shepard*,[434] involved a public weigher which had negligently overstated the weight of a shipment of beans, to the detriment of the purchaser. The court there held that because the defendant knew the identity of the plaintiff-purchaser, knew that the plaintiff would rely on the certificate of weight in paying the seller who had arranged for the weighing, and had in fact sent a copy of the certificate to the plaintiff, it was fair to impose liability. In the words of Judge Benjamin N. Cardozo's opinion for the New York Court of Appeals, the purchase by the plaintiff was the "end and aim" of the transaction for "whose benefit and guidance" the information was supplied. The occurrence and extent of the plaintiff's reliance was no surprise to the defendant.

In the next case, *Jaillet v. Cashman*,[435] a customer in a stockbroker's office had relied to his detriment upon erroneous information about a Supreme Court decision[436] which the defendant had sent over a ticker. The plaintiff's identity was unknown to the defendant; he was merely one of a potentially vast number of persons who might possibly have been reached by the information. The nature and extent of the transactions in which plaintiff might rely on the erroneous information were completely unknown to the defendant. Moreover, the plaintiff's trust in the information was not, in any sense, the "end and aim of" the transaction. Not surprisingly, the court refused to impose liability.

---

[432] *Id.* at 322–23.

[433] *Privity* is an elusive term, more easily used than defined or understood. According to BALLENTINE'S LAW DICTIONARY (3d ed., LEXIS 2009), it means "an identity of interest between persons, so that the interest of the one is measured by the same legal right." According to BLACK'S LAW DICTIONARY (9th ed. 2009), *privity* is "[t]he connection or relationship between two parties, each having a legally recognized interest in the same subject matter (such as a transaction, proceeding, or piece of property); mutuality of interest."

[434] 135 N.E. 275 (N.Y. 1922).

[435] 139 N.E. 714 (N.Y. 1923).

[436] The Supreme Court decision which gave rise to the dispute was *Eisner v. Macomber*, 252 U.S. 189 (1920), an important tax case. The initial misunderstanding of Justice Mahlon Pitney's opinion, presented orally from the bench, was widespread. I have heard this story, which may be true: Justice Louis D. Brandeis needed to leave for a funeral. Though he had written a dissent, Brandeis was permitted to speak first. Pitney then delivered the majority opinion. This departure from customary practice of the majority opinion being announced first confused the reporters in the courtroom. As soon as they heard Brandeis say who should win, they ran out to put the news on the wire, because the tax issue was one of great importance. The reporters got it wrong because they did not wait to listen to Pitney, thinking that he was the dissent.

In the third case, *Ultramares v. Touche, Niven & Co.*,[437] Cardozo, by then Chief Judge of the New York Court of Appeals, wrote an opinion that has become a great landmark in this area of the law. The case involved an accounting firm. Fearful of exposing accountants to liability "in an indeterminate amount for an indeterminate time to an indeterminate class" as a result of momentary carelessness, Cardozo wrote that a corporation which had lent money to a company on the basis of misstatements contained in a certified balance sheet could not recover for negligent misrepresentation. While 32 copies of that balance sheet had been supplied (and while this would have been enough to establish reason to expect communication and reliance under the deceit count in the complaint, which was permitted to stand), the character of the persons to be reached and influenced and the nature and extent of the contemplated transaction were unknown to the defendant.

Guided by these three precedents, the same court, more than fifty years later, decided two appeals, both involving accounting firms, in *Credit Alliance Corp. v. Arthur Andersen & Co.*[438] In one case, the audited statements had been passed indirectly to the plaintiff by the audited party. The court held there was no liability. In the other case, where the auditors had been in frequent direct communication with the plaintiff, the court held that the plaintiff could sue for negligent misrepresentation. The court reasoned that auditors are liable for negligent preparation of financial reports only to those in privity of contract with them, or to those whose relationship with the auditors is "so close as to approach that of privity."[439] Judge Matthew Jasen wrote: "Before accountants may be held liable in negligence to noncontractual parties who rely to their detriment on inaccurate financial reports, certain prerequisites must be satisfied: (1) the accountants must have been aware that the financial reports were to be used for a particular purpose or purposes; (2) in the furtherance of which a known party or parties was intended to rely; and (3) there must have been some conduct on the part of the accountants linking them to that party or parties, which evinces the accountants' understanding of that party or parties' reliance."[440]

Near-Privity by Statute. New Jersey, which once subscribed to a foreseeability rule,[441] has legislatively adopted a near-privity rule. A New Jersey statute now provides in part:

> b. Notwithstanding the provisions of any other law, no accountant shall be liable for damages for negligence arising out of and in the course of rendering any professional accounting service unless:
>
> (1)   The claimant against the accountant was the accountant's client; or
>
> (2)   The accountant:
>
>   (a)   knew at the time of the engagement by the client, or agreed with the client after the time of the engagement, that the professional

---

[437] 174 N.E. 441 (N.Y. 1931).

[438] 483 N.E.2d 110 (N.Y. 1985).

[439] *Id.* at 115.

[440] *Id.* at 118.

[441] *See H. Rosenblum, Inc. v. Adler*, 461 A.2d 138, 153 (N.J. 1983).

accounting service rendered to the client would be made available to the claimant, who was specifically identified to the accountant in connection with a specified transaction made by the claimant;

   (b)   knew that the claimant intended to rely upon the professional accounting service in connection with that specified transaction; and

   (c)   directly expressed to the claimant, by words or conduct, the accountant's understanding of the claimant's intended reliance on the professional accounting service; or

  (3)   In the case of a bank claimant, the accountant acknowledged the bank's intended reliance on the professional accounting service and the client's knowledge of that reliance in a written communication.[442]

In *Cast Art Industries, LLC v. KPMG, LLP*,[443] the New Jersey Supreme Court held that the plaintiff failed to establish that the defendant accounting firm: (1) knew its accounting services for a client would be made available to the plaintiff, (2) knew that the plaintiff intended to rely on that information in a specified transaction; and (3) expressed to the plaintiff, by words or conduct, its understanding of the plaintiff's intended reliance. The plaintiff therefore failed to satisfy the requisite elements of the state Accountant Liability Act. The defendant accounting firm was entitled to judgment in its favor.

The Restatement's View: Intended Reliance by a Member of Limited Group. The third view on the scope of liability for purely economic losses caused by negligent misrepresentation is the *Restatement* view. That view takes an intermediate position, holding that liability for a negligent misstatement requires proof of something more than foreseeability of reliance, but not necessarily privity or near-privity between the plaintiff and defendant.

> According to the *Restatement*, liability for negligent misrepresentation extends only to "the person or one of a limited group of persons for whose benefit and guidance [the defendant] intends to supply the information or knows that the recipient intends to supply it," and even then only where the reliance is in a transaction substantially similar to the one the defendant intended to influence or knew the recipient intended to influence.[444] While it is not essential that the maker of the statement know the identity of the person for whose guidance the information is supplied, it "may be vitally important" that he be aware of the "number and character of the persons to be reached and influenced, and the nature and extent of the transaction for which guidance is furnished," because those factors define the "risk of liability to which the supplier subjects himself by undertaking to give the information."[445] Put differently, one of the fundamental principles of modern tort

[handwritten margin note: Restatement view on scope of liability]

---

[442] N.J. Stat. Ann. 2A:53A-25 (LEXIS 2014).

[443] 36 A.3d 1049 (N.J. 2012).

[444] Restatement (Second) of Torts § 552(2) (1977).

[445] *Id.* § 552(2) cmt. h.

law is that liability should not only be based on fault, but limited in proportion to fault. Unless one is aware of the magnitude of the harm that might result from mere carelessness, and thus has the opportunity and incentive to take adequate precautions, it is unfair to impose extensive liability.

It often makes a great deal of difference to plaintiffs and defendants which view a jurisdiction follows with respect to the scope of liability for negligent misrepresentation.

PROBLEM 2-14: THE SOLAR ENERGY TAX SHELTER

William Arnold and Nathaniel Bale promoted a great tax shelter in which $15,000 investments would produce an immediate tax credit of $30,000, a deduction of $15,000, and the opportunity to reap profits from a solar energy business, Sunny Days, Ltd. Two hundred persons invested their money, some as little as $15,000 and others as much as $2.5 million. Later the Internal Revenue Service disallowed the deductions and credits. The IRS then assessed interest and penalties against the individual investors.

Arnold and Bale wasted the money that had been invested in Sunny Days, Ltd. Subsequently, they were prosecuted for criminal fraud and went to prison. Arnold and Bale have no personal assets that can be reached by aggrieved investors. Sunny Days, Ltd. is now bankrupt.

The investors have consulted you about whether it is possible for them to sue Victoria Lamont and her law firm. Lamont had helped Arnold and Bale attract investors by writing a legal opinion letter. Addressed "To Whom It May Concern," the letter stated that investors in the solar energy venture would be entitled under the Internal Revenue Code to the credits and deductions that Arnold and Bale touted. Lamont gave the promoters the opinion letter for use in promoting investments in Sunny Days, Ltd.

The opinion letter recited "facts" that made the venture look legitimate: namely, that the corporation was structured in a certain way to protect investors rights; that equipment would be bought and sold at market prices; that certain operations were bonded; and that particular facilities were already in operation. Lamont had gotten all of this information from Arnold and Bale.

The opinion letter told readers that based upon the stated facts, the IRS would be unable to deny investors a $30,000 credit and $15,000 deduction per $30,000 unit of investment. If the facts in the letter had been true, this would have been correct. However, the "facts" the letter recited were nonexistent.

None of the investors were clients of, or personally dealt with, Lamont or her law firm. Most of the investors who remember receiving the letter say that it was provided to them by Arnold or Bale. A few say that they got the letter from a friend who had gotten the letter from Arnold or Bale.

Lamont now says that she told an associate at her law firm to conduct a "due diligence" inquiry before writing the opinion letter for her to sign. The associate recalls things differently. In fact, the associate is willing to testify that Lamont said that she would check the facts personally. Regardless of whether the lack of inquiry was attributable to a mistake or to indifference, there was no verification of the facts. The factual statements in the letter were false. Worse yet, the letter said that the law firm had made an independent investigation to verify the facts.

Please evaluate whether the investors can state a claim for fraud or negligent misrepresentation against Lamont and her law firm.

4.   Damages for Negligent Misrepresentation

Emotional Distress.   In   appropriate   cases,   damages   for   negligent misrepresentation (or for fraud) may include amounts for emotional distress and harm to reputation. For example, in *Spagnola v. Town of Morristown*,[446] a woman who was the victim of alleged sexual harassment by town officials, stated a claim for negligent misrepresentation against the town's outside law firm and a member of the firm. The court explained:

> To establish a cause of action for negligent misrepresentation . . . a plaintiff must establish "that the defendant negligently made an incorrect statement of a past or existing fact, that the plaintiff justifiably relied on it and that his reliance caused a loss or injury.". . . .
>
> The first element . . . may be satisfied by Plaintiff's contentions that Defendant Rich "deliberately misled and misinformed" her about her rights regarding sexual harassment. . . . Plaintiff also alleges . . . that Defendant Rich: ["told Plaintiff that Morristown had no policy which had been violated by Maurer's conduct"; "misled plaintiff into believing that defendant Morristown had no duty to protect her, foreseeably leading to her continued exposure to sexually offensive materials"; and "affirmatively misled plaintiff about her rights against sexual harassment, stating in part that there had been no sexual harassment because there had been no sexual touching or sexual language directed at her personally."]. . . .
>
> . . . Taking Plaintiff's remaining allegations as true, the Court finds that Plaintiff may also satisfy the second element. . . . Plaintiff alleges . . . that Defendant Rich's representation that the Town of Morristown had no duty to protect her caused Plaintiff to remain in her position and continue to be exposed to sexually offensive materials. . . . The third element requires Plaintiff to demonstrate that her reliance caused a loss or injury. Here, Plaintiff alleges that her repeated exposure to the sexual materials caused Plaintiff economic loss, emotional distress, psychological injury, pain and suffering, humiliation and damage to her reputation.[447]

---

[446] 2006 U.S. Dist. LEXIS 88431 (D.N.J. Dec. 7, 2006).

[447] *Id.* at *21–*24.

5.   Defenses and Other Obstacles to Recovery

a.   Comparative Negligence

Negligent misrepresentation is merely a particular type of negligence. It is therefore not surprising that courts hold that a comparative negligence defense may be raised by the defendant in such an action. For example, in *Staggs v. Sells*,[448] the defendants' agent had incorrectly represented that certain residential property, where the defendants had never lived, was not prone to flooding. The court allowed the buyers to recover for negligent misrepresentation, but reduced the damages by 40% because the buyers had not followed their appraiser's advice to have a surveyor evaluate the property for flooding. The court found no inconsistency between the doctrine of comparative negligence and the requirement that a plaintiff alleging negligent misrepresentation must have justifiably relied upon the defendant's misstatement.[449]

C.   STRICT LIABILITY FOR MISREPRESENTATION

Two (or Three) Categories. A nonculpable misrepresentation triggers strict liability for damages in at least two situations. The first is where the misrepresentation occurs in a sale, lease, or exchange transaction which would be subject to rescission as a result of the misrepresentation. The second is an aspect of products liability law which holds that damages are available where a misrepresentation relating to a product proximately causes physical harm. A possible third category of strict liability for misrepresentation deals with what is sometimes called "constructive fraud." Constructive fraud is discussed in Part D of this chapter.

1.   Sale, Lease, and Exchange Transactions

Preventing Unjust Enrichment. Cases imposing strict liability for inaccurate statements of fact typically involve defendants who sold or leased property. For example, in *Richard v. A. Waldman and Sons, Inc.*,[450] a plot plan misrepresented the location of a house, which in fact did not comply with set-back requirements. According to the Supreme Court of Connecticut:

> At the time of the closing, the defendant delivered to the plaintiffs a plot plan prepared by a registered engineer and land surveyor. This plan showed a sideyard of twenty feet on the southerly boundary of the lot which was in compliance with . . . zoning regulations.
>
> . . . Approximately four months after the delivery of the deed to the plaintiffs, the defendant discovered, when it set pins defining the boundaries of the premises, that the southeast corner of the foundation of the plaintiffs' house was only 1.8 feet from the southerly boundary of the lot. At this time, it was found that trespass upon adjoining property occurred in

[448] 86 S.W.3d 219 (Tenn. Ct. App. 2001).
[449] *Id.* at 224.
[450] 232 A.2d 307 (Conn. 1967).

entering and leaving the plaintiffs' back door and stoop. Prior to this discovery, the parties were unaware that there was a violation of the zoning regulations as to sideyard requirements. . . .

. . . [T]he plaintiffs had reasonable grounds upon which to attribute to the defendant accurate knowledge of what it represented as to the location of the structure on the lot. . . . It would be unjust to permit the defendant under these circumstances to "retain the fruits of a bargain induced by" a material misrepresentation upon which the plaintiffs relied. . . .[451]

The court held that the plaintiff was entitled to recover damages, notwithstanding the fact that the statement was made without fault. As the language in *Waldman* suggests, these kinds of decisions prevent a defendant's misrepresentations, even though entirely innocent, from enriching the defendant at the plaintiff's expense.

ALI Formulation. The *Restatement* describes the general rule for this category of cases as applying to any "sale, rental or exchange transaction," including transactions involving "land, chattels, securities or anything else of value, such as copyrights, patents and other valuable intangible rights."[452] According to the *Restatement*, damages are limited to the difference between what the plaintiff gave up and what the plaintiff got in exchange, which is to say "out of pocket" damages.[453] Note, however, the purchaser could recover "benefit of the bargain" damages by casting the material misrepresentation not as a tort, but as a contractual breach of warranty.[454] In that case, contract law defenses would apply.

Significantly, the *Restatement* provision on strict liability for material misrepresentations in sale, lease, or exchange transactions has been cited by relatively few courts. Some cases have noted that the rule was never adopted in their jurisdiction.[455]

Elements Similar to Fraud and Negligent Misrepresentation. Of course, claims falling within this category of strict liability share some of the same requirements as fault-based misrepresentation actions. There must be a misrepresentation of fact that is material and intended to induce reliance.[456] Moreover, proof of reliance is essential. In *Gibson v. Campano*,[457] the presence of a disclaimer clause in a real estate contract barred an innocent misrepresentation claim relating to termite damage.

No Liability to Third Parties. Third parties to a transaction can never recover under this strict liability rule. The plaintiff must have been a party to the transaction in which there was a material misrepresentation.[458] Thus, suppose that

---

[451] *Id.* at 309–10.

[452] RESTATEMENT (SECOND) OF TORTS § 552C & cmt. c (1977).

[453] *See id.* § 552C(2).

[454] *See id.* § 552C cmt. b.

[455] *See Growall v. Maietta*, 931 A.2d 667 (Pa. Super. Ct. 2007).

[456] RESTATEMENT (SECOND) OF TORTS § 552C cmt. e (1977).

[457] 699 A.2d 68 (Conn. 1997).

[458] *See* RESTATEMENT (SECOND) OF TORTS § 552C cmt. d (1977).

A, relying on a misrepresentation made by *B*, buys property at an inflated price from *C*. If the misrepresentation was fraudulent, *A* can recover from *B* — at the least if there was special reason to expect reliance.[459] If it was negligent, *A* can recover from *B* if *B* had a financial interest in the transaction[460] and *A* satisfies the requirements of the applicable view on scope of liability. If the misrepresentation was entirely innocent, *A* cannot recover from *B*.

Damages Versus Rescission. Because even an innocent misrepresentation of material fact will allow a purchaser to rescind a contract,[461] the major benefit to allowing a purchaser to commence an action for damages under tort principles for innocent misrepresentation is to permit the purchaser to keep the property. Rescission would require the purchaser to return what was received in the rescinded transaction.

Strict Liability by Statute. In some states, a result similar to common law strict liability is achieved by statute. Thus, a Texas statute dispenses with the need to prove *scienter* in real estate and stock transactions and offers other advantages to plaintiffs. Thus, § 27.01 of the Texas Business and Commerce Code provides:

(a)   Fraud in a transaction involving real estate or stock in a corporation or joint stock company consists of a

    (1)   false representation of a past or existing material fact, when the false representation is (A) made to a person for the purpose of inducing that person to enter into a contract; and (B) relied on by that person in entering into that contract; or

    (2)   false promise to do an act, when the false promise is (A) material; (B) made with the intention of not fulfilling it; (C) made to a person for the purpose of inducing that person to enter into a contract; and (D) relied on by that person in entering into that contract.

(b)   A person who makes a false representation or false promise commits the fraud described in Subsection (a) of this section and is liable to the person defrauded for actual damages.

(c)   A person who makes a false representation or false promise with actual awareness of the falsity thereof commits the fraud described in Subsection (a) of this section and is liable to the person defrauded for exemplary damages. Actual awareness may be inferred where objective manifestations indicate that a person acted with actual awareness.

(d)   A person who (1) has actual awareness of the falsity of a representation or promise made by another person and (2) fails to disclose the falsity of the representation or promise to the person defrauded, and (3) benefits from the false representation or promise commits the fraud described in Subsection (a) of this section and is liable to the person defrauded for exemplary damages. Actual awareness may be inferred where objective

---

[459] *See* Part A-3 of this Chapter.

[460] *See* Part B of this Chapter.

[461] *See* Restatement (Third) of Restitution & Unjust Enrichment § 13(1) and cmt. c (2011).

manifestations indicate that a person acted with actual awareness.

(e)   Any person who violates the provisions of this section shall be liable to the
      person defrauded for reasonable and necessary attorney's fees, expert
      witness fees, costs for copies of depositions, and costs of court.[462]

2.   Misrepresented Products That Cause Physical Harm

Under § 402B of the *Restatement (Second) of Torts*,[463] which has been adopted
in several jurisdictions, a seller of goods who, by advertising, labeling, or otherwise,
misrepresents to the public a material fact is strictly liable to a consumer for
physical injury caused by the erroneous statement. Thus, a seller who incorrectly
says that a shampoo is safe for use on hair, that glass is shatterproof, or that rope
has a certain strength, will be liable for physical injuries resulting to one who could
reasonably have been expected to use the product, even though the victim was not
the purchaser of the item and the statement was not made intentionally, recklessly,
or negligently.

For example, *Ladd v. Honda Motor Co., Ltd.*,[464] was an action by a boy who
became paralyzed when he lost control of an all-terrain vehicle. The Tennessee
Court of Appeals held that a manufacturer's advertisements for an entire product
line, and not solely for the model of ATV used by the plaintiff, could provide the
basis for establishing liability based on innocent misrepresentation. Similarly, in
Crocker v. Winthrop Labs.,[465] the Texas Supreme Court found a drug manufacturer
liable under § 402B for misrepresenting that the drug "was free and safe from all
dangers of addiction."

Under the second *Restatement's* formulation of this strict liability rule, liability
is limited to physical harm to a person or property and does not extend to purely
economic loss. As a model, § 402B of the second *Restatement* has now been
replaced by § 9 of the *Restatement (Third) of Torts: Products Liability*, which
provides that:

> One engaged in the business of selling or otherwise distributing products
> who, in connection with the sale of a product, makes a fraudulent, negligent,
> or innocent misrepresentation of material fact concerning the product is
> subject to liability for harm to persons or property caused by the
> misrepresentation.[466]

Of course, it is essential to link the misrepresentation to the resulting harm. In
Miller v. Pfizer Inc.,[467] parents alleged that misrepresentations about an antide-
pressant medication had caused their 13-year-old son to commit suicide. A federal
district court in Kansas rejected the claim due, in part, to the fact that the plaintiffs

---

[462] Tex. Bus. & Com. Code Ann. § 27.01 (LEXIS 2014).

[463] *See* Restatement (Second) of Torts § 402B (1965).

[464] 939 S.W.2d 83 (Tenn. Ct. App. 1996).

[465] 514 S.W.2d 429, 432–33 (Tex. 1974).

[466] Restatement (Third) of Torts: Products Liab. § 9 (1998).

[467] 196 F. Supp. 2d 1095 (D. Kan. 2002), *aff'd*, 356 F.3d 1326 (10th Cir. 2004).

failed to show that the prescribing physician on whom they relied had himself relied on any alleged misrepresentations made by the defendant.

D.   CONSTRUCTIVE FRAUD

Easing the Requirements of Fraud. "Constructive fraud" is a doctrine more frequently employed by courts than carefully examined or explained by scholars. In some cases, the doctrine appears to dispense with or dilute one or more of the requirements of fraud. To that extent, constructive fraud imposes liability for innocent misrepresentation, or at least some form of liability more strict than the standard fraud action. These issues are discussed below.

However, other cases that use the term "constructive fraud" appear to have little or nothing to do with misrepresentation. For example, in *LaSalle National Trust, N.A. v. Board of Directors of the 1100 Lake Shore Drive Condominium,*[468] the plaintiff alleged that a condominium board's failure to cooperate with her plans to renovate her penthouse house was "constructive fraud," and a resulting judgment was affirmed in relevant part, even though there was no evidence of misrepresentation in the usual sense.

Imprecise Legal Reasoning. The cases in which "constructive fraud" deals with liability for misrepresentation are often maddeningly imprecise as to whether and how the elements of fraud are relaxed under the doctrine. In general, the term "constructive fraud" means one of three things. First, the term may simply mean that nondisclosure is actionable. Thus, it might be said that a person under a legal duty to disclose information (*see* Part A-2(b) of this chapter), who does not do so, engages in conduct which amounts to "constructive fraud." When the term is used in this way, there is no change in the elements of fraud. The speaker has merely signaled that nondisclosure is as readily actionable as an affirmative misstatement. The second and third meanings of "constructive fraud" relate to the *scienter* element of fraud. The cases sometimes say that under the doctrine of constructive fraud the plaintiff does not need to prove "intent to defraud." Statements like this appear to indicate that the plaintiff is relieved from proving *scienter.* As discussed below, the alternatives are that the requirement of establishing that the defendant acted with knowledge of falsity or reckless disregard for the truth is replaced either by strict liability or by a requirement of negligence as to falsity.

Making Innocent Misrepresentation Actionable. Some cases are reasonably clear in discussing constructive fraud (although whether they are fully accurate is another question). For example, in *Community Bank & Trust Co. of Virginia v. Bohannon,*[469] the Virginia Circuit Court wrote:

> Constructive fraud is the innocent misrepresentation of a material fact with the intent that a person will rely on it, which he does and is thereby damaged. The Amended Counterclaim alleges . . . that "at no time did [the bank's officer] state that . . . [promised] funding was tentative." Assuming for the purposes of the demurrer that the pleadings are true, defendant

---

[468] 677 N.E.2d 1378 (Ill. App. Ct. 1997).

[469] 1988 Va. Cir. LEXIS 338 (Mar. 15, 1988).

claims he was told the zero coupon bond would be forthcoming and was not aware that the arrangements were tentative at best. If proven, this type of innocent or mistaken misrepresentation is material and would be grounds for a claim of constructive fraud.[470]

Basing Liability on Negligence. Other cases seem to mean simply that if you cannot prove fraud, you can sometimes sue for negligent misrepresentation. Consider *Michel v. Moore & Associates, Inc.*,[471] where the California Court of Appeal wrote:

Mike Kirkpatrick was a real estate agent working for . . . [respondent Moore]. . . . [H]e inspected a home in Rolling Hills Estates owned by a friend's parents. Hoping to become the listing agent if the parents decided to sell their house, he took notes of the property's defects, including possible water leaks, cracked interior walls, and damage to the pool. If he won the listing, he planned to use his notes to identify needed repairs and possible disclosure to potential buyers.

About six months later . . . the house was on the market. Kirkpatrick, who had not received the sellers' listing, showed the house to appellants Carl and Sydne Michel, who were represented by agent Nicola Lagudis, a colleague of Kirkpatrick also working for respondent Moore. During the home tour, Kirkpatrick did not point out any of the defects from his notes. . . .

Appellants and the sellers shortly thereafter agreed on the terms of sale and entered escrow. . . . Lagudis visually inspected the property and gave appellants her obligatory transfer disclosure statement (TDS). . . . The TDS did not . . . disclose other defects listed in Kirkpatrick's notes. . . .

One of Kirkpatrick's tasks as respondent's "transaction coordinator" was reviewing the sales files of respondent's agents to ensure a sale's paperwork was in order before escrow closed. Accordingly, Kirkpatrick reviewed Lagudis's TDS to appellants. Although mindful of his notes as he reviewed the TDS, he did not tell Lagudis about them, nor did he augment her TDS with anything from those notes. . . .

Starting with the first winter rains about a month after appellants moved into their new home, cracks emerged in interior walls, which appellants repeatedly patched. Around that time, appellants started remodeling their backyard and pool. To do so, they needed a permit, which required a soil engineer to inspect their property. The engineer discovered poor topsoil and fill had caused significant instability and ground movement on the property. He found the movement had tilted the house's foundation about 3.5 inches from level. . . . To stabilize the house, he recommended placing caissons under its foundation down to solid bedrock.

---

[470] *Id.* at 540.

[471] 156 Cal. App. 4th 756 (2007).

Upset by the engineer's report, appellants met with Kirkpatrick in January 2001. They told him about the soil instability and cracks in the walls, which would likely cost about half a million dollars to fix. Kirkpatrick replied he had seen during his inspection before the house was put on the market cracks big enough to slip a coin into. Hearing about his notes for the first time, appellants asked for a copy, which Kirkpatrick gave them.[472]

The Michels subsequently sued the Moore agency for fraudulent concealment and violation of obligations under a state statute (which is not relevant here). In finding for the agency, the jury determined that the agency had not concealed or suppressed any fact. The trial court had instructed the jury that to prove fraudulent concealment the Michels had to establish that the agency "intentionally concealed facts with the intent to defraud them."[473] The trial court also declined to submit the plaintiff's negligent nondisclosure claim to the jury on the grounds that it was duplicative of the statutory claim. In reversing the judgment, the appellate court wrote:

> A broker has a fiduciary duty to its client. . . .
>
> A fiduciary must tell its principal of all information it possesses that is material to the principal's interests. . . . A fiduciary's failure to share material information with the principal is constructive fraud, a term of art obviating actual fraudulent intent. . . . Constructive fraud is a unique species of fraud applicable only to a fiduciary or confidential relationship. . . . [A]s a general principle constructive fraud comprises any act, omission or concealment involving a breach of legal or equitable duty, trust or confidence which results in damage to another even though the conduct is not otherwise fraudulent. Most acts by an agent in breach of his fiduciary duties constitute constructive fraud. The failure of the fiduciary to disclose a material fact to his principal which might affect the fiduciary's motives or the principal's decision, which is known (or should be known) to the fiduciary, may constitute constructive fraud. . . . Appellants' negligent nondisclosure/constructive fraud theory relieved them of the burden of needing to prove respondent intended to defraud them, a much easier row to hoe than proving actual intent to defraud for fraudulent concealment.
>
> . . . [T]he court did not instruct on constructive fraud's connection to fiduciary relationships. Instead, the court told the jury that appellants needed to prove respondent intentionally concealed or suppressed information with the intent to defraud. By imposing the tougher evidentiary challenge of proving actual fraudulent intent, the court derailed appellants from the easier evidentiary route to liability through constructive fraud, which does not require actual fraudulent intent. Thus, the court's fiduciary instruction did not provide appellants the legal benefit to which they were entitled.[474]

---

[472] *Id.* at 799–801.

[473] *Id.* at 801.

[474] *Id.* at 802–03 (internal quotation marks omitted).

The court remanded the case for "further proceedings only on appellants' cause of action for negligent nondisclosure."[475] Thus, the court held that constructive fraud means that a person who is owed fiduciary duties can sue for negligent misrepresentation when there is nondisclosure of material facts. Obviously, this is a very different interpretation of the doctrine than the one reached by the Virginia trial court in *Bohannon* (discussed above). That court said that constructive fraud imposes liability for innocent misrepresentation.

The Term "Constructive Fraud" as Encompassing Negligent and Innocent Misrepresentation. It is perhaps not surprising that some decisions have said that constructive fraud includes both innocent and negligent misrepresentation. *Supervalu, Inc. v. Johnson*,[476] made that point and also clarified that certain doctrinal principles well-established in the law of fraud apply also to claims under the doctrine of constructive fraud:

> To prevail on a constructive fraud claim, a plaintiff must show by clear and convincing evidence that the defendant negligently or innocently made a false representation of material fact, and that the plaintiff suffered damage as a result of his reliance upon that misrepresentation.

> Because fraud must involve a misrepresentation of a present or a preexisting fact, fraud ordinarily cannot be predicated on unfulfilled promises or statements regarding future events. . . . Nevertheless, if a defendant makes a promise that, when made, he has no intention of performing, that promise is considered a misrepresentation of present fact and may form the basis for a claim of actual fraud. . . .

> Under no circumstances, however, will a promise of future action support a claim of constructive fraud. . . . The rationale underlying this rule is plain. If unfulfilled promises, innocently or negligently made, were sufficient to support a constructive fraud claim, every breach of contract would potentially give rise to a claim of constructive fraud.[477]

Constructive Fraud Beyond Fiduciary Relationships. The constructive fraud doctrine is generally limited to cases where one party owes the other fiduciary obligations. Indeed, in some cases, the absence of a fiduciary relationship has been deemed fatal to a constructive fraud claim. For example, in *Joyce v. Morgan Stanley & Co., Inc.*,[478] the Seventh Circuit held that shareholders and option holders of an acquired corporation could not sue the acquired corporation's financial advisor for constructive fraud because there was no fiduciary relationship between the parties, as required by Illinois law. However, there are other cases which apply constructive fraud to a wider range of transactions not involving fiduciary obligations.

In *Mattingly v. First Bank of Lincoln*,[479] the purchaser of a service station sued a bank which lent him money to finance the transaction. He alleged that the bank

---

[475] *Id.* at 804.

[476] 666 S.E.2d 335 (Va. 2008).

[477] *Id.* at 341–42.

[478] 58 F.3d 797, 802–03 (7th Cir. 2008).

[479] 947 P.2d 66 (Mont. 1997).

had failed to disclose that it knew about underground contamination of the service station property. The plaintiff alleged negligence, negligent misrepresentation, and constructive fraud. In reversing a grant of summary judgment for the bank, the Montana Supreme Court wrote:

> The presence of a legal duty is an essential element of a claim for constructive fraud. Section 28-2-406, MCA, defines constructive fraud as:
>
>> (1) any breach of duty which, without an actually fraudulent intent, gains an advantage to the person in fault or anyone claiming under him by misleading another to his prejudice or to the prejudice of anyone claiming under him; or
>>
>> (2) any such act or omission as the law especially declares to be fraudulent, without respect to actual fraud.
>
> Thus, in addressing First Bank's motion for summary judgment with respect to Mattingly's claim for constructive fraud, this Court must first determine whether the lower court erred in concluding First Bank owed no duty to Mattingly to disclose any information it may have had regarding the contamination.
>
> Whether or not a legal duty exists is a question of law for the court's determination. . . . Although the legal duty which often exists in constructive fraud cases is a fiduciary one, this Court has previously held that Montana's constructive fraud statute "does not require that the plaintiff demonstrate a fiduciary relationship, [but] merely requires the establishment of a duty." . . . Under certain "special circumstances," neither a confidential nor a fiduciary relationship is necessary for a finding of constructive fraud.
>
> This Court has held special circumstances may exist where one party has acted to mislead the other in some way. Specifically, this Court has determined that constructive fraud may be present "[w]here sellers [of real property], by words or conduct, create a false impression concerning serious impairment or other important matters and subsequently fail to disclose the relevant facts." . . .
>
> . . . Similarly, in [*Moschelle v. Hulse*, 622 P.2d 155 (Mont. 1980)], we held special circumstances supporting a claim for constructive fraud existed where sellers made misleading statements regarding the physical condition of the property and the income generated from the business. . . .
>
> A duty sufficient to support a claim for constructive fraud may arise in a commercial transaction. . . . Whether First Bank, by its words or conduct, created a false impression concerning the contamination, and subsequently failed to disclose relevant facts, is a question of material fact. Special circumstances giving rise to a duty on the part of First Bank may exist should a trier of fact find that First Bank misrepresented the value of the property in light of the contamination, and that Mattingly relied upon this representation in purchasing the property.

Furthermore, First Bank had peculiar knowledge of the environmental hazard. Mattingly contracted with First Bank to borrow money, unaware of the duties and financial obligations he was assuming by becoming an owner of environmentally damaged property. A jury may well conclude that such facts would constitute special circumstances in this case.

Based on the foregoing, we conclude that the District Court erred in summarily finding no special circumstances giving rise to a duty on the part of First Bank to disclose any information it may have had regarding the ground contamination to Mattingly.[480]

The scope of the rule in *Mattingly* is unclear. Nevertheless, lawyers cannot ignore the pronouncements of a state supreme court. In advising clients, lawyers must take into account the uncertainties of existing law and be prepared to make responsible arguments for coherently construing precedent. One possibility, as suggested above, is the view that invocation of the doctrine of "constructive fraud" does not change anything about the usual principles governing tort liability other than to clarify that nondisclosures are sometimes actionable, or that a plaintiff may be entitled to recover from a defendant who was only negligent as to the falsity of a representation or, in some cases, subject to strict liability for the misstatement.

PROBLEM 2-15: THE LEAKY BASEMENT

Sam Soretski sold a house to Katherine Chinchaulk for $80,000. The house had been owned by Sam's sister, Dahlia Defeau, for 38 years prior to her death. The residence had been vacant for four years while Defeau was in a nursing home. The house and other property passed to Soretski under the terms of Defeau's will. Soretski immediately put the house up for sale at an attractive price because he did not want to be bothered with taking care of the property. Soretski never lived in the house, and had not even visited there. The house was located in a small town on the other side of the state. As siblings, Soretski and Defeau were not close, but Soretski inherited her property only because he was Defeau's last surviving kin.

Incidental to the closing of the sale of the house, Sam signed the Property Disclosure Form required by state law. Under the jurisdiction's Residential Property Disclosure Act ("RPDA"), "Any seller who intends to transfer any interest in real property shall disclose to the buyer any material defects with the property known to the seller by completing all applicable items in a property disclosure statement."

Paragraph 4(b) of the disclosure statement asked, "Are you aware of any water leakage, accumulation or dampness within the basement, garage or crawl space?" Soretski marked "no" as the answer. Paragraph 4(c) of the disclosure statement asked, "Do you know of any repairs or other attempts to control any water or dampness problem in the basement, garage or crawl space?" Soretski again marked "no" as the answer.

According to the RPDA:

---

[480] *Id.* at 71–73.

A seller is not obligated . . . to make any specific investigation or inquiry in an effort to complete the property disclosure statement. In completing the property disclosure statement, the seller shall not make any representations that the seller or the agent for the seller knows or has reason to know are false, deceptive or misleading and shall not fail to disclose a known material defect.

Soon after the closing, Chinchaulk became aware of a water leakage problem in the basement apartment. Specifically, water came out from under the baseboard onto the floor when the first floor apartment's toilet was flushed. A plumber told Chinchaulk that it would cost roughly $20,000 to repair the problem, which must have existed for some period of time.

Except for the leak in the basement, Chinchaulk liked the house, and she knew that she had gotten a good deal on it. A similar house on the same street sold for $115,000 at the same time she bought the Defeau house. However, Chinchaulk does not think she should have to pay for the plumbing repairs. She has no evidence that Soretski lied when he filled out the Property Disclosure Form, and she knew that he had never visited the house he inherited from his sister. Please advise Chinchaulk about the likelihood of recovering damages in a tort action for misrepresentation.

E. REVIEW

By way of review, consider the issues posed by erroneous scoring of standardized tests. The material below addresses whether mis-scoring could give rise to liability for fraud and negligent misrepresentation. The "review" sections of later chapters reference the same problem for the purpose of considering the viability of claims for defamation, false light invasion of privacy, tortious interference with contract or prospective advantage, or injurious falsehood.

Standardized Tests, Erroneous Scores, and Tort Liability.[481] Hopes and dreams often hinge upon the accuracy of standardized test scores. Results frequently determine, or greatly influence, whether a student progresses to the next grade level, attains a diploma, gains admission to a college or university, or can practice a profession after graduation.

Common Ground. There are endless disputes over the merits of standardized testing. Yet, everyone agrees that if standardized tests are given, they should be scored consistently and accurately. If answer "C" is the "right" choice for a question, then "C" must be the right choice for every student who answers that question. If a hundred students all select identical answers on the same standardized test, they should all receive the same scores.

The Vast Expansion of Standardized Testing. Although standardized tests have been used in America since at least the 1920s, the field of standardized test preparation, administration, and scoring grew "enormously" after President

---

[481] This following material is based on, and language is borrowed from, Vincent R. Johnson, *Standardized Tests, Erroneous Scores, and Tort Liability*, 38 RUTGERS L.J. 655, 656–98 (2007). Supporting citations can be found in the article.

George W. Bush signed the No Child Left Behind Act in 2002, catalyzing the demand for such evaluative instruments at the state level.

Given the volume of standardized testing, it is not surprising that errors occur, either in scoring tests or reporting results (collectively referred to hereinafter as "scoring errors" or "mis-scoring"). Yet, when those failings are publicized by the media, they are not dismissed as inevitable glitches in an otherwise sound system. Sometimes the revelation of mis-scoring precipitates lawsuits, such as recent cases arising from mis-scoring of the SAT and the teacher test PRAXIS. Occasionally, there are even legislative investigations.

Spectacular Mis-Scoring. In recent years, there have been spectacular instances of standardized test scoring errors. One recent failure involved the National Conference of Bar Examiners' (NCBE) distribution of results from the Multistate Bar Examination (MBE). The scoring error related to a "keying error" involving only one of two hundred questions on the exam, but affecting the scores of almost 8,000 of the roughly 20,000 law school graduates who took the bar exam. Based on the scores initially reported, some applicants for admission to the practice of law were told they had passed the bar examination, and others were told they had failed — although in some states applicants had not yet been notified when the error became known. After some successful test-takers had already been sworn in as new lawyers, the NCBE acknowledged that some of the test scores were wrong. For days, the magnitude of the problem was unclear, and the consequences for the bar applicants were uncertain. At least one state "uncertified" a new lawyer that it had already sworn in.

Mis-Scoring the SAT. More recently, the College Board mis-scored more than 5,000 of the 495,000 exams from the October 2005 Scholastic Aptitude Test (SAT). The vast majority of the erroneous scores were off by 100 points, but some students received scores that were as much as 450 points too low on the 2,400 scale. About 600 of the students received scores 50 points too high. The problem with the test results was discovered by the College Board in January 2006 after the College Board asked the Pearson Measurement Company, which originally scored the examinations, to hand score some tests. However, the error was not made public until March 2006. Ultimately, the College Board decided that it would report to colleges and universities higher scores for students whose exams had been scored too low, but that it would not lower the scores of students whose tests had been scored too high. This solution did not please everyone. Students whose initial scores were erroneously low feared that, during the interim, they had been denied admissions opportunities and scholarships to which they were rightfully entitled. Students whose exams had been scored accurately worried that they had been disadvantaged by being forced to compete with some applicants whose scores were erroneously too high and never corrected. Colleges and universities were forced to address a myriad of inquiries and, in many instances, to review applicant files yet another time as the truth played out in the critical winter-spring time period of the admissions season. Because many offers of admission or scholarship assistance had been made and accepted between December and March, it was likely that the erroneous information had an impact on some of those decisions. Ultimately a class action was filed and later settled.

Mis-scoring the Teacher Test (PRAXIS). In yet another case, the Educational Testing Service acknowledged that it had graded some essay answers on PRAXIS, a teacher test, too stringently. About 27,000 people who took the exam received lower scores than they should have. Roughly, 4,100 of them were erroneously told they had failed. The resulting class action was eventually settled by creation of an $11.1 million fund to provide cash payments to plaintiffs to compensate for lost wages, decreased earning capacity, and other losses.

There are other reports of standardized test scoring errors. Such problems have occurred, for example, in California, Minnesota, New Jersey, New York, Virginia, and Washington. According to one count, there were at least 137 publicly disclosed cases of large-scale testing errors, most of them relatively recent.

Litigation Follows Innovation. It is not surprising, or necessarily undesirable, that erroneous standardized test scores are beginning to generate tort litigation. This is the natural course of development in America. Innovation is frequently followed by litigation because new or expanded practices often cause harm. When losses occur as a result of such developments, lawsuits offer a public mechanism for compensating injured persons, forcing innovators to internalize the costs of their endeavors, and creating incentives for measures that minimize future harm by reducing activity levels or increasing precautions. Within proper limits, litigation can, and frequently does, provide a healthy check on market excesses by forcing persons who benefit from selling goods or services to bear the burden of incidental losses or at least to spread those losses broadly among those who enjoy the goods or services.

In the early and mid-twentieth century, mass production of automobiles was soon followed by car-accident lawsuits, and mass-marketing of consumer goods gave rise to products-liability litigation. More recently, the widespread use of computerized databases has produced lawsuits related to data security and identity theft, and the expansion of international education programs is now generating claims by students injured while studying in foreign countries. It is entirely natural, from the perspective of more than a century of American legal history, for the recent vast expansion of standardized testing to be followed by lawsuits seeking to balance the sometimes conflicting goals of compensating victims and deterring bad practices, with the need to craft liability rules that facilitate the types of innovative practices and products that promote growth and progress and assist societal achievement and personal fulfillment.

Forcing Businesses to Examine Harmful Practices. Tort litigation, like litigation generally, often serves useful purposes. To begin with, it forces companies and other enterprises to examine harmful practices that might otherwise receive inadequate attention. For example, the College Board's president dismissively said that it "did not really matter" why SAT exams became wet before they were mis-scored. But preventing losses in the future often depends on determining precisely why a certain type of problem occurred in the first instance.

Tort litigation also plays a vital role in addressing problems that are left unresolved by legislatures and administrative agencies. Indeed, without a fair forum in which to litigate disputes about conduct that causes harm, or other governmental avenues for redress, victims of intentional or accidental injuries might resort to violence and other undesirable practices, as they sometimes do in other countries. For example, in China, students who had been defrauded by a university recently rioted because China presently has no tort system or other mechanism offering a realistic opportunity for resolving such disputes.

Possible Tort Remedies. An array of tort claims might arise from erroneous scoring of standardized tests, including misrepresentation, defamation, false-light invasion of privacy, tortious interference with prospective advantage, and injurious falsehood. While some of these theories will rarely offer a viable avenue for recovery, other theories, on particular facts, may provide a basis for relief.

Damages in Erroneous Scoring Cases. Standardized test scoring errors cause many types of losses, not all of which will be equally compensable under tort law. The key variables in determining whether a particular element of damages will be awarded are the strength of the causal link between the mis-scoring and the alleged harm, and whether the amount of the loss can be quantified with reasonable certainty. If there is serious doubt as to either causation or amount, recovery of an element of damages may be denied.

Foreseeable "Out of Pocket" Expenditures. The fact and magnitude of some mis-scoring losses can be established with a high degree of certainty if the losses are the direct result of foreseeable out-of-pocket expenditures. For example, a test-taker who receives an erroneously low score may quite predictably spend readily ascertainable amounts of money on: securing a re-scoring of the initial exam; registering to take the test again; enrolling in a test preparation course; purchasing study aids; securing professional tutoring or diagnostic assistance; traveling to the repeat test site; or perhaps even enrolling in test-related academic offerings.

Quantifying Losses. Certain other types of losses, involving reduced income rather than expenditures, may be so likely to result from an erroneously low score that their legitimacy cannot readily be doubted. The only uncertainty in such cases will reside in fixing the amount, but even then the jury may find guidance in what many would regard as reliable evidence, such as average earnings figures for new employees in a particular field. Reduced income for a test-taker who is the victim of erroneous scoring may result in a variety of ways, including: time away from work to sit for the repeat test or to take related courses; denial of necessary professional certification or licensing; and otherwise delayed entry into the job market.

Reduced income resulting from lost scholarships will often be easy to quantify. Several states employ merit scholarship programs that use SAT scores to determine the amount of awards. Also, at many colleges and universities, scholarships are awarded based simply on a matrix formula, where the variables are grade point average (GPA) and test score. At a particular school, an admitted law student with an LSAT score of 160 and an undergraduate GPA of 3.5, might be routinely awarded a $10,000 scholarship, since that is the amount awarded to every student in the matrix category. However, a student with the same undergraduate GPA and a test score of 155 might be normally awarded $5,000, according to the matrix. If a law student who is the victim of erroneous standardized test scoring can point to such evidence, it may be possible for the student to quantify the student's economic loss with sufficient persuasiveness to permit recovery of that element of damages. Of course, if a college or university is the plaintiff, it should be able to use similar evidence to show that, but for the test score error, it would have offered a student a lower scholarship.

There may be other cases of compelling evidence that the plaintiff suffered economic harm. A student might be able to show, for example, that but for a test score error, the student would have fallen into the "presumptive admit" category at the state university, and that by enrolling there the student would have saved a certain amount of money each year by qualifying for in-state tuition. If the student in fact applied to the state university, this type of argument may be quite reasonable and sufficient to support a jury award.

Unquantifiable Losses. Some of the losses that undoubtedly result from standardized test scoring errors may be so difficult to quantify that the law will be reluctant to permit recovery. Into this category may fall compensation for the value of: missing a graduation ceremony; suffering embarrassment and other forms of emotional distress; and (depending on the precise facts) losing the opportunity to attend an educational program to which the test-taker either applied and was rejected or decided not to apply because the erroneous score appeared not to be competitive.

Losses Not Proximately Caused. Finally, some asserted losses may be so dubiously linked to standardized test scoring errors that it will be difficult or impossible for a court to find, by a preponderance of the evidence, that but for the mis-scoring, the loss would not have occurred. This may be true, for example, where a test-taker argues that because of an erroneous score a job offer was not extended. Similarly, a student who contends that, but for a defendant's misrepresentation, the student would have been admitted to a better school, gotten a better job, and made higher lifetime earnings will be hard pressed to establish the requisite level of certainty to sustain an award of those damages.

Contract Law Remedies. If a test-taker whose score is reported incorrectly paid a fee to take the test, the mis-scoring could be treated as a breach of an express or implied contractual promise to correctly grade the exam, and the test-taker could then sue for contract damages. However, in many instances, the test-taker does not pay a fee, as when students in a public school system are required to pass a state-mandated achievement test. In that case, no breach-of-contract claim is feasible. Similarly, test-score-recipients, such as colleges and universities, typically have no contract with testing agencies. Except perhaps on a third-party-beneficiary theory, contract law offers those institutions no relief for losses they sustain as a result of incorrect scores.

Even if a contract claim is available to persons harmed by erroneous standardized test results, that may not foreclose a tort-law analysis, except, possibly, under the economic-loss rule. In many areas of the law, such as products liability, a plaintiff has the option of asserting a breach-of-contract claim, or tort claims based on negligence or strict liability, or all of those theories. Similarly, a client harmed by the conduct of a lawyer ordinarily may sue for breach of contract, as well as for the torts of negligence, fraud, or breach of fiduciary duty. The categorization of the claim will have many important consequences. It will determine, for example, the applicable statute of limitations, pertinent defenses, dischargeability of a judgment in bankruptcy, insurance coverage, and the appropriate standards for calculating damages. However, American law has often recognized that relief afforded by contract law (expectation, or reliance, damages) is sometimes inadequate in comparison to tort principles, and there is certainly no general rule that, merely because a contract claim can be stated, tort law remedies are unavailable. Thus, it is not surprising that in the PRAXIS teacher-test mis-scoring litigation, the plaintiffs alleged multiple claims for breach of contract, negligence, and negligent misrepresentation.

Tort Theories of Recovery. When standardized tests are mis-scored, there may be more than one potential defendant. For example, an entity that administers a test may sub-contract the scoring of the results to a separate independent entity, and then rely upon those scores in reporting results to various recipients. Tort liability frequently turns upon facts relating to what a defendant did or did not do, and the culpability associated with that action or omission (*e.g.*, intent, recklessness, or negligence), and other related considerations. It is important to remember that not all defendants will be similarly situated. On a particular theory, one defendant may be subject to liability and another may not.

In a limited range of cases, erroneous standardized test results might support claims for misrepresentation. In thinking about this subject, it is useful to differentiate two distinct misrepresentation theories (fraud and negligent misrepresentation) and two potential groups of plaintiffs (test-takers and other test-score recipients).

Mis-Scoring Liability Based on Fraud. The chief obstacle to a fraud claim will be proving *scienter*. Presumably, it will be nearly impossible for a plaintiff to prove that a testing agency knowingly distributed erroneous results. However, establishing *scienter* based on recklessness will be easier, and sometimes possible. When the maker of a statement knowingly lacks confidence in the truth that a statement implies, the statement, if false, is fraudulently made. Thus, if a testing agency has doubts about the correctness of test results, but nevertheless distributes those results without disclosing its concerns, the agency acts with *scienter* and could be sued for fraud, if the test results are erroneous and cause harm by inducing reliance.

Failure to Correct Disseminated Results. There is a well-recognized tort duty to correct false statements that, although believed to have been true when made, are later discovered to be false. The duty to correct continues until the recipient of the information is no longer able to protect his or her own interests by avoiding reliance upon the utterance that the speaker has discovered to be erroneous. This theory of liability would be applicable to cases where a testing agency discovers errors in previously distributed test results, but neglects to disclose those errors in a timely fashion.

Privilege to Investigate. Suppose that test results distributed in November are discovered in December to contain errors, but the problem is not disclosed to test-takers or other score recipients until March. Is the nondisclosure of the errors between December and March the basis for a lawsuit? Presumably, a testing agency would have a conditional privilege to delay revelation of the suspected errors long enough to conduct an investigation of the facts. The investigation might take weeks or months. For example, when the College Board was alerted to possible problems with the October 2005 SAT, it launched an investigation of not merely the October test, but the subsequent exams in November, December, and January, for a total of 1.5 million investigated exams in all. A privilege to delay revelation of information about possible scoring errors long enough to investigate the facts would help to prevent the type of harm that could be caused by erroneous reports about suspect results, and would also be consistent with the testing agency's own legitimate interest in taking reasonable steps to protect its reputation. However, once the error has been or should have been verified, it is incumbent upon the testing agency to promptly disclose the information — provided that the reliance on the erroneous information could still be avoided.

Feasibility of Remedial Action. On the posited facts concerning failure to correct, is there anything a test-taker or other score recipient could do to prevent erroneous test results from causing harm? In many cases, "yes." A test-taker who has applied for admission to a college or university could advise that institution of the unreliability of the results. A student who eschewed application to another educational program because the erroneous results appeared uncompetitive might still apply there for admission. And a student might forebear incurring the costs of preparing for and retaking the standardized test until correct results are available. In addition, an educational institution informed of documented or potential errors might be able to delay admissions decisions or scholarship offers, or might re-consider the files of students who were previously rejected. It seems possible that, in some cases, liability may be imposed under the duty-to-correct theory. This is particularly true if there is evidence not merely of non-disclosure of the errors, but that the testing agency hid that information or unreasonably hoped that the problem would not be discovered.

Mis-scoring Liability Based on Negligent Misrepresentation. Actions for negligent misrepresentation (as opposed to fraud) would likely follow a similar analysis in cases against commercial providers of testing services, since liability for negligent misrepresentation extends to persons who fail to exercise care in statements made in the course of business operations. The scope of liability for negligent misrepresentation is often more tightly limited than for deceit. However, those limitations would not affect aggrieved paying test-takers or most other score-recipients. Cases that limit the scope of negligent-misrepresentation liability more strictly than by a rule of foreseeable reliance generally do either of two things. The cases either follow the *Restatement* approach or they impose a requirement of privity or "near-privity." Under the *Restatement (Second) of Torts*, liability extends only to a "person or [a member] of a limited group of persons for whose benefit and guidance [the defendant] intends to supply the information or knows that the recipient intends to supply it,"[482] and only with respect to "reliance in a transaction that [the defendant] intends the information to influence or knows that the recipient so intends or in a substantially similar transaction."[483]

---

[482] Restatement (Second) of Torts § 552(2)(a) (1977).

[483] *Id.* § 552(2)(b).

The educational institutions that receive standardized test results related to admissions applications would readily qualify as plaintiffs under the *Restatement* test, since in such cases it would be clear both that they might rely, and what type of reliance might occur. In addition, such direct recipients of erroneous test scores would probably also satisfy a privity or near-privity test. In cases involving the direct transmission of an erroneous document, there is the kind of one-to-one dealing that substitutes for privity.

A test-taker who pays a fee to take an exam would also have no trouble satisfying a scope-of-liability requirement. The payment would place the test-taker in privity with the testing agency and would thus satisfy any type of standing requirement for negligent misrepresentation (foreseeability of reliance, intended reliance under the *Restatement* rule by a member of a limited group in a known or similar transaction, or privity/near-privity).

Non-Paying Test-Takers. A different analysis would be required in cases of non-paying test-takers, such as elementary students who take state-required standardized examinations. First, those test-takers might only be able to establish foreseeable reliance, not intended reliance (under the *Restatement* rule) or privity/near-privity. Second, there would also be an important issue relating to duty. Some cases — such as suits dealing with drug testing and other medical examinations — have held that the party administering the test owes no duty of care to the test subject, but only to the party paying for the test. Without a duty to exercise care on the part of the defendant, a plaintiff would be unable to sue for negligent misrepresentation, since duty is an essential element of any negligence-based claim.

However, a number of cases are to the contrary and hold that a testing agency, even if employed by a third-party, owes a duty of care to the test-taker. One lawsuit with apparent relevance to tort liability for erroneous scoring of standardized tests is *Merrick v. Thomas*.[484] There, the Supreme Court of Nebraska held that a merit commission owed a duty to a job applicant to score a test accurately. The plaintiff, after receiving an offer of employment from the sheriff's department, resigned her full-time job at her former place of employment. However, she was subsequently terminated by the sheriff's department following discovery that her hiring was the result of an incorrect test score. The court wrote:

> The merit commission could foresee that Merrick, by the act of applying, desired the job and would rely on the results of a prerequisite test for that job. It is reasonably foreseeable that an inaccurate passing score could result in Merrick's name being given to the sheriff as a qualified applicant and that, approximately 6 months after taking the test, Merrick would be offered a job that she was not qualified for. Last, it is reasonably foreseeable that acceptance of the offer would, with a high degree of certainty, cause injury when officials discovered the true test score. The defendants argue that the only duty owed is to the sheriff who receives the test score. [However], the duty owed Merrick is rooted in common law.[485]

---

[484] 522 N.W.2d 402 (Neb. 1994).

[485] *Id.* at 406–07.

Of course, even if a duty of reasonable care is owed to a test-taker, there is another obstacle to recovery. If the claim is framed as negligent misrepresentation, it is essential to prove the plaintiff relied upon the negligently false statement. Sometimes, it will be difficult or impossible to establish such reliance by a preponderance of the evidence.

Chapter 3

DEFAMATION

A. TRADITIONAL RULES AND CONSTITUTIONAL TRANSFORMATION

A Matter of Honor. There may be a few topics in tort law to which people are indifferent, but defamation is certainly not one of them. People intuitively know what it means to be defamed, and they react just as viscerally as when they are defrauded. Indeed, the average person's emotional reaction to defamation may be even stronger and more heated than the typical response to fraud. Fraud is disgusting, but it usually involves only money. Defamation, in contrast, is generally a matter of honor. The natural inclination of one whose character and good name have been attacked is to want to hire a lawyer, file a lawsuit, and win vindication in court. So, it is not surprising that there are more news reports about suits for defamation (which encompasses the torts of libel and slander[1]) than about any other subject in the expansive field of torts.

Difficult to Win. The fact that there are many defamation claims does not mean that it is easy for a plaintiff to win. In fact, the reality is quite the contrary. All things considered, it is extremely hard to prevail in an action for libel or slander. Dozens of rules conspire to favor defamation defendants. For society as a whole, perhaps this is a good thing. The difficulty of winning a defamation claim tends to ensure that speech and press are legally unfettered to a very large extent. However, it also means that victims of false and defamatory statements are often left without effective remedies. Suits against the media are particularly challenging. Media outlets are repeat players in this area of the law. They have a vested interest in ensuring that adverse precedent is not established and in resisting settlement demands. Such cases are especially hard-fought because media defendants are typically represented by experienced counsel who have defended many defamation claims.

Frustrated Plaintiffs. Not only do defamation plaintiffs typically not win enforceable money judgments, they also usually get nothing close to a judicial declaration that the offensive statements were false. Moreover, the cumbersome path of litigation may prolong the victim's mental agony for years through round after endless round of pleadings, discovery requests, meetings with counsel, and depositions. If a case makes it to trial, the plaintiff is often then subjected to grueling cross-examination, sometimes intended to show that the plaintiff had such a bad reputation that, even if an actionably false statement was made, it caused no

---

[1] Generally speaking, *libel* is written defamation and *slander* is oral defamation. These topics are discussed in greater detail in Part B of this chapter.

damage. Of course, litigation sometimes attracts the attention of the press, and the present configuration of defamation law means that the media, with relative impunity, may repeat and circulate even more widely the original defamatory charges or related embarrassing information. Moreover, in cases where a defamatory statement is posted on the Internet, it is often actually or virtually impossible to expunge those libelous assertions.

Claims by Victims of Truth. In some cases, defamation plaintiffs win. For example, a judge who was defamed by false charges that he told a rape victim to "get over it," was awarded more than $2 million.[2] Nevertheless, the overall statistics are sobering for anyone thinking of filing suit. Of course, a libel or slander claim sometimes has settlement value, even if the true prospects of prevailing in litigation are dim. It should be remembered that not all defamation plaintiffs are innocent victims of maliciously uttered falsehoods; some are the casualties of truth. Defamation law is often a refuge for underperformers, such as employees who are let go because of lack of productivity, poor skills, or for other legitimate reasons. Terminated employees frequently allege that they lost their jobs because supervisors and co-workers defamed them. Crafting business practices to anticipate the likelihood of defamation claims by unhappy present or former employees is now a major aspect of good preventative lawyering for all types of institutions. This includes not only entities in the profit-making sector, but also nonprofit enterprises, such as private colleges and universities.

The Struggle Over What Is Actionable. The difficulty of prevailing in a defamation lawsuit does not mean that suits for libel and slander are going away anytime soon. Persons who believe that they have been wronged by attacks on their character want justice. In the United States, that often means going to court. Anglo-American law and its precursors have grappled with the questions of when and how to compensate victims of defamatory statements at least since the time of the Roman Empire. Indeed, within the last fifty years, the entire corpus of American defamation law has been transformed by dedicated efforts to reconcile common law principles (which often favored plaintiffs) with the demands of the First Amendment (which often favors defendants). There is no reason to think that the struggle to "re-form" defamation law will cease in the near future. Indeed, with the ability to electronically transmit defamatory statements to ever wider audiences, one might expect an increase in defamation litigation and related tort jurisprudence.

Reformation by Constitutional Litigation, Not Tort Reform. The type of "tort reform" legislation which in recent decades has reshaped many areas of tort law, such as medical malpractice law, rarely addresses the topics of libel and slander. This is due in part to the fact that many of the requirements of defamation law are constitutionally mandated by the United States Supreme Court's interpretation of the Federal Constitution. The law of defamation has been radically restructured in the past half century, but virtually all of the major developments have come from the marble temple that architect Cass Gilbert built at One First Street, N.E., in Washington, DC, not from state capitols, such as Albany, Harrisburg, Austin, or

---

[2] *See Murphy v. Boston Herald, Inc.*, 865 N.E.2d 746 (Mass. 2007).

Sacramento. Moreover, even when state legislatures act, what they do must be consistent with the First Amendment.

An Immensely Complex and Challenging Field. Today, the American law of libel and slander is immensely complex. Anyone who likes triple-layered legal analysis, fraught with razor-edge distinctions, unanswered critical questions, and legal standards that can be interpreted in a half dozen ways, will be comfortable in this area of the law. On the other hand, the lawyers who only occasionally "dabble" in defamation law should be sure to keep their legal malpractice premiums paid. Of course, many good lawyers who have taken the time to master the law of libel and slander regard the principles of defamation law as an intellectually challenging labyrinth that calls into action their best lawyering skills. Some of these lawyers have become recognized as champions of First Amendment principles, particularly as they apply to the media or the Internet.

The Elements of a Defamation Claim. It makes sense to begin the study of libel and slander with a quick sketch of the elements of a *prima facie* case for defamation. As will soon become apparent, the complexity starts here because the requirements of a defamation suit are a variable (and occasionally uncertain) mixture of traditional common law principles and more recently ascendant constitutional rules.

In general, there must be a (1) defamatory statement of fact, (2) culpably published by the defendant, (3) who (in many or all cases) acted with fault as to the falsity of the statement that (4) caused damages to the plaintiff (which sometimes the plaintiff must prove and in other cases are "presumed").[3]

Three Categories. The third and fourth elements of a defamation claim vary in their requirements according to the status of the plaintiff and whether the statement in question relates to a "matter of public concern" or a "matter of private concern." Under the United States Supreme Court's present expression of constitutional principles, there are ultimately three categories.

(a) Public Officials and Public Figures. First, "public officials" and "public figures" who are suing with regard to a statement relating to a matter of public concern, such as their conduct or fitness, have the heaviest burden of proof and must show that the defendant acted with "actual malice," meaning knowledge of the falsity of the defamatory statement or reckless disregard for the truth. It is often extremely difficult to prove actual malice. If that standard is satisfied, plaintiffs in this category may recover "presumed damages" and punitive damages in certain kinds of cases.

(b) Private Persons Suing with Regard to Matters of Public Concern. Second, "private persons" suing with regard to a matter of public concern must, as a constitutional requirement, prove at least that the defendant acted negligently as to the falsity of the statement, although states are free to set the standard of culpability higher. In the absence of proof of actual malice, presumed damages and punitive damages may not be recovered, and compensation may be awarded only for proven actual losses.

---

[3] *Cf.* RESTATEMENT (SECOND) OF TORTS § 558 (1977) (listing four elements).

(c) Matters of Private Concern. Third, any person suing in regard to a matter of private concern stands in the most favored category. The Supreme Court has not yet decided whether these plaintiffs must prove that the defendant was at least negligent as to the falsity of the defamatory statement — although many states recognize that requirement. At least so far as constitutional restrictions are concerned, plaintiffs in the "private concern" category may recover presumed damages in certain kinds of defamation cases without proof of actual loss.

Proving Falsity, as Well as Fault as to Falsity. Generally speaking, if a plaintiff must prove that the defendant acted with fault as to the falsity of the defamatory statement (*i.e.*, negligence or actual malice), the plaintiff must also prove that the statement was false. Falsity is not presumed. However, there are still some unanswered questions about whether the old rule — that truth is an affirmative defense to be pleaded and proved by the defendant — has been entirely jettisoned.

B.   LIBEL AND SLANDER

Libel and Slander Distinguished. In general, written defamation is "libel" and oral defamation is "slander."[4] This distinction is important for two reasons. First, lawyers and judges use the terms precisely, rather than interchangeably. They do not speak of a "slanderous article" in the newspaper or a "libelous speech" at a public meeting. Second, and more importantly, libel and slander are treated differently with respect to the issue of damages.

At common law, libel was regarded as more serious than slander. This was probably due to the fact that the rules emerged at a time when few persons could read or write. Written defamation was regarded as having special potency with respect to causing harm. A written defamatory statement was potentially permanent and it could be handed from person to person in the exact same form. Slander, in contrast, was evanescent. Presumably, oral defamation would someday be forgotten. Even before that point was reached, it was likely that any extensive repetition of oral statements would so transform them that they would become unrecognizable, or at least undependable. To that extent, it was harder for a recipient to place credence in repeated oral assertions, and therefore less justification for holding the original speaker accountable.

Libel Per Se and Presumed Damages. At common law, all libel was actionable *per se*, which means without proof of damages.[5] Damages were presumed to result from written defamation. A jury could simply look to the nastiness of the defamatory falsehood and the extent of its dissemination and award a substantial amount in compensation for presumed losses. If this seems odd, or perhaps even breath-taking, it is. Nowhere else in all of tort law are presumed compensatory damages awarded. Plaintiffs must always prove their losses, except in the few cases in which a nominal award is made to vindicate the plaintiff's technical right.

---

[4] *See id.* § 568.

[5] *See id.* § 569.

Nevertheless, courts still follow the rule that damages are presumed in cases involving libel. For example, in *LeBlanc v. Skinner*,[6] the New York Appellate Division wrote:

> [A]ny written article is "actionable without alleging special damages if it tends to expose the plaintiff to public contempt, ridicule, aversion or disgrace . . .". . . . The published allegation that the plaintiff put a severed horse head in a Town Board member's swimming pool constituted defamation *per se* under this standard and, therefore, did not require the plaintiff to plead special damages . . . .[7]

Some states limit the rule on presumed damages to cases in which the libel, on its face, is defamatory *of the plaintiff* or to certain types of libelous statements (such as statements which, if oral, would fall with the slander *per se* categories discussed below). In Iowa, "libel *per se* is available only when a private figure plaintiff sues a nonmedia defendant for certain kinds of defamatory statements that do not concern a matter of public importance."[8]

Slander Per Se and Presumed Damages. Traditionally, slander was actionable "*per se*," that is, without proof of damages, only if the statement accused the plaintiff of:

(1) Committing a serious crime;

(2) Having a "loathsome disease";

(3) Being incompetent or dishonest in practicing a business, trade, or profession; or

(4) Being an unchaste woman.[9]

Serious Crime. A false accusation of crime will generally support an award of presumed damages only if the crime would be punishable by imprisonment or involves moral turpitude.[10] Finding these principles inapplicable, a New York trial court ruled that a "charge of stealing a $6.95 order of chicken wings . . . hardly constitutes . . . [an accusation] of a serious crime."[11]

In *TC v. Valley Central School District*,[12] a federal court in New York found that any allusion to an unnamed crime, which the plaintiff deduced from his suspension from high school, was too attenuated to be considered slander *per se* and qualify as actionable.

---

[6] 103 A.D.3d 202 (N.Y. App. Div. 2012).

[7] *Id.* at 401 (N.Y. App. Div. 2012).

[8] *Bierman v. Weier*, 826 N.W.2d 436, 448 (Iowa 2013).

[9] *See* Lisa R. Pruitt, *"On the Chastity of Women All Property in the World Depends": Injury from Sexual Slander in the Nineteenth Century*, 78 IND. L.J. 965 (2003).

[10] RESTATEMENT (SECOND) OF TORTS § 571 (1977).

[11] Andrew Kershner, *Attorney Accused of Stealing Chicken Wings Loses Bid to Sue Bar*, N.Y.L.J., Nov. 7, 2012.

[12] 777 F. Supp. 2d 577 (S.D.N.Y. 2011).

Loathsome Disease. The "loathsome disease" category was always the slander *per se* category least litigated. It covered things such as accusation of leprosy or a venereal disease, and might today include HIV or AIDS. According to the *Restatement*, the disease must be of a lingering or chronic variety to permit an award of presumed damages.[13] Thus, the exception never applied to smallpox, which quickly ran its course.

Accusing a person of extreme racism is not the same thing as stating that the person has a loathsome disease. As a federal court in New York explained:

> No matter whether racism is a mental illness, it does not constitute a "disease" under defamation law. The requirement that the disease be communicable ensures that the defamatory comment serves to isolate the person. . . . Labeling an individual a racist does not isolate an individual as the law contemplates.[14]

Incompetence or Dishonesty in Business Trade or Profession. The category of slander *per se* dealing with incompetence or dishonesty in business, trade, or profession is particularly broad. Consider the many varieties of vocational deficiency, such as lack of knowledge, inadequate skills, poor judgment, deficient experience, and ignorance of, or disregard for, business or professional ethics. Today, false charges of sexual harassment in the workplace are defamatory *per se*,[15] presumably because they fall within this category. In one case that settled for a large amount, the defendant accused the plaintiff beer distributorship of selling repackaged, out-of-date beer.[16] This was a charge of dishonesty in business.

Some cases are careful to point out that there must be a clear linkage between the alleged deficiency and special aspects of the plaintiff's business, trade or profession. For example in *Hancock v. Variyam*,[17] "in a letter sent to colleagues and others, a physician accused a fellow physician of lacking veracity and speaking in half truths, resulting in an award of $90,000 in actual damages for mental anguish and loss of reputation and $85,000 in exemplary damages."[18] The Texas Supreme Court reversed and rendered judgment against the plaintiff. As the court explained:

> A statement constitutes defamation *per se* if it "injures a person in his office, profession, or occupation." . . . Hancock argues, among other things, that his statements that Variyam lacks veracity and deals in half truths did not uniquely injure Variyam in his profession as a physician and thus were not defamatory *per se*. Variyam responds that the statements were intended to, and did, injure him in his profession because the letter was circulated to other physicians and a failure to be truthful would impact his patient care, teaching, research, and publishing. We agree with Hancock

---

[13] RESTATEMENT (SECOND) OF TORTS § 572 cmt. c (1977).

[14] *TC v. Valley Cent. School Dist.*, 777 F. Supp. 2d 577 (S.D.N.Y. 2011).

[15] *See Fox v. Parker*, 98 S.W.3d 713, 726 (Tex. App. 2003).

[16] *See Anheuser-Busch, Maris Family Settle for $120M*, NAT'L L.J., Aug. 29, 2005, at 16.

[17] 400 S.W.3d 59 (Tex. 2013).

[18] *Id.* at 62.

that the statements did not injure Variyam in his profession as a physician and thus were not defamatory *per se*.

The *Restatement* more fully defines a statement that injures one in her profession as a statement that "ascribes to another conduct, characteristics or a condition that would adversely affect his fitness for the proper conduct of his lawful business, trade or profession, or of his public or private office, whether honorary or for profit. . . ." *Restatement (Second) of Torts* § 573 (1977). Examples provide guidance of what injury to a person in her profession actually means. Comments to the applicable section of the *Restatement* provide:

> When peculiar skill or ability is necessary, an imputation that attributes a lack of skill or ability tends to harm the other in his business or profession. Statements that a physician is a drunkard or a quack, or that he is incompetent or negligent in the practice of his profession, are actionable. So too, a charge that a physician is dishonest in his fees is actionable, *although an imputation of dishonesty in other respects does not affect his character or reputation as a physician.*
>
> . . . .
>
> Disparagement of a general character, equally discreditable to all persons, is not enough unless the particular quality disparaged is of such a character that it is peculiarly valuable in the plaintiff's business or profession. . . . Thus, a statement that a physician consorts with harlots is not actionable *per se*, although a charge that he makes improper advances to his patients is actionable; the one statement does not affect his reputation as a physician whereas the other does so affect it.

Id. § 573 cmt. c, e (emphasis added).

. . . Variyam accused Hancock of violating Division policy on transferring patients. In response, Hancock accused Variyam of lacking veracity and dealing in half-truths. Variyam argues, and the court of appeals agreed, that having a reputation for untruthfulness would "affect his relationship with other physicians that might send him business or work." . . . The court of appeals noted that "[l]ike lawyers and bankers, a physician such as Variyam, by definition, depends greatly on his reputation." . . . But the inquiry is not whether a reputation is necessary for a profession. If that were true — because all professions require reputations of some sort — all statements defaming professionals would be defamatory *per se*. Rather, the proper inquiry is whether a defamatory statement accuses a professional of lacking a peculiar or unique skill that is necessary for the proper conduct of the profession. . . .

The specific trait of truthfulness is not peculiar or unique to being a physician. . . . Accordingly, the allegations that Variyam lacked veracity and dealt in half truths do not adversely affect his fitness for proper conduct as a physician. . . .

Variyam also asserts that a reputation for untruthfulness hinders his relations with his peers and his ability to research and publish. But few trades, businesses, and professions involve no human interaction. If an accusation of untruthfulness is defamatory *per se* for a physician in her profession, it would likewise be defamatory *per se* for other trades, businesses, and professions that rely on human interaction. In short, Hancock's charges do not adversely affect Variyam's fitness for the proper conduct of being a physician and are not defamatory *per se*.[19]

Serious Sexual Misconduct. The *Restatement* now says that the unchastity category of slander *per se* covers "serious sexual misconduct" by a plaintiff of either sex.[20] State statutes sometimes take the same position. For example, an Illinois statute provides that false charges of fornication or adultery are actionable.[21]

Policy Basis of Presumed Damages. "The rationale for presuming damages in certain defamation actions . . . [is] that requiring proof of actual reputational harm would be unfair because 'the effect of defamatory statements is so subtle and indirect that it is impossible directly to trace the effects thereof in loss to the person defamed.'"[22]

Broadcast Defamation in a YouTube World. There is certainly reason to question whether written defamation is more damaging today than oral statements. Which is more harmful, a YouTube video that goes viral, or a written entry on a blog? The *Restatement* allows the possibility that libel includes not only a written or printed defamatory statement but "its embodiment in physical form or by any other form of communication that has the potentially harmful qualities characteristic of written or printed words."[23] In addition, the *Restatement* takes the position that "[b]roadcasting of defamatory matter by means of radio or television is libel, whether or not it is read from a manuscript."[24] However, some states classify broadcast defamation as slander by statute, presumably as a result of lobbying on behalf of radio and television networks and stations.[25] It remains to be seen whether the law will treat videos on the Internet as libel or slander. The comments posted on YouTube are presumably libel.

Presumed Damages Today. As discussed later, the Constitution prohibits an award of presumed damages in a case involving a matter of public concern absent proof of "actual malice." There are no constitutional restrictions on presumed damages in cases involving matters of private concern,[26] but as discussed later, some states have departed from the traditional common law rules.

---

[19] *Id.* at 66–68.

[20] RESTATEMENT (SECOND) OF TORTS § 574 (1977).

[21] *See* 740 ILL. COMP. STAT. 145/1 (LEXIS 2014).

[22] Kevin P. Allen, *The Oddity and Odyssey of "Presumed Damages" in Defamation Actions Under Pennsylvania Law*, 42 DUQ. L. REV. 495, 496 (2004) (citing RESTATEMENT (FIRST) OF TORTS § 621 cmt. a (1938)).

[23] RESTATEMENT (SECOND) OF TORTS § 568(1) (1977).

[24] *Id.* § 568A.

[25] *See* RODNEY A. SMOLLA, 1 LAW OF DEFAMATION § 1:14 (2008).

[26] *See Dun & Bradstreet, Inc. v. Greenmoss Builders, Inc.*, 472 U.S. 749 (1985).

The "Special Damages" Requirement. In cases where libel or slander was not actionable *per se* (without proof of damages), it was traditionally necessary for the plaintiff to prove that the defamation caused special damages of a pecuniary or economic nature.[27] Notably, "special damages" did not include emotional distress. For example, in an old New York case, *Terwilliger v. Wands*,[28] the plaintiff was orally accused of beating a path to the neighbor-lady's house for the purpose of engaging in sex with her while her husband was in prison. The only injury the plaintiff proved was that he was so upset that he could not attend to business; there was no evidence that anyone had treated him differently. The court affirmed a judgment for the defendant because the slander did not fall within the four *per se* categories and there was no proof of special damages. If the suit had been brought by a woman, or if the accusation had been made in writing, there would have been no need to prove special damages.

Although cases still say that a plaintiff must prove that a statement that is not actionable *per se* caused damage, modern constitutional precedent recognizes that states are free to allow (and typically do permit) compensation for emotional distress as a variety of actual loss.

C. WHAT STATEMENTS ARE DEFAMATORY?

1.   Disgrace Is Essential

Defamation Defined. Defamation is defined largely by reference to how others will act in response to a statement. A statement is defamatory if it tends to harm the plaintiff's reputation and diminish the respect, goodwill, confidence, or esteem in which the plaintiff is held by members of the community or deter others from associating or dealing with the plaintiff.[29] According to a much-repeated definition, a defamatory utterance is one which holds the plaintiff up to scorn, hatred, ridicule, or contempt. Thus, if a law book publisher identifies two law professors as the authors of a poorly researched update to their treatise, they may sue for defamation.[30] The same is true if the plaintiff is falsely accused of "being a thief and distributing cocaine"[31] or if the wife of a former congressman is accused of verbally attacking her husband's intern.[32] "[A] statement, which accuses someone of pulling a fire alarm in the middle of a busy workday, when no fire has actually occurred, is a statement that tends to lower that individual's estimation in the community," and is therefore actionable under the law of defamation.[33]

---

[27] RESTATEMENT (SECOND) OF TORTS § 575 cmt. b (1977).

[28] 17 N.Y. 54 (1858).

[29] *See* RESTATEMENT (SECOND) OF TORTS § 559 (1977).

[30] *See Rudovsky v. West Publ'g Corp.*, 2010 U.S. Dist. LEXIS 71062 (E.D. Pa. July 15, 2010).

[31] *Integrated Sec. Solutions, LLC v. Sec. Tech. Sys.*, LLC, 2007 Conn. Super. LEXIS 2397 (Sept. 10, 2007).

[32] *See Condit v. Nat'l Enquirer, Inc.*, 248 F. Supp. 2d 945, 948 (E.D. Cal. 2002).

[33] *Ciemniecki v. Parker McCay P.A.*, 2012 U.S. Dist. LEXIS 552, at *17 (D.N.J. Jan. 4, 2012).

Disgrace or Discredit. It is essential that the allegedly defamatory statement carry with it the sting of disgrace or discredit. Saying that a judge accepts bribes is defamatory; saying that the judge is overly-intellectual is not defamatory. An article calling a Democrat a Republican is not actionable, but one asserting that a Democrat is a member of Al-Qaeda can form the basis for a libel lawsuit.

Judge and Jury. It is for the judge to determine in the first instance whether a statement could be understood as defamatory. Then, if reasonable minds could differ, it is for the jury to determine whether the plaintiff was in fact defamed.

In *Damon v. Moore*,[34] a serviceman, who was seriously injured in Iraq and lost parts of both arms, was pictured for sixteen seconds in an anti-war documentary by producer Michael Moore. The serviceman alleged that the documentary was an attack on the integrity of the Commander-in-Chief and that the serviceman's unwitting appearance in the film defamed him by portraying him as sharing, adopting, and endorsing the filmmaker's views. The First Circuit held that the district court properly dismissed the complaint because no one could possibly have viewed the plaintiff as being disloyal to the United States. The court noted that in the sixteen-second segment the plaintiff spoke exclusively about the pain he was suffering and the efficacy of his pain treatment, and that the plaintiff was only one of "approximately fifty individuals whose interviews were taken out of their original packaging and inserted into the documentary in order to further Moore's message."[35] Many of those persons, including the President, Vice-President, and Secretary of Defense, presumably, disagreed with the film's message.

Homosexuality. In *Stern v. Cosby*,[36] a federal court in New York held that calling someone a homosexual is not defamation *per se*. As stated by the court:

> The New York Court of Appeals . . . has never held that a statement imputing homosexuality constitutes defamation *per se*. Accordingly, this Court must predict what New York's highest court would do were the issue before it. . . .
>
> . . . [W]hether a statement is defamatory *per se* can evolve from one generation to the next.[37]
>
> The question . . . is whether the New York Court of Appeals, in 2009, would hold that a statement imputing homosexuality connotes the same degree of "shame, obloquy, contumely, odium, contempt, ridicule, aversion, ostracism, degradation or disgrace," . . . as statements accusing someone of serious criminal conduct, impugning a person in his or her trade or profession, implying that a person has a "loathsome disease," or imputing unchastity to a woman. I conclude that it would not.

---

[34] 520 F.3d 98 (1st Cir. 2008).

[35] *Id.* at 106.

[36] 645 F. Supp. 2d 258 (S.D.N.Y. 2009).

[37] [n.8] It is, for example, unlikely that the New York Court of Appeals would today hold that it is libelous *per se* to state that a white man is "colored" or a "negro," but that is precisely what the Court held in 1926. *See Sydney v. MacFadden Newspaper Publ'g Corp.*, 151 N.E. 209, 211 (N.Y. 1926).

The past few decades have seen a veritable sea change in social attitudes about homosexuality. First, and perhaps most importantly, in 2003 the United States Supreme Court, in a sweeping decision, invalidated laws criminalizing intimate homosexual conduct, holding that such laws violate the Fourteenth Amendment's Due Process Clause. *Lawrence v. Texas*, 539 U.S. 558, 578 (2003). . . .

Second, in 2009, the "current of contemporary public opinion" does not support the notion that New Yorkers view gays and lesbians as shameful or odious. . . . [A]ccording to a recent opinion poll from Quinnipiac University . . . New York State residents support gay marriage 51 to 41 percent. . . .

Finally, the New York Court of Appeals has not, in its most recent opinion touching on social attitudes toward homosexuality, given any indication that it perceives widespread disapproval of homosexuality in New York. In *Hernandez v. Robles*, a majority of the Court of Appeals rejected the argument that the New York Constitution compels recognition of same-sex marriage. 7 N.Y.3d 338, 356 (2006). The plurality opinion clearly recognized, however, that social attitudes toward gay and lesbian New Yorkers had changed dramatically in the past few years, . . . and that the New York legislature could permit same-sex marriage if it chose to. . . .[38]

Judge McMahon, in 2008, considered this issue and reached the opposite conclusion. *See Gallo v. Alitalia-Linee Aeree Italiane-Societa Per Azioni*, 585 F. Supp. 2d 520, 549–50 (S.D.N.Y. 2008). Her carefully-considered decision was based largely on the fact that prejudice still exists against gays and lesbians in our society. . . . While I certainly agree that gays and lesbians continue to face prejudice, I respectfully disagree that the existence of this continued prejudice leads to the conclusion that there is a widespread view of gays and lesbians as contemptible and disgraceful. . . .

Thus, I hold that Statements 1 and 2 are not defamatory *per se* merely because they impute homosexuality to Stern. They are, however, nonetheless susceptible to a defamatory meaning. Therefore, a jury will decide whether they are defamatory.

Statement 1 alleges that Stern engaged in a sexual act with Birkhead at a party. . . . A reasonable jury could find that engaging in oral sex at a party is shameful or contemptible, and the fact that this conduct may not be illegal does not alter this conclusion. . . . Moreover, it also appears from the record that, at the time this alleged incident took place in 2005 . . . , Smith was dating Birkhead and/or still involved in a relationship with Stern. . . . Thus, to the extent that the Statement implies that Stern was unfaithful to Smith, this would be further reason for a jury to find that the Statement is defamatory.

---

[38] [Ed. note:] New York's Marriage Equality Act was signed into law in 2011 allowing same-sex couples to marry in New York.

Statement 2 alleges that Stern made a sex tape with Birkhead. This allegation would expose Stern to contempt among most people — even if, arguably, not among the social circles in which he and Smith traveled. . . .

. . . Accordingly, Stern will have to prove special damages as to each of these Statements.[39]

2.   Defamatory in Whose Eyes?

In *Damon v. Moore, supra,* the plaintiff argued that, in determining whether his depiction in the documentary was defamatory, the facts had to be viewed not from the perspective of a reasonable person, but through the eyes of his military brethren. The court did not find this point critical for it concluded that "there . . . [was] no reason to believe that a reasonable member of the military or veteran community would conclude that Damon's appearance in the documentary conveyed a defamatory meaning."[40] Nevertheless, the underlying point is important. In whose eyes must the plaintiff be defamed? The eyes of "right-thinking" people? "Reasonable" people? A majority of people?

Any Considerable and Respectable Segment of the Community. In *Grant v. Reader's Digest Association,*[41] Judge Learned Hand addressed this question. In that case, the defendant had published a statement implying that the plaintiff was a Communist sympathizer. An action was stated because some persons, not clearly irresponsibly, would have thought less of the plaintiff as a result of the statement. For the Second Circuit, Judge Hand wrote:

> A man may value his reputation even among those who do not embrace the prevailing moral standards; and it would seem that the jury should be allowed to appraise how far he should be indemnified for the disesteem of such persons. . . . That is the usual rule. *Peck v. Tribune Co.,* . . . [214 U.S. 185 (1909)]; *Restatement of Torts,* § 559. . . . [T]he opinions at times seem to make it a condition that to be actionable the words must be such as would so affect "right-thinking people" . . . and it is fairly plain that there must come a point where that is true. As was said in *Mawe v. Piggot,* Irish Rep. 4 Comm. Law, 54, 62, among those "who were themselves criminal or sympathized with crime," it would expose one "to great odium to represent him as an informer or prosecutor or otherwise aiding in the detection of crime"; yet certainly the words would not be actionable. Be that as it may, in New York if the exception covers more than such a case, it does not go far enough to excuse the utterance at bar. *Katapodis v. Brooklyn Spectator, Inc.,* . . . [38 N.E.2d 112 (N.Y. 1941)], held that the imputation of extreme poverty might be actionable; although certainly "right-thinking" people ought not shun, or despise, or otherwise condemn one because he is poor. . . . We do not believe, therefore, that we need say whether "right-

---

[39] 645 F. Supp. 2d 258, 266–268 (S.D.N.Y. 2009). *See also Yonaty v. Mincolla,* 97 A.D.3d 141 (N.Y. App. Div. 2012) (holding that statements falsely describing a person as lesbian, gay, or bisexual does not constitute slander *per se* and that special damages must be proved).

[40] 520 F.3d at 108 (1st Cir. 2008).

[41] 151 F.2d 733 (2d Cir. 1945).

thinking" people would harbor similar feelings toward a lawyer, because he had been an agent for the Communist Party, or was a sympathizer with its aims and means. It is enough if there be some, as there certainly are, who would feel so, even though they would be "wrong-thinking" people if they did. . . ."[42]

Suits Based on Literally True Statements. Note that in *Grant* the statement at issue was literally true: the lawyer has served as a legislative agent for the Communist Party. What was allegedly false and defamatory was the implied innuendo that the lawyer was a Communist sympathizer. Actions for libel and slander can be based on literally true statements. However, it is often hard to convince a jury that there was an implied defamatory assertion that meets all of the requirements of a cause of action.

3.   Rules of Construction

The "Whole Publication" Rule. It is often said that a defamatory writing must be read as a whole and that a particular phrase will not be viewed in isolation. Sometimes this means that a statement, which by itself might seem to be defamatory, is not actionable. For example, in *James v. Gannett Co., Inc.*,[43] the New York Court of Appeals held that a statement that a belly dancer sold her time to lonely old men was not libelous in light of other statements that she did so just to sit with them, to be nice to them, and to talk. Similarly, in *Treutler v. Meredith Corp.*, the Eighth Circuit found that a statement that a political candidate's company was charged with selling obscene books was not actionable because other statements explained that the charges were false.[44]

Conversely, sometimes an apparently innocent statement takes on a defamatory connotation in light of other parts of the text or conversation. Thus, in *LaBozzo v. Brooks Bros., Inc.*,[45] a New York trial court wrote:

> [S]tatements to the effect that the plaintiff was incompetent and unprofessional might, if taken alone, be protected as pure [nonactionable] opinion. However, in the context of his charges that plaintiff had been billing Brooks for hours during which she was either not working at all or was working for other clients, they are tantamount to an accusation that plaintiff was stealing from her employer.[46]

Headlines and Illustrations. There is an important question as to how attention-grabbing parts of an article, such as headlines and illustrations, should be treated.[47] Some courts have gone to great lengths to ensure that the whole publication is considered in determining whether the plaintiff has been defamed.

---

[42] *Id.* at 734–35.

[43] 353 N.E.2d 834 (N.Y. 1976).

[44] 455 F.2d 255 (8th Cir. 1972).

[45] 2002 N.Y. Misc. LEXIS 605, at *1 (Apr. 25, 2002).

[46] *Id.* at *10–*11.

[47] *See generally* Joseph H. King, Jr., *Defining the Internal Context for Communications Containing Allegedly Defamatory Headline Language*, 71 U. Cin. L. Rev. 863 (2003).

For example, in *Ross v. Columbia Newspapers, Inc.*,[48] the South Carolina Supreme Court found that an erroneous headline, which asserted that the plaintiff was a suspect in the death of his wife, was rendered innocuous by the last sentence of the article which said that the wife was in serious condition in the hospital.

A more practical approach is to say that bold face type deserves greater weight than fine print in determining whether someone has been defamed. Many persons read only the headlines and never consider every part of an article.

For example, *Kaelin v. Globe Communications Corp.*[49] was a case related to the saga of former sports star O.J. Simpson. After Simpson was acquitted of the murder of his wife, a tabloid ran a story saying that the police were considering charging Kato Kaelin, a witness in the trial, with perjury. The headline screamed "Cops Think Kato Did It!"; a clarifying article was buried on page 17. The Ninth Circuit held that Kaelin's defamation claim could go forward. As the court explained, "headlines are not . . . liability-free zones."[50] There was evidence that the publisher had acted with "actual malice" because an editor admitted at a deposition that he was concerned that the headline "did not accurately reflect the content of the article."[51]

"Mitior Sensus" and the Innocent Construction Rule. In an effort to cope with an avalanche of slander lawsuits in the sixteenth and seventeenth centuries, English courts adopted the doctrine of "*mitior sensus*," under which statements were to be construed in their more lenient sense. Thus, calling someone a forger was not actionable because the term could simply mean that the plaintiff was a metal-worker. This doctrine effectively closed the courthouse doors to a wide range of cases.

The doctrine of *mitior sensus* is now rejected in England, and never had much impact in the United States. However, there are some decisions that seem to be jurisprudentially related. For example, in *Liberty Mutual Fire Insurance Co. v. O'Keefe*,[52] an attorney representing a client in a suit against an insurance company placed an advertisement for evidence which stated: "If anyone has any information regarding Liberty Mutual Fire Insurance Company's delay or failure to pay claims or losses, please contact the undersigned." The Wisconsin Court of Appeals held that the ad was not defamatory as a matter of law because "there are many legitimate reasons why an insurance company would not immediately pay all claims."[53]

More importantly, Illinois sometimes follows what is called the "innocent construction rule," with respect to which there is a great deal of precedent. Under this rule, "words allegedly libelous that are capable of being read innocently must

---

[48] 221 S.E.2d 770 (S.C. 1976).

[49] 162 F.3d 1036 (9th Cir. 1998).

[50] *Id.* at 1040.

[51] *Id.* at 1037.

[52] 556 N.W.2d 133, 134 (Wis. Ct. App. 1996).

[53] *Id.* at 135.

be so read and declared nonactionable as a matter of law."[54] For example, in *Rasky v. Columbia Broadcasting System, Inc.*,[55] the Illinois Appellate Court used dictionary definitions of "landlord" and "slum" to hold that calling someone a "slumlord" might have meant only that he was the landlord of a building located in a part of town that is a slum, and was therefore not actionable.

In *Lott v. Levitt*,[56] an author sued for defamation based on a statement in the best-selling book *Freakonomics*, which asserted that other scholars had been unable to replicate the results of his crime study. The author argued that the statement implied that he had falsified his results. In affirming a dismissal of the plaintiff's claim, the Seventh Circuit wrote:

> Using an academic definition of "replicate," Lott maintains that the passage means that others repeated, to a tee, his technical analysis but were unable to duplicate his results, suggesting that he either faked his data or performed his analysis incompetently.

> But this technical reading is not the only reasonable interpretation of the passage. . . . [*Freakonomics*] takes into account the lay reader, breaking down technical terms into easily understandable, if imprecise, ideas. . . . The book relies on anecdotal evidence and describes with only the broadest strokes the statistical methodologies used. In this context, it is reasonable to read "replicate" in more generic terms. That is, the sentence could mean that scholars tried to reach the same conclusion as Lott, using different models, data, and assumptions, but could not do so. This reading does not imply that Lott falsified his results or was incompetent; instead, it suggests only that scholars have disagreed with Lott's findings about the controversial relationship between guns and crime. . . . [57]

Some cases say that the Illinois innocent construction rule does not apply to cases where "a plaintiff not only must allege extrinsic facts to prove the defamatory nature of the statement but also must plead and must prove special damages."[58] However, a detailed exploration of the Illinois innocent construction rule is beyond the scope of this book. Two things must be remembered. First, if one is litigating a defamation case to which Illinois law applies, it is essential to research the current interpretation of this special doctrine which differs greatly from principles applicable under the law of most other states. Second, care needs to be exercised in citing Illinois defamation precedent dealing with the issue of how potentially defamatory language should be construed.

---

[54] *John v. Tribune Co.*, 181 N.E.2d 105 (Ill. 1962).

[55] 431 N.E.2d 1055 (Ill. App. Ct. 1981).

[56] 556 F.3d 564 (7th Cir. 2009).

[57] *Id.* at 569.

[58] *Fedders Corp. v. Elite Classics*, 279 F. Supp. 2d 965, 970 (S.D. Ill. 2003).

4.   Pleading Extrinsic Facts to Prove Defamation

Libel Per Se Versus Libel Per Quod. If a written statement, by its own terms, clearly defames the plaintiff, it is sometimes called libel *per se*. For example, an article charging that "John Smith stole money from the cash register" is libelous *per se*.

(Note that this is the third way in which the term *per se* has been used in this chapter. Sometimes *per se* means that a defamatory statement is actionable without proof of special damages and that presumed damages may be recovered. Sometimes *per se* means that there is no doubt that a statement is defamatory and that the question is decided by the court as a matter of law and not by the jury as a matter of fact. And sometimes *per se* means that a statement clearly refers to and defames the plaintiff. Thus, whenever someone says that something is defamatory *per se*, it is important to analyze or inquire into the meaning of the term *per se*.)

Colloquium, Inducement, and Innuendo. If it is necessary to plead additional facts to show that a written statement defames the plaintiff, it is libelous *per quod*. Thus, it may be necessary to plead facts establishing "colloquium" (that the statement referred to the plaintiff), "inducement" (the predicate for the defamatory meaning), or "innuendo" (the defamatory charge). Consider the words "He's dating Alexandra." On its face, the statement might seem to be innocent. However, if "he" refers to Claudius (colloquium), and if Claudius is a Roman Catholic priest (inducement), the statement implies that Claudius is a religious hypocrite (innuendo).

State law typically imposes strict pleading requirements on plaintiffs suing with respect to statements that are not defamatory on their face. In *Gibney v. Fitzgibbon*,[59] the Third Circuit applied Pennsylvania law to a defamation claim arising from an employment context. The plaintiff, Gibney, contacted Merck & Co., Inc., alleging that his employer (Evolution, Inc.) had overbilled Merck and that the matter needed to be investigated. FitzGibbon, an in-house lawyer for Merck, responded to Gibney in a letter that was copied to other persons. The letter stated:

> While I note your "request" for an audit, we see no need for any such audit. As far as Merck is concerned, the alleged overbilling has been investigated, the allegations have been determined to be unfounded and the matter is now closed and warrants no further action by Merck.[60]

In a subsequent defamation action against Merck and FitzGibbons, Gibney claimed that FitzGibbon had "falsely stated that the allegations were 'unfounded' and that he suffered substantial and permanent harm to his reputation. . . ."[61] Rejecting the defamation claim, the Third Circuit wrote:

> The statement in question here that "[a]s far as Merck is concerned, the alleged overbilling has been investigated, [and] the allegations have been determined to be unfounded" — says nothing about Gibney himself or his

---

[59] 2013 U.S. App. LEXIS 19907 (3d Cir. Sept. 30, 2013).

[60] *Id.* at *2.

[61] *Id.* at *3.

character, yet he claims that it "conveys that [he] made false or unsubstantiated accusations about [Evolution]." However, innuendo "cannot be used
to introduce new matter, or to enlarge the natural meaning of the words,
and thereby give to the language a construction which it will not bear." . . .
FitzGibbon was simply answering Gibney's letter "providing Gibney with
the result of the investigation that Gibney's letter had initiated." Gibney
asks us to read meaning into the statement which clearly is not there. While
Gibney was dissatisfied with FitzGibbon's statement that his allegations
were unfounded, even if that statement were untrue, it would not "lower
him in the estimation of the community or . . . deter third parties from
associating or dealing with him." . . . We therefore agree with the District
Court that FitzGibbon's statement was not capable of a defamatory
meaning as a matter of law.[62]

PROBLEM 3-1: THE TEENAGE SEX EPIDEMIC

Gerard and Nanette Pasteur were shocked with disbelief when they opened the
Sunday magazine section of their newspaper and found that a picture of their
daughter Claudette had been used to illustrate an article on "The Teenage Sex
Epidemic."

The cover of the magazine section included a reference to the article. It said
"Wild and Sexually Loose Teens at Edgewood High. Page 8."

The article, which ran from pages 8 to 13, began with a double-page spread. The
initial page of the article was entirely taken up by a photo of two girls and three
boys. One the girls was Claudette. The photo showed the teens dressed in formal
attire. It must have been taken at the high school's spring dance. Claudette was
standing closest to the camera, so she was the largest figure in the picture. She was
clearly visible and identifiable, although neither she nor any of the other students
were named.

On the facing page (page 9), there were two headlines, both in large font. The
largest headline said "Teens 'Hook Up' Frequently." The second headline read
"They May Know More About Sex Than Their Parents." Below the headlines,
which dominated the page, were two paragraphs of text. At the bottom of the page
was the author's byline. And below that, in font smaller than the fonts used for the
article's text or the byline, were two more sentences which read:

> The photos on these pages were taken by award-winning photojournalist
> Amadeo Carette as part of a documentary project on "Contemporary
> Teens," which will be aired on PBS this coming winter. The individuals
> pictured are unrelated to the people or events described in the story.

The remaining pages of the article laid out anecdotal and statistical evidence
indicating that teens today are much more sexually active than even a decade ago.
The article explained that "hook up" is a flexible term that could refer to kissing or
any of several kinds of sex. The article suggested that one of the most significant
reasons that teens today are more sexually active is that parents, especially in

---

[62] *Id.* at *6–*7.

two-income families, devote insufficient time to supervision of their children.

Upon being questioned by her parents, Claudette denied having had sex with the other students pictured in the article or anyone else for that matter.

Gerard and Nanette Pasteur and their daughter have asked whether you will represent them in a defamation suit against the newspaper. They believe that the article has caused serious harm to Claudette's reputation, and that it has also defamed them as her parents. Both of them are working professionals who are well-known in the community. Please prepare an analysis of whether the article constitutes a defamatory statement about each of the three potential plaintiffs. Also identify other issues that you anticipate being significant factors if a lawsuit is filed.

D. FALSITY REQUIREMENT

1.   Assertion of Fact

A statement is not actionable under the law of libel or slander unless it includes a provably false assertion of defamatory fact. The landmark case is *Milkovich v. Lorain Journal Co.*[63]

a.   *Milkovich v. Lorain Journal Co.*

Alleged Lies About a Wrestling Match. Describing the facts of the *Milkovich* dispute, Chief Justice William H. Rehnquist wrote:

> . . . Petitioner Milkovich, now retired, was the wrestling coach at Maple Heights High School. . . . [H]is team was involved in an altercation at a home wrestling match with a team from Mentor High School. Several people were injured. In response to the incident, the Ohio High School Athletic Association (OHSAA) held a hearing at which Milkovich and H. Don Scott, the Superintendent of Maple Heights Public Schools, testified. Following the hearing, OHSAA placed the Maple Heights team on probation for a year. . . . Thereafter, several parents and wrestlers sued OHSAA in the Court of Common Pleas of Franklin County, Ohio, seeking a restraining order against OHSAA's ruling. . . . Both Milkovich and Scott testified in that proceeding. The court overturned OHSAA's probation and ineligibility orders on due process grounds.
>
> The day after the court rendered its decision, respondent Diadiun's column appeared in the News-Herald. . . . The column bore the heading "Maple beat the law with the 'big lie,'" beneath which appeared Diadiun's photograph and the words "TD Says." The carryover page headline announced ". . . Diadiun says Maple told a lie." The column contained the following passages:

---

[63] 497 U.S. 1 (1990).

. . . a lesson was learned (or relearned) yesterday by the student body of Maple Heights High School, and by anyone who attended the Maple-Mentor wrestling meet of last Feb. 8.

A lesson which, sadly, in view of the events of the past year, is well they learned early.

It is simply this: If you get in a jam, lie your way out.

If you're successful enough, and powerful enough, and can sound sincere enough, you stand an excellent chance of making the lie stand up, regardless of what really happened.

. . . .

Anyone who attended the meet, whether he be from Maple Heights, Mentor, or impartial observer, knows in his heart that Milkovich and Scott lied at the hearing after each having given his solemn oath to tell the truth.

But they got away with it.

Is that the kind of lesson we want our young people learning from their high school administrators and coaches?

I think not . . .[64]. . . .[65]

The Rulings of the Ohio Courts. Milkovich commenced a defamation action against respondents in the county court, alleging that the column accused him of committing the crime of perjury, damaged him in his occupation of teacher and coach, and constituted libel *per se*. Ultimately, the trial court granted summary judgment for respondents. The Ohio Court of Appeals affirmed, considering itself bound by the state Supreme Court's determination in Superintendent Scott's separate action against respondents that, as a matter law, the article was a constitutionally protected expression of opinion.

The *Scott* court decided that the proper analysis for determining whether utterances are fact or opinion was set forth in the decision of the United States Court of Appeals for the D.C. Circuit in *Ollman v. Evans*, [750 F.2d 970 (1984)]. . . . Under that analysis, four factors are considered to ascertain whether, under the "totality of circumstances," a statement is fact or opinion. These factors are: (1) "the specific language used"; (2) "whether the statement is verifiable"; (3) "the general context of the statement"; and (4) "the broader context in which the statement appeared." . . . The court

---

[64] [n.2] [The entire text of the article was set forth. The article included this passage:]

. . . .

I was among the 2,000-plus witnesses of the meet at which the trouble broke out, and I also attended the hearing before the OHSAA, so I was in a unique position of being the only non-involved party to observe both the meet itself and the *Milkovich-Scott* version presented to the board.

Any resemblance between the two occurrences is purely coincidental.

. . . .

[65] 497 U.S. at 3–5.

found that application of the first two factors to the column militated in favor of deeming the challenged passages actionable assertions of fact. . . . That potential outcome was trumped, however, by the court's consideration of the third and fourth factors. With respect to the third factor, the general context, the court explained that "the large caption 'TD Says' . . . would indicate to even the most gullible reader that the article was, in fact, opinion." . . . As for the fourth factor, the "broader context," the court reasoned that because the article appeared on a sports page — "a traditional haven for cajoling, invective, and hyperbole" — the article would probably be construed as opinion. . . .[66]

Defamatory Opinions at Common Law and Fair Comment. Turning to the development of the common law of defamation, Chief Justice Rehnquist explained:

> Defamation law developed not only as a means of allowing an individual to vindicate his good name, but also for the purpose of obtaining redress for harm caused by such statements. . . . As the common law developed in this country, apart from the issue of damages, one usually needed only allege an unprivileged publication of false and defamatory matter to state a cause of action for defamation. . . . The common law generally did not place any additional restrictions on the type of statement that could be actionable. Indeed, defamatory communications were deemed actionable regardless of whether they were deemed to be statements of fact or opinion. . . .
>
> However, due to concerns that unduly burdensome defamation laws could stifle valuable public debate, the privilege of "fair comment" was incorporated into the common law as an affirmative defense to an action for defamation. "The principle of 'fair comment' afforded legal immunity for the honest expression of opinion on matters of legitimate public interest when based upon a true or privileged statement of fact." . . . As this statement implies, comment was generally privileged when it concerned a matter of public concern, was upon true or privileged facts, represented the actual opinion of the speaker, and was not made solely for the purpose of causing harm. . . . Thus under the common law, the privilege of "fair comment" was the device employed to strike the appropriate balance between the need for vigorous public discourse and the need to redress injury to citizens wrought by invidious or irresponsible speech.[67]

Constitutional Protection of Hyperbole and Satire. Rehnquist then turned to the Supreme Court's earlier decisions in defamation cases. He discussed its holdings in *New York Times Co. v. Sullivan*,[68] *Curtis Publishing Co. v. Butts*,[69] *Rosenbloom v. Metromedia, Inc.*,[70] and *Gertz v. Robert Welch, Inc.*,[71] which, as discussed later in this chapter, preclude the imposition of strict liability for false

---

[66] *Id.* at 8–9.

[67] *Id.* at 12–14.

[68] 376 U.S. 254 (1964).

[69] 388 U.S. 130 (1967).

[70] 403 U.S. 29 (1971).

[71] 418 U.S. 323 (1974).

defamatory statements in a wide range of contexts.

Still later, in *Philadelphia Newspapers, Inc. v. Hepps*, . . . [475 U.S. 767 (1986)], we held that "the common-law presumption that defamatory speech is false cannot stand when a plaintiff seeks damages against a media defendant for speech of public concern." . . . In other words, the Court fashioned "a constitutional requirement that the plaintiff bear the burden of showing falsity, as well as fault, before recovering damages." . . .

We have also recognized constitutional limits on the type of speech which may be the subject of state defamation actions. In *Greenbelt Cooperative Publishing Assn., Inc. v. Bresler*, . . . [398 U.S. 6 (1970)], a real estate developer had engaged in negotiations with a local city council for a zoning variance on certain of his land, while simultaneously negotiating with the city on other land the city wished to purchase from him. A local newspaper published certain articles stating that some people had characterized the developer's negotiating position as "blackmail," and the developer sued for libel. Rejecting a contention that liability could be premised on the notion that the word "blackmail" implied the developer had committed the actual crime of blackmail, we held that "the imposition of liability on such a basis was constitutionally impermissible — that as a matter of constitutional law, the word 'blackmail' in these circumstances was not slander when spoken, and not libel when reported in the Greenbelt News Review." . . . Noting that the published reports "were accurate and full," the Court reasoned that "even the most careless reader must have perceived that the word was no more than rhetorical hyperbole, a vigorous epithet used by those who considered [the developer's] negotiating position extremely unreasonable." . . . *See also Hustler Magazine, Inc. v. Falwell*, . . . [485 U.S. 46, 50 (1988)] (First Amendment precluded recovery under state emotional distress action for ad parody which "could not reasonably have been interpreted as stating actual facts about the public figure involved"); *Letter Carriers v. Austin*, . . . [418 U.S. 264, 284–286 (1974)] (use of the word "traitor" in literary definition of a union "scab" not basis for a defamation action under federal labor law since used "in a loose, figurative sense" and was "merely rhetorical hyperbole, a lusty and imaginative expression of the contempt felt by union members").

The Court has also determined "that in cases raising First Amendment issues . . . an appellate court has an obligation to 'make an independent examination of the whole record' in order to make sure that 'the judgment does not constitute a forbidden intrusion on the field of free expression.' " . . .

Respondents would have us recognize, in addition to the established safeguards discussed above, still another First Amendment-based protection for defamatory statements which are categorized as "opinion" as opposed to "fact." For this proposition they rely principally on the following dictum from our opinion in *Gertz*:

Under the First Amendment there is no such thing as a false idea. However pernicious an opinion may seem, we depend for its correction not on the conscience of judges and juries but on the competition of other ideas. But there is no constitutional value in false statements of fact. . . .

Judge Friendly appropriately observed that this passage "has become the opening salvo in all arguments for protection from defamation actions on the ground of opinion, even though the case did not remotely concern the question." *Cianci v. New Times Publishing Co.*, 639 F.2d 54, 61 (CA2 1980). . . .

. . . [W]e do not think this passage from *Gertz* was intended to create a wholesale defamation exemption for anything that might be labeled "opinion." . . . Not only would such an interpretation be contrary to the tenor and context of the passage, but it would also ignore the fact that expressions of "opinion" may often imply an assertion of objective fact.[72]

No Special Protection for Opinions That Imply False Facts. Rehnquist then explored the subject of implicit statements of fact:

If a speaker says, "In my opinion John Jones is a liar," he implies a knowledge of facts which lead to the conclusion that Jones told an untruth. Even if the speaker states the facts upon which he bases his opinion, if those facts are either incorrect or incomplete, or if his assessment of them is erroneous, the statement may still imply a false assertion of fact. Simply couching such statements in terms of opinion does not dispel these implications; and the statement, "In my opinion Jones is a liar," can cause as much damage to reputation as the statement, "Jones is a liar." As Judge Friendly aptly stated: "[It] would be destructive of the law of libel if a writer could escape liability for accusations of [defamatory conduct] simply by using, explicitly or implicitly, the words 'I think.' ". . . .

. . . [Appellants] contend that in every defamation case the First Amendment mandates an inquiry into whether a statement is "opinion" or "fact," and that only the latter statements may be actionable. They propose that a number of factors developed by the lower courts (in what we hold was a mistaken reliance on the *Gertz* dictum) be considered in deciding which is which. But we think the "breathing space" which "freedoms of expression require in order to survive," . . . is adequately secured by existing constitutional doctrine without the creation of an artificial dichotomy between "opinion" and fact.

Foremost, we think *Hepps* stands for the proposition that a statement on matters of public concern must be provable as false before there can be liability under state defamation law, at least in situations, like the present, where a media defendant is involved. Thus, unlike the statement, "In my opinion Mayor Jones is a liar," the statement, "In my opinion Mayor Jones shows his abysmal ignorance by accepting the teachings of Marx and Lenin," would not be actionable. *Hepps* ensures that a statement of opinion

---

[72] 497 U.S. at 16–18.

relating to matters of public concern which does not contain a provably false factual connotation will receive full constitutional protection.[73]

Next, the *Bresler-Letter Carriers-Falwell* line of cases provides protection for statements that cannot "reasonably [be] interpreted as stating actual facts" about an individual. . . . This provides assurance that public debate will not suffer for lack of "imaginative expression" or the "rhetorical hyperbole" which has traditionally added much to the discourse of our Nation. . . .

The *New York Times-Butts-Gertz* culpability requirements further ensure that debate on public issues remains "uninhibited, robust, and wide-open." . . . Thus, where a statement of "opinion" on a matter of public concern reasonably implies false and defamatory facts regarding public figures or officials, those individuals must show that such statements were made with knowledge of their false implications or with reckless disregard of their truth. Similarly, where such a statement involves a private figure on a matter of public concern, a plaintiff must show that the false connotations were made with some level of fault as required by *Gertz*. . . .

We are not persuaded that . . . an additional separate constitutional privilege for "opinion" is required to ensure the freedom of expression guaranteed by the First Amendment. . . .[74]

An Implied Assertion That the Coach Perjured Himself. Turning back to the facts of the *Milkovich* dispute, Rehnquist explained:

The dispositive question . . . then becomes whether or not a reasonable factfinder could conclude that the statements in the Diadiun column imply an assertion that petitioner Milkovich perjured himself in a judicial proceeding. We think this question must be answered in the affirmative. As the Ohio Supreme Court itself observed: "the clear impact in some nine sentences and a caption is that [Milkovich] 'lied at the hearing after . . . having given his solemn oath to tell the truth.' " . . . This is not the sort of loose, figurative or hyperbolic language which would negate the impression that the writer was seriously maintaining petitioner committed the crime of perjury. Nor does the general tenor of the article negate this impression.

We also think the connotation that petitioner committed perjury is sufficiently factual to be susceptible of being proved true or false. A determination of whether petitioner lied in this instance can be made on a core of objective evidence by comparing, *inter alia*, petitioner's testimony before the OHSAA board with his subsequent testimony before the trial court. As the *Scott* court noted regarding the plaintiff in that case: "Whether or not H. Don Scott did indeed perjure himself is certainly verifiable by a perjury action with evidence adduced from the transcripts and witnesses present at

---

[73] [n.7] We note that the issue of falsity relates to the defamatory facts implied by a statement. . . .

[74] 497 U.S. at 18–21.

the hearing. Unlike a subjective assertion the averred defamatory language is an articulation of an objectively verifiable event." . . . So too with petitioner Milkovich.[75]

The judgment of the Ohio Court of Appeals was reversed and the case remanded for further proceedings. Chief Justice Rehnquist's opinion was joined by six other justices (White, Blackmun, Stevens, O'Connor, Scalia, and Kennedy, JJ.).

Brennan and Marshall Dissent. Justice Thurgood Marshall joined the dissenting opinion of Justice William J. Brennan, Jr., which stated:

> Diadiun's assumption that Milkovich must have lied at the court hearing is patently conjecture. The majority finds Diadiun's statements actionable, however, because it concludes that these statements imply a factual assertion that Milkovich perjured himself at the judicial proceeding. I disagree. Diadiun not only reveals the facts upon which he is relying but he makes it clear at which point he runs out of facts and is simply guessing. Read in context, the statements cannot reasonably be interpreted as implying such an assertion as fact. . . .[76]

b.   Applying *Milkovich*

Triable Issues of Fact. Statements of opinion have been found to raise triable issues with respect to whether they implied false facts in cases where the host of a call-in talk show repeatedly accused a judge of being "corrupt";[77] a professional organization's directory described an attorney as an "ambulance chaser";[78] a supervisor stated that "he had reason to believe" that the plaintiff had sabotaged a computer;[79] and a work labeled "fiction" characterized the plaintiff as a "slut."[80]

In *Williams v. Garraghty*,[81] an employee alleged that a prison warden was guilty of sexual harassment. Rejecting the argument that the statements were constitutionally protected expressions of opinion, the Virginia Supreme Court found that supporting statements in the memorandum, relating to an alleged incident at the plaintiff's house and certain "derogatory notes," were clearly factual in nature, and therefore could serve as the basis for a defamation lawsuit.

Opinions Incapable of Implying False Facts. Opinions which have been found to be incapable of implying false facts include statements labeling a physician a "real tool"; [82] calling a union's attorney "a very poor lawyer";[83] labeling a scholar a

---

[75] *Id.* at 21–22.

[76] *Id.* at 28.

[77] *See Bentley v. Bunton*, 94 S.W.3d 561 (Tex. 2002).

[78] *See Flamm v. American Ass'n of Univ. Women*, 201 F.3d 144 (2d Cir. 2000).

[79] *See Staples v. Bangor Hydro-Elec. Co.*, 629 A.2d 601 (Me. 1993).

[80] *See Bryson v. News Am. Pubs., Inc.*, 672 N.E.2d 1207 (Ill. 1996).

[81] 455 S.E.2d 209, 215 (Va. 1995).

[82] *McKee v. Laurion*, 825 N.W.2d 725, 733 (Minn. 2013).

[83] *See Sullivan v. Conway*, 157 F.3d 1092 (7th Cir. 1998).

"crank" for having taken a "wrongheaded" position;[84] and characterizing the chairman of an election board a "lying asshole."[85]

Colorful Hyperbole. In *Imperial Apparel, Ltd. v. Cosmo's Designer Direct, Inc.*,[86] a defamation dispute between competing retailers arising from an advertisement, the Supreme Court of Illinois wrote:

> The gist of the ad, taken as a whole, is simply this: plaintiffs copied Cosmo's "3 for 1" sale idea, plaintiffs were wrong to do so and should stop, and while most customers realize the difference between the companies offering the sales, those who might not should not be deceived — you get more for your money in Cosmo's 3 for 1 sale. To be sure, the language Cosmo's used to convey these concepts was unflattering. The ad employed terms such as "rags," "flea market style warehouse," "dried cream cheese," "low rent," and "a hooker's come on." It also likened plaintiffs to the Iraqi Information Minister and claimed they "inflate prices and compromise quality." In our view, however, these are merely subjective characterizations lacking precise and readily understood meaning. In the context of discount clothing sales, no reasonable person would regard them as anything other than colorful hyperbole aimed at capturing the reader's interest and attention.[87]

In *Seaton v. TripAdvisor LLC*,[88] a resort sued for defamation after being placed on TripAdvisor's "2011 Dirtiest Hotels List." The Sixth Circuit held that the resort failed to state a cause of action for two reasons:

> First, TripAdvisor's use of "dirtiest" amounts to rhetorical hyperbole. Second, the general tenor of the "2011 Dirtiest Hotels" list undermines any impression that TripAdvisor was seriously maintaining that Grand Resort is, in fact, the dirtiest hotel in America.[89]

In *Varrenti v. Gannett Co., Inc.*,[90] a New York trial court ruled that anonymous comments posted on a newspaper website were not actionable even though they suggested that the police department was not properly serving village citizens. As the court explained:

> [B]ased on the over-all context in which the alleged defamatory statements were made, a reasonable reader would conclude that the statements were the opinions of the anonymous John/Jane Doe defendants. . . . The tone of the comments was sarcastic, hyperbolic, and based on rumors that the anonymous posters heard around the Village of Brockport and about the Department. Moreover, the apparent purpose of the comments made by

---

[84] *See Dilworth v. Dudley*, 75 F.3d 307, 311 (7th Cir. 1996).

[85] *See Greenhalgh v. Casey*, 67 F.3d 299 (6th Cir. 1995).

[86] 882 N.E.2d 1011 (Ill. 2008).

[87] *Id.* at 1023–24.

[88] 728 F.3d 592 (6th Cir. 2013).

[89] *Id.* at 598.

[90] 33 Misc. 3d 405 (N.Y. Sup. Ct. 2011).

the John/Jane Doe defendants was to call for an investigation into the Department's practices.[91]

Unverifiable Assertions. Some opinions are found to be nonactionable because they imply nothing that could be verified. For example, in *Seelig v. Infinity Broadcasting Corp.*,[92] the California Court of Appeal held that the terms "chicken butt," "local loser," and "big shank" were too vague to be capable of being proven true or false. Similar conclusions have been reached with respect to nonspecific allegations that a person was "cheating the city"[93] or a "crook."[94]

In *Jefferson County School District v. Moody's Investor's Services, Inc.*,[95] a school district's bond offering did well at first, but then turned sour after Moody's published an article saying that the outlook on the district's obligation debt was "negative" and that the district was under "ongoing financial pressures" because of state underfunding. Consequently, the district was forced to re-offer the bonds at a higher interest rate, which caused a significant financial loss. The Tenth Circuit held that the vagueness of the phrases "negative outlook" and "ongoing financial pressures" rendered them protected expressions of opinion.

In *Palestine Herald-Press Co. v. Zimmer*,[96] the Texas Court of Appeals held that a sports editor's statement that a coach made an obscene gesture was not actionable. The court explained:

> Tyler's statement that the gesture Zimmer made with his arms was "obscene," without further description, is subjective and indefinite. The answer to the question of whether something is "obscene" varies from state to state, from community to community, and from person to person. . . . It is an individual judgment that rests solely in the eye of the beholder and, as such, is not an objectively verifiable statement of fact. . . .[97]

Postings on Internet Bulletin Boards. In *Mathis v. Cannon*,[98] the Supreme Court of Georgia found that three inflammatory messages posted on an Internet bulletin board fell short of the constitutional fact requirement that is a prerequisite to a defamation cause of action. One of the messages read:

> cannon a crook
>
> by: duelly41
>
> > hey cannon why u got fired from calton company? ? ? ? why does cannon and lt governor mark taylor think that crisp county needs to be dumping ground of the south? ? ? u be busted man crawl under a rock

---

[91] *Id.* at 677.

[92] 97 Cal. App. 4th 798 (2002).

[93] *See Schivarelli v. CBS, Inc.*, 776 N.E.2d 693, 699 (Ill. App. Ct. 2002).

[94] *See Dubinsky v. United Airlines Master Exec. Coun.*, 708 N.E.2d 441 (Ill. App. Ct. 1999).

[95] 175 F.3d 848 (10th Cir. 1999).

[96] 257 S.W.3d 504 (Tex. App. 2008).

[97] *Id.* at 512.

[98] 573 S.E.2d 376 (Ga. 2002).

and hide cannon and poole!!!! if u deal with cannon u a crook too!!!!!!! so stay out of crisp county and we thank u for it[99]

Disposing of the claim, the court wrote:

> Although the messages accused Cannon of being a crook and a thief and asked why he had been fired from a specific company, these accusations were made as part of the ongoing debate about the garbage disposal dispute in Crisp County. . . . [A]ny person reading the postings on the message board — written entirely in lower case replete with question marks, exclamation points, misspellings, abbreviations, and dashes — could not reasonably interpret the incoherent messages as stating actual facts about Cannon, but would interpret them as the late night rhetorical outbursts of an angry and frustrated person opposed to the company's hauling of other people's garbage into the county.[100]

While such electronic venting is sometimes not actionable, that does not prevent lawsuits from being filed. *National Law Journal* reported that a Chicago woman's tweet ("Who said sleeping in a moldy apartment was bad for you? Horizon realty thinks it's OK"), triggered a $50,000 claim for defamation of business reputation.[101]

Attempted Humor and the Importance of Context. In *Knievel v. ESPN*,[102] the Ninth Circuit held that statements made in an attempt at humor were not actionable. Describing the facts, the court wrote:

> Famed motorcycle stuntman Evel Knievel and his wife Krystal were photographed when they attended ESPN's Action Sports and Music Awards in 2001. The photograph depicted Evel, who was wearing a motorcycle jacket and rose-tinted sunglasses, with his right arm around Krystal and his left arm around another young woman. ESPN published the photograph on its "extreme sports" website with a caption that read "Evel Knievel proves that you're never too old to be a pimp." The Knievels brought suit against ESPN . . . contending that the photograph and caption were defamatory because they accused Evel of soliciting prostitution and implied that Krystal was a prostitute.[103]

In affirming dismissal of the action, the court stated:

> ESPN argued . . . that viewers accessing the website could not help but to see at least some of the surrounding web pages in order to view the photograph and caption that the Knievels allege to be defamatory. . . . [W]e found that in order to access the photograph, one must first view, at minimum, the nine photographs that precede it and the EXPN.com home page. . . .

---

[99] *Id.* at 379.

[100] *Id.* at 383.

[101] Tresa Baldas, *Putting the "Twit" in Twitter*, Nat'l L.J., Aug. 17, 2009, at 3.

[102] 393 F.3d 1068 (9th Cir. 2005).

[103] *Id.* at 1070.

Our first inquiry is into the "broad context" of the statement, which includes "the general tenor of the entire work, the subject of the statements, the setting, and the format of the work." . . . The . . . content of the EXPN.com main page is lighthearted, jocular, and intended for a youthful audience. . . . The page directs the viewer to "[c]heck out what the rockstars and prom queens were wearing," and offers a "behind the scenes look at all the cool kids, EXPN-style." Most importantly, . . . the page features slang phrases such as "[d]udes rollin' deep" and "[k]ickin' it with much flavor," neither of which is susceptible to a literal interpretation. . . .

Next, we examine the "specific context and content of the statements, analyzing the extent of figurative or hyperbolic language used and the reasonable expectations of the audience in that particular situation." . . . The web pages immediately preceding and following the Knievel photo use slang words such as "hardcore" and "scoping," and slang phrases such as "throwing down a pose," "put a few back," and "hottie of the year," none of which is intended to be interpreted literally. . . .

. . . Read in the context of the satirical, risque, and sophomoric slang found on the rest of the site, the word "pimp" cannot be reasonably interpreted as a criminal accusation.[104]

Application to Torts Other Than Libel and Slander. The excerpts from *Milkovich* set forth above in the text briefly mention *Hustler Magazine v. Falwell*.[105] *Falwell* stands for the proposition that it is impossible to circumvent the false fact requirement of a defamation action by framing the claim as a suit for intentional infliction of emotional distress. In *Falwell*, an obscene parody, which was presented as fiction, depicted the plaintiff, a well-known minister, as engaging in an incestuous rendezvous in an out-house. The idea was so outlandish that few readers could have believed that it had actually taken place. A jury denied recovery on the plaintiff's libel claim, finding that the parody could not be taken as describing facts, but it awarded him damages for intentional infliction of emotional distress. Relying on defamation precedent, the Supreme Court reversed. It ruled that the First Amendment interest in uninhibited debate on public issues precludes a public figure from recovering against a publisher for intentional infliction of emotional distress, unless the publication contained a false statement of fact made with knowledge of its falsity or reckless disregard for its truth.

PROBLEM 3-2: THE EX-GOVERNOR'S DIVORCE

In August 2009, numerous news sources reported that Sarah and Todd Palin were getting a divorce. A few days earlier, Sarah Palin, the 2008 Republican vice presidential candidate, had resigned the governorship of Alaska. According to an article in *Alaska Report*, Palin's lawyer threatened to sue the owner of the "highly trafficked 'ImmoralMinority' blog" unless he removed an offending article about the supposed divorce and posted a retraction. According to the article, the plan was to serve libel action papers on the blog owner at a kindergarten. Is saying that

---

[104] *Id.* at 1076–79.

[105] 485 U.S. 46 (1988).

someone is getting a divorce actionable under the law of defamation?

2.   Defamation Based on Conduct

Some defamation suits are based on conduct, rather than on written or spoken words. For example, in *Tyler v. Macks Stores of S.C., Inc.*,[106] the South Carolina Supreme Court found that a cause of action was stated where the defendant allegedly discharged an employee immediately following a polygraph test. Likewise, in *Morrison v. National Broadcasting Co.*,[107] the New York Court of Appeals allowed an action where an unwitting plaintiff had been duped into being a contestant on a rigged television game show.

Difficulty in Ascertaining the Factual Assertion. Certain courts have declined to recognize a suit for libel or slander based solely on conduct. For example, in *Bolton v. Department of Human Services*,[108] a former employee brought an action for defamation based on his former supervisor's accompanying the employee to the exit door, without a spoken word, immediately following the employee's discharge. The Minnesota Supreme Court concluded, as a matter of law, that the plaintiff had not been defamed, stating that:

> In most other states that have allowed an action for defamation by conduct, the behavior has tended to rise to the level of "dramatic pantomime": that is, an interplay of words and conduct that provide a clearly discernible account of the making of a false statement about the aggrieved to a third party.[109]

The *Bolton* court appears to have been influenced by the fact that even in a defamation suit based on conduct, it is necessary to prove a false statement of fact. The court noted the heightened difficulty in a defamatory conduct case of applying applicable legal tests in a suit based on a communication "that can be interpreted by the declarant to have one meaning but to have quite a different one to the recipient."[110]

3.   Substantial Truth

An action will not lie if an allegedly defamatory statement is true or substantially true. For example, in the movie *Bowling for Columbine*, producer Michael Moore said that "Terry and James [Nichols] were both arrested in connection to the bombing"[111] of the Oklahoma City federal building. In fact, James was neither charged nor arrested regarding the Oklahoma City bombing. Although he was later indicted for possession of unregistered firearms, he "was arrested only days after the bombing and his arrest was brought about by the

---

[106] 272 S.E.2d 633 (S.C. 1980).

[107] 227 N.E.2d 572 (N.Y. 1967).

[108] 540 N.W.2d 523, 525–26 (Minn. 1995).

[109] *Id.* at 525.

[110] *Id.*

[111] *Nichols v. Moore*, 477 F.3d 396, 398 (6th Cir. 2007).

FBI's investigation into Timothy McVeigh's and Terry Nichols's roles in the bombing."[112] Nevertheless, in *Nichols v. Moore*, the Sixth Circuit concluded that a defamation action by James was barred because Moore's statement was substantially true.[113]

Similarly, in *Alleman v. Vermilion Publishing Corp.*,[114] a "letter to the editor" charged that the plaintiff doctor had refused to see the defendants' child because the child was the patient of another doctor. In fact, the doctor might have said that he refused to provide treatment because another doctor had been called and was on his way to the hospital. No one could remember exactly what was said. The court held that the published statement was a substantially accurate reflection of the events which took place — namely that the doctor had refused to provide services to an injured child — and that therefore no action would lie.

Other cases have reached similar conclusions without using the term "substantial truth." Thus, in *Sykes v. Hengel*,[115] the board of managers of a limited liability corporation issued a memorandum detailing why the corporation was in bad shape financially and indicating that the chief executive officer had been replaced. The memorandum stated in part that "[t]his action . . . was deemed necessary because of a series of key operational and management deficiencies that have occurred over the course of the last 12 to 15 months."[116] A federal court in Iowa ruled that the dismissed CEO failed to state a cause of action for defamation. Observing that the facts about the corporation's financial plight were true, the court wrote:

> Stripped of innuendo, the Memorandum does not state anything defamatory about Sykes. . . . While a businessperson may feel bruised by statements suggesting business failure on his watch, accurate statements of the condition of the company during that period do not support a cause of action on this theory of liability.[117]

The "Gist" of the Statement. Whether a statement is "substantially true" depends upon whether the "gist" of the statement is accurate. For example, in *Gustafson v. City of Austin*,[118] the Texas Court of Appeals held that an e-mailed statement was not actionable. The gist of what was said (namely, that a CPR teacher was no longer a valid heart association CPR instructor and his instructor status had been officially revoked by the association) was not substantially worse than the literal truth (namely, that the teacher was no longer a valid heart association CPR instructor, and while he could still teach CPR courses, the courses were not sanctioned by the heart association).

---

[112] *Id.* at 401.

[113] *Id.* at 402.

[114] 316 So. 2d 837 (La. Ct. App. 1975).

[115] 394 F. Supp. 2d 1062 (S.D. Iowa 2005).

[116] *Id.* at 1068.

[117] *Id.* at 1075.

[118] 110 S.W.3d 652 (Tex. App. 2003).

Greater Opprobrium or Sting. In assessing substantial truth, some courts ask whether the truth would have carried less sting or less opprobrium than the false statement. Under this standard, saying that the plaintiff, while drunk, hit and killed a pedestrian is probably not actionable if the plaintiff, while drunk, struck and killed a motorist.

In *UTV of San Antonio, Inc. v. Ardmore, Inc.*,[119] the Texas Court of Appeals held that a statement that an inspector had found roaches at a daycare center during a follow-up inspection was not more damaging than would have been true of an accurate statement that the inspector had noted allegations by staff members of roaches on a cup, a crockpot, and a counter, but that no roaches were found on the day of a specific inspection.

Suppose that a lawyer was previously reprimanded by disciplinary authorities for engaging in an impermissible business transaction with a client and for representing multiple clients with conflicting interests. If an unhappy litigation opponent sends e-mails to third parties saying that the lawyer was "nearly disbarred," is a successful defamation claim precluded by the substantial truth rule? Reprimand is one of the lightest forms of sanctions imposed on errant lawyers, and disbarment is the most severe. However, most lay persons know little about lawyer discipline. A substantial truth defense was not raised in *Baldinger v. Ferri*[120] and the Third Circuit affirmed a million dollar default judgment for the plaintiff.[121]

Minor Details. Minor details are often irrelevant. It is probably not actionable to say inaccurately that a person stole a red purse, rather than a blue one, or that the person swindled a customer on the sale of a new Ford, rather than on the sale of a new Chevy. In the former case, the gist of the statement is that the actor stole a purse, and the color of the purse has nothing to do with how the person is viewed by others. In the latter case, the gist of the statement is that a customer was swindled while purchasing a new car. The truth about the make of the car has nothing to do with the sting that attaches to the statement.

Note, however, that a different result might be reached if the plaintiff is falsely charged with stealing something last week, when the theft actually occurred ten years earlier. Recent misconduct often carries a higher degree of opprobrium than a relatively ancient infraction of the same nature.

Specific Allegations Versus General Allegations. Some charges are specific and others are general. If specific allegations are made, then the focus of the substantial truth inquiry is clear. The question is whether the person did what was charged or something very similar. If the answer to those questions is no, it makes little difference that the person committed other bad acts on different occasions.

A speaker who alleges that a teacher accepted a bribe from a student in exchange for a passing grade does not establish substantial truth by proving that the teacher submitted fraudulent invoices to the school for reimbursement of travel expenses.

---

[119] 82 S.W.3d 609 (Tex. App. 2002).

[120] 2013 U.S. App. LEXIS 19790 (3d Cir. Sept. 27, 2013).

[121] Mary Pat Gallagher, *Third Circuit Affirms Damages for Lawyer Defamed by Litigation Rival,* N.J. L.J., Oct. 1, 2013.

However, proof of other bad acts may be allowed into evidence as bearing upon the plaintiff's reputation and how much it has been damaged by the defendant's false allegations.

Guccione v. Hustler Magazine, Inc.[122] involved a charge that was general, rather than specific. The plaintiff was accused of participating in an ongoing adulterous relationship. In fact, the plaintiff had lived in adultery for thirteen of the preceding seventeen years, but the adultery had ceased when his wife divorced him. The court held that the statement could not be read to mean that the marriage and the cohabitation had existed simultaneously for only a moment or brief interval prior to the publication. Rather, the only reasonable construction of the statement was that the marriage and cohabitation had existed simultaneously throughout an undefined span of time that included the period immediately prior to publication. The facts showed this to be substantially true, because the plaintiff's adultery had continued over the course of many years. Because the published statement would not have had a worse effect on the mind of the reader than the truth, the complaint failed to state a claim.

Excusing Inaccuracies. Some cases have been generous in excusing inaccuracies. For example, in *Steele v. Spokesman-Review*,[123] the Idaho Supreme Court held that statements in an article, which alleged that an attorney had relocated from California to Idaho at about the same time as members of a white supremacist group, were substantially true, even though two years separated their moves. In *Swindall v. Cox Enterprises, Inc.*,[124] the Georgia Court of Appeals found that an editorial's assertion that a former Congressman had "lied about drug-money laundering" was substantially true, even though he had only been convicted of concealing from a grand jury his involvement in discussions about money laundering. And, in *Provencio v. Paradigm Media, Inc.*,[125] the Texas Court of Appeals held that a postcard identifying the plaintiff as a registered sex offender was substantially true, even though the card bore a misleading return address implying that it had been sent by the government rather than by a news organization.

Technically Inaccurate Terminology. Courts routinely make allowances for the use of technically inaccurate lay terminology.[126] In *Rouch v. Enquirer & News of Battle Creek, Michigan*,[127] the Supreme Court of Michigan found that an article using the word "charge" to describe an arrest and booking was not defamatory, even though no formal arraignment had occurred. In *Rosen v. Capital City Press*,[128] the Louisiana Court of Appeal excused the incorrect use of term "narcotics" to encompass depressants and stimulants.

---

[122] 800 F.2d 298 (2d Cir. 1986).

[123] 61 P.3d 606 (Idaho 2002).

[124] 558 S.E.2d 788 (Ga. Ct. App. 2002).

[125] 44 S.W.3d 677 (Tex. App. 2001).

[126] *See* RESTATEMENT (SECOND) OF TORTS § 581A cmt. f (1977).

[127] 487 N.W.2d 205 (Mich. 1992).

[128] 314 So. 2d 511 (La. Ct. App. 1975).

Questions of Fact May Preclude Summary Judgment. In *Neely v. Wilson*,[129] a physician (Neely) appealed a grant of summary judgment to media defendants in a suit stemming from their investigative broadcast involving the physician. After the broadcast aired, the physician's medical practice collapsed. The Texas Supreme Court wrote:

> Whether Neely raised a fact issue regarding the truth or falsity of the underlying statements is the primary issue in this appeal. We have developed the substantial truth doctrine to determine the truth or falsity of a broadcast: if a broadcast taken as a whole is more damaging to the plaintiff's reputation than a truthful broadcast would have been, the broadcast is not substantially true and is actionable. . . .

> Assessing a broadcast's gist is crucial. A broadcast with specific statements that err in the details but that correctly convey the gist of a story is substantially true. . . . On the other hand, a broadcast "can convey a false and defamatory meaning by omitting or juxtaposing facts, even though all the story's individual statements considered in isolation were literally true or non-defamatory." . . . We determine a broadcast's gist or meaning by examining how a person of ordinary intelligence would view it. . . .

> The broadcast at issue began by asking listeners if they would want to know "if your surgeon had been disciplined for prescribing himself and taking dangerous drugs." The broadcast discusses the Jetton and Wu cases and then states that the Board "did discipline Neely." After discussing the Order, the broadcast contains the following statement by Paul Jetton:

>> Narcotics, opiates, I mean it's just things that, I mean things that they don't even let people operate machinery or drive cars when they're, when they're taking them and this guy's doing brain surgery on people. I mean it's just, even now I'm just, it's just incredulous, you just can't even believe that it even happened.

> . . . We agree with Neely that a person of ordinary intelligence could conclude the gist of the broadcast was that Neely was disciplined for operating on patients while using dangerous drugs or controlled substances.

> . . . [T]he government investigation (here from the Board Order) does not indicate that this allegedly defamatory statement was correct. . . . [T]he Order reflects that Neely was disciplined for self-prescribing dangerous drugs or controlled substances, not for taking them.

> In addition, Neely brought forth evidence that he was not operating on patients while taking or using dangerous drugs or controlled substances. . . .

> Based on Neely's responsive evidence, we hold that there is a fact issue regarding the truth or falsity of the gist that Neely was disciplined for operating on patients while taking or using dangerous drugs or controlled

---

[129] 2013 Tex. LEXIS 511 (June 28, 2013).

substances. . . . [B]ecause the factfinder may conclude that the gist was more damaging to Neely's reputation than a truthful and accurate broadcast would have been, the substantial truth defense cannot support the trial court's summary judgment.[130]

4.   Burden of Proof on Falsity

In *Neely v. Wilson*,[131] *supra*, the Texas Supreme Court stated that defamation actions are subject to a "defense of truth," but observed that:

> The United States Supreme Court and this Court long ago shifted the burden of proving the truth defense to require the plaintiff to prove the defamatory statements were false when the statements were made by a media defendant over a public concern.[132]

The court noted that "[t]his distinction is less material at the summary judgment stage where, as here, the media defendant is the movant"[133] and must demonstrate that there is no issue of material fact in order to prevail on the ground that an allegedly defamatory statement is substantially true.

E.   COLLOQUIUM REQUIREMENT: "OF AND CONCERNING THE PLAINTIFF"

A plaintiff can sue for libel or slander only if the allegedly defamatory statement refers to the plaintiff. Thus, cases often say that the defamation must be "of and concerning the plaintiff."

In *Prince v. Out Publishing Inc.*,[134] a magazine published an article which referred to illegal drug use and unsafe sex and included photographs of the plaintiff and others at "circuit parties." The court held that the plaintiff failed to satisfy the "of and concerning" requirement, reasoning:

> The photographs published in the Article establish that there were many people at the party. In addition, the text refers to parties attended by thousands of people. There is nothing in the text of the Article to suggest that the general statements about illegal drug use and unsafe sex apply to plaintiff.[135]

---

[130] *Id.* at *21–*33.

[131] 2013 Tex. LEXIS 511 (June 28, 2013) (citing *Philadelphia Newspapers, Inc. v. Hepps*, 475 U.S. 767, 777 (1986)).

[132] *Id.* at *6.

[133] *Id.*

[134] 2002 Cal. App. Unpub. LEXIS 5189 (Jan. 3, 2002).

[135] *Id.* at *20.

1.　　　Group Defamation

Does a defamatory statement referring to a group (*e.g.*, doctors, Democrats, or alumni of a university) defame some or all of the individuals associated with the group? In many instances, the answer is no, for there is little reason to think that the defamatory innuendo would harm particular individuals. Thus, an assertion that members of Congress cheat on their taxes does not entitle every member of the House of Representatives to sue.

Size of Group, Inclusiveness of Language, Special Circumstances. It is impossible to state a definite rule for group defamation. In each case, it is important to consider the circumstances surrounding the statement, such as the size of the group, the inclusiveness of the language (*e.g.*, "one," "some," "many," "most," "all," "every single one"), and special circumstances (*e.g.*, whether the plaintiff was the only member of the defamed group who was present or whether the defendant looked directly at the plaintiff while making the statement). Naturally, the smaller the group, the more inclusive the language, and the more focused the charge, the easier it is to allow a member of the group to state a cause of action. Defamation of a group with more than twenty-five members has rarely been found to be actionable. However, there is no magic to that number.

In *Neiman-Marcus v. Lait*,[136] defamatory statements were made charging that: (1) "some" of the models at a particular store were call girls; (2) "the salesgirls" were less expensive and "not as snooty as the models"; and (3) "[m]ost of" the male sales staff were homosexuals. The plaintiffs in the suit were all nine of the store's models, 15 of its 25 salesmen, and 30 of its 382 saleswomen. The plaintiffs who were models and salesmen belonged to relatively small groups. Despite the fact that the language referring to them was not all-inclusive, the statements reflected upon them sufficiently that each model and salesman was permitted to sue. None of the salesgirls stated a cause of action because they belonged to a very large group and there were no special circumstances singling out members of that group.

In *Diaz v. NBC Universal, Inc.*,[137] the Second Circuit addressed similar issues relating to group defamation. The court wrote:

> Appellants filed the complaint on behalf of . . . approximately 400 present and former special agents of the federal DEA who were employed . . . during the period from 1973 through 1985. They alleged . . . that a legend . . . appearing at the end of the feature film *American Gangster* . . . which both describes itself as based on a true story and as a fictionalized version of events, defamed Diaz, Korniloff, and Toal, and all members of their putative class. The legend . . . stated that the "collaboration" of Richard Roberts, a New Jersey police officer, and Frank Lucas, a major narcotics trafficker in the New York City area, "led to the convictions of three quarters of New York City's Drug Enforcement Agency."

> . . . Under the group libel doctrine, a plaintiff's claim is insufficient if the allegedly defamatory statement referenced the plaintiff solely as a member

---

[136] 13 F.R.D. 311 (S.D.N.Y. 1952).

[137] *Diaz v. NBC Universal, Inc.*, 2009 U.S. App. LEXIS 15653 (2d Cir. July 16, 2009).

of a group, unless the plaintiff can show that the circumstances of the publication reasonably give rise to the conclusion that there is a particular reference to the plaintiff. . . .

Appellants cannot make this showing. . . . [W]e first note that the "group" defined by the legend is New York City's DEA in its entirety. . . . In view of the large size of this group (consisting of 400 individuals, or even potentially 233, as appellants characterized the group post-complaint), and that the legend makes reference only to three-quarters of the group, i.e., "some" of its members, appellants' claim is incapable of supporting a jury's finding that the allegedly libelous statements refer to them as individuals. . . .[138]

In *Harvest House Publishers v. Local Church*,[139] the Texas Court of Appeals wrote:

Under the group libel doctrine, a plaintiff has no cause of action for a defamatory statement directed to some or less than all of the group when there is nothing to single out the plaintiff. . . . *Wright v. Rosenbaum*, 344 S.W.2d 228, 231–33 (Tex. Civ. App. — Houston 1961, no writ) (holding that statement that "one of the four ladies" stole dress, but not naming guilty person, was not slanderous of any particular person); *Bull v. Collins*, 54 S.W.2d 870, 871–72 (Tex. Civ. App. — Eastland 1932, no writ) (holding that statement that either A or B stole the money, without specifying guilty party, not slanderous); *Harris v. Santa Fe Townsite Co.*, 58 Tex. Civ. App. 506, 125 S.W. 77, 80 (1910, *writ ref'd*) (holding that statement that an unnamed "band of nine women" from South Silsbee cut a fence was not libelous because 15 women lived in South Silsbee).[140]

The *Harvest House Publishers* suit was based on a book which included the plaintiff church in a list of 50 "cults." The court rejected the plaintiff's defamation claim stating:

[W]e cannot conclude that a reasonable reader could believe that all groups named in the book participate in the criminal activities that plaintiffs claim as the basis of their libel action. No reasonable reader could conclude that the book accuses the church, and, in fact, every other church named in the book, of rape, murder, child molestation, drug smuggling, etc. As such, the allegedly libelous statements in the Introduction are not "of and concerning the church" and are not actionable.[141]

---

[138] *Id.* at 95–96.

[139] 190 S.W.3d 204 (Tex. App. 2006).

[140] *Id.* at 213.

[141] *Id.* at 214.

2.   Fictional Portrayals

Plaintiffs sometimes argue that they were the basis of a fictionalized portrayal which defamed them. In these kinds of cases, the question is simply whether the defamatory depiction could reasonably be understood as referring to the plaintiff. Labeling something as "fiction" does not necessarily mean that it is not actionable.

For example, in *Muzikowski v. Paramount Pictures Corp.*,[142] the Seventh Circuit held that a Little League baseball coach stated a claim for defamation based on the movie "Hardball" starring Keanu Reeves. Although the character had a different name, there were many similarities. Unlike the plaintiff, the character committed theft and lied about being a licensed securities broker.

Similarly, in *Bindrim v. Mitchell*,[143] a psychologist who conducted nude group therapy sessions claimed that he was the basis for a character in a novel who conducted the same type of sessions, and that he was defamed by the unflattering rendering of that character. Because the evidence was conflicted on the question of whether the plaintiff and the character were the same person, the California Court of Appeal held that the issue was properly for the jury. An award to the plaintiff was upheld, perhaps because the evidence showed that the author of the novel had been a participant in the plaintiff's sessions.

In *Cullum v. White*,[144] the defendant in a defamation suit involving statements made in emails and on a website tried to avoid liability by arguing that statements on the website were fiction. A Texas appellate court rejected that argument because the jury could have found otherwise. According to the opinion by Justice Sandee Bryan Marion:

> As to the website, it included information that anyone acquainted with White would understand it referred to the Ranch and infer it related to White. The evidence demonstrated White had a long reputation as a Mary Kay representative and the webpage referred to a cosmetic connection. The webpage referred to a hunting ranch, to the FBI, animal abuse, murder, pathological liars, and alcohol sickness, all of which is similar to the information included in the emails. At trial, Cullum attempted to explain his comments as merely referring to a fictional book he was writing, but he admitted some of the ideas came from his time working at the Ranch. The jury could infer from Cullum's reference to the website in the Raglin email that it referred to White and the Ranch.[145]

Unbelievable Fiction. What saves many fiction writers from liability for defamation is the false-fact requirement (*see* Part D of this chapter). If the demeaning portrayal is so fantastic that it would not be believed, it may be impossible to establish that there was a provably false assertion of fact.

---

[142] 322 F.3d 918 (7th Cir. 2003).

[143] 92 Cal. App. 3d 61 (1979).

[144] 399 S.W.3d 173 (Tex. App. 2011).

[145] *Id.* at 182–83.

In *Pring v. Penthouse International, Ltd.*,[146] a real Miss Wyoming brought a suit based on a story about a fictional Miss Wyoming which described certain sexual activities. The court reversed a multi-million-dollar award to the plaintiff on the ground that the work, which described unbelievable events (*e.g.*, oral sex resulting in levitation), was a complete fantasy and could not possibly be understood as a statement of fact.

3. Institutional Plaintiffs

Business Reputation. A corporation or other business enterprise can be defamed with respect to its institutional characteristics, such as credit worthiness, efficiency, honesty, or fairness to customers. Thus, a manufacturer's allegations that a competitor pirated its designs may give the competitor a claim for defamation.[147] So, too, it is actionable to state falsely that a business has filed for bankruptcy.[148]

Direct Defamatory Innuendo. To be actionable, a statement must directly reflect on the institutional character of the plaintiff. Thus, in *Fairyland Amusement Co. v. Metromedia, Inc.*,[149] a federal court in Missouri held that a news report that there were increasing numbers of rapes in certain neighborhoods, did not defame an amusement park located in one of those areas. The court explained:

> A mere report of immoral or illegal activities "in and around" the premises cannot be fairly interpreted to mean that the business either negligently or purposefully encourages or acquiesces in such conduct. . . . [The report] did not cast any aspersion on the integrity or manner in which the corporate plaintiffs conduct their business. It did not suggest, for example, that they were insolvent, . . . that they were cheating their customers, . . . or that they were guilty of racial discrimination.[150]

Indirect Defamatory Innuendo. Statements about persons sometimes reflect adversely on the entities with which they are associated, and vice versa. In general, "words written about a corporate officer give no right of action to the corporation unless spoken or written in direct relation to the trade or business of the corporation."[151] Similarly, statements about an institutional entity do not defame its officers, directors, or employees, unless there is reason to conclude that the defamatory innuendo directly reflects on the performance and competence of such persons.

---

[146] 695 F.2d 438 (10th Cir. 1982).

[147] *See Fedders Corp. v. Elite Classics*, 279 F. Supp. 2d 965, 970–71 (S.D. Ill. 2003).

[148] *See Dun & Bradstreet, Inc. v. Greenmoss Builders, Inc.*, 472 U.S. 749 (1985).

[149] 413 F. Supp. 1290, 1295 (W.D. Mo. 1976).

[150] *Id.* at 1294–95.

[151] *Palm Springs Tennis Club v. Rangel*, 73 Cal. App. 4th 1, 5 (1999).

4.   Criticism of Ideas

It is difficult to prove that criticism of an idea amounts to defamation of a person who holds or advocates the idea. For example, in *Ezrailson v. Rohrich*,[152] the Texas Court of Appeals held that a medical research article, which criticized the creative research ideas behind a test relating to breast implant leakage, was not capable of a defamatory meaning as a matter of law. The court further explained that the author of the criticized article could not maintain a libel action because the defendant's article discussed the medical research test in question, rather than the plaintiff personally.

Of course, imputing an idea to a person may be defamatory, if subscription to the idea carries with it the sting of disgrace. Labeling someone a Holocaust-denier might be actionable; stating that a person is an environmentalist is not actionable.

5.   Defamation of the Dead

Defamation of the dead does not allow the decedent's estate to sue for libel or slander. Moreover, courts are reluctant to find that statements about deceased family members say something defamatory about the character of survivors.

For example, in *Rose v. Daily Mirror, Inc.*,[153] a newspaper article stated erroneously that the decedent, the father or husband of the plaintiffs, was "Baldy Jack Rose," a "self-confessed murderer" who had "lived in constant fear that emissaries of the underworld . . . would catch up with him and execute gang vengeance."[154] The plaintiffs were named by the article as the decedent's survivors, but nothing else was said about them. The New York Court of Appeals rejected the plaintiffs' claims for libel because "a libel or slander upon the memory of a deceased person which makes no direct reflection upon his relatives gives them no cause of action for defamation."[155]

6.   Unintended Reference to the Plaintiff

There are some cases which hold that unintended reference to the plaintiff is sufficient to satisfy the colloquium requirement. For example, in *Allied Marketing Group, Inc. v. Paramount Pictures Corp.*,[156] the television program aired a segment about a sweepstakes scam. According to the opinion of the Texas Court of Appeals:

> Paramount intended to use a fictional company name in connection with the . . . segment and thought that "Sweepstakes Clearing House" was a fictional name. However, unknown to Paramount, Allied had been using the name "Sweepstakes Clearinghouse" since 1984 in connection with a direct mail offer business. . . .

---

[152] 65 S.W.3d 373 (Tex. App. 2001).

[153] 31 N.E.2d 182 (N.Y. 1940).

[154] *Id.* at 182.

[155] *Id.*

[156] 111 S.W.3d 168 (Tex. App. 2003).

The court found that the program's segment on sweepstakes scams, which was not an obvious work of fiction, was "of and concerning" the sweepstakes company for purposes of a defamation action. Persons who knew the plaintiff could have concluded that the defamatory matter referred to the plaintiff. The show's fictional company name was identical to that of the real company, which was actually in the business of conducting sweepstakes contests. Moreover, one of the plaintiff's contests was very similar to the show's "scam" sweepstakes. The program segment did not indicate to viewers that the show's fictional company did not exist. The court concluded that "[b]ecause the test is based on the reasonable understanding of the viewer of the publication, it is not necessary for the plaintiff to prove that the defendant intended to refer to the plaintiff." Note, however, that while the court found that the colloquium requirement was satisfied, a plaintiff in this type of action may have difficulty establishing that the defendant acted with the requisite degree of fault as to the falsity of the defamatory statement. See Part G of this chapter.

PROBLEM 3-3: THE POOR BAR PASS RATE

The graduates of William Howard Taft School of Law have had trouble passing the state bar examination for many years. Despite the best efforts of the dean and law faculty, the school's passing rate for first-time test takers has hovered at roughly 40%, far behind the typical statewide average of 82%. Dean Alf Tilden, now in his fourth year as head of the school, has made improving bar passage the primary goal of his administration. All of the resources of the law school have been mobilized for the purpose of ensuring that graduates of Taft pass the bar on the first attempt in numbers exceeding the statewide average. By outlining a persuasive ten-point plan, Dean Tilden convinced many of the school's alumni to support his efforts with donations to a scholarship fund that help to ensure that students can focus on their studies and have the money they need to enroll in bar review courses between graduation and taking the bar.

When the results of the July bar examination were released, they showed that Taft graduates had made progress. The 100 first-time test takers from Taft passed the bar examination at a rate of 49%. The test results were not great, but they were a step in the right direction. However, when the local newspaper published an article about the bar results, it got some of the numbers wrong. The article said that 89% of all test takers had passed; in fact, the number was 82%. The article also said that only 34% of Taft graduates had passed the examination, rather than 49%. Who, if anyone, has been defamed by the erroneous report of the July bar results?

F. PUBLICATION

Communication to One Person Who Understands. In the law of defamation, "publication" is a term of art. It has nothing in particular to do with rolling the printing presses or preparing a manuscript for sale. Rather, it simply denotes communication of defamatory matter to a third person (other than the plaintiff) who understands. Thus, whispering in the ear of a friend, sending a text message, or posting a note on a public bulletin board can constitute publication.

There is a quaint old case that nicely illustrates what publication means. In *Economopoulos v. A. G. Pollard Co.*,[157] when one clerk accused the plaintiff in English of stealing a handkerchief, no one was present. When a second clerk made a similar accusation in Greek, the persons present (other than the plaintiff) did not understand Greek. The Supreme Judicial Court of Massachusetts held that no cause of action for defamation was stated because of lack of publication.

Communication solely to the plaintiff does not constitute an actionable publication. Libel and slander are mainly concerned with the loss of esteem and regard in the eyes of others.

Culpability Required. To be actionable, publication must be attributable to fault on the part of the defendant. There is no strict liability for defamatory information that is communicated when someone unforeseeably overhears a conversation or reads a private letter. The defendant must have intended to publish the information to the recipient or done so carelessly (*i.e.*, negligently or recklessly).

Disclosure by the Plaintiff with Knowledge of the Defamatory Content. In some cases, it is foreseeable to the originator of a written defamatory statement that the recipient will communicate the statement to a third person. Whether the originator will be held liable for the publication generally depends upon whether the recipient was aware of the libelous nature of the statement. If the recipient is *unaware* of what the statement says, and if transmission of the statement is foreseeable to the originator, the originator may be found to have published the statement to the third person. The *Restatement* offers illustrations of a letter sent to a blind person, who gives it to a family member to read to the blind person,[158] and of a letter written in a foreign language, which is given to a translator.[159] In these kinds of cases, it is fair to hold the originator liable when the third person learned of the defamatory content.

In contrast, if the recipient is *aware* of the defamatory content of the originator's statement, but repeats it or shows it to another person, the recipient is deemed to be responsible for the communication and the originator is not the publisher.[160] This is true even if the originator can foresee the plaintiff's repetition or transmission of the defamatory material.

Liability for Republication by Persons Other Than the Plaintiff. New York follows a strict rule that limits the liability of the originator of defamation for harm caused by repetition of that statement by others. In *Geraci v. Probst*,[161] Chief Judge Jonathan Lippman wrote for the New York Court of Appeals:

> Our republication liability standard has been consistent for more than one hundred years.

---

[157] 105 N.E. 896 (Mass. 1914).

[158] RESTATEMENT (SECOND) OF TORTS § 577 illus. 10 (1977).

[159] *Id.* illus. 11 (1977).

[160] *Id.* cmt. m (1977).

[161] 938 N.E.2d 917 (N.Y. 2010).

"It is too well settled to be now questioned that one who utters a slander, or prints and publishes a libel, is not responsible for its voluntary and unjustifiable repetition, without his authority or request, by others over whom he has no control and who thereby make themselves liable to the person injured, and that such repetition cannot be considered in law a necessary, natural and probable consequence of the original slander or libel" . . .

The rationale behind this rule is that each person who repeats the defamatory statement is responsible for the resulting damages. . . .

Applying this standard, we find that the defendants are not responsible for any harm plaintiff may have suffered from the 2005 *Newsday* article and that the article should not have been admitted into evidence. Plaintiff failed to demonstrate that Probst had any connection whatsoever with the *Newsday* article. Notably, the article was published more than three years after Probst wrote the letter to the Board. There is no evidence that Probst contacted anyone at *Newsday* in order to induce them to print his allegations. Nor is there evidence that anyone at *Newsday* contacted Probst regarding the story. Finally, there is no indication that Probst had any control over whether or not *Newsday* published the article. "[A]bsent a showing that [defendant] approved or participated in some other manner in the activities of the third-party republisher" (*Karaduman v. Newsday, Inc.*, 416 N.E.2d 557 [N.Y. 1980]), there is no basis for allowing the jury to consider the article containing the republished statement as a measure of plaintiff's damages attributable to defendants.

Plaintiff asserts that defendants should be liable for the damages caused by the *Newsday* article because republication was to be reasonably expected. Specifically, plaintiff argues that when allegations of this type of misconduct are made against a public official, it is reasonable as a matter of law to expect that those allegations will be newsworthy and that it would then be a matter for the factfinder as to whether it would be objectively reasonable to expect republication in the media under the facts of a particular case.

It is true that in dicta in *Karaduman* we left open the possibility that three reporters could have been held legally responsible for the republication of their article in book form "had plaintiff been able to demonstrate that they participated in the original publication with knowledge or a reasonable expectation that republication was likely". . . . This standard also appears in the *Restatement* (*see Restatement [Second] of Torts* § 576[c] ["The publication of a libel or slander is a legal cause of any special harm resulting from its repetition by a third person if, but only if, . . . the repetition was reasonably to be expected"]).

But the *Restatement* "foreseeability" standard is not nearly as broad as plaintiff or the dissent suggest. Comment d explains that a republication may be foreseeable "[i]f the defamation is repeated by a person to whom it is published" if the originator of the statement "had reason to expect that it would be so repeated." The obvious example is when a person makes a defamatory statement to a newspaper reporter who, in turn, repeats it in a newspaper article. . . . The second example in comment d occurs when the originator of a statement "widely disseminated the defamation and thus intimated to those who heard it that he [or she] is not unwilling to have it known to a large number of people." Neither of these circumstances is present here: Probst never made any statements to *Newsday* reporters (and *Newsday* apparently did not contact him before publishing the story), nor did Probst "widely disseminate" the allegations concerning plaintiff. Thus, even if we were to adopt the *Restatement's* foreseeability standard, it would not lead us to the conclusion urged by plaintiff.[162]

1.   "Compelled" Self-Publication

Occasional decisions have recognized a theory of "compelled" self-publication. These cases have usually reasoned that an employee was "compelled" to publish a defamatory statement by a former employer to a prospective employer to explain a change of jobs. For example, in *Kuechle v. Life's Companion P.C.A., Inc.*,[163] the Minnesota Court of Appeals held that because a nurse was told that her former employer had reported her alleged misconduct to the Nurse's Board, the nurse had no reasonable means to avoid self-publishing the statement to a new employer, even though she was not asked about the reasons for her termination. Quoting an earlier decision of the Minnesota Supreme Court, the intermediate tribunal explained:

> The concept of compelled self-publication does no more than hold the originator of the defamatory statement liable for damages caused by the statement where the originator knows, or should know, of circumstances whereby the defamed person has no reasonable means of avoiding publication of the statement or avoiding the resulting damages. . . .[164]

Generally Rejected. Many courts have rejected the concept of "compelled" self-publication[165] or expressed hostility to it. For example, in *White v. Blue Cross and Blue Shield of Massachusetts, Inc.*,[166] the Supreme Judicial Court of Massachusetts noted that the highest courts of four states (Iowa, Minnesota, Missouri, and North Carolina) had recognized the doctrine, but found support for this theory of publication was far from unanimous. In an opinion rejecting the concept of "compelled" self-publication, the Chief Justice Margaret H. Marshall wrote:

> We recognize the conundrum faced by discharged employees who are required by prospective employers to explain the circumstances of their discharge. But as the leading authority on defamation has explained, compelled self-publication defamation in the employment context is "troubling conceptually." [1 *R.D. Sack, Libel, Slander, and Related Problems* § 2.5.2, at 2-84 (3d ed. 1994 & Supp. 2003).] "It is the termination and the

---

[162] *Id.* at 919–22.

[163] 653 N.W.2d 214, 219–20 (Minn. Ct. App. 2002).

[164] *Id.* at 219 (quoting *Lewis v. Equitable Life Assur. Soc'y*, 389 N.W.2d 876, 886 (Minn. 1986)).

[165] *See, e.g., Gonsalves v. Nissan Motor Corp.*, 58 P.3d 1196 (Haw. 2002).

[166] 809 N.E.2d 1034 (Mass. 2004).

reasons for it, not the communication, about which the plaintiff is actually complaining. . . ." . . . Any harm arising from the employee's discharge is more appropriately dealt with under principles of employment law, and not under the law of libel and slander. . . .[167]

In *Olivieri v. Rodriguez*,[168] a federal constitutional action involving a probationary police officer, the Seventh Circuit wrote:

> The [plaintiff's] position resembles the largely discredited doctrine of "compelled republication" or (more vividly) "self-defamation," which allows the victim of a defamation to satisfy the requirement of publication by publishing it himself, for example to prospective employers as in the present case. . . . The doctrine is inconsistent with the fundamental principle of mitigation of damages. . . . Most states . . . reject self-defamation as a basis for a tort claim, and it would be odd for federal constitutional law to embrace this questionable doctrine.

Legislative Barriers. Some states have legislatively rejected "compelled" self-publication. Thus, a Colorado statute provides:

> No action for libel or slander may be brought or maintained unless the party charged with such defamation has published, either orally or in writing, the defamatory statement to a person other than the person making the allegation of libel or slander. Self-publication, either orally or in writing, of the defamatory statement to a third person by the person making such allegation shall not give rise to a claim for libel or slander against the person who originally communicated the defamatory statement.[169]

Minnesota has not legislatively rejected the "compelled" self-publication theory which has been recognized by Minnesota courts. However, the legislature has passed a law which addresses the issue of grounds for termination. The statute provides:

> *Subdivision 1. Notice required.*
>
> An employee who has been involuntarily terminated may, within fifteen working days following such termination, request in writing that the employer inform the employee of the reason for the termination. Within ten working days following receipt of such request, an employer shall inform the terminated employee in writing of the truthful reason for the termination.

---

[167] *Id.* at 1037.

[168] 122 F.3d 406 (7th Cir. 1997).

[169] Colo. Rev. Stat. Ann. § 13-25-125.5 (LEXIS 2014).

Subdivision 2. Defamation action prohibited.

No communication of the statement furnished by the employer to the employee under subdivision 1 may be made the subject of any action for libel, slander, or defamation by the employee against the employer.[170]

It is hard to see how this law, which has rarely been cited by courts, does anything more than say that one cannot bring a defamation action based on truth. Another Minnesota law limits the use of the "compelled" self-publication theory in defamation actions involving communications obtained by an employee based on review of the employee's personnel records.[171]

2.   Distributors of Defamatory Publications

Publishers Versus Distributors. The law draws a distinction between "publishers" and "distributors." Whereas a "publisher" of defamation is subject to liability, a mere "distributor" is not.

Bookstores and Libraries. Conduits of information, such as bookstores, libraries, printers, and newspaper deliverers, which are unaware of the defamatory content of the materials they disseminate, are often classified as "distributors." On that ground, they escape liability for libel and slander, since either form of defamation action requires "publication."

Of course, a bookstore or other information conduit that purveys materials that it knows to be false and defamatory is likely to be treated as a "publisher." It will therefore be subject to liability.

The term "distributor" reflects an interpretation of the second requirement of a defamation action — publication — in a way that anticipates the third requirement of a defamation action — fault as to falsity. It will be difficult or impossible to show that an information conduit that was unaware of the content of defamatory material acted with fault as to the falsity of those statements. No one reasonably expects information conduits, such as bookstores, to read all of their volumes to determine if any contain defamation. Practically speaking, the only way to show fault as to falsity is to prove that the information conduit was aware of the false contents.

Editorial Control. Publishers of newspapers and magazines exercise editorial control over the content of their publications. Therefore, they do not qualify as mere distributors and are subject to liability. For example, in *Flowers v. Carville*,[172] a federal court in Nevada held that the plaintiff stated a cause of action against a publisher who allegedly knew that a book contained false and defamatory statements about the plaintiff's alleged affair with a former President.

---

[170] Minn. Stat. Ann. § 181.933 (LEXIS 2014).

[171] *Id.* § 181.962 Subd. 2 (LEXIS 2014).

[172] 266 F. Supp. 2d 1245 (D. Nev. 2003).

3.   Statements on the Internet

Not a "Publisher." The Communications Decency Act insulates various potential defendants from liability by addressing the issue of "publication." Under the Act, "No provider or user of an interactive computer service shall be treated as the publisher or speaker of any information provided by another information content provider."[173] The Communications Decency Act is discussed in Part I-1 of this chapter.

4.   Intra-Entity and Fellow Agent Communications

Some states hold that communications between constituents of the same entity (*e.g.*, between officers or employees of a corporation)[174] or between agents of the same principal (*e.g.*, between a client's lawyer and accountant) are not "publications" for the purposes of the law of defamation. Under this view, the corporation or principal is merely communicating with itself, not with a third party.

The *Restatement*[175] and many states[176] take a contrary position. They reason that a corporation's constituent members (*e.g.*, officers, directors, and employees) and a principal's co-agents are individuals distinct from the entity or principal, and those individuals have personal views which may be affected by the intra-entity or co-agent communications of defamatory matter. Thus, in *Bals v. Verduzco*,[177] the Indiana Supreme Court labeled the no-publication view an "unacceptable legal fiction."

The better view is to treat intra-entity or co-agent communications as publications, but recognize that a cause of action may be barred by a qualified privilege. (Qualified privileges are discussed in Part I-4 of this chapter.) In *Staples v. Bangor Hydro-Elec. Co.*,[178] the Supreme Judicial Court of Maine endorsed this approach, noting that "damage to one's reputation within the corporate community may be as devastating as that outside" and that "the defense of qualified privilege provides adequate protection."

PROBLEM 3-4: THE BOTCHED COVER LETTER

Seeking to find a better position as an executive corporate assistant, Carolyn Mason hired an Internet-based job search firm, Talent Ltd., to assist her in locating the right potential employer. For $1500, Talent Ltd. promised to revise Mason's resume into a letter format and then mail the resume to 500 "key decision-makers" in large corporations who were likely to know of, and have the authority to fill, non-advertised employment opportunities.

---

[173] 47 U.S.C.S. § 230(c)(1) (LEXIS 2014).

[174] *See Starr v. Pearle Vision, Inc.*, 54 F.3d 1548 (10th Cir. 1995) (Oklahoma law).

[175] *See* RESTATEMENT (SECOND) OF TORTS § 577 cmt. i (1977).

[176] *See Popko v. Continental Cas. Co.*, 823 N.E.2d 184 (Ill. App. Ct. 2005); *Simpson v. Mars, Inc.*, 929 P.2d 966 (Nev. 1997).

[177] 600 N.E.2d 1353, 1356 (Ind. 1992).

[178] 629 A.2d 601, 604 (Me. 1993).

After Talent Ltd. prepared the letter, Mason approved its text. The first sentence of the letter read: "Currently seeking new challenges as a corporate executive assistant, I am a detail-oriented professional possessing 20 years of related leadership experience."

Following the mailing of the letter to 500 prospective employers, Mason was given a CD. A cover letter said that the disk contained files with all of the merge-printed correspondence, as well as an Excel spreadsheet with the employers' names. Mason could use the spreadsheet to keep track of acknowledgment correspondence and other follow-up contacts.

Mason did not examine the CD immediately. However, after three weeks had passed and she had not heard from any potential employer, she opened the files on the CD. She found that every letter contained a serious typographical error. The first sentence of each letter read, "Currently seeking new challenges as a 70 E.S1 B,EWI.5391 position, I am a detail-oriented professional possessing 20 years of related leadership experience." That was not the text she had approved.

Mason believes that she has been defamed to 500 excellent prospective employers and that her career prospects have been seriously harmed. Please prepare an analysis of the issues Mason will face in a libel suit against Talent Ltd.

G. FAULT AS TO FALSITY UNDER CONSTITUTIONAL PRINCIPLES

Three Varieties of Fault. The term "fault as to falsity" relates to the purported falsity of the defamatory statement. "Fault as to falsity" comes in at least three varieties. The most culpable variety is knowledge of falsity. The next variety — reckless disregard for the truth — is treated as just as bad as knowledge of falsity, at least if "reckless" means that the defendant acted with subjective awareness of the defamatory statement's probable falsity. The least blameworthy variety of fault as to falsity is negligence. Whether fault as to falsity must be proved in a libel or slander action, and if so, to what degree, depends on the way that the case is categorized.

As alluded to earlier in this chapter, the current configuration of constitutional precedent indicates that there are three types of defamation cases: (1) cases where public officials or public figures are suing with respect to matters of public concern; (2) cases where private persons are suing with respect to matters of public concern; and (3) cases where anyone is suing with respect to a matter of private concern.

[handwritten margin note: Types of const. defam. cases]

1. Category I: Public Officials and Public Figures Suing with Respect to Matters of Public Concern

Anyone who plays a large role in the life of the community is likely to be required to meet what is commonly referred to as the *New York Times* "actual malice" standard when bringing a suit for libel or slander. The evolution of this standard and its application are considered below.

a. Strict Liability at Common Law

At common law, it was unnecessary to show that the defendant knew or should have known that a statement was false. Moreover, the defendant did not even have to be aware that the statement referred to the plaintiff or that it was defamatory. For example, in an English case, *Cassidy v. Daily Mirror Newspapers, Ltd.*,[179] a newspaper article said that a Mr. Cassidy was engaged to a woman pictured in the paper. Both had consented to allow the paper to announce their engagement. The newspaper did not know that Cassidy was already married. In a subsequent defamation suit by Cassidy's wife, the court held that she had been libeled by the newspaper. Her acquaintances testified that they inferred from the article that Mrs. Cassidy was not in fact married to Cassidy, with whom she was living — which at the time was thought to cause serious harm to her reputation.

Thus, under traditional rules, libel and slander did not require proof of fault on the part of a defendant who published defamatory information. It was accurate to say that "[a]t common law, libel was a strict liability tort that did not require proof of falsity, fault, or actual damages."[180] This is no longer true. The rules began to change in 1964 in *New York Times Co. v. Sullivan*.[181]

b. *New York Times v. Sullivan*

By any fair standard, the United States Supreme Court's decision in *New York Times Co. v. Sullivan*[182] is a true landmark. It began the process of reconciling traditional defamation law with the constitutional demands of the First Amendment. So powerful has been the force of *New York Times Co. v. Sullivan* that the decision and its progeny have utterly transformed the law of defamation. It is impossible to think about any libel or slander claim in a complete way without positioning the facts within the matrix of principles that have evolved from *New York Times Co. v. Sullivan* and later decisions. Those cases today exert a dominant force on the analysis of whether, and to what extent, the plaintiff must prove that the defendant was at fault with respect to the falsity of the defamatory statement, and whether damages may be presumed rather than proved.

An Advertisement in Support of the Civil Rights Movement. Justice William J. Brennan, Jr. delivered the opinion of the Court in *New York Times Co. v. Sullivan*.[183] As he explained the suit, he said that the Court was required "to determine for the first time the extent to which the constitutional protections for speech and press limit a State's power to award damages in a libel action brought by a public official against critics of his official conduct."[184] Turning to the facts of the lawsuit, Justice Brennan wrote:

---

[179] 2 K.B. 331 (1929).

[180] *Mathis v. Cannon*, 573 S.E.2d 376, 380 (Ga. 2002).

[181] 376 U.S. 254 (1964).

[182] *Id.* at 254.

[183] *Id.*

[184] *Id.* at 256.

Respondent L. B. Sullivan is one of the three elected Commissioners of the City of Montgomery, Alabama. [His duties included supervision of the Police Department.]. . . . He brought this civil libel action against the four individual petitioners, who are Negroes and Alabama clergymen, and against petitioner the New York Times Company, a New York corporation which publishes . . . a daily newspaper. A jury in the Circuit Court of Montgomery County awarded him damages of $500,000, the full amount claimed, against all the petitioners, and the Supreme Court of Alabama affirmed. . . .

Respondent's complaint alleged that he had been libeled by statements in a full-page advertisement . . . [relating to the civil rights movement for racial equality.]. . . .

The text appeared over the names of 64 persons, many widely known for their activities in public affairs, religion, trade unions, and the performing arts. . . .

Of the 10 paragraphs of text in the advertisement, the third and a portion of the sixth were the basis of respondent's claim of libel. . . .

. . . .

It is uncontroverted that some of the statements contained in the two paragraphs were not accurate descriptions of events which occurred in Montgomery. . . . Although the police were deployed near the campus in large numbers on three occasions, they did not at any time "ring" the campus, and they were not called to the campus in connection with the demonstration on the State Capitol steps, as the third paragraph implied. Dr. King had not been arrested seven times, but only four; and although he claimed to have been assaulted some years earlier in connection with his arrest for loitering outside a courtroom, one of the officers who made the arrest denied that there was such an assault.

[Respondent was not mentioned by name.] On the premise that the charges in the sixth paragraph could be read as referring to him, respondent was allowed to prove that he had not participated in the events described. . . .[185]

Traditional Libel Law. Turning, then, to the proceedings in the Alabama courts, Justice Brennan explained:

The trial judge submitted the case to the jury under instructions that the statements in the advertisement were "libelous *per se*" and were not privileged, so that petitioners might be held liable if the jury found that they had published the advertisement and that the statements were made "of and concerning" respondent. . . .

---

[185] *Id.* at 256–59.

Under Alabama law as applied in this case . . . [o]nce "libel *per se*" has been established, the defendant has no defense as to stated facts unless he can persuade the jury that they were true in all their particulars. . . .[186]

"Uninhibited, Robust and Wide-Open." Justice Brennan then began to lay the intellectual foundations on which the modern of law defamation would be built. He stated:

The First Amendment, said Judge Learned Hand, "presupposes that right conclusions are more likely to be gathered out of a multitude of tongues, than through any kind of authoritative selection. To many this is, and always will be, folly; but we have staked upon it our all." . . . Mr. Justice Brandeis, in his concurring opinion in *Whitney v. California*, [274 U.S. 357 (1927)], gave the principle its classic formulation:

Those who won our independence believed . . . that public discussion is a political duty; and that this should be a fundamental principle of the American government. They recognized the risks to which all human institutions are subject. But they knew that order cannot be secured merely through fear of punishment for its infraction; that it is hazardous to discourage thought, hope and imagination; that fear breeds repression; that repression breeds hate; that hate menaces stable government; that the path of safety lies in the opportunity to discuss freely supposed grievances and proposed remedies; and that the fitting remedy for evil counsels is good ones. Believing in the power of reason as applied through public discussion, they eschewed silence coerced by law — the argument of force in its worst form. Recognizing the occasional tyrannies of governing majorities, they amended the Constitution so that free speech and assembly should be guaranteed.

Thus we consider this case against the background of a profound national commitment to the principle that debate on public issues should be uninhibited, robust and wide-open, and that it may well include vehement, caustic, and sometimes unpleasantly sharp attacks on government and public officials. . . . The present advertisement, as an expression of grievance and protest on one of the major public issues of our time, would seem clearly to qualify for the constitutional protection. The question is whether it forfeits that protection by the falsity of some of its factual statements and by its alleged defamation of respondent.

. . . As Madison said, "Some degree of abuse is inseparable from the proper use of every thing; and in no instance is this more true than in that of the press." . . . In *Cantwell v. Connecticut*, 310 U.S. 296, the Court declared:

In the realm of religious faith, and in that of political belief, sharp differences arise. In both fields the tenets of one man may seem the rankest error to his neighbor. To persuade others to his own point of view, the pleader, as we know, at times, resorts to exaggeration, to

---

[186] *Id.* at 262–67.

vilification of men who have been, or are, prominent in church or state, and even to false statement. But the people of this nation have ordained in the light of history, that, in spite of the probability of excesses and abuses, these liberties are, in the long view, essential to enlightened opinion and right conduct on the part of the citizens of a democracy.

[The] erroneous statement is inevitable in free debate, and . . . it must be protected if the freedoms of expression are to have the "breathing space" that they "need . . . to survive". . . .[187]

The Defense of Truth Is Not Sufficient. Justice Brennan then turned to the question of what these principles of free expression mean to the law of defamation, writing:

> What a State may not constitutionally bring about by means of a criminal statute is likewise beyond the reach of its civil law of libel. The fear of damage awards under a rule such as that invoked by the Alabama courts here may be markedly more inhibiting than the fear of prosecution under a criminal statute. . . . Presumably a person charged with violation of [a criminal libel] statute enjoys ordinary criminal-law safeguards such as the requirements of an indictment and of proof beyond a reasonable doubt. These safeguards are not available to the defendant in a civil action. The judgment awarded in this case — without the need for any proof of actual pecuniary loss — was one thousand times greater than the maximum fine provided by the Alabama criminal statute. . . . And since there is no double jeopardy limitation applicable to civil lawsuits, this is not the only judgment that may be awarded against petitioners for the same publication. Whether or not a newspaper can survive a succession of such judgments, the pall of fear and timidity imposed upon those who would give voice to public criticism is an atmosphere in which the First Amendment freedoms cannot survive. . . .
>
> The state rule of law is not saved by its allowance of the defense of truth. . . . A rule compelling the critic of official conduct to guarantee the truth of all his factual assertions — and to do so on pain of libel judgments virtually unlimited in amount — leads to a comparable "self-censorship." Allowance of the defense of truth, with the burden of proving it on the defendant, does not mean that only false speech will be deterred. . . . Under such a rule, would-be critics of official conduct may be deterred from voicing their criticism, even though it is believed to be true and even though it is in fact true, because of doubt whether it can be proved in court or fear of the expense of having to do so. . . . The rule thus dampens the vigor and limits the variety of public debate. It is inconsistent with the First and Fourteenth Amendments.[188]

The "Actual Malice" Standard. Justice Brennan's opinion for the court then laid down the rule for which *New York Times Co. v. Sullivan* has become famous:

---

[187] *Id.* at 270–73.

[188] *Id.* at 277–79.

The constitutional guarantees require, we think, a federal rule that prohibits a public official from recovering damages for a defamatory falsehood relating to his official conduct unless he proves that the statement was made with "actual malice" — that is, with knowledge that it was false or with reckless disregard of whether it was false or not. An oft-cited statement of a like rule, which has been adopted by a number of state courts, is found in the Kansas case of *Coleman v. MacLennan*, 78 Kan. 711, 98 P. 281 (1908). . . . On appeal the Supreme Court of Kansas, in an opinion by Justice Burch, reasoned as follows:

> [I]t is of the utmost consequence that the people should discuss the character and qualifications of candidates for their suffrages. The importance to the state and to society of such discussions is so vast, and the advantages derived are so great that they more than counterbalance the inconvenience of private persons whose conduct may be involved, and occasional injury to the reputations of individuals must yield to the public welfare, although at times such injury may be great. The public benefit from publicity is so great and the chance of injury to private character so small that such discussion must be privileged.

. . . .

We hold today that the Constitution delimits a State's power to award damages for libel in actions brought by public officials against critics of their official conduct. Since this is such an action, the rule requiring proof of actual malice is applicable. . . .[189]

Failure to Meet the Standard. The court then returned to the facts of the pending case to measure them against the constitutional standard:

> . . . [W]e consider that the proof presented to show actual malice lacks the convincing clarity which the constitutional standard demands, and hence that it would not constitutionally sustain the judgment for respondent under the proper rule of law. The case of the individual petitioners requires little discussion. Even assuming that they could constitutionally be found to have authorized the use of their names on the advertisement, there was no evidence whatever that they were aware of any erroneous statements or were in any way reckless in that regard. The judgment against them is thus without constitutional support.
>
> As to the Times, we similarly conclude that the facts do not support a finding of actual malice. The statement by the Times' Secretary that, apart from the padlocking allegation, he thought the advertisement was "substantially correct," affords no constitutional warrant for the Alabama Supreme Court's conclusion that it was a "cavalier ignoring of the falsity of the advertisement. . . . Z" The statement does not indicate malice at the time of the publication; even if the advertisement was not "substantially correct" — although respondent's own proofs tend to show that it was — that opinion was at least a reasonable one, and there was no evidence to

---

[189] *Id.* at 279–83.

impeach the witness' good faith in holding it. The Times' failure to retract upon respondent's demand, although it later retracted upon the demand of Governor Patterson, is likewise not adequate evidence of malice for constitutional purposes. Whether or not a failure to retract may ever constitute such evidence, there are two reasons why it does not here. First, the letter written by the Times reflected a reasonable doubt on its part as to whether the advertisement could reasonably be taken to refer to respondent at all. Second, it was not a final refusal, since it asked for an explanation on this point — a request that respondent chose to ignore. Nor does the retraction upon the demand of the Governor supply the necessary proof. It may be doubted that a failure to retract which is not itself evidence of malice can retroactively become such by virtue of a retraction subsequently made to another party. But in any event that did not happen here, since the explanation given by the Times' Secretary for the distinction drawn between respondent and the Governor was a reasonable one, the good faith of which was not impeached.

Finally, there is evidence that the Times published the advertisement without checking its accuracy against the news stories in the Times' own files. The mere presence of the stories in the files does not, of course, establish that the Times "knew" the advertisement was false, since the state of mind required for actual malice would have to be brought home to the persons in the Times' organization having responsibility for the publication of the advertisement. With respect to the failure of those persons to make the check, the record shows that they relied upon their knowledge of the good reputation of many of those whose names were listed as sponsors of the advertisement, and upon the letter from A. Philip Randolph, known to them as a responsible individual, certifying that the use of the names was authorized. There was testimony that the persons handling the advertisement saw nothing in it that would render it unacceptable under the Times' policy of rejecting advertisements containing "attacks of a personal character"; their failure to reject it on this ground was not unreasonable. We think the evidence against the Times supports at most a finding of negligence in failing to discover the misstatements, and is constitutionally insufficient to show the recklessness that is required for a finding of actual malice. . . .

We also think the evidence was constitutionally defective in another respect: it was incapable of supporting the jury's finding that the allegedly libelous statements were made "of and concerning" respondent. . . . There was no reference to respondent in the advertisement, either by name or official position. A number of the allegedly libelous statements . . . did not even concern the police. . . . The statements upon which respondent principally relies as referring to him are the two allegations that did concern the police or police functions: that "truckloads of police . . . ringed the Alabama State College Campus" after the demonstration on the State Capitol steps, and that Dr. King had been "arrested . . . seven times." These statements were false only in that the police had been "deployed near" the campus but had not actually "ringed" it and had not gone there in connection with the State Capitol demonstration, and in that Dr. King had been arrested only four times. The ruling that these discrepancies between what was true and what was asserted were sufficient to injure respondent's reputation may itself raise constitutional problems, but we need not consider them here. Although the statements may be taken as referring to the police, they do not on their face make even an oblique reference to respondent as an individual. . . .

. . . The present proposition would sidestep this obstacle by transmuting criticism of government, however impersonal it may seem on its face, into personal criticism, and hence potential libel, of the officials of whom the government is composed. . . . We hold that such a proposition may not constitutionally be utilized to establish that an otherwise impersonal attack on governmental operations was a libel of an official responsible for those operations. . . .[190]

The Vote: 9-0. Five justices (Warren, C.J., and Clark, Harlan, Stewart, and White, JJ.) joined Justice Brennan's opinion, which reversed the judgment of the Alabama Supreme Court and remanded the case for further proceedings. Justices Hugo Black and Arthur Goldberg filed concurring opinions, each of which would have categorically denied any action for defamation to a public official based on public conduct. Justice William O. Douglas joined in both of the concurring opinions.

c. Who Is a Public Official?

"Public Official" Versus "Public Employee." The "actual malice" requirement does not apply to every defamation plaintiff who is on the government payroll. Thus, not every "public employee" is a "public official." For example, in *Anaya v. CBS Broadcasting Inc.*,[191] a federal court in New Mexico held that a procurement agent employed by a government-run defense lab was not a public official.

The Test for Defining "Public Official." "It is clear . . . that the 'public official' designation applies at the very least to those among the hierarchy of government employees who have, or appear to the public to have, substantial responsibility for or control over the conduct of governmental affairs."[192] Thus, the term may apply to the executive director of a housing authority[193] or of a lottery.[194]

The Test. Ultimately, the test is whether the "position in government has such apparent importance that the public has an independent interest in the qualifications and performance of the person who holds it, beyond the general public interest in the qualifications and performance of all governmental employees."[195]

---

[190] *Id.* at 285–92.

[191] 626 F. Supp. 2d 1158 (D.N.M. 2009).

[192] *Rosenblatt v. Baer*, 383 U.S. 75, 85 (1966).

[193] *See Ortego v. Hickerson*, 989 So. 2d 777 (La. Ct. App. 2008).

[194] *See Cloud v. McKinney*, 228 S.W.3d 326 (Tex. App. 2007).

[195] *Rosenblatt v. Baer*, 383 U.S. 75, 86 (1966).

Expansive Interpretation. Courts have often interpreted the public official category expansively, including such persons as a physician who served on a state medical board.[196] Police officers of all varieties are routinely classified as public officials.[197] Depending on the facts, lower echelon employees, such as a county surveyor,[198] a teacher who is also the school's athletic director,[199] a state university's director of the Office of Community Standards,[200] or a child protective services specialist,[201] may all be deemed to be public officials.

Former Public Officials. A former public official may be subject to the actual malice requirement. This is true at least if the allegedly defamatory statement relates to the former public official's performance while in office.[202]

Relationship to Public Performance. The actual malice rule applies to public officials only if the defamatory statement relates to the official's qualifications. "[A] statement that the governor drinks himself into a drunken stupor at home every night much more clearly affects his qualifications than a statement that a tax assessor keeps a secret collection of pornographic pictures."[203]

d.   Treating Public Figures the Same as Public Officials

Soon after *New York Times Co. v. Sullivan* was decided, the actual malice rule was expanded to cover not only "public officials," but also "public figures." As recounted in *Mathis v. Cannon*[204] by the Supreme Court of Georgia:

> [I]n *Curtis Publishing Co. v. Butts*, [388 U.S. 130 (1967)] a majority of the Court applied the *New York Times* rule on actual malice to criticism of "public figures," defined as individuals who are "intimately involved in the resolution of important public questions or, by reason of their fame, shape events in areas of concern to society at large." The Court found that Wally Butts, the University of Georgia athletic director, had attained his status as a public figure by his position alone; the second plaintiff, a retired army officer, had achieved public figure status "by his purposeful activity amounting to a thrusting of his personality into the 'vortex' of an important public controversy," the racial integration of the University of Mississippi. The rationale for extending the constitutional privilege to protect criticism of public figures was the increasingly blurred distinctions between the

---

[196] *See Hotze v. Miller*, 361 S.W.3d 707 (Tex. App. 2012).

[197] *See Smith v. Huntsville Times Co., Inc.*, 888 So. 2d 492 (Ala. 2004); *Tomkiewicz v. Detroit News, Inc.*, 635 N.W.2d 36 (Mich. Ct. App. 2001).

[198] *See Foster v. Laredo Newspapers, Inc.*, 541 S.W.2d 809, 814 (Tex. 1976).

[199] *See Johnson v. Southwestern Newspapers Corp.*, 855 S.W.2d 182, 186–87 (Tex. App. 1993).

[200] *See Fiacco v. Sigma Alpha Epsilon Fraternity*, 528 F.3d 94 (1st Cir. 2008).

[201] *See Villarreal v. Harte-Hanks Communications, Inc.*, 787 S.W.2d 131, 133–35 (Tex. App. 1990).

[202] *Rosenblatt v. Baer*, 383 U.S. 75 (1966). *See* Joseph H. King, *Whither the "Paths of Glory": The Scope of the New York Times Rule in Defamation Claims by Former Public Officials and Candidates*, 38 VERMONT L. REV. 275 (2013).

[203] RESTATEMENT (SECOND) OF TORTS § 580A cmt. b (1977).

[204] 573 S.E.2d 376, 381 (Ga. 2002).

governmental and private sectors: "In many situations, policy determinations which traditionally were channeled through formal political institutions are now originated and implemented through a complex array of boards, committees, commissions, corporations, and associations, some only loosely connected with the Government."[205]

PROBLEM 3-5: THE LAW CLERK AT THE STATE SUPREME COURT

Jordan Kelly thought that he had landed a great job when he was offered a clerkship by a justice of the state supreme court. The pay was low, about one-third of what a top law school graduate could make at a big law firm. But the prestige was high.

Clerking for a supreme court justice meant assisting the justice with research and writing in the cases that came before the court, and recommending how disputed issues should be decided. A top-flight judicial clerkship was the best credential anyone could earn right out of law school. A clerkship at the state high court had long-term cachet. And after the one year of economic sacrifice while clerking, clerks who accepted offers from big firms were phased in at second-year associate salaries and sometimes were paid handsome "signing bonuses." That was a great plus, but it is also where the problem started.

Kelly started working at the court the Tuesday after Labor Day. During the first week, he never came close to thinking about a pending case. The entire four days were taken up with an "orientation" program for the fourteen new clerks who would work for the seven justices on the supreme court. The program focused on judicial ethics, online legal research, judicial writing styles, data security, and court protocol.

The following day (Saturday), a story broke in the state's leading newspaper, The Capital Bulletin, which claimed that several supreme court clerks had accepted obscenely large signing bonuses from large law firms that had cases pending before the state supreme court. It was not clear whether the clerks who were involved were members of the last clerkship "class" (who had just finished their clerkship year) or members of the new clerkship class (who were just starting). The paper did not name names, but it quoted anonymous "reliable sources." The story quickly triggered a weekend blizzard of criticism that ended up being directed mainly at the justices of the state supreme court, although the justices' clerks were condemned, too.

Bloggers and talk show hosts had a field day. Kelly received an endless stream of calls and text messages from former classmates wanting to know what was going on. He said that he did not know who was involved, or even whether there was any truth to the allegations.

On Monday, Kelly found his picture and photos of the other thirteen new law clerks on the front page of The Capital Bulletin. Apparently the names of the clerks had been assembled from a press release the court had issued about the diversity of the new clerkship class. The photos seemed to have been gathered from

---

[205] *Id.* at 381.

Facebook and MySpace, or perhaps from the "Entering Class" booklets that had been published at some of the law schools the clerks had attended. The Monday article stuck to its original story, but it still did not name names as to which clerks had accepted the enormous signing bonuses.

As a result of these events, Kelly's year at the supreme court started out with a fiasco. All of his former classmates and professors were speculating about whether he was involved in the scandal. Kelly has not yet lined up a post-clerkship job, and he now realizes that it will not be as easy as he thought it would be. Rather than the luster of an honorable supreme court clerkship, he will be tainted by association with a corruption scandal.

If Kelly sues the Bulletin for defamation, will he be able to prove that its stories defamed him? And, if so, will he have to prove that the editors acted with actual malice?

e.   Proving "Actual Malice"

(1)   The Meaning of "Actual Malice"

Focus on the Defendant's Subjective State of Mind. Actual malice is a state of mind about the falsity of a defamatory statement. The only way to establish actual malice is to prove that the defendant knew that the statement was false or consciously acted with reckless disregard for whether or not it was false. In either case, the test is subjective. "Knowledge" of falsity means that the defendant subjectively knew that the statement was false. It is not enough that a reasonably prudent person would have known, or should have known, that the statement was false. Likewise, recklessness in the context of actual malice is a subjective test. Only persons who publish defamation with subjective "awareness of probable falsity" are reckless.[206]

A defamation case litigated in Texas settled after one day of trial when the plaintiff produced an e-mail showing that the defendant had expressly threatened to defame the plaintiff. That documentary evidence, coupled with the stark disparity between the defamatory communication and a favorable contemporaneous performance evaluation authored by the defendant, would have been enough to prove actual malice.

Erroneous Beliefs Honestly Held. The statement of an erroneous belief that is honestly held, which has some factual support, cannot ordinarily be found to have been uttered with actual malice. For example, in *Peter Scalamandre & Sons, Inc. v. Kaufman,*[207] the defendant asserted that the plaintiff conducted "an illegal haul and dump operation" and that the "people of Texas are being poisoned." Because statements were shown at trial to be the defendant's honest beliefs and were not so without basis as to constitute reckless disregard for the truth, the Fifth Circuit held that the plaintiff's cause of action failed.

---

[206] *St. Amant v. Thompson*, 390 U.S. 727, 731 (1968).

[207] 113 F.3d 556, 562 (5th Cir. 1997).

Similarly, in *Sparks v. Peaster*,[208] the Georgia Court of Appeals held that a city manager did not act with actual malice when he said that a resident had a serious cocaine habit. The evidence showed that the plaintiff was confrontational and sometimes irrational, and that police officers had given the manager reason to believe that the plaintiff had a problem with drugs.

Inattention to the Truth. One consequence of focusing defamation litigation on the issue of actual malice is that attention shifts from whether the statement was true or false to what the defendant subjectively knew. This may make it impossible for the plaintiff to clear his or her name by obtaining a ruling on falsity.

Disruption of the Editorial Processes. In cases involving media defendants, litigation of the actual malice issue may be highly disruptive to editorial processes. The publisher's state of mind must normally be inferred from circumstantial evidence. Consequently, plaintiffs often seek discovery of information about such matters as communications between reporters and editors, facts known but not used in a story, the pressures under which the work was prepared, and the identity and credibility of the defendant's sources.

"Actual Malice," Not "Express" or "Common-Law" Malice. "Actual malice," as used in defamation cases, is a term of art which must be clearly distinguished from "express" or "common-law" malice. The fact that statements are uttered with spite, ill will, vindictiveness, or motives of revenge says nothing about whether those statements are true or false. Therefore, a showing that the defendant was actuated by bad motives (sometimes called "express malice" or "common-law malice") is not, by itself, sufficient to satisfy the actual-malice requirement.

Jury instructions may not permit a finding of actual malice to be based merely upon proof of hatred, enmity, desire to injure, or the like. As the United States Supreme Court observed in *Garrison v. State of Louisiana*,[209] a criminal defamation case:

> [T]he great principles of the Constitution which secure freedom of expression . . . preclude attaching adverse consequences to any except the knowing or reckless falsehood. Debate on public issues will not be uninhibited if the speaker must run the risk that it will be proved in court that he spoke out of hatred; even if he did speak out of hatred, utterances honestly believed contribute to the free interchange of ideas and the ascertainment of truth. Under a rule . . . permitting a finding of [actual] malice based on an intent merely to inflict harm, rather than to inflict harm through falsehood, "it becomes a hazardous matter to speak out against a popular politician, with the result that the dishonest and incompetent will be shielded." . . . Moreover, "[i]n the case of charges against a popular political figure . . . it may be almost impossible to show freedom from ill-will or selfish political motives." . . .
>
> . . . [O]nly those false statements made with the high degree of awareness of their probable falsity demanded by *New York Times* may be the subject

---

[208] 581 S.E.2d 579 (Ga. Ct. App. 2003).

[209] 379 U.S. 64 (1964).

of either civil or criminal sanctions. . . . [The Constitution protects even] vehement, caustic, and sometimes unpleasantly sharp attacks on government and public officials.[210]

Of course, in many instances, if evidence of express malice is coupled with facts showing that the defendant lacked an honest belief in the truth of the statements, there may be "actual malice" sufficient to support a finding of liability, as well as facts that encourage a jury to return a large judgment.

Lack of Thorough Investigation. Failing to thoroughly investigate a story may be negligence, but it does not, by itself, amount to actual malice. For example, in *St. Amant v. Thompson,*[211] the Supreme Court held that relying on a single, perhaps unreliable, source without attempting to verify the accuracy of statements was not "reckless" within the meaning of the "actual malice" standard. However, the *St. Amant* Court did acknowledge that:

> Professions of good faith will be unlikely to prove persuasive, for example, where a story is fabricated by the defendant, is the product of his imagination, or is based wholly on an unverified anonymous telephone call. Nor will they be likely to prevail when the publisher's allegations are so inherently improbable that only a reckless man would have put them in circulation. Likewise, recklessness may be found where there are obvious reasons to doubt the veracity of the informant or the accuracy of his reports.[212]

Failure to Consult the Plaintiff or Present an Objective View. There is ordinarily no obligation on the defendant to talk to the subject of the defamatory communication to obtain that person's version of the events described.[213] Nor is actual malice proved by the fact that the defendant failed to present an objective picture of events.[214]

Departure from Journalistic Standards. In *Harte-Hanks Communications, Inc. v. Connaughton,*[215] the Supreme Court explained that "a public figure plaintiff must prove more than an extreme departure from professional standards and . . . a newspaper's motive in publishing a story — whether to promote an opponent's candidacy or to increase its circulation — cannot provide a sufficient basis for finding actual malice."[216] Thus, it is not surprising that factual inaccuracies alone do not prove actual malice,[217] nor does evidence that the reporting behind an article was speculative or even sloppy.[218]

---

[210] *Id.* at 73–75.

[211] 390 U.S. 727 (1968).

[212] *Id.* at 732.

[213] *See Rosenbloom v. Metromedia, Inc.*, 403 U.S. 29 (1971).

[214] *See New York Times Co. v. Connor*, 365 F.2d 567, 576 (5th Cir. 1966).

[215] 491 U.S. 657 (1989).

[216] *Id.* at 665.

[217] *See Time, Inc. v. Pape*, 401 U.S. 279 (1971).

[218] *See Oliver v. Village Voice, Inc.*, 417 F. Supp. 235, 238 (S.D.N.Y. 1976).

Anticipation of Financial Gain. The fact "[t]hat a defendant publishes statements anticipating financial gain [by itself] . . . fails to prove actual malice" for "a profit motive does not strip communications of constitutional protections."[219]

Failure to Retract. A defendant's subsequent conduct often does not establish the defendant's earlier state of mind. Thus, as the opinion in *New York Times v. Sullivan, supra,* indicates, a failure to retract an allegedly defamatory statement may be insufficient to establish actual malice, particularly where it is dubious that the statement referred to the plaintiff. The same analysis may apply if there has been no request for a retraction. Thus, in *Dongguk University v. Yale University,*[220] the Second Circuit reasoned that:

> Dongguk never requested a retraction from Yale after Yale had discovered its error. Thus, Dongguk's evidence of Yale's failure to expeditiously correct its earlier misstatements fails to provide any further support that any officials at Yale acted with actual malice at the time Reinstein's statements were made.[221]

However, if a defendant who refuses to retract was aware at the time of the original publication that its assertions were wrong, an action will lie. For example, in *Golden Bear Distributing Systems of Texas, Inc. v. Chase Revel, Inc.,*[222] an author's notes showed that she knew her article was incorrect.

Use of Recanted Statements. In *WJLA-TV v. Levin,*[223] an orthopedist was accused of sexually assaulting his female patients and using inappropriate medical procedures. The court held that the television station's use of the statements of a physician, which the station knew the physician had retracted, was sufficient to support a jury finding of actual malice. A $2 million award of presumed damages was upheld.

Disregard of Red Flags. In some instances, the presence of multiple red flags will show that the defendant acted in reckless disregard of the truth, and therefore with actual malice. For example, in *Young v. Gannett Satellite Information Network, Inc.,*[224] the Sixth Circuit explained the basic facts of the case before it:

> [T]he Miami Township police department fired Police Sergeant James Young for allegedly forcing sex on a woman he was said to be involved with. However, the termination was overturned by an arbitrator. The arbitrator stated that it was unclear what happened on the day in question but that the police department had not proven its allegations. The arbitrator's report also mentioned that DNA samples from the scene did not match Young and found that the complainant lacked credibility. Thirteen years later, a Gannett newspaper published the statement "Young had sex with a woman while on the job" in an article commenting on a local debate about

---

[219] *See Peter Scalamandre & Sons, Inc. v. Kaufman,* 113 F.3d 556, 561 (5th Cir. 1997).

[220] 734 F.3d 113 (2d Cir. 2013).

[221] *Id.* at 126.

[222] 708 F.2d 944 (5th Cir. 1983).

[223] 564 S.E.2d 383 (Va. 2002).

[224] 734 F.3d 544 (6th Cir. 2013).

the suspension of a different police officer. Young sued Gannett for defamation and obtained a $100,000 verdict. . . .[225]

The court concluded that "[t]here was sufficient evidence for a jury to decide that Gannett's editor knew that the accusation was probably false and that the editor published it regardless."[226] As the court explained:

> The jury could have properly relied upon the inclusion in the arbitrator's report of several statements that Herron should have seen as red flags. First, the report noted that the semen found on Phillips's carpet did not match Young's DNA. Second, the report cast serious doubts on Phillips's credibility. Third, it mentioned only a single incident that occurred while Young was on duty. As to that incident, the arbitrator noted that Phillips's accusation that Young forced her to perform oral sex "is not supported by the evidence" and that "[t]he lack of truthfulness by both parties . . . prevents any reasonable assessment of what happened." . . .

> Armed with that knowledge, Herron nevertheless published the statement "Young had sex with a woman while on the job" as if it were fact. This is reckless disregard of the truth at best, and is sufficient for the jury to have found that Gannett published the statement with actual malice. A newspaper cannot publish an accusation that it knows has no evidence behind it as a fact to fit its desired storyline and then cloak itself in the First Amendment.[227]

Conversely, the absence of red flags can help to show that a statement was not made with actual malice. For example, in *Trump v. O'Brien*,[228] a billionaire brought a libel action against the author of a book which understated his wealth. In affirming summary judgment for the defendant on the ground that the plaintiff failed to establish actual malice, a New Jersey appellate court noted:

> [W]e find no evidence to support Trump's conclusion that the confidential sources utilized by O'Brien were fictitious. . . . Further we find . . . no basis for Trump's argument that O'Brien had "obvious reasons to doubt the veracity of [his] informants or the accuracy of [their] reports." . . . There were no significant internal inconsistencies in the information provided by the confidential sources, nor was there "reliable" information that contradicted their reports. . . . Nothing suggests that O'Brien was subjectively aware of the falsity of his source's figures or that he had actual doubts as to the information's accuracy.[229]

Fabricated Statements. Suppose that a person knowingly files false criminal charges against another for the purpose of gaining leverage in a business dispute. The accusations are defamatory because they accuse another of crime and, because

---

[225] *Id.* at 545.

[226] *Id.*

[227] *Id.* at 547–48.

[228] 29 A.3d 1090 (N.J. Super. App. Div. 2011).

[229] *Id.* at 1101.

they are fabricated, they are published with actual malice.[230]

(2)   Standard of Proof and Judicial Review

Clear and Convincing Evidence of Actual Malice. Although other issues in a defamation action, such as proof of damages, are normally subject to a preponderance-of-the-evidence standard of proof,[231] actual malice must be established by clear and convincing evidence as matter of constitutional requirements.[232] This heightened standard of proof applies not only to jury determinations, but to preliminary rulings on motions for summary judgment.[233] Therefore, it is difficult for a plaintiff to survive a defendant's motion for summary disposition, for it is necessary to adduce evidence from which actual malice could be found by clear and convincing evidence.

Appellate Review of Actual Malice Findings. Whether the evidence supports a finding of actual malice is a question of law. In determining whether the constitutional standard is satisfied, the trial court and every reviewing court must consider the factual record in full to ascertain whether there is clear and convincing evidence.[234] Thus, a finding of actual malice is not entitled to the deference normally extended to findings of fact. This rule confers its substantial benefits exclusively on defendants because independent appellate review occurs only when the jury finds for the plaintiff. The no-deference rule, coupled with the clear-and-convincing-evidence standard, may do more to provide "breathing space" for free expression than the actual malice standard itself.

The independent review requirement does not extend to all elements of a defamation cause of action. For example, a jury's finding of falsity or substantial truth must be accepted if supported by substantial evidence.[235]

(3)   Applying Supreme Court Principles

(a)   Example: *Freedom Newspapers of Texas v. Cantu*

A typical state court decision applying United States Supreme Court principles is *Freedom Newspapers of Texas v. Cantu*.[236] *Cantu* nicely illustrates the challenges of proving actual malice in reporting. In that case, there was a debate between the candidates for sheriff in a predominantly Hispanic, south Texas county. The Democratic candidate (Cantu) was Hispanic and the Republican candidate (Vinson) was Anglo. The Democratic candidate urged during the debate

---

[230] *See Cluse v. H & E Equipment Services, Inc.*, 34 So. 3d 959, 971 (La. Ct. App. 2010).

[231] *But see Hornberger v. Am. Broad. Companies, Inc.*, 799 A.2d 566, 578 (N.J. Super. Ct. App. Div. 2002).

[232] *See Harte-Hanks Communications, Inc. v. Connaughton*, 491 U.S. 657, 661 n.2 (1989).

[233] *See Anderson v. Liberty Lobby, Inc.*, 477 U.S. 242, 255–56 (1986).

[234] *See Bose Corp. v. Consumers Union of the U.S., Inc.*, 466 U.S. 485 (1984).

[235] *See Lundell Mfg. Co., Inc. v. Am. Broad. Companies, Inc.*, 98 F.3d 351 (8th Cir. 1996).

[236] 168 S.W.3d 847 (Tex. 2005).

that he was the best candidate, stating in part:

> Mr. Vinson is a nice man, but he is an instructor, he is not a sheriff. You have
> to have the right character to be a sheriff and you have to delegate
> authority and it does not stop there. You have to be bi-cultural to
> understand what is going on in our neighborhoods, where there is a lot of
> burglaries, how are you going to relate to these people — in Spanish — and
> make them understand that they need to stop or we are going to put a stop
> to it in their neighborhoods. . . . You have to be able to understand, you
> have to have grown up here to understand that.[237]

The Offending Headline. Afterwards, a newspaper article about the debate
carried the following provocative headline:

> Cantu: No Anglo can be sheriff of Cameron County.[238]

Cantu took exception to the article and its headline because he had never used
the word "Anglo." In response to his protest, the newspaper published a second
article with a clarifying headline stating, "Sheriff candidate says racial issue wasn't
the point."[239] After winning the election, Cantu sued the newspaper for defamation.
Eventually, a unanimous Texas Supreme Court concluded that:

> The summary judgment record before us establishes as a matter of law
> that the Herald's reporter thought he was reporting the gist of what Cantu
> said. Accordingly, any error in the Herald's articles evidences at most
> negligence, not actual malice. We reverse the court of appeals' judgment
> and render judgment that Cantu take nothing.[240]

Words Never Used. In explaining its decision, the Texas Supreme Court first
concluded, consistent with United States Supreme Court precedent, that the fact
that the sheriff did not use the exact words attributed to him was not evidence of
actual malice. The court wrote:

> From the day the articles appeared through oral arguments in this Court,
> Cantu's primary complaint is that he never used the words attributed to
> him by the Herald in its initial headline and first sentence. The Herald
> concedes this is true. The court of appeals concluded this was some
> evidence of malice, as "Pierce attended the debate and heard the candi-
> date's comments, and knew that Cantu did not say that 'No Anglo can be
> sheriff of Cameron County.'"
>
> But unlike the court of appeals, the Herald did not put this last phrase in
> quotation marks. While some of Cantu's statements at the debate were
> placed in quotation marks, this one was not. Cantu discounts this distinc-
> tion, arguing the colon used in the headline is the "equivalent" of quotation
> marks.

---

[237] *Id.* at 850.

[238] *Id.*

[239] *Id.* at 851.

[240] *Id.* at 859.

In *Masson v. New Yorker Magazine, Inc.*,[241] the United States Supreme Court held that placing a reporter's words in a speaker's mouth may be evidence of malice in some circumstances. As the Court noted:

> In general, quotation marks around a passage indicate to the reader that the passage reproduces the speaker's words verbatim. They inform the reader that he or she is reading the statement of the speaker, not a paraphrase or other indirect interpretation by an author.

But the Court rejected the notion that every alteration of a speaker's words was some evidence of actual malice. The Court noted that reporters who rely on notes must often reconstruct a speaker's statements, and even those who rely on recordings can print statements verbatim "in only rare circumstances" due to space limitations and editorial judgments.

Instead, the Court held that an altered statement could constitute some evidence of actual malice if a reasonable reader could understand the passage as the speaker's actual words (not a paraphrase), and the alteration was material. . . .

In this case, three rather apparent clues would lead a reasonable reader to conclude the Herald was interpreting Cantu's remarks rather than quoting them verbatim. First, such a reader would note that quotation marks were placed around eight of Cantu's statements in the first article, but not the one at issue.

Second, a reasonable reader could not miss the pattern of the articles, in which a summary of what each candidate said appears in one paragraph . . . followed by one or two paragraphs of explicit quotations to support the summary. In this context, a reasonable reader would understand the first headline and sentence to be a paraphrase of Cantu's remarks, with his actual statements following in quotations.

Finally, while both articles were allegedly defamatory, the Herald's second article reported Cantu's response that "I did not say that an Anglo could not be sheriff." Nothing in the follow-up article contradicts that claim. To the contrary, the report that "some observers believe" Cantu had made "discriminating remarks" at the debate clarified that the issue was the implicit rather than explicit meaning of what he said.

Based on the entire context of the articles Cantu claims were defamatory, we hold that a reasonable reader would have understood the Herald's reports to be a paraphrase or interpretation of Cantu's remarks. Accordingly, proof that he did not make the exact remark attributed to him, standing alone, is no evidence of actual malice.[242]

Rational Interpretation of Ambiguities. Elaborating on the same theme, the Texas Supreme Court explained:

---

[241] [n.15] 501 U.S. 496, 519–20 (1991).

[242] 168 S.W.3d at 854–55.

Of course, deliberately attributing a statement to a public figure that the latter never made may be defamatory whether or not it is in quotation marks. . . .

Cantu argues that the Herald made a deliberate and material change in meaning when it converted his remarks about his bilingual and bicultural attributes into remarks about racial and ethnic ones. For summary judgment purposes, we assume the truth of Cantu's assertion that he intended only the former. Further, we agree with Cantu that reasonable jurors could conclude from the Herald's report that he was accused of intending the latter, and that the difference between the two is material.

But evidence that the Herald's report was mistaken, even negligently so, is no evidence of actual malice. Cantu must present some evidence that the Herald misinterpreted his remarks on purpose, or in circumstances so improbable that only a reckless publisher would have made the mistake. "An understandable misinterpretation of ambiguous facts does not show actual malice."

In *Time, Inc. v. Pape*, the Supreme Court addressed a similar defamation claim in which the words of a source were undisputed but their meaning was ambiguous.[243] In that case, a report on police brutality by the U.S. Commission on Civil Rights cited allegations from a civil lawsuit asserting misconduct by Chicago police. In its article on the Commission's report, Time magazine stated the allegations as fact, omitting the word "alleged" that appeared in the report.

But while the Commission's report did list the incident as "alleged," in fact the report was "extravagantly ambiguous" about whether the allegations were true. The Commission summarized the contents of the report as "the alleged facts of 11 typical cases of police brutality," though of course none could be "typical cases" of brutality unless they were true. While the report stated that the truth of each incident was a matter for the courts, the Commission cited no other evidence of brutality to support the changes it recommended. In this context, the Supreme Court held that reporting the Chicago incident as factual was a rational interpretation of what the Commission's report impliedly said:

> Time's omission of the word "alleged" amounted to the adoption of one of a number of possible rational interpretations of a document that bristled with ambiguities. The deliberate choice of such an interpretation, though arguably reflecting a misconception, was not enough to create a jury issue of "malice" under *New York Times*. To permit the malice issue to go to the jury because of the omission of a word like "alleged," despite the context of that word in the Commission Report and the external evidence of the Report's overall meaning, would be to

---

[243] [n.25] 401 U.S. 279 (1971).

impose a much stricter standard of liability on errors of interpretation or judgment than on errors of historic fact.[244]

In this case, Cantu's remarks at the debate also "bristled with ambiguities." Cantu argues that his comments had nothing to do with race, as anyone can be both bilingual and bicultural. But the context here was a debate in which Cantu was distinguishing himself from his opponent. Cantu conceded at his deposition that he knew his opponent was not Hispanic, but did not know whether he spoke Spanish; at the least, this might suggest he was using "bilingual" to indicate the former rather than latter. And Cantu does not explain why his opponent was not "bicultural," despite claiming many more years of experience in law enforcement in the Rio Grande Valley than Cantu.

. . . .

While Cantu never used the explicit words stated in the Herald's initial article, the standard is whether that summary was a rational interpretation of what he said.[245] Pleas for ethnic solidarity or racial prejudice are not always made in explicit terms. As Justice Peeples noted in analyzing such a plea in the context of a jury argument, "[t]o permit the sophisticated ethnic plea while condemning those that are open and unabashed would simply reward counsel for ingenuity in packaging."[246] Similarly, holding that headlines like the one here are actionable unless candidates make an explicit ethnic plea would reward candidates who make implicit ones by punishing the press for reporting on it.

. . . The difference in the candidates' ethnic backgrounds were apparently obvious to those who attended the debate, and as we have noted the terms Cantu used to distinguish himself are similar to those sometimes used for ulterior purposes. Further, while the record does not reflect the composition of the audience at the debate, the wider audience is a matter of record — according to the U.S. Census taken in the year of the election, 84.3% of Cameron County residents were persons of Hispanic or Latino origin. If Cantu's only purpose was to emphasize his community ties, he could have chosen less ambiguous terms.

. . . Based on the entire context of the debate, we hold that the Herald's articles were a rational interpretation of Cantu's remarks at the debate. Accordingly, the articles standing alone were not evidence of actual malice.[247]

---

[244] [n.31] *Id.* at 290.

[245] [n.33] *Pape*, 401 U.S. at 290.

[246] [n.34] *Tex. Employers' Ins. Ass'n v. Guerrero*, 800 S.W.2d 859, 862–63 (Tex. App. — San Antonio 1990, writ denied) (holding that argument by plaintiff's counsel that "by golly there comes a time when we have got to stick together as a community" was incurable when plaintiff and 11 members of jury had Spanish surnames).

[247] 168 S.W.3d at 855–57.

Evidence of Dislike for the Plaintiff. The Texas Supreme Court next concluded that out-of-court statements indicating that the officers of the newspaper disliked Cantu were not evidence of actual malice.

> . . . Cantu detailed several out-of-court statements by Herald reporters to the effect that the officers of the paper "don't like you" and "had it out" for him. Assuming the truth of this hearsay, it only establishes ill will, which is not proof of actual malice. Jurors cannot impose liability on the basis of a defendant's "hatred, spite, ill will, or desire to injure."[248] "[E]vidence of pressure to produce stories from a particular point of view, even when they are hard-hitting or sensationalistic, is no evidence of actual malice." "[A]ctual malice concerns the defendant's attitude toward the truth, not toward the plaintiff." While a personal vendetta demonstrated by a history of false allegations may provide some evidence of malice, free-floating ill will does not.[249]

Rejection of Alternative Interpretation. The Texas Supreme Court also dismissed the idea that rejection of an alternative interpretation of the events is evidence of actual malice. The court explained:

> . . . [T]he court of appeals pointed to the second Herald article as proof that the paper changed nothing after learning of Cantu's objections and receiving an audiotape of the debate. "The mere fact that a defamation defendant knows that the public figure has denied harmful allegations or offered an alternative explanation of events is not evidence that the defendant doubted the allegations." In the world of politics, "such denials are so commonplace . . . they hardly alert the conscientious reporter to the likelihood of error."[250] The Herald's prompt follow-up article quoting Cantu's version of his remarks and the opinions of his supporters is evidence of the absence of actual malice, not the opposite. . . .[251]

Subsequent Events. The court next found that subsequent events had little significance to the issue of actual malice. It wrote:

> [The court of appeals] . . . pointed to the questions [that the newspaper editor] Cox raised after reading the first article as some evidence that the newspaper entertained doubts about its veracity. But "the focus of the actual-malice inquiry is the defendant's state of mind during the editorial process. Evidence concerning events after an article has been printed and distributed, has little, if any, bearing on that issue."[252]

Expert Opinions on Reporting Bias. Finally, the Texas Supreme Court concluded that expert opinions on whether reporting is biased are not useful. It explained:

---

[248] [n.39] *Letter Carriers v. Austin*, 418 U.S. 264, 281 (1974).

[249] 168 S.W.3d at 857–58.

[250] [n.44] *Harte-Hanks Communications, Inc. v. Connaughton*, 491 U.S. 657, 692 n.37 (1989).

[251] 168 S.W.3d at 858.

[252] *Id.*

. . . [T]he court of appeals pointed to the opinions of an "expert journalist" criticizing the Herald's handling of the story and finding a consistent pattern of biased reporting regarding Cantu. But actual malice inquires only into the mental state of the defendant, and the expert claimed no particular expertise in that field. Nor was his opinion based on anything other than the articles themselves and the circumstantial evidence already discussed. Even assuming this evidence was competent, his opinions cannot show that the Herald knew its articles were not a rational interpretation of Cantu's remarks.[253]

The Role of the Press in the Internet Age. In summary, the Texas Supreme Court explained:

> "[P]erhaps the largest share of news concerning the doings of government appears in the form of accounts of reports, speeches, press conferences, and the like." While an increasing number of such "doings" can be viewed in full by those with Internet access and sufficient time, most members of the public rely on the myriad of other news outlets — traditional and otherwise — to provide them with a summary. As a result, press reports generally must include not a transcript of what was said but a distillation and analysis of its implications.

> "Any departure from full direct quotation of the words of the source, with all its qualifying language, inevitably confronts the publisher with a set of choices." Since the founding of the nation, political candidates have complained that those choices sometimes appear to adopt the most unflattering and controversial interpretation possible. But nothing in the Constitution requires the press to adopt favorable attitudes toward public figures.[254]

PROBLEM 3-6: THE RACIAL PROFILING STORY

The producers of a television "news magazine" decided to do a show on racial profiling. They hired three African-American teenagers to drive a new Lincoln Town Car after dark on the largely vacant downtown streets of a large city. The objective was to see if the teenagers would be stopped by police and how they would be dealt with.

When the Lincoln changed lanes without signaling, it was pulled over by two white police officers in a cruiser. Another police car with two more white officers soon arrived. The officers asked the teenagers for identification. Things were said by the officers and the teenagers. Ultimately, the teenagers were ordered out of the car and frisked. A search of the vehicle ensued, which included the opening of the trunk and of packages located in the backseat. No contraband was found. After that, the teenagers were released. Most of these events were captured by two cameras hidden in the Lincoln and by a third camera in a van which photographed the events at a distance.

---

[253] *Id.* at 858–59.

[254] *Id.* at 859.

The footage relating to the stop comprised about nine minutes of the 22-minute segment of the televised program which dealt with racial profiling. The segment was called "Driving While African-American." While the video of the stop was shown on the program, it was narrated by the program host, Benjamin Franklin Bernstein, an "investigative journalist" who had gained a reputation for "over the top" reporting and use of inflammatory language. As the footage was shown, a professor from Joseph Story School of Law discussed the action. The comments were recorded sometime after the actual police stop but before the show was televised. The professor had seen only part of the footage related to the stop. On the program segment that was aired, the professor said that the search of the car was illegal under the Fourth Amendment and that the footage appeared to be a casebook example of racial profiling. Bernstein likewise opined, "police target African-Americans when they are driving simply because they are black." Viewers were told about how the producers had hired the teenagers to drive the Lincoln as an "experiment" to see how the police would react.

The material about the stop and search of the Lincoln was sandwiched between two other segments of the program which offered egregious examples of racial profiling. In the one instance, an African-American teenager was killed during a traffic stop. In the other case, police shot an African-American husband when they were called to a home to investigate domestic violence that was in progress.

After the program aired, it was widely discussed on the web and in the press. Many experts took the position that the Lincoln was stopped and investigated lawfully. Other experts asserted that the police officers had acted unconstitutionally and that a car full of white teenagers would not have been stopped for changing lanes without signaling.

The four officers involved in the search of the Lincoln were not named on the program, although the city and the police department to which the officers belonged were named. The images of the search were sufficiently clear that the officers could be identified by persons who knew them.

After the program aired, the police department conducted an investigation of the stop. That action caused the officers considerable distress and embarrassment. Although no disciplinary action was taken against the officers, it seems clear that their connection to the racial profiling story has hurt their careers.

As a result of their fathers' roles in the events in question, children of three of the four officers have been subjected to abuse by other students at schools where they are enrolled.

The officers have consulted you about whether they can bring a suit for fraud or defamation against the producers of the news magazine or persons associated with that production. Please prepare a preliminary analysis of the issues.

2.   Category II: Private Persons Suing with Respect to Matters of Public Concern

After the *New York Times* actual-malice requirement was extended to public figures, a plurality of the court voted to go even further. *Rosenbloom v. Metromedia, Inc.*[255] held that actual malice had to be proved in any case involving a "matter of public concern." However, *Rosenbloom* was soon repudiated in *Gertz v. Robert Welch, Inc.*[256]

a.   *Gertz v. Robert Welch, Inc.*

A Lawyer Defamed as a "Communist-Fronter." In *Gertz*, a youth (Nelson) was shot and killed by a police officer (Nuccio), who was later convicted of homicide. The youth's family retained attorney Elmer Gertz (later the "petitioner") to represent them in civil litigation arising from the death. In this capacity, Gertz attended the coroner's inquest into the boy's death and initiated actions for damages. However, he neither discussed Officer Nuccio with the press nor played any part in the criminal proceeding.

Notwithstanding Gertz's minor connection with the criminal prosecution of Nuccio, an article in respondent's magazine (American Opinion) portrayed him as an architect of a plan to "frame" the police officer. American Opinion was an outlet for the views of the anti-communist John Birch Society.

The article contained serious inaccuracies. The implication that petitioner had a criminal record was false. There was no evidence that he or an organization to which he belonged had taken any part in planning the 1968 demonstrations in Chicago. There was also no basis for the charge that petitioner was a "Leninist" or a "Communist-fronter." Moreover, he had never been a member of the "Marxist League for Industrial Democracy" or the "Intercollegiate Socialist Society." The managing editor of American Opinion had made no effort to verify or substantiate the charges against petitioner, but had nevertheless appended an editorial introduction stating that the author had "conducted extensive research into the Richard Nuccio Case."

The District Court denied the defendant's motion to dismiss petitioner's libel action. After the evidence was presented, it "ruled in effect that petitioner was neither a public official nor a public figure," and it submitted the issue of damages to the jury, which awarded $50,000. On further reflection, the District Court concluded that the *New York Times* standard applied and entered judgment for defendant notwithstanding the jury verdict. This action was affirmed by the Court of Appeals for the Seventh Circuit, on the basis of *Rosenbloom v. Metromedia, Inc.*[257]

The Standard for Public Persons. Justice Lewis F. Powell, Jr. delivered the opinion for the Court. The opinion charted a new direction for an important range

[255] 403 U.S. 29 (1971).
[256] 418 U.S. 323 (1974).
[257] 403 U.S. 29 (1971).

of cases in defamation law. Justice Powell wrote:

> The principal issue in this case is whether a newspaper or broadcaster that publishes defamatory falsehoods about an individual who is neither a public official nor a public figure may claim a constitutional privilege against liability for the injury inflicted by those statements. . . .

> The legitimate state interest underlying the law of libel is the compensation of individuals for the harm inflicted on them by defamatory falsehood. We would not lightly require the State to abandon this purpose, for, as Mr. Justice Stewart has reminded us, the individual's right to the protection of his own good name "reflects no more than our basic concept of the essential dignity and worth of every human being — a concept at the root of any decent system of ordered liberty. . . ."

> Some tension necessarily exists between the need for a vigorous and uninhibited press and the legitimate interest in redressing wrongful injury.
> . . .

> The *New York Times* standard defines the level of constitutional protection appropriate to the context of defamation of a public person. Those who, by reason of the notoriety of their achievements or the vigor and success with which they seek the public's attention, are properly classified as public figures and those who hold governmental office may recover for injury to reputation only on clear and convincing proof that the defamatory false-hood was made with knowledge of its falsity or with reckless disregard for the truth. This standard administers an extremely powerful antidote to the inducement to media self-censorship of the common-law rule of strict liability for libel and slander. And it exacts a correspondingly high price from the victims of defamatory falsehood. Plainly many deserving plain-tiffs, including some intentionally subjected to injury, will be unable to surmount the barrier of the *New York Times* test. Despite this substantial abridgment of the state law right to compensation for wrongful hurt to one's reputation, the Court has concluded that the protection of the *New York Times* privilege should be available to publishers and broadcasters of defamatory falsehood concerning public officials and public figures. . . . We think that these decisions are correct. . . . For reasons stated below, we conclude that the state interest in compensating injury to the reputation of private individuals requires that a different rule should obtain with respect to them.[258]

Reasons for Treating Private Persons Differently. Justice Powell then explained why private persons stand on different footing than public persons:

> The first remedy of any victim of defamation is self-help — using available opportunities to contradict the lie or correct the error and thereby to minimize its adverse impact on reputation. Public officials and public figures usually enjoy significantly greater access to the channels of effective communication and hence have a more realistic opportunity to counteract

---

[258] 418 U.S. at 332–43.

false statements than private individuals normally enjoy. Private individuals are therefore more vulnerable to injury, and the state interest in
protecting them is correspondingly greater.

More important . . . , there is a compelling normative consideration
underlying the distinction between public and private defamation plaintiffs.
An individual who decides to seek governmental office must accept certain
necessary consequences of that involvement in public affairs. He runs the
risk of closer public scrutiny than might otherwise be the case. . . .

Those classed as public figures stand in a similar position. Hypothetically,
it may be possible for someone to become a public figure through no
purposeful action of his own, but the instances of truly involuntary public
figures must be exceedingly rare. For the most part those who attain this
status have assumed roles of especial prominence in the affairs of society.
Some occupy positions of such persuasive power and influence that they are
deemed public figures for all purposes. More commonly, those classed as
public figures have thrust themselves to the forefront of particular public
controversies in order to influence the resolution of the issues involved. In
either event, they invite attention and comment.

Even if the foregoing generalities do not obtain in every instance, the
communications media are entitled to act on the assumption that public
officials and public figures have voluntarily exposed themselves to increased risk of injury from defamatory falsehood concerning them. No such
assumption is justified with respect to a private individual. He has not
accepted public office or assumed an "influential role in ordering society."
. . . He has relinquished no part of his interest in the protection of his own
good name, and consequently he has a more compelling call on the courts
for redress of injury inflicted by defamatory falsehood. Thus, private
individuals are not only more vulnerable to injury than public officials and
public figures; they are also more deserving of recovery.

For these reasons we conclude that the States should retain substantial
latitude in their efforts to enforce a legal remedy for defamatory falsehood
injurious to the reputation of a private individual. . . .[259]

Rejection of Rosenbloom. Justice Powell then explained why the Court's
decision in *Rosenbloom* had erred.

The extension of the *New York Times* test proposed by the *Rosenbloom*
plurality would abridge this legitimate state interest [in compensating
harm to reputation] to a degree that we find unacceptable. And it would
occasion the additional difficulty of forcing state and federal judges to
decide on an *ad hoc* basis which publications address issues of "general or
public interest" and which do not — to determine, in the words of Mr.
Justice Marshall, "what information is relevant to self-government." . . .
We doubt the wisdom of committing this task to the conscience of judges.
Nor does the Constitution require us to draw so thin a line between the

---

[259] *Id.* at 344–46.

drastic alternatives of the *New York Times* privilege and the common law of strict liability for defamatory error. The "public or general interest" test for determining the applicability of the *New York Times* standard to private defamation actions inadequately serves both of the competing values at stake. On the one hand, a private individual whose reputation is injured by defamatory falsehood that does concern an issue of public or general interest has no recourse unless he can meet the rigorous requirements of *New York Times*. This is true despite the factors that distinguish the state interest in compensating private individuals from the analogous interest involved in the context of public persons. On the other hand, a publisher or broadcaster of a defamatory error which a court deems unrelated to an issue of public or general interest may be held liable in damages even if it took every reasonable precaution to ensure the accuracy of its assertions. And liability may far exceed compensation for any actual injury to the plaintiff, for the jury may be permitted to presume damages without proof of loss and even to award punitive damages.[260]

New Rule for Private Persons Suing with Respect to Matters of Public Concern. Justice Powell then set the standards for what have become known as *Gertz*-type cases, defamation suits involving private persons and matters of public concern:

> [S]o long as they do not impose liability without fault, the States may define for themselves the appropriate standard of liability for a publisher or broadcaster of defamatory falsehood injurious to a private individual. . . . .
>
> . . . [W]e endorse this approach in recognition of the strong and legitimate state interest in compensating private individuals for injury to reputation. But this countervailing state interest extends no further than compensation for actual injury. For the reasons stated below, we hold that the States may not permit recovery of presumed or punitive damages, at least when liability is not based on a showing of knowledge of falsity or reckless disregard for the truth.
>
> The common law of defamation is an oddity of tort law, for it allows recovery of purportedly compensatory damages without evidence of actual loss. Under the traditional rules pertaining to actions for libel, the existence of injury is presumed from the fact of publication. Juries may award substantial sums as compensation for supposed damage to reputation without any proof that such harm actually occurred. The largely uncontrolled discretion of juries to award damages where there is no loss unnecessarily compounds the potential of any system of liability for defamatory falsehood to inhibit the vigorous exercise of First Amendment freedoms. Additionally, the doctrine of presumed damages invites juries to punish unpopular opinion rather than to compensate individuals for injury sustained by the publication of a false fact. . . . [S]tates have no substantial interest in securing for plaintiffs such as this petitioner gratuitous awards of money damages far in excess of any actual injury.

---

[260] *Id.* at 346.

. . . We need not define "actual injury," as trial courts have wide experience in framing appropriate jury instructions in tort actions. Suffice it to say that actual injury is not limited to out-of-pocket loss. Indeed, the more customary types of actual harm inflicted by defamatory falsehood include impairment of reputation and standing in the community, personal humiliation, and mental anguish and suffering. . . . [T]here need be no evidence which assigns an actual dollar value to the injury.

. . . Like the doctrine of presumed damages, jury discretion to award punitive damages unnecessarily exacerbates the danger of media self-censorship, but, unlike the former rule, punitive damages are wholly irrelevant to the state interest that justifies a negligence standard for private defamation actions. They are not compensation for injury. . . . In short, the private defamation plaintiff who establishes liability under a less demanding standard than that stated by *New York Times* may recover only such damages as are sufficient to compensate him for actual injury.[261]

Application to the Facts in Gertz. Justice Powell then turned to an analysis of the facts in *Gertz* under the new rules:

[R]espondent contends that we should affirm the judgment below on the ground that petitioner is either a public official or a public figure. There is little basis for the former assertion. Several years prior to the present incident, petitioner had served briefly on housing committees appointed by the mayor of Chicago, but at the time of publication he had never held any remunerative governmental position. Respondent admits this but argues that petitioner's appearance at the coroner's inquest rendered him a "*de facto* public official." Our cases recognize no such concept. Respondent's suggestion would sweep all lawyers under the *New York Times* rule as officers of the court and distort the plain meaning of the "public official" category beyond all recognition. We decline to follow it.

Respondent's characterization of petitioner as a public figure raises a different question. . . .

Petitioner has long been active in community and professional affairs. He has served as an officer of local civic groups and of various professional organizations, and he has published several books and articles on legal subjects. Although petitioner was consequently well known in some circles, he had achieved no general fame or notoriety in the community. None of the prospective jurors called at the trial had ever heard of petitioner prior to this litigation, and respondent offered no proof that this response was atypical of the local population. We would not lightly assume that a citizen's participation in community and professional affairs rendered him a public figure for all purposes. Absent clear evidence of general fame or notoriety in the community, and pervasive involvement in the affairs of society, an individual should not be deemed a public personality for all aspects of his life. It is preferable to reduce the public-figure question to a more

---

[261] *Id.* at 346–50.

meaningful context by looking to the nature and extent of an individual's participation in the particular controversy giving rise to the defamation.

In this context it is plain that petitioner was not a public figure. He played a minimal role at the coroner's inquest, and his participation related solely to his representation of a private client. He took no part in the criminal prosecution of Officer Nuccio. Moreover, he never discussed either the criminal or civil litigation with the press and was never quoted as having done so. He plainly did not thrust himself into the vortex of this public issue, nor did he engage the public's attention in an attempt to influence its outcome. We are persuaded that the trial court did not err in refusing to characterize petitioner as a public figure for the purpose of this litigation.

We therefore conclude that the *New York Times* standard is inapplicable to this case and that the trial court erred in entering judgment for respondent. Because the jury was allowed to impose liability without fault and was permitted to presume damages without proof of injury, a new trial is necessary. We reverse and remand for further proceedings in accord with this opinion.[262]

A Bare Majority That Reconfigured the Law Nationally. Justice Powell's opinion was joined by Potter Stewart, Thurgood Marshall, Harry Blackmun and William Rehnquist, JJ. Justice Blackmun stated in a concurrence that he found some difficulties with the majority opinion, but that he joined in it to attain a "definitive ruling." Chief Justice Warren Burger dissented in an opinion which indicated that he disapproved of the requirement of negligence for private defamation. Justice William O. Douglas dissented on the basis of his absolute-privilege theory, and would have at least retained the *Rosenbloom* rule. Justice William J. Brennan, Jr. dissented and would have retained the *Rosenbloom* rule. Justice Byron White dissented and would have retained strict liability for private defamation.

b.   Applying the *Gertz* standards

Actual Malice Versus Negligence in Gertz-type Cases. The great majority of jurisdictions have accepted *Gertz's* invitation to require only a showing of negligence in cases brought by private persons suing with respect to matters of public concern. For example, in *Rudloe v. Karl*,[263] Florida State University was sued for publishing in the "Alumni Notes" section of its magazine material submitted by one alumnus which insinuated that another alumnus had stolen a priceless aquatic specimen from a professor and had later offered it for sale. In reversing dismissal of the claim, the Florida District Court of Appeal wrote:

> Sovereign immunity [under Florida law] is no bar to appellants' negligent defamation claim. "First, for there to be governmental tort liability, there must be either an underlying common law or statutory duty of care with respect to the alleged negligent conduct." . . . Here, because of the

---

[262] *Id.* at 351–52.

[263] 899 So. 2d 1161 (Fla. Dist. Ct. App. 2005).

common law duty publishers owe non-public figures, the . . . complaint adequately stated a claim for relief against FSU in alleging that FSU negligently published defamatory material about Mr. Rudloe and Gulf Specimen.[264]

However, occasional decisions have mandated a greater showing of fault as to falsity. For example, there is authority that in Indiana a *Gertz*-type plaintiff must prove actual malice.[265]

The New York Variation of the Culpability Requirement. New York has articulated the culpability requirement for *Gertz*-type cases against media defendants in unusual terms. When defamation involves a matter of public concern, a private plaintiff must prove that the media defendant "acted in a grossly irresponsible manner without due consideration for the standards of information gathering and dissemination ordinarily followed by responsible parties."[266]

Equating Negligent Reference to the Plaintiff with Negligence as to Falsity. Some cases take the position that negligent reference to the plaintiff is the same as negligence as to the falsity of the allegedly defamatory statement. For example, in *Stanton v. Metro Corp.*,[267] an article gave the allegedly false impression that a teenage girl (Stanton), who was pictured in a photograph, was sexually promiscuous. In holding that the girl stated a cause of action for defamation because the article could be understood to defame her, the court wrote that "private persons . . . may recover compensation (assuming proof of all other elements of a claim for defamation) on proof that the defendant was negligent in publishing defamatory words which reasonably could be interpreted to refer to the plaintiff."[268]

Public Figure Status is a Question of Law. Whether the plaintiff is a public figure is a question of law for the court to decide. Although *Gertz* makes clear that some persons may be public figures for all purposes, the relevant issue is normally whether the plaintiff is a limited-purpose public figure, which means a public figure with respect to the subject matter of the defamatory statement.

Time, Inc. v. Firestone. In *Time, Inc. v. Firestone*,[269] a weekly magazine had inaccurately reported that a wealthy couple had been granted a divorce because of the plaintiff's adultery and cruelty. In fact, the basis for the ruling was "lack of domestication" on the part of both spouses. In addressing the issue of whether the former wife (the "respondent") was a public figure, then-Justice William H. Rehnquist wrote for a majority of the Court:

> Respondent did not assume any role of especial prominence in the affairs of society, other than perhaps Palm Beach society, and she did not thrust

---

[264] *Id.* at 1164.

[265] *See Poyser v. Peerless*, 775 N.E.2d 1101 (Ind. Ct. App. 2002).

[266] *Huggins v. Moore*, 726 N.E.2d 456, 460 (N.Y. 1999) (quoting *Chapadeau v. Utica Observer Dispatch*, 341 N.E.2d 569, 571 (N.Y. 1975)).

[267] 438 F.3d 119 (1st Cir. 2006).

[268] *Id.* at 131–32.

[269] 424 U.S. 448 (1976).

herself to the forefront of any particular public controversy in order to influence the resolution of the issues involved in it.

Petitioner contends that because the Firestone divorce was characterized by the Florida Supreme Court as a "cause célèbre," it must have been a public controversy and respondent must be considered a public figure. But in so doing petitioner seeks to equate "public controversy" with all controversies of interest to the public. Were we to accept this reasoning, we would reinstate the doctrine advanced in the plurality opinion in Rosenbloom v. Metromedia, Inc., 403 U.S. 29 (1971), which concluded that the *New York Times* privilege should be extended to falsehoods defamatory of private persons whenever the statements concern matters of general or public interest. In *Gertz*, however, the Court repudiated this position. . . .

Dissolution of a marriage through judicial proceedings is not the sort of "public controversy" referred to in *Gertz*, even though the marital difficulties of extremely wealthy individuals may be of interest to some portion of the reading public. Nor did respondent freely choose to publicize issues as to the propriety of her married life. She was compelled to go to court by the State in order to obtain legal release from the bonds of matrimony. . . .[270] We hold respondent was not a "public figure" for the purpose of determining the constitutional protection afforded petitioner's report of the factual and legal basis for her divorce.[271]

Examples of Public Figures. Courts have classified as public figures: a politically active city resident;[272] a public restaurant;[273] a Holocaust survivor who authorized a biography;[274] a security guard who granted interviews before he became a suspect;[275] a professional football player;[276] a former U.S. Senate candidate;[277] a Playboy playmate who posed for a photograph;[278] a research scientist and bioterrorism expert who was a frequent commentator on anthrax mailings that killed five persons;[279] and a college dean.[280]

---

[270] [n.3] Nor do we think the fact that respondent may have held a few press conferences during the divorce proceedings in an attempt to satisfy inquiring reporters converts her into a "public figure." Such interviews should have no effect upon the merits of the legal dispute between respondent and her husband or the outcome of that trial, and we do not think it can be assumed that any such purpose was intended. Moreover, there is no indication that she sought to use the press conferences as a vehicle by which to thrust herself to the forefront of some unrelated controversy in order to influence its resolution. . . .

[271] 424 U.S. at 453–55.

[272] *See Sparks v. Peaster*, 581 S.E.2d 579 (Ga. Ct. App. 2003).

[273] *See Pegasus v. Reno Newspapers, Inc.*, 57 P.3d 82 (Nev. 2002).

[274] *See Thomas v. L.A. Times Comm'ns*, 2002 U.S. App. LEXIS 18465 (9th Cir. Sept. 6, 2002).

[275] *See Atlanta-Journal Constitution v. Jewell*, 555 S.E.2d 175 (Ga. Ct. App. 2001).

[276] *See Chuy v. Philadelphia Eagles Football Club*, 595 F.2d 1265, 1280 (3d Cir. 1979).

[277] *See Williams v. Pasma*, 656 P.2d 212, 216 (Mont. 1982).

[278] *See Vitale v. National Lampoon, Inc.*, 449 F. Supp. 442 (E.D. Pa. 1978).

[279] *See Hatfill v. New York Times Co.*, 532 F.3d 312 (4th Cir. 2008).

[280] *See Byers v. Southeastern Newspaper Corp.*, 288 S.E.2d 698 (Ga. Ct. App. 1982).

Narrow Definition of Public Figure. Some decisions, often quite sensibly, have construed the "public figure" category narrowly. For example, in *Franklin Prescriptions, Inc. v. New York Times Co.*,[281] a federal court in Pennsylvania held that a pharmacy, which used the Internet for informational purposes only and did not take orders over the Internet, was not a limited-purpose public figure in the context of a public controversy about online pharmacies making expensive drugs more accessible.

In *Lundell Manufacturing Co. v. American Broadcasting Companies*,[282] the Eighth Circuit held that a manufacturer of a garbage recycling machine was not a public figure. Although garbage disposal was a matter of public concern, the manufacturer's entry into a contract for the mere sale of the machine to a county was not the injection of the manufacturer into a controversy for the purpose of influencing a public issue. Moreover, the defendant network's conduct in televising the issue did not render the manufacturer a public figure.

In *Bochetto v. Gibson*,[283] a well-known attorney (Bochetto), who had once run for mayor of Philadelphia, alleged that he had been defamed by another attorney, who had filed a legal malpractice complaint against Bochetto and faxed a copy of the complaint to a reporter who wrote a story. The complaint asserted that Bochetto had committed malpractice by failing to disclose an adverse report to a client who was defending two real property quiet-title actions. In discussing whether the faxing of the complaint to the reporter was protected by a qualified privilege, the Pennsylvania Court of Common Pleas wrote:

> [T]he particular controversy giving rise to the defamation claim was a private lawsuit brought against Bochetto by his former client. That Malpractice Action does "not involve a matter of public controversy with foreseeable and substantial ramifications for the members of the general public." . . . Since the Malpractice Action against Bochetto does not rise to the level of a public controversy, it does not implicate Bochetto as a public figure, and he is a private person for purposes of this litigation.[284]

Involuntary Public Figures. Courts have employed such a bewildering array of tests in grappling with the elusive idea of "involuntary public figure" status that it is difficult to say anything useful about this category.[285] The label rarely seems to fit. In *Neely v. Wilson*,[286] the Texas Supreme Court wrote:

> The [United States Supreme] Court's forecast that it would be "exceedingly rare" for a person to become a public figure involuntarily has proven true:

---

[281] 267 F. Supp. 2d 425 (E.D. Pa. 2003).

[282] 98 F.3d 351 (8th Cir. 1996).

[283] 2006 Phila. Ct. Com. Pl. LEXIS 310 (July 27, 2006).

[284] *Id.* at *14.

[285] *See* Joseph H. King, Jr., *Deus ex Machina and the Unfulfilled Promise of New York Times v. Sullivan: Applying the Times for All Seasons*, 95 Ky. L.J. 649, 657 (2007) ("The hirsute contours of the public figure-private figure dichotomy have been especially vague for the involuntary public figure subcategory").

[286] 2013 Tex. LEXIS 511 (June 28, 2013).

neither the United States Supreme Court nor this Court has found circumstances in which a person involuntarily became a limited-purpose public figure. . . .

On these facts [involving a physician who was allegedly defamed by an investigative report], we cannot say this is the exceedingly rare case in which a person has become a limited-purpose public figure against his will. Before the broadcast in question, Neely was mentioned in a 1996 newspaper article about settling a malpractice lawsuit and a December 2003 newspaper statement that Neely was placed on probation for self-prescribing medications. Neely was not quoted in either article. Neely also refrained from talking to Wilson [the investigative reporter] regarding the broadcast at issue. Because Neely is not a limited-purpose public figure, he need not prove actual malice. . . .[287]

Private Enterprisers Who Assist or Disrupt the Government. In *Mathis v. Cannon*,[288] the Georgia Supreme Court considered the rules relating to limited-purpose public figures. Addressing the facts before it, the court wrote:

The [Georgia] court of appeals has adopted a three-part analysis used in federal cases to determine whether an individual is a limited-purpose public figure. Under this analysis, a court "must isolate the public controversy, examine the plaintiff's involvement in the controversy, and determine whether the alleged defamation was germane to the plaintiff's participation in the controversy."

Applying this analysis, we conclude that Cannon [the majority owner and president of TransWaste Services, Inc., a private entity] is a limited-purpose public figure in the controversy surrounding the recycling facility and landfill in Crisp County. The public controversy concerns the Solid Waste Management Authority of Crisp County's financially unsuccessful operation of its solid waste recovery facility and resulting strain on the county's resources and its taxpayers. After 18 months of operation, the plant was not able to process the solid waste or produce the recyclable materials and commercial compost as projected. As a result, a large amount of solid waste that was collected from other locations for processing at the authority's plant was instead being diverted to the county landfill. The county commission voted to raise property taxes to deal with the costs related to disposing of the county's own waste and expand the county-owned landfill to accommodate the additional solid waste that TransWaste was bringing into the county under its contract with the authority.

In reviewing Cannon's role, we find that he was involved in the public controversy in Crisp County in at least three ways. First, he was a crucial actor in helping the authority obtain the commitments from other county and city governments in south Georgia to provide solid waste for the authority's facility. . . .

---

[287] *Id.* at *45–*46.

[288] 573 S.E.2d 376 (Ga. 2002).

Second, Cannon represented the authority in a variety of ways that far exceeded the terms of TransWaste's contract to collect and haul solid waste to Crisp County. As he explained in his deposition, the authority in 1996 was still "just a shell of an authority developing a concept," with no funding, lines of credit, or buildings. "TransWaste would step in to try to help the Authority in whatever way they could, and there are many, many instances of that." . . . Using his personal contacts with city and county officials developed from selling them heavy-duty equipment, Cannon solicited business for the authority; this solicitation helped generate business for TransWaste as the authority's exclusive hauler. He negotiated the authority's contracts with local governments who provided waste, borrowed money through TransWaste and wrote a check directly to the City of Warner Robins for equipment that the authority had agreed to purchase, wrote and signed correspondence on authority letterhead in his capacity as its solid waste hauler, and participated in some of the authority's executive sessions.

Third, Cannon precipitated the financial crisis in November 1999 by filing a lawsuit against the authority and then temporarily halting deliveries to the solid waste recovery plant. . . . Cannon knew, or should have known, that suing the authority for payment for services rendered would affect the county as the other major participant in the project.

Based on Cannon's role in developing the project, representing the authority, and accelerating the crisis, we conclude that he voluntarily injected himself into the controversy or, at a minimum, became drawn into the public controversy over the operation of the authority's facility and county's landfill. . . . Having blurred the distinction between his work for his private business and his more public efforts in helping develop the quasi-governmental project, he should not be able to erect a barrier to public criticism of his role once the project failed to perform as planned.

. . . [W]e conclude that the nature and extent of Cannon's participation in the local controversy concerning solid waste disposal has made him a limited-purpose public figure. . . .[289]

c. Defamation in Politics

Candidates, political action committees, and others sometime disseminate extreme characterizations of the records or proposals of political opponents. These statements are not exempt from the law of defamation. A candidate for public office is a current public official or an aspiring public figure who must prove actual malice in order to prevail in suit for libel or slander. That is a formidable obstacle which may take years to surmount, but sometimes the standard can be met.

In *Boyce & Isley, PLLC v. Cooper*,[290] the person who was elected state attorney general had run a commercial alleging that his opponent's law firm had "sued the state" and had charged the taxpayers an hourly rate of $28,000, "more than a police

---

[289] *Id.* at 381–83.

[290] 568 S.E.2d 893 (N.C. Ct. App. 2002).

officer's salary for each hour's work." In fact, the fee had been pursued not by the plaintiff, but by the plaintiff's father, in a contingent-fee class action before the plaintiff ever joined the law firm. The statements, which implied unethical billing practices, were found to be libelous *per se*. Moreover, claims were stated by all four members of the opponent's law firm and by the firm itself. The plaintiffs were able to prove actual malice, in part because the successful candidate had refused to pull the ad after demands for its discontinuance.

In *Flowers v. Carville*,[291] the Ninth Circuit held that a claim was stated against former presidential advisors based on their repetition of CNN news reports stating that tape recordings made by the plaintiff had been "doctored" or "selectively edited." The court acknowledged that the plaintiff might not be able to prove actual malice, noting that "[o]ne who repeats what he hears from a reputable news source, with no individualized reason external to the news report to doubt its accuracy, has not acted recklessly."[292] However, the "[d]efendants were not uninvolved third parties who clearly lacked access to the facts behind the published reports."[293]

Problem 3-7: The Defamed Telemarketer

AmeriTel Marketers, Inc. is a telemarketer of a wide range of business products and services. At any given time, it serves hundreds or thousands of clients. Annually, its representatives (or its machines) make several million phone calls.

AmeriTel was hired by Midland Ventures, an oil and gas company, to market investments in oil and gas exploration to persons in middle and upper income categories. It was not difficult for AmeriTel to target the right prospective purchasers because its databases contained the names of millions of individuals, along with direct or indirect information about the assets, earnings, and investments of many of those persons.

Ultimately, Midland was disappointed by AmeriTel's services and terminated their contract. Many purchasers complained to Midland that they had been misled by statements made by AmeriTel representatives. Subsequently, a Midland employee posted unflattering comments about AmeriTel on an online business rating website. Those statements related to the types of deceptive sales pitches that AmeriTel representatives employed in talking to prospective customers.

Despite demands from AmeriTel, Midland has refused to remove the allegedly defamatory statements from the website. Corporate counsel for AmeriTel needs to advise company executives on the prospects for success if a defamation action is filed against Midland. The first question is whether AmeriTel will have to prove actual malice. You are a law clerk in the office of corporate counsel. Please prepare an analysis of the factors that will bear upon judicial resolution of that issue and the likely result.

---

[291] 310 F.3d 1118 (9th Cir. 2002).

[292] *Id.* at 1130.

[293] *Id.*

3.   Category III: Anyone Suing with Respect to Matters of Private Concern

The development of the constitutional principles applicable to actions for libel and slander took an unexpected turn with the 1985 ruling in *Dun & Bradstreet, Inc. v. Greenmoss Builders, Inc.*[294]

a.   *Dun & Bradstreet, Inc. v. Greenmoss Builders, Inc.*

In *Dun & Bradstreet,*[295] a credit report erroneously stated that a business had declared bankruptcy. The United States Supreme Court, noting the limited circulation of the report to only a small number of subscribers, concluded that the defamatory statement did not involve a matter of "public concern." Because that was the case, the Court found that state libel law, which allowed the plaintiff to recover presumed and punitive damages without proof of actual malice, did not violate the First Amendment.

A Surprising Distinction. It was surprising that the Court drew a distinction between matters of public concern and matters of private concern. In 1971, *Rosenbloom v. Metromedia, Inc.*[296] had embraced that distinction in deciding how far to extend the actual-malice standard. However, just three years later, *Gertz v. Robert Welch, Inc.*[297] repudiated *Rosenbloom* on the ground that judges should not be called upon to decide what is or is not a matter of public concern. That reasoning was no longer found to be persuasive in *Dun & Bradstreet,* and the distinction between public and private matters has endured ever since.

Not All Speech is Equally Important. In his plurality opinion in *Dun & Bradstreet* (which Justices William H. Rehnquist and Sandra Day O'Connor joined), Justice Lewis F. Powell explained the basis for distinguishing between private and public matters. He wrote:

> We have long recognized that not all speech is of equal First Amendment importance. It is speech on "matters of public concern" that is "at the heart of the First Amendment's protection." . . .

> . . . In contrast, speech on matters of purely private concern is of less First Amendment concern. . . . As a number of state courts . . . have recognized, the role of the Constitution in regulating state libel law is far more limited when the concerns that activated *New York Times* and *Gertz* are absent. In such a case,

> "[t]here is no threat to the free and robust debate of public issues; there is no potential interference with a meaningful dialogue of ideas concerning self-government; and there is no threat of liability causing a reaction of self-censorship by the press. . . ."

---

[294] 472 U.S. 749 (1985).

[295] *Id.*

[296] 403 U.S. 29 (1971).

[297] 418 U.S. 323 (1974).

While such speech is not totally unprotected by the First Amendment, . . . its protections are less stringent. In *Gertz*, we found that the state interest in awarding presumed and punitive damages was not "substantial" in view of their effect on speech at the core of First Amendment concern. . . . This interest, however, is "substantial" relative to the incidental effect these remedies may have on speech of significantly less constitutional interest. The rationale of the common-law rules has been the experience and judgment of history that "proof of actual damage will be impossible in a great many cases where, from the character of the defamatory words and the circumstances of publication, it is all but certain that serious harm has resulted in fact." . . . As a result, courts for centuries have allowed juries to presume that some damage occurred from many defamatory utterances and publications. *Restatement of Torts* § 568, Comment b, p. 162 (1938) (noting that Hale announced that damages were to be presumed for libel as early as 1670). This rule furthers the state interest in providing remedies for defamation by ensuring that those remedies are effective. In light of the reduced constitutional value of speech involving no matters of public concern, we hold that the state interest adequately supports awards of presumed and punitive damages — even absent a showing of "actual malice."[298]

The Unresolved Issue: Fault as to Falsity in "Private Matter" Cases. Justice Powell's opinion in *Dun & Bradstreet* was silent on whether a plaintiff, in a defamation suit involving a private matter, must prove that the defendant was at least negligent as to the falsity of the statement. Chief Justice Warren Burger, in a separate concurrence, asserted that the rules announced in *Gertz* were limited to cases involving matters of public concern. Justice Byron White, in another concurrence, opined that *Dun & Bradstreet* had rejected the *Gertz* rule that liability cannot be imposed without fault, as well as *Gertz's* holding that awards of presumed or punitive damages require actual malice. In contrast, Justice William J. Brennan, speaking in dissent for himself and three other justices (Thurgood Marshall, Harry Blackmun, and John Paul Stevens, JJ.), argued that the holding in *Dun & Bradstreet* was narrow and that the parties did not question the requirement of fault as a prerequisite to obtaining a judgment and actual damages.

Subsequent federal and state court decisions "run the gamut from assertions that *Dun & Bradstreet* swept away all First Amendment requirements in private-private suits to unequivocal declarations that the case affected nothing but the fault requirement for presumed and punitive damages."[299] At least one U.S. Court of Appeals (the Fifth Circuit), three federal district courts, and four states' appellate courts have interpreted *Dun & Bradstreet* as eliminating constitutional restrictions in cases involving private persons suing with respect to matters of private concern.[300] For example, in *Imperial Apparel, Ltd. v. Cosmo's Designer Direct,*

---

[298] 472 U.S. at 758–61.

[299] Ruth Walden & Derigan Silver, *Deciphering Dun & Bradstreet: Does the First Amendment Matter in Private Figure-Private Concern Defamation Cases*, 14 Comm. L. & Pol'y 1, 15–16 (2009).

[300] *Id.* at 16–21.

Inc.,[301] a defamation suit involving competing retailers, the Supreme Court of Illinois wrote:

> [N]o claim has been made that the statements made in the disputed advertisement addressed a matter of public concern. . . . [Therefore], the special standards for fault, falsity, and punitive damages imposed by the first amendment in defamation actions therefore have no application to the claims asserted by Imperial and the Rosengartens against Cosmo's. Those claims are subject to the normal common law fault, falsity and punitive damage principles followed in Illinois in defamation cases. . . . Illinois does not impose liability without fault in defamation cases. . . .[302]

Many States Require Negligence. Despite the fact that the issue of fault has not been definitively resolved by the United States Supreme Court, many states apply a negligence standard to cases involving private persons, even if they involve issues of private concern.[303]

b. Distinguishing Private Concern from Public Concern

Dun & Bradstreet provides little guidance for distinguishing matters of private concern from matters of public concern. Indeed, the Court's application of the law to the facts then before it seems counter-intuitive and erroneous. The defendant's credit report said that a corporation had voluntarily declared bankruptcy. It could certainly be argued that whether a business has failed financially is a matter of public concern, at least if the business employs numerous workers, has many creditors, and pays taxes.

Limited Dissemination. Justice Powell's opinion placed weight on the fact that the erroneous credit report was given limited dissemination and that the five subscribers who received the report were contractually precluded from further disseminating its contents. The Court also suggested that the reporting of "objectively verifiable information" deserved less constitutional protection than other kinds of speech, and that market forces gave credit-reporting agencies an incentive to be accurate, "since false credit reporting is of no use to creditors."[304] Summarizing the conclusion that the report was a matter of private concern, Justice Powell wrote:

> [The credit report] was speech solely in the individual interest of the speaker and its specific business audience. . . . This particular interest warrants no special protection when — as in this case — the speech is wholly false and clearly damaging to the victim's business reputation. . . .

---

[301] 882 N.E.2d 1011 (Ill. 2008).

[302] *Id.* at 1021.

[303] *Cf. Neely v. Wilson*, 2013 Tex. LEXIS 511 (June 28, 2013) ("to recover defamation damages in Texas, a plaintiff must prove the media defendant: (1) published a statement; (2) that defamed the plaintiff; (3) while either acting with actual malice (if the plaintiff was a public official or public figure) or negligence (if the plaintiff was a private individual) regarding the truth of the statement").

[304] 472 U.S. at 762–63.

Moreover, since the credit report was made available to only five subscribers, who, under the terms of the subscription agreement, could not disseminate it further, it cannot be said that the report involves any "strong interest in the free flow of commercial information." . . . There is simply no credible argument that this type of credit reporting requires special protection to ensure that "debate on public issues [will] be uninhibited, robust, and wide-open."[305]

Other Supreme Court Guidance. In *Snyder v. Phelps*,[306] the U.S. Supreme Court reversed awards of compensatory and punitive damages in a tort action for intentional infliction of emotional distress arising from picketing at a military funeral that was intended to protest homosexuality, particularly in the military. The Court wrote that "[g]iven that Westboro's [the picketers'] speech was at a public place on a matter of public concern, that speech is entitled to "special protection" under the First Amendment. As the Court explained:

> Whether the First Amendment prohibits holding Westboro liable for its speech in this case turns largely on whether that speech is of public or private concern, as determined by all the circumstances of the case. "[S]peech on 'matters of public concern' . . . is 'at the heart of the First Amendment's protection.' " . . .

> We noted a short time ago, in considering whether public employee speech addressed a matter of public concern, that "the boundaries of the public concern test are not well defined." *San Diego v. Roe*, 543 U.S. 77, 83, (2004) (per curiam). Although that remains true today, we have articulated some guiding principles, principles that accord broad protection to speech to ensure that courts themselves do not become inadvertent censors.

> Speech deals with matters of public concern when it can "be fairly considered as relating to any matter of political, social, or other concern to the community," . . . or when it "is a subject of legitimate news interest; that is, a subject of general interest and of value and concern to the public," . . . The arguably "inappropriate or controversial character of a statement is irrelevant to the question whether it deals with a matter of public concern." . . .

> Our opinion in *Dun & Bradstreet*, on the other hand, provides an example of speech of only private concern. . . . To cite another example, we concluded in *San Diego v. Roe* that, in the context of a government employer regulating the speech of its employees, videos of an employee engaging in sexually explicit acts did not address a public concern; the videos "did nothing to inform the public about any aspect of the [employing agency's] functioning or operation." . . .

> Deciding whether speech is of public or private concern requires us to examine the "content, form, and context" of that speech, "as revealed by the

---

[305] *Id.* at 762.

[306] 131 S. Ct. 1207 (2011).

whole record." . . . [I]t is necessary to evaluate all the circumstances of the speech, including what was said, where it was said, and how it was said.

The "content" of Westboro's signs plainly relates to broad issues of interest to society at large, rather than matters of "purely private concern." . . . The placards read "God Hates the USA/Thank God for 9/11," "America is Doomed," "Don't Pray for the USA," "Thank God for IEDs," "Fag Troops," "Semper Fi Fags," "God Hates Fags," "Maryland Taliban," "Fags Doom Nations," "Not Blessed Just Cursed," "Thank God for Dead Soldiers," "Pope in Hell," "Priests Rape Boys," "You're Going to Hell," and "God Hates You." . . . While these messages may fall short of refined social or political commentary, the issues they highlight — the political and moral conduct of the United States and its citizens, the fate of our Nation, homosexuality in the military, and scandals involving the Catholic clergy — are matters of public import. The signs certainly convey Westboro's position on those issues, in a manner designed, unlike the private speech in *Dun & Bradstreet*, to reach as broad a public audience as possible. And even if a few of the signs — such as "You're Going to Hell" and "God Hates You" — were viewed as containing messages related to Matthew Snyder or the Snyders specifically, that would not change the fact that the overall thrust and dominant theme of Westboro's demonstration spoke to broader public issues.

. . . Westboro's signs, displayed on public land next to a public street, reflect the fact that the church finds much to condemn in modern society. Its speech is "fairly characterized as constituting speech on a matter of public concern," . . . and the funeral setting does not alter that conclusion.

. . . .

. . . [T]he jury verdict imposing tort liability on Westboro for intentional infliction of emotional distress must be set aside.[307]

The Speaker's Intent About Privacy or Publicness. Is it a fair reading of *Dun & Bradstreet* and *Snyder* to say that speech that is intended to be private is likely to be a matter of private concern, and that speech that is intended to be public is likely to be a matter of public concern?

Deference to the Media. In *Huggins v. Moore*,[308] the New York Court of Appeals wrote that the fact that an article "has been published in a newspaper is not conclusive that its subject matter warrants public exposition." Nevertheless, in *Moore*, statements contained in a gossip column about an acrimonious celebrity divorce were found to be matters of genuine social concern. The opinion for an unanimous court stated:

Plaintiff Charles Huggins is the former husband of Melba Moore, a popular actress. . . . Plaintiff brought this defamation action as a result of three articles written by defendant Linda Stasi and published in the "Hot Copy"

---

[307] 131 S. Ct. at 1215–19.

[308] 726 N.E.2d 456, 460 (N.Y. 1999).

column of defendant Daily News. . . . The articles concerned Moore's allegations of plaintiff's betrayal of trust in their personal and financial relationships during the dissolution of their marriage. The series reported how Moore began to speak out as a self-described victim of "economic spousal abuse," because she believed her husband had cheated her out of her interest in the entertainment management company they had built together, leaving her destitute.

. . . [T]he articles themselves show the greater significance of Moore's personal story, a tragic downfall from a position of stardom and wealth. Moore was given a platform for speaking out as a victim of an allegedly pervasive modern phenomenon of economic spousal abuse. Manifestly, what Stasi [the author of the articles] identified as the "important social issue" of "economic spousal abuse" was at least arguably within the sphere of legitimate public concern. . . .

. . . [W]e will not second-guess Stasi's editorial determination that Moore's "personal saga" was reasonably related to this matter of social concern to the community. . . . [A]lthough "not conclusive," the editorial determination of newsworthiness of the subject "may be powerful evidence of the hold those subjects have on the public's attention". . . . In this case, the evidence was powerful indeed. The record establishes that Moore's downfall, and her claim of plaintiff's betrayal, was reported nationwide across the entire spectrum of print and broadcast media.

In ruling to the contrary, the Appellate Division did not accord the deference to editorial judgment our decisions require. That the "core" of the dispute between Moore and plaintiff was a divorce is not conclusive. The articles also portrayed Moore's alleged victimization by her financial as well as marital partner to the point of economic and career ruination. It is this episode of human interest that reflected a matter of genuine social concern. . . . [T]he allegedly defamatory text here was not so remote from the matter of public concern as to constitute an abuse of editorial discretion. . . .[309]

Allegations of Fraud. In *Senna v. Florimont*,[310] an arcade game barker used a public address system to tell boardwalk walkers that a competitor was "dishonest" and "a crook," and to say that he "ran away and screwed all of his customers in Seaside" and would do it all again. Finding that the resulting defamation action only required proof of negligence as to falsity, the Supreme Court of New Jersey wrote:

Defendants would have us conclude that whenever one business tars its competitor with the canard of consumer fraud, the accusation, even if false, involves a matter of public concern. However, this was not a case of disinterested investigative reporting by a newspaper, using a variety of sources, to demonstrate that customers were being defrauded by a service-oriented business, as was true in [*Turf Lawnmower Repair, Inc. v.*

---

[309] *Id.* at 458–62.

[310] 958 A.2d 427 (N.J. 2008).

Bergen Record Corp., 655 A.2d 417 (N.J. 1995)]. Defendants' employees were basically scaring customers away from plaintiff. Their accusations were not more highly valued speech because they charged their rival with consumer fraud rather than a peccadillo. It cannot be that, in the competition of the marketplace, the bigger the lie the more free speech protection for the publisher of the lie. Businesses have an obligation to act with due care before calling the services rendered by a rival crooked or fraudulent.[311]

The Significance of Being Regulated by the Government. Senna v. Florimont, supra, addressed whether being regulated by the government makes an entity's activities a matter of public concern:

Defendants also claim that Fascination parlors are highly regulated businesses and therefore their employees' false and disparaging broadcasts about their competitor do not render them liable, even if they were negligent, because they fall within the safe harbor of the actual-malice standard. Defendants unmoor the term "highly regulated industry" from its conceptual settings. . . . There is a difference between a newspaper publishing an investigative report about the questionable loan practices of a bank, which is part of a highly regulated industry, and a highly regulated Fascination parlor using its public address system in an attempt to put out of business its competitor's highly regulated Fascination parlor. . . .

The invocation of the term "highly regulated industry" is not talismanic, giving every speaker immunity for his negligent, false, and harmful speech. In New Jersey, not just banks and arcade games, but professions (*e.g.*, law, medicine, and accountancy), trades, and many other businesses are highly regulated by the government. The critical inquiry in determining whether speech involves a matter of public interest is the content, form, and context of the speech. For example, when one accountant wrongly and falsely accuses another accountant of overcharging clients, and disseminates those accusations to clients, the public interest is not served by shielding the speaker from the consequences of his negligence. The same holds true for Fascination parlors.

So long as one business tells the truth about another, or does not publish a falsehood negligently, that business will not be exposed to liability. . . . The speech in this case no more involves the public interest than the false credit report in *Dun & Bradstreet*. . . . In balancing the respective interests at stake here, including plaintiff's right to enjoy his reputation free of unfair and false aspersions, the negligence standard adequately protects defendants' free speech rights.[312]

---

[311] *Id.* at 445.

[312] *Id.* at 445–46.

(1)   Example: *Quigley v. Rosenthal*

In *Quigley v. Rosenthal*,[313] the Tenth Circuit struggled with the task of distinguishing matters of public concern from matters of private concern. In *Quigley*, homeowners (the Quigleys) sued a civil rights group (the Anti-Defamation League) and its attorney (Rosenthal) on defamation and other theories of liability based on statements the defendants had made relating to allegedly anti-Semitic behavior on the part of the homeowners against their Jewish neighbors (the Aronsons). Discussing the defamation claim, the court wrote:

> Consistent with *Gertz*, the Colorado Supreme Court has extended the . . . "actual malice" standard of liability to cases where "a defamatory state-ment has been published concerning one who is not a public official or a public figure, but the matter involved is of public or general concern."[314]
> . . .
>
> Defendants do not dispute that the Quigleys [the plaintiffs] were private individuals at the time the alleged defamatory statements were made. Instead, defendants assert that the statements involved matters of public or general concern since they concerned a civil lawsuit alleging "that the Quigleys had conspired with others to deprive [their neighbors] the Aronsons of their constitutional rights on the basis of their religion and race." . . . The district court rejected defendants' arguments, concluding that defendants' statements did not relate to a matter of public or general concern:
>
> > [T]he bulk of the allegedly defamatory statements were based on excerpts of private telephone conversations between the Quigleys and other third parties which the Aronsons surreptitiously intercepted. In this regard, the Quigleys' position contrasts to that of the plaintiffs in . . . [*Diversified Mgmt., Inc. v. The Denver Post, Inc.*, 653 P.2d 1103 (Colo. 1982)], in which the court found that alleged widespread and ongoing land-development schemes of questionable propriety consti-tuted a matter of public concern strictly because the matter still had the potential to affect future buyers of lots which were yet-unsold. Similarly, in . . . [*Lewis v. McGraw-Hill Broadcasting Co.*, 832 P.2d 1118 (Colo. Ct. App. 1992)], the court found a matter of public interest existed in part because the plaintiff filed a civil lawsuit to "protest[ ] racially motivated policies of a large retail establishment which allegedly had been directed against her." Thus, in *Lewis*, in addition to the fact that the plaintiff had essentially thrust herself into a public debate through her lawyer's public commentary at a local meeting, the court relied on the fact that resolution of the issues could have an [effect] on other patrons of a commercial entity.

---

[313] 327 F.3d 1044 (10th Cir. 2003).

[314] [n.4] Under Colorado law, if a private individual is involved and the matter is not one of "public or general concern," the plaintiff merely needs to establish fault amounting to negligence on the part of the defendant. . . .

At the time of the allegedly defamatory statements in this case, Rosenthal [the civil rights group's attorney] had received merely one unsolicited request from the press based on the filing of the [civil] lawsuit, as compared to the "immediate and widespread publicity from the various media organizations" which the filing of the underlying lawsuit in *Lewis* prompted. It was defendants' decision (arguably along with the Aronsons'), not the Quigleys', to amplify the matter by calling a press conference under the ADL name. Because, at the time of the press conference . . . [the original publication of the allegedly defamatory statements] the dispute between the Aronsons and the Quigleys was still essentially private, I conclude that . . . Rosenthal's statements about them are, accordingly, not subject to the higher [actual malice] standard [of fault].[315]

Striking the Balance in Favor of Private Matter. The *Quigley* court suggested that, at least in Colorado, there is a preference for classifying matters as "private" rather than "public," for that tends to permit redress of defamatory harm. The Tenth Circuit wrote:

Unfortunately, Colorado law provides no clear set of guidelines for determining whether a matter is of "public concern." . . . At best, the Colorado courts have indicated that "a matter is of public concern whenever 'it embraces an issue about which information is needed or is appropriate,' or when 'the public may reasonably be expected to have a legitimate interest in what is being published.' " . . . Further, the Colorado courts have indicated that "the balance should be struck in favor of a private plaintiff if his or her reputation has been injured by a non-media defendant in a purely private context." . . .

Applying these general standards to the facts presented here, it is apparent that the statements were made by a non-media defendant (Rosenthal) and concerned private plaintiffs (the Quigleys), rather than public officials or public figures. To that extent, the balance would seem to tip in favor of concluding that the matter was of private, rather than public, concern.[316]

Civil Litigation: Content is the Critical Factor. Addressing the relevance of pending civil litigation, the Tenth Circuit wrote:

[D]efendants note that Rosenthal was discussing allegations made in a civil lawsuit filed against the Quigleys. . . . it appears that defendants are suggesting that civil litigation is always a matter of public concern.

. . . [I]t is far from certain that all civil litigation is considered to be a matter of public concern under Colorado law. Perhaps the most analogous Colorado case is *Lewis*, where private plaintiffs sued media defendants for falsely reporting during a newscast that one of the plaintiffs previously had been arrested for obstruction of justice, indecent exposure, and prostitution. The Colorado Court of Appeals concluded that the incorrect statements "involved a subject matter of . . . public concern." . . . In reaching

---

[315] 327 F.3d at 1058–59.

[316] *Id.* at 1059–60.

this conclusion, the court noted "that the newscast emerged in the context of a persistent and concededly public controversy over [a major retailer's] policies towards minorities, a controversy triggered by publicity surrounding plaintiffs' $15 million lawsuit and their allegations of racially discriminatory policies by [the retailer]." . . . Although the existence of a civil lawsuit was a relevant factor in *Lewis*, nothing in the court's opinion suggests that the mere filing of a civil lawsuit, by itself, is sufficient to trigger "public concern." Rather, it appears clear that the content of the lawsuit is the critical factor. . . .[317]

The Impermissible Discrimination Factor. The court next addressed whether allegations of discrimination are always a matter of public concern.

According to defendants, any type of discrimination, including religious and ethnic discrimination, is necessarily a matter of public concern.

. . . The defendants appear to be on stronger ground here. In *Connick v. Myers*, 461 U.S. 138, 148 n.8, (1983), the Court stated that "racial discrimination," at least in the context of public-employment, is "a matter inherently of public concern." . . .

Notwithstanding this case law, two factors unique to this case weigh against the conclusion that the allegations in the Aronsons' lawsuit were a matter of public concern. First, unlike the cases cited above, the allegations of discrimination asserted in the Aronsons' lawsuit were not asserted against a public employer, nor were they asserted against any entity or person with which the general public had contact (*e.g.*, the major retailer in *Lewis*). Thus, there was no concern that the public's tax dollars were supporting discrimination (*e.g.*, as in the instance of a public employer charged with discrimination), nor was there a concern that members of the public were likely to be harmed or discriminated against (*e.g.*, as in the instance of a major retailer charged with discrimination). *See Saulpaugh v. Monroe Cmty. Hosp.*, 4 F.3d 134, 143 (2d Cir. 1993) (concluding that employee's complaints of sex discrimination did not implicate matters of public concern because they did not implicate "system-wide discrimination" and instead "were motivated by and dealt with her individual employment situation"); *cf. [Williams v. Continental Airlines, Inc.*, 943 P.2d 10, 18 (Colo. Ct. App. 1996)] (concluding public concern was not implicated where there was "no claim or evidence that plaintiff [was] an unsafe or less skilled pilot because he allegedly raped or attempted to rape women during off-duty hours," nor any evidence "that members of the flying public [we]re in danger of being sexually assaulted by plaintiff").[318]

The Baseless Allegations Factor. Finally, the court found it significant that the underlying controversy was known by the defendants to lack merit. The Tenth Circuit wrote:

---

[317] *Id.* at 1060.

[318] *Id.* at 1060–61.

[I]mportantly, Rosenthal and the ADL were intimately familiar with the Aronsons and their allegations, having talked and met with the Aronsons . . . on numerous occasions. . . . Unlike a third-party (*e.g.*, newspaper reporter) unfamiliar with the parties to a lawsuit or its underlying facts, Rosenthal and the ADL were in a position to know, and indeed knew or should have known, that the allegations in the Aronsons' lawsuit were baseless. Accordingly, we are unable to conclude that Rosenthal's comments at the press conference and on the radio show involved matters of "public concern" since Rosenthal and the ADL knew or should have known that the Aronsons' allegations of racial discrimination/harassment were not colorable. *See Kemp v. State Bd. of Agric.*, 803 P.2d 498, 504 (Colo. 1990) ("When an employee alleges a *colorable claim* that a university is guilty of racial discrimination, it is a matter of public concern.") (emphasis added); *see generally* . . . *Snead v. Redland Aggregates, Ltd.*, 998 F.2d 1325, 1330 (5th Cir. 1993) ("A speaker cannot turn his speech into a matter of public concern simply by issuing a press release."). We agree with the district court that the statements made by Rosenthal at the press conference and during the radio show did not involve matters of public concern.[319]

c.   Doubts About Presumed Damages Today

State Precedent Limiting Presumed Damages. It is useful to remember that, when it was decided in 1974, the Supreme Court's decision in *Gertz v. Robert Welch, Inc.*[320] appeared to hold that presumed damages were not available in *any case* absent actual malice. Thus, the *Restatement (Second) of Torts*, in 1977, embraced a general rule requiring proof of actual harm resulting from defamation.[321] Eleven years later, in 1985, the Supreme Court made clear, in *Dun & Bradstreet, Inc. v. Greenmoss Builders, Inc.*,[322] that the Constitution does not preclude an award of presumed damages without proof of actual malice in a case involving a private matter. However, during the period between the decisions in *Gertz* and *Dun & Bradstreet*, the original interpretation of *Gertz* influenced the development of the law at the state level. For example, decisions in Pennsylvania greatly restricted the availability of presumed damages.[323] Similar precedent limiting the common law rules on presumed damages exists in other jurisdictions, notwithstanding the fact that *Dun & Bradstreet* retreated from the original interpretation of *Gertz*. Thus, in *Smith v. Durden*,[324] the New Mexico Supreme Court held that as a matter of state law all defamation plaintiffs, "irrespective of the plaintiff's and communication's classification as public or private, . . . [must] prove actual injury to reputation and actual resulting damages."

However, other states continue to recognize the concept of presumed damages,

---

[319] *Id.* at 1061.

[320] 418 U.S. 323 (1974).

[321] RESTATEMENT (SECOND) OF TORTS § 621 and caveat (1977).

[322] 472 U.S. 749 (1985).

[323] *See Agriss v. Roadway Exp., Inc.*, 483 A.2d 456, 474 (Pa. Super. Ct. 1984).

[324] 276 P.3d 943 (N.M. 2012).

although sometimes only in restricted ways. In *W.J.A. v. D.A.*,[325] the high court of New Jersey, held that "presumed damages continue to play a role in our defamation jurisprudence in private plaintiff cases that do not involve matters of public concern." As the court explained, in New Jersey, "[w]here a plaintiff does not proffer evidence of actual damage to reputation, the doctrine of presumed damages permits him to survive a motion for summary judgment and to obtain nominal damages, thus vindicating his good name," however recovery of compensatory damages requires "proof of actual damage to reputation." Traditionally, the concept of presumed damages has been used by states to justify very substantial awards, not merely as a basis for nominal damages.

In *Bierman v. Weier*,[326] the Iowa Supreme Court held that "libel *per se* is available only when a private figure plaintiff sues a nonmedia defendant for certain kinds of defamatory statements that do not concern a matter of public importance." The court noted, with abundant citations to authority, that "Iowa is not the only state to continue to apply common law *per se* presumptions in private plaintiff/private concern cases involving (at least) nonmedia defendants."[327]

PROBLEM 3-8: THE FIRED PROFESSOR

Two stories aired on a local radio station last week. The story on Monday reported that:

> A lawsuit filed by a former Nathanael Greene University law professor could set a precedent. George Redeck was fired after he received tenure, in so many words, a job for life. His attorney, Linda Wong, says the university sees tenure as something that's conditional. Wong says that if she wins the case, it will mean that professors like Redeck will have job security when granted tenure. She says tenured professors like Redeck could only be fired for just cause. Wong said: "Several professors were dismissed with George Redeck, all of whom happen to be Anglo and male."

On Tuesday, the second story stated:

> According to Robert Garza, attorney for Nathanael Greene University, "George Redeck was never granted tenure by the university. The dean of the law school voted against granting him tenure. The other deans as a body voted against granting him tenure. And on these recommendations, the president of the university denied him tenure. In the spring of last year, the university notified professor Redeck that his application for tenure was denied and that his contract to teach at the university would not be renewed. Redeck's contract has since expired." Garza further stated: "George Redeck is not the only professor who has been denied tenure at the university in recent years. Contrary to the assertion made on this station on Monday that all of the other professors denied tenure 'happen to

---

[325] 43 A.3d 1148 (N.J. 2012).

[326] 826 N.W.2d 436, 448 (Iowa 2013).

[327] *Id.* at 455.

be Anglo and male,' two of the most recent disappointed applicants are female."

Ever since the stories aired, the university president has been besieged by phone calls from angry alumni because Redeck was a popular professor. Some of the alumni have accused the university of incompetence and discrimination in firing Redeck. Many alums have threatened to terminate their contributions to the university's annual fund. As assistant university counsel, please prepare an analysis of whether the university can state a cause of action for defamation against the radio station, Wong, or Redeck.

H.   DAMAGES AND INJUNCTIVE RELIEF

1.   Emotional Distress

Seeking Only Emotional Distress Damages. A defamation plaintiff may wish to avoid litigating the issue of damage to reputation, in order to avoid potentially brutal discovery requests, cross-examination, and testimony by others on that issue. In that case, the plaintiff may waive damages to reputation and seek compensation only for emotional distress. For example, in *Time, Inc. v. Firestone*,[328] a libel action arising from an erroneous report about a divorce, then-Justice William H. Rehnquist wrote:

> Petitioner has argued that because respondent withdrew her claim for damages to reputation on the eve of trial, there could be no recovery consistent with *Gertz* . . . [However, in *Gertz*] we made it clear that States could base awards on elements other than injury to reputation, specifically listing "personal humiliation, and mental anguish and suffering" as examples of injuries which might be compensated consistently with the Constitution upon a showing of fault. Because respondent has decided to forgo recovery for injury to her reputation, she is not prevented from obtaining compensation for such other damages that a defamatory falsehood may have caused her.
>
> . . . Several witnesses testified to the extent of respondent's anxiety and concern over Time's inaccurately reporting that she had been found guilty of adultery, and she herself took the stand to elaborate on her fears that her young son would be adversely affected by this falsehood when he grew older. The jury decided these injuries should be compensated by an award of $100,000. We have no warrant for re-examining this determination. . . .[329]

Establishing the Extent of Emotional Loss. Of course, a plaintiff seeking to recover emotional distress damages must always prove with reasonable certainty the extent of those losses. In *El-Khoury v. Kheir*,[330] a suit between two residents of

---

[328] 424 U.S. 448 (1976).

[329] *Id.* at 460–61.

[330] 241 S.W.3d 82 (Tex. App. 2007).

a village in Lebanon, the plaintiff proved the defendant defamed him by accusing him of not paying a debt relating to the transfer of an interest in a car dealership business with two locations in Houston. The jury awarded no damages for harm to reputation, $25,000 for emotional distress, and $147,000 in punitive damages. On appeal, the Texas Court of Appeals wrote:

> [T]he jury awarded nothing for the following elements of claimed damages: lost profits; harm to Kheir's "good name and character among his . . . friends, neighbors, or acquaintances"; his "good standing in the community"; or his "personal humiliation." The only damages awarded were for Kheir's "mental anguish and suffering," which the jury assessed at $25,000. . . . El-Khoury contends that the evidence is legally insufficient to support the jury's $25,000 award. . . .[331]

Mental anguish damages are recoverable in a defamation case. *Bentley v. Bunton*, 94 S.W.3d 561, 604 (Tex. 2002) (*Bentley I*). In *Bentley I*, the supreme court applied the legal-sufficiency test to mental anguish damages awarded as compensation for injuries and mental strain arising from damage to reputation and good name stemming from accusations of corruption by a media defendant. . . . Though a majority of the court agreed that Bentley had provided legally sufficient evidence of some amount of mental anguish, . . . a four-judge plurality concluded there was legally insufficient evidence to support $7 million in mental anguish damages. . . . On remand to consider that award, the Tyler Court of Appeals concluded that the $7 million mental anguish award was "unsupported by the evidence" and "so large as to be contrary to reason"; determined from the trial record that $150,000 would be "reasonable compensation"; and suggested a $6,850,000 remittitur. . . .

In addressing the remitted award in *Bunton v. Bentley*, 153 S.W.3d 50 (Tex. 2004) (*Bentley II*), the supreme court concluded that legally sufficient evidence supported awarding $150,000 to Bentley as compensatory damages for his mental anguish. . . . Citing *Bentley I*, the court noted that "the ordeal" of his defamation had cost Bentley time, deprived him of sleep, caused him embarrassment in the community in which he had spent almost all of his life, disrupted his family, and distressed his children at school. . . . Moreover, evidence from Bentley's friends showed that he had become depressed, that his honor and integrity had been impugned, and that his family's related suffering added to his own distress; in short, "he would never be the same." . . . In Bentley's own words, the experience of being accused of corruption was "the worst of his life." . . .

---

[331] Kheir contended on appeal that, because El-Khoury's statements constituted slander *per se*, he was not required to prove his damages. However, the court found that Kheir waived that argument by failing to object to certain questions submitted to the jury. Query: would the plaintiff's lawyer be subject to liability for malpractice based on failure to timely assert that the statement was actionable without proof of actual losses? That argument seems plausible. *See* Chapter 2 of Susan Saab Fortney & Vincent R. Johnson, Legal Malpractice Law: Problems and Prevention (2008) (discussing lawyers' liability for negligence).

Both *Bentley* decisions reflect the concerns initially expressed by the supreme court in *Saenz v. Fidelity & Guar. Ins. Underwriters*, 925 S.W.2d 607 (Tex. 1996), and *Parkway Co. v. Woodruff*, 901 S.W.2d 434 (Tex. 1995), that legally sufficient proof support mental anguish awards in order to "ensure" that recovery for such non-economic damages constitute compensation for actual injuries to the plaintiff rather than "a disguised disapproval of the defendant." . . .

> According to the definition derived from *Parkway*, mental anguish implies a relatively high degree of mental pain and distress. It is more than mere disappointment, anger, resentment or embarrassment, although it may include all of these. It includes a mental sensation of pain resulting from such painful emotions as grief, severe disappointment, indignation, wounded pride, shame, despair and/or public humiliation.

. . . Recognizing the "somewhat unwieldy" nature of the definition, the supreme court acknowledged that the definition nonetheless requires the jury to distinguish between "lesser" reactions and degrees of emotions, for example, disappointment, embarrassment, and anger, for which there is no compensation, and more extreme degrees of emotions, for example, severe disappointment, wounded pride, and indignation, which may be compensable in a proper case . . . on a further showing that these emotions substantially disrupted the plaintiff's daily routine. . . .

Evidence of "adequate details" to assess mental anguish may derive from the claimant's own testimony, the testimony of third parties, or testimony by expert witnesses. . . .

In addition to evidence of compensable mental anguish, under the standards just stated, some evidence must justify the amount awarded as compensation. . . . Consistent with the language of the standard jury charge used in this case, juries may not "simply pick a number and put it in the blank," but must determine an amount that "fairly and reasonably" compensates for mental anguish "that causes 'substantial disruption in . . . daily routine' or a 'high degree of mental pain and distress.' " . . .

. . . [W]e agree with El-Khoury that the evidence in this case is not legally sufficient to support the jury's awarding Kheir $25,000 as "fair" and "reasonable" compensation for mental anguish and suffering from allegedly defamatory statements by El-Khoury. . . .

Kheir and his wife provided the only testimony concerning his claim of mental anguish. There was no testimony by third parties and no expert testimony. Kheir generally attested to "stress" and "anxiety," and also stated that he lost weight, experienced headaches, and had difficulty sleeping that sometimes required him to take a sleeping pill. Though Kheir's wife stated that he was "half the man he was," the only specifics she provided were that he was "very stressed" and had difficulty sleeping. Neither Kheir nor his wife described a "high degree" of pain or distress that "substantially" disrupted Kheir's daily routine. . . . In addition, neither Kheir nor his wife attempted to establish a causal connection between the defamatory statements allegedly made by El-Khoury and Kheir's stress and anxiety.

To the contrary, Kheir's testimony consistently linked his stress to damage to his reputation or lack of respect among the 3,000 to 4,000 people in the Lebanese village where he lived and had his business. Yet, the jury rejected any amount of damages, either for harm, if any, to Kheir's "good name and character among his . . . friends, neighbors, and acquaintances," or harm, if any, to his "good standing in the community." . . .

Kheir also referred to his inability to obtain credit for a planned expansion of his business and stated that vendors and suppliers discontinued their previous practice of permitting him to pay accumulated invoices at the end of a season. But, the record establishes that Kheir's credit problems resulted from a lien that was automatically imposed on some of Kheir's property after El-Khoury filed suit in Lebanon to enforce the agreement to transfer. As the record further demonstrates, news of lawsuits appears in newspapers in Lebanon. Yet, Kheir bases his claims in this lawsuit on El-Khoury's allegedly defamatory statements to others, rather than on allegations in his lawsuit, which would be privileged regardless and, thus, not actionable. . . .

Finally, the record lacks any evidence from which the jury might have derived the $25,000 amount awarded to Kheir as fair and reasonable compensation for his claimed mental anguish. . . .

. . . [W]e hold that the evidence from the trial of this case would not enable reasonable and fair-minded people to arrive at the verdict reached by the jury here in awarding Kheir $25,000 for mental anguish and suffering. . . .

. . . .

Well-settled law [in Texas, but not in all states] holds that a party may not recover punitive, or exemplary, damages unless the party recovers actual damages. . . . Having concluded that Kheir may not recover the only actual damages awarded by the jury, we are compelled to hold that Kheir may not recover punitive damages. . . .[332]

The court remanded the case for a new trial on both liability and damages.

2.   Limitations on Punitive Damages

First Amendment Limitations. As discussed above, under the First Amendment, punitive damages are available in cases involving matters of public concern only if the plaintiff proves actual malice. That requirement does not apply to matters of purely private concern.

Due Process and State Limitations. However, any punitive damages award must comply with limitations imposed by state law and with the Due Process

---

[332] 241 S.W.3d at 85–89 (Tex. App. 2007).

requirements of the Fourteenth Amendment. Those restrictions, including the constitutional limitations recognized in *State Farm Mutual Automobile Insurance Co. v. Campbell*[333] and related cases, are discussed in Chapter 2 Part A-5-e.

3.   Injunctions Against Defamation

Temporary Versus Permanent Injunctions. In *Hill v. Petrotech Resources Corp.*,[334] the Supreme Court of Kentucky vacated a circuit court's temporary injunction against allegedly defamatory speech because it was an impermissible prior restraint on speech. The court carefully explained its reasons:

> Aside from the First Amendment's heavy presumption against prior restraints, courts have long held that equity will not enjoin a libel. . . . "Although the rule has been severely criticized by legal scholars, and the courts have occasionally deviated therefrom in extreme cases or where a collateral ground of equity jurisdiction could be found, it appears to be clearly established by the large majority of the cases upon this question that equity will not grant an injunction against the publication of a personal libel or slander in the absence of some independent ground for the invocation of equitable jurisdiction." . . .

> The traditional rule against enjoining defamation is of long-standing effect, having been first established in eighteenth-century England. . . . [W]hile there appears to be an emerging modern trend toward permitting such injunctions upon a final adjudication that the speech under question is false, there nevertheless remain staunch advocates of the traditional rule that a prior restraint on speech is unacceptable under any circumstances. . . .

> . . . Professor [Erwin] Chemerinsky argues that even after a judicial determination that the speech at issue is false, "[t]he injunction means that a person can only speak by going before the judge and getting permission. That is the very essence of a prior restraint." . . . In his view, it is always the case that "damages, not injunctions, are the appropriate remedy in a defamation action," . . . "even in the case of the "judgment proof defendant". . . .

> The recognition that false, defamatory speech is unprotected by the First Amendment has resulted in the development of a modern, superseding rule concerning the enjoining of defamatory speech. Under the modern rule, once a judge or jury has made a final determination that the speech at issue is defamatory, the speech determined to be false may be enjoined.

> The emergence of the modern rule was anticipated by now U.S. District Judge William O. Bertelsman in his 1971 law review article, Injunctions Against Speech and Writing: A Re-evaluation, 59 *Ky. L.J.* 319 (1971). In the article, Judge Bertelsman suggested that the traditional view . . . should be reevaluated, and that injunctions could be constitutionally granted in defamation and privacy cases under a standard similar to the rule as stated

---

[333] 538 U.S. 408 (2003).

[334] 325 S.W.3d 302 (Ky. 2010).

above. More recently, in *Lassiter v. Lassiter*, 456 F. Supp. 2d 876, 882 (E.D. Ky. 2006), Judge Bertelsman addressed the matter further.

In *Lassiter*, . . . Judge Bertelsman noted that this Court had not addressed the issue, but he surmised that when afforded the opportunity to rule on the propriety of injunctive relief against defamation or invasion of privacy, we would, if we permitted an injunction at all, do so only under the following standards:

> 1. That the injunction be clearly and narrowly drawn so as not to prohibit protected expression;
>
> 2. That the falsity or illegality of the expression be finally adjudicated prior to the issuance of the injunction;
>
> 3. That the falsity or illegality be established by at least clear and convincing evidence;
>
> 4. That the enjoined expression not be political in nature, or otherwise protected by the First Amendment, or on a subject so imbued with the public interest that its publication outweighs the social policy in the protection of reputation and privacy; and
>
> 5. That the usual equitable requirements for an injunction be met. . . .

We generally agree with the formulation suggested by Judge Bertelsman, and adopt all of it except the requirement that the falsity of the speech at issue be proven by clear and convincing evidence.[335] . . .

Thus, as a matter of first impression, we adopt the modern rule that defamatory speech may be enjoined only after the trial court's final determination by a preponderance of the evidence that the speech at issue is, in fact, false, and only then upon the condition that the injunction be narrowly tailored to limit the prohibited speech to that which has been judicially determined to be false.

. . . .

Upon application of the modern rule as described above to the circumstances of the present case, we need go no further than to note that the speech alleged to be false and defamatory by the Respondents has not been finally adjudicated to be, in fact, false. . . . Only upon such a determination could the speech be ascertained to be constitutionally unprotected, and therefore subject to injunction against future repetition. . . .[336]

---

[335] [n2:] We emphasize at this point that the discussion herein excludes injunctions that may relate to media defendants, public figures, and matters of public interest. An entirely separate set of rules is implicated when the litigation involves these parties and issues. *See New York Times v. Sullivan*, 376 U.S. 254 and its progeny.

[336] *Id.* at 306–11.

4.   Duty to Mitigate

The duty to mitigate damages applies broadly throughout American law. Texas has a special statute applicable to libel and slander actions called the "Defamation Mitigation Act."[337] That law imposes important limitations on the maintenance of any action for defamation and on the availability of punitive damages:

§ 73.052. Purpose

The purpose of this subchapter is to provide a method for a person who has been defamed by a publication or broadcast to mitigate any perceived damage or injury.

. . . .

§ 73.054. Applicability

(a) This subchapter applies to a claim for relief, however characterized, from damages arising out of harm to personal reputation caused by the false content of a publication.

(b) This subchapter applies to all publications, including writings, broadcasts, oral communications, electronic transmissions, or other forms of transmitting information.

§ 73.055. Request for Correction, Clarification, or Retraction

(a) A person may maintain an action for defamation only if:

(1) the person has made a timely and sufficient request for a correction, clarification, or retraction from the defendant; or

(2) the defendant has made a correction, clarification, or retraction.

(b) A request for a correction, clarification, or retraction is timely if made during the period of limitation for commencement of an action for defamation.

(c) If not later than the 90th day after receiving knowledge of the publication, the person does not request a correction, clarification, or retraction, the person may not recover exemplary damages.

(d) A request for a correction, clarification, or retraction is sufficient if it:

(1) is served on the publisher;

(2) is made in writing, reasonably identifies the person making the request, and is signed by the individual claiming to have been defamed or by the person's authorized attorney or agent;

(3) states with particularity the statement alleged to be false and defamatory and, to the extent known, the time and place of publication;

(4) alleges the defamatory meaning of the statement; and

---

[337] Tex. Civ. Prac. & Rem. Code § 73.051 *et seq.* (Lexis 2014).

(5) specifies the circumstances causing a defamatory meaning of the statement if it arises from something other than the express language of the publication.

(e) A period of limitation for commencement of an action under this section is tolled during the period allowed by Sections 73.056 and 73.057.

§ *73.056. Disclosure of Evidence of Falsity*

(a) A person who has been requested to make a correction, clarification, or retraction may ask the person making the request to provide reasonably available information regarding the falsity of the allegedly defamatory statement not later than the 30th day after the date the person receives the request. Any information requested under this section must be provided by the person seeking the correction, clarification, or retraction not later than the 30th day after the date the person receives the request.

(b) If a correction, clarification, or retraction is not made, a person who, without good cause, fails to disclose the information requested under Subsection (a) may not recover exemplary damages, unless the publication was made with actual malice.

§ *73.057. Timely and Sufficient Correction, Clarification, or Retraction*

(a) A correction, clarification, or retraction is timely if it is made not later than the 30th day after receipt of:

(1) the request for the correction, clarification, or retraction; or

(2) the information requested under Section 73.056(a).

(b) A correction, clarification, or retraction is sufficient if it is published in the same manner and medium as the original publication or, if that is not possible, with a prominence and in a manner and medium reasonably likely to reach substantially the same audience as the publication complained of and:

(1) is publication of an acknowledgment that the statement specified as false and defamatory is erroneous;

(2) is an allegation that the defamatory meaning arises from other than the express language of the publication and the publisher disclaims an intent to communicate that meaning or to assert its truth;

(3) is a statement attributed to another person whom the publisher identifies and the publisher disclaims an intent to assert the truth of the statement; or

(4) is publication of the requestor's statement of the facts, as set forth in a request for correction, clarification, or retraction, or a fair summary of the statement, exclusive of any portion that is defamatory of another, obscene, or otherwise improper for publication.

(c) If a request for correction, clarification, or retraction has specified two or more statements as false and defamatory, the correction, clarification, or retraction may deal with the statements individually in any manner provided by Subsection (b).

(d) Except as provided by Subsection (e), a correction, clarification, or retraction is published with a prominence and in a manner and medium reasonably likely to reach substantially the same audience as the publication complained of if:

(1) it is published in a later issue, edition, or broadcast of the original publication;

(2) publication is in the next practicable issue, edition, or broadcast of the original publication because the publication will not be published within the time limits established for a timely correction, clarification, or retraction; or

(3) the original publication no longer exists and if the correction, clarification, or retraction is published in the newspaper with the largest general circulation in the region in which the original publication was distributed.

(e) If the original publication was on the Internet, a correction, clarification, or retraction is published with a prominence and in a manner and medium reasonably likely to reach substantially the same audience as the publication complained of if the publisher appends to the original publication the correction, clarification, or retraction.

§ *73.058. Challenges to Correction, Clarification, or Retraction or to Request for Correction, Clarification, or Retraction*

(a) If a defendant in an action under this subchapter intends to rely on a timely and sufficient correction, clarification, or retraction, the defendant's intention to do so, and the correction, clarification, or retraction relied on, must be stated in a notice served on the plaintiff on the later of:

(1) the 60th day after service of the citation; or

(2) the 10th day after the date the correction, clarification, or retraction is made.

(b) A correction, clarification, or retraction is timely and sufficient unless the plaintiff challenges the timeliness or sufficiency not later than the 20th day after the date notice under Subsection (a) is served. If a plaintiff challenges the timeliness or sufficiency, the plaintiff must state the challenge in a motion to declare the correction, clarification, or retraction untimely or insufficient served not later than the 30th day after the date notice under Subsection (a) is served on the plaintiff or the 30th day after the date the correction, clarification, or retraction is made, whichever is later.

(c) If a defendant intends to challenge the sufficiency or timeliness of a request for a correction, clarification, or retraction, the defendant must state the challenge in a motion to declare the request insufficient or untimely served not later than the 60th day after the date of service of the citation.

(d) Unless there is a reasonable dispute regarding the actual contents of the request for correction, clarification, or retraction, the sufficiency and timeliness of a request for correction, clarification, or retraction is a question of law. At the earliest appropriate time before trial, the court shall rule, as a matter of law, whether the request for correction, clarification, or retraction meets the requirements of this subchapter.

§ 73.059. *Effect of Correction, Clarification, or Retraction*

If a correction, clarification, or retraction is made in accordance with this subchapter, regardless of whether the person claiming harm made a request, a person may not recover exemplary damages unless the publication was made with actual malice.

§ 73.060. *Scope of Protection*

A timely and sufficient correction, clarification, or retraction made by a person responsible for a publication constitutes a correction, clarification, or retraction made by all persons responsible for that publication but does not extend to an entity that republished the information.

[Other parts of the act have been omitted: § 73.061 ("Admissibility of Evidence of Correction, Clarification, or Retraction") and § 73.062. ("Abatement").]

PROBLEM 3-9: THE ALUMNI MAGAZINE

North American University endeavors to maintain the fond regard of its 97,000 alumni by publishing a quarterly magazine. The magazine contains news about the university and its graduates, including a "Class Notes" section with short entries about university alumni, arranged by class year. The entries listed in Class Notes, which are never more than a paragraph long, are typically based on information that alumni submit to the magazine about their professional accomplishments and family developments. Some entries are composed from stories found in news-wire services, press releases, and newspapers.

The spring issue of the alumni magazine contained the following information in the Class Notes section:

> Ross Lamont, BS 2001, was named chief operating officer of the Gay Rights League, a non-profit organization which lobbies for legal recognition of gay and lesbian rights. He married his life-partner, Brett Rile, BA 2002, on June 11, 2009, in Boston. Lamont and Rile are both employed at Citibank in Manhattan and live in Greenwich Village.

You are assistant counsel to North American University. Lamont and Rile have each threatened to sue. They are not gay, not married, not employed at Citibank, and do not live in Greenwich Village. The Gay Rights League is a nonexistent entity.

The university Alumni Affairs Office, which compiles the Class Notes section of the magazine, has no record of the source of the information for the Lamont/Rile entry. The director of the office has acknowledged that the office has no standardized fact-checking process for verifying Class Notes entries. The director emphasized, however, that nothing like this has ever happened before at the university.

Prepare to advise the university president on the legal risks posed by the threatened suit and to recommend a course of action. Assume that applicable state law includes a statute similar to the Texas Defamation Mitigation Act quoted above.

I. DEFENSES AND OBSTACLES TO RECOVERY

1. The Communications Decency Act of 1996

Cases against Internet service providers (ISPs) originally focused on whether an ISP exercised editorial control. In an early, much-noted case, *Stratton Oakmont, Inc. v. Prodigy Services Co.*,[338] the court wrote:

> First, Prodigy held itself out to the public and its members as controlling the content of its computer bulletin boards. Second, Prodigy implemented this control through its automatic software screening program, and the Guidelines which Board Leaders are required to enforce. By actively utilizing technology and manpower to delete notes from its computer bulletin boards on the basis of offensiveness and "bad taste," for example, Prodigy is clearly making decisions as to content . . . and such decisions constitute editorial control. . . . [T]his Court is compelled to conclude that for the purposes of plaintiffs' claims in this action, Prodigy is a publisher rather than a distributor.[339]

Some persons feared that decisions like *Stratton Oakmont* would inhibit the growth and use of the Internet. In response to those concerns, Congress passed the Communications Decency Act of 1996, which now greatly limits the liability of ISPs and many other potential defendants.

a. The Congressional Language

Under the Communications Decency Act, "[n]o provider or user of an interactive computer service shall be treated as the publisher or speaker of any information provided by another information content provider."[340] Because a clear understanding of the reach of this language is crucial in a wide range of tort litigation, it is useful to look at this provision in its legislative context, including the Act's statements of purpose and definitions. The relevant provision is 47 U.S.C. § 230, which states in full:

(a) Findings

The Congress finds the following:

---

[338] 1995 N.Y. Misc. LEXIS 229 (May 26, 1995).

[339] *Id.* at *10–*11.

[340] 47 U.S.C.S. § 230(c)(1) (LEXIS 2014).

(1) The rapidly developing array of Internet and other interactive computer services available to individual Americans represent an extraordinary advance in the availability of educational and informational resources to our citizens.

(2) These services offer users a great degree of control over the information that they receive, as well as the potential for even greater control in the future as technology develops.

(3) The Internet and other interactive computer services offer a forum for a true diversity of political discourse, unique opportunities for cultural development, and myriad avenues for intellectual activity.

(4) The Internet and other interactive computer services have flourished, to the benefit of all Americans, with a minimum of government regulation.

(5) Increasingly Americans are relying on interactive media for a variety of political, educational, cultural, and entertainment services.

(b) Policy

It is the policy of the United States—

(1) to promote the continued development of the Internet and other interactive computer services and other interactive media;

(2) to preserve the vibrant and competitive free market that presently exists for the Internet and other interactive computer services, unfettered by Federal or State regulation;

(3) to encourage the development of technologies which maximize user control over what information is received by individuals, families, and schools who use the Internet and other interactive computer services;

(4) to remove disincentives for the development and utilization of blocking and filtering technologies that empower parents to restrict their children's access to objectionable or inappropriate online material; and

(5) to ensure vigorous enforcement of Federal criminal laws to deter and punish trafficking in obscenity, stalking, and harassment by means of computer.

(c) Protection for "good samaritan" blocking and screening of offensive material

(1) Treatment of publisher or speaker

No provider or user of an interactive computer service shall be treated as the publisher or speaker of any information provided by another information content provider.

(2) Civil liability

No provider or user of an interactive computer service shall be held liable on account of—

(A) any action voluntarily taken in good faith to restrict access to or availability of material that the provider or user considers to be obscene, lewd, lascivious, filthy, excessively violent, harassing, or otherwise objectionable, whether or not such material is constitutionally protected; or

(B) any action taken to enable or make available to information content providers or others the technical means to restrict access to material described in paragraph (1).

(d) Obligations of interactive computer service

A provider of interactive computer service shall, at the time of entering an agreement with a customer for the provision of interactive computer service and in a manner deemed appropriate by the provider, notify such customer that parental control protections (such as computer hardware, software, or filtering services) are commercially available that may assist the customer in limiting access to material that is harmful to minors. Such notice shall identify, or provide the customer with access to information identifying, current providers of such protections.

(e) Effect on other laws

(1) No effect on criminal law

Nothing in this section shall be construed to impair the enforcement of section 223 or 231 of this title, chapter 71 (relating to obscenity) or 110 (relating to sexual exploitation of children) of Title 18, or any other Federal criminal statute.

(2) No effect on intellectual property law

Nothing in this section shall be construed to limit or expand any law pertaining to intellectual property.

(3) State law

Nothing in this section shall be construed to prevent any State from enforcing any State law that is consistent with this section. No cause of action may be brought and no liability may be imposed under any State or local law that is inconsistent with this section.

(4) No effect on Communications Privacy law

Nothing in this section shall be construed to limit the application of the Electronic Communications Privacy Act of 1986 or any of the amendments made by such Act, or any similar State law.

(f) Definitions

As used in this section:

(1) Internet

The term "Internet" means the international computer network of both Federal and non-Federal interoperable packet switched data networks.

(2) Interactive computer service

The term "interactive computer service" means any information service, system, or access software provider that provides or enables computer access by multiple users to a computer server, including specifically a service or system that provides access to the Internet and such systems operated or services offered by libraries or educational institutions.

(3) Information content provider

The term "information content provider" means any person or entity that is responsible, in whole or in part, for the creation or development of information provided through the Internet or any other interactive computer service.

(4) Access software provider

The term "access software provider" means a provider of software (including client or server software), or enabling tools that do any one or more of the following:

(A) filter, screen, allow, or disallow content;

(B) pick, choose, analyze, or digest content; or

(C) transmit, receive, display, forward, cache, search, subset, organize, reorganize, or translate content.[341]

b.   Internet Service Providers and Distributor Liability

Section 230 of the Communications Decency Act has been broadly interpreted as banning defamation and other claims against Internet services. For example, in *Blumenthal v. Drudge*,[342] a federal court for the District of Columbia found that an Internet service provider was immune from defamation liability based on a gossip column, even though the provider paid the columnist, promoted the column as a new source of unverified instant gossip, and had certain editorial rights.

In *Barrett v. Rosenthal*,[343] the Supreme Court of California recounted the decision of the Fourth Circuit in *Zeran v. America Online, Inc.*,[344] which rejected the theory of distributor liability as applied to defamation on the Internet. *Barrett* agreed with *Zeran* that Congress did not intend to create such an exception to the immunity conferred by § 230 of the Communications Decency Act of 1996. The *Barrett* court wrote:

Kenneth Zeran was bombarded with angry and derogatory telephone calls, including death threats, after an unidentified person posted a message on

---

[341] 47 U.S.C.S. § 230 (LEXIS 2014).

[342] 992 F. Supp. 44 (D.D.C. 1998).

[343] 146 P.3d 510 (Cal. 2006).

[344] 129 F.3d 327 (4th Cir. 1997).

an America Online, Inc. (AOL) bulletin board. The message advertised t-shirts with offensive slogans referring to the Oklahoma City bombing of the Alfred P. Murrah Federal Building, and instructed prospective purchasers to call Zeran's home telephone number. Zeran notified AOL of the problem, and the posting was eventually removed. However, similar postings appeared, and an Oklahoma radio announcer aired the contents of the first message. Zeran was again inundated with threatening phone calls. He sued AOL for unreasonable delay in removing the defamatory messages, refusing to post retractions, and failing to screen for similar postings.

AOL successfully moved for judgment on the pleadings. . . . The Fourth Circuit Court of Appeals affirmed, holding that the plain language of section 230 "creates a federal immunity to any cause of action that would make service providers liable for information originating with a third-party user of the service. Specifically, § 230 precludes courts from entertaining claims that would place a computer service provider in a publisher's role. Thus, lawsuits seeking to hold a service provider liable for its exercise of a publisher's traditional editorial functions — such as deciding whether to publish, withdraw, postpone or alter content — are barred." . . .

. . . While original posters of defamatory speech do not escape accountability, Congress "made a policy choice . . . not to deter harmful online speech [by] imposing tort liability on companies that serve as intermediaries for other parties' potentially injurious messages." . . . This policy reflects a concern that if service providers faced tort liability for republished messages on the Internet, they "might choose to severely restrict the number and type of messages posted." . . .

Zeran made the same argument adopted by the Court of Appeal here: that Congress intended to distinguish between "publishers" and "distributors," immunizing publishers but leaving distributors exposed to liability. . . . Zeran contended that because Congress mentioned only the term "publisher" in section 230, it intended to leave "distributors" unprotected. He claimed that once he gave AOL notice that it was posting defamatory statements on its bulletin board, AOL became liable as a "distributor." . . .

The *Zeran* court held that the publisher/distributor distinction makes no difference for purposes of section 230 immunity. Publication is a necessary element of all defamation claims, and includes every repetition and distribution of a defamatory statement. . . . Although "distributors" become liable only upon notice, they are nevertheless included in "the larger publisher category." . . . [Zeran] "simply attaches too much importance to the presence of the distinct notice element in distributor liability. . . . [O]nce a computer service provider receives notice of a potentially defamatory posting, it is thrust into the role of a traditional publisher. The computer service provider must decide whether to publish, edit, or withdraw the posting. In this respect, Zeran seeks to impose liability on AOL for assuming the role for which § 230 specifically proscribes liability — the publisher role." . . .

Subjecting service providers to notice liability would defeat "the dual purposes" of section 230, by encouraging providers to restrict speech and abstain from self-regulation. . . . A provider would be at risk for liability each time it received notice of a potentially defamatory statement in any Internet message, requiring an investigation of the circumstances, a legal judgment about the defamatory character of the information, and an editorial decision on whether to continue the publication. "Although this might be feasible for the traditional print publisher, the sheer number of postings on interactive computer services would create an impossible burden in the Internet context." . . .

"More generally, notice-based liability for interactive computer service providers would provide third parties with a no-cost means to create the basis for future lawsuits. Whenever one was displeased with the speech of another party conducted over an interactive computer service, the offended party could simply 'notify' the relevant service provider, claiming the information to be legally defamatory. . . . Because the probable effects of distributor liability on the vigor of Internet speech and on service provider self-regulation are directly contrary to § 230's statutory purposes, we will not assume that Congress intended to leave liability upon notice intact." . . .

The *Zeran* court's views have been broadly accepted, in both federal and state courts. Before the Court of Appeal issued its opinion below, two other California Courts of Appeal had followed *Zeran*. In *Kathleen R. v. City of Livermore* (2001) 87 Cal. App. 4th 684, 104 Cal. Rptr. 2d 772, a taxpayer sued after her son obtained sexually explicit photographs through an Internet connection at a public library. She sought injunctive relief on various theories of liability. . . . The *Kathleen R.* court held that the state law causes of action were barred by section 230. . . .

In *Gentry v. eBay, Inc.* (2002) 99 Cal. App. 4th 816, 121 Cal. Rptr.2d 703, the plaintiffs used eBay's on-line marketing services to purchase sports memorabilia. Claiming the items bore forged autographs, they sued eBay for negligence, unfair trade practices, and violation of Civil Code section 1739.7, which regulates the sale of such collectibles. . . . The *Gentry* court ruled that section 230 immunized eBay from liability on all the plaintiffs' claims. It . . . reasoned that the plaintiffs were trying to hold eBay responsible for disseminating information provided by the individual sellers who used its service. . . .[345]

The *Barrett* court agreed with *Zeran* that § 230 provides immunity to distributors as well as other publishers.

---

[345] 146 P.3d at 515–18.

c.   Website Operators

In many cases, protection under the Act extends to website operators. Thus, in *Doe v. Friendfinder Network, Inc.*,[346] a federal court in New Hampshire held that the operator of a "sex and swinger" website was immune from various state law tort claims even though "certain features of the AdultFriendFinder service facilitated the submission of false or unauthorized profiles." And in *Schneider v. Amazon.com, Inc.*[347] the Washington Court of Appeals concluded that an online bookseller was not liable for defamatory comments posted about an author's books. Immunity is not lost simply because the website operator exercises the option to edit or delete some of the information that has been posted.[348] Thus, in *Batzel v. Smith*,[349] the Ninth Circuit ruled that the operator of an anti-art-theft website, who posted an allegedly defamatory e-mail authored by a third party, and who did no more than select and make minor alterations to the e-mail, could not be considered a content provider subject to liability under the CDA.

d.   Individual "Users" of the Internet

In *Barrett v. Rosenthal*,[350] section 230 immunity was "invoked by an individual who had no supervisory role in the operation of the Internet site where allegedly defamatory material appeared."[351] As the facts were described by the Supreme Court of California:

> Plaintiffs, Dr. Stephen J. Barrett and Dr. Terry Polevoy, operated Web sites devoted to exposing health frauds. Defendant Ilena Rosenthal directed the Humantics Foundation for Women and operated an Internet discussion group. Plaintiffs alleged that Rosenthal and others committed libel by maliciously distributing defamatory statements in e-mails and Internet postings, impugning plaintiffs' character and competence and disparaging their efforts to combat fraud. They alleged that Rosenthal republished various messages even after Dr. Barrett warned her they contained false and defamatory information.
>
> . . . The [trial] court determined that the only actionable statement appeared in an article Rosenthal received via e-mail from her codefendant Tim Bolen. This article, subtitled "Opinion by Tim Bolen," accused Dr. Polevoy of stalking a Canadian radio producer. Rosenthal posted a copy of this article on the Web sites of two newsgroups devoted to alternative health issues. . . .[352]

Turning to the issue of whether Rosenthal's republication of the Bolen article was

---

[346] 540 F. Supp. 2d 288, 294–95 (D.N.H. 2008).

[347] 31 P.3d 37 (Wash. Ct. App. 2001).

[348] *See Ben Ezra, Weinstein, and Company, Inc. v. America Online, Inc.*, 206 F.3d 980 (10th Cir. 2000).

[349] 333 F.3d 1018 (9th Cir. 2003).

[350] 146 P.3d 510 (Cal. 2006).

[351] *Id.* at 515.

[352] *Id.* at 513–14.

immune from suit, the court considered the question of "user" liability. It wrote:

> Individual Internet "users" like Rosenthal, . . . are situated differently from institutional service providers with regard to some of the principal policy considerations discussed by the *Zeran* court and reflected in the Congressional Record. In particular, individuals do not face the massive volume of third-party postings that providers encounter. Self-regulation is a far less challenging enterprise for them. Furthermore, service providers, no matter how active or passive a role they take in screening the content posted by users of their services, typically bear' less responsibility for that content than do the users. Users are more likely than service providers to actively engage in malicious propagation of defamatory or other offensive material. These considerations bring into question the scope of the term "user" in section 230, and whether it matters if a user is engaged in active or passive conduct for purposes of the statutory immunity.

> "User" is not defined in the statute, and the limited legislative record does not indicate why Congress included users as well as service providers under the umbrella of immunity granted by section 230(c)(1). The standard rules of statutory construction, however, yield an unambiguous result. We must begin with the language employed by Congress and the assumption that its ordinary meaning expresses the legislative purpose. . . . [The term "user"] plainly refers to someone who uses something, and the statutory context makes it clear that Congress simply meant someone who uses an interactive computer service.

> Section 230(c)(1) refers directly to the "user of an interactive computer service." Section 230(f)(2) defines "interactive computer service" as "any information service, system, or access software provider that provides or enables computer access by multiple users to a computer server, including specifically a service or system that provides access to the Internet. . . ." Section 230(a)(2) notes that such services "offer users a great degree of control over the information that they receive," and section 230(b)(3) expresses Congress's intent "to encourage the development of technologies which maximize user control over what information is received by individuals, families, and schools who use the Internet and other interactive computer services." Thus, Congress consistently referred to "users" of interactive computer services, specifically including "individuals" in section 230(b)(3).

> There is no reason to suppose that Congress attached a different meaning to the term "user" in section 230(c)(1). . . . Rosenthal used the Internet to gain access to newsgroups where she posted Bolen's article about Polevoy. She was therefore a "user" under the CDA, as the parties conceded below. Nor is there any basis for concluding that Congress intended to treat service providers and users differently when it declared that "[n]o provider or user of an interactive computer service shall be treated as [a] publisher or speaker. . . ." (§ 230(c)(1).) We cannot construe the statute so as to render the term "user" inoperative. . . .

Polevoy urges us to distinguish between "active" and "passive" Internet use, and to restrict the statutory term "user" to those who engage in passive use. He notes that subdivisions (a)(2) and (b)(3) of section 230 refer to information "received" by users. He also observes that the caption of subdivision (c) is "Protection for 'good samaritan' blocking and screening of offensive material." From these premises, Polevoy reasons that the term "user" must be construed to refer only to those who receive offensive information, and those who screen and remove such information from an Internet site. He argues that those who actively post or republish information on the Internet are "information content providers" unprotected by the statutory immunity. "Information content provider" is defined as "any person or entity that is responsible, in whole or in part, for the creation or development of information provided through the Internet or any other interactive computer service. . . ." (§ 230(f)(3).)

Polevoy's view fails to account for the statutory provision at the center of our inquiry: the prohibition in section 230(c)(1) against treating any "user" as "the publisher or speaker of any information provided by another information content provider." A user who merely receives information on a computer without making it available to anyone else would be neither a "publisher" nor a "speaker." Congress obviously had a broader meaning in mind. Nor is it clear how a user who removes a posting may be deemed "passive" while one who merely allows a posting to remain online is "active." Furthermore, Congress plainly did not intend to deprive all "information content providers" of immunity, because the reference to "another" such provider in section 230(c)(1) presumes that the immunized publisher or speaker is also an information content provider. . . .[353]

We conclude there is no basis for deriving a special meaning for the term "user" in section 230(c)(1), or any operative distinction between "active" and "passive" Internet use. By declaring that no "user" may be treated as a "publisher" of third party content, Congress has comprehensively immunized republication by individual Internet users.

. . . .

We share the concerns of those who have expressed reservations about the *Zeran* court's broad interpretation of section 230 immunity. The prospect of blanket immunity for those who intentionally redistribute defamatory statements on the Internet has disturbing implications. . . .

Plaintiffs are free under section 230 to pursue the originator of a defamatory Internet publication. Any further expansion of liability must await congressional action.[354]

---

[353] [n.19] At some point, active involvement in the creation of a defamatory Internet posting would expose a defendant to liability as an original source. Because Rosenthal made no changes in the article she republished on the newsgroups, we need not consider when that line is crossed. We note, however, that many courts have reasoned that participation going no further than the traditional editorial functions of a publisher cannot deprive a defendant of section 230 immunity. . . .

[354] 146 P.3d at 526–29.

e.   Anonymous Postings on the Internet

Subpoenas to Disclose Identities. Because providers of defamatory content can be held liable for defamation posted on the Internet, it often becomes critical for a plaintiff to discover the identity of the author of anonymously posted statements.

(1)   Example: *Krinsky v. Doe No. 6*

In *Krinsky v. Doe 6*,[355] a corporate officer allegedly defamed on the Internet sued ten "Doe" defendants and served a subpoena on Yahoo!, Inc., a message-board host, seeking information on the identities about the pseudonymous posters. Doe No. 6 unsuccessfully moved to quash the subpoena. On appeal, Doe No. 6 argued that the trial court had erred because there is a constitutional right to speak anonymously on the Internet.

Constitutional Right to Speak Anonymously. Addressing the right to speak anonymously in *Krinsky*, the California Court of Appeal wrote:

> The use of a pseudonymous screen name offers a safe outlet for the user to experiment with novel ideas, express unorthodox political views, or criticize corporate or individual behavior without fear of intimidation or reprisal. In addition, by concealing speakers' identities, the online forum allows individuals of any economic, political, or social status to be heard without suppression or other intervention by the media or more powerful figures in the field.

> Yet no one is truly anonymous on the Internet, even with the use of a pseudonym. Yahoo! warns users of its message boards that their identities can be traced, and that it will reveal their identifying information when legally compelled to do so. . . .

> When vigorous criticism descends into defamation, however, constitutional protection is no longer available. "[I]t is well understood that the right of free speech is not absolute at all times and under all circumstances. There are certain well-defined and narrowly limited classes of speech, the prevention and punishment of which has never been thought to raise any Constitutional problem. These include the lewd and obscene, the profane, the libelous, and the insulting or 'fighting' words — those which by their very utterance inflict injury or tend to incite an immediate breach of the peace. It has been well observed that such utterances are no essential part of any exposition of ideas, and are of such slight social value as a step to truth that any benefit that may be derived from them is clearly outweighed by the social interest in order and morality." . . .

> Corporate and individual targets of . . . online aspersions may seek redress by filing suit against their unknown detractors. Once notified of a lawsuit by the website host or ISP, a defendant may then assert his or her First Amendment right to speak anonymously through an application for a

---

[355] 159 Cal. App. 4th 1154 (2008).

protective order or, as here, a motion to quash the subpoena. The present action for defamation and interference with business relationships is but one example of such confrontations.[356]

Tests to Determine Whether a Subpoena Will Be Enforced. The *Krinsky* court then turned to the question of what test should be used to determine whether the interests of the person allegedly harmed by improper communications should take precedence over the interest of the anonymous speaker. The court discussed four options: (1) a "good faith" test; (2) balancing the plaintiff's *prima facie* case against the defendant's First Amendment rights; (3) whether there are facts sufficient to defeat a motion for summary judgment or a motion to dismiss; and (4) simply whether the plaintiff has stated a *prima facie* case.

Option #1: The Good Faith Test. Addressing the first option, the *Krinsky* court wrote:

> Federal and state courts have made valiant efforts to devise a fair standard by which to balance the interests of the parties involved in disputes over Internet speech. The most deferential to plaintiffs are those applying a "good faith" standard. (*See, e.g., In re Subpoena Duces Tecum to America Online, Inc.* (2000) 52 Va. Cir. 26, 37, 2000 WL 1210372 [ISP required to disclose Doe identities upon corporate plaintiff's "legitimate, good faith basis" for alleging actionable conduct and the necessity of the information to advance the claim].) Plaintiff does not urge us to adopt such a low threshold for disclosure, nor would we do so; it offers no practical, reliable way to determine the plaintiff's good faith and leaves the speaker with little protection.[357]

Option #2: Balancing Prima Facie Case Against First Amendment Rights. Turning to the second option, the court explained:

> Other courts have exercised greater scrutiny of the plaintiff's cause of action before allowing the speaker to be identified. In *Dendrite International Inc. v. John Doe No. 3* (2001) 342 N.J. Super. 134, 775 A.2d 756, for example, a corporation alleged defamation by multiple Doe defendants on a Yahoo! message board and then sought expedited discovery in order to learn their identities. The New Jersey appellate court set forth a four-part test, to ensure that plaintiffs do not use discovery to "harass, intimidate or silence critics in the public forum opportunities presented by the Internet." . . . First, the plaintiff must make an effort to notify the anonymous poster that he or she is the subject of a subpoena or application for a disclosure order, giving a reasonable time for the poster to file opposition. The plaintiff must also set forth the specific statements that are alleged to be actionable. Third, the plaintiff must produce sufficient evidence to state a *prima facie* cause of action. If this showing is made, then the final step should be undertaken: to balance the strength of that *prima facie* case against the defendant's First Amendment right to speak anonymously. . . . In *Den-*

---

[356] *Id.* at 237–39.

[357] *Id.* at 241.

drite, the appellate court affirmed the trial court's denial of the discovery application, as the corporate plaintiff had failed to produce evidence that any decline in its stock price had been caused by the offensive messages.[358]

Option #3: Facts Sufficient to Defeat Summary Judgment or Dismissal. The court then explained but rejected the third option:

> Neither party advocates a third line of analysis set forth in *Doe v. Cahill*, [884 A.2d 451 (Del. 2005)], a case involving political speech about a public figure. In *Cahill* the Doe defendant was sued for defamation after criticizing a town councilman on an Internet blog. . . .
>
> . . . The *Cahill* court . . . adopted a standard applicable to a plaintiff opposing summary judgment. Thus, the plaintiff "must support his defamation claim with facts sufficient to defeat a summary judgment motion." . . .[359] . . .
>
> *Cahill* was followed by trial courts in various jurisdictions. . . . In *Lassa v. Rongstad* (2006) 294 Wis.2d 187 [718 N.W.2d 673], however, the Wisconsin Supreme Court rejected the Delaware court's summary judgment standard in favor of a motion-to-dismiss standard. The "silly or trivial libel claims" that would survive a motion to dismiss in a notice-pleading state such as Delaware would be adequately tested on a motion to dismiss in Wisconsin, where the statement constituting libel must be set forth in the complaint. The majority opinion did not, however, explain how (or if) a motion to dismiss would incorporate a balancing of the parties' competing interests.
>
> Other courts have utilized a motion-to-dismiss standard in weighing the need of injured parties to discover the identity of libelous Doe defendants against the rights of those defendants to speak anonymously. . . .
>
> We find it unnecessary and potentially confusing to attach a procedural label, whether summary judgment or motion to dismiss, to the showing required of a plaintiff seeking the identity of an anonymous speaker on the Internet. California subpoenas in Internet libel cases may relate to actions filed in other jurisdictions, which may have different standards governing pleading and motions. . . .
>
> We agree with the Delaware Supreme Court that . . . [requiring the plaintiff to attempt to notify the defendant] does not appear to be unduly burdensome. . . . We recognize, however, that an Internet Web site, chat room, or message board may no longer exist or be active by the time the plaintiff brings suit; consequently, it would be unrealistic and unprofitable to insist, as did the *Cahill* court, that a plaintiff "post a message notifying the anonymous defendant of the plaintiff's discovery request on the same message board where the allegedly defamatory statement was originally posted." . . . Moreover, when ISPs and message-board sponsors (such as

---

[358] *Id.*

[359] [n.9] The court made an exception for the element of malice in a case involving a public figure, a showing that depends on whether the defendant had knowledge that his or her statement was false or made it with reckless disregard as to its truth. . . .

Yahoo!) themselves notify the defendant that disclosure of his or her identity is sought, notification by the plaintiff should not be necessary. And in the procedural posture presented here, where the defendant is moving to quash the subpoena, the notification requirement benefits no one. Obviously Doe 6 has already learned of the subpoena or he would not be seeking protection.[360]

Option #4: The Prima Facie Showing Test. The California Court of Appeal then explained why it was adopting the fourth option:

> Common to most courts considering the issue is the necessity that the plaintiff make a *prima facie* showing that a case for defamation exists. Requiring at least that much ensures that the plaintiff is not merely seeking to harass or embarrass the speaker or stifle legitimate criticism. . . .
>
> Plaintiff objects to the requirement of a *prima facie* showing. She contends that it infringes a party's due process right because it does not include a reasonable opportunity to obtain evidence a plaintiff would need to establish a *prima facie* case. She does not, however, explain why she would necessarily be deprived of such an opportunity in the context of a motion to quash. . . . In an Internet libel case, that burden should not be insurmountable; here, for example, plaintiff knows the statement that was made and produced evidence of its falsity and the effect it had on her.
>
> We therefore agree with those courts that have compelled the plaintiff to make a *prima facie* showing of the elements of libel in order to overcome a defendant's motion to quash a subpoena seeking his or her identity. Where it is clear to the court that discovery of the defendant's identity is necessary to pursue the plaintiff's claim, the court may refuse to quash a third-party subpoena if the plaintiff succeeds in setting forth evidence that a libelous statement has been made.[361] When there is a factual and legal basis for believing libel may have occurred, the writer's message will not be protected by the First Amendment. . . . Accordingly, a further balancing of interests should not be necessary to overcome the defendant's constitutional right to speak anonymously.[362]

Turning to the facts of the case, the *Krinsky* court concluded that the subpoena to discover Doe No. 6's identity should have been quashed because his Internet postings, which fell into the category of crude, satirical hyperbole, compelled the conclusion that they were not actionable.

---

[360] 159 Cal. App. 4th 1154 at 1168–70 (2008).

[361] [n.14] "Prima facie evidence is that which will support a ruling in favor of its proponent if no controverting evidence is presented. . . . It may be slight evidence which creates a reasonable inference of fact sought to be established but need not eliminate all contrary inferences. . . ."

[362] 159 Cal. App. 4th 1154 at 1170–72 (2008).

PROBLEM 3-10: THE SBA SURVEY

Charles Evans Hughes School of Law was not a happy place. Students fiercely disagreed with many of the law school's policies, including class attendance rules, the grading curve, and the large number of required courses. The law school administration was widely perceived as insensitive to student concerns. As a means of documenting student discontent for the purpose of effecting "change," the Student Bar Association conducted an online survey. To do this, the SBA used Survey Monkey,[363] a service which distributed the survey to law students by e-mail, compiled the results in anonymous form, and then returned the results to the SBA.

The narrative answers to the free-style question about "other concerns" ranged from "disgruntled" to "angry" and "rabid." A number of charges were levied against Dean Priscilla Klink, including accusations that she had been publicly intoxicated at the school's law journal banquet a few months earlier and had recently spent law school funds on landscaping and maintenance of her home, ten miles from campus.

As he had promised, when the survey results arrived in PDF format, the SBA president, Dennis Calmer, with the help of other SBA officers, e-mailed copies of the results to the students who had participated in the survey. The officers also made extra copies of the survey available in the SBA office on campus.

Calmer delivered a hard copy of the survey in a sealed envelope to the dean's secretary, Carolyn Cason, with a request for a meeting with the dean at her earliest convenience. Cason opened the survey envelope, because she opened all of the dean's mail, stamped the contents of each envelope with a "received" date, and delivered the contents to Dean Klink's office. The staff at the law school had heard rumors about an SBA survey. When Cason saw that the contents of the envelope dealt with the survey, she read the results. Cason did not believe what the survey said, but she knew that Dean Klink would be angry.

"Angry" did not begin to describe the dean's reaction. She was furious. She called the SBA officers into her office and she read them the "riot act." She told them that they had libeled her and that such conduct was not befitting persons seeking admission to the bar. Dean Klink told the officers that she was reporting each of them to the Character and Fitness Committee of the State Board of Law Examiners, and that they could expect to be called upon to explain why they had published false and defamatory statements about her and why that was not evidence of bad character.

Dean Klink also said that she would do everything possible to discover the identities of the students who had anonymously submitted the false and defamatory comments about her to Survey Monkey. And, the dean promised, those persons would be dealt with appropriately.

SBA president Calmer has recognized that he is in big trouble and has hired you to assist him with legal difficulties that may arise in the bar admissions process. In the meantime, Calmer cannot sleep because he is not even sure whether he did

---

[363] http://www.surveymonkey.com.

anything wrong, and he is afraid that he has gotten some of his classmates in trouble. Calmer does not know if the facts make him or anyone else liable for defamation. Please prepare a legal analysis of the facts so that you can explain to Calmer where he stands.

f. Exceptions to Communications Decency Act Immunity

Fraud and Negligent Misrepresentation. Courts sometimes find narrow exceptions to the Communications Decency Act (CDA). For example, in *Anthony v. Yahoo! Inc.*,[364] the plaintiff alleged that the operator of an online dating service created false user profiles to trick new members into joining and to stop current members from leaving. A federal court in California found that claims for fraud and negligent misrepresentation were not barred by the CDA's publisher-immunity provision.

(1) Example: *Barnes v. Yahoo! Inc.*

In *Barnes v. Yahoo! Inc.*,[365] the Ninth Circuit addressed "whether the Communications Decency Act of 1996 protects an Internet service provider from suit where it undertook to remove from its website material harmful to the plaintiff but failed to do so."[366] Describing the facts of the case, the court wrote:

> . . . Cecilia Barnes broke off a lengthy relationship with her boyfriend . . . [H]e responded by posting profiles of Barnes on a website run by Yahoo!, Inc. ("Yahoo"). . . .

> . . . The profiles contained nude photographs of Barnes and her boyfriend, taken without her knowledge, and some kind of open solicitation . . . to engage in sexual intercourse. The ex-boyfriend then conducted discussions in Yahoo's online "chat rooms," posing as Barnes and directing male correspondents to the fraudulent profiles he had created. . . . Before long, men whom Barnes did not know were peppering her office with emails, phone calls, and personal visits, all in the expectation of sex.

> In accordance with Yahoo policy, Barnes mailed Yahoo a copy of her photo ID and a signed statement denying her involvement with the profiles and requesting their removal. One month later . . . Barnes again asked Yahoo by mail to remove the profiles. Nothing happened. The following month, Barnes sent Yahoo two more mailings. During the same period, a local news program was preparing to broadcast a report on the incident. A day before the initial air date of the broadcast, Yahoo broke its silence; its Director of Communications, a Ms. Osako, called Barnes and asked her to fax directly the previous statements she had mailed. Ms. Osako told Barnes that she would "personally walk the statements over to the division responsible for stopping unauthorized profiles and they would take care of it." Barnes

---

[364] 421 F. Supp. 2d 1257 (N.D. Cal. 2006).

[365] 570 F.3d 1096 (9th Cir. 2009).

[366] *Id.* at 1098.

claims to have relied on this statement and took no further action regarding the profiles and the trouble they had caused. Approximately two months passed without word from Yahoo, at which point Barnes filed this lawsuit against Yahoo in Oregon state court. Shortly thereafter, the profiles disappeared from Yahoo's website, apparently never to return.[367]

Turning to the dispute before it, the Ninth Circuit summarized the case:

> Barnes' complaint against Yahoo . . . appears to allege two causes of action. . . . First, the complaint suggests a tort for the negligent provision or non-provision of services which Yahoo undertook to provide. . . . Oregon has adopted section 323 of the *Restatement (Second) of Torts* (1965), which describes the elements of this claim. . . . Barnes also refers in her complaint and in her briefs to Yahoo's "promise" to remove the indecent profiles and her reliance thereon to her detriment. We construe such references to allege a cause of action under section 90 of the *Restatement (Second) of Contracts* (1981).
>
> . . . Yahoo contended that section 230(c)(1) of the Communications Decency Act ("the Act") renders it immune from liability in this case. *See* 47 U.S.C. § 230(c)(1). The district court granted the motion to dismiss. . . .[368]

Addressing the merits of the appeal, the Ninth Circuit then began its analysis of the federal law in question.

> Section 230 of the Act [quoted earlier in this chapter], also known as the Cox-Wyden Amendment ("the Amendment"), protects certain internet-based actors from certain kinds of lawsuits. . . .
>
> . . . The operative section of the Amendment is section 230(c) ["Protection for 'good samaritan' blocking and screening of offensive material."] . . .
>
> Section 230(c) has two parts. . . . Looking at the text, it appears clear that neither this subsection nor any other declares a general immunity from liability deriving from third-party content, as Yahoo argues it does. "Subsection (c)(1) does not mention 'immunity' or any synonym." . . .
>
> . . . [O]ne notices that subsection (c)(1), which after all is captioned "Treatment of publisher or speaker," precludes liability only by means of a definition. "No provider or user of an interactive computer service," it says, "*shall be treated* as the publisher or speaker of any information provided by another information content provider." . . . Subsection 230(e)(3) makes explicit the relevance of this definition, for it cautions that "[n]o cause of action may be brought and no liability may be imposed under any State or local law that is inconsistent with this section." Bringing these two subsections together, it appears that subsection (c)(1) only protects from liability (1) a provider or user of an interactive computer service (2) whom

---

[367] *Id.* at 1098–99.

[368] *Id.* at 1099.

a plaintiff seeks to treat, under a state law cause of action, as a publisher or speaker (3) of information provided by another information content provider.

. . . The flashpoint in this case is the meaning of the "publisher or speaker" part of subsection (c)(1). . . .

The cause of action most frequently associated with the cases on section 230 is defamation. . . .

But . . . the language of the statute does not limit its application to defamation cases. Indeed, many causes of action might be premised on the publication or speaking of what one might call "information content." A provider of information services might get sued for violating anti-discrimination laws . . . ; for fraud, negligent misrepresentation, and ordinary negligence . . . ; for false light [invasion of privacy] . . . ; or even for negligent publication of advertisements that cause harm to third parties. . . . Thus, what matters is not the name of the cause of action — defamation versus negligence versus intentional infliction of emotional distress — what matters is whether the cause of action inherently requires the court to treat the defendant as the "publisher or speaker" of content provided by another. . . .

We have indicated [in a prior case] that publication involves reviewing, editing, and deciding whether to publish or to withdraw from publication third-party content. . . .[369]

Negligent Performance of an Undertaking. The court then rejected the plaintiff's tort cause of action for negligent performance of an undertaking. The court wrote:

The Oregon law tort that Barnes claims Yahoo committed derives from section 323 of the *Restatement (Second) of Torts*, which states:

One who undertakes, gratuitously or for consideration, to render services to another which he should recognize as necessary for the protection of the other's person or things, is subject to liability to the other for physical harm resulting from his failure to exercise reasonable care to perform his undertaking, if (a) his failure to exercise such care increases the risk of such harm, or (b) the harm is suffered because of the other's reliance upon the undertaking.

Barnes argues that this tort claim would not treat Yahoo as a publisher. She points to her complaint, which acknowledges that although Yahoo "may have had no initial responsibility to act, once [Yahoo,] through its agent, undertook to act, [it] must do so reasonably." According to Barnes, this makes the undertaking, not the publishing or failure to withdraw from publication, the source of liability. . . .

We are not persuaded. . . . The word "undertaking," after all, is meaning-less without the following verb. That is, one does not merely undertake; one

---

[369] *Id.* at 1099–1102.

undertakes *to do* something. And what is the undertaking that Barnes alleges Yahoo failed to perform with due care? The removal of the indecent profiles that her former boyfriend posted on Yahoo's website. But removing content is something publishers do, and to impose liability on the basis of such conduct necessarily involves treating the liable party as a publisher of the content it failed to remove. . . .[370]

Defamation Liability Based on Failure to Remove. The Ninth Circuit reinforced its conclusion that negligent performance of an undertaking was not actionable under the CDA because a person can sometimes become liable as a publisher of defamatory content based on failure to remove a libelous statement from the person's premises:

> . . . [W]e note that Yahoo could be liable for defamation for precisely the conduct of which Barnes accuses it. Defamation law sometimes imposes "an affirmative duty to remove a publication made by another." *Prosser and Keaton on Torts* § 113, at 803. Courts have applied this principle, including in a case that reads like a low-tech version of the situation before us. In *Hellar v. Bianco*, 244 P.2d 757, 758 (Cal. Ct. App. 1952), a woman received a phone call from a man who sought to arrange an unconventional, but apparently amorous, liaison. . . . After being rebuffed, the man informed the woman that her phone number appeared on the bathroom wall of a local bar along with writing indicating that she "was an unchaste woman who indulged in illicit amatory ventures.". . . . The woman's husband promptly called the bartender and demanded he remove the defamatory graffito, which the bartender said he would do when he got around to it. . . . Shortly thereafter, the husband marched to the bar . . . and discovered the offending scrawl still gracing the wall. . . . He defended his wife's honor by suing the bar's owner.

> The California Court of Appeal held that it was "a question for the jury whether, after knowledge of its existence, [the bar owner] negligently allowed the defamatory matter to remain for so long a time as to be chargeable with its republication.". . . .

> . . . [W]e hold that section 230(c)(1) bars Barnes' claim, under Oregon law, for negligent provision of services that Yahoo undertook to provide. . . .[371]

Promissory Estoppel. The court then turned to the plaintiff's contract law claim based on promissory estoppel.

> [W]e [must] inquire whether Barnes' theory of recovery under promissory estoppel would treat Yahoo as a "publisher or speaker" under the Act.

> . . . In a promissory estoppel case, as in any other contract case, the duty the defendant allegedly violated springs from a contract — an enforceable promise — not from any non-contractual conduct or capacity of the defendant. . . . Barnes does not seek to hold Yahoo liable as a publisher or

---

[370] *Id.* at 1102–03.

[371] *Id.* at 1103–05.

speaker of third-party content, but rather as the counter-party to a contract, as a promisor who has breached.

How does this analysis differ from our discussion of liability for the tort of negligent undertaking?. . . . To undertake a thing, within the meaning of the tort, *is* to do it.

Promising is different because it is not synonymous with the performance of the action promised. That is, whereas one cannot undertake to do something without simultaneously doing it, one can, and often does, promise to do something without actually doing it at the same time. Contract liability here would come not from Yahoo's publishing conduct, but from Yahoo's manifest intention to be legally obligated to do something, which happens to be removal of material from publication. Contract law treats the outwardly manifested intention to create an expectation on the part of another as a legally significant event. . . .

Furthermore, a court cannot simply infer a promise from an attempt to de-publish of the sort that might support tort liability under section 323 of the *Restatement (Second) of Torts*. For, as a matter of contract law, the promise must "be as clear and well defined as a promise that could serve as an offer, or that otherwise might be sufficient to give rise to a traditional contract supported by consideration." . . . . [The formation of a contract] "requires a meeting of the minds of the parties, a standard that is measured by the objective manifestations of intent by both parties to bind themselves to an agreement.". . . . Thus a general monitoring policy, or even an attempt to help a particular person, on the part of an interactive computer service such as Yahoo does not suffice for contract liability. This makes it easy for Yahoo to avoid liability: it need only disclaim any intention to be bound. . . .

One might also approach this question from the perspective of waiver. The objective intention to be bound by a promise . . . also signifies the waiver of certain defenses. . . . [O]nce a court concludes a promise is legally enforceable according to contract law, it has implicitly concluded that the promisor has manifestly intended that the court enforce his promise. By so intending, he has agreed to depart from the baseline rules (usually derived from tort or statute) that govern the mine-run of relationships between strangers. Subsection 230(c)(1) creates a baseline rule: no liability for publishing or speaking the content of other information service providers. Insofar as Yahoo made a promise with the constructive intent that it be enforceable, it has implicitly agreed to an alteration in such baseline.

Therefore, we conclude that, insofar as Barnes alleges a breach of contract claim under the theory of promissory estoppel, subsection 230(c)(1) of the Act does not preclude her cause of action. Because we have only reviewed the affirmative defense that Yahoo raised in this appeal, we do not reach the question whether Barnes has a viable contract claim or whether Yahoo has an affirmative defense under subsection 230(c)(2) of the Act.

. . . [W]e affirm in part, reverse in part, and remand for further proceedings. . . .[372]

Barnes' holding that a tort claim based on voluntary undertaking was barred by the terms of the Communications Decency Act is very much in accord with other precedent which has construed the Act broadly. Whether the *Barnes* decision, to allow the plaintiff's promissory estoppel claim to proceed, will withstand the test of time is open to question. (The court's brief discussion of whether Yahoo! waived its rights under the Act is probably the most persuasive rationale for permitting the contract claim to stand.) Nevertheless, *Barnes* nicely illustrates the issues with which courts must grapple relating to defamation on the Internet.

2.   **Retraction Statutes**

Effect on Punitive Damages. Some states have passed retraction statutes which, like the Texas Defamation Mitigation Act quoted earlier in this chapter, bear on the issue of punitive damages. For example, in Georgia, a statute provides that any plaintiff who did not ask for a retraction is generally not entitled to punitive damages.[373]

Occasionally, retraction statutes antedate important Supreme Court decisions. It is therefore important to ask what (if anything) they add to the considerable constitutional protections that have already been recognized by the Supreme Court. For example, a Mississippi statute, adopted in 1962 (two years before *New York Times Co. v. Sullivan*), provides as follows:

> (1) Before any civil action is brought for publication, in a newspaper domiciled and published in this state or authorized to do business in Mississippi so as to be subject to the jurisdiction of the courts of this state, of a libel, or against any radio or television station domiciled in this state, the plaintiff shall, at least ten (10) days before instituting any such action, serve notice in writing on the defendant at its regular place of business, specifying the article, broadcast or telecast, and the statements therein, which he alleges to be false and defamatory.

> (2) If it appears upon the trial that said article was published, broadcast or telecast in good faith, that its falsity was due to an honest mistake of the facts, and there were reasonable grounds for believing that the statements in said article, broadcast or telecast were true, and that within ten (10) days after the service of said notice a full and fair correction, apology and retraction was published in the same edition or corresponding issues of the newspaper in which said article appeared, and in as conspicuous place and type as was said original article, or was broadcast or telecast under like conditions correcting an honest mistake, and if the jury shall so find, the plaintiff in such case shall recover only actual damages. The burden of proof of the foregoing facts shall be affirmative defenses of the defendant and pled as such.

---

[372] *Id.* at 1106–09.

[373] *See Mathis v. Cannon*, 573 S.E.2d 376, 385 (Ga. 2002).

(3) This section shall not apply to any publication concerning a candidate for public office made within ten (10) days of any primary, general or special election in which such candidate's candidacy for or election to public office is to be determined, and this section shall not apply to any editorial or to any regularly published column in which matters of opinions are expressed.[374]

Problem 3-11: The Dangerous School Teacher

On a website named "Dangerous Teachers," there was a link to a document (the "Document") about Sam McGlynn, a shop class teacher at Chestnut Ridge High School. The Document appeared to be an official reprimand of McGlynn, who had been found guilty of making improper use of the Internet to access pornographic materials via school computers.

A comment (the "Comment") posted by a reader under the website's link for the McGlynn Document stated: "What did you expect of a burned out teacher married to a woman who spent five years in a mental institution?"

Soon after the postings appeared on the "Dangerous Teachers" website, local radio talk show hosts began discussing the allegations made in both the Document and the Comment. The local television then ran a story which repeated the substance of the Document posted on the web, but said nothing about the Comment. The television reporter in the televised segment said that both Chestnut Ridge High School and Sam McGlynn had been asked to respond to the allegations, but that both refused to discuss the matter.

The Document posted on the web about McGlynn was fabricated. There is no truth to the allegations in the Document or the Comment.

Sam McGlynn and his wife, Nancy McGlynn, have hired a lawyer, Grace Hammerstein. Hammerstein has explained that under the Communications Decency Act there is little chance of recovering tort damages from the operator of the "Dangerous Teachers" website if the operator did not originate the posted material. However, Hammerstein said that it may be possible to recover damages from persons who posted the Document and Comment on the website and from the radio and television stations whose broadcasts discussed the allegations.

If defamation actions against the broadcasters are governed by a retraction statute identical to the Mississippi retraction statute quoted above, must Hammerstein request a retraction before commencing litigation against the potential defendants? In addition, if a retraction is made by a defendant, what effect will that have on the McGlynns' defamation claims?

3.   Absolute Privileges

"Absolute" privileges are absolute. If an absolute privilege applies, it generally makes no difference what the defendant knew or should have known, or why the defendant uttered the defamatory statement. In contrast, "qualified" or

---

[374] Miss. Code Ann. § 95-1-5 (Lexis 2014).

"conditional" privileges (discussed later in this chapter) may be negated by various forms of improper conduct by a defendant.

a.   Judicial Proceedings Privilege

The "judicial proceedings privilege" is sometimes called the "litigation privilege." Pursuant to this rule, statements made by judges, lawyers, parties, witnesses, or jurors in connection with pending or contemplated litigation are absolutely privileged.[375]

Bars Defamation and Other Claims. In *Jones v. Coward*,[376] the defendant attorney asked a potential witness "Did you hear that [plaintiff] got run out of town for drugs?" or stated, "[Plaintiff] got run out of town for drugs."[377] The North Carolina Court of Appeals held "that an attorney's statement or question to a potential witness regarding a suit in which that attorney is involved, whether preliminary to trial, or at trial, is privileged and immune from civil action for defamation," unless it is "palpably irrelevant" to the case.[378] The court further held that the judicial proceedings privilege also barred an action for intentional infliction of emotional distress based on the same facts, because otherwise "the privilege . . . would be eviscerated, and the public policy providing advocates the security to zealously pursue cases on behalf of their clients would be completely undermined."[379]

In *Atkinson v. Affronti*,[380] a union attorney sent a letter to a general contractor alleging that its superintendent had stabbed a large, inflatable rat used by union picketers, and that the union intended to hold the general contractor responsible. In finding that a defamation claim by the supervisor against the union attorney was barred by the judicial proceedings privilege, the Appellate Court of Illinois noted that the privilege "affords complete immunity, irrespective of the attorney's knowledge of the statement's falsity or the attorney's motives in publishing the defamatory matter."[381]

Advertising for Clients or Evidence. In *Simpson Strong-Tie Co., Inc. v. Stewart, Estes & Donnell*,[382] an attorney ran a newspaper ad and a website announcement. The newspaper ad said:

Attention: Wood Deck Owners

If your deck was built after January 1, 2004 with galvanized screws manufactured by Phillips Fastener Products, Simpson Strong-Tie or Grip-Rite, you may have certain legal rights and be entitled to monetary

---

[375] *See* RESTATEMENT (SECOND) OF TORTS §§ 585–589 (1977).

[376] 666 S.E.2d 877 (N.C. Ct. App. 2008).

[377] *Id.* at 878.

[378] *Id.* at 880.

[379] *Id.*

[380] 861 N.E.2d 251 (Ill. App. Ct. 2006).

[381] *Id.* at 256.

[382] 232 S.W.3d 18 (Tenn. 2007).

compensation, and repair or replacement of your deck. Please call if you would like an attorney to investigate whether you have a potential claim. . . .[383]

The announcement on the law firm's website read:

Class Action Investigations

Phillips Screws and Fasteners and/or Simpson's Screws and Fasteners — We are investigating the accelerated corrosion due to defectively manufactured screws and fasteners caused by pressure treated wood.[384]

In addressing the question of whether the litigation privilege "encompasses an attorney's solicitous statements made prior to the filing of a lawsuit," the Supreme Court of Tennessee rejected the plaintiff's argument that recognition of such a privilege would give "attorneys 'unfettered license . . . to troll for clients via . . . indiscriminate advertising portraying possible defendants in any defamatory light advantageous to securing new' business for the attorney."[385] The court wrote:

We are persuaded that the litigation privilege applies to attorney solicitations published prior to the start of litigation. Specifically, the communication at issue is protected by the privilege if (1) the communication was made by an attorney acting in the capacity of counsel, (2) the communication was related to the subject matter of the proposed litigation, (3) the proposed proceeding must be under serious consideration by the attorney acting in good faith, and (4) the attorney must have a client or identifiable prospective client at the time the communication is published. The privilege will not apply unless each of these elements is satisfied.[386]

Quoting the *Restatement*, the court cautioned that the "bare possibility that the proceeding might be instituted is not to be used as a cloak to provide immunity for defamation when the possibility is not seriously considered."[387] Nevertheless, the court broadly framed the rule, which it found to be supported by cases in other jurisdictions. The court wrote:

. . . The plaintiff argues that the privilege should not apply to circumstances such as those presented here because rather than limiting the defamatory communications to persons having a potential claim against the plaintiff, the defendant "indiscriminately circulated them to the entire world." According to the plaintiff, the defendant had not consulted with a client or potential client about any claim against the plaintiff but broadly scattered its defamatory statements to everyone with access to the Tennessean newspaper and the Internet. Relying upon cases finding that a defamatory communication is protected only if it is published to persons with an interest in the proposed litigation, *see, e.g., Andrews v. Elliot*, 109

---

[383] *Id.* at 20.

[384] *Id.* at 21.

[385] *Id.* at 23–24.

[386] *Id.* at 24.

[387] *Id.* at 24 (quoting Restatement (Second) of Torts § 586 cmt. e (1977)).

N.C. App. 271, 426 S.E.2d 430, 433 (N.C. Ct. App. 1993), the plaintiff maintains that untargeted communications by an attorney should fall outside the permissible scope of the privilege to safeguard against abuse.

. . . .

While we are not unsympathetic with the plaintiff's position, limiting the privilege in the manner suggested by the plaintiff could, in our view, inhibit potential parties or witnesses from coming forward and impede the investigatory ability of litigants or potential litigants, thereby undermining the reasons for the privilege. In some situations, attorneys may have no practical means of discerning in advance whether the recipients of the communication have an interest in the proposed proceeding. In that event, the attorney can only communicate with those having the ability and desire to join the proposed litigation by publishing the statement to a wider audience, which may include unconnected individuals. When the prerequisites of the privilege are satisfied, the privilege should not be lost based on this fact alone. We note, however, that unnecessary defamatory publications to recipients unconnected with the proposed proceeding would not be privileged. . . . For example, if the attorney has a feasible way of discerning which recipients have an interest in the case, but nevertheless publishes the defamatory communication to those having no interest in the case, the privilege would not apply.

. . . .

We also observe that, even if the requirements of the privilege are satisfied, an attorney who exceeds the bounds of permissible conduct may face collateral consequences. For example, an attorney who makes false and defamatory statements which result in a baseless lawsuit may face a malpractice action by the client or a malicious prosecution action by the party defamed, or both. . . . An attorney who institutes meritless litigation or files suit for an improper purpose may also face sanctions imposed by the courts under Rule 11 of the Tennessee Rules of Civil Procedure. In addition, an attorney may be disciplined by the Board of Professional Responsibility for violating ethical requirements which prohibit the filing of frivolous claims or soliciting employment by means of fraud or false or misleading statements. . . . These alternative remedies for attorney misconduct present "the risk of punishment for the errant lawyer . . . real enough to require that lawyer to beware." . . . In light of these alternative remedies, coupled with the limitations we have placed on the privilege itself, we are satisfied that the privilege cannot be exploited as an opportunity to defame with impunity.[388]

---

[388] *Id.* at 25–27.

(1) Example: *Cassuto v. Shulick*

The breadth of the judicial proceedings privilege is illustrated by a case which should give great comfort to lawyers who mistakenly hit the "reply all" button when sending e-mail. *Cassuto v. Shulick*[389] involved a fee dispute between a Pennsylvania attorney (Shulick), who was lead counsel for a client (Stone), and a New York attorney (Cassuto), who was hired to serve as local counsel for the client, but had been dismissed. Describing the facts, a federal court in New York wrote:

> Cassuto emailed many of the parties involved in the Stone matter notifying them of his charging lien and demanding that his name be included on any and all settlement documents "as attorney," and on the settlement check. Among the parties copied on this email were Shulick, Eric Kades, a named plaintiff in the *Stone* matter, and Craig Miller, the CEO of Stone Commercial Brokerage, and the attorneys who represented the defendant in the *Stone* matter. . . .

> In response, Shulick hit "reply all" and wrote the following sentence . . . [implying that Cassuto's claim] ". . . evidenc[ed] that he is still, apparently, as . . . previously suspected, under the influence of substances that caused him to act so irratically [sic] previously [sic] — the reason for his termination." Cassuto claims this statement constitutes libel *per se*. . . .[390]

Pertinence, Broadly Defined, is a Question of Law. Addressing the merits of the defamation claim, the court wrote:

> The judicial proceedings privilege is an absolute bar to defamation suits arising out of statements pertinent to judicial proceedings made by any party related to those proceedings. Whether statements of an allegedly defamatory nature are pertinent for purposes of the judicial proceedings privilege is a question of law for the court to decide.

> In determining whether a statement is pertinent to judicial proceedings for purposes of the privilege, courts apply an "extremely liberal" test, asking whether the statement is "at all pertinent to the litigation." The measure of a statement's pertinence to judicial proceedings is whatever a reasonable person would think is "connected" to the case. Thus, any doubts are to be resolved in favor of finding a statement to be pertinent to a judicial proceeding. "The barest rationality, divorced from any palpable or pragmatic degree of probability, suffices to establish the offending statement's pertinence to the litigation." The privilege embraces anything that may possibly be pertinent, including disputes over legal fees between attorneys. Additionally, a statement made during the course of judicial proceedings is only actionable where the statement is "so outrageously out of context as to permit one to conclude, from the mere fact that the statement was uttered, that it was motivated by no other desire than to defame."[391]

[handwritten margin note: Liberal test for what is pertinent]

---

[389] 2007 U.S. Dist. LEXIS 42638 (S.D.N.Y. June 11, 2007).

[390] *Id.* at *3–*5.

[391] *Id.* at *8–*9.

Wholly Unrelated Statements. The *Cassuto* court further explained:

> While the privilege does not extend to statements made by persons "wholly unrelated" to the relevant litigation, "no strained or close construction will be indulged in to exempt a [person] from the protection of privilege." The privilege is not destroyed simply because a participant to the judicial proceedings no longer represents a party. The privilege is only inapplicable where the statement is made by someone who has no involvement whatsoever in the pending litigation or was never involved in the proceedings. Moreover, it is irrelevant for purposes of applying the privilege that third parties inadvertently heard or read an allegedly defamatory statement.[392]

Pertinence is Evaluated in Context. The court continued:

> In determining whether a statement is pertinent to a judicial proceeding, the statement must be read in context. Here, Cassuto initiated the discussion in issue. Cassuto entitled his initial email to Shulick "SETTLEMENT-*Stone Commercial Brokerage, Inc. v. Organic, Inc. et al.*" As evidenced by the subject line, the email pertained to the *Stone* lawsuit. Nonetheless, Cassuto contends the email is not pertinent to a judicial proceeding because it related to the Fee Agreement, not to the lawsuit. Cassuto is simply wrong. The statement related to the lawsuit as it arose from Cassuto's representation in the *Stone* matter. In response to Cassuto's request for fees, Shulick sent an email rejecting Cassuto's claim, stating that "he would be happy to litigate the fees."

> Frustrated with his failing efforts to obtain payment from Shulick, Cassuto filed a lien against any *Stone* settlement. While Cassuto contends the fee dispute was not pertinent to the *Stone* litigation, his decision to file a lien against the settlement proceeds and to alert all parties and counsel of that decision proves the contrary.

> . . . .

> Cassuto contends that his status as former counsel should preclude any application of the judicial proceedings privilege. But when former counsel to litigation continue to involve themselves in actual proceedings, the privilege still applies. As discussed above, Cassuto sent an email to opposing counsel in *Stone* demanding his name be included on settlement papers with the designation "as attorney.". . . .

> Cassuto relies on *Silverman v. Clark* [822 N.Y.S.2d 9 (App. Div. 2006)] in which the privilege did not apply to an attorney formerly involved in litigation. But this case is inapposite. The attorney in *Silverman* merely contacted his former client to suggest that she proceed with her new attorney cautiously, or alternatively, return to his firm. The attorney made no statement pertinent to a pending litigation as was the case here.

---

[392] *Id.* at *10.

Finally, Cassuto contends that the immunity should not apply because Shulick copied his secretary and paralegal on subsequent emails, including the string of emails containing the allegedly defamatory statements. However, as noted earlier, the privilege is not extinguished simply because third parties have been exposed to the allegedly defamatory statements.[393]

The Second Circuit affirmed the district court's ruling in *Cassuto*, in a summary order which stated simply, "For substantially the reasons stated by the District Court, we agree that the e-mail was privileged. We have considered all of Cassuto's arguments and find them to be without merit."[394]

(2)   Quasi-Judicial Proceedings

Statements relating to a *quasi-judicial* proceeding are often absolutely privileged. For example, in *Sullivan v. Smith*,[395] the Alabama Court of Civil Appeals held that the statements of a crime victim's parents to the state Board of Pardons and Paroles could not form the basis for a slander action.

Quasi-judicial proceedings come in many varieties. In *Craig v. Stafford Const., Inc.*,[396] the Supreme Court of Connecticut held that an investigation conducted by a police department's internal affairs division constituted a quasi-judicial proceeding. Therefore, a defamation action, based on a complaint to the division about a police officer's alleged racial bias, was barred by an absolute privilege. The court noted that, in determining whether a proceeding is quasi-judicial in nature, it is appropriate to consider the following factors: "whether the body has the power to: (1) exercise judgment and discretion; (2) hear and determine or to ascertain facts and decide; (3) make binding orders and judgments; (4) affect the personal property rights of private persons; (5) examine witnesses and hear the litigation of the issues on a hearing; and (6) enforce decisions or impose penalties."[397]

Complaints to Government Agencies. In *5-State Helicopters, Inc. v. Cox*,[398] a defamation claim arose from two letters of complaint sent to the Federal Aviation Administration (FAA). In holding that the suit was barred by an absolute privilege, Chief Justice John Cayce wrote for the Texas Court of Appeals:

> A proceeding is quasi-judicial in nature if it is conducted by a governmental executive officer, board, or commission that has the authority to hear and decide the matters coming before it or to redress the grievances of which it takes cognizance. . . .
>
> . . . [T]he rationale for extending the absolute privilege to statements made during quasi-judicial proceedings rests in the public policy that every citizen should have the unqualified right to appeal to governmental agencies

---

[393] *Id.* at *11–*15.

[394] 2008 U.S. App. LEXIS 27429 (2d Cir. Mar. 5, 2008).

[395] 925 So. 2d 972 (Ala. Civ. App. 2005).

[396] 856 A.2d 372 (Conn. 2004).

[397] *Id.* at 377 (quoting *Kelley v. Bonney*, 606 A.2d 693, 704 (Conn. 1992)).

[398] 146 S.W.3d 254 (Tex. App. 2004).

for redress "without the fear of being called to answer in damages" and that the administration of justice will be better served if witnesses are not deterred by the threat of lawsuits. . . . The absolute privilege is intended to protect the integrity of the process and ensure that the quasi-judicial decision-making body gets the information it needs. . . .

Whether an alleged defamatory statement is related to a proposed or existing judicial or quasi-judicial proceeding, and is therefore absolutely privileged, is a question of law. . . .

In this case, FAA's quasi-judicial status is not in dispute. The FAA Administrator may reinspect and reexamine any civil aircraft at any time to ensure that the aircraft is in compliance with federal air safety laws. . . . If it appears that a person may be in violation of federal aviation statutes or regulations, the FAA is authorized to initiate an investigation and decide whether any violations have occurred. . . . The FAA may, among other things, hold administrative hearings, issue orders of compliance, assess civil penalties, seize noncompliant aircraft, or bring a civil enforcement action in federal district court. . . . If . . . as a result of the investigation, the FAA determines that a violation has occurred that does not require legal enforcement action, an appropriate official in the FAA field office responsible for processing the enforcement case "may take administrative action in disposition of the case.". . . . Such administrative actions include issuing a warning notice to the alleged violator.[399]

Quasi-Judicial Status Depends on Authority, Not Adjudication. In *5-State Helicopters, supra,* the court emphasized that a governmental entity's status depends on the entity's authority:

> The mere fact that the FAA's investigation did not culminate in a full-blown administrative hearing or a "formal adjudication" did not alter its quasi-judicial nature. It is undisputed that the FAA had the authority to conduct such a hearing and adjudication if it had determined that such measures were necessary. A proceeding's quasi-judicial status depends on whether the governmental entity has the authority to investigate and decide the matters at issue, not on the length, complexity, or outcome of the proceeding. . . .

> . . . [T]o adopt the narrow view of quasi-judicial proceedings that appellees urge would result in a rule that private citizens' communications to a quasi-judicial body about a matter that the entity was authorized to investigate and resolve would not be privileged unless and until the proceeding reached the administrative hearing stage. Such a rule would have a chilling effect on the free flow of information and deter rather than aid the decision-making body's efforts to obtain necessary information. . . .[400]

---

[399] *Id.* at 257–58.
[400] *Id.* at 258–59.

Attorney Disciplinary Matters. In many states, persons reporting alleged attorney misconduct to disciplinary authorities enjoy an absolute privilege.[401] In some jurisdictions, the privilege is an extension of the judicial proceedings privilege to attorney disciplinary hearings, which are quasi-judicial in nature.

Mixter v. Farmer[402] was a dispute between two lawyers in which Mixter alleged, in part, that Farmer had defamed him. According to a Maryland appellate court "Farmer sent twenty letters to various Maryland attorneys discussing . . . [Mixter's] 'unprofessional behavior' in . . . [a particular case], and seeking information about other lawyers' negative experiences with Mixter for a potential complaint with the Attorney Grievance Commission of Maryland (AGC)." In concluding that the defamation claim was barred by absolute privilege the court wrote:

> The trial court found that Farmer's letters . . . had a specific and rational relationship to the anticipated proceedings before the AGC, and thus were absolutely privileged. . . .
>
> Mixter contends that the sixteen-month delay between Farmer's writing the letters and filing the grievance establishes that appellee did not intend originally to file a grievance, but only used this later filing as an excuse, after appellant sued him. . . . We disagree. . . . The record shows that Farmer's letters specifically mentioned that he was seeking information for a bar counsel complaint. Although the delay in filing a grievance was lengthy, we agree with the trial court that it was not long enough to sever the clearly stated connection to the AGC complaint. Anyone reporting a grievance to the AGC is allowed time to gather evidence for his or her claims. . . .
>
> Mixter contends that Farmer's lack of particularity in his AGC complaint, coupled with his inability at deposition to point to any specific professional rule violations, exposes his real purpose to be to disparage Mixter's reputation in the legal community. We find this argument unpersuasive for two reasons: first, there is no requirement that an AGC complaint allege specific rule violations; and secondly, under Maryland law, even a meritless complaint is privileged and the complainant's motive is immaterial.
>
> Mixter next contends that the trial court's ruling harms the public policy underlying absolute judicial privilege because it allows Farmer to disparage him continuously and without recourse. While we acknowledge that the AGC process potentially may allow defamation against a specific lawyer, this outcome is weighed against the greater need to protect the public from unethical lawyers.[403]

Other Professional Boards. In *Sobol v. Alarcon*,[404] the court concluded that an absolute privilege barred a defamation action by a certified legal document

---

[401] *See* TEX. GOV'T CODE ANN. T.2, SUBT. G, APP. A-1 § 15.8 (LEXIS 2014).

[402] 81 A.3d 631 (Md. 2013).

[403] *Id.* at 635–36.

[404] 131 P.3d 487 (Ariz. Ct. App. 2006).

preparer. In that case, an attorney sent a letter to the State Bar accusing a certified legal document preparer of the unauthorized practice of law. Thereafter, the State Bar forwarded the letter to the Board of Legal Document Preparers. In disposing of a suit against the attorney who made the report, the Arizona Court of Appeals wrote:

> This court has afforded absolute immunity to individuals who have filed complaints with the State Bar against attorneys accusing them of unethical conduct. . . . We have done so to encourage the public to report alleged unethical lawyer behavior without fear of reprisal and free from the threat of civil litigation. Application of the privilege also ensures the State Bar, as the entity authorized by the Supreme Court of Arizona to regulate attorney conduct, receives the information it needs to accomplish its disciplinary role. . . .
>
> In Arizona, a [certified] legal document preparer . . . may perform specified legal services without being supervised by an attorney in good standing with the State Bar. In light of the role now permissibly played by certified legal document preparers in working with the public and providing the public with certain legal services, just as with the legal profession, public policy demands that absolute immunity be extended to members of the public who report alleged unethical behavior by certified legal document preparers. We can conceive of no reason why a person who reports allegedly unethical conduct by a lawyer should be protected by absolute immunity while a person who reports allegedly unethical conduct by a certified legal document preparer should be subjected to the risk of civil liability. Given the public's need for access to legal services and the importance of regulating those who provide such services, there should be no distinction. . . .[405]

University Sexual Harassment Procedures. In *Hartman v. Keri*,[406] the Supreme Court of Indiana held that statements charging a university professor with sexual harassment were absolutely privileged. The court explained its reasoning as follows:

> [Anti-harassment policies] . . . similar to Purdue's are commonly found in institutions of higher education. At least three states [New York, California, and Maryland] have held that communications to school authorities raising complaints against educators enjoy the same absolute privilege the law accords to statements in judicial proceedings. . . . In reaching this conclusion courts have described the processes of the educational institutions as quasi-judicial. . . . This view of the issue, adopted by Justice Rucker's separate opinion, invokes a body of law that analyzes the availability of the privilege in terms of the degree to which court-like procedures are available. Thus, courts have examined whether proceedings are under oath, whether there is subpoena power, whether discovery is available, and the like. . . . Purdue's processes do not establish such a

---

[405] *Id.* at 490.

[406] 883 N.E.2d 774 (Ind. 2008).

formal apparatus. But to the extent Keri has a complaint about the adequacy or fullness of the process, it is a complaint with Purdue, not Hartman and Swinehart [the complainants]. That complaint has been asserted in federal court and has been resolved there adversely to Keri. At least in the context of educational institutions, as long as the process is reasonably transparent and fair and affords the subject an opportunity to respond, we think the ultimate issue focuses less on the particular process and more on the recognition of the institution's interest in assuring a proper educational environment.

Hartman and Swinehart acted under the procedure Purdue established. Protecting their complaints with anything less than an absolute privilege could chill some legitimate complaints for fear of retaliatory litigation. . . . A university should be given the latitude to tailor its processes to the educational environment without degrading the protection the law gives to complaints of misconduct in the educational setting. . . .

Citizens reporting suspected criminal activity to law enforcement enjoy only a qualified privilege, which subjects them to the risk of retaliatory civil litigation for malicious or unfounded charges. *E.g.*, *Holcomb v. Walter's Dimmick Petrol., Inc.*, 858 N.E.2d 103, 106 (Ind. 2006) (*citing Conn v. Paul Harris Stores, Inc.*, 439 N.E.2d 195, 200 (Ind. Ct. App. 1982)). At first blush it may seem anomalous to grant a higher degree of protection to complaints made in the educational setting. But a current student is subject to academic discipline for abuse of the process. In practical terms this is a substantial deterrent to false reporting. Moreover, the need for protection is greater in the educational setting because the subject of the complaint — the educator — is in a position of authority over the student, so fear of retaliation presents a potential obstacle to open airing of grievances. . . .

Finally, we think it is relevant that the Indiana General Assembly has given state higher educational institutions the power to govern conduct on institution property and to "prevent unlawful or objectionable acts," of the institution's students, faculty, and employees "wherever the conduct might occur." Ind. Code Ann. §§ 21-39-2-2 to -3 (West 2008). This includes the power to "dismiss, suspend, or otherwise punish any student, faculty member, or employee of the state educational institution who violates the institution's rules or standards of conduct, after determination of guilt by lawful proceedings." . . . These statutes authorize educational institutions to construct their own disciplinary procedures in a way that protects the needs of the participants and also serves the educational goals of the institution. Although Purdue's procedure may lack the trappings of a traditional court proceeding, it is orderly and reasonably fair, requires "appropriate discipline" for those who file knowingly false or malicious complaints, and promises reasonable efforts to restore the reputation of anyone charged with discrimination or harassment that proves unsubstantiated. If Keri has been unfairly treated, his complaint is against Purdue

University as the architect and implementer of the policy and procedures, not the students who invoked the process.[407]

(3) Limits of the Judicial Proceedings Privilege

Publication to the Press or Other Audiences of Statements Related to Litigation. Occasionally courts find that statements connected to litigation are not protected by the absolute judicial proceedings privilege. One such case was *Bochetto v. Gibson.*[408] In that case, an attorney (Bochetto) was sued for legal malpractice based on conduct which allegedly occurred in connection with the defense of a client in quiet-title actions. In the legal malpractice action, the client was represented by a new attorney (Gibson). The legal malpractice complaint alleged that Bochetto had breached his fiduciary obligations by failing to disclose important information (an expert report) to the client and by other misconduct related to the procurement of a substitute expert report. After filing the legal malpractice complaint for the client, Gibson faxed a copy to a reporter with the Legal Intelligencer (Dudick), which resulted in a story which Bochetto claimed was false and defamatory. In a defamation suit by Bochetto against Gibson and his firm, the defendants argued that the claim was barred by the judicial proceedings privilege. In addressing that issue, the Supreme Court of Pennsylvania wrote:

> Pursuant to the judicial privilege, a person is entitled to absolute immunity for "communications which are issued *in the regular course of judicial proceedings* and which are *pertinent and material to the redress or relief sought."* *Post v. Mendel*, 510 Pa. 213, 507 A.2d 351, 355 (1986) (emphasis in original). . . .
>
> In *Post*, this Court was asked to decide whether the judicial privilege protected an attorney from liability for statements he made in a letter detailing alleged acts of misconduct by his opposing attorney, which was not only sent to the opposing attorney, but was also sent as copies to the judge trying the case, the Disciplinary Board of this Court, and the attorney's client. Although we found that the letter had been issued during the course of the trial and referred to matters that occurred during the trial, we nevertheless concluded that it was not: (1) issued as a matter of regular course of the proceedings; or (2) pertinent and material to the proceedings.[409] Accordingly, . . . we held that . . . [the letter] was not "within the

---

[407] *Id.* at 777–79.

[408] 860 A.2d 67 (Pa. 2004).

[409] [n.13] In finding that the letter did not satisfy these two criteria, we explained as follows:

> The letter did not state or argue any legal position, and it did not request any ruling or action by the court. Nor did the communication request that anything contained in it should even be considered by the court. The letter was clearly not a part of the judicial proceedings to which it made reference, and merely forwarding a copy of the letter to the court did not make it a part of those proceedings. Likewise, forwarding copies of the letter to plaintiff's alleged client . . . and to the Disciplinary Board . . . did not render the letter a part of the trial proceedings, and transmittal of those copies would not logically have been expected to affect the course of trial.

Post, 507 A.2d at 356.

sphere of [communications] which judicial immunity was designed to protect" and that the attorney was not absolutely immune from liability for his statements in the letter. . . .

In . . . the instant case, we initially note that Gibson's publication of the complaint to the trial court was clearly protected by the privilege. . . . However, the fact that the privilege protects this first publication does not necessarily mean that it also protects Gibson's later act of republishing the complaint to Dudick. *See Pawlowski v. Smorto*, 403 Pa. Super. 71, 588 A.2d 36, 41 n.3 (1991) ("[E]ven an absolute privilege may be lost through overpublication. . . . In the case of the judicial privilege, overpublication may be found where a statement initially privileged because made in the regular course of judicial proceedings is later republished to another audience outside of the proceedings."); *Barto v. Felix*, 250 Pa. Super. 262, 378 A.2d 927, 930 (1977) (although allegations in attorney's brief were protected by judicial privilege, attorney's remarks concerning contents of brief during press conference were not likewise protected by privilege). Indeed, this later act may only be protected by the judicial privilege if it meets the two elements that we held in *Post* are critical for the privilege to apply, *i.e.*, (1) it was issued during the regular course of the judicial proceedings; and (2) it was pertinent and material to those proceedings. As Gibson's act of sending the complaint to Dudick was an extrajudicial act that occurred outside of the regular course of the judicial proceedings and was not relevant in any way to those proceedings, it is plain that it was not protected by the judicial privilege.[410]

The court noted in a footnote that while Gibson is not absolutely immune from liability for faxing the complaint to the reporter, he might nevertheless be entitled to a qualified privilege. As discussed later in this chapter, qualified privileges are "abused," and therefore afford no protection, if the defendant acts with knowledge of a statement's falsity or for improper motives, such as spite, ill-will, or vindictiveness.

PROBLEM 3-12: THE ACCUSED CATERER

Soon after the City of St. Loyal (the City) adopted a new ethics code (the Code), a complaint was filed with the Ethics Review Board (the Board) by Raphael's Catering (Raphael's). The complaint related to the City's solicitation of bids for a lucrative, five-year, exclusive-rights catering contract at the Convention Center.

Raphael's had submitted a bid for the contract. One of the competing bids was submitted by Raphael's old nemesis, Child's Comestibles (Child's). In the complaint to the Board, Raphael's alleged that the owners of Child's had made improper campaign contributions to certain members of City Council, and was therefore ineligible to bid on the Convention Center catering contract.

The new Code provided that neither the filing of a complaint nor any official action relating to a complaint would be public information unless and until the

---

[410] 860 A.2d at 71–73 (Pa. 2004).

Board made a finding that the complaint had merit. Unfortunately, because the provisions of the Code were new and city officials were unfamiliar with them, the complaint filed by Raphael's against Child's was erroneously distributed to the press in response to an open records request.

The resulting news stories attracted great public attention. Reporters researching the story were able to document a history of "bad blood" and animosity between Raphael's and Child's. Media scrutiny also focused on whether members of City Council were in compliance with campaign finance laws.

The Board, which consisted of eleven members approved by City Council, offered Child's the opportunity to present a defense to the charges stated in Raphael's complaint. Applicable provisions in the Code prohibited *ex parte* communications with members of the Board. The Code also required all witnesses to be sworn and provided that all questioning of witnesses was to be conducted by the members of the Board. Under the Code, a person charged with unethical conduct had a right to attend a hearing and to present witnesses, but no right to be accompanied by legal counsel. No standard of proof was stated in the Code.

The Board had the power to make a finding that the Code had been violated and to recommend to City Council what sanction should be imposed. However, the Board's findings and recommendations were not binding on City Council, which had plenary power to review any finding of fact *de novo* and to disregard any recommendation of the Board.

The proceedings relating to the complaint against Child's were closed to the public. Ultimately, the Board found that there was no violation and recommended that City Council take no further action. City Council followed that recommendation.

After the Convention Center catering contract was awarded to a bidder unrelated to the ethics complaint, Child's filed suit against Raphael's alleging that the statements made in the complaint to the Board were false and defamatory, without any factual basis, and maliciously intended to cause Child's not to be awarded the catering contract. Raphael's has moved to dismiss the defamation complaint on the ground that its ethics complaint to the Board was absolutely privileged. No prior case or legislative enactment has addressed this question. How should the court rule?

b.   Legislative and Executive Branch Absolute Privileges

Legislative Proceedings. It is not at all surprising that, in a country with a three-branch government, the judicial proceedings privilege is paralleled by privileges relating to the legislative and executive branches. Thus, as a matter of common law, utterances by legislators and legislative witnesses, if published in connection with legislative functions, are immune from suit.[411]

---

[411] *See* RESTATEMENT (SECOND) OF TORTS §§ 590 & 590A (1977).

In *Riddle v. Perry*,[412] the Supreme Court of Utah held that the statement of a legislative witness, which implied that the sponsor of a bill had been bribed, was related to the hearing and therefore absolutely privileged. This was true even though both the committee parliamentarian and the legislative witness both acknowledged that the statement was out of order.

Legislative Capacity Versus Supervisory or Administrative. Some courts have drawn a critical distinction based on whether the legislative body is acting in a legislative capacity, on the one hand, or merely a supervisory or administrative capacity, on the other hand. For example, in *Isle of Wight County v. Nogiec*,[413] the Virginia Supreme Court recognized the concept of legislative absolute privilege, but found it inapplicable to the facts before it. As the court explained:

> [W]hether a communication made by an assistant county administrator to a member of a county's board of supervisors during a board meeting is absolutely privileged is a question of first impression in this Court.

> Small urges us to adopt the *Restatement's* approach . . . The *Restatement* clarifies that legislative proceedings include not only those held by the "highest legislative body of a State," but also those held by "subordinate legislative bodies to which the State has delegated legislative power, such as a city council or county board." . . .

> Just as in judicial proceedings, we think that absolute privilege in legislative proceedings serves the public interest. In particular, it encourages individuals who participate in such proceedings to speak freely on issues relating to "the operation of the government." . . . That public interest, however, must be balanced against "the right of an individual to enjoy his reputation free from defamatory attacks." . . . We therefore believe that application of the privilege should be limited to proceedings before a legislative body in which the public interest in free speech outweighs the potential harm to an individual's reputation. In our view, this only occurs when the legislative body is acting in its legislative capacity — *i.e.*, when it is creating legislation — rather than in its supervisory or administrative capacity.

> . . . The General Assembly has granted certain powers to county boards of supervisors. The broadest of these powers is a general police power. . . . In accordance with that power, a county, through its board of supervisors, "may adopt such measures as it deems expedient to secure and promote the health, safety and general welfare of its inhabitants which are not inconsistent with the general laws of the Commonwealth." . . . Not all powers given to boards of supervisors, however, are legislative in nature; some are supervisory or administrative. Under Code § 15.2–1409, for example, boards of supervisors "may make such investigations relating to its government affairs as it deems necessary." And, pursuant to Code

---

[412] 40 P.3d 1128 (Utah 2002).

[413] 704 S.E.2d 83 (Va. 2011).

§ 15.2–1230, they "may require monthly financial reports from any officer or office of the county."

Assuming, without deciding, that absolute privilege is afforded to subordinate legislative bodies, the creation of legislation is the nexus that supports the application of the privilege. Absolute privilege therefore does not attach to communications made by participants in proceedings conducted by a board of supervisors that do not concern the creation of legislation.

. . . [The] evidence does not demonstrate that the Board was acting in a legislative capacity when Small gave his report. On the contrary, it shows that the Board was acting in a supervisory or administrative capacity. The Board had convened to receive a report on the efforts being undertaken to repair County property (*i.e.*, the museum), not to create legislation. Thus, because the Board was not acting in a legislative capacity when it received Small's report, its meeting was not a legislative proceeding to which the public interest supports the attachment of an absolute privilege. We therefore conclude that Small's statements were not absolutely privileged.

While Small's statements were not entitled to an absolute privilege, they were entitled to a qualified privilege because, as an assistant administrator for the County, Small had a duty to report the status of the museum repairs to the Board. . . . [A] qualified privilege afforded Small sufficient protection from liability for defamation because the statements, whether compelled or volunteered, were only actionable if Nogiec was able to prove that they were made with malice. Hence, the circuit court properly submitted to the jury the issue of whether the statements were made with malice. Accordingly, we hold that the circuit court did not err in denying Small's motions to strike and set aside the verdict on Nogiec's defamation claim.[414]

Executive Branch Communications. Statements by high level executive branch officials in the federal or state government are absolutely privileged, under common law principles, if made in connection with the performance of official duties.[415] At the state level, the absolute privilege for executive branch communications extends at least to high level officials, such as the governor, attorney general, and heads of state departments. Whether lesser state officials enjoy a qualified, rather than absolute, privilege depends on state law.[416]

Statements in Search Warrants. In *Smith v. Danielczyk*,[417] the Maryland Court of Appeals held that police officers were entitled to only qualified immunity with respect to defamatory statements contained in a search warrant application. Interestingly, the court also noted that the judicial proceedings privilege was not applicable to the facts, which involved a search of the lockers of fellow police officers. The court wrote:

---

[414] *Id.* at 89–90.

[415] *See* RESTATEMENT (SECOND) OF TORTS § 591 (1977).

[416] *See id.* § 591 cmt. c.

[417] 928 A.2d 795 (Md. 2007).

An application for a search warrant may be said to be in the nature of a judicial proceeding because the application must be made to a judge and because the issuance of a warrant is a judicial act. On the other hand, . . . an application for search warrant, at least in the ordinary case, is not made in the course of an existing judicial proceeding and does not inaugurate or necessarily lead to one. . . . Moreover, the presentation of a search warrant application is almost always *ex parte*, often occurring at the judge's home during the evening hours, with little or no ability to test the accuracy of the affiant's averments. Absent some knowledge to the contrary, the judge necessarily assumes good faith and truthfulness on the part of the affiant and looks to see only whether those averments, assuming them to be true, suffice to establish probable cause to believe that incriminating evidence will be found at the place or on the person to be searched. . . .

The normal trappings of . . . [an adversarial] judicial proceeding are thus lacking. In that regard, the presentation of an application for search warrant may be more akin to an investigatory proceeding rather than a judicial one. . . .

A critical underpinning to allowing an absolute privilege for statements made in the course of a judicial proceeding is that, because such a proceeding is normally adversarial in nature, there is usually the ability to test the veracity of those statements and to publicly rebut them. Witnesses can be cross-examined; contradictory evidence can be presented. A neutral fact-finder, after examining all of the evidence presented, can decide what is believable and what is not. . . . Even in sub-proceedings that may themselves be *ex parte* in nature, such as requests for temporary restraining orders, the opportunity exists later in the case to expose and sanction false statements. . . .

That counterweight simply does not exist with respect to search warrant applications. . . .

The rationale for being cautious about extending an absolute privilege to an *ex parte* search warrant proceeding was well-stated in *Franks v. Delaware*, [438 U.S. 154, 168 (1978)]: "[t]he requirement that a warrant not issue 'but upon probable cause, supported by Oath or affirmation,' would be reduced to a nullity if a police officer was able to use deliberately falsified allegations to demonstrate probable cause, and, having misled the magistrate, then was able to remain confident that the ploy was worthwhile."[418]

Rights Under the Petition Clause. Persons communicating with executive branch officers do not enjoy an absolute privilege that would defeat a defamation action. The guarantees of the Petition Clause of the Federal Constitution have been found to be coextensive with those articulated in *New York Times Co. v. Sullivan*[419] and its progeny. Thus, in *McDonald v. Smith*,[420] the United States Supreme Court

---

[418] *Id.* at 811–13.

[419] 376 U.S. 254 (1964).

[420] 472 U.S. 479 (1985).

held that letters addressed to the President, concerning the plaintiff's qualifications to become a United States Attorney, could give rise to liability if actual malice was proved.

Similarly, in *Clark v. Jenkins*,[421] the Texas Court of Appeals held that a civil rights group and its president were not absolutely immune from a defamation suit based on the group's distribution of a memorandum to the Justice Department and a Congressman requesting certain action. The memorandum stated that a member of city council was a convicted felon who had served time for prostitution and drug-related offenses. A jury verdict was upheld because there was clear and convincing evidence that the defendants acted with actual malice.

State Constitutional Protections. State law sometimes provides greater protection than the Federal Constitution. In *Kashian v. Harriman*,[422] the California Court of Appeal held that the state statutory absolute privilege for statements made in connection with an "official proceeding," defeated a defamation claim based on a letter urging a division of the Office of the Attorney General to institute an investigation of the tax-exempt status being claimed by a certain health care provider.

c.   Westfall Act and Federal Officers and Employees

Any reference to the application of judicial, legislative, or executive branch absolute privileges at the federal level is incomplete without some discussion of the protections afforded to federal employees under the Westfall Act. In *Wuterich v. Murtha*,[423] a U.S. Marine sued a Congressman for defamation based on the Congressman's statements to the press. The D.C. Circuit wrote:

> This case involves an important question concerning the scope of absolute immunity under the Westfall Act. *See* 28 U.S.C. § 2679. The Westfall Act "accords federal employees absolute immunity from common-law tort claims arising out of acts they undertake in the course of their official duties." *Osborn v. Haley*, 549 U.S. 225, 229 (2007). . . . [If] "a federal employee is sued for wrongful or negligent conduct, the Act empowers the Attorney General to certify that the employee 'was acting within the scope of his office or employment at the time of the incident out of which the claim arose.' Upon the Attorney General's certification, the employee is dismissed from the action, and the United States is substituted as defendant in place of the employee." . . .

> In this case, U.S. Marine Frank D. Wuterich sued Congressman John Murtha, alleging that the Congressman made false and defamatory statements to the press about the role of Wuterich's squad in the deaths of civilians in Haditha, Iraq in 2005. Congressman Murtha invoked the protections of the Westfall Act and the Attorney General's designee certified that the Congressman was acting within the scope of his employ-

---

[421] 248 S.W.3d 418 (Tex. App. 2008).

[422] 98 Cal. App. 4th 892 (2002).

[423] 562 F.3d 375 (D.C. Cir. 2009).

ment at the time he uttered the contested statements. . . . Congressman
Murtha and the United States now appeal the District Court's denial of the
Attorney General's certification.[424]

Addressing the framework of the Westfall Act, the *Wuterich* court explained:

> [Once] the federal employee is dismissed from the case and the United
> States is substituted as the defendant in place of the employee . . . the suit
> is governed by the Federal Tort Claims Act ("FTCA") and is subject to all
> of the FTCA's exceptions for actions in which the Government has not
> waived sovereign immunity. . . . When one of these exceptions applies, the
> Attorney General's certification converts the tort suit into a FTCA action
> over which the federal court lacks subject matter jurisdiction and has the
> effect of altogether barring plaintiff's case.[425]

The FTCA bars an action against the federal government for many types of
intentional torts, including libel and slander.[426] Thus, the viability of the plaintiff's
claim hinged upon whether the Congressman's statements were within the scope of
his office or employment. If so, the Congressman was immune and sovereign
immunity precluded the plaintiff from suing the federal government. Addressing
the key issue, the *Wuterich* court wrote:

> The *Restatement* provides:
>
> Conduct of a servant is within the scope of employment if, but only if:
>
> (a) it is of the kind he is employed to perform;
>
> (b) it occurs substantially within the authorized time and space limits;
>
> (c) it is actuated, at least in part, by a purpose to serve the master, and
>
> (d) if force is intentionally used by the servant against another, the use
> of force is not unexpectable by the master.
>
> *Restatement (Second) of Agency* § 228(1). . . .
>
> Wuterich argues that Congressman Murtha's statements to the media fell
> outside the scope of his employment because they were neither conduct "of
> the kind he is employed to perform," . . . nor were they "actuated, at least
> in part, by a purpose to serve the master,". . . . Wuterich alleged in his
> complaint that Congressman Murtha's "comments were made outside of
> the scope of his employment as a U.S. Congressman and [were] intended to
> serve his own private purposes and interests.". . . . Wuterich additionally
> maintained at the motion hearing before the District Court that Congress-
> man Murtha's comments fell outside the scope of his official duties because
> they were intended to embarrass Defense Secretary Rumsfeld. Taken
> together and generously construed under the liberal pleading standard of

[handwritten margin note: Westfall Act Test]

---

[424] *Id.* at 377–78.

[425] *Id.* at 380.

[426] *See* 28 U.S.C. 2680(h) (LEXIS 2014).

Rule 8(a), Wuterich has failed to allege facts that, taken as true, establish that Congressman Murtha's actions exceeded the scope of his employment.

The analysis of Wuterich's allegations is controlled by this court's decision in *Council on American Islamic Relations v. Ballenger*, 444 F.3d 659 (D.C. Cir. 2006). In that case, the Council on American-Islamic Relations sued Congressman Cass Ballenger for defamation and slander after Congressman Ballenger remarked that the organization was the "fund-raising arm for Hezbollah" during a conversation with a reporter about his separation from his wife. . . . The District Court upheld the Government's Westfall Act certification and dismissed the case. . . . In affirming the District Court, this court explained that the proper test under *Restatement* § 228(1)(a) is whether the "[underlying conduct] — not the allegedly defamatory sentence — was the kind of conduct Ballenger was employed to perform." . . .

Applying this test, the court in *Ballenger* held that the Congressman's conduct was of the kind he was employed to perform, because "[s]peaking to the press during regular work hours in response to a reporter's inquiry falls within the scope of a congressman's 'authorized duties.' " . . . Further, the court was quite clear in stating that, even though the allegedly defamatory statement was made in the course of a conversation about Congressman Ballenger's marital difficulties, his "conduct was motivated — at least in part — by a legitimate desire to discharge his duty as a congressman" within the meaning of *Restatement* § 228(1)(c). . . . This was so, the court explained, because a congressman's "ability to do his job as a legislator effectively is tied, as in this case, to the Member's relationship with the public and in particular his constituents and colleagues in the Congress." . . .

. . . [I]t is clear that Wuterich has not alleged any facts that even remotely suggest that Congressman Murtha was acting outside the scope of his employment when he spoke about the Haditha incident. . . . [T]he underlying conduct — interviews with the media about the pressures on American troops in the ongoing Iraq war — is unquestionably of the kind that Congressman Murtha was employed to perform as a Member of Congress. This is especially true in the case of Congressman Murtha, who was the Ranking Member of the Appropriations Committee's Subcommittee on Defense and had introduced legislation to withdraw American troops from Iraq. . . .

. . . Wuterich's claim that Congressman Murtha desired to "embarrass" Defense Secretary Rumsfeld, even if true, surely would not take his actions outside the scope of his employment.

As this court emphasized in *Ballenger*, "The *Restatement*'s text reveals that even a partial desire to serve the master is sufficient." . . . Attacking the credibility of Defense Secretary Rumsfeld, the man who was the public face of the war in Iraq, was . . . part and parcel of Congressman Murtha's job as a legislator charged with overseeing military affairs and of his efforts to serve his constituents by advancing legislation to bring home American troops stationed in Iraq.

. . . .

. . . [W]e hereby vacate the District Court's order. . . . Wuterich's case is barred by sovereign immunity. . . .[427]

d.   State Sovereign Immunity and State Officers and Employees

Libel and slander claims against states as entities are typically barred by sovereign immunity. In *White v. Trew*,[428] the Supreme Court of North Carolina considered whether sovereign immunity also barred "a libel suit by a tenured public university professor against his department head for an unfavorable annual review."[429] The court held that because the action failed to state whether the department head was being sued in official or individual capacity, the claim was barred by sovereign immunity.

e.   Other Absolute Privileges

Spousal Communications. The publication of defamatory material between a husband and wife is absolutely privileged.[430]

Consent by the Plaintiff. The maxim *volenti non fit injuria* applies as readily to libel and slander actions as in other areas of tort law. To one who is willing, no harm is done. If the plaintiff consents to the defendant's publication of defamatory material, the plaintiff cannot complain.[431]

Publications Required by Law. A statement uttered under legal compulsion generally is not actionable. Thus, if a broadcaster is required to afford a political candidate an equal chance to be heard, and has no right of censorship, the broadcaster cannot be held liable for dissemination of defamatory statements by the candidate that are broadcast in compliance with that legal obligation.[432]

Various statutes create both a duty to report and a privilege to protect the reporter from tort liability. For example, a section in the Texas Finance Code entitled "Reports of Apparent Crime," provides that:

> A state trust company that is . . . [the] victim of an apparent or suspected misapplication of its corporate or fiduciary funds or property in any amount by a director, manager, managing participant, officer, or employee shall . . . [make a report] to the banking commissioner within 48 hours. . . . The state trust company or a director, manager, managing participant, officer,

---

[427] *Wuterich*, 562 F.3d at 383–87.

[428] 736 S.E.2d 166 (N.C. 2013).

[429] *Id.* at 166.

[430] *See* RESTATEMENT (SECOND) OF TORTS § 592 (1977).

[431] *See id.* § 583.

[432] *See id.* § 592A cmt. a.

employee, or agent is not subject to liability for defamation or another charge resulting from information supplied in the report.[433]

The California Child Abuse and Neglect Reporting Act provides that "[n]o mandated reporter shall be civilly or criminally liable for any report required or authorized by this article."[434]

Reports of Criminal Activity to the Police. In *Hagberg v. California Federal Bank FSB*,[435] the California Supreme Court, relying on a state statute that immunizes statements in official proceedings, held that "when a citizen contacts law enforcement personnel to report suspected criminal activity and to instigate law enforcement personnel to respond, the communication . . . enjoys an unqualified privilege." The privilege defeated the plaintiff's claims alleging slander and other theories of tort liability. The plaintiff in *Hagberg* had argued that the only explanation the defendant called the police was racial or ethnic prejudice based on the fact that she was Hispanic. In response, the court wrote:

> Because our review of the record raises a serious question whether the evidence . . . was sufficient even to raise a triable issue of fact on the question whether Cal Fed or its employees were motivated by racial or ethnic prejudice in their treatment of plaintiff or followed a policy of singling out persons of certain races or ethnic backgrounds for discriminatory treatment, we have concluded that this is not an appropriate case in which to resolve the broad legal question whether proof that a business establishment has called for police assistance (or has a policy of calling for police assistance) based on racial or ethnic prejudice could give rise to liability under the Unruh Civil Rights Act notwithstanding the provisions of section 47(b) [the statutory official proceedings privilege]. . . .[436]

Suspected Child Abuse. Some states hold that reports relating to suspected child abuse are absolutely privileged. For example, California law imposes on certain persons a duty to report evidence of suspected child abuse, then further provides:

> No mandated reporter shall be civilly or criminally liable for any report required or authorized by this article. . . . Any other person reporting a known or suspected instance of child abuse or neglect shall not incur civil or criminal liability as a result of any report authorized by this article unless it can be proven that a false report was made and the person knew that the report was false or was made with reckless disregard of the truth or falsity of the report, and any person who makes a report of child abuse or neglect known to be false or with reckless disregard of the truth or falsity of the report is liable for any damages caused. . . .[437]

---

[433] TEX. FINANCE CODE § 183.113(a) (LEXIS 2014).

[434] CAL. PENAL CODE § 11172 (LEXIS 2014).

[435] 81 P.3d 244 (Cal. 2004).

[436] *Id.* at 260.

[437] CAL. PENAL CODE § 11172(a) (LEXIS 2014).

There are many statutory variations in other jurisdictions relating to reports of suspected child abuse.[438]

PROBLEM 3-13: THE BAR ADMISSION APPLICANT

When Kayla Quince applied for admission to practice after graduating from law school, she found that the process required a lot of paperwork. Among other things, she had to furnish the bar examiners with the names and contact information of all of her supervisors at every place she had ever worked.

After her first year of law school, Quince had interned at the law firm of Sorenson & Porter, where she was supervised by Andy Clark. Quince therefore listed Clark on her application materials. She also signed the "Authorization and Release" form that she had received from the State Bar. The form, after she filled in her name, stated in relevant part:

> I, Kayla Quince, hereby give my consent to the Board of Law Examiners to conduct an investigation as to my moral character and fitness and to make inquiries and request such information from third parties as, in the sole discretion of the Board, is necessary to such investigation. . . .
>
> I authorize every person having opinions about me or knowledge or control of information pertaining to me to reveal, furnish, and release to the Board of Law Examiners any such opinions, knowledge, information, documents, records, or other data. . . .
>
> I hereby release, discharge, and hold harmless the Board of Law Examiners and any person, firm, company, corporation, employer, or other third-party, and their agents, from any and all liability of every nature and kind arising out of the furnishing, inspection, and use of such opinions, knowledge, documents, or other data. . . .

The statement was signed by Quince before a Notary Public and notarized.

When Quince worked at Sorenson & Porter, she had made some mistakes. However, she thought that Clark would give her a positive report if he was contacted by the bar examiners. Quince was seriously wrong.

Some of the errors that Quince had made at the law firm had seriously embarrassed Clark and had potentially subjected the firm to malpractice liability. When Clark was contacted by the bar examiners, he was provided with a copy of the Authorization and Release Form. In response to the inquiry about Quince, Clark provided a full and unflattering account of Quince's errors at the firm. In fact, what Clark wrote was even worse than the truth because Clark confused Quince with Karen Curren, another intern who worked for the law firm the same summer. Andy Clark's letter to the Board of Law Examiners attributed some of Curren's errors and unprofessional conduct to Quince.

As a result of Clark's letter, the Board of Law Examiners conducted a full investigation into the matter, which delayed Quince's admission to the bar for six

---

[438] *See, e.g.,* COLO. REV. STAT. ANN. § 19-3-309 (LEXIS 2014).

months. During that period, the firm by which Quince was hired for a job after graduation paid her at the same agreed salary that she continued to receive after becoming fully licensed. Please evaluate whether Quince has a viable defamation claim against Clark and his law firm.

4.   Qualified Privileges

Legal issues relating to "conditional" or "qualified" privileges fall into two basic categories. The first concerns when such privileges arise, and the second relates to the circumstances under which such privileges are lost.[439]

Types of Interests Protected. In general, a qualified privilege may arise in any situation in which there is good reason for the law to encourage or permit a person to speak or write about a potential defamation plaintiff, even though the speaker is not certain about the accuracy of the information relayed. Thus, the *Restatement* contains specific qualified privilege rules relating to protection of: (1) the publisher's own interests;[440] (2) the interests of the recipient of a communication or a third party;[441] (3) a common interest of the publisher and recipient;[442] (4) the interests of family members;[443] and (5) the public interest (including communications with public officials or peace officers[444] and communications by inferior state officers who are not entitled to an absolute privilege[445]).

In general, a communication is more likely to be qualifiedly privileged than would otherwise be the case: if there is a relationship between the publisher and the recipient; if the communication concerns a risk that could be avoided or mitigated through reliance on the information provided; if the statement was solicited, rather than volunteered; and if the allegedly defamed person previously engaged in some form of related wrongful conduct.

when a comm. will likely be privileged

In *Havlik v. Johnson & Wales University*,[446] the First Circuit held that a university, which reasonably but erroneously believed that it was required by federal law to issue a crime report about one student's assault on another, was protected by a qualified privilege from a defamation suit based on the contents of the report. Moreover, the fact that a university vice president had "accused the plaintiff of prevarication" relating to the underlying events and "may have harbored some hostility toward the plaintiff" was irrelevant for purposes of determining whether the report was privileged.[447] This was true because there was no evidence that the vice president played any part in the preparation of that document.

---

[439]   *See* Restatement (Second) of Torts § 593 (1977).

[440]   *Id.* § 594.

[441]   *Id.* § 595.

[442]   *Id.* § 596.

[443]   *Id.* § 597.

[444]   *Id.* § 598.

[445]   *Id.* § 598A.

[446]   509 F.3d 25 (1st Cir. 2007).

[447]   *Id.* at 34.

Moral Duties. Duties that are "moral," rather than "legal," may be sufficient to create a qualified privilege. In *Chandok v. Klessig*,[448] the Second Circuit stated:

> A statement is generally "subject to a qualified privilege when it is fairly made by a person in the discharge of some public or private duty, legal or moral." . . .

> In addition, a "qualified[ ] privilege extends to a communication made by one person to another upon a subject in which both have an interest." . . . In some instances the common-interest privilege may overlap the moral-duty privilege, for one may have a "moral duty to communicate . . . knowledge and information about a person in whom the [speaker] ha[s] an interest to another who also has an interest in such person," . . . Thus, in *Buckley*, Dr. Litman, the physician who believed his assistant had stolen patient files, had a qualified privilege for communicating that information to a fellow physician who had handled the practice of Dr. Litman while the latter was away and with whom the assistant was seeking employment. . . .

> Within this framework, we conclude that all of Klessig's Statements were protected by one or more state-law privileges. Several were subject to qualified privileges for statements that Klessig had a legal and/or moral obligation to make. As to legal obligations, the fact that some of the NOS research was funded by federal moneys meant that Klessig was required to inform the pertinent agencies of suspicions of scientific misconduct. . . . Thus, when Klessig wrote to officials of NIH [National Institutes of Health] and NSF [National Science Foundation] stating that "[e]vidence [had] recently emerged that strongly suggests that [Chandok] falsified" some, most, or all of her reported data . . . he was fulfilling a legal obligation. Similarly, when Klessig formally filed his allegations against Chandok with the Scientific Misconduct Investigation Committee, he was complying with the reporting requirement, for the regulations required an immediate inquiry and/or investigation into allegations of possible misconduct . . . .

> Moreover, in light of the facts that Klessig had twice applied to NIH for, and twice failed to be awarded, federal funds for his NOS [nitric oxide synthase] research, and that NIH granted Klessig's laboratory funds (in excess of $1 million) for NOS research only after receiving his third application, which was cowritten by Chandok and consisted almost exclusively of Chandok's reported data, we conclude that even had there been no federal reporting regulations, Klessig would have had a moral obligation to inform NIH of the possible fabrication of the data on which, clearly, it had relied.

> Further, Klessig plainly had a moral obligation to share his concerns about Chandok's reported results with BTI's [Boyce Thompson Institute for Plant Research's] president Stern, with BTI's responsible personnel officer Pola, with the Cell and PNAS [Proceedings of the National Academy of Sciences] articles' coauthors Ekengren, who was a BTI scientist, and Martin, Ytterberg, and van Wijk, who were members of the faculty at

---

[448] 632 F.3d 803 (2d Cir. 2011).

Cornell. The reputations and credibility of both institutions and all of these individual scientists were imperiled by the fact that they were explicitly associated with scientific articles that may have been predicated on fabricated research results or fraudulent reporting. The moral-obligation qualified privilege applies to at least the nine Statements sent to one or more of these BTI and Cornell recipients. . . .

We note also that Klessig's Imputed Statement to the PNAS editor and the formal retraction sent to PNAS too fell within the qualified privilege for statements that Klessig had a moral obligation to make. Having caused PNAS to publish the article, and having developed serious doubts about the accuracy or veracity of its contents, Klessig and his coauthors who shared those doubts rightly felt that they owed it to PNAS — and to any fellow scientist who might otherwise base his or her research on those reported data — to make known their views of the Cell and PNAS articles' unreliability.

. . . .

Thus, all of Klessig's Statements were privileged under New York law in the absence of a showing by Chandok that they were motivated by "actual" or common-law malice.[449]

Credit Reporting Agencies. Credit reporting agencies are usually held to have a qualified privilege with respect to communications to their subscribers.

a.   Privileges of Employers and Employees

Current Employers. "[A]n employer has a conditional or qualified privilege that attaches to communications made in the course of an investigation following a report of employee wrongdoing."[450]

Co-Employees. Comments by one employee about another employee may enjoy a qualified privilege, for example, if they are made at a board of directors' corporate grievance hearing[451] or are published to management with respect to another's job performance.[452] Thus, in *Bals v. Verduzco*,[453] the Indiana Supreme Court held that an action by a current employee based upon a supervisor's allegedly defamatory evaluation was barred by a qualified privilege. Likewise, in *DeNardo v. Bax*,[454] the Supreme Court of Alaska found that an employee's statements that she was being stalked by a co-worker were qualifiedly privileged because they expressed her legitimate concern for personal safety.

Former Employers. A former employer's statements, made in good faith about a former employee to a state workforce commission, are qualifiedly privileged

---

[449] *Id.* at 814–17.

[450] *Randall's Food Markets, Inc. v. Johnson*, 891 S.W.2d 640, 646 (Tex. 1995).

[451] *See Hagebak v. Stone*, 61 P.3d 201 (N.M. Ct. App. 2002).

[452] *See Sheehan v. Anderson*, 263 F.3d 159 (3d Cir. 2001).

[453] 600 N.E.2d 1353 (Ind. 1992).

[454] 147 P.3d 672 (Alaska 2006).

because the speaker and the recipient have a common interest.[455] Likewise, if the plaintiff's former employer is asked about the plaintiff's job performance by a prospective new employer, most jurisdictions would say that the former employer has a qualified privilege.

Nevertheless, former employees sometimes sue former employers who provide unflattering information to prospective employers, arguing that any qualified privilege was vitiated by abuse. This risk has caused some former employers to refuse to give prospective employers any information about their former employees other than job titles and dates of employment. Such a practice has a number of bad consequences. Able employees, who would receive good references if employers could comment freely, may not get the praise they deserve. New employers are deprived of the use of pertinent information in making hiring decisions. And, occasionally, even third parties may be harmed, as when a former employer, fearing litigation, does not disclose a job applicant's history of actual or threatened violence.

Some states have enacted legislation to make it harder for former employees to bring defamation actions. Thus, a Kansas statute provides:

(a) Unless otherwise provided by law, an employer, or an employer's designee, who discloses information about a current or former employee to a prospective employer of the employee shall be qualifiedly immune from civil liability.

(b) Unless otherwise provided by law, an employer who discloses information about a current or former employee to a prospective employer of the employee shall be absolutely immune from civil liability. The immunity applies only to disclosure of the following: (1) date of employment; (2) pay level; (3) job description and duties; (4) wage history.

(c) Unless otherwise provided by law, an employer who responds in writing to a written request concerning a current or former employee from a prospective employer of that employee shall be absolutely immune from civil liability for disclosure of the following information to which an employee may have access:

(1) written employee evaluations which were conducted prior to the employee's separation from the employer and to which an employee shall be given a copy upon request; and

(2) whether the employee was voluntarily or involuntarily released from service and the reasons for the separation. . . .[456]

Note that the Kansas statute covers only information furnished to a prospective employer.

---

[455] *See Patrick v. McGowan*, 104 S.W.3d 219 (Tex. App. 2003).

[456] KAN. STAT. ANN. Ch. 44, Art. 1, § 44-119a (LEXIS 2014).

b.   Fair Comment

The qualified privilege of fair comment once played a major role in libel and slander litigation. Pursuant to the privilege, a person who accurately reported the facts could offer an opinion about a related subject of public interest without risk of liability. However, the privilege was lost if the facts were erroneously stated, unless the statement itself was privileged.

The constitutionalization of the law of defamation, which began with *New York Times v. Sullivan*,[457] has in many respects eclipsed the privilege of fair comment because in numerous situations a false statement of fact, or even a negligently false statement of fact, will not give rise to liability. However, courts still occasionally discuss the privilege of fair comment.

For example, in *Magnusson v. New York Times Co.*,[458] a plastic surgeon, who was the subject of an unflattering "In Your Corner" consumer report on television, sued the broadcasting station and reporter. The court held that a common law fair comment privilege could be asserted as a defense. The Oklahoma Supreme Court wrote:

> Under the common law defense of fair comment, a statement is generally privileged when it: 1) deals with a matter of public concern; 2) is based on true or privileged facts; and 3) represents the actual opinion of the speaker, but is not made for the sole purpose of causing harm. In making the privilege determination, courts look to the phrasing of the statement, the context in which it appears, the medium through which it is disseminated, the circumstances surrounding its publication, and a consideration of whether the statement implies the existence of undisclosed facts.

> First, there is no question that the opinions expressed in the broadcasts involved a matter of public concern. Public health is clearly a matter of public consonance. Furthermore, the availability and skills of surgeons constitute matters relating to a community's public health.

> Second, Magnusson does not allege that the stories were false in the sense that they did not accurately report the patients' complaints. . . . Here, all the patients interviewed by Edwards and included in the KFOR broadcasts were clearly basing their statements about the doctor's professionalism . . . on their individual experiences and the opinions or conclusions they developed therefrom.

> Third, it is for the court to determine whether a statement is one of fact or opinion. The statements here cannot reasonably be interpreted as stating actual facts about the doctor. Rather, they are in the nature of nonactionable "judgmental statements", opinionative but not factual in nature. Furthermore, where the tone of the broadcast is pointed, exaggerated and heavily laden with emotional rhetoric and moral outrage, listeners are put on notice to expect speculation and personal judgment. References to

---

[457] 376 U.S. 254 (1964).

[458] 98 P.3d 1070 (Okla. 2004).

"botched" surgeries and "devastating" scars clearly fall within this category rather than being statements which could reasonably be interpreted as stating actual facts.

Finally, the reports were presented as part of the "In Your Corner" series — clearly identified as investigations into claims by patients in which both negative and positive disclosures were made about Magnusson and to which the doctor was given the opportunity to respond. There was nothing about the broadcasts indicating that facts were being withheld. . . .

. . . Applying the standards of the common law fair comment privilege and considering the statements' phrasing, their context, the medium through which they were presented, the circumstances surrounding their publication, and a determination of whether the statements imply the existence of undisclosed facts, we have little difficulty determining that the broadcasts here, both of which were focused on alleged complications arising from plastic surgery and the conditions associated therewith, meet the requirements for application of the common law fair comment privilege.[459]

c.   Abuse of Qualified Privileges

A qualified privilege is defeasible in the sense that the law *does care about* what the defendant knew, who the defendant told, and why the defendant made the statement. Thus, a qualified privilege may be lost or "abused" in a variety of ways, such as by excessive publication, improper motives (such as spite, ill will, or vindictiveness), or fault on the part of the defendant as to the falsity of the communication.

Excessive Publication. Excessive publication occurs when a person with good reasons to communicate potentially defamatory information tells other recipients who do not need to know. This amounts to an abuse of privilege, and the excessive publication is actionable.

Of course, whether the defendant has engaged in excessive publication is usually a question of fact. In *McCoy v. Neiman Marcus Group, Inc.,*[460] a federal court in Texas held that a company did not abuse its qualified privilege by holding a department meeting to explain to remaining employees that the plaintiff was terminated for fraud and that systems were in place to detect such fraud.

Lack of Good Faith and Disregard for the Plaintiff's Rights. Some courts say that, in order to be qualifiedly privileged, a statement must be made in good faith. For example, in *Kuechle v. Life's Companion P.C.A., Inc.,*[461] the Minnesota Court of Appeals held that an employer, who said that an employee had been discharged for allegedly violating a direct order, did not have a qualified privilege because the employer had made only a cursory investigation of the underlying facts, failed to interview the plaintiff, and ignored a supervisor's statement that she had made a request of the plaintiff, rather than given a direct order.

---

[459] *Id.* at 1076–77.

[460] 1997 U.S. Dist. LEXIS 2136 (N.D. Tex. Feb. 5, 1997).

[461] 653 N.W.2d 214 (Minn. Ct. App. 2002).

Intent to Injure or Disregard of Rights. In *Popko v. Continental Casualty Co.*,[462] a suit by a former employee relating to the reasons for his termination, the Appellate Court of Illinois articulated the abuse of privilege issue in slightly different terms. The court wrote:

> A corporation has an unquestionable interest in investigating and correcting a situation where one of its employees may be engaged in suspicious conduct within the company. . . . Thus, a qualified privilege exists for communications made concerning such investigation.

> However, even on such occasion, the communication may still be actionable if the privilege is abused, *i.e.*, if there is a direct intention to injure the plaintiff or a reckless disregard of the plaintiff's rights. . . .[463]

Negligence or Actual Malice. Traditionally, in many states, negligence with respect to the falsity of a defamatory statement destroyed a qualified privilege. Obviously, continued adherence to this rule, in light of *New York Times Co. v. Sullivan* and its progeny, would have meant that the concept of qualified privilege would have virtually vanished from American defamation law in those jurisdictions. Not surprisingly, the second *Restatement* endorsed the view, long followed in some states, that only actual malice, not negligence, destroys a qualified privilege. Thus qualified privileges continue to play a role in cases not involving public officials and public figures.

It is not surprising that in *Wiggins v. Mallard*,[464] the Supreme Court of Alabama ruled that "a private-party-defamation plaintiff may overcome a qualified-immunity defense with testimony indicating that the defendant intentionally lied about the plaintiff." Intentional lying constitutes actual malice.

In *Martin v. State Department of Public Safety and Corrections*,[465] a Louisiana appellate court likewise held that only fault amounting to actual malice vitiates a qualified privilege. The court explained the application of the rule to the facts of the case as follows:

> The plaintiff sued the State of Louisiana, Department of Public Safety and Corrections, Office of State Police, for defamation damages arising out of a news release by Troop E of the Louisiana State Police regarding a fatal automobile accident. The news release named the plaintiff, "John Martin, Jr., (W/M 37yrs)" as the driver of a pick-up truck on La. Hwy. 156 in Winn Parish, of which he lost control and rolled several times, ejecting his passenger, who was killed when struck by an oncoming vehicle. The report also stated that "alcohol usage is suspected of Mr. Martin, Jr." The evidence at trial established that the driver was actually the plaintiff's father, of the same name but absent the suffix "Jr." No explanation was forthcoming from the evidence as to how the mix-up occurred. The court held that the State

---

[462] 823 N.E.2d 184 (Ill. App. Ct. 2005).

[463] *Id.* at 180–81.

[464] 905 So. 2d 776, 788 (Ala. 2004).

[465] 109 So. 3d 442 (La. Ct. App. 2013).

was liable for defamation. After granting a new trial on the issue of damages, the court awarded the plaintiff $10,000 in damages with interest from date of judicial demand. . . .

The only part of the trial court's reasons for judgment that indicate that it might have considered the qualified or conditional privilege defense raised by the state was the initial statement by the court that publication of the report was a matter of public interest. . . . The evidence in this case indicates that the mistake was very likely a clerical error, given the fact that the driver and the plaintiff have the same name, except for the suffix, which was not on several documents, the fatality victim in the accident was a "Jr.," and the radio communication from Tpr. Nugent in which he said "vehicle*452 #1 was a junior," coupled with the urgency with which these reports are made. The error is at most, simple inadvertence or negligence, but certainly not rising to the level of recklessness required to show abuse of privilege in order to defeat the qualified privilege afforded to the defendant in this case. . . .

We therefore conclude that the trial court erred as a matter of law in not applying the qualified privilege to the circumstances in this case, and it was clearly wrong in not finding that the plaintiff failed to show that the defendant abused the privilege in this case.[466]

In *American Future Systems, Inc. v. Better Business Bureau of Eastern Pennsylvania*,[467] the Supreme Court of Pennsylvania refused to endorse the view that only fault amounting to actual malice, not negligence, destroys a qualified privilege. The court appeared to conclude, perhaps appropriately, that because it is easy to raise an issue of conditional privilege, private plaintiffs would often be required to prove actual malice to prevail in a defamation action.

Federal law recognizes what amounts to a qualified privilege — defeasible by proof of actual malice — related to airline threats. In *Air Wisconsin Airlines Corp. v. Hoeper*,[468] the United States Supreme Court rejected a defamation claim by a pilot against an airline. As the Court explained:

In 2001, Congress created the Transportation Security Administration (TSA) to assess and manage threats against air travel. . . . To ensure that the TSA would be informed of potential threats, Congress gave airlines and their employees immunity against civil liability for reporting suspicious behavior. . . . But this immunity does not attach to "any disclosure made with actual knowledge that the disclosure was false, inaccurate, or misleading" or "any disclosure made with reckless disregard as to the truth or falsity of that disclosure."[469]

The Limited Value of Qualified Privileges. The fact that a qualified privilege may be lost by abuse limits the potency of qualified privileges. It is easy to raise a

---

[466] *Id.* at 445–52.

[467] 923 A.2d 389 (Pa. 2007).

[468] 134 S. Ct. 852 (2014).

[469] *Id.* at 857–58.

fact issue as to whether abuse of a qualified privilege occurred. Therefore, summary judgment is often denied to a defendant asserting a qualified privilege.[470] For example, *Gray v. HEB Food Store No. 4*[471] involved these facts:

> Betty Gray was grocery shopping at appellee's store. Upon completing her shopping, she went to pay for her groceries at a check-out operated by HEB checker Esmi Cantu. As this occurred, Yvette Rodriguez, an assistant service manager, approached the check-out counter and made several statements directed to Cantu and appellant. Gray alleged that Rodriguez asked Cantu, "What are you giving this lady free?" Gray further alleged that Rodriguez then turned to Gray and asked Gray, "Ma'am, what are you getting free today?" According to Gray, Rodriguez repeated these questions several times.[472]

The grocery store argued that it had a qualified privilege to make inquiries to investigate alleged theft from the store. However, the grocery store was denied summary judgment on the defamation claim because the store's evidence was insufficient to show that the statement was made without malice.

PROBLEM 3-14: THE SUSPECTED PLAGIARIST

Anca Engles and Kevin Stensley had been academic competitors in their engineering program for several semesters. In terms of grade point average, Kevin was number one in the class, outranking Anca every semester by a mere fraction of a point. When word quietly spread throughout the class that Kevin had submitted for course credit a research paper that he had purchased online, Anca was secretly delighted. The only thing she could think of was that she would finally rank number one, *if* the news reached the school administrators and *if* they took action. However, neither of those conditions was certain to occur.

Feigning concern for academic standards and the reputation of the school, Anca discussed with her husband, John Hatch, and her best friend, Marcie Reusch, whether she had a duty to report what she knew to the dean or associate dean of the engineering program. John cautioned her not to do anything because she really had no "facts." Marcie said that the widespread rumor was a "fact" and that she should report it, but do so anonymously.

Anca delivered an unsigned letter to the office of the associate dean, by sliding it under the door after hours. The associate dean would normally have ignored an anonymous complaint, but these charges concerned the top student in the class. The associate dean decided that he had to raise the issue with the dean, in order to get directions on whether it was necessary to make some kind of inquiry.

---

[470] *See Ciemniecki v. Parker McCay P.A.*, 2012 U.S. Dist. LEXIS 552 (D.N.J. Jan. 4, 2012) ("Given the genuine disputes of material fact that have been raised regarding the Parker Defendants' motives for accusing Plaintiff of raising a false public alarm, Court finds that the Parker Defendants have failed to establish the applicability of the qualified privilege at this stage").

[471] 941 S.W.2d 327 (Tex. App. 1997).

[472] *Id.* at 328.

The dean told the associate dean that the school could be greatly embarrassed if a story came out establishing that the best student had been given credit for a "plagiarized" paper, purchased on the Internet, after the administration knew of that risk. The dean instructed the associate dean not to convene an honor court hearing but instead to make a confidential inquiry to see if Kevin would admit or deny wrongdoing if confronted with the anonymous report.

The associate dean located a cell phone number for Kevin and called him. Kevin did not answer, but a recording of Kevin's voice said to leave a message. Thinking that only Kevin would pick up messages on Kevin's cell phone, the associate dean said, "Kevin, I have very bad news. There is a rumor circulating on campus that you submitted a plagiarized research paper. I need to talk to you as soon as possible."

Unfortunately, the message was picked up by Kevin's roommate, Riley West, who had borrowed Kevin's cell phone and had been expecting a call. Riley had already heard about the rumor on campus. He did not know if it was true and had not discussed the rumor with Kevin. Listening to the associate dean's message impressed Riley with the gravity of the situation. With embarrassment, Riley relayed the message to Kevin.

Kevin immediately called the associate dean, who was not available. Distraught and unwilling to wait until he could reach the associate dean, Kevin called the dean. He told the dean what the associate dean had said on the message, and denied that he had purchased a research paper online or submitted anything other than his own work in fulfillment of course requirements.

Although the rumor was wholly unfounded, it caused serious harm to Kevin's reputation, at least on campus. If Kevin can prove all of the above facts, can he prevail in a defamation action against any of the persons who repeated the false charges?

5.   Fair Report Privilege

Reports of Official Actions and Proceedings. The "fair report" privilege (sometimes called the "reporter's privilege") is neither "absolute" nor "qualified" as those terms are used to describe other defamation privileges. Rather, the privilege hinges on the subject matter, fairness, and accuracy of the report.

Knowledge of Falsity is Usually Irrelevant. Under common law principles, a fair and accurate report about official actions or proceedings, or about a meeting open to the public on matters of public concern, is privileged even if the person making the report knows that the report contains false defamatory information.[473] However, under Texas legislation which has codified the fair report privilege, the "privilege does not extend to the republication of a matter if it is proved that the matter was republished with actual malice after it had ceased to be of public concern."[474]

---

[473] *See* RESTATEMENT (SECOND) OF TORTS § 611 (1977).

[474] TEX. CIV. PRAC. & REM. CODE ANN. § 73.002(a) (LEXIS 2014).

Under the fair report privilege, a newspaper can accurately quote what a police department press release says about an arrest without any obligation to investigate the facts. In *Goss v. Houston Community Newspapers*,[475] the defendants were sued for defamation based on publication of a newspaper article:

> The story, entitled "Drag racers arrested by deputy," stated that Goss and another man had been arrested after a Harris County Sheriff's Deputy observed that their vehicles appeared to be racing. The story further reported that appellant was placed into custody for possession of a controlled substance while the other man was charged with racing on a highway.[476]

In fact, "Goss was never charged with drag racing, and the controlled substance charge was later dismissed."[477] Nevertheless, a libel claim was barred by the fair report privilege because the Texas Court of Appeals found that, although some of the information was arranged in a different order, the story quoted nearly verbatim large portions of the sheriff's department's news release and fairly summarized other portions.

Privilege Hinges on "Substantial" Fairness and Accuracy, Not Absence of Abuse. In *Alpine Industries Computers, Inc. v. Cowles Pub. Co.*,[478] a retailer (Alpine) brought a defamation action against a newspaper publisher (Cowles) based on an article asserting that Alpine sold counterfeit software. Alpine contended that the reporter's privilege did not apply to the story or that, if it did, the privilege was abused. Addressing the dispute, the Washington State Court of Appeals wrote:

> Washington has long afforded news media defendants a privilege for reporting on official actions and proceedings. . . .
>
> . . . [T]he more recent Washington opinions discussing the fair reporting privilege rely to some degree on Section 611 of *Restatement (Second) of Torts* . . . [which states]:
>
> > "The publication of defamatory matter concerning another in a report of an official action or proceeding or of a meeting open to the public that deals with a matter of public concern is privileged if the report is accurate and complete or a fair abridgement of the occurrence reported."
>
> . . . .
>
> The purpose of the fair reporting privilege is to serve the public's interest in obtaining information as to what transpires in official proceedings and public meetings. . . . The "privilege is not intended as merely a convenient method of shielding the press from tort liability, but instead is intended to ensure that information is made available to the public concerning what occurs in official proceedings." . . .

---

[475]   252 S.W.3d 652 (Tex. App. 2008).

[476]   *Id.* at 654.

[477]   *Id.*

[478]   57 P.3d 1178 (Wash. Ct. App. 2002), *amended* 64 P.3d 49 (Wash. Ct. App. 2003).

Significantly, the fair reporting privilege is "somewhat broader in its scope" than the conditional privileges set forth in Sections 594 through 598A of [the] *Restatement (Second) of Torts*. . . . The fair reporting privilege may protect the publisher even if the publisher does not believe defamatory statements contained in the official report to be true or even knows the defamatory statements to be false. . . .

. . . [T]he fair reporting privilege is not subject to the same abuse analysis as conditional privileges. . . .

. . . [T]he fair reporting privilege extends to reports of official actions, including actions arising from judicial proceedings. . . . Here, the challenged statements are easily traceable to the District Court's proceedings as reflected by Microsoft's complaint [against Alpine], the court order signed by Mr. Le [the owner of Alpine] and reported in the story, and the District Court's memorandum decision. Given the record, we conclude as a matter of law that the challenged statements are attributable to an official proceeding. . . .

For a report to be a fair abridgment of an official proceeding, surgical precision is not required so long as the report is substantially accurate and fair. *Restatement, supra*, § 611 cmt. f. "It is not necessary that it be exact in every immaterial detail or that it conform to that precision demanded in technical or scientific reporting." *Id.* "It is enough that it conveys to the persons who read it a substantially correct account of the proceedings." *Id.*
. . . .

. . . Under this standard, the publisher must not edit and delete an otherwise accurate report so as to misrepresent the proceeding and thus mislead the reader. *Restatement, supra*, § 611 cmt. f. And the publisher must not add material so as to cast a person in a defamatory light. . . . To determine the fairness of the report, we must read the article as a whole.
. . .

Here, a passage in the . . . story states the District Court ordered Alpine to pay damages for the sales of both Office Pro and Windows 95 counterfeit software after December 1998. The passage is partially inaccurate; the sales at issue were of Windows 95 counterfeit software alone. But if the story is read in its entirety, the error is not substantial. The story contained two references to Mr. Le's claim that he stopped selling Office Pro after the cease and desist letter from Microsoft. Moreover, the story contains a direct quote from the District Court order regarding "Le's decision to continue buying Windows 95. . . ." Viewed in context with the entire story, the challenged passage is substantially accurate and fair as a matter of law.[479]

Press Releases and On-the-Record Comments Made by Public Officials. The fair report privilege sometimes extends to reports about informal comments made

---

[479] *Id.* at 1185–87.

by public officials. In *Hudak v. Times Pub. Co., Inc.*,[480] a federal court in Pennsylvania wrote:

> . . . Pennsylvania courts give a somewhat broad interpretation to the concept of "reports of an official action or proceeding," as set forth in the *Second Restatement*. We conclude that the reported remarks of Mr. Foulk, which Plaintiff challenges in this case, should likewise be viewed as a "report" of "official action" giving rise to a privileged occasion. Here, it is undisputed that, following Plaintiff's formal arrest on criminal charges, Defendant Thompson went to the District Attorney's office in her capacity as a reporter for the Times for the express purpose of eliciting an official comment on the charges. . . . She met with Mr. Foulk, face-to-face, in his office, asked him to officially comment on the case for purposes of publication, and recorded his statement directly. . . . Mr. Foulk, as District Attorney of Erie County, is the chief law enforcement officer of the county. . . . While his on-the-record comments were made in the context of an informal, one-on-one meeting with Ms. Thompson, they served the same purpose as a press release or press conference. Accordingly, Defendant Thompson's report of Mr. Foulk's comments constitute a "report of an official action or proceeding" for purposes of the fair report privilege. . . .
>
> Finally, our conclusion that the fair report privilege conditionally applies to the reported comments of Mr. Foulk is supported by case law from other jurisdictions. . . . *See, e.g.,* . . . Alsop v. The Cincinnati Post, 2001 U.S. App. LEXIS 23808, at *2 (6th Cir. Oct. 30, 2001) (privilege applied to newspaper's statement that plaintiff sold crack cocaine to informants at his store, where challenged statement was based on information obtained from U.S. Attorney's press release); . . . *Thomas v. Telegraph Pub. Co.*, 155 N.H. 314, 929 A.2d 993, 1010 (2007) (suggesting that the privilege would not automatically protect reports of all private conversations between police officers and reporters but would protect reports that bear sufficient indicia of accuracy and that are based upon press conferences, interviews with a police chief, or other types of official conversations). . . .
>
> . . . The touchstone of the fair report privilege seems to be whether there exist sufficient indicia of "officialdom" in the reported communication. The record here supports but one conclusion: though Mr. Foulk's remarks to Ms. Thompson occurred in a casual setting, they constituted an official, on-the-record report concerning governmental action undertaken within the scope of Mr. Foulk's office.[481]

Government Informants and Unofficial Sources. Information obtained from government informants is not protected by the fair report privilege because the information is not obtained as the result of an official act or proceeding.[482] As the Tennessee Court of Appeals explained:

---

[480] 534 F. Supp. 2d 546 (W.D. Pa. 2008).

[481] *Id.* at 572–73.

[482] *Lewis v. NewsChannel 5 Network, L.P.*, 238 S.W.3d 270 (Tenn. Ct. App. 2007).

The prevailing view is that the fair report privilege should not be extended to apply to the "myriad types of informal reports and official and unofficial investigations, contacts, and communications of law enforcement personnel at all levels of the state and federal bureaucracy with local, regional, and national media."... . It should be applied only to reports of official actions or proceedings involving responsible, authoritative decision-makers who assume legal and political responsibility for their actions. . . . Unofficial, off-the-record statements, especially when the source remains confidential, lack the dignity and authoritative weight of official actions and proceedings and, therefore, reports of these statements should not be protected by the fair report privilege. . . .

The American Law Institute has addressed how far the scope of "official action" extends into the domain of arrests and the underlying facts associated with the arrests by differentiating between reports of an arrest and statements regarding the underlying facts that precipitated the arrest. The *Restatement (Second) of Torts* states that "[a]n arrest by an officer is an official action, and a report of the fact of the arrest or of the charge of crime made by the officer in making or returning the arrest" is within the fair report privilege; however, "statements made by the police or by the complainant or other witnesses or by the prosecuting attorney as to the facts of the case or the evidence expected to be given are not yet part of the judicial proceeding or of the arrest itself" are not. . . .[483]

Policy Basis: Agency, Public Supervision, and Public Interest. The fair report privilege, as formulated by the *Restatement*, is so well established that it is difficult to find a detailed exploration of the policy basis of the rule. Addressing those concerns, in *Medico v. Time, Inc.*,[484] the Third Circuit explained:

> Three policies underlie the fair report privilege. . . . Initially, an agency theory was offered to rationalize a privilege of fair report: one who reports what happens in a public, official proceeding acts as an agent for persons who had a right to attend, and informs them of what they might have seen for themselves. The agency rationale, however, cannot explain application of the privilege to proceedings or reports not open to public inspection.

[handwritten margin note: policy behind the fair report privilege]

A theory of public supervision also informs the fair report privilege. Justice Holmes, applying the privilege to accounts of courtroom proceedings, gave the classic formulation of this principle:

> (The privilege is justified by) the security which publicity gives for the proper administration of justice. . . . It is desirable that the trial of causes should take place under the public eye, not because the controversies of one citizen with another are of public concern, but because it is of the highest moment that those who administer justice should always act under the sense of public responsibility and that every citizen should

---

[483] *Id.* at 286–87.

[484] 643 F.2d 134 (3d Cir. 1981).

be able to satisfy himself with his own eyes as to the mode in which a public duty is performed.

Cowley v. Pulsifer, 137 Mass. 392, 394 (1884). . . .

A third rationale for the fair report privilege rests, somewhat tautologically, on the public's interest in learning of important matters. . . . [However,] "mere curiosity in the private affairs of others is of insufficient importance to warrant granting the privilege," . . .

Some jurisdictions rely on the informational rationale to extend the privilege to accounts of the proceedings of public meetings of private, nongovernmental organizations, as long as the meeting deals with matters of concern to the public. . . .

Care must be taken, of course, to ensure that the supervisory and informational rationales not expand into justifications for reporting any defamatory matter maintained in any government file. . . .[485]

The Reliability Rationale and Reports About Actions of Foreign Governments. Some cases invoke reliability as one of the policy foundations of the fair report privilege. For example, in *OAO Alfa Bank v. Center for Public Integrity*,[486] two Russian businessmen sued a public interest organization and its reporters for publishing defamatory statements linking the plaintiffs to organized crime and narcotics trafficking. In deciding the case in favor of the defendants, a federal court in the District of Columbia held that the fair report privilege did not apply to reports about the actions of a foreign government. The reasoning of the court suggests that the supposed reliability or unreliability of official information may sometimes play a role in the application of the doctrine. The court wrote:

The Fourth Circuit . . . in *Lee v. Dong-A Ilbo*, 849 F.2d 876 (4th Cir. 1988), . . . refused to extend the privilege to a United States news agency report of a South Korean government press release. Reasoning that "[w]e are familiar with the workings of our government and consider it to be open and reliable," while "[f]oreign governments, like nongovernmental sources of information, are not necessarily familiar, open, reliable, or accountable," the Fourth Circuit declined to "provide a blanket privilege to those who report the activities of foreign governments.". . . . The court then held that applying "the privilege in a piecemeal fashion would be extremely difficult," placing the court in the untenable position of attempting to determine whether a foreign state exhibits the "openness and reliability that warrant an extension of the privilege." . . . The court therefore concluded that the privilege should not apply to reports on the acts of foreign governments.

This Court agrees. . . . Indeed, the *Restatement* adopts the same approach, explicitly limiting the compass of the privilege to reports of the proceedings or actions of "the government of the United States, or of any State or of any of its subdivisions," *Restatement (Second) of Torts* § 611

---

[485] *Id.* at 140–42.

[486] 387 F. Supp. 2d 20 (D.D.C. 2005).

cmt. d (1977). . . . [E]ven if the better course would be to assess the application of the privilege to a foreign state on a case-by-case basis, the defendants in this case allege that Russia during this period [the 1990s] was a "corrupt system run by crony capitalists," . . . hardly the showing of "openness and reliability" one would presumably look for in extending the privilege.[487]

Inaccurate Reports. In *Myers v. The Telegraph*,[488] the Illinois Appellate Court found that a news report was substantially inaccurate and therefore not protected by the fair report privilege. Newspaper accounts had reported that a criminal had pled guilty to a felony and was placed on probation. However, according to official reports, the felony charges that were initially brought against the criminal were dismissed, and he pled guilty only to a misdemeanor and was given a conditional discharge.

Similarly, in *Edwards v. Paddock Publications, Inc.*,[489] the fair report privilege was found not to apply because, while the defendants accurately reported that Christopher Edwards had been arrested, they published an accompanying photograph of another Christopher Edwards, a high school football star, who had no connection to the arrest.

Embellishments. In some cases, embellishment of a report with other facts or expressions of the speaker's opinion means that the speaker is not protected by the fair report privilege. In *Quigley v. Rosenthal*,[490] the Tenth Circuit found that the fair report privilege did not apply to the defamation claim before it. The court wrote:

> [I]t is clear that [defendant] Rosenthal's statements at the press conference and on the Greg Dobbs Show went well beyond merely reporting the allegations in the Aronsons' complaint [in a lawsuit against their neighbors]. . . . It is apparent from Rosenthal's statements that he was asserting, as a matter of fact, that the allegations in the Aronsons' complaint were true, and that he, the . . . [Anti-Defamation League], and the Aronsons had substantial evidence to support those allegations. Further, on several occasions, Rosenthal's comments went well beyond the allegations of the complaint.[491]

PROBLEM 3-15: THE EMPLOYER WHO SUBORNED PERJURY

Olympus is a small town where news travels fast. When Sally Tarnett, a former employee of Seguin Valley Farm (the Farm), filed a petition seeking a protective order against the Farm's manager, Steven Klapp, people were soon talking. They did not know the details of the request for an injunction, but they remembered all of the high points in the turbulent relationship between Tarnett and Klapp.

---

[487] *Id.* at 41–42.

[488] 773 N.E.2d 192 (Ill. App. Ct. 2002).

[489] 763 N.E.2d 328, 336 (Ill. App. Ct. 2001).

[490] 327 F.3d 1044 (10th Cir. 2003).

[491] *Id.* at 1062.

For almost a decade, Tarnett and Klapp had dated on and off, with periods of romantic bliss punctuated by several spectacular break-ups. Sometimes passionate, sometimes vengeful, the relationship played out, more or less, in full public view. There was no shortage of melodrama. It was just another episode in the saga when Tarnett quit her job at the Farm and then named Klapp in the petition for a protective order.

In the petition, Tarnett alleged that Klapp had attempted to induce her to commit perjury in a lawsuit brought by the Farm against one of its business partners. According to the petition, Klapp sent certain key employees at the Farm two letters. Attachments to the petition purported to be true and correct photocopies of those letters. The first letter described the pending lawsuit filed on behalf of the Farm. The letter stated that employees had to decide, before lawyers came to talk to them, "whether you consider yourself part of the Farm or whether you think you can find a better employer and more generous pay, benefits, perks, flexibility, and working conditions somewhere else in the valley." The second letter contained the following passage:

> You needn't concern yourself about whether what you say is accurate or may subsequently be proved false; you are asked only to testify to what you believe to the best of your knowledge is true. . . . If we find that you are equivocal or unwilling to become involved on behalf of Seguin Valley Farm, and that damages the case our legal team has worked hard to build, then I will have to make the determination whether it is workable for me to run the Farm with only the staff members who can be counted on when the Farm really needs them.

The petition seeking a protective order alleged that, after Tarnett received the letters, Klapp threatened to physically harm her if she refused to cooperate.

Peter Woodward, a reporter for the Valley Tribune, a local newspaper, read the court pleadings with wide-eyes. He knew that a story about Tarnett and Klapp would sell papers. However, Woodward was unable to confirm that any other employee at the Farm had received either of the letters which, according to the petition, had been delivered not just to Tarnett, but to several other key employees. This disturbed him because Woodward also remembered that, only a year earlier, Tarnett had sued Klapp for assault. However, she had dismissed the action soon after Klapp received a dose of bad publicity.

While he was trying to check out the facts alleged in Tarnett's petition, Woodward heard a more detailed version of the story. From at least two sources he learned that Klapp had threatened to harm not just Tarnett, but also her ten-month-old son. Many persons in Olympus thought that Klapp was the father of the boy.

An article was soon published in the Tribune under Woodward's byline. It reported that Tarnett had sought a protective order against Klapp after he had allegedly threatened her and her son with violence unless she committed perjury. The article quoted the language in the second letter which stated: "You needn't concern yourself about whether what you say is accurate or may subsequently be proved false." However, it omitted the part that said, "you are asked only to testify to what you believe to the best of your knowledge is true."

At a hearing held after publication of the article, the judge refused to issue a protective order because he found that the facts asserted by the petitioner were not credible. Tarnett did not appeal that ruling.

Klapp has sued Woodward and the Tribune for defamation. Please prepare an analysis of how the Tribune can defend against the claim.

6.   Neutral-Reportage Privilege

As presently configured, the neutral-reportage privilege is a minor tributary of the river of defamation law. In *Edwards v. National Audubon Soc'y, Inc.*,[492] the New York Times reported that a publication by a prominent conservation group had criticized certain scientists as "paid liars" because of their support of the chemical industry in a controversy over a pesticide. In finding for the newspaper, Chief Judge Irving Kaufman said that even if actual malice had been established (which it was not), a constitutional privilege of neutral republication protected the Times. Thus, the court ruled that the public interest in being informed about ongoing controversies justified creating a privilege to republish allegations made by a responsible organization against a public figure, if the republication is done accurately and neutrally in the context of an existing controversy.

Some courts have rejected the neutral-reportage privilege.[493] A few have endorsed it.[494] The Supreme Court has not ruled on whether such privilege is constitutionally mandated. Professor David Anderson of the University of Texas has written that:

> If the President of the United States baselessly accused the Vice President of plotting to assassinate him . . . most courts surely would hold that the media could safely report the President's accusation even if they seriously doubted its truth.[495]

7.   SLAPP Laws (Strategic Lawsuits Against Public Participation)

Suits for libel or slander are often filed not to win, but to silence critics who may be coerced to back down rather than face the expenses and risks of litigation. Not surprisingly, many legislatures have sought to curb such abuses, at least insofar as they threaten to diminish discussion of public issues. These states have passed what are called "SLAPP" laws, so named because they apply to Strategic Lawsuits Against Public Participation. Twenty-eight states and the District of Columbia

---

[492] 556 F.2d 113 (2d Cir. 1977).

[493] *See Hogan v. Herald Co.*, 444 N.E.2d 1002 (N.Y. 1982); *Norton v. Glenn*, 860 A.2d 48 (Pa. 2004); *see also Khawar v. Globe Int'l, Inc.*, 965 P.2d 696 (Cal. 1998) (declining to apply the privilege to the case of a private person accused of killing Robert Kennedy).

[494] *See April v. Reflector-Herald, Inc.*, 546 N.E.2d 466, 469 (Ohio Ct. App. 1988).

[495] David A. Anderson, *Is Libel Law Worth Reforming?*, 140 U. Pa. L. Rev. 487, 504 (1991).

have enacted anti-SLAPP (Strategic Lawsuit Against Public Participation) statutes which make it relatively easy to dismiss meritless retaliatory defamation charges.[496]

In *Dove Audio Inc. v. Rosenfeld, Meyer & Susman*,[497] the son of the late actress Audrey Hepburn asked lawyers to look into why one of his mother's charities had received so little in the way of royalties from one of her audio recordings. The lawyers contacted other celebrities who had participated in the recordings and their charities, informing them of the problem and stating an intention to file a complaint with the Attorney General. Dove Audio then sued the law firm for defamation and tortious interference. (Tortious interference is discussed in Chapter 5.) Finding that the law firm was immune under both the absolute litigation privilege and the SLAPP statute, the California Court of Appeal wrote:

> In general terms, a SLAPP suit is "a meritless suit filed primarily to chill the defendant's exercise of First Amendment rights.". . . . Under [Code Civ. Proc.] section 425.16, subdivision (b), "A cause of action against a person arising from any act of that person in furtherance of the person's right of petition or free speech under the United States or California Constitution in connection with a public issue shall be subject to a special motion to strike, unless the court determines that the plaintiff has established that there is a probability that the plaintiff will prevail on the claim."
>
> Subdivision (e) provides: "As used in this section, 'act in furtherance of a person's right of petition or free speech under the United States or California Constitution in connection with a public issue' includes any written or oral statement or writing made before a legislative, executive, or judicial proceeding, or any other official proceeding authorized by law; any written or oral statement or writing made in connection with an issue under consideration or review by a legislative, executive, or judicial body, or any other official proceeding authorized by law; or any written or oral statement or writing made in a place open to the public or a public forum in connection with an issue of public interest."
>
> . . . .
>
> RM & S's communication raised a question of public interest: whether money designated for charities was being received by those charities. The communication was made in connection with an official proceeding authorized by law, a proposed complaint to the Attorney General seeking an investigation. . . .
>
> . . . Once the party moving to strike the complaint makes that threshold showing, the burden shifts to the responding plaintiff to establish a probability of prevailing at trial. Appellant did not, and cannot do so. . . . RM & S's communications were absolutely privileged under Civil Code section 47, subdivision (b). That privilege is applicable to both causes of

---

[496] *See* State Anti-SLAPP Laws, Public Participation Project, http://www.anti-slapp.org (2014).

[497] 47 Cal. App. 4th 777 (1996).

action alleged by appellant, defamation and interference with economic relationship. . . . The trial court did not err in granting RM & S's special motion to strike under section 425.16.

Lack of a Public Issue. In some cases, dismissal pursuant to a SLAPP law is denied because there is no pending public issue. For example, in *Hariri v. Amper*,[498] an environmental group was sued for defamation by a landowner who wanted to operate an airport on his property. The New York Appellate Division held that the group was not entitled to relief under the state SLAPP law because the landowner had never formally requested a zoning variance and was therefore not a "public applicant or permittee."

8.   Statutes of Limitations

Short Period for Filing. Actions for defamation are typically subject to a short statute of limitations. For example, the Illinois statute provides:

> Actions for slander, libel or for publication of matter violating the right of privacy, shall be commenced within one year next after the cause of action accrued.[499]

The decision in *Serrano v. Ryan's Crossing Apartments*[500] illustrates the operation of a similar statute. In *Serrano*, the Texas Court of Appeals wrote:

> A "slander claim accrues on the date of the communication or publication and not on the date of the consequences or *sequelae*." . . .
>
> . . . Serrano has not articulated with specificity the particular slanderous comments in issue. We construe her argument to be that Ryan's Crossing slandered her name by falsely filing an affidavit which ultimately resulted in her criminal prosecution for theft by check. The affidavit, dated February 5, 2003, alleged that Serrano wrote a rent check for $670 which was not paid due to insufficient funds. Serrano filed suit for slander on December 15, 2004, well past the one-year statute of limitations. . . . Summary judgment was properly granted [to defendant Ryan's Crossing] on the slander claims.[501]

Affirmative Defense. The argument that a defamation claim is barred by the statute of limitations is an affirmative defense. The defendant bears the burden of pleading and proving the applicability of this statutory obstacle to recovery. However, if the plaintiff asserts on appeal that the trial court improperly held that a libel or slander claim was untimely, the plaintiff is required to muster the evidence to show that the trial court erred.

---

[498] 51 A.D.3d 146 (N.Y. App. Div. 2008).

[499] 735 ILL. COMP. STAT. ANN. 5/13-201 (LEXIS 2014).

[500] 241 S.W.3d 560 (Tex. App. 2007).

[501] *Id.* at 563.

For example, in *Lesher v. Doescher*,[502] the plaintiffs alleged that they were "the victims of a vicious cyber-defamation campaign that was waged on www.topix.com." Specifically, the plaintiffs asserted that for approximately a year and a half, through over 25,000 posts on the web site, the defendants wrongfully accused the plaintiffs of sexually assaulting defendant Shannon Coyel and made other disparaging statements about them relating to drugs, diseases, sexual perversion and other matters. The jury awarded the plaintiffs almost $14 million. However, the trial court granted the defendants' motion for judgment notwithstanding the verdict without specifying its reasons for doing so.

On appeal, a Texas appellate court affirmed the trial court's entry of a take-nothing judgment, explaining as follows:

> The record clearly establishes that . . . [defendants] sought a judgment notwithstanding the jury's verdict on the ground that . . . [plaintiffs' appellants' claims were barred by the one-year [statute of limitations]. . . . On appeal, . . . [i]n the part of the brief where . . . [plaintiffs] state the issues that they are raising, they list six of them, with the final issue being that the trial court "erred in granting the judgment notwithstanding the verdict because Defendants waived any claim that limitations barred recovery." No other part of the brief, however, contains any discussion or legal authorities . . . .

> The conclusory, unsupported title of the sixth issue in one sentence contained in a preliminary section of the brief, without any discussion of the issue in the argument section, is insufficient to raise an argument regarding limitations in this court. . . .

> Because appellants have failed to adequately challenge appellees' limitations argument, which was an independent ground for judgment notwithstanding the verdict that appellees raised in the trial court, we affirm the trial court's judgment without addressing the merits of the limitations argument or . . . of appellants' five properly raised and briefed issues. . . .[503]

Public Entities and Employees. In some states, defamation actions against a public entity or public employee are governed by a special statute of limitations, not by the one that usually applies to defamation actions.[504] That type of statute of limitations may also be short.

The Discovery Rule and "Inherently Secretive" Publications. In some cases, the running of the statute of limitations on a libel or slander claim is tolled pursuant to a discovery rule. For example, in *Manguso v. Oceanside Unified School District*,[505] the California Court of Appeal held that a claim filed 16 years after the defendant placed an allegedly defamatory letter in the plaintiff's personnel file was not too late, because the plaintiff could not reasonably have been expected to

---

[502] 2013 Tex. App. LEXIS 12655 (Oct. 10, 2013).

[503] *Id.* at *6–*9.

[504] *See, e.g., Dube v. Likins*, 167 P.3d 93, 108 (Ariz. Ct. App. 2007).

[505] 88 Cal. App. 3d 725 (1979).

discover the basis for her cause of action before then. However, in a later case, *Hebrew Academy of San Francisco v. Goldman*,[506] the California Supreme Court made clear that discovery rules may be applied only to a narrow range of cases. The court stated that:

> [C]ourts uniformly have rejected the application of the discovery rule to libels published in books, magazines, and newspapers, stating that although application of the discovery rule may be justified when the defamation was communicated in confidence, that is, in an inherently secretive manner, the justification does not apply when the defamation occurred by means of a book, magazine, or newspaper that was distributed to the public. . . .[507]

Extending that line of precedent to the limit, the *Hebrew Academy* decision ruled that the discovery rule did not apply in a case involving a transcript of an oral history that had an extremely limited circulation of less than ten copies distributed to religious libraries, because the book was not published in an "inherently secretive manner."[508]

The Discovery Rule and Due Diligence. In *Cole v. Ferranti*,[509] the Third Circuit held that an inmate's claim for defamation was barred by Pennsylvania's one-year statute of limitations, stating:

> We do not decide whether Pennsylvania's discovery rule broadly operates in the context of mass-media defamation claims because we conclude that in this case Cole could not have been "reasonably unaware that an injury has been sustained" during the limitations period. . . . Cole acknowledges that he received a letter from Ferranti in 2007 asking if he would be willing to add anything to a book Ferranti was writing called *Street Legends*, which included passages about Cole's affiliation with the Junior Black Mafia. Cole asserts that he replied by letter to Ferranti stating that he did not want his name to be included in the book, and thereafter assumed that the matter was resolved. It was not until June 2009, Cole maintains, that he learned about the publication of *Street Legends* when he was told by fellow inmates that a book which made unflattering references to him was circulating among the inmate population. According to Cole, he did not decide to read the book until six months later, in December 2009, and did not file his complaint in the District Court for another two months.
>
> Cole had advance notice of the book's imminent publication before the one-year limitations period on defamation claims began to run. Although his incarceration may have required him to exercise more diligence in discovering that *Street Legends* was published before the limitations period expired in April 2009, there is no evidence to suggest that Cole acted in a reasonable manner to preserve his rights after corresponding with Ferranti. On the contrary, he admits that after informing Ferranti that he did

---

[506] 173 P.3d 1004 (Cal. 2007).

[507] *Id.* at 1009 (quotation marks and citations omitted).

[508] *Id.* at 1010.

[509] 2013 U.S. App. LEXIS 17794 (3d Cir. Aug. 26, 2013).

not wish to be in the book, he assumed the matter was over. Cole did not act to preserve his rights even after learning that *Street Legends* was circulating in his prison, waiting until December 2010 to obtain a copy and read it. Under these circumstances, we cannot conclude that application of Pennsylvania's equitable discovery rule is appropriate.[510]

a.   The Single-Publication Rule

Defamation defendants sometimes escape liability by arguing that a claim was filed too late under the terms of the single-publication rule. That rule, which is reflected in § 577A of the *Restatement (Second) of Torts*, provides that any one edition of a book or newspaper, or any one radio or television broadcast, is a single publication, with respect to which only one action may be brought for all damages resulting from the publication. According to the California Supreme Court in *Shively v. Bozanich*,[511] a publication generally is said to occur on the "first general distribution of the publication to the public." Thus, a plaintiff may not bring an action every time a book is sold, and in every jurisdiction in which a sale takes place. The single-publication rule addresses the concern that, if every sale or reading of a book were a publication, there would be no effective statute of limitations in libel cases. The rule also helps plaintiffs by allowing the collection of all damages in a single litigation.

Under the single-publication rule, suppose that this book was published in 2015, purchased in 2016, read by a student in 2017, and sold second-hand to another student in 2018. Absent tolling pursuant to a discovery rule, the period of limitations applicable to a person defamed in the book began to run in 2015. However, if a paperback edition of this book is published in 2019, that event is a separate publication which starts the running of the statute of limitations anew.

(1)   Application to Internet Publications

There is an important question as to how the statute of limitations applies to defamatory statements on the Internet. For example, does every change to a website constitute a republication of defamatory material on the website? In addition, what about transmission at different times of the same statement via the Internet, as where the same report is sent to different subscribers?

Selective Limited Dissemination. In *Pendergrass v. ChoicePoint, Inc.*,[512] a federal court in Pennsylvania considered some of these issues. In that case, when the plaintiff was dismissed from employment with Rite Aid, Rite Aid submitted a report to a ChoicePoint service called Esteem, an employment screening database. According to the court:

> After his termination, Plaintiff interviewed with CVS Pharmacy and Walgreens Pharmacy for permanent full-time positions. . . . Although he was approved for hiring at both CVS and Walgreens, he was told on or

---

[510] *Id.* at 206–07.

[511] 80 P.3d 676 (Cal. 2003) (quoting *Belli v. Roberts Bros. Furs*, 240 Cal. App. 2d 284, 289 (1966)).

[512] 2008 U.S. Dist. LEXIS 99767 (E.D. Pa. Dec. 10, 2008).

about November 30, 2006 that a "bad report" in his employment history prevented his hiring. . . . According to Plaintiff, the "bad report" was the report Rite Aid submitted to the Esteem database describing the January 11, 2006 incident at Rite Aid as "Cash Register Fraud and Theft of Merchandise," with a total theft amount of $ 7,313.00. . . . On July 25, 2007, after unsuccessfully attempting to correct the inaccurate Esteem report with ChoicePoint, Plaintiff received a letter from the retail chain Target that denied his employment application based on a copy of the Esteem report. . . .

Plaintiff alleges . . . that ChoicePoint "did in fact republish the defamatory report, repeatedly, to its other Esteem subscribers, including but not limited to the said communications to CVS, Walgreens and Target.". . . . As a result, "Plaintiff has been branded a thief in the eyes of almost every potential employer in his field" and has experienced difficulty finding full-time employment. . . .[513]

On January 10, 2008, Plaintiff sued Rite Aid alleging defamation and other claims. Rite Aid moved to dismiss the defamation count based on failure to file within the one-year statute of limitations. Addressing that issue, the *Pendergrass* court wrote:

Rite Aid argues that Plaintiff's defamation claim arises from the publication of the allegedly false theft report to ChoicePoint, which Plaintiff discovered on or about November 30, 2006 when he received the letter from Walgreens. . . . Even assuming that the one-year statute of limitations period did not begin until Plaintiff discovered the existence of the publication on or about November 30, 2006, Rite Aid argues that the Complaint is barred because it was filed in January 2008, well beyond the one-year statute of limitations period. . . .

. . . Plaintiff argues that each viewing of the defamatory report in the Esteem database constitutes a separate tort, each with its own statute of limitations. Because the original defamer may be held liable for repetition of the defamatory statement if the repetition was authorized or expected, *see Restatement (Second) of Torts § 576* (1977), Plaintiff contends that Rite Aid is liable for the foreseeable repetition of the incident report by ChoicePoint. Thus, according to Plaintiff, Rite Aid is liable for each "republication" of the Esteem report, including the July 2007 viewing by Target and any other republications occurring within the statutory limitations period. Therefore, Plaintiff contends, only the portion of his defamation claim that stems from any publication or republication occurring prior to January 10, 2007 is subject to dismissal on statute of limitations grounds.[514]

The *Pendergrass* court then turned to the question of whether the single-publication rule was applicable to the case, noting that:

---

[513] *Id.* at *3–*4.

[514] *Id.* at *5–*6.

Pennsylvania has adopted the Uniform Single Publication Act by statute. *See* 42 Pa. Cons. Stat. § 8341(b) ("No person shall have more than one cause of action for damages for libel or slander, or invasion of privacy, or any other tort founded upon any single publication, or exhibition, or utterance, such as any one edition of a newspaper, or book, or magazine, or any one presentation to an audience, or any one broadcast over radio or television, or any one exhibition of a motion picture.").[515]

Material Not Available to the Public. The *Pendergrass* court then elaborated on application of the rule:

> Courts considering the single publication rule in internet-based defamation cases generally have found it applicable to postings made on websites accessible to the general public. As the New York Court of Appeals has explained, "[c]ommunications posted on Web sites may be viewed by thousands, if not millions, over an expansive geographic area for an indefinite period of time. Thus, a multiple publication rule would implicate an even greater potential for endless retriggering of the statute of limitations, multiplicity of suits and harassment of defendants." *Firth v. State*, 775 N.E.2d 463, 466 (N.Y. 2002); *see also Oja v. U.S. Army Corps of Eng'rs*, 440 F.3d 1122, 1131 (9th Cir. 2006). . . .
>
> In cases where, as here, the allegedly defamatory electronic report was not made available to the public but only to subscribing members of a database, the risks of an infinite limitations period and multiple suits are reduced significantly. . . . In [*Swafford v. Memphis Individual Practice Ass'n*, 1998 Tenn. App. LEXIS 361, at *23 (Tenn. Ct. App. 1998)], the Tennessee Court of Appeals found that the single publication rule did not apply to allegedly defamatory information that the defendants supplied to a national medical practitioner database that was later accessed by database subscribers. . . . Because the database was not accessible to the general public, the court found it "unlikely that more than a handful of individuals or entities would gain access to information stored in the data base," and therefore, the defendants' report was not an "aggregate publication" justifying the single publication rule. . . .
>
> Numerous courts have rejected the theory that providing allegedly defamatory or inaccurate information to a consumer reporting agency is equivalent to a mass publication of that information. . . . These courts have concluded, therefore, that each transmission of the defamatory information is a separate republication of that material, giving rise to a new cause of action. . . . The Court finds these cases persuasive, as Rite Aid did not circulate the report to a wide audience; instead, it transmitted it to ChoicePoint with the knowledge that it would be made available to subscribing Esteem customers upon request.
>
> . . . Unlike a single publication that reaches many viewers through circulation of the original material, information in the Esteem database is viewed on separate, distinct occasions by subscribing members. . . . The

---

[515] *Id.* at *8–*9 n.2.

risks of an infinite statute of limitations resulting from widespread circulation of a single publication are not present in the instant case. . . . Because the risks justifying the rule are not present, the Court finds that Pennsylvania courts would not apply the single publication rule to the facts of this case.[516]

The court therefore rejected Rite Aid's statute of limitations defense.

Updating Websites. Observing that "communications accessible over a public Web site resemble those contained in traditional mass media, only on a far grander scale," the New York Court of Appeals held, in *Firth v. State*,[517] that the single-publication rule applies to publications on the Internet. It found that updating a website usually does not constitute a new publication of defamatory material contained on the website:

> The mere addition of unrelated information to a Web site cannot be equated with the repetition of defamatory matter in a separately published edition of a book or newspaper . . . for it is not reasonably inferable that the addition was made either with the intent or the result of communicating the earlier and separate defamatory information to a new audience.
>
> . . . [M]any Web sites are in a constant state of change, with information posted sequentially on a frequent basis. . . . A rule applying the republication exception . . . [to unrelated changes] would either discourage the placement of information on the Internet or slow the exchange of such information. . . . These policy concerns militate against a holding that any modification to a Web site constitutes a republication of the defamatory communication itself.[518]

Linking Another Website. In *In re Philadelphia Newspapers, LLC*,[519] the Third Circuit considered whether a person who creates a link to another website is liable for republishing defamatory material on that website. As the court explained:

> [I]n a case with facts similar to this appeal, the Court held that a link and reference to an allegedly defamatory article did not amount to a republication of the article. In *Salyer v. Southern Poverty Law Center, Inc.*, 701 F. Supp. 2d 912 (W.D. Ky. 2009) (Heyburn II, J.), the defendant posted an allegedly defamatory article to his website. Between the time of the initial posting and the defendant's removal of the article from the website, the defendant linked to the article while referencing it several times in other articles posted on the website. None of the references mentioned the plaintiff by name or restated the allegedly defamatory comments. The Court analyzed the link and reference separately, holding that neither amounted to republication. As to the link, it cautioned that "to find that a new link to an unchanged article posted long ago on a website republishes that article would result in a continual retriggering of the limitations

---

[516] *Id.* at *9–*16.

[517] 775 N.E.2d 463, 464 (N.Y. 2002).

[518] *Id.* at 72–73.

[519] 690 F.3d 161 (3d Cir. 2012).

period," and thus held that a link "is simply a new means for accessing the referenced article," not a republication. . . . As to the reference, it noted that "[w]hile [a reference] may call the existence of the article to the attention of a new audience, it does not present the defamatory contents of the article to the audience. Therefore, a reference, without more, is not properly a republication." . . .

We agree with the distinction in these cases. The single publication rule advances the statute of limitations' policy of ensuring that defamation suits are brought within a specific time after the initial publication. Websites are constantly linked and updated. If each link or technical change were an act of republication, the statute of limitations would be retriggered endlessly and its effectiveness essentially eliminated. A publisher would remain subject to suit for statements made many years prior, and ultimately could be sued repeatedly for a single tortious act the prohibition of which was the genesis of the single publication rule. . . . Additionally, under traditional principles of republication, a mere reference to an article, regardless how favorable it is as long as it does not restate the defamatory material, does not republish the material. . . . These traditional principles are as applicable to Internet publication as traditional publication, if not more so. Publishing a favorable reference with a link on the Internet is significantly easier. Taken together, though a link and reference may bring readers' attention to the existence of an article, they do not republish the article.[520]

PROBLEM 3-16: THE NEWSPAPER'S ONLINE ARCHIVE

The Afternoon News ran an article in its daily newspaper on December 18, 2009, with the headline "Former Valley Mayor Reaches Plea Agreement." The Associated Press ("AP") then picked up and altered the Afternoon News article by changing its title to "Former Valley Mayor Guilty of Illegally Importing Elephant Tusks." The Afternoon News website then automatically incorporated the text of the AP article into the website, so that both the original article and the AP article appeared on the Afternoon News website.

After protests by the former mayor, Bob Raub, the Afternoon News ran a retraction on February 2, 2010, in the print version of the newspaper. The retraction stated that the original story misidentified the party who pled guilty. Legal action had been taken against a company of which Raub was the president, not against Raub personally, for illegal importation of elephant tusks. All charges against Raub had been dismissed. The company, not Raub, had pled guilty.

The retraction never appeared on the Afternoon News website. Sometime in November 2010, the original and AP versions of the online story were removed from the "free" portion of the Afternoon News website. Both articles then continued to be available in the website's "archive" for a fee. It is impossible to establish whether anyone accessed the articles between November 2010 and October 2011 because a computer virus destroyed both the archive and the relevant billing files at the Afternoon News main office.

---

[520] *Id.* at 175.

The online "archive" (but not the billing files) had been backed up at a remote location and could be re-created. However, because the pay-per-view arrangement for viewing the archive had not been financially successful, future charges for specific articles were eliminated. Beginning in October 2011, all previously "archived" materials were available free of charge to the 38,000 subscribers of the printed version of the Afternoon News. In November 2011, the subject matter of the original article became an issue in Valley politics, and Raub, who continued to be politically active, was accused by a candidate for mayor of having been previously convicted of illegally importing parts of animals that were gathered from endangered species.

In January 2012, former mayor Raub consulted you to determine whether it is too late to sue the Afternoon News for defamation. If it is not too late, Raub wants to know whether he can prevail. The applicable statute of limitations is two years. Please advise.

9.   The Libel-Proof Plaintiff Doctrine

The libel-proof plaintiff doctrine has extremely limited application. According to the doctrine, some plaintiffs have such a bad reputation that they cannot be damaged by false statements, and therefore they should not be permitted to sue for defamation. It makes sense that an infamous dictator or terrorist, such as Aldolf Hitler, Saddam Hussein, or Osama bin Laden, should not be permitted to waste the time of the courts (not to mention opposing parties) litigating a claim for defamation. However, in cases not so extreme, courts are likely to reject this defense to liability.

In *Stern v. Cosby*,[521] plaintiff Howard K. Stern, the former lawyer for and companion of the late Anna Nicole Smith, sued the author and publisher of a best-selling book. Stern contended that the defendants defamed him by falsely stating or suggesting, among other things, that "he had engaged in sex with the father of Smith's child, 'pimped' Smith to as many as fifty men a year, and played a role in Smith's death."[522] The defendants argued that Stern was "libel-proof." A federal court in New York rejected this argument, stating:

> The libel-proof doctrine is predicated on the notion that "a plaintiff's reputation with respect to a specific subject may be so badly tarnished that he cannot be further injured by allegedly false statements on that subject.".
> . . . While the doctrine is most often applied to plaintiffs with criminal convictions, it is not limited to plaintiffs with criminal records. . . .
>
> The Second Circuit has cautioned that the libel-proof plaintiff doctrine is to be sparingly applied, as it is unlikely that many plaintiffs will have such tarnished reputations that their reputations cannot sustain further damage. . . .
>
> There is some question, as the parties acknowledge, as to whether the libel-proof plaintiff doctrine is valid in the wake of the Supreme Court's

---

[521] 2009 U.S. Dist. LEXIS 70912 (S.D.N.Y. Aug. 12, 2009).

[522] *Id.* at *1.

decision in *Masson v. New Yorker Magazine, Inc.*, 501 U.S. 496, 523 (1991), where the Court held that the incremental harm doctrine — the "cousin" of the libel-proof doctrine — is not properly grounded in the First Amendment, and therefore not valid under federal law. . . .

Whether a plaintiff is libel-proof is a question of law for the Court to decide. . . .

. . . I conclude that it does not bar Stern's suit.

First, Stern should not be precluded from seeking damages for being defamed by the Book merely because he was the subject of critical discussion on tabloid television and in celebrity gossip magazines. Even assuming, for example, that Geraldo Rivera and other celebrity journalists and talk show hosts suggested that Stern had a hand in Smith's death, Stern denies these accusations. If indeed the accusations are false, the fact that Stern might have been falsely accused before does not mean that he could not be further injured if he was falsely accused again. . . . Moreover, there is a qualitative difference between comments made on a tabloid television show and written statements in a book purporting to be the product of legitimate "investigative journalism," written by — as appears on the cover of the Book — an "Emmy-Award Winning Journalist." . . .

Second, much of the conduct detailed in the Book is fundamentally different from the conduct that was the subject of the allegations swirling in the tabloid media. None of the media reports prior to the publication of the Book referenced Stern engaging in oral sex with Birkhead or making a video of himself and Birkhead doing so. The general thrust of the media reports prior to publication of the Book was that Stern was a member of Smith's bizarre inner circle who exploited Smith for money and fame. This is different in kind from many of the allegations in the Book, and thus Stern's reputation could sustain further damage. . . . As then-Judge Scalia aptly put it, "[i]t is shameful that Benedict Arnold was a traitor; but he was not a shoplifter to boot, and one should not have been able to make that charge while knowing its falsity with impunity." *Liberty Lobby v. Anderson*, 746 F.2d 1563, 1568 (D.C. Cir. 1984), *rev'd on other grounds*, 477 U.S. 242 (1986). So, too, here.

Similarly, the criminal complaint filed against Stern in California does not alter this conclusion. While it undoubtedly does some damage to Stern's reputation, it is only an accusation and he is obviously presumed innocent in the matter. Moreover, the subject matter of the criminal complaint is different from most of the Statements at issue in this case. The criminal complaint charges Stern with playing a role in obtaining prescription drugs for Smith. It says nothing about promiscuous homosexual sex, "pimping," or any of the other Statements at issue here.

Finally, the fact that Stern was seen on certain episodes of The Anna Nicole Show in a negative light likewise does not render him libel-proof. Although the show was a "reality show," Stern contends that much of it was staged, and many viewers undoubtedly watched the show with some skepticism.

More importantly, the allegations in the Statements are significantly different and much more serious than the conduct Stern engaged in on the show.[523]

10.   The Employment-at-Will Doctrine

Some states adhere to an employment-at-will doctrine under which an employee can be terminated for any reason or no reason at all. Because many defamation claims arise from job termination, questions logically arise as to whether remedies under the law of defamation are limited in any way by the employment-at-will doctrine.

In *Exxon Mobil Corp. v. Hines*,[524] two employees (plaintiffs/appellees) were terminated based on conduct relating to a charitable contribution matching plan. In a subsequent defamation action, the jury awarded the former employees damages for emotional distress, harm to reputation, and, in each case, $100,000 in past and future lost income and lost unemployment benefits. Addressing the last element of the damages awards, the Texas Court of Appeals wrote:

> Under the at-will employment doctrine, an employer may generally terminate an at-will employee without fear of legal repercussions for a good reason, a bad reason, or no reason at all. . . . Additionally, as a corollary to the doctrine, Texas does not recognize a cause of action for "negligent investigation" in the employment context. . . . Based on these two principles, Exxon argues that appellee's economic damages are barred because they resulted from the employment terminations and not directly from the defamation. . . .[525]

> We begin by noting that appellees do not allege, and there is no evidence to suggest, that Exxon ever communicated the substance of the September 23 and October 23 presentations to anyone outside the company. Consequently, under appellees' theory, the internal communication of the reason for the terminations (*i.e.*, the alleged defamation) enables them to recover the damages caused by the terminations. This would clearly violate the at-will employment doctrine — and its general prohibition against wrongful termination claims by at-will employees — by creating liability where at law none may exist (*i.e.*, by allowing monetary recovery when the employer terminates the employee for a "bad reason").[526] . . . We reject appellees'

---

[523] *Id.* at *6–*8.

[524] 252 S.W.3d 496 (Tex. App. 2008).

[525] [n.4] Based on their defamation finding, the jury awarded economic damages to appellees for lost income and lost employment benefits suffered in the past and likely to be sustained in the future. . . . [T]here is no evidence in the record to suggest that these damages were caused by any Exxon conduct other than the termination of appellees.

[526] [n.6] Thus, the situation before us is distinctly different from cases wherein a plaintiff alleges two alternative but not legally prohibited causes of action such as design defect and breach of warranty in the products liability context. In that situation, a plaintiff can recover under one cause of action (assuming he or she can muster the requisite proof) without violating a prohibition against the other claim. Here, recovery of lost wages and employment benefits due to termination violates the at-will employment doctrine.

argument and hold that a terminated employee may not recover damages resulting from employment termination simply because the reason for the termination (even if defamatory) may have been internally communicated within the employing company.

Our holding should not be construed as suggesting that an employer can never defame an employee in Texas or that an employee can never recover defamation damages from his or her employer (whether the defamation was communicated only internally or also externally); it merely means that an employee cannot recover as defamation damages those damages caused by employment termination. . . .[527]

11.   Separation of Church and State

In *Harvest House Publishers v. Local Church*,[528] a church had been listed as a cult in a book. The Texas Court of Appeals held that "being labeled a 'cult' is not actionable because the truth or falsity of the statement depends upon one's religious beliefs, an ecclesiastical matter which cannot and should not be tried in a court of law."[529]

12.   Due Care Statutes

In *Neely v. Wilson*,[530] the Texas Supreme Court noted that:

[T]he [Texas] Legislature has . . . added the due care provision for broadcasters, shielding them from liability unless the plaintiff proves the broadcaster failed to exercise due care to prevent publication of a defamatory statement. . . . [Tex. Civ. Prac. & Rem. Code § 73.004.] The provision requires that:

A broadcaster is not liable in damages for a defamatory statement published or uttered in or as a part of a radio or television broadcast by one other than the broadcaster unless the complaining party proves that the broadcaster failed to exercise due care to prevent the publication or utterance of the statement in the broadcast.

. . . We have previously commented that, under the due care provision, "[b]roadcasters are generally not liable in defamation for broadcasts made by third parties." . . . A number of other jurisdictions have enacted a due care provision, although some states require the defendant broadcaster to prove it used due care (as opposed to our statute, which requires the plaintiff to prove the defendant broadcaster did not use due care).

It is unlikely that these kinds of laws add much to the law of defamation. Virtually all states require culpable (*i.e.*, negligent, reckless, or intentional) publication of the

---

[527] 252 S.W.3d at 502–03.

[528] 190 S.W.3d 204 (Tex. App. 2006).

[529] *Id.* at 212.

[530] 2013 Tex. LEXIS 511 (June 28, 2013).

defamatory matter. And plaintiffs are constitutionally required to prove negligence as to falsity or actual malice in a wide range of cases.

PROBLEM 3-17: THE ERRONEOUSLY DISBARRED ATTORNEY

All of the lawyers in the state are required to belong to the State Bar. One of the benefits that members receive in exchange for their dues is a monthly magazine called "Lawyers." A regular feature in the magazine is a section devoted to disciplinary actions. Any lawyers who have been disbarred, suspended from practice, or otherwise publicly disciplined because of misconduct are listed in that section, along with a brief description of the basis on which discipline was imposed.

The August issue of Lawyers carried an entry in the disciplinary action section which read as follows:

Correction

An article provided by the Board of Disciplinary Appeals for "Disciplinary Actions" in the July issue of Lawyers was inaccurate:

Page 730: The board entered an interlocutory order of suspension against Bernard Dolze (#5372625); it did not disbar him as indicated. Dolze was convicted in United States District Court of 12 counts of mail fraud and of aiding and abetting an intentional crime. He was sentenced to 90 months in prison. Upon release, Dolze will be placed on supervised release for three additional years. He was ordered to make immediate restitution in the amount of $1,008,316. Dolze has appealed his conviction. In the event that the conviction becomes final, Dolze will be disbarred.

Can Dolze state a viable claim for defamation against anyone involved in the publication of the erroneous report in the July issue of Lawyers?

J. REVIEW

Recall the excerpt in the "review" section of Chapter 2, discussing whether economic harm caused by erroneous scoring of standardized tests might be actionable under the law of deceit or negligent misrepresentation. Does the law of defamation offer an additional remedy or a better alternative?

A statement is not defamatory unless it carries with it the sting of disgrace. To be actionable as libel or slander, an utterance must adversely reflect on the personal character of the plaintiff, such as by subjecting the plaintiff to "hatred, ridicule or contempt." A defamatory statement must so tend to "harm the reputation of another as to lower him in the estimation of the community or to deter third persons from associating or dealing with him." Communications falling short of this standard will not support a libel or slander claim.

Many standardized test score errors are of a minor magnitude. A report understating a test-taker's performance by twenty-five, or perhaps even fifty, points on the 2400-point SAT, is so unlikely to subject the test-taker to the opprobrium of the community that a court should not entertain a resulting defamation claim. *De minimis non curat lex*. Defamation actions seeking to redress a minor scoring error may be dismissed under the substantial-truth rule, which bars recovery based on statements that, though literally false, are substantially correct.

A scoring error of greater magnitude will warrant more extensive judicial consideration, such as test results on the 2400-point SAT that are under-stated by, say, 200, 300, or 400 points. At some juncture, the magnitude of the error will be so great as to disgrace the test-taker and cause others to think less of him or her. Statements that impute incompetence in business, trade, or profession are readily actionable as libel and slander. Mis-scoring plaintiffs may be able to invoke successfully this type of precedent to mount defamation claims in cases involving sizeable scoring errors. This line of reasoning will be particularly appealing where an erroneous score precipi-tates clear harm, such as causing a student to be denied a diploma, degree, or essential professional credential. In such cases, a defendant testing agency publishes to those to whom it disseminates test scores false facts purporting to show that the test-taker is not "competent."

The "publication" requirement for libel and slander is satisfied by inten-tional or negligent communication of the false statement to a third person who understands the defamatory utterance. This standard is satisfied where a testing agency provides test results directly to a person other than the test-taker. It is even possible that a testing agency may be held liable for republication of an erroneous score by the test-taker. While the originator of a defamatory statement is generally not responsible for its republication by the subject of the false and defamatory statement, that is because the subject is normally aware of the defamatory content, and has a duty to avoid or mitigate damages. However, retransmission by the plaintiff of a known falsehood should be distinguished from cases of unwitting transmission of a defamatory message whose falsehood is unknown. "If the defamed person's transmission of the communication to the third person was made without an awareness of the [false and] defamatory nature of the matter, and if the circumstances indicated that communication to a third party would be likely, a publication may properly be held to have occurred."

. . . .

Whether a defamation suit by a test-taker whose score is seriously understated is treated as involving a private person suing with respect to a matter of public concern (a *Gertz* case), or simply a person suing with respect to a matter of private concern (a *Dun & Bradstreet* case), has important implications not only with respect to culpability, but whether damages must be proved. At common law, all libel (generally written defamation) was actionable *per se*, as were four categories of slander (generally oral defamation, including statements imputing incompetence in business, trade or profession). This meant that a jury could award "presumed damages," without proof of actual losses. Under the rule of presumed damages — which was a great departure from the usual standards of tort liability — the jury could look to the nastiness of the statement, and the degree of its dissemination, and presume an amount of damages that would fairly compensate the plaintiff. Thus, many sizeable awards were made without any precise proof of what losses actually occurred. During the process of reconciling the ancient law of libel and slander with the demands of the First Amendment, . . . [the] Supreme Court held that a *Gertz*-type plaintiff (a private person suing with regard to a matter of public concern) could not recover presumed damages without proof of actual malice. In contrast, a *Dun & Bradstreet*-type plaintiff (a person suing with respect to a matter of purely private concern) was still allowed to recover presumed damages under the traditional rules, even in the absence of actual malice. Consequently, damages issues relating to a defamation claim in standardized test mis-scoring cases may be greatly affected by whether the false statement is viewed as a matter of purely private concern, rather than a matter of public concern. In that situation, proof of actual losses will frequently not be required.

What qualifies as a matter of private concern is often unclear, and many persons doubt whether courts can or should attempt to define what matters are legitimately of concern to the public. In *Dun & Bradstreet*, the Supreme Court re-embraced the public concern/private concern dichotomy that it had rejected just a few years earlier, and surprisingly held that an erroneous statement about whether a major employer in the community was going bankrupt was a matter of private concern because the statement was contained in a credit report that was distributed to a very limited number of subscribers. In light of that ruling, standardized test results reported confidentially to a small number of private schools — in contrast to standardized testing results in the public education, which are often publicly available — might fall within that "private concern" category. . . .

As yet, there is little guidance from courts directly addressing defamation . . . claims based on standardized test scoring errors, although a recent case declined to hold as a matter of law that "misreported test scores can never give rise to a claim for defamation." One of the unresolved questions is whether a claim for libel or slander against a testing agency can be defeated by a qualified privilege. Regardless of the attacks on standardized testing, many would argue that such evaluative instruments serve a useful purpose, and therefore a testing agency's good faith communication of test scores — even if erroneous — should be qualifiedly privileged. A qualified privilege is lost when the privilege is abused. One form of abuse is dissemination of a statement with knowledge of its falsity or with reckless disregard for its truth. This means that qualified privileges will play no role in cases alleging defamation or false-light against testing agencies, if the plaintiff must prove actual malice. That is, proof of the plaintiff's *prima facie* case would, by necessity, destroy a qualified privilege. However, as explained above, it is likely that in many libel or slander mis-scoring suits the plaintiff will qualify as a "private" person, and will therefore only need to prove that the defendant testing agency acted with negligence as to the falsity of the report. In such cases, it may be possible for a qualified privilege to defeat the plaintiff's proof of a *prima facie* case.[531]

---

[531] Vincent R. Johnson, *Standardized Tests, Erroneous, Scores, and Tort Liability*, 38 RUTGERS L.J. 655, 698–708 (2007).

Chapter 4

INVASION OF PRIVACY

A. OVERVIEW

Four Kinds of Actions. It is generally agreed that there are four kinds of tort actions for invasion of privacy: unauthorized use of name or likeness; intrusion upon private affairs; publicity placing one in a highly offensive "false light"; and public disclosure of private matters. Viewed from the perspective of plaintiffs, these torts vary greatly in their effectiveness.

Appropriation of Name Or Likeness. Unauthorized use of name or likeness (also known as "appropriation") is a mighty theory of liability. Such claims are frequently litigated, and the tort often enables plaintiffs to win injunctive or monetary relief. The appropriation action is so vibrant that it flourishes as a tort claim and begins to shade off into principles that animate other areas of law, such as unfair competition and intellectual property. Some persons say that appropriation has more to do with protecting property rights (in one's name or image) than with privacy.

Intrusion Upon Private Affairs. Intrusion upon private affairs is another highly viable tort cause of action. It plays an important role in preserving some measure of personal privacy in modern life. Actionable intrusions take many forms, including physical presence and electronic monitoring. The requirements of the tort are demanding, but not impossible to meet. Many intrusion claims succeed.

False Light. False light is a weak tort cause of action. It overlaps with defamation, is fraught with demanding requirements, and rarely provides relief that could not be won on other theories of liability. Although a number of states have recognized this difficult-to-win cause of action, other jurisdictions have declined to do so, finding the action to be duplicative of other remedies or addressing matters of too little importance to warrant judicial relief.

Disclosure of Private Matters. The privacy action for disclosure addresses nearly universal concerns about improper revelation of personal information. It is therefore not surprising that there is a wealth of precedent relating to this tort. However, the requirements are so formidable that disclosure claims rarely succeed. This does not mean that disclosure is an unimportant action. Rather, the law governing disclosure liability is simply more important to defendants, in protecting their freedom of action, than to plaintiffs, in providing compensation for harm caused by unwanted publicity.

Multiple Or Alternative Causes of Action. Plaintiffs often allege that a single course of conduct violated their privacy on several grounds. For example, in

Gleason v. Smolinski,[1] a man mysteriously disappeared. The defendant then investigated a woman with whom the man had been involved and published an unflattering story about her, which revealed embarrassing facts and was illustrated by a picture of the woman. In a subsequent lawsuit, the plaintiff (unsuccessfully) claimed that the defendant had committed all four privacy torts, and other torts as well. Often privacy claims are raised in actions alleging libel, slander, or intentional or negligent infliction of emotional distress.

In many cases, it is important to consider whether a claim that would fail on one privacy theory might succeed on another. Some states recognize only some of the four privacy causes of action.

The Restatement. The literature relating to tort liability for invasion of privacy is voluminous. The seminal article, published in the late nineteenth century by Charles D. Warren and Louis D. Brandeis, argued that the law should protect not just interests in life, health, property, and reputation, but also privacy.[2] However, the modern landmark is the *Restatement (Second) of Torts*, which endorsed the idea of four separate causes of action.[3]

Courts addressing invasion of privacy disputes almost inevitably turn to the language of the *Restatement*. Therefore, the *Restatement* formulations of the four privacy actions will be given adequate attention in this chapter. However, it must be remembered that those rules were written in a different world — a world before video recorders, cable channels, personal computers, fax machines, digital cameras, the Internet, and ubiquitous databases. The *Restatement* rules may not be adequate to the challenge of providing legal protection for privacy in the 21st century. Nevertheless, there is little evidence of change. Claims arising from postings on social networking websites or from the contents of e-mail attachments are routinely scrutinized in terms of the language found in the second *Restatement*.

The Shrinking Realm of Privacy. To say that the sphere for personal privacy has been greatly diminished by recent advances in transportation, communications and other technologies is to state the obvious. It remains to be seen whether one or more of the four privacy actions will simply wither away under the assault of modern life. Perhaps the law needs new paradigms for legal protection of privacy interests.

Privacy Rights Under the Federal Constitution. The common law and statutory legal principles governing tort liability for invasion of privacy must be clearly distinguished from privacy rights under the United States Constitution. The Constitution limits the power of states to interfere with certain intimately personal decisions, such as use of contraceptives[4] or having an abortion.[5] Those limitations are referred to as the constitutional "right of privacy," but they generally have little to do with the causes of action described in this chapter. Nevertheless, other

---

[1] 2009 Conn. Super. LEXIS 1982 (July 20, 2009).

[2] Charles D. Warren & Louis D. Brandeis, *The Right to Privacy*, 4 Harv. L. Rev. 193 (1890).

[3] Restatement (Second) of Torts §§ 652A–652I (1977).

[4] *See Griswold v. Connecticut*, 381 U.S. 479 (1965).

[5] *See Roe v. Wade*, 410 U.S. 113, 152–53 (1973).

constitutional provisions, particularly freedom of speech and freedom of the press, often play an important role in tort actions alleging invasion of privacy.

Privacy Rights Under State Constitutions. Some jurisdictions, such as California,[6] have a right of privacy that is rooted in their state constitution. California's constitutional right of privacy will support an action for tort damages on appropriate facts.[7]

Statutory Versus Common Law Privacy. In most states, the tort principles governing liability for invasion of privacy have evolved as a matter of common law. However, in some states, the relevant provisions are statutory. For example, in Rhode Island, legislation articulates four categories of invasion of privacy which closely parallel the actions recognized by the *Restatement.*[8]

Privileged Invasions of Privacy. The absolute and conditional privileges that will defeat an action for defamation (*see* Chapter 3) generally apply to the publication of any matter that is alleged to be an invasion of privacy.[9] Thus, if the fair report privilege defeats a libel action, it will defeat a false light claim based on the same facts.[10]

B. DISCLOSURE OF PRIVATE FACTS

Elements. According to the *Restatement* section entitled "Publicity Given To Private Life":

> One who gives publicity to a matter concerning the private life of another is subject to liability to the other for invasion of his privacy, if the matter publicized is of a kind that (a) would be highly offensive to a reasonable person, and (b) is not of legitimate concern to the public.[11]

[handwritten margin note: Elements of disclosure of private facts]

This basis for liability is sometimes referred to as the "disclosure" or "private-facts" tort.

Policy Basis. In *Cowles Publishing Co. v. State Patrol*, the Supreme Court of Washington explained the considerations underlying tort liability for disclosure:

> Every individual has some phases of his life and his activities and some facts about himself that he does not expose to the public eye, but keeps entirely to himself or at most reveals only to his family or to close personal friends. Sexual relations, for example, are normally entirely private matters, as are family quarrels, many unpleasant or disgraceful or humiliating illnesses, most intimate personal letters, most details of a man's life in his home, and some of his past history that he would rather forget. When these intimate details of his life are spread before the public gaze in a manner

---

[6] *See* CAL. CONST. Art. 1, § 1 (LEXIS 2014) (stating that privacy is an inalienable right).

[7] *See Egan v. Schmock*, 93 F. Supp. 2d 1090 (N.D. Cal. 2000).

[8] *See, e.g.*, R.I. GEN. LAWS 9-1-28.1 (LEXIS 2014).

[9] RESTATEMENT (SECOND) OF TORTS § 652F & 652G (1977).

[10] *See Milligan v. United States*, 644 F. Supp. 2d 1020, 1038–1040 (M.D. Tenn. July 21, 2009).

[11] RESTATEMENT (SECOND) OF TORTS § 652D (1977).

highly offensive to the ordinary reasonable man, there is an actionable invasion of his privacy, unless the matter is one of legitimate public interest.[12]

Antiquated View? One can question whether these statements are still valid in a world where many persons blog about the most personal aspects of their lives, where "sexting" is not unheard-of among teens, and where some persons broadcast their every move via webcams. Yet, such practices are still the exceptions which prove the rule. The fact that some persons seem to have little interest in privacy does not mean that others should be deprived of whatever protection the law may provide.

1.   Liability for Telling the Truth

Unlike actions for misrepresentation or defamation, which require proof of a false or misleading statement, the privacy action for disclosure imposes liability for *dissemination of the truth*. This should give one pause because, as the previous chapters have explained, there are many cases in which even publication of a falsehood, let alone truth, is not actionable.

Trade Secrets and Confidential Information. Nevertheless, the issue must be placed in context. There are many cases where telling the truth will give rise to liability for damages. For example, if an employee discloses a company's trade secrets, or if a doctor or lawyer reveals a patient or client's confidential information, the person making the revelation will often be held liable for resulting harm. It is no defense to say that the disclosed statements were true. Consequently, it may be possible to reconcile a privacy action's imposition of tort liability for disclosure of true private facts with the demands of free speech and free press.

Florida Star v. B.J.F. In *Florida Star v. B.J.F.*,[13] the United States Supreme Court declined an "invitation to hold broadly that truthful publication may never be punished consistent with the First Amendment." In that case, the Court held that a newspaper could not be liable for damages based on publishing the name of a rape victim obtained from a publicly released police report. A Florida statute (§ 794.03) made it unlawful to "print, publish, or broadcast . . . in any instrument of mass communication" the name of the victim of a sexual offense. The Court wrote:

> We hold only that where a newspaper publishes truthful information which it has lawfully obtained, punishment may lawfully be imposed, if at all, only when narrowly tailored to a state interest of the highest order, and that no such interest is satisfactorily served by imposing liability under § 794.03 to appellant under the facts of this case.[14]

---

[12] 748 P.2d 597, 602 (Wash. 1988) (quoting RESTATEMENT (SECOND) OF TORTS § 652D cmt. b (1977)).

[13] 491 U.S. 524 (1989).

[14] *Id.* at 541.

Applying the Florida Star Standard. In *Bowley v. City of Uniontown Police Dept.*,[15] the Third Circuit addressed the question of whether a newspaper could be held liable for publishing the name of the 15-year-old perpetrator, rather than the 7-year-old victim, of an alleged rape. A Pennsylvania law prohibited disclosure of law enforcement records concerning a child 14 years of age or older under the facts of the case. The court wrote:

> [I]n order to determine whether the First Amendment permits the imposition of civil liability upon the Herald Standard for publishing the article concerning Bowley's arrest, we must consider: (A) whether the information was truthful and lawfully obtained; (B) whether the information concerned a matter of public significance; and (C) whether the imposition of liability would be the most narrowly tailored way to serve a state interest of the highest order.
>
> . . . [T]he truthfulness of the article is not in dispute. . . .
>
> . . . In light of the allegations in the Complaint, . . . Bowley can prove no set of facts establishing that the Herald Standard obtained the information unlawfully.
>
> According to the Complaint, Officer Balsley informed the Herald Standard of Bowley's arrest. . . . Although Balsley violated Pennsylvania law prohibiting the release of juvenile arrest records by doing so, . . . his unlawful release of the information does not make receipt of that information by the Herald Standard unlawful. Section 6308 prohibits only the disclosure of juvenile law enforcement information, not the receipt of such information.
> . . .
>
> Moreover, the Supreme Court held in *Florida Star* that failure by the police to comply with a Florida statute prohibiting the release of a rape victim's name did not render unlawful a newspaper's resultant receipt of the protected information. . . . The Court explained, "[n]or does the fact that the Department apparently failed to fulfill its obligation under . . . [the non-disclosure statute] make the newspaper's ensuing receipt of this information unlawful.". . . .
>
> . . . Although this case is somewhat complicated by the fact that the alleged offender was himself a minor, we think the legitimacy of public concern regarding the rape of a minor cannot seriously be doubted, regardless of the age of the accused.
>
> . . . .
>
> Because the information published by the Herald Standard was truthful, lawfully obtained, and concerning a matter of public significance, the First Amendment shields the Herald Standard from civil liability unless the imposition of liability is narrowly tailored to serve an interest of the highest order. . . . [W]e hold that subjecting the Herald Standard to civil liability is not the most narrowly tailored means of serving that interest.

---

[15] 404 F.3d 783 (3d Cir. 2005).

The Supreme Court has held that when the government itself inappropriately releases otherwise-confidential information "the imposition of damages against the press for its subsequent publication can hardly be said to be a narrowly tailored means of safeguarding anonymity.". . . . Indeed, when the government has stewardship over confidential information, not releasing the information to the media in the first place will more narrowly serve the interest of preserving confidentiality than will punishing the publication of the information once inappropriately released. . . .

. . . Bowley, therefore, cannot seek civil damages against the Herald Standard consistent with the First Amendment. . . .[16]

The Third Circuit affirmed the district court's grant of the Herald Standard's motion to dismiss.

Conflict with the First Amendment *or State Constitutional Provisions*. At least one state — North Carolina, in *Hall v. Post*[17] — has declined to recognize the private-facts tort because of its potential for conflict with the First Amendment to the Federal Constitution. Also, in *Doe v. Methodist Hospital*,[18] the Indiana Supreme Court declined to recognize disclosure actions, noting that "torts involving disclosure of truthful but private facts . . . [encounter] a considerable obstacle in the truth-in-defense provisions of the Indiana Constitution."

2.   Private Versus Public

Expectation of Privacy. For disclosure to be actionable, there must be a reasonable expectation of privacy. In *Pontbriand v. Sundlun*,[19] the Rhode Island Supreme Court held that whether depositors had a reasonable expectation of privacy in their bank records, and whether disclosure would be offensive to a reasonable person, were questions of fact that precluded summary judgment.

Employers increasingly monitor outbound e-mails to protect trade secrets and other information.[20] This would seem to mean that employees have less reason to expect that the e-mails they write at work are private.

Blogging, Sexting, Webcaming, and Social Networking Websites. Conduct such as blogging, sexting, webcaming, or posting information on a social networking website relinquishes one's expectation of privacy and will typically bar a privacy action. Those forms of conduct might be deemed to be a defense in the nature of consent, assumption of the risk, waiver, or perhaps even estoppel. At a more basic level, such revelations simply mean that the facts in question are no longer private, and therefore not protected by the privacy action for disclosure.

---

[16] *Id.* at 786–89.

[17] 372 S.E.2d 711 (N.C. 1988).

[18] 690 N.E.2d 681 (Ind. 1997).

[19] 699 A.2d 856 (R.I. 1997).

[20] *See* Tresa Baldas, *More Companies Read E-mail Over Employees' Shoulders*, NAT'L L.J., Sept. 28, 2009.

Sandler v. Calcagni[21] was a case arising from revelations made in a "print on demand" book about a former high school cheerleader. A federal court in Maine concluded that, because the plaintiff admitted that "she revealed her decision to seek psychological help during college on her publicly accessible myspace.com webpage," the defendant's disclosure of that information was "not actionable as it does not reveal a private fact."[22]

Matters of Public Record. Disseminating information about matters of public record, such as birth dates, marriages, military service, lawsuit filings, or professional licenses will not give rise to liability.[23] In *Cox Broadcasting Corp. v. Cohn*,[24] the Supreme Court held that the publication of a rape victim's name — which appeared in official records open to the public — was constitutionally protected. Although disclosure of the identity of the victim was prohibited by state law, the Court found that by "placing the information in the public domain on official court records, the state must be presumed to have concluded that the public interest was thereby being served."

Readily Observable Matters. Facts that can be easily observed by others are ordinarily classified as public rather than private. For example, in *John Doe 2 v. Associated Press*,[25] the Fourth Circuit concluded that a reporter was not liable for disclosing the name of a sexual assault victim who testified in open court, even though the judge had instructed reporters not to do so. As the Fourth Circuit explained:

> Plaintiff points to no case . . . suggesting any circumstance under which there might be a privacy interest in information disclosed in an open courtroom. Anyone was free to sit in the courtroom and listen to plaintiff's testimony: the sentencing hearing was public and open to both ordinary members of the public and representatives of the press. Neither plaintiff's complaint nor the record suggests that the trial judge closed the courtroom or restricted attendance in any way. . . .
>
> . . . The nature of the information disclosed here does not change our legal analysis: "if a person, whether willingly or not, becomes an actor in an event of public or general interest, then the publication of his connection with such an occurrence is not an invasion of his right to privacy." . . .[26]

Photographs Taken in Public. Normally, a privacy action for disclosure of true facts or intrusion upon seclusion cannot be based upon photographs of the plaintiff taken in a public place. The reason is generally that the plaintiff has voluntarily chosen to appear in a place visible to others, so that taking and using the photographs does not invade a privacy interest.[27] Thus, no action will lie based on

---

[21] 565 F. Supp. 2d 184 (D. Me. 2008).

[22] *Id.* at 197.

[23] RESTATEMENT (SECOND) OF TORTS § 652D cmt. b (1977).

[24] 420 U.S. 469 (1975).

[25] 331 F.3d 417 (4th Cir. 2003).

[26] *Id.* at 421–22.

[27] *But see* Andrew Jay McClurg, *Bringing Privacy Law Out of the Closet: A Tort Theory of Liability*

the publication of pictures of a party-goer dancing naked from the waist up on an elevated platform[28] or of a man sitting on a porch.[29] For the same reasons, recordings made by seemingly ubiquitous video cameras now found in public locations are unlikely to give rise to a disclosure action if the recorded contents are publicized.[30]

In *Neff v. Time, Inc.*,[31] Sports Illustrated published a photograph of a football fan aping at a camera while his fly was open. In ruling for the defendant, a federal court in Pennsylvania wrote:

> Neff's picture was taken in a public place with his knowledge and with his encouragement; he was catapulted into the news by his own actions; nothing was falsified; a photograph taken at a public event which everyone present could see, with the knowledge and implied consent of the subject, is not a matter concerning a private fact. A factually accurate public disclosure is not tortious when connected with a newsworthy event even though offensive to ordinary sensibilities. The constitutional privilege protects all truthful publications relevant to matters of public interest.[32]

A notable decision to the contrary is *Daily Times-Democrat Co. v. Graham*.[33] According to the Supreme Court of Alabama:

> The appellee entered the Fun House with her two boys and as she was leaving her dress was blown up by the air jets and her body was exposed from the waist down, with the exception of that portion covered by her "panties."

> At this moment the appellant's photographer snapped a picture of the appellee in this situation. This was done without the appellee's knowledge or consent. Four days later the appellant published this picture on the front page of its newspaper.[34]

In affirming a judgment for the plaintiff, the court explained its reasoning as follows:

> We can see nothing of legitimate news value in the photograph. Certainly it discloses nothing as to which the public is entitled to be informed. . . .

> To hold that one who is involuntarily and instantaneously enmeshed in an embarrassing pose forfeits her right of privacy merely because she happened at the moment to be part of a public scene would be illogical, wrong, and unjust.

---

for Intrusions in Public Places, 73 N.C. L. REV. 989 (1995) (arguing that expecting to be seen in public and expecting to be photographed for the front page of the paper are not the same thing).

[28] *See Prince v. Out Publ'g Inc.*, 2002 Cal. App. Unpub. LEXIS 5189 (Jan. 3, 2002).

[29] *See Floyd v. Park Cities People, Inc.*, 685 S.W.2d 96 (Tex. Ct. App. 1985).

[30] *Cf. Key v. Compass Bank, Inc.*, 826 So. 2d 159 (Ala. Civ. App. 2001).

[31] 406 F. Supp. 858 (W.D. Pa. 1976).

[32] *Id.* at 861.

[33] 162 So. 2d 474 (Ala. 1964).

[34] *Id.* at 476.

One who is a part of a public scene may be lawfully photographed as an incidental part of that scene in his ordinary status. Where the status he expects to occupy is changed without his volition to a status embarrassing to an ordinary person of reasonable sensitivity, then he should not be deemed to have forfeited his right to be protected from an indecent and vulgar intrusion of his right of privacy merely because misfortune overtakes him in a public place. . . .[35]

PROBLEM 4-1: THE UNFORTUNATE FOOTBALL PLAYER

A newspaper published an article about a high school football game. The article was accompanied by a photograph of Ed McCarthy, a high school senior, which was taken after he had recovered a fumble during the game and was running full stride for the goal line. The picture showed McCarthy's genitalia, which happened to be exposed at the exact moment that the photograph was taken. McCarthy's pants had split unexpectedly, and he was not wearing the customary athletic supporter.

McCarthy has been greatly embarrassed by the publication and intends to sue the newspaper for invasion of privacy. In advance of a meeting with McCarthy and his parents, please prepare an analysis of these facts in light of the requirements of a disclosure action. Be prepared to discuss potential obstacles to recovery.

3.   Publicity Versus Publication

a.   In General

The "publicity" requirement of a privacy action for disclosure (and for false light) differs greatly from the "publication" requirement in defamation (*see* Chapter 3). Whereas, in defamation, a publication occurs any time a statement is communicated to a third person who understands its content, "publicity" for purposes of invasion of privacy means:

> that the matter is made public, by communicating it to the public at large, or to so many persons that the matter must be regarded as substantially certain to become one of public knowledge. . . .[36]

In *Biederman's of Springfield, Inc. v. Wright*,[37] the Supreme Court of Missouri held that oral publication over a three-day period in a public restaurant, where numerous customers were present, satisfied the publicity requirement.

Lack of "Publicity." Under the "publicity" standard, a letter sent to a creditor of the plaintiff will not give rise to liability.[38] Nor will a lender's disclosure of an applicant's negative credit rating to one person from whom the applicant intended to make a purchase.[39] The same is true even if the defendant discloses to a limited

---

[35] *Id.* at 477–78.

[36] RESTATEMENT (SECOND) OF TORTS § 652D cmt. a. (1977).

[37] 322 S.W.2d 892, 898 (Mo. 1959).

[38] RESTATEMENT (SECOND) OF TORTS § 652D cmt. a & illus. 1 (1977).

[39] *See Robins v. Conseco Fin. Loan Co.*, 656 N.W.2d 241 (Minn. Ct. App. 2003).

number of co-workers that plaintiff underwent psychiatric treatment.[40] In each case, "publicity" is lacking.

In *Hargrave v. GE Aviation Systems, LLC*,[41] an employer disclosed an employee's blood test results to three persons who were part of a company hired to determine whether the plaintiff's exposure to toxic substances was work-related. A federal court in Florida found that such limited revelation was not publicity for purposes of a disclosure claim.

Foreseeable Versus Unforeseeable Republication. The teachings of defamation law suggest that it would be fair to hold the initial disseminator of private facts liable for foreseeable republication of that matter. However, if it is *unforeseeable* that the matter will become public knowledge, there is no liability, even if that occurs. For example, in *Swinton Creek Nursery v. Edisto Farm Credit, ACA*,[42] the Supreme Court of South Carolina rejected the argument that, if information eventually became public, a party who disclosed the information to only one person by private letter could be held liable for "sparking the flame" of publicity.

b.   Two Types of Publicity

Public Versus Private Communications. Some cases, but certainly not all, have been careful to differentiate two kinds of publicity. The distinction is drawn between public communications and private communications.

(1)   Example: *Yath v. Fairview Clinics, N.P.*

Communication to the Public at Large Versus Selected Individuals. In *Yath v. Fairview Clinics, N.P.*,[43] the Court of Appeals of Minnesota addressed the question of whether posting private information on a MySpace webpage was "publicity" for purposes of a disclosure action. The court wrote:

> "Publicity," for the purposes of an invasion-of-privacy claim, means that "the matter is made public, by communicating it to the public at large, or to so many persons that the matter must be regarded as substantially certain to become one of public knowledge." . . . [*Restatement (Second) of Torts* § 652D cmt. a (1977).] In other words, there are two methods to satisfy the publicity element of an invasion-of-privacy claim: the first method is by proving a single communication to the public, and the second method is by proving communication to individuals in such a large number that the information is deemed to have been communicated to the public.[44]

Faxing Information Versus Posting on MySpace. Elaborating on these two varieties of publicity, the court explained:

---

[40] *See Eddy v. Brown*, 715 P.2d 74 (Okla. 1986).

[41] 2009 U.S. Dist. LEXIS 65456 (M.D. Fla. July 29, 2009).

[42] 514 S.E.2d 126 (S.C. 1999).

[43] 767 N.W.2d 34 (Minn. App. 2009).

[44] *Id.* at 42.

The [Minnesota] supreme court's analysis and application in . . . [*Bodah v. Lakeville Motor Express, Inc.*, 663 N.W.2d 550, 553 (Minn. 2003)] is illuminating. The *Bodah* court held that the publicity element was not satisfied when an employer disseminated employee names and social security numbers to sixteen managers in six states. . . . The employer disseminated the information by private means, specifically, by facsimile. The private rather than public nature of this communication caused the *Bodah* court to consider whether the communication was to a large enough number of recipients to support a determination of "publicity" under the second method. It held that dissemination of information to the relatively small group of individuals did not satisfy the publicity element because the disseminated information could not "be regarded as substantially certain to become public." . . .

. . . [I]n reaching the conclusion, the supreme court explained the type of communication that would constitute publicity under the first method. It approvingly acknowledged the *Restatement of Torts* explanation that "any publication in a newspaper or a magazine, even of small circulation . . . or any broadcast over the radio, or statement made in an address to a large audience," would meet the publicity element of an invasion-of-privacy claim. . . . It also relied on the *Restatement* for the proposition that posting private information in a shop window viewable by passers-by constitutes "publicity." . . . The *Restatement* explains that "[t]he distinction . . . is one between private and public communication." . . . This explanation informs our judgment that the challenged communication here constitutes publicity under the first method, or publicity *per se*. Unlike *Bodah*, where the private information went through a private medium to reach a finite, identifiable group of privately situated recipients, Yath's private information was posted on a public MySpace.com webpage for anyone to view. This Internet communication is materially similar in nature to a newspaper publication or a radio broadcast because upon release it is available to the public at large.[45]

Number of "Friends" Is Irrelevant to "Publicity." In *Yath*, the MySpace page in issue stated (accurately) that the plaintiff had a sexually transmitted disease. "The page listed six 'friends,' indicating that by then at least those six people had accessed the page."[46] Addressing the significance of that small number of "friends," the court wrote:

The district court appears to have accepted . . . [defendants'] argument that the publicity element was not satisfied because Yath proved only that a small number of people actually viewed the MySpace.com webpage and that the webpage was available only 24 to 48 hours. A similar argument could be made about a newspaper having only a small circulation, or a radio broadcast at odd hours when few were listening. The district court therefore mistakenly analyzed "publicity" using the second method, which

---

[45] *Id.* at 42–43.

[46] *Id.* at 39.

applies only to privately directed communication and requires an assessment based on the number of actual viewers. But when the communication is made by offering the information in a public forum, the first method applies and the tort is triggered when the discloser makes the private information publicly available, not when some substantial number of individuals actually get the information. Like the temporary posting of information in a shop window, the MySpace.com webpage put the information in view of any member of the public — in large or small numbers — who happened by. The number of actual viewers is irrelevant. . . .[47]

Focus on the Medium, Not the Message. The court then considered whether a social networking webpage is a private communication. The court reasoned:

> [Defendant] Fairview argues that posting information on a "social networking" website such as MySpace.com should be treated only as a private communication because Myspace.com webpages are not of "general interest" like online newspaper websites. But *Bodah's* analysis of the publicity element renders this claimed distinction meaningless. The determination does not depend on whether the content offered through the medium is of general interest to the public, but on whether the content is conveyed through a medium that delivers the information directly to the public. The supreme court's other example of publicity, albeit offered in *dicta*, is consistent with this approach. The court expressly opined that the posting of private employee information on the Internet would constitute "publicity." . . . By focusing on the number of people who were exposed to the information, the district court revealed that it erroneously treated the nature of the medium as private, which would constitute publicity only if the information would likely be retold publicly. We hold that the publicity element of an invasion-of-privacy claim is satisfied when private information is posted on a publicly accessible Internet website.[48]

The Significance of Password Protection. The *Yath* court did not decide the legal significance of password protected material posted on the Internet. However, it touched on the issue tangentially. The court wrote:

> The MySpace.com webpage that triggers Yath's claim was . . . [a publicly accessible website]. Access to it was not protected, as some webpages are, by a password or some other restrictive safeguard. It was a window that Yath's enemies propped open for at least 24 hours allowing any internet-connected voyeur access to private details of her life. The claim therefore survives the "publicity" challenge.
>
> . . . .
>
> It is true that mass communication is no longer limited to a tiny handful of commercial purveyors and that we live with much greater access to information than the era in which the tort of invasion of privacy developed. A town crier could reach dozens, a handbill hundreds, a newspaper or radio

---

[47] *Id.* at 43.

[48] *Id.* at 43–44.

station tens of thousands, a television station millions, and now a publicly accessible webpage can present the story of someone's private life, in this case complete with a photograph and other identifying features, to more than one billion Internet surfers worldwide. This extraordinary advancement in communication argues for, not against, a holding that the MySpace posting constitutes publicity.[49]

Number of Actual Recipients is Relevant to Damages. Elaborating on communications to the public, the court explained:

> Contrary to the concurring opinion, as the *Restatement* examples illustrate, publicity under the first theory occurs at the point when the communication is made to the public at large, not to a large number of the public: "any *publication* in a newspaper or a magazine, even of small circulation" (not *any information that a large number of persons actually read in the newspaper*); "in a handbill distributed to a large number of persons" (not *a handbill actually read by a large number of persons*); "any broadcast over the radio" (not *any broadcast actually heard by a significant audience*). *Restatement (Second) of Torts* § 652D cmt. a. "Publicity" therefore occurs on the act that disseminates the information "to the public at large," which is the printing, distribution, or utterance in the public forum. Although the damages calculation for invasion of privacy might be influenced by the extent to which the publicity was effective, . . . a determination that publicity occurred does not require a large actual audience.

> We acknowledge that some public webpages might get little actual attention. But the same may be said of a card posted on the door of a residence or a poster displayed in a shop window, each of which constitutes publicity. . . . The unrestricted MySpace.com webpage posting likewise constitutes publicity.[50]

Despite finding that there had been publicity of the private matter, the *Yath* court affirmed a grant of summary judgment to the defendants because there was no evidence that they had been involved in creating the MySpace.com webpage.

c.   Special Relationship Exception

Some cases have recognized what is called a "special relationship" (or "confidential relationship") exception to the usual publicity requirements applicable in a disclosure action. For example, in *Pachowitz v. Le Doux*,[51] the Washington Court of Appeals wrote that "[w]hen a special relationship exists, the public can include one person or small groups such as fellow employees, club members, church members, family or neighbors." The court cited cases which have so held and declined to state that disclosure to one person or a small group, as a matter of law, fails to satisfy the publicity requirement. The judgment in *Pachowitz*

---

[49] *Id.* at 44.

[50] *Id.* at 44–45.

[51] 666 N.W.2d 88, 96 & n. 9 (Wis. Ct. App. 2003).

affirmed, in relevant part, an award based on disclosure to one person whom the defendant knew had "loose lips."

d.   Publicity in the Twenty-First Century

A Keystroke to Reach a Billion People. In *Peterson v. Moldofsky*,[52] the defendant e-mailed nude pictures of the plaintiff to her mother, ex-husband, ex-in laws, current boyfriend, boss, and coworkers. In addressing whether the plaintiff adequately alleged publicity for purposes of her disclosure claim, a federal court in Kansas wrote:

> Defendant contends that he is entitled to summary judgment . . . because he emailed the pictures to only . . . [a small number of] people, which he claims is an insufficient number to satisfy the "publicity" requirement of this tort. . . .

> . . . [T]he Court disagrees with Defendant's contention that comment a of the *Restatement (Second) of Torts* § 652D, which states that "it is not an invasion of the right to privacy . . . to communicate a fact . . . to a single person, or even to a small group of people," controls this issue. The Court is not persuaded that the Kansas Supreme Court would follow comment *a* in a case involving the transmission of sexually explicit material over the Internet. To begin with, unlike the cases that have quoted comment *a*, this case does not involve a traditional form of communication, such as paper mail or an oral conversation. This distinction is significant because the Internet enables its users to "quickly and inexpensively surmount" the barriers to generating publicity that were inherent in the traditional forms of communication. Furthermore, the Court finds significant the fact that comment *a* was published at a time when few, if any, contemplated the fact that a single, noncommercial, individual could distribute information, including personal information, "to anyone, anywhere in the world" in just a matter of seconds. Today, unlike 1977, the year that the American Law Institute officially adopted the *Restatement (Second)*, due to the advent of the Internet, "the barriers of creating publicity are slight." Consequently, as is true of the existing Kansas case law, the *Restatement* offers little to no assistance to the Court. . . .

> In regards to the tort of publicity of private facts, it is well established that the purpose behind recognizing the tort is to protect an individual from the unwarranted distribution of private facts. To ensure that this purpose is not undermined, a growing number of jurisdictions have adopted flexible standards for determining whether publication has occurred. One standard that has been adopted by many courts throughout the country is the confidential relation standard, a standard that holds that the publication requirement may be met when the defendant discloses private information to people with whom the plaintiff has a special relationship. The Court finds that this trend of flexibility is instructive on the question of whether a court

---

[52] 2009 U.S. Dist. LEXIS 90633 (D. Kan. Sept. 29, 2009).

can find, consistent with the *Restatement's* dictates, that the distribution of private information to a small group of people can constitute publication.

Cognizant of the purpose behind recognizing the tort of publicity of private facts, the trend in sister jurisdictions, the prevalence of the Internet, and the relative ease in which information can be published over the Internet, the Court concludes that Kansas does not, as a matter of law, preclude a privacy claim simply because the defendant communicated the private fact to a small group of people. . . .

Here, Defendant emailed sexually explicit material to a handful of Plaintiff Piper's family and friends. While the Court agrees that it is unlikely that Piper's mother will distribute the incriminating photos to the public, the Court cannot, as a matter of law, say that her ex-husband, or any of the other recipients for that matter, will not. With one simple keystroke, a recipient of the email could, at least theoretically, disclose the pictures to over a billion people. Therefore, in light of this fact, the Court finds that a genuine issue of fact exists as to whether the contents of the email are substantially certain to become public knowledge.[53]

PROBLEM 4-2: THE ADULT BOOKSTORE PATRON

Erick Lamont, a married man with three children in elementary school, had never stopped at the Adult Bookstore before. He had thought about doing so because signs for the store, screaming "Exit Here! Live Girls!," were clearly visible from the Interstate. But he had never done it.

When Erick pulled off to find the store, he discovered to his relief that the property, which was located about a half mile from the Interstate, was surrounded by a large privacy fence. Cars parked at the store could not easily be seen by passersby.

Two days after his visit to the store, a message was left on the answering machine at the Lamont house. The message said that the listener would find a video posted on YouTube to be very interesting. The video, apparently bearing a correct date and time, showed Erick's car pulling into the Adult Bookstore parking lot and Erick walking into the store.

Whoever posted the video apparently has targeted the store and its customers for humiliation. It is unclear how the responsible parties pieced together Erick's license plate and home phone number — perhaps by unauthorized access to records of the motor vehicle department or by buying information on the Internet.

Erick's family has not seen the video on YouTube, but he is frantic that they might. Whoever posted the video and called his house the first time seems likely to call again. Erick has consulted you about his legal options. Please advise.

---

[53] *Id.* at *15–*21.

4.   Highly Offensive to a Reasonable Person

A disclosure of private facts is not an actionable invasion of privacy unless disclosure of the matter would be highly offensive to a reasonable person. There is generally no basis for persons to be highly offended that others observe and talk about their comings and goings and other facts readily visible to the public.

Shame is Not the Issue. In *Haynes v. Alfred A. Knopf, Inc.*,[54] Chief Judge Richard Posner wrote for the Seventh Circuit:

> Even people who have nothing rationally to be ashamed of can be mortified by the publication of intimate details of their life. Most people in no wise deformed or disfigured would nevertheless be deeply upset if nude photographs of themselves were published in a newspaper or a book. They feel the same way about photographs of their sexual activities, however "normal," or about a narrative of those activities, or about having their medical records publicized. Although it is well known that every human being defecates, no adult human being in our society wants a newspaper to show a picture of him defecating. The desire for privacy illustrated by these examples is a mysterious but deep fact about human personality. It deserves and in our society receives legal protection. . . .[55]

Disclosure of Confidential Information. The mere fact that the information disclosed about the plaintiff was confidential does not necessarily mean that disclosure would be highly offensive to a reasonable person. For example, in *Bratt v. IBM*,[56] the First Circuit held that revelation that the plaintiff had frequently used a confidential open-door process for resolving work-related grievances was not an actionable invasion of privacy.

Highly Offensive Matter Versus Highly Offensive Conduct? What must be highly offensive, the facts disclosed to the public or the defendant's conduct in making the disclosure? The language of the *Restatement* seems clear. Liability will not be assessed unless "the matter publicized is of a kind that . . . would be highly offensive to a reasonable person."[57] Many cases are consistent with this view. For example, in *International Union v. Garner*,[58] a federal court in Tennessee held that no action would lie where police officers had noted the license plate numbers of cars parked in front of the location of a meeting organizing a union, traced the license plates to automobile registrations, and then reported that information to the plaintiffs' employer. As the court explained:

> [T]he "matter publicized" is not highly offensive to a reasonable person. Rather, . . . what may be deemed offensive in this case is the manner of dissemination of the publicity. The plaintiffs assert that the Pulaski Police Department was responsible for conducting surveillance on citizens who

---

[54] 8 F.3d 1222 (7th. Cir 1993).

[55] *Id.* at 1229.

[56] 785 F.2d 352, 359 (1st Cir. 1986).

[57] Restatement (Second) of Torts § 652D (1977).

[58] 601 F. Supp. 187 (M.D. Tenn. 1985).

sought to engage in legitimate activities. The matter publicized itself, however, is not highly offensive nor is it private. A reasonable person would not be offended by the revelation that another person was engaged in union organization activity.

. . . [T]he plaintiffs' proper cause of action is not one for invasion of privacy, but rather one which challenges the method and purpose of the surveillance conducted by the public officials.[59]

However, some cases have focused not on the subject matter of the disclosure, but on the defendant's conduct leading to the disclosure. For example, in *Four Navy Seals v. Associated Press*,[60] a reporter discovered photos on the Internet appearing to depict military personnel engaged in abuse of Iraqi prisoners. As described by a federal court in California:

> In some photos, the military personnel appear to be mugging or grinning for the camera. In other photos, the military personnel are shown to be sitting on, lying atop, or stepping on detainees, some of whom are hooded. Finally, a few photos show military personnel pointing a firearm at a prisoner's bloody head at point blank range.[61]

The photos had unexpectedly been made available to the public. As the court explained:

> Jane Doe [the wife of one of the SEALS] had uploaded the digital photographs to her "smugmug" account believing that they would not be available to the general public. Hettena [a reporter who conducted an Internet search via Google] downloaded thirteen of the photos depicting Navy SEALs with Iraqi captives, and immediately printed copies without the necessity of keying any password, entering a code, or incurring a monetary charge. . . . Nor had Hettena observed any notice of privacy or requirement of permission when he had accessed the account.[62]

In discussing the disclosure claim by the plaintiffs (Jane Doe and four navy SEALS), the court wrote:

> Plaintiffs fail to adequately plead that Defendants [the reporter and Associated Press] engaged in the type of conduct "highly offensive to a reasonable person" required for the disclosure of private facts tort. . . .

> In this case, locating photos posted on the internet and writing an accompanying story about potential Iraqi prisoner abuse is not the type of offensive conduct typically associated with the tort of publication of private facts. The degree of intrusion was minimal; Hettena merely conducted a search on the internet, and used no deception in locating and downloading the images. The context of the search, Defendants' effort to report on potential abuse of Iraqi prisoners in the wake of the Abu Ghraib scandal,

---

[59] *Id.* at 190.

[60] 413 F. Supp. 2d 1136 (S.D. Cal. 2005).

[61] *Id.* at 1141.

[62] *Id.*

also demonstrates that Hettena's actions were not offensive. The setting into which Defendants intruded, a publicly-accessible website, was one in which a reasonable person would not expect privacy. The Associated Press merely distributed a truthful story, with photos that depict a topic of great public interest. As a matter of law, Defendants' alleged conduct was not offensive.[63]

If, in *Four Navy SEALS*, the court erred in focusing on whether the defendant's conduct, rather than the matter disclosed, was highly offensive, the error was likely harmless. There were good grounds for concluding both that the photos posted on the Internet and searchable via Google were not actionable because they were not private and they also related to a subject matter of public concern.

5.   Not of Legitimate Concern to the Public

Many disclosure actions fail because the publicized subject matter was of legitimate concern to the public. On this ground, reference to a person as a suspect in a serial murder investigation has been found not to be an invasion of privacy.[64]

a.   In General

Newsworthiness. Some courts talk about whether information was of legitimate concern to the public in terms of whether the material disclosed was "newsworthy." For example, in *Capra v. Thoroughbred Racing Association*,[65] a man who was convicted of fixing horse races was given a new identity under the federal witness protection program, in exchange for providing useful testimony. The man's wife and son also received new identities, but the family was still in danger because organized crime figures had reportedly offered large sums of money for information about the husband's new name and whereabouts. After the man's wife applied to the racing board, in her new name and her son's new name, for licenses to purchase and race horses, the board issued a press release disclosing the identity and location of the husband and wife. In a privacy action by the husband, wife, and son, the Ninth Circuit applied a three-part test for newsworthiness, stating:

> On the record before us, a reasonable jury . . . could find that the press release was not newsworthy as to one or more of the plaintiffs. First, the jury must consider the social value of the facts published in light of the public's interest in protecting persons willing to testify. . . . While the federal witness protection program cannot by itself overcome the First Amendment, the program possesses some social values that weight against unlimited free speech under the general balancing test. . . . Second, the jury must consider the seriousness of the intrusion caused by the publication. Finally, the jury must consider the extent to which parties voluntarily exposed themselves to public notoriety. In this respect, . . . [the husband],

---

[63] *Id.* at 1145.

[64] *See Wilson v. Freitas*, 121 Haw. 120, 214 P.3d 1110, 1120 (Ct. App. 2009).

[65] 787 F.2d 463, 464–65 (9th Cir. 1986).

who was convicted, his wife . . . , who made the application, and their son
Kevin, whose name was placed on the application, are not all similarly
situated.[66]

Reviving Interest in Prior Conduct. It is usually permissible to revive public
interest in someone who was once a public figure.[67] For example, in *Sidis v. F-R
Publishing Corporation*,[68] the plaintiff, who led a reclusive life, had once been a
famous child prodigy. The defendant's publishing of an article, which recounted the
plaintiff's earlier accomplishments and described his present life in detail, was held
not to be actionable by the Second Circuit.

In *Melvin v. Reid*,[69] the California Court of Appeal reached a contrary result in
a case involving a former prostitute who, after her acquittal on a murder charge,
had led a conventional life. She sued because the defendants produced a motion
picture about her early life. The court held that the plaintiff's activities had ceased
to be a matter of public concern and allowed her privacy claim to proceed. However,
in a later case, *Forsher v. Bugliosi*,[70] the California Supreme Court opined that
Melvin might come out differently under modern constitutional principles.

Victims of Accidents or Crimes. Published photographs of the victims of
accidents or crimes are typically not actionable invasions of privacy, even if the
victim is in agony or without clothes. Thus, in *Anderson v. Fisher Broad. Co., Inc.*,[71]
the Supreme Court of Oregon held that televising pictures of the plaintiff, an
accident victim who was bleeding and in pain, was not an invasion of privacy.

One way to explain these holdings is by saying that the accurate illustrations of
news stories are "newsworthy." Another explanation is to draw a parallel to the
treatment of "involuntary public figures" (which includes victims) under defamation
law. (*See* Chapter 3.) Involuntary public figures are held to the demanding actual
malice requirement of proof, even though they typically did nothing to inject
themselves into a public controversy or otherwise assume the risk of being defamed.
Of course, holding so does not foreclose relief entirely. It just makes the path to
recovery difficult. In contrast, disclosure actions by victims fail entirely if the
subject matter is newsworthy.

b.   Limits on "Legitimate Public Interest."

Plastic Surgery. In *Vassiliades v. Garfinckel's, Brooks Brothers*,[72] the District
of Columbia Court of Appeals affirmed a finding of liability in a disclosure action
against a plastic surgeon, but reversed in part for a new trial on damages. The
plaintiff's plastic surgeon had used "before" and "after" pictures of her during a
department store presentation on plastic surgery and on a related television show.

---

[66] *Id.*

[67] *See* Restatement (Second) of Torts § 652D cmt. k (1977).

[68] 113 F.2d 806 (2d Cir. 1940).

[69] 112 Cal. App. 285 (1931).

[70] 608 P.2d 716 (Cal. 1980).

[71] 712 P.2d 803 (Or. 1986).

[72] 492 A.2d 580 (D.C. 1986).

Noting that there was nothing uncomplimentary or unsavory about the pictures, the court held that the publicity could have been found by a jury to be "highly offensive to a reasonable person," and therefore actionable. Addressing the issue of whether the publicity concerned a matter of legitimate public interest, the court wrote:

> It is a defense to a claim of invasion of privacy that the matter publicized is of general public interest. . . . [T]his defense or privilege is not limited to dissemination of news about current events or public affairs, but also protects "information concerning interesting phases of human activity and embraces all issues about which information is needed or appropriate so that individuals may cope with the exigencies of their period." . . .

> Nevertheless, the privilege to publicize matters of legitimate public interest is not absolute. . . . Certain private facts about a person should never be publicized, even if the facts concern matters which are, or relate to persons who are, of legitimate public interest. . . . We thus find persuasive the distinction Mrs. Vassiliades draws between the private fact of her reconstructive surgery and the fact that plastic surgery is a matter of legitimate public interest.

> The conflict between the public's right to information and the individual's right to privacy requires a balancing of the competing interests. . . . [U]pon balancing the two interests, we hold that Mrs. Vassiliades had a higher interest to be protected. Although Dr. Magassy and Garfinckel's may well have performed a public service by making the presentations about plastic surgery, and the public undoubtedly has an interest in plastic surgery, it was unnecessary for Dr. Magassy to publicize Mrs. Vassiliades' photographs. Publication of her photographs neither strengthened the impact nor the credibility of the presentations nor otherwise enhanced the public's general awareness of the issues and facts concerning plastic surgery. . . . Dr. Magassy's presentations could have been just as informative by using either photographs of other patients or photographs from medical textbooks. . . . We hold, therefore, that Dr. Magassy invaded Mrs. Vassiliades' privacy by giving publicity to private facts. . . .[73]

Contrast *Vassiliades* with *Sandler v. Calcagni*.[74] In *Sandler*, a federal court in Maine wrote:

> Plaintiff alleges that two statements in . . . [a book] regarding plastic surgery on her nose are actionable invasions of her privacy. . . . First, the Court questions whether this matter is truly private: cosmetic surgery on one's face is by its nature exposed to the public eye. . . . In addition, Plaintiff argues only generally that the disclosure of her plastic surgery would be highly offensive. The *Restatement* notes that, "[t]he protection afforded to the plaintiff's interest in his privacy must be relative to the customs of the time and place. . . . Complete privacy does not exist in this

---

[73] 492 A.2d at 588–90.

[74] 565 F. Supp. 2d 184 (D. Me. 2008).

world except in a desert, and anyone who is not a hermit must expect and endure the ordinary incidents of the community life of which he is a part." . . . In this day and age, the Court finds that Plaintiff has failed to generate a triable issue as to whether the disclosure was highly offensive.[75]

In Vitro Fertilization. In *Y.G. & L.G. v. Jewish Hospital of St. Louis,*[76] the plaintiffs sued a hospital and television station for public disclosure of private facts after the station filmed the plaintiffs' participation in an event at the hospital commemorating the success of the hospital's *in vitro* fertilization program, in which they had participated. The Missouri Court of Appeals held that the plaintiffs stated a cause of action for invasion of privacy, writing:

> The plaintiffs alleged in their petition that they were "assured" that "no publicity nor public exposure" would occur, that they twice refused interviews or to be filmed, and made every reasonable effort to avoid being filmed, and that no one knew of their reproductive process other than Y.G.'s mother. . . .

> While the modern medical, technical process of *in vitro* fertilization may be of great interest to the public generally, publicizing the individual persons who undergo such medical "miracle," without their consent and without waiver states a claim upon which relief may be granted. . . .

> The defendants contend that the plaintiffs waived any right to privacy they had by attending the function. . . . [W]e hold that there was no waiver. Plaintiffs were assured that the function would be private, they twice refused an interview, and by merely attending the function there was no express voluntary waiver of a known right.

> KSDK's motion alleged that appellants waived their right to privacy by attending the party because they disclosed their *in vitro* program participation to the other attendees. . . . There are numerous cases holding that matters of public record or events taking place in a public location may be publicized without invasion of privacy. . . .

> The mere fact that an event takes place where others are present does not waive the right to privacy. . . .

> In the case at bar, the allegations of the petition show that appellants were assured that the persons invited would include only other persons involved in the IVF program, and would not be open to the public or the media. By attending such a function, appellants clearly chose to disclose their participation to only the other *in vitro* couples. By so attending this limited gathering, they did not waive their right to keep their condition and the process of *in vitro* private, in respect to the general public.[77]

---

[75] *Id.* at 198.

[76] 795 S.W.2d 488 (Mo. Ct. App. 1990).

[77] *Id.* at 501–02.

Problem 4-3: The Abortion Clinic Protesters

Legionnaires for Life is a religiously affiliated anti-abortion group. One aspect of their program is to promote respect for life by picketing abortion clinics and persuading pregnant mothers not to have abortions.

Jared Thomas is an active Legionnaires member. By rummaging through a recycling container outside of an abortion clinic, Thomas found a discarded piece of paper showing that a woman named Ingalill Alstrom had an appointment at the clinic later the same week, presumably to have an abortion.

When Alstrom arrived at the clinic on the day in question, she was stunned to be met by protesters carrying large placards bearing her name. One of the signs read, "Ingalill Alstrom — Save Your Baby — Don't Have an Abortion — God Wants you to Cancel Your Appointment." Other signs were similar.

When Alstrom saw the signs she broke down in tears. Passersby stopped and tried to help her, but she was frantic. Members of the Legionnaires then attempted to approach Alstrom, but were pushed back by the passersby. Eventually, Alstrom was escorted to her car and left the scene.

You have been asked to meet with Alstrom to discuss whether her legal rights have been violated. Please prepare to discuss whether she can state a viable claim for public disclosure of private affairs.

6.   Damages

Duration, Identification, Impact on Others, and Personal Reaction. In *Vassiliades v. Garfinckel's, Brooks Brothers,*[78] the District of Columbia Court of Appeals held that the trial court did not abuse its discretion in finding that damage awards were against the weight of the evidence in a case involving unauthorized use of photos of the plaintiff by her plastic surgeon in department store and television presentations. In ordering a new trial on damages, the court wrote:

> The evidence at trial relating to the extent of the injury suffered by Mrs. Vassiliades showed that her photograph was on television for less than 40 seconds, her name was not mentioned and the person in the photograph was referred to only as a patient in her forties. Only one person who saw the television program identified her and that person told one of Mrs. Vassiliades' former coworkers about her surgery. Although most of Mrs. Vassiliades' testimony focused on the television presentation, she also offered evidence that seventy-nine people saw her photograph at the department store presentation. However, her name was not mentioned; only one person at the store presentation knew her, and there was no evidence that anyone recognized her photographs. There was also evidence that a neighbor, who was also a former coworker, knew about her surgery before Dr. Magassy's presentations. Mrs. Vassiliades did not offer evidence of the impact of the publicity on the persons who saw her photographs, but only described her own mental and behavioral reactions. Her husband

---

[78] 492 A.2d 580 (D.C. 1986).

corroborated her behavioral reactions, but no medical evidence was offered to support her claim of severe depression. The jury was instructed that Mrs. Vassiliades sought recovery for only a sixty-day period, was cautioned to base its verdict solely on the evidence before it, and was told that it could not award any speculative damages.

. . . [W]hen the question of excessiveness is close, appellate courts give the benefit of every doubt to the trial court's judgment. . . . Upon consideration of the nature of Mrs. Vassiliades' evidence and her stipulated limitation on her claim for damages, we cannot say the trial court's grant of a new trial was so beyond the range of reason as to require reversal. The verdicts for a sixty-day period of $350,000 against Dr. Magassy and $250,000 against Garfinckel's are at least at the outer limits of the maximum range of a reasonable verdict.[79]

7.   Special Issues

a.   Actions Against Churches

When invasion of privacy claims are asserted against churches, the usual issues arise as to whether the protections afforded by the religion clauses of the First Amendment preclude imposition of tort liability. In *Guinn v. Church of Christ of Collinsville*,[80] a former church member who was denounced for "fornication" sued the church, alleging invasion of privacy and intentional infliction of emotional distress. The Supreme Court of Oklahoma held that the church elders' continued denunciation of a former member after she had withdrawn from the church was not protected by the First Amendment.

b.   Waiver

Voluntary Relinquishment of a Known Right. Waiver is typically defined as the "voluntary relinquishment or abandonment — express or implied — of a legal right."[81] A waiver of privacy rights will bar a cause of action for disclosure. However, courts are often reluctant to find that a voluntary relinquishment of rights has occurred.

Partial Waiver. In *Diaz v. Oakland Tribune, Inc.*,[82] the defendant revealed that the president of the student body at her college had once been a man, and had a sex-change operation before going to college. The California Court of Appeal held that although the plaintiff had waived her right to privacy about her public conduct by seeking to become president of the student body, this did not "warrant that her entire private life be open to public inspection," especially because the public arena she entered was so small.

---

[79] *Id.* at 594–95.

[80] 775 P.2d 766 (Okla. 1989).

[81] Black's Law Dictionary (9th ed. 2009).

[82] 139 Cal. App. 3d 118 (1983).

c.　　Consent

Actual Consent, Apparent Consent, and Ostensible Agency. Consent will bar any action for invasion of privacy, provided that the conduct is within the scope of the consent.[83] Either actual consent[84] or apparent consent[85] will suffice. In addition, it seems likely that conduct by one acting with ostensible agency will defeat a privacy cause of action, if the principal has cloaked the agent with apparent authority to consent to revelation of what would otherwise be private matters.[86]

In *Vassiliades v. Garfinckel's, Brooks Brothers*,[87] the plaintiff's plastic surgeon told a department store that he had permission to use the plaintiff's "before" and "after" pictures in a store presentation on plastic surgery. That was not correct. In holding that the store, unlike the surgeon, was not liable for disclosure of private facts, the Court of Appeals for the District of Columbia wrote:

> The undisputed evidence is that Dr. Magassy had unqualifiedly assured Garfinckel's that he had obtained his patients' consent. Clear evidence of consent will insulate a party from liability. . . . Thus, the issue is whether Garfinckel's was justified in relying on Dr. Magassy's oral assurance. Garfinckel's decision to ask Dr. Magassy to participate in its program was based on its understanding that he was a reputable professional; Garfinckel's director of public relations testified about Dr. Magassy's prior complimentary public exposure. Before the television program, Garfinckel's director examined each of the slides on a view finder and, upon finding some to be not particularly pleasant, asked Dr. Magassy if he had obtained permission from his patients to use the slides. Based on Dr. Magassy's assurance that he had, the director did not inquire about consent prior to the department store presentation. No evidence was presented to suggest that Garfinckel's had any reason to doubt Dr. Magassy's statement.
>
> Under these circumstances, we hold that Garfinckel's was justified in relying on Dr. Magassy's assurances that he had Mrs. Vassiliades' consent and that Mrs. Vassiliades has failed to meet her burden to prove Garfinckel's liability for invasion of her privacy. . . .[88]

Relationship of Consent to Fault. The ruling in *Vassiliades* is probably better explained by lack of fault than by consent. There was no actual consent on the part of the plaintiff, which is why the plastic surgeon was held liable for public disclosure of private facts. There was nothing *in the plaintiff's conduct* which gave the store the appearance that the plaintiff consented, and therefore apparent consent can be ruled out as a reason for holding the store not liable. It also seems unlikely that the surgeon was cloaked with apparent authority to allow the use of the photographs.

---

[83] *See* RESTATEMENT (SECOND) OF TORTS § 652F (1977).

[84] *See id.* § 892(1).

[85] *See id.* § 892(2).

[86] *See* RESTATEMENT (THIRD) OF AGENCY § 2.03 (2006).

[87] 492 A.2d 580 (D.C. 1986).

[88] *Id.* at 590.

Unauthorized statements by an agent do not enlarge the scope of the agent's authority.[89] The *plaintiff did nothing* to give the store the impression that the doctor was authorized to consent to disclosure. Moreover, that is not what the surgeon said: he said that the plaintiff had consented (which was not true), not that he was consenting on her behalf.

The best explanation of the court's ruling is that the store had acted reasonably in relying upon the assurances of a respected professional. Thus, the only way to hold the store liable would be to impose liability without fault. This raises an important issue relating to the *Restatement*'s[90] formulation of the blackletter rule on liability for disclosure of private facts, quoted at the beginning of this section of the chapter. The rule says that "[o]ne who gives publicity to a matter concerning the private life of another is subject to liability."[91] There is no indication in the blackletter rule as to what level of culpability on the part of the defendant, if any, is required before liability may be assessed. Presumably, intentionally giving publicity to a private matter is actionable. Whether recklessly or negligently giving publicity to a private matter will suffice is less certain, but there are cases so holding.[92] Thus, the Sixth Circuit remarked in *Yoder v. Ingersoll-Rand Co.*,[93] "it is far from clear that the Ohio Supreme Court would hold that the tort of public disclosure requires an intentional disclosure." When one remembers the rulings in the defamation field, it seems highly dubious that strict liability for disseminating the truth would be imposed. Defamation plaintiffs are routinely required to prove fault as to falsity with respect to *false* defamatory statements.

d.   The Disclosure Tort and Open Records Laws

Although plaintiffs rarely seem to succeed in tort actions alleging public disclosure of private facts, the principles governing disclosure liability sometimes play an important role in the interpretation of open records laws. This is true because "freedom of information" acts often contain a privacy exception that will defeat a request for public access. Courts often rely upon tort principles when interpreting the scope of such privacy provisions. This is significant because immunizing information from revelation under an open records law may be as valuable to a plaintiff as a monetary judgment seeking to compensate harm caused by a revelation that has already occurred.

Interpreting Privacy Exceptions. In *Bellevue John Does 1-11 v. Bellevue School Dist. #405*,[94] public school teachers sought injunctive relief to prevent a school district from releasing their names in response to a public records request for information about teachers alleged to have committed sexual misconduct against students. In concluding that certain teachers' identities were exempt from disclosure, the Supreme Court of Washington interpreted the public records law's

---

[89] *See* RESTATEMENT (THIRD) OF AGENCY § 2.03 cmt. c (2006).

[90] RESTATEMENT (SECOND) OF TORTS § 652D (1977).

[91] *Id.*

[92] *See Prince v. St. Francis-St. George Hosp., Inc.*, 20 Ohio App. 3d 4, 484 N.E.2d 265 (1985).

[93] 1998 U.S. App. LEXIS 31993, at *12–*13 (6th Cir. Dec. 22, 1998).

[94] 189 P.3d 139 (Wash. 2008).

privacy exception by reference to the requirements of a tort action for disclosure of private facts. The court wrote:

> [W]e previously determined that when a complaint regarding misconduct during the course of public employment is substantiated or results in some sort of discipline, an employee does not have a right to privacy in the complaint. We have also held performance evaluations are protected by the right of privacy. The remaining issue is whether a person has a right to privacy in false or unsubstantiated allegations of misconduct.

> . . . The fact that a teacher is accused of sexual misconduct is a "matter concerning the private life" [of the teacher] within . . . the scope of the right to privacy. . . .

> . . . . It is undisputed that disclosure of the identity of a teacher accused of sexual misconduct is highly offensive to a reasonable person. . . .

> The . . . question is whether the identities of teachers who are the subjects of unsubstantiated allegations of sexual misconduct are a matter of legitimate public concern. "[L]egitimate" means "reasonable.". . . . One "factor bearing on whether information is of legitimate concern to the public is whether the information is true or false." . . . Generally, "the public . . . has no legitimate interest in finding out the names of people who have been falsely accused." . . .

> As a preliminary matter, we choose to address whether the public has a legitimate concern in the identities of teachers who are the subjects of unsubstantiated claims of sexual misconduct rather than patently false claims. Making a distinction between "unsubstantiated" and "patently false" is vague and impractical. Placing the burden on agencies and courts to determine whether allegations are patently false rather than simply unsubstantiated is unworkable, time consuming, and, absent specific rules and guidelines, likely to lead to radically different methods and conclusions. . . .

> Precluding disclosure of the identities of teachers who are subjects of unsubstantiated allegations will not impede the public's ability to oversee school districts' investigations of alleged teacher misconduct. . . .

> When an allegation is unsubstantiated, the teacher's identity is not a matter of legitimate public concern. . . . The public can continue to access documents concerning the nature of the allegations and reports related to the investigation and its outcome, all of which will allow concerned citizens to oversee the effectiveness of the school districts' responses. The identities of the accused teachers will simply be redacted to protect their privacy interests. . . .

> . . . . We hold a teacher's identity should be released under the PDA [public disclosure act] only when alleged sexual misconduct has been substantiated or when that teacher's conduct results in some form of discipline, even if only a reprimand. Letters of direction and related documents must be disclosed under the PDA, but where a letter simply

seeks to guide future conduct, does not identify an incident of substantiated misconduct, and does not subject the teacher to any form of restriction or discipline, a teacher's name and other identifying information must be redacted.[95]

e.   Relatives of Deceased Family Members

Family members may have a privacy right in the photographic records relating to deceased relatives. In *Reid v. Pierce County*,[96] county employees had allegedly shown various persons photographs of corpses that were taken by a medical examiner's office. The Supreme Court of Washington held that relatives of the decedents pictured in the photos could maintain an invasion of privacy action against the county.

In *Catsouras v. Department of California Highway Patrol*,[97] two police officers allegedly e-mailed pictures of the decedent's decapitated corpse to persons not involved in an accident investigation, apparently as a Halloween prank. "Those photographs were strewn about the Internet and spit back at the family members [the plaintiffs], accompanied by hateful messages."[98] In holding that the family members' invasion of privacy action was improperly dismissed, the California Court of Appeal wrote:

> California law clearly provides that surviving family members have no right of privacy in the context of written media discussing, or pictorial media portraying, the life of a decedent. Any cause of action for invasion of privacy in that context belongs to the decedent and expires along with him or her. . . . The publication of death images is another matter, however. . . . The dissemination of death images can only affect the living. As cases from other jurisdictions make plain, family members have a common law privacy right in the death images of a decedent, subject to certain limitations.[99]

In *Katz v. National Archives & Records Administration*,[100] an author sought disclosure of autopsy photographs of President John F. Kennedy under the Freedom of Information Act. In interpreting a privacy exception to disclosure obligations under the Act, a federal court in the District of Columbia opined:

> [T]he Kennedy family has a clear privacy interest in preventing the disclosure of both the x-rays and the optical photographs taken during President Kennedy's autopsy. . . .
>
> . . . [A]llowing access to the autopsy photographs would constitute a clearly unwarranted invasion of the Kennedy family's privacy.[101]

---

[95] *Id.* at 147–53.

[96] 961 P.2d 333 (Wash. 1998).

[97] 181 Cal. App. 4th 856 (2010).

[98] *Id.* at 357.

[99] *Id.* at 358.

[100] 862 F. Supp. 476 (D. D.C. 1994), *aff'd*, 68 F.3d 1438 (D.C. Cir. 1995).

[101] *Id.* at 485–86.

f.   Statutory Rights Relating to Disclosure of Private Facts

Information About H.I.V. In some states, statutes expressly create a cause of action for harm resulting from certain types of disclosure of information. For example, § 50-b of the New York Civil Rights Law, with exceptions, provides in relevant part:

> The identity of any victim of a sex offense . . . or of an offense involving the alleged transmission of the human immunodeficiency virus, shall be confidential. No report, paper, picture, photograph, court file or other documents, in the custody or possession of any public officer or employee, which identifies such a victim shall be made available for public inspection. No such public officer or employee shall disclose any portion of any police report, court file, or other document, which tends to identify such a victim except as provided in subdivision two of this section.[102]

A provision for enforcing the specified obligations then provides:

> If the identity of the victim of an offense defined in subdivision one of section fifty-b of this article is disclosed in violation of such section, any person injured by such disclosure may bring an action to recover damages suffered by reason of such wrongful disclosure. In any action brought under this section, the court may award reasonable attorney's fees to a prevailing plaintiff.[103]

PROBLEM 4-4: THE ABUSIVE TEACHER

Linda Hawley, an elementary school teacher, was involved in an incident with a student, Martha Burd. Burd and her parents filed a complaint with the school and, before the complaint was acted upon, contacted the local television station. In an interview that was broadcasted on the evening news, Burd alleged that Hawley attacked her. During the broadcast, Hawley's picture was repeatedly shown to viewers.

Hawley believes that the Burds and the television station have invaded her privacy. Please advise Hawley whether she can state a claim for public disclosure of private facts if she can prove that the assault allegations were false and unsubstantiated.

C.   INTRUSION UPON SECLUSION OR PRIVATE AFFAIRS

Elements. According to the *Restatement* section entitled "Intrusion Upon Seclusion":

> One who intentionally intrudes, physically or otherwise, upon the solitude or seclusion of another or his private affairs or concerns, is subject to

---

[102] N.Y. CIV. RIGHTS LAW § 50-b (LEXIS 2014).

[103] *Id.* at § 50-c.

liability to the other for invasion of his privacy, if the intrusion would be highly offensive to a reasonable person.[104]

The Defendant Must Intrude. In *Gleason v. Smolinski*,[105] the defendant published a newspaper article about a man who had mysteriously disappeared. The article discussed the plaintiff, a woman who had been romantically involved with the missing man and was suspected to know something about his disappearance. In addressing the plaintiff's claim for intrusion, the Superior Court of Connecticut wrote:

> The plaintiffs' complaint quotes several excerpts from Murray's newspaper article, but it fails to allege an actual intrusion, physical or otherwise. It has been said that, "[t]he invasion may be by physical intrusion into a place in which the plaintiff has secluded himself, as when the defendant forces his way into the plaintiff's room in a hotel or insists over the plaintiff's objection in entering his home. It may also be by the use of the defendant's senses, with or without mechanical aids, to oversee or overhear the plaintiff's private affairs, as by looking into his upstairs windows with binoculars or tapping his telephone wires. It may be by some other form of investigation or examination into his private concerns, as by opening his private and personal mail, searching his safe or his wallet, examining his private bank account, or compelling him by a forged court order to permit an inspection of his personal documents. . . ." *See . . . [Restatement (Second) of Torts]* § 652B, comment (b). The plaintiffs do not allege facts concerning how Murray obtained any of this information and therefore, there is no allegation of any form of offensive investigation or other intrusion into Gleason's life by invading her privacy. Publication of private information alone is not legally sufficient to sustain this particular cause of action, which is concerned with the methods used when obtaining private information, rather than its subsequent dissemination. . . . Accordingly, the defendant's motion to strike . . . is granted.[106]

Intrusion Statutes. Some states have adopted statutory provisions that parallel the common law principles governing intrusion. For example, the Nebraska statute varies from the language of the *Restatement* and emphasizes the potential connection between intrusion and trespass. The Nebraska law provides:

> Any person, firm, or corporation that trespasses or intrudes upon any natural person in his or her place of solitude or seclusion, if the intrusion would be highly offensive to a reasonable person, shall be liable for invasion of privacy.[107]

The Right to Be Left Alone. Many court decisions and writers have discussed the privacy action for intrusion as legal recognition of the "right to be left alone." Whatever such right there is, it is probably shrinking. Because of advances in

---

[104] Restatement (Second) of Torts § 652B (1977).

[105] 2009 Conn. Super. LEXIS 1982 (July 20, 2009).

[106] *Id.* at *7–*9.

[107] Neb. Rev. Stat. § 20-203 (LEXIS 2014).

communication and technology, affairs are less private, solitude is more rare, and seclusion is harder to find.

1.   Intentional Intrusion, Physical or Otherwise

Publicity and Newsworthiness Are Not Key Issues*.* An intrusion is actionable even if facts relating thereto are not revealed to anyone else by the intruder. Thus, unlike an action for disclosure of private facts, intrusion does not require publicity of information. Moreover, because publicity is not necessary, courts addressing intrusion claims rarely are asked to consider whether facts discovered as a result of intrusion were of legitimate concern to the public.

a.   Culpability

Intentional Intrusion*.* Intrusion cases seldom focus on whether an intrusion was sufficiently intentional to give rise to liability because in many cases the intentional nature of the intrusion is obvious. However, in *Mauri v. Smith*,[108] the Supreme Court of Oregon considered what "intentional intrusion" meant in a lawsuit arising from the entry of police officers into an apartment. The court wrote:

> Although courts in other jurisdictions often use the phrase "intentional intrusion" in this context, few define it. A notable exception is *O'Donnell v. U.S.*, 891 F.2d 1079 (3d Cir. 1989). The plaintiff in that case, a former patient of the Veterans Administration (VA), sued the VA for intrusion upon seclusion when it released a summary of his psychiatric treatment to his employer without having received authorization. . . . The trial court granted the VA's motion for summary judgment. . . .
>
> On appeal, the Third Circuit set out to define "intentional intrusion." It gave "intent" the meaning stated in *Restatement (Second) of Torts* § 8A (1965): "that the actor desires to cause the consequences of his act, or that he believes that the consequences are substantially certain to result from it.". . . . Because the *Restatement* does not define "intrusion," the court looked to its ordinary meaning; the dictionary "defines 'intrude' to mean to thrust oneself in without invitation, permission, or welcome." . . . The court then analyzed the *Restatement's* discussion of intrusion upon seclusion in the light of those definitions:
>
> "The comments and illustrations to Section 652B disclose that an 'intrusion upon seclusion' claim usually involves a defendant who does not believe that he has either the necessary personal permission or legal authority to commit the intrusive act." *O'Donnell*, 891 F.2d at 1083.
>
> The court then held that there was no intrusion, primarily because it was undisputed that the VA believed that it had the plaintiff's permission to release the disputed record. . . . To similar effect, see *Gilmore v. Enogex*,

---

[108] 929 P.2d 307 (Or. 1996).

Inc., 878 P.2d 360, 366 (Okla. 1994) ("intentional intrusion" in this tort means a *nonconsensual* intrusion).[109]

Desire to Cause Unauthorized Entry or Substantial Certainty Thereof. The *Mauri* court then focused on state of mind as it relates to nonconsensual entry. The court explained:

> . . . [W]e are in general accord. . . . A person intrudes by thrusting himself or herself in without invitation, permission, or welcome. A person acts intentionally when he or she either desires to cause the consequence of an act or believes that the consequence is substantially certain to result from the act. By definition, then, an actor commits an intentional intrusion if the actor either desires to cause an unauthorized intrusion or believes that an unauthorized intrusion is substantially certain to result from committing the invasive act in question.[110]

> A plaintiff bears the burden to establish each element of a tort. That principle applies equally to elements that involve a defendant's state of mind. . . .

> . . . Viewed in the light most favorable to plaintiffs, the record reasonably can be read to establish (a) that the officers lacked plaintiffs' consent to enter their apartment or had consent to enter, but only for a particular purpose, and (b) that the officers either desired to cause an unauthorized intrusion or believed that an unauthorized intrusion was substantially certain to result from their entry. On the issue of "intentional intrusion," then, the record is sufficient to create a question of fact for the jury.[111]

Inadvertent Viewing. Because intrusion is an intentional tort, inadvertent viewing of sexual conduct in a bathroom stall is not actionable.[112]

PROBLEM 4-5: THE STOLEN LAPTOP

Ceana MacKenzie is the vice president for human relations at GlobalBank, a financial institution with offices in seven countries. Her duties include oversight and management of the retirement portfolios of GlobalBank employees.

GlobalBank company policy prohibits employees from transporting confidential data files on laptops or thumb drives without encryption. However, the encryption process is slow and inconvenient, and management is aware that the policy is often disregarded.

In violation of the encryption policy, MacKenzie took a laptop home with her knowing that it contained unencrypted information relating to the retirement

---

[109] *Id.* at 310–11.

[110] [n.5] We emphasize that the parties have brought the case to us only on a theory of consent. Defendant police officers and their employer have not argued before us that they had a separate justification — such as law-enforcement authority — for the initial entry, in the absence of consent. . . .

[111] 929 P.2d at 311.

[112] *See Hougum v. Valley Mem. Homes*, 574 N.W.2d 812 (N.D. 1998).

accounts of over 15,000 employees. During a burglary of MacKenzie's home, the laptop was stolen and never recovered.

Because the unencrypted information on the laptop contained social security numbers and other personal information, the affected employees are now at an increased risk of becoming victims of identity theft. GlobalBank has offered to provide those employees with a free subscription to a credit-monitoring service for two years. Daily alerts, based on the tracking of reports from the three major credit reporting agencies, will alert subscribers to changes in the credit histories, such as new accounts or loans taken out in their names. This information enables subscribers to take prompt action to minimize harm from identity theft.

A group of affected employees has concluded that the offer of free credit-monitoring services is an insufficient response to the problem that GlobalBank has created. They have consulted you about whether it is possible for them to sue GlobalBank, possibly as representatives of a large class of affected employees. Please evaluate whether the employees can state a colorable privacy claim based upon intrusion into private affairs.

b.   Actionable Intrusions

Prying, Physical Entry, Forced Revelation, and Disruption. The tort of intrusion may be committed in many ways. Some cases involve conduct that amounts to prying, such as hacking into an e-mail account or computer files,[113] tapping a phone, looking through a window, or reading personal correspondence or bank statements. Other cases involve unauthorized physical entry into a protected sphere, such as a home, an office, a hospital room, or hotel accommodations. Other cases have found there to be an intrusion where the plaintiff is forced to reveal facts, as may be true where a person is compelled to submit to a search or a drug test. In some instances, disruptive noises, such as numerous phone calls, have been deemed to be actionable intrusions.

Some cases involve multiple forms of intrusion. For example, in *Tompkins v. Cyr*,[114] the Fifth Circuit held that anti-abortion activists invaded the privacy of a physician and his spouse by: watching their house using binoculars; using a bull-horn to preach during demonstrations at the plaintiffs' home; making repeated harassing phone calls to the plaintiffs; and rattling their gate while they were eating Thanksgiving dinner.

In *Wolfson v. Lewis*,[115] a federal court in Pennsylvania held that the CEO of a health insurer and his family were entitled to a preliminary injunction against television reporters, barring them from violating the family's privacy rights. There was evidence that the reporters had: placed the exterior of the family's house under surveillance with telescopes, zoom lens video cameras, and ultra-sensitive microphones; followed the daughter and son-in-law to work and attempted to film

---

[113] *Coalition for an Airline Passengers' Bill of Rights v. Delta Air Lines, Inc.*, 693 F. Supp. 2d 667 (S.D. Tex. 2010).

[114] 202 F.3d 770 (5th Cir. 2000).

[115] 924 F. Supp. 1413 (E.D. Pa. 1996).

them entering a building; followed the family to Florida, where they went for seclusion; and established a surveillance boat in public waters as close as possible to the CEO's house. This was all done for the purpose of forcing the CEO to reconsider an earlier decision not to appear on camera for an interview regarding allegedly high salaries paid to executives of the insurer.

Annoying Phone Calls. Courts are reluctant to hold that unwanted phone calls, by themselves, amount to an actionable intrusion on privacy. For example, in *Baker v. Caribbean Cruise Line, Inc.*,[116] a federal court in Arizona wrote:

> The only conduct alleged is calls made to Plaintiff's cell phone. The complaint fails to allege in more than a conclusory fashion the frequency or content of the calls or to specify what was highly offensive about them. . . . Therefore, the complaint fails to state a claim on which relief can be granted. . . .[117]

However, where the facts are compelling, an action will lie. Thus, in *Imagine Medispa, LLC v. Transformations, Inc.*,[118] a federal court in West Virginia quoted language in the *Restatement* indicating that while "occasional telephone calls cannot constitute an intrusion upon seclusion, repeated, persistent calls at inconvenient hours can."[119] Addressing the facts before it, the court stated:

> Here, the plaintiffs' allege that the defendants created the advertisement for the [plaintiff's] Camaro and posted it on Craigslist, that the advertisement caused Rubio to receive scores of calls from strangers "at all hours of the day and night," and that the calls caused "annoyance and inconvenience," and were "disruptive" to Rubio's personal life and business. . . . These allegations are sufficient at this stage to state a claim for intrusion upon seclusion.[120]

Secret Viewing Devices. In *Koeppel v. Spiers*,[121] the defendant was sued for invasion of privacy based on his installation of a video camera in a uni-sex bathroom at his business. Because there was no evidence that the defendant ever used the camera to view anyone using the bathroom, the district court granted the defendant's motion for summary judgment. On appeal, the Iowa Supreme Court held that the district court had erred. As the court explained:

> In this case, the parties do not dispute that placing a camera in a bathroom would be highly objectionable to a reasonable person, nor do they dispute that a bathroom is a place where a reasonable person expects to be left alone. Instead, the parties disagree about the proof necessary to show the act of intrusion occurred. Koeppel [the plaintiff] primarily argues the installation of the camera in the bathroom with the intent to view is sufficient. . . .

---

[116] 2014 U.S. Dist. LEXIS 28960 (D. Ariz. March 6, 2014).

[117] *Id.* at *4.

[118] 2014 U.S. Dist. LEXIS 24287 (S.D.W. Va. Feb. 26, 2014).

[119] *Id.* at *10.

[120] *Id.*

[121] 808 N.W.2d 177 (Iowa 2011).

. . . Courts across the nation are divided on the question whether a person can intrude without actually viewing or recording the victim. Some courts conclude the installation of surveillance equipment in a private place is sufficient to show an intrusion. . . .

On the other hand, other courts have adopted a standard of intrusion requiring a defendant either see or hear another person's private activities. . . . In deciding a standard for Iowa, we think it is important to keep in mind that the tort protects against acts that interfere with a person's mental well-being by intentionally exposing the person in an area cloaked with privacy. . . . The point of disagreement among courts across the nation essentially boils down to whether the harm sought to be remedied by the tort is caused by accessing information from the plaintiff in a private place or by placing mechanisms in a private place that are capable of doing so at the hand of the defendant. Both perspectives clearly have support in other jurisdictions. However, we find the . . . secret use of an electronic listening or recording device is abhorrent to the interests sought to be protected by the tort. . . . [T]he comments and illustrations contained in the *Restatement (Second) of Torts* make no suggestion that the intrusion into solitude or seclusion requires someone to actually see or hear the private information. . . . Finally, the minority rule fails to provide full protection to a victim, while giving too much protection to people who secretly place recording devices in private places. Direct evidence that an actual viewing occurred can be difficult to establish, and a person who is inclined to secretly place a camera in a private area can easily incapacitate the camera when it is not in use so as to minimize any responsibility upon discovery. A plaintiff who learns a camera was placed in a private place should not be forced to live with the uncertainty of whether an actual viewing occurred. . . .

. . . It would be inconsistent with the policy of the tort to find an intrusion when the privacy of the plaintiff could not have been exposed in any way. . . . Accordingly, proof the equipment is functional is an ingredient in the inquiry. . . .

. . . [W]e agree with Speirs [the defendant] that our law does not recognize a tort of attempted invasion of privacy. . . . However, the act of intrusion is complete once it is discovered by the plaintiff because acquisition of information is not a requirement. . . . [H]arm from intrusion arises when the plaintiff reasonably believes an intrusion has occurred. . . .

An electronic invasion occurs under the intrusion on solitude or seclusion component of the tort of invasion of privacy when the plaintiff establishes by a preponderance of evidence that the electronic device or equipment used by a defendant could have invaded privacy in some way.[122]

Stalking. A privacy action may be based upon stalking. In *Summers v. Bailey,*[123]

---

[122] *Id.* at 181–85.

[123] 55 F.3d 1564 (11th Cir. 1995).

the defendant parked outside of the plaintiff's grocery store for hours, exhibited a large gun, followed her when she ran errands, and often parked near her house. In finding that a cause of action for intrusion was stated, the Eleventh Circuit opined:

> Traditionally, watching or observing a person in a public place is not an intrusion upon one's privacy. However, Georgia courts have held that surveillance of an individual on public thoroughfares, where such surveillance aims to frighten or torment a person, is an unreasonable intrusion upon a person's privacy.[124]

c.   Conduct Not Amounting to Intrusions

Distributing Photos Is Not Intrusion. In *Peterson v. Moldofsky*,[125] the defendant took photographs of the plaintiff while she was engaged in various sexual acts with other persons. When the relationship between the plaintiff and defendant soured, the defendant distributed copies of the photos to various persons, including friends, family members, and co-workers of the plaintiff. In a subsequent lawsuit, a federal court in Kansas rejected the plaintiff's intrusion claim, writing:

> Plaintiff does not allege that the photographs that were distributed were taken against her will or were otherwise wrongfully obtained; rather, she merely claims that the *distribution* of the explicit photographs constitutes an intrusion. . . . [T]his contention is contrary to Kansas law, as the act of distribution does not constitute an intrusion sufficient to make out a claim for invasion of privacy under the theory of intrusion upon seclusion.[126]

Compiling and Renting Information. In *Dwyer v. American Express Co.*,[127] credit cardholders brought suit based on the defendants' practice of renting information regarding cardholders' spending habits. The Illinois Appellate Court held that the plaintiffs failed to state an action for intrusion:

> The alleged wrongful actions involve the defendants' practice of renting lists that they have compiled from information contained in their own records. By using the American Express card, a cardholder is voluntarily, and necessarily, giving information to defendants that, if analyzed, will reveal a cardholder's spending habits and shopping preferences. We cannot hold that a defendant has committed an unauthorized intrusion by compiling the information voluntarily given to it and then renting its compilation.[128]

Lawful Receipt and Use of Information. Even if information is of a private nature, lawful receipt thereof generally does not amount to intrusion. For example,

---

[124] *Id.* at 1566.

[125] 2009 U.S. Dist. LEXIS 90633 (D. Kan. Sept. 29, 2009).

[126] *Id.* at *14–*15.

[127] 652 N.E.2d 1351 (Ill. App. Ct. 1995).

[128] *Id.* at 1354.

in *Mayes v. LIN Television of Texas, Inc.*,[129] a television station broadcast a recording of a secretly taped phone conversation involving the plaintiff, who was a member of the city council. A federal court in Texas held that the station was not liable for intrusion because the station did not make the secret recording and had legally obtained the tape. Moreover, the tape had already been disseminated to the public by other media organizations.

Compelled Disclosure. Sometimes there is a difference between intrusion and compelled disclosure. In *Jensen v. State*,[130] the Supreme Court of Idaho held that a state requirement that a contractor seeking to renew a license disclose any criminal conviction "even if the conviction was sealed, expunged or the judgment withheld," did not constitute an actionable intrusion into privacy.

2. Solitude, Seclusion, and Private Affairs

Potentially Broad Scope. The *Restatement* says that intentional intrusion is actionable if the defendant invades "the solitude or seclusion of another or his private affairs or concerns."[131] Thus, at least in theory, the potential scope of liability is broad.

Reasonable Expectations of Privacy. Many decisions have emphasized that for an action to lie there must be intrusion into a place where the plaintiff has a reasonable expectation of solitude, seclusion, or privacy. In *Sabrah v. Lucent Technologies, Inc.*, the Fifth Circuit recognized that a jury could find such an expectation in a case where an employer opened several packages of an employee's mail, including one labeled "private," and removed their contents.[132] In *Mauri v. Smith*,[133] the Supreme Court of Oregon reached the same conclusion where police officers entered an apartment without authorization. Similarly, in *Hoskins v. Howard*,[134] the Idaho Supreme Court found that there was an issue of fact as to whether cordless telephone users had a legitimate expectation of privacy in their phone conversation, which precluded summary judgment for the defendant.

No Reasonable Expectations of Privacy. In many cases, intrusion actions have failed because the plaintiff had no legitimate expectation of privacy. For example, *Parkstone v. Coons*,[135] a federal court in Delaware held that the defendant's alleged intrusion into computerized data was not actionable because, every time the plaintiff logged on to the computer, the plaintiff checked a box acknowledging that the computer system could be monitored by his employer.

---

[129] 1998 U.S. Dist. LEXIS 15088 (N.D. Tex. Sept. 23, 1998).

[130] 72 P.3d 897 (Idaho 2003).

[131] RESTATEMENT (SECOND) OF TORTS § 652B (1977).

[132] 1998 U.S. Dist. LEXIS 17906, at *38–*39 (N.D. Tex. Nov. 9, 1998), aff'd, 200 F.3d 815 (5th Cir. 1999).

[133] 929 P.2d 307 (Or. 1996).

[134] 971 P.2d 1135 (Idaho 1998).

[135] 2009 U.S. Dist. LEXIS 33765 (D. Del. Apr. 20, 2009).

Similarly, in *Tagouma v. Investigative Consultant Services, Inc.*,[136] the court held that the plaintiff failed to show that he had an expectation of privacy while praying in public. Therefore, he failed to state a privacy claim against an investigator hired by his employer's workers' compensation carrier, who videotaped him worshiping at an Islamic Center. The Pennsylvania Superior Court explained its reasoning as follows:

> First, Appellant had a diminished expectation of privacy because of his workers' compensation claim. Second, it is undisputed that the Islamic Center was open to the public and Appellant was praying directly in front of a plate glass window. Appellant contends that the act of worship is entitled to a reasonable expectation of privacy because "even though he participated in the worship service with others, he sought to keep the service free from interference of the world[,] and in particular to keep his prayers to his god private to himself" . . . . Such an argument is a red herring. In essence, Appellant asks this Court to create a privacy expectation based on religion, but ignores the fact that he was in public at the time of surveillance. However, merely assigning a purpose to the activity cannot save Appellant's claim for intrusion upon seclusion. For purposes of the tort, Appellant's physical activities and not his thoughts, prayers, or even expressions of prayer were viewed. Witnessing Appellant kneeling in the Al-Hikmeh Institute would be no different than viewing someone kneeling in another public forum. . . .

> In his second issue presented, Appellant argues that Zeigler's use of vision enhanced photographic equipment was impermissible. . . . He contends that the Islamic Center was secluded because: (1) it was set back from Carlisle Pike behind two buildings that partially obstructed it on either side; (2) was located at a much lower elevation than the main road; (3) there was no parking or a sidewalk on Carlisle Pike, thereby limiting pedestrian observers; (4) the speed limit was 40 miles per hour on Carlisle Pike, making it virtually impossible for drivers to get more than a quick glimpse of the Center; (5) all of the surrounding businesses were closed; and (6) the parking lot across the street where Zeigler took photos was 82 yards away. . . . Appellant maintains that "the permissible distance for videotaping [should] be the same distance that the human eye can see" otherwise the privacy standards of the Commonwealth "would be the horrors of George Orwell's novel 1984." . . .

> In this case, it is undisputed that Zeigler was standing at a lawful vantage point in the parking lot across the street from the Islamic Center. His use of a zoom lens, similar to using binoculars, was not unreasonable. Moreover, the Islamic Center was not completely obstructed from the view from the street. Zeiger could have just as easily walked down the public driveway and taken photos from directly outside the window. Further, as the trial court aptly noted:

---

[136] 4 A.3d 170 (Pa. Super. Ct. 2010).

While some individuals might expect a certain level of privacy in a house of worship, the specific intrusion here concerned observation of [Appellant] that any member of the non-trespassing public could have observed simply by driving up to the building in which [Appellant] was located. As such, a reasonable person videotaped under similar circumstances could not have considered such conduct "highly offensive" or have taken "serious offense" to it.

. . . [W]e conclude that Appellant failed to establish his right to privacy, even with Zeigler's use of vision-enhanced photographic equipment. . . .[137]

In *People for the Ethical* Treatment *of Animals v. Bobby Berosini, Ltd.*,[138] the Supreme Court of Nevada found that an animal trainer had no expectation of privacy backstage while preparing animals for a performance. The trainer therefore could not state a privacy claim against a worker who videotaped the trainer striking animals.

In *Remsburg v. Docusearch*, Inc.,[139] the Supreme Court of New Hampshire considered whether a person has a cause of action for intrusion upon seclusion when an investigator obtains the person's work address by placing a pretextual phone call. The court found that "where a person's work address is readily observable by members of the public, the address cannot be private and no intrusion upon seclusion action can be maintained."[140]

Gender-Specific Expectations of Privacy. In *Soliman v. Kushner Companies, Inc.*,[141] the landlord and managers of a commercial building, and others, were sued for invasion of privacy based on cameras installed in two male and two female public bathrooms, ostensibly in response to complaints about vandalism and damage to the facilities. The video monitoring and recording equipment was concealed inside smoke detectors. According to the opinion issued by a New Jersey appellate court:

> Defendants claimed the cameras were positioned to monitor or focus only on the "common area" of the bathrooms, where the washbasins are located . . . [and not] the toilet stalls and therefore did not invade or violate plaintiffs' expectation of privacy.[142]

In holding that the privacy claims were improperly dismissed by the trial court, the appellate court wrote:

> In our view, a rational jury could find that shielding the cameras from detection by placing them inside facially innocuous, yet ubiquitous safety devices, such as smoke detectors, is more suggestive of a sinister voyeuristic purpose than a good faith reasonable attempt at combating vandalism. This plausible conclusion by a jury is further supported by defendants'

---

[137] *Id.* at 176–178

[138] 895 P.2d 1269 (Nev. 1995).

[139] 816 A.2d 1001 (N.H. 2003).

[140] *Id.* at 1009.

[141] 77 A.3d 1214, 1248 (N.J. Super. Ct. App. Div. 2013).

[142] *Id.* at 1218.

decision to disregard the suggestions made by the Fair Lawn Police Department to place a sign on the bathroom doors alerting all who entered that the bathroom's so-called "common areas" were monitored by video cameras.

However, even assuming a good faith motive, a rational jury could find that the approach adopted by defendants here is *per se* unreasonable because: (1) the clandestine nature of the surveillance operation negated the deterrent effect defendants allegedly sought to create; (2) acts of vandalism to bathrooms do not justify the installation of a covert video surveillance system to monitor inherently private areas like bathrooms; (3) although all areas of a bathroom are deemed private, bathrooms intended to be used exclusively by women and girls are inherently more susceptible to invasion of privacy claims. Plaintiffs can present evidence to a jury that women and girls utilize public bathrooms, including areas outside the toilet stalls, with the reasonable expectation that their private grooming activities will only be visible to fellow female users who may be present at the time; and (4) both men and women may have used the so-called quasi-public areas of the bathrooms to perform personal grooming or other private activities when no one else was visibly present that they would have otherwise refrained from performing even in the presence of members of their own gender.[143]

Would *Soliman* have turned out differently if a sign had been posted notifying bathroom users of surveillance? *Lewis v. Dayton Hudson Corp.*[144] turned aside an invasion of privacy claim based on hidden cameras in the fitting room of a store. The Michigan Court of Appeals reasoned that "where, as here, signs are clearly posted notifying customers that they are under surveillance while inside the fitting room of a retail establishment, the 'modicum of privacy' the fitting room appears to afford does not include freedom from overhead observation by a store security guard who is of the same sex as the customer."[145] Is there a legally significant difference between a bathroom and a fitting room?

Information Already Known to Others. *Myrick v. Barron*[146] was a case where the defendant conducted an investigation by asking persons questions about a well-known president *pro tem* of the State Senate. The Alabama Supreme Court held that the inquiries did not amount to intrusion. The investigation resulted only in disclosure of information already known by others, and information that other people know cannot be protected as "private."

Concerns About Remedy Duplication. In deciding how far the scope of liability for intrusion extends, some courts have expressed concerns about duplicating remedies found in other areas of the law. For example, in *Allstate Ins. Co. v. Ginsberg*,[147] the Supreme Court of Florida considered whether touching someone in a sexual manner and making sexually offensive comments could form the basis for

---

[143] *Id.* at 1219–20.

[144] 339 N.W.2d 857 (Mich. Ct. App. 1983).

[145] *Id.* at 861.

[146] 820 So. 2d 81 (Ala. 2001).

[147] 863 So. 2d 156 (Fla. 2003).

an intrusion of privacy action. The court answered that question in the negative, writing:

> The intrusion . . . [must be] into a "place" in which there is a reasonable expectation of privacy and [this] is not referring to a body part. . . . [T]he tort of invasion of privacy was not intended to be duplicative of some other tort. Rather, this is a tort in which the focus is the right of a private person to be free from public gaze.[148]

PROBLEM 4-6: THE NAKED PHOTOS

Jeffrey Smith stayed at the apartment of his friend Jaylan Dunn, while Dunn was out of town. While using Dunn's desktop computer, Smith stumbled onto a file containing naked photographs of Dunn with another person who was also naked.

Smith could not believe what he had found. Smith told the story of his discovery to another friend, Bob Parana, by phone. Parana persuaded Smith to send him a copy of the digital photos as e-mail attachments, which Smith did.

Can Smith or Parana be held liable to Dunn in an action for intrusion?

a.   Privacy in the Workplace

(1)   Example: *Hernandez v. Hillsides, Inc.*

Privacy Expectations Are Not Binary. In *Hernandez v. Hillsides, Inc.*,[149] the California Supreme Court reviewed decisions addressing whether there is a legitimate expectation of privacy in the workplace. The court wrote:

> [W]hile privacy expectations may be significantly diminished in the workplace, they are not lacking altogether. In [*Sanders v. American Broadcasting Companies*, 978 P.2d 67 (Cal. 1999)], a reporter working undercover for a national broadcasting company obtained employment alongside the plaintiff as a telepsychic, giving "readings" to customers over the phone. The reporter then secretly videotaped and recorded interactions with the plaintiff and other psychics using a small camera hidden in her hat and a microphone attached to her brassiere. The taping occurred in a large room containing 100 cubicles that were open on one side and on top, and from which coworkers could be seen and heard nearby. Visitors could not enter this area without permission from the front desk. Ultimately, the plaintiff sued the reporter and the broadcasting company for violating his privacy after one of his secretly taped conversations aired on television. A jury verdict in the plaintiff's favor was reversed on appeal. The appellate court concluded that the plaintiff could not reasonably expect that actions and statements witnessed by coworkers would remain private and not be disclosed to third parties. . . .

---

[148] *Id.* at 162.

[149] 47 Cal. 4th 272 (2009).

. . . [W]e disagreed with the Court of Appeal in *Sanders*, and reversed the judgment. This court emphasized that privacy expectations can be reasonable even if they are not absolute. "[P]rivacy, for purposes of the intrusion tort, is not a binary, all-or-nothing characteristic. There are degrees and nuances to societal recognition of our expectations of privacy: the fact that the privacy one expects in a given setting is not complete or absolute does not render the expectation unreasonable as a matter of law.". . . .[150]

Identity of the Intruder and Nature of the Intrusion as Relevant Factors. The *Hernandez* court then addressed factors bearing upon whether workplace conduct amounts to intrusion on private affairs. The court wrote:

. . . *Sanders* highlighted various factors which, either singly or in combination, affect societal expectations of privacy. One factor was the identity of the intruder. . . . We noted that the plaintiff in that case, and other employees, were deliberately misled into believing that the defendant reporter was a colleague, and had no reason to suspect she worked undercover to secretly tape their interactions for use in a national television program. . . .

Also relevant . . . was the nature of the intrusion . . . meaning . . . both the extent to which the subject interaction could be "seen and overheard" and the "means of intrusion." . . . These factors weighed heavily in the plaintiff's favor: "[T]he possibility of being overheard by coworkers does not, as a matter of law, render unreasonable an employee's expectation that his or her interactions within a nonpublic workplace will not be videotaped in secret by a journalist." . . .[151]

A Spectrum of Expectations. The *Hernandez* court then explained that, in the workplace, there is a wide spectrum of privacy expectations.

At one end of the spectrum are settings in which work or business is conducted in an open and accessible space, within the sight and hearing not only of coworkers and supervisors, but also of customers, visitors, and the general public. (*See Wilkins v. National Broadcasting Co.* (1999) 71 Cal. App. 4th 1066, 1072–73, 1078, 84 Cal. Rptr. 2d 329 [holding for purpose of common law intrusion tort that businessmen lacked privacy in lunch meeting secretly videotaped on crowded outdoor patio of public restaurant]; *see also Acosta v. Scott Labor LLC* (N.D. Ill. 2005) 377 F. Supp. 2d 647, 649, 652 [similar conclusion as to employer secretly videotaped by disgruntled employee in common, open, and exposed area of workplace]; *Melder v. Sears, Roebuck and Co.* (La. Ct. App. 1999) 731 So. 2d 991, 994, 1001 [similar conclusion as to department store employee captured on video cameras used to monitor customers as they shopped].)

At the other end of the spectrum are areas in the workplace subject to restricted access and limited view, and reserved exclusively for performing bodily functions or other inherently personal acts. (*See Trujillo v. City of*

---

[150]　*Id.* at 1074.

[151]　*Id.* at 1074–75.

Ontario (C.D. Cal. 2006) 428 F. Supp. 2d 1094, 1099–1100, 1103, 1119–22 (*Trujillo*) [recognizing that employees have common law and constitutional privacy interests while using locker room in basement of police station, and can reasonably expect that employer will not intrude by secretly videotaping them as they undress]; *see also Doe by Doe v. B.P.S. Guard Services, Inc.* (8th Cir. 1991) 945 F.2d 1422, 1424, 1427 (*Doe*) [similar conclusion as to models who were secretly viewed and videotaped while changing clothes behind curtained area at fashion show]. . . .)

. . . [Other cases fall between the extremes.] (*Cf. Sacramento County Deputy Sheriffs' Assn. v. County of Sacramento* (1996) 51 Cal. App. 4th 1468, 1482, 1487, 59 Cal. Rptr. 2d 834 [rejecting common law intrusion claim of jail employee secretly videotaped while handling inmate property based on accessibility of his office to others and heightened security concerns inherent in custodial setting]; *see also Marrs v. Marriott Corp.* (D. Md. 1992) 830 F. Supp. 274, 283 [similar conclusion as to security guard secretly videotaped while breaking into colleague's locked desk in open office used as common area by entire staff].)[152]

b.   Privacy in Marriage

(1)   Example: *In re Marriage of Tigges*

In re Marriage of Tigges[153] was an intrusion action by a wife against a husband relating to surreptitious videotaping in their marital bedroom. The claim was asserted in answer to her husband's petition for dissolution of the marriage. A key issue in the case was whether the wife had a legitimate expectation of privacy vis-a-vis her husband. Explaining the factual background of the dispute, the Supreme Court of Iowa wrote:

> Jeffrey surreptitiously installed recording equipment and recorded Cathy's activities during the marriage in the marital home. The equipment included a video cassette recorder positioned above a ceiling, a camera concealed in an alarm clock located in the bedroom regularly used by Cathy, and a motion sensing "optical eye" installed in the headboard of the bed in that room. Cathy discovered her activities in the bedroom had been recorded when she observed Jeffrey retrieving a cassette from the recorder. . . .

> . . . When she viewed the tape, Cathy discovered it revealed nothing of a graphic or demeaning nature. . . . [I]t recorded the "comings and goings" from the bedroom she regularly used. Notwithstanding the unremarkable activities recorded on the tape, Cathy suffered damage as a consequence of Jeffrey's actions. She felt violated, fearing Jeffrey had placed, or would place, other hidden cameras in the house.[154]

---

[152] *Id.* at 1075.

[153] 758 N.W.2d 824 (Iowa 2008).

[154] *Id.* at 825–26.

Expectations of Privacy During a Marriage. The *Tigges* court then addressed the issue of whether the plaintiff had a legitimate expectation of privacy:

> In *Miller v. Brooks*, 472 S.E.2d 350 (N.C. App. 1996), a wife hired private investigators to install a hidden camera in the bedroom of her estranged husband's separate residence. . . . The husband discovered the hidden equipment and sued both his wife and her agents who assisted her in its installation. . . . [T]he North Carolina Court of Appeals noted the expectation of privacy "might, in some cases, be less for married persons than for single persons," but that "such is not the case . . . where the spouses were estranged and living separately.". . . . [T]he appellate court reversed the summary judgment [which had been granted to the defendants], concluding issues of fact remained for trial in the husband's claims against his wife and her agents. . . .
>
> . . . [I]n the case before this court the record is unclear whether Jeffrey installed the equipment and accomplished the recording of Cathy's activities before or after the parties separated. . . . Whether or not Jeffrey and Cathy were residing together in the dwelling at the time, we conclude Cathy had a reasonable expectation that her activities in the bedroom of the home were private when she was alone in that room. Cathy's expectation of privacy at such times is not rendered unreasonable by the fact Jeffrey was her spouse at the time in question, or by the fact that Jeffrey may have been living in the dwelling at that time.[155]

The Right of Privacy Is Not Limited to Unmarried Individuals. The Iowa Supreme Court found that its conclusion in *Tigges* was consistent with the decision of the Texas Court of Appeals in *Clayton v. Richards*,[156] a case where Mrs. Clayton hired Richards to install video equipment in the bedroom shared by Mrs. Clayton and her husband. In a privacy action against the wife and installer, the *Clayton* court wrote:

> A spouse shares equal rights in the privacy of the bedroom, and the other spouse relinquishes some of his or her rights to seclusion, solitude, and privacy by entering into marriage, by sharing a bedroom with a spouse, and by entering into ownership of the home with a spouse. *However, nothing in the . . . common law suggests that the right to privacy is limited to unmarried individuals.*
>
> *When a person goes into the privacy of the bedroom, he or she has a right to the expectation of privacy in his or her seclusion. A video recording surreptitiously made in that place of privacy at a time when the individual believes that he or she is in a state of complete privacy could be highly offensive to the ordinary reasonable person.* The video recording of a person without consent in the privacy of his or her bedroom *even when done by the other spouse* could be found to violate his or her rights of privacy.

---

[155] *Id.* at 826–27.

[156] 47 S.W.3d 149 (Tex. App. 2001).

As a spouse with equal rights to the use and access of the bedroom, it would not be illegal or tortious as an invasion of privacy for a spouse to open the door of the bedroom and view a spouse in bed. It could be argued that a spouse did no more than that by setting up a video camera. . . . It is not generally the role of the courts to supervise privacy between spouses in a mutually shared bedroom. *However, the videotaping of a person without consent or awareness when there is an expectation of privacy goes beyond the rights of a spouse because it may record private matters, which could later be exposed to the public eye. The fact that no later exposure occurs does not negate that potential and permit willful intrusion by such technological means into one's personal life in one's bedroom.*[157]

Offensiveness Does Not Depend on Videotaped Content. Finding *Miller* and *Clayton* persuasive, the Iowa high court concluded that "Cathy did not forfeit through marriage her expectation of privacy as to her activities when she was alone in the bedroom." Affirming an award of damages to Cathy, the court disposed of a remaining argument:

Jeffrey contends the judgment in favor of Cathy must be reversed because the videotaping captured nothing that would be viewed as highly offensive to a reasonable person. He emphasizes the videotape captured nothing of a "private" or "sexual" nature in the bedroom. This contention is without merit, however, because the content of the videotape is not determinative of the question of whether Jeffrey tortiously invaded Cathy's privacy. . . . The intentional, intrusive, and wrongful nature of Jeffrey's conduct is not excused by the fact that the surreptitious taping recorded no scurrilous or compromising behavior. The wrongfulness of the conduct springs not from the specific nature of the recorded activities, but instead from the fact that Cathy's activities were recorded without her knowledge and consent at a time and place and under circumstances in which she had a reasonable expectation of privacy.[158]

3.   Highly Offensive to a Reasonable Person

A privacy action for intrusion, like one for disclosure, will lie only for an invasion that would be highly offensive to a reasonable person. In *Alderson v. Bonner*,[159] the Idaho Court of Appeals permitted recovery because even though "standing on another's front porch and looking through a window in the door is not normally offensive," "[w]hen an uninvited man lurks at the front door at night, peering in the window at a young female, with video camera in hand and without announcing his presence, such conduct is objectionable."[160]

---

[157] *Id.* at 827–28 (italics inserted by *Tigges*).

[158] *Id.* at 829–30.

[159] 132 P.3d 1261 (Idaho App. 2006).

[160] *Id.* at 1267.

In *Pendleton v. Fassett*,[161] a federal court in Kentucky allowed an intrusion claim to go to trial because there was a factual dispute over whether the search of a student for drugs rose to the level of being highly offensive. According to one version of the evidence, the student was made to bare her breasts during the search.

In contrast, in *Denton v. Chittenden Bank*,[162] the Supreme Court of Vermont held that a supervisor did not commit an invasion of privacy when he came to an employee's home during a birthday party for the employee's daughter. After arriving uninvited, the supervisor asked questions, which were overheard by the employee's family and friends, about the employee's physical condition, his doctor, whether he was taking medication, and when he would be coming back to work. Although the questions were unusual and possibly rude, they would not be highly offensive to a reasonable person.

PROBLEM 4-7: THE OFFICE WITH THE HIDDEN CAMERA

Our Lady of Sorrows is a large church that operates an elementary school which enrolls more than a thousand students. Until recently, Alina Antonescu was employed at the school. She had a small enclosed office where she performed clerical work during business hours. The office had two windows on exterior walls. Blinds on the windows could be opened and closed. The office also had a door that could be locked. Several persons, besides Antonescu, had keys to the office, including at least five administrators, plus custodial staff persons.

John Hikock, the principal of the school, learned from a log produced by the school's computer center that late at night, after Antonescu had left the premises, an unknown person often used a computer in her office to access the Internet and view pornographic websites. Those activities conflicted with church policy and with the school's goal of providing a wholesome learning environment for children.

Concerned that the culprit might be a staff member who worked with the children, Hikock set up a hidden camera in Antonescu's office, without notifying her. The camera could be operated from a remote location, at any time of day or night, to permit either live or recorded viewing of activities at the targeted workstation.

It is undisputed that the camera was not operated for either of these purposes during business hours. As a consequence, plaintiffs' activities in the office were never viewed or recorded by means of the surveillance system.

Before it was discovered, the camera was operated intermittently over a three-week period. The camera was discovered because a red light on the motion detector flashed and Antonescu saw it. The cord attached to the camera was plugged into an electrical outlet and was warm to the touch. Shocked by the discovery, Antonescu immediately reported the matter to two supervisors. The camera was promptly removed.

---

[161] 2009 U.S. Dist. LEXIS 78322 (W.D. Ky. Sept. 1, 2009).

[162] 163 Vt. 62, 655 A.2d 703 (1994).

Antonescu was distressed, in part, because she used her office to change clothes before and after she went out to run at lunch. Antonescu has quit her job at the school because she is unwilling to work at a place that monitors employees with hidden cameras. She has asked you to advise her about whether she can successfully sue the church (as operator of the school) for invasion of privacy. Please prepare to brief her about the legal issues that will arise in such a case.

4.   Damages

The general rule in American law is that a plaintiff must always prove that the defendant's tortious conduct caused damage. Exceptions to this principle are rare. Thus, it was not surprising that in *LaMartiniere v. Allstate Ins. Co.*[163] the Louisiana Court of Appeal held that peeping over a wall to see furniture that had been stored by suspected arsonists was not an actionable invasion of privacy because it caused no damage. However, some cases have held that an award of nominal damages is available in intrusion cases not resulting in actual loss.[164]

5.   Special Issues

a.   First Amendment Considerations

News Gathering as a Defense. Intrusion cases rarely raise First Amendment concerns because the tort usually does not involve speech or press. However, in *Miller v. NBC*,[165] a television news crew entered an apartment to film the activities of paramedics called to rescue a man who had suffered a fatal heart attack. The film was used on the nightly news without anyone's consent. In finding that the widow had stated claims for trespass, intrusion, and outrage, the California Court of Appeal rejected NBC's argument that liability was precluded by its constitutional right to gather news. It found that "the obligation not to make unauthorized entry into the private premises of individuals . . . does not place an impermissible burden on newsgatherers, nor is it likely to have a chilling effect on the exercise of First Amendment rights."[166]

The California Supreme Court followed *Miller* in *Shulman v. Group W Productions Co.*[167] The court allowed the plaintiff to get to a jury on an *intrusion* claim against the employer of a television cameraman who had videotaped conversations between the plaintiff and a nurse while on board a rescue helicopter that was taking the plaintiff to a hospital after an accident. In contrast, the court held that the plaintiff's claim for *disclosure of private facts* failed because the facts were newsworthy.

---

[163] 597 So. 2d 1158 (La. Ct. App. 1992).

[164] *See Sabrina W. v. Willman*, 540 N.W.2d 364 (Neb. Ct. App. 1995).

[165] 187 Cal. App. 3d 1463 (1986).

[166] *Id.* at 685.

[167] 955 P.2d 469 (Cal. 1998).

b.   Consent

An intrusion action is barred by consent. This is often true even if the plaintiff felt morally or economically coerced into giving consent.

In *Harbolt v. Steel of West Virginia, Inc.*,[168] a worker whose pockets, locker, and car were searched for drugs sued for intrusion upon his private affairs. A federal court in West Virginia wrote:

> [O]ne of Plaintiff's co-workers reported to Defendant management that he had purchased pain pills from Plaintiff while on company property. The co-worker supported these allegations with a signed written statement and, later, a sworn, notarized affidavit. His allegations were specific in regards to the price paid for the pills and reasonably specific in regards to the number of pills purchased. . . .

> . . . Plaintiff acknowledged that he was "[n]ot physically" forced to empty his pockets, that he was "the one that emptied [his] pockets[,]" and that "[t]hey didn't reach into [his] pockets.". . . . He agreed that he never told Mr. McMellon or Mr. Artrip that he refused to empty his pockets. He also agreed that he emptied his pockets, at least in part, because he "wanted to show them that [he] had nothing to hide." . . .

> . . . At his deposition, Plaintiff acknowledged that he "consent[ed] to the search of [his] locker," stating, "I was fine with that.". . . . Like the search of Plaintiff's pockets, the search of his locker revealed no drugs.

> Mr. McMellon and Mr. Artrip then told Plaintiff that "they wanted to go to [his] vehicle.". . . . Plaintiff replied, "No . . . I don't want you all in my vehicle," but Mr. McMellon insisted: "Yeah, we are going to get in your vehicle, . . . because it is on our property." . . . At that point, Plaintiff stated, "If you're looking for my prescriptions that the company doctor gave me yesterday, they're in my arm console thing. . . . I'll get it.". . . . While Plaintiff was retrieving the drugs, Mr. McMellon apparently searched Plaintiff's trunk, and he may have opened Plaintiff's back door. However, the only drugs recovered were those Plaintiff got from his console.

> . . . While Plaintiff maintains he did not give his consent because he felt he "really had no choice," what Plaintiff really alleges here is that he faced a choice between two undesirable options. . . . Although Plaintiff may have been terminated, he could have refused to consent to the search, notwithstanding his assertions to the contrary.

> To the extent that Mr. McMellon searched Plaintiff's vehicle, it appears that Plaintiff did not consent. However, Mr. McMellon's acts were wholly unlike, for example, a person entering the residence of another over that person's objections. . . . Plaintiff had been accused of selling drugs on company property. His car was parked on company property. The investigation was not into his "private affairs or concerns," but rather dealt with an issue

---

[168] 2009 U.S. Dist. LEXIS 63131 (S.D.W. Va. July 6, 2009).

closely linked to workplace safety. . . . The search of Plaintiff's car under these circumstances, even without his consent, would not "be highly offensive to a reasonable person." . . . For these reasons, summary judgment should be granted.[169]

c.   Proximate Causation

Some intrusion cases raise important issues relating to causation. For example, in *Leang v. Jersey City Board of Education*,[170] one teacher (Leang) told another (Ashworth) either that "my doctor said the amount of stress in my body could have killed some people" or "I'm so stressed out that I can kill twenty-two people."[171] Based on whatever statement was made, Ashworth reported Leang to school administrators as being a threat to the safety of the school children. The police came, and Leang was taken to the hospital and examined. In discussing the intrusion claim that arose from these events, the Supreme Court of New Jersey wrote:

> Plaintiff's invasion of privacy claim is based on two specific events, which she has referred to as the "strip search," by which she means the physical examination conducted by the hospital doctors, and the psychiatric evaluation she underwent. The claim therefore must be analyzed within the parameters of the tort of intrusion on seclusion. . . .
>
> . . . In order to recover on either version of this tort, plaintiff must first demonstrate that the physical and psychiatric examination at the hospital was "highly offensive to a reasonable person." However, because both of these examinations took place at the hospital and at the direction of hospital personnel, plaintiff can only recover if she can prove a causal link between them and defendants' actions. . . .
>
> Generously read, plaintiff's invasion of privacy claim rests on her assertion that Ashworth, seeking revenge [for her having spurned his unwanted advances], intentionally and falsely reported that plaintiff had uttered a threat, with the . . . intent that she would be taken to the hospital and subjected to examinations that would be highly offensive to an ordinary person, and that his false report caused those events to occur. As to Bruno [the school principal], plaintiff's invasion of privacy claim must rest on the assertion that she shared or joined in Ashworth's plan . . . knowing that his claim about the threat was false.
>
> Our careful review of the record convinces us that plaintiff simply cannot meet these proof requirements as to Bruno, because there is no evidence that Bruno acted with the requisite intent or that she thought that the report of a threat was false. Although the question is a closer one as to Ashworth, there is evidence that he did not accurately report what plaintiff said and that he would have been aware that under . . . [the "Uniform

---

[169] *Id.* at *39–*44.

[170] 969 A.2d 1097 (N.J. 2009).

[171] *Id.* at 1104.

State Memorandum of Agreement Between Education and Law Enforcement Officials"] his report would trigger a call to the police or a mental
health evaluation. We find in those assertions the bare minimum needed for
plaintiff to be able to proceed on her claim against Ashworth for invasion of
privacy.

We caution the trial court . . . [that] in order to succeed on this claim,
plaintiff will be required to demonstrate that Ashworth's report was not
simply inaccurate, but that he knew it to be false and willfully reported it
as true. Moreover, plaintiff will also be required to prove that the medical
and psychiatric examinations were "highly offensive to a reasonable
person" and that Ashworth, rather than the police or EMTs, was the
proximate cause of those two discrete events on which her invasion of
privacy claim is based.[172]

d.   Statutory Actions

Anti-Recording Laws. Some jurisdictions have special statutes that address
particular types of invasion of privacy. For example, in *Dillon v. Seattle Deposition
Reporters, LLC,*[173] a Washington appellate court explained:

Washington's privacy act provides, in relevant part:

   (1)   Except as otherwise provided in this chapter, it shall be unlawful
for any individual, partnership, corporation, association, or the
state of Washington, its agencies, and political subdivisions to
intercept, or record any:

     (a)   Private communication transmitted by telephone, telegraph,
radio, or other device between two or more individuals between
points within or without the state by any device electronic or
otherwise designed to record and/or transmit said communication regardless how such device is powered or actuated, without
first obtaining the consent of all the participants in the communication;

     (b)   Private conversation, by any device electronic or otherwise
designed to record or transmit such conversation regardless how
the device is powered or actuated without first obtaining the
consent of all the persons engaged in the conversation.

RCW 9.73.030(1). Violation of the privacy act is a gross misdemeanor, and
is also actionable in tort. . . . There must be proof of, "(1) a private
communication transmitted by a device, which was (2) intercepted by use of
(3) a device designed to record and/or transmit, (4) without the consent of
all parties to the private communication." . . . [174]

The *Dillon* court held that there were triable questions of fact as to whether a

---

[172] *Id.* at 1116–17.

[173] 316 P.3d 1119 (Wash. Ct. App. 2014).

[174] *Id.* at 1127–28.

corporate officer of an entity involved in litigation reasonably believed that his conversations with lawyers for the opposing party were private. The court further held that a tort action under the state privacy act was not barred by the state SLAPP statute.[175] The opinion of the court stated:

> Washington's anti-SLAPP statute protects persons who engage in "action[s] involving public participation and petition" from having to defend against a claim based on those actions. The recording of telephone conversations is not such an action. This is so even when such recording is designed to gather evidence for a lawsuit between private parties. The anti-SLAPP statute does not operate to transform unprotected activity into protected activity simply because it is undertaken during the course of a lawsuit.[176]

Problem 4-8: The Salesman at the Physical Exam

Amalia Kovar was a patient of Federico Silliman, an oncologist. Dr. Silliman allowed Bob Rattini, a medical device salesperson, who had once failed out of medical school, to be present in the room during his physical examination of Kovar. As part of the examination, Kovar was required to undress.

Dr. Silliman did not disclose to Kovar the fact that Rattini was a salesman. Nor did Kovar inquire into Rattini's status. If all of these facts are true, can Kovar state a claim against Rattini or Kovar for intrusion upon private affairs?

D.   FALSE LIGHT

Elements. According to the *Restatement* section entitled "Publicity Placing Person in False Light":

> One who gives publicity to a matter concerning another that places the other before the public in a false light is subject to liability to the other for invasion of his privacy, if
>
> (a) the false light in which the other was placed would be highly offensive to a reasonable person, and
>
> (b) the actor had knowledge of or acted in reckless disregard as to the falsity of the publicized matter and the false light in which the other would be placed.[177]

False Position. Various sources have explained the relationship between libel and slander, on the one hand, and false light invasion of privacy, on the other:

> The interest protected by this Section is the interest of the individual in not being made to appear before the public in an objectionable false light or

---

[175] SLAPP laws (dealing with Strategic Lawsuits Against Public Participation) are discussed in Chapter 3, Part I-7.

[176] *Id.* at 1123.

[177] *Roe v. Heap*, 2004 Ohio App. LEXIS 2093, at *62–*63 (May 11, 2004) (quoting *Restatement (Second) of Torts* § 652E cmt. b (1977)).

false position, or in other words, otherwise than as he is. In many cases to which the rule stated here applies, the publicity given to the plaintiff is defamatory, so that he would have an action for libel or slander . . . In such a case the action for invasion of privacy will afford an alternative or additional remedy, and the plaintiff can proceed upon either theory, or both, although he can have but one recovery for a single instance of publicity.

It is not, however, necessary to the action for invasion of privacy that the plaintiff be defamed. It is enough that he is given unreasonable and highly objectionable publicity that attributes to him characteristics, conduct or beliefs that are false, and so is placed before the public in a false position. When this is the case and the matter attributed to the plaintiff is not defamatory, the rule here stated affords a different remedy, not available in an action for defamation.[178]

Statements Found to Be Actionable. In *Kolegas v. Heftel Broadcasting Corp.*,[179] the Supreme Court of Illinois held that a complaint stated a claim for false light. The defendants allegedly said that the plaintiff and his wife must have been married in a "shotgun wedding," which they were not, and that the plaintiff's wife and child had abnormally large heads as a result of Elephant Man's disease, although their heads were not of abnormal size.

In *Duncan v. Peterson*,[180] a minister (Duncan) and the church for which he was the pastor (Hope Church) "alleged that defendants invaded Duncan's privacy by sending false and misleading letters stating that Duncan could no longer act as a minister and could no longer accept the title of 'Reverend,' 'Pastor,' or any other title that would imply that Duncan had credentials for spiritual leadership and ministry."[181] The Appellate Court of Illinois found that Duncan stated a cause of action for false light, but that the church had no right to sue because the allegations related to Duncan.[182] The court found that the pastor's claims were not barred by the doctrine of ecclesiastical abstention because they could be resolved without inquiry into religious principles since the defendants "agreed that defendants did not have the authority to decide who could minister for Hope Church and that only the leadership of Hope Church had the authority to decide who could be a minister or a pastor for their church."[183]

Corporations May Not Sue for False Light or Other Invasions of Privacy. Many cases have held that corporations cannot sue for false light invasion of privacy. In *Oberweis Dairy, Inc. v. Democratic Congressional Campaign Committee, Inc.*,[184] a false light claim was based on statements in a political ad indicating that

---

[178] *Id.*

[179] 607 N.E.2d 201 (Ill. 1992).

[180] 835 N.E.2d 411 (Ill. App. Ct. 2005).

[181] *Id.* at 414.

[182] *Id.* at 419.

[183] *Id.* at 423.

[184] 2009 U.S. Dist. LEXIS 18514 (N.D. Ill. Mar. 11, 2009).

"illegal immigrants were found working at the plaintiff's dairy stores."[185] The defendant moved to dismiss on the ground that the corporation lacked standing. In granting the motion, a federal court in Illinois wrote:

> [A]lthough Defendant has not pointed to any Illinois case that expressly holds that corporations lack standing to sue for false light, neither has Plaintiff cited *any* cases holding that corporations do have standing to sue for false light.
>
> The single case Plaintiff cites in support of its position, *Pullman Standard Car Mfg. Co. v. Local Union No. 2928 of United Steelworkers of America*, 152 F.2d 493 (7th Cir. 1945), is a libel case recognizing that a corporation's business reputation is protected by law. But the tort of false light invasion of privacy does not protect a party's reputation; it protects an individual's personal privacy interest to be free from false publicity. . . . Corporations do not have such a privacy interest. . . .
>
> . . . The *Restatement* has long recognized that corporations do not have standing to sue for false light. *Restatement (Second) of Torts* § 652I and cmt. c (1977) ("A corporation . . . has no personal right of privacy. It has therefore no cause of action for any of the four forms of invasion covered by §§ 652B to 652E."). . . . Even in jurisdictions not relying on the *Restatement*, courts have found that corporations lack standing to sue for privacy torts, including false light. . . .
>
> The Court finds that . . . the Supreme Court of Illinois would hold that Plaintiff has failed to state a claim under Illinois law.[186]

Similar issues arise under federal law. In *FCC v. AT&T Inc.*,[187] Chief Justice John Roberts explained:

> The Freedom of Information Act requires federal agencies to make records and documents publicly available upon request, unless they fall within one of several statutory exemptions. One of those exemptions covers law enforcement records, the disclosure of which "could reasonably be expected to constitute an unwarranted invasion of personal privacy." 5 U.S.C. § 552(b)(7)(C). The question presented is whether corporations have "personal privacy" for the purposes of this exemption.[188]

The Chief Justice's opinion for a unanimous court concluded that the "protection in [the] FOIA against disclosure of law enforcement information on the ground that it would constitute an unwarranted invasion of personal privacy does not extend to corporations."[189] The opinion quipped, "[w]e trust that AT&T will not take it personally."[190]

---

[185] *Id.* at *1.

[186] *Id.* at *3–*5 (emphasis in original).

[187] 131 S. Ct. 1177 (2011).

[188] *Id.* at 1180.

[189] *Id.* at 1185.

[190] *Id.*

1.   Defamation Distinguished

Because of the potential overlap of false light and defamation, many persons have questioned the necessity for this form of privacy action. This is particularly true in that doctrinal and procedural limits crafted for libel and slander claims (such as the requirement of a provably false assertion of fact[191]) are typically applied to false light suits.

Falsity Not Involving Disgrace. Some statements that cast one in a false light may be highly offensive, yet do not carry with them the sting of disgrace that is essential to defamation. The classic example is an inferior poem, article, or book attributed to a famous author. The author may be highly offended by the misrepresentation, even though the work is not so bad as to subject the author to the hatred, scorn, or ridicule that is the gist of a defamation action.

In *Patterson v. Grant-Herms*,[192] the Tennessee Court of Appeals explained the nature of the dispute before it as follows:

> . . . [An operations] agent employed by Southwest Airlines brought an action against a passenger for posting allegedly false and defamatory statements on Twitter and Facebook regarding actions taken by the agent when the passenger attempted to board a flight. The trial court granted the passenger's motion for summary judgment, holding that the statements did not rise to the level of defamation, that the language could not be construed to hold the agent up to public ridicule, and that the language was not highly offensive to a reasonable person. We affirm the grant of summary judgment on the defamation claim and reverse the grant of summary judgment on the claim for invasion of privacy; we remand the case for further proceedings.[193]

Explaining its decision, the court wrote:

> . . . Ms. Grant–Herms argues that the words are not offensive because "[t]he appellant works for an airline. As this court is surely aware, airlines are notorious for bad customer service. The statements that were made by the appellee in this case are not only not highly offensive, they are sentiments that have likely been uttered by airline passengers for decades." This argument, however, does not address the threshold question of whether the statements themselves put Ms. Patterson in a false light; that is, was there such a "major misrepresentation of [her] activities that serious offense may reasonably be expected to be taken." . . .
>
> The materials filed by Ms. Grant–Herms did not specifically address the elements of the false light invasion of privacy claim. To the extent she relied upon the words themselves to negate the "highly offensive to a reasonable person element" of the claim, construing the words in a light most favorable to Ms. Patterson and affording her all reasonable inferences, we believe

---

[191] *See, e.g., State v. Carpenter*, 171 P.3d 41, 53 (Alaska 2007).

[192] 2013 Tenn. App. LEXIS 675 (Oct. 8, 2013).

[193] *Id.* at *1–*2.

that a reasonable person could find, under the entire circumstances of the incident, that Ms. Grant–Herms' posting of selective facts placed Ms. Patterson in a false light by implying that Ms. Patterson was rude and a bad service agent, one who was more concerned with adherence to the airline rules and procedures than the welfare of the child, and that these implications caused injury to her. Considering the record, Ms. Grant–Herms has not shown she is entitled to summary judgment on the false light invasion of privacy claim.[194]

In *Douglass v. Hustler Magazine*,[195] photographs of an actress who had posed nude for Playboy were published in Hustler without her consent. In finding that the actress stated a claim for false light invasion of privacy, Judge Richard Posner wrote for the Seventh Circuit:

> We cannot say that it would be irrational for a jury to find that in the highly permissive moral and cultural climate prevailing in late twentieth-century America, posing nude for Playboy is consistent with respectability for a model and actress but that posing nude in Hustler is not (not yet, anyway), so that to portray Robyn Douglass as voluntarily posing nude for Hustler could be thought to place her in a false light even though she had voluntarily posed nude for Playboy.[196]

Addressing the differences between defamation and false light, the court explained:

> Part of Douglass's claim is that Hustler insinuated that she is a lesbian; and such a claim could of course be the basis for an action for defamation. But the rest of her claim fits more comfortably into the category of offensive rather than defamatory publicity. The difference is illustrated by *Time, Inc. v. Hill*, . . . [385 U.S. 374 (1967)]. Life magazine had presented as true a fictionalized account of the ordeal of a family held hostage by escaped convicts. The members of the family were shown being subjected to various indignities that had not actually occurred. The article did not defame the family members in the sense of accusing them of immoral, improper, or other bad conduct, and yet many people would be upset to think that the whole world thought them victims of such mistreatment. The false-light tort, to the extent distinct from the tort of defamation . . . , rests on an awareness that people who are made to seem pathetic or ridiculous may be shunned, and not just people who are thought to be dishonest or incompetent or immoral. . . .

> The question whether [plaintiff] . . . was also being depicted in a degrading association with Hustler invites attention to the difference between libel and false light. It would have been difficult for Douglass to state this claim as one for libel. For what exactly is the imputation of saying (or here, implying) of a person that she agreed to have pictures of herself appear in a vulgar and offensive magazine? That she is immoral? This would be too

---

[194] *Id.* at *12–*16.

[195] 769 F.2d 1128 (7th Cir. 1985).

[196] *Id.* at 1137.

strong a characterization in today's moral climate. That she lacks good
taste? This would not be defamatory. . . . The point is, rather, that to be
shown nude in such a setting before millions of people — the readers of the
magazine — is degrading in much the same way that to be shown beaten up
by criminals is degrading. . . .[197]

a.   Judicial Reluctance to Recognize False Light

A number of states have rejected actions for false light. For example, in
Bilodeau-Allen v. American Media, Inc.,[198] a federal court in Massachusetts
declined to recognize an action for false light in a suit based on an article that said
that a woman's child was the illegitimate son of a U.S. senator.

Concerns About Usefulness. In *Jews For Jesus, Inc. v. Rapp*,[199] an article
stated that a woman, who was Jewish, had accepted Christian beliefs. In refusing
to recognize an action for false light, the Florida Supreme Court wrote:

> Although we acknowledge that a majority of the states have recognized the
> false light cause of action, we are struck by the fact that our review of these
> decisions has revealed no case, nor has one been pointed out to us, in which
> a judgment based solely on a false light cause of action was upheld. . . .
>
> . . . [R]ecognizing the tort would apparently not open the proverbial
> floodgates to false light claims. Yet, the fact that we can find no judgment
> that has been upheld by an appellate court solely on the basis of false light
> leads us to conclude that the absence of false light does not create any
> significant void in the law.[200]

The *Rapp* court further held that a statement is actionable as defamation if a
"substantial and respectable minority" of the community would regard it as
defamatory. The court expressed no opinion about the facts before it and remanded
the case for further proceedings. On remand, the district court of appeal found that
Rapp stated a claim for defamation.[201]

Concerns About Procedural Safeguards. In *Cain v. Hearst Corp.*, the Texas
Supreme Court refused to recognize false light invasion of privacy because
defamation encompasses most false light claims and false light "lacks many of the
procedural limitations that accompany actions for defamation, thus unacceptably
increasing the tension that already exists between free speech constitutional
guarantees and tort law."[202] The court rejected the solution of some jurisdictions —
application of the defamation restrictions to false light — because any benefit to
protecting nondefamatory false speech was outweighed by the chilling effect on free
speech.

---

[197] *Id.* at 1133–35.

[198] 549 F. Supp. 2d 129 (D. Mass. 2008).

[199] 997 So. 2d 1098 (Fla. 2008).

[200] *Id.* at 1113.

[201] 1 So. 3d 1284 (Fla. Dist. Ct. App. 2009).

[202] 878 S.W.2d 577 (Tex. 1994).

Recognition of Only Nondefamatory False Light. Georgia, like Missouri,[203] recognizes false light only to the extent that the action does not overlap with defamation. For example, in *Smith v. Stewart*,[204] an author was sued by a former longtime friend based on an unflattering portrayal of a character in a novel, which was allegedly patterned on the facts of the former friend's life. The Georgia Court of Appeals wrote:

> Stewart's false light claim is based upon Smith's description of SuSu (and, consequently, her) as an "atheist and right wing reactionary who engages in frequent, tawdry sex and drinks to alcoholic excess." According to Stewart's complaint, she is not an atheist, right-wing reactionary, or promiscuous alcoholic. . . . In order to survive as a separate cause of action, "a false light claim must allege a nondefamatory statement. If the statements alleged are defamatory, the claim would be for defamation only, not false light invasion of privacy." . . .
>
> Having reviewed Stewart's claims, we conclude that her false light invasion of privacy claim is encompassed by her defamation claim, which is based upon the same allegations. . . . Therefore, the trial court is directed to grant summary judgment to the defendants on this claim upon remand.[205]

Statutory Omission of False Light. "Virginia, New York, and Wisconsin [have] refused to recognize the common law tort of false light because their state legislatures adopted privacy statutes that do not expressly include the tort."[206]

Recent Recognition of False Light. Some recent decisions have bucked whatever trend there is against false light. Thus, in *Welling v. Weinfeld*,[207] the Supreme Court of Ohio recognized the viability of the false light action in a case based on distribution of handbills that suggested that the neighbors' son might have thrown a rock through a window.

PROBLEM 4-9: THE TEENAGE RIFT

Bryer Medvedik, a high school sophomore, is gay. After he told that fact to his friends and parents (Peter and Adela Medvedik), some tensions began to develop in his relationships at school.

Bryer had a big argument in the school cafeteria with his longtime friend, Evelyn Swartz. Evelyn was raised very conservatively by her parents, Harry and Rose Swartz. In Evelyn's view, being "gay" was simply an immoral, totally unacceptable, choice.

Bryer and Evelyn had been part of the same circle of friends. However, when the rift between them developed, the group split up. Most of their friends sided with Bryer, and Evelyn was left pretty much out in the cold.

---

[203] *See Cockram v. Genesco, Inc.*, 680 F.3d 1046, 1056–57 (8th Cir. 2012).

[204] 660 S.E.2d 822 (Ga. Ct. App. 2008).

[205] *Id.* at 834.

[206] *West v. Media General Convergence, Inc.*, 53 S.W.3d 640 (Tenn. 2001).

[207] 866 N.E.2d 1051 (Ohio 2007).

The consequences of the break-up played out every day at school and every night at the Swartz home. Evelyn reported to her mother, blow by blow, every real or perceived way in which she had been slighted by Bryer or his friends.

Rose Swartz is not a woman to stand by quietly if her daughter is being mistreated. Rose went to the high school on several occasions to complain to school administrators about how her daughter was being victimized by obscene gestures, foul language, and even threats. Rose demanded that the school suspend Bryer. In pleading her daughter's case, Rose made several derogatory statements about Bryer's sexual orientation, and seemed to be obsessed with the issue. School administrators conducted several investigations into numerous allegations of misconduct, particularly the charge that Bryer had threatened Evelyn with a gun. The administrators found nothing to corroborate any of the charges.

One of the complaints that Rose made was that Bryer had brought pornographic pictures to school and showed them to other students. The school administrators determined that there was no pornography. Bryer had simply shown a few friends pictures of him and two guys taken at a gay dance. There was nothing obscene about the contents of the photos. Not surprisingly, Rose and her daughter Evelyn had never actually seen the pictures.

When school administrators failed to take the steps that Rose demanded to suspend Bryer from school, Rose went to the police. In person at the police department, she informed police officers that Bryer was distributing pornography at the high school and had threatened her daughter with a gun. The police conducted a full investigation, interviewing students and administrators at the high school. The officers found no evidence whatsoever to corroborate Rose's charges.

On these facts, can Bryer Medvedik successfully state a claim against Rose Swartz for false light invasion of privacy?

2.   Constitutional Limitations

Because of the duplicative coverage of actions for defamation and false light, it is reasonable to ask whether the constitutional limitations that have shaped the law of defamation also apply to false light. If that is not true, it might be possible to circumvent such restrictions by suing for false light, rather than libel or slander. Not surprisingly, the courts have been loath to permit such manipulation when First Amendment interests are at stake. Nevertheless, there are still some unanswered questions.

a.   Actual Malice or Other Fault

An Issue Unresolved by the Supreme Court. It is still not clear what degree of fault must, *as a matter of constitutional law*, be proved in a false light action.

Time, Inc. v. Hill,[208] decided in 1967, was the case involving a magazine article about a play. The play was based on a crime in which the plaintiffs had been taken hostage for nineteen hours. Although the ordeal ended peacefully, the plaintiffs

---

[208] 385 U.S. 374 (1967).

were depicted as having been subjected to violent and brutal treatment. Noting the differences between false light and defamation, the United States Supreme Court held that both theories required proof of actual malice.

The *Time* decision was reaffirmed by the Supreme Court in 1974 in *Cantrell v. Forest City Publishing Co.*[209] In *Cantrell*, the survivors of a man killed in the Silver Bridge disaster were portrayed as impoverished, and his widow was described as continually wearing a "mask of non-expression." The Supreme Court held that there was adequate evidence of actual malice to support the false light claim. Though acknowledging that its ruling that same year in *Gertz v. Robert Welch, Inc.*[210] had modified the constitutional standards applicable to defamation actions, the Court found it unnecessary to address whether, in a false light action by a private person, a state can set the standard for proving fault as to falsity at the level of ordinary negligence. Thus far, the Supreme Court has never resolved this issue.

A Majority of States Require Actual Malice. In *Meyerkord v. Zipatoni Co.*[211] the Missouri Court of Appeals held that false light was actionable in that state, but that the tort required proof of actual malice. As the court described the facts of that case:

> . . . Meyerkord was employed by Zipatoni, a Missouri corporation that provides marketing services to businesses, and was listed as the "registrant" for Zipatoni's account with Register.com for the purpose of the registration of websites. Meyerkord's employment with Zipatoni ended in 2003.

> In 2006, Zipatoni registered www.alliwantforxmasisapsp.com through Register.com. Meyerkord was listed as the registrant for www.alliwantforxmasisapsp.com, but had no involvement in the creation, registration, or marketing of the website, which was used during a viral marketing campaign initiated by Sony to sell its Play Station Portable ("PSP"). Shortly after the PSP campaign became active, bloggers, consumers, and consumer activist groups began voicing on blogs and websites their concern, suspicion, and accusations over the campaign and those associated with it, including Zipatoni and Meyerkord.

> Thereafter, Meyerkord filed an action against Zipatoni for false light invasion of privacy because Zipatoni failed to remove him as the registrant for its account with Register.com and registered www.alliwant forxmasis apsp.com with Meyerkord listed as the registrant when he no longer worked for Zipatoni. . . .[212]

The *Meyerkord* court found that "adhering to the actual malice standard in the *Restatement* for all types of cases strikes the best balance between allowing false

---

[209] 419 U.S. 245 (1974).

[210] 419 U.S. 323 (1974).

[211] 276 S.W.3d 319 (Mo. Ct. App. 2008).

[212] *Id.* at 321–22.

light claims and protecting First Amendment rights."[213] The court then disposed of the claim before it, stating:

> In his petition, Meyerkord alleged Zipatoni was "negligent and careless" in failing to remove him as the registrant for its account with Register.com and in registering www.alliwant forxmasis apsp. com with Meyerkord listed as the registrant. Because we have . . . found that the proper standard for liability is actual malice, we find Meyerkord has failed to plead the essential elements for a claim of false light invasion of privacy. . . .[214]

Actual Malice Is Difficult to Prove. As the earlier chapter on defamation makes clear, it is difficult to prove that a defendant acted with actual malice. In *Durando v. Nutley Sun*,[215] the Supreme Court of New Jersey explained the facts of the dispute before it:

> [A] regional weekly newspaper inaccurately printed a front-page "teaser," reporting that "two local men," plaintiffs — whose names were not mentioned in the teaser — had been arrested for stock fraud. The two men were charged with illicit stock manipulation in a complaint filed by the Securities and Exchange Commission, but they had not been arrested. Readers who turned to the article on page eleven learned that plaintiffs were the subject of a civil complaint alleging that they had bilked unsuspecting investors of nine million dollars. No word or phrase in the article itself suggested that plaintiffs had been arrested.[216]

The court affirmed a grant of summary judgment to the defendant on the plaintiff's failure to introduce evidence of actual malice to support its false light claim. As the court explained:

> On the summary-judgment record before us, Milo, the then-executive editor of *The Nutley Sun* for four months, was undoubtedly careless in composing the erroneous front-page teaser, "Local men arrested in 'pump and dump' scheme, page 11." After all, Lynn's article [which was being reprinted] never indicated that Durando or Dotoli were arrested or being criminally prosecuted. But in determining whether the false-light claim survives summary judgment, we are not guided by the standard of how the reasonably prudent editor would have performed the task. Rather, we must determine whether, from the record, a reasonable jury could conclude that Milo — despite his admitted mistake — entertained serious doubts about the truth of the teaser when he published it. That is, could a reasonable jury conclude that Milo's conduct was so reckless that it "approache[d] the level of publishing a knowing, calculated falsehood?" . . . [T]he answer to that question is no. . . .

> One does not have to condone Milo's shoddy editing to understand how he might have made the mistake in preparing the teaser, a day after he had

---

[213] *Id.* at 325.

[214] *Id.* at 326.

[215] 37 A.3d 449 (N.J. 2012).

[216] *Id.* at 452.

read Lynn's article. Clearly, the article spoke about the civil complaint filed by the SEC against Durando and Dotoli, and Milo knew the difference between civil and criminal actions. But the language of the SEC complaint, as reflected in the article, also bespeaks criminality. The article stated that three men, including plaintiffs, "pumped up the price of a worthless stock, then dumped it on unsuspecting investors in a $9 million scheme." . . .

Had Milo read the actual SEC complaint, perhaps, the chance of a mistake would have been magnified. The complaint charged Durando and Dotoli with violations of federal securities laws, including the commission of "illegal insider trading" and the filing of "reports containing false and misleading statements." Under the New Jersey Code of Criminal Justice, a person commits the crime of theft "if he purposely obtains property of another by deception." . . . That bears mentioning not because plaintiffs were charged with committing a crime, but because the language of the article sounded like a crime. . . .

This record does not permit us to conclude that Milo's professions — that he made a mistake — are inherently incredible or improbable. He was a harried editor, responsible for a staff of ten and reading hundreds of pieces of correspondence, racing to meet a printing deadline. Somehow, he mistakenly reconfigured the headline of the article, "Local men charged in stock scheme," to the front-page teaser, "Local men arrested. . . ."

Not much can be made of Milo's deleting the last three paragraphs of Lynn's article to fit within the space requirements of his weekly newspaper. While it is true that one of those paragraphs noted again that the SEC complaint was a "civil case," another omitted paragraph included the damning information that the complaint "alleges fraud and violations of various securities laws." The editing does not suggest that Milo attempted to mislead the reader.

. . . Given the heightened protections for free speech and a free press under the actual-malice standard, and the failure of plaintiffs to establish by clear and convincing evidence a jury issue, we come to the same conclusion as the trial court and the Appellate Division — summary judgment must be granted.[217]

Some States Require Private Persons to Prove Only Negligent Falsity. A few states have held that negligence as to falsity may sometimes serve as the basis for liability in a false light action. For example, in *West v. Media General Convergence, Inc.*,[218] the Supreme Court of Tennessee held that false light invasion of privacy is actionable if a private person, suing with regard to a matter of private concern, proves that the publisher was negligent in placing the plaintiff in a false light. As the court explained:

In *Memphis Publishing Co. v. Nichols*, 569 S.W.2d 412 (Tenn. 1978), this Court adopted negligence as the standard for defamation claims asserted

---

[217] *Id.* at 461–62.

[218] 53 S.W.3d 640 (Tenn. 2001).

by private individuals about matters of private concern. Our decision to adopt a simple negligence standard in private plaintiff/private matter false light claims is the result of our conclusion that private plaintiffs in false light claims deserve the same heightened protection that private plaintiffs receive in defamation cases. Therefore, when false light invasion of privacy claims are asserted by a private plaintiff regarding a matter of private concern, the plaintiff need only prove that the defendant publisher was negligent in placing the plaintiff in a false light. For all other false light claims, we believe that the actual malice standard achieves the appropriate balance between First Amendment guarantees and privacy interests.[219]

b.   Provably False Assertion of Fact

In a suit for false light invasion of privacy the plaintiff must prove that the defendant made a provably false assertion of fact. Absent such a showing, the action for false light will fail.[220]

For example, in *Wilson v. Freitas*,[221] the defendant stated that it was "widely accepted as fact" that the plaintiff was the suspected serial killer who had committed various crimes. The Hawaii Court of Appeals concluded that the defendant publishers and authors were entitled to summary judgment on a defamation claim because the statement in question was not provably false, and in any event the plaintiff had not presented competent evidence to prove the statement false. For the same reasons, the court concluded that the plaintiff's false light claim could not stand.

Literally True Statements. Just as literally true statements that imply false facts are actionable as libel or slander, so too the literal truth of publicized facts is no defense to a false light cause of action. As the Supreme Court of Tennessee explained in *West v. Media General Convergence, Inc.*:[222]

> The facts may be true in a false light claim. However, the angle from which the facts are presented, or the omission of certain material facts, results in placing the plaintiff in a false light. "Literal accuracy of separate statements will not render a communication 'true' where the implication of the communication as a whole was false." . . .[223]

Substantial Truth. If a statement is substantially true, it is not actionable as either defamation or false light. For example, in *Burns v. Chapman*,[224] a police chief made statements to the press about the private life of a police officer, who was married to another officer (Dominguez) at the time he committed suicide. The Superior Court of Connecticut found that claims for defamation and false light were

---

[219] *Id.* at 647–48.

[220] *See Stien v. Marriott Ownership Resorts, Inc.*, 944 P.2d 374 (Utah Ct. App. 1997).

[221] 214 P.3d 1110 (Haw. Ct. App. 2009).

[222] 53 S.W.3d 640 (Tenn. 2001).

[223] *Id.* at 645 n.5.

[224] 2008 Conn. Super. LEXIS 3228 (Dec. 12, 2008).

barred by the substantial truth of the police chief's comments. The court stated in part:

> The first allegedly libelous statement . . . is that the plaintiff and Dominguez "could not get it together personally." The evidence shows that the plaintiff and Dominguez had lived together until Dominguez left after a few months because of conflicts with the plaintiff's mother. After his return to the plaintiff's home in November 2003, Dominguez apparently threatened to leave on a number of occasions. . . . The court finds the statement of the defendant to be essentially truthful.
>
> The second allegedly libelous statement is that the plaintiff's relationship with Dominguez was "very stormy." In her testimony the plaintiff conceded that Dominguez had a stormy personality, but denied that their relationship was stormy. The plaintiff testified that her note of January 18, 2004 . . . was an attempt to make an honest appraisal of her relationship with Dominguez and then use the note as a basis for a discussion with him.
>
> That note describes a relationship which could be accurately characterized as stormy. "I try to talk to you and you just yell. I try to tell you I don't like something and you point out many things you don't like about me. You are always miserable or it seems that way. We fight and nothing gets resolved. You call me ungrateful." . . . The court finds that the defendant's statement that the plaintiff had a very stormy relationship with Dominguez was truthful.
>
> The third alleged libelous statement was that the plaintiff and Dominguez were engaged in a "domestic dispute . . . apparently over child support." The plaintiff testified that there was no discussion of child support on the evening of January 18, 2004 or at any other time. However, there can be no doubt that there was a domestic dispute between them. . . .
>
> . . . Beihn testified that Dominguez told her that his dispute with the plaintiff included demands from her that he contribute to the support of his infant daughter. . . . The court finds that it is more likely than not that child support was, in fact, one of the issues in the dispute between the plaintiff and Dominguez.
>
> . . . .
>
> Since none of the defendant's statements were false or untrue in any meaningful respect, the court finds the issues on the first count [libel] for the defendant.[225]

The court concluded that, because the disputed statements were "essentially true" and could not support a defamation claim, "the plaintiff cannot prevail on her claim of being placed in a false light."[226]

---

[225] *Id.* at *32–*39.

[226] *Id.* at *47.

3.   Publicity

False light invasion of privacy requires "publicity" in the same sense that the term is used in connection with actions for disclosure of private facts. Consequently, the false portrayal ordinarily must be communicated to the public at large or to so many persons that the matter is substantially certain to become one of public knowledge. Thus, in *Andrews v. Stallings*, the New Mexico Court of Appeals held that a newspaper reporter's alleged disclosure to the IRS regarding a village council member's corporation's tax filings did not amount to publicity that would support a false light claim.[227]

Similarly, in *L-S Industries, Inc. v. Matlack*,[228] a federal court in Tennessee held that communication of information about a former employee, in a letter addressed to a single person and in an e-mail directed to three persons, was not publicity.

In contrast, in *Rossi v. Schlarbaum*,[229] a federal court in Pennsylvania found that phone calls to employees of the strip clubs where the plaintiff had worked was publicity that would support a false light claim based on alleged statements that the plaintiff was a prostitute with a criminal record.

Even if a false statement eventually reaches a large number of persons, the originator of the statement will only be liable for publicity if the wide dissemination of the statement was foreseeable. In *Bean v. Gutierrez*,[230] disparaging statements made in a private conversation eventually appeared in a business newsletter that was distributed to 2,800 persons. The District of Columbia Court of Appeals held that there was no publicity because the speaker was just gossiping and had no reason to believe that the recipient would publish the information.

Special Relationship Exception. Some courts adjudicating false light claims have recognized a special relationship exception to the usual rules governing proof of publicity. The exception is similar to the one that some jurisdictions apply in actions for public disclosure of private affairs (discussed earlier in this chapter).

For example, in *Duncan v. Peterson*,[231] a false light claim was based on dissemination of a letter to three church members. The Appellate Court of Illinois wrote:

> In *Poulos v. Lutheran Social Services of Illinois, Inc.*, . . . [728 N.E.2d 547 (Ill. App. Ct. 2000)], the court noted that although it had never been determined what evidence was sufficient to establish the element of "before the public" for a false light action, the publicity element for a closely related action, public disclosure of private facts, had been previously defined. The publicity element for public disclosure of private facts has been defined as

---

[227] 892 P.2d 611 (N.M. Ct. App. 1995).

[228] 2009 U.S. Dist. LEXIS 9721 (E.D. Tenn. Feb. 9, 2009).

[229] 600 F. Supp. 2d 650 (E.D. Pa. 2009).

[230] 2009 D.C. App. LEXIS 447 (Sept. 10, 2009).

[231] 835 N.E.2d 411 (Ill. App. Ct. 2005).

"communication . . . 'to the public at large, or to so many persons that the matter must be regarded as substantially certain to become one of public knowledge.' ". . . .

The *Poulos* court also noted that an exception to this publicity element has been recognized. . . . Publicity may be established by a showing that the disclosure was made to a person or persons with whom the plaintiff has a special relationship. . . . The court in *Miller v. Motorola*, . . . [560 N.E.2d 900 (Ill. App. Ct. 1990)] . . . provided that a special relationship is present in situations when the communication was made to a particular public such as employees, club members, church members, family, or neighbors. The reasoning for the special relationship exception is that disclosure to a limited number of persons may be just as devastating as disclosure to the general public. . . . The *Poulos* court found this reasoning persuasive, and it adopted the exception for false light actions. . . .

The *Poulos* court then found that a special relationship existed between the plaintiff, a teacher, and the chairman of the board of trustees of the school board for which he worked. . . . [In the present case], the May 9, 2000, letter was sent by defendants to three former board members of Hope Church, *i.e.*, Dickman, Nader, and Puccinelli. . . . Neither the evidence nor the complaint was clear as to what relationship Dickman, Nader, and Puccinelli had with Hope Church in May 2000. Nevertheless, publicity to these three men, who within a short period of time had been leaders in Hope Church, would have been just as devastating as publication to the general public because of their close ties to the congregation. We therefore find that there was a special relationship between the recipients of the letter and Duncan. Accordingly, the element of "before the public" is satisfied.[232]

4.   Highly Offensive to a Reasonable Person

To be actionable under the tort of false light, a false portrayal must be of a kind that would be highly offensive to a reasonable person. This standard was met in *Bojko v. Lima*.[233] The Connecticut Superior Court affirmed a judgment, based in part on false light, against a parent who conducted an e-mail campaign against a teacher, which portrayed the teacher as an abuser and pedophile. The court found that the offending statements were such a major misrepresentation of the teacher's character that it was reasonable to expect the teacher to take serious offense to such statements.

Not Highly Offensive. Many false light actions fail because the portrayal was not highly offensive. For example, in *Straub v. Scarpa*,[234] the Florida District Court of Appeal wrote:

---

[232] *Id.* at 423–24.

[233] 2009 Conn. Super. LEXIS 1359 (May 12, 2009).

[234] 967 So. 2d 437 (Fla. Dist. Ct. App. 2007).

The lawsuit was based on a letter Scarpa sent to the members of Southfields Homeowners Association. Straus is on the Association's board of directors. Scarpa's letter solicited other homeowners and association members to provide her with proxy rights to vote for a slate of directors in an upcoming election. The letter contained these paragraphs:

> If you feel as we do that the property owners would be better represented by those of us who actually live here and that we will present a fair operating budget containing only *necessary* expenditures to maintain our community thus our property values, then please fill out your proxy giving me the permission to vote our slate. . . .

> Our assessments have doubled this past year and probably will triple with this upcoming budget. It will no doubt contain very expensive items that have nothing to do with the operation of our community. The only recourse we have is to elect responsible homeowners and rein in this unnecessary spending.[235]

In rejecting the false light claim, court explained:

> No reasonable person "would be justified in the eyes of the community in feeling seriously offended and aggrieved" by the letter. . . . In a residential community governed by a homeowners association, vigorous debate over community expenditures is a value to be encouraged, not a pathway to litigation. To encourage tort litigation in a case such as this is to stifle discussion and place political power in the hands of those wealthy and aggressive enough to finance a lawsuit.[236]

5.   Special Issues

a.   Statutes of Limitations

A false-light plaintiff may encounter procedural challenges relating to the statute of limitations. In many states, the statute of limitations governing false light actions is short, and some courts are disinclined to toll the running of the statutory period by applying a discovery rule.

Tolling Under a Discovery Rule in Cases Involving Spoken Words. In *Daniel v. Taylor*,[237] the plaintiff was incarcerated for nine years after pleading guilty to various offenses. Upon being released, he inspected the district attorney's file in his criminal case. He discovered that false statements had been made about him by four individuals. The plaintiff then sued for slander and false light. In finding that the claims were time-barred, the Tennessee Court of Appeals wrote:

> The statute of limitations for a slander claim is only six months. . . . In . . . [*West v. Media General Convergence, Inc.*, 53 S.W.3d 640 (Tenn. 2001)], . . .

---

[235] *Id.* at 439.

[236] *Id.* As noted above in the text, subsequent to Straus, the Supreme Court of Florida held that false light is not a viable cause of action in that state.

[237] 2009 Tenn. App. LEXIS 110 (Mar. 25, 2009).

the Court also held that . . . [false light] would have the same statute of limitations as a corresponding defamation claim, . . . [because] application of different statutes of limitation for false light and defamation cases could undermine the effectiveness of limitations on defamation claims. . . .

Thus, Plaintiff's slander and false light invasion of privacy claims both have a six month statute of limitations. . . .

. . . [T]he question then becomes whether the discovery rule applies to these two claims as argued by Plaintiff. . . .

. . . [T]he policies upon which statutes of limitations are based, *i.e.*, preventing stale claims and preserving evidence, are especially applicable to slander actions because of the intangible nature of the evidence, spoken words, and of the injury itself, damage to character and reputation. . . .

. . . Identical concerns are present with regard to false light invasion of privacy claims based upon spoken words. . . . Plaintiff's slander and false light invasion of privacy claims against defendants Lambert and Brown were properly dismissed based on the statute of limitations.[238]

PROBLEM 4-10: THE ALTERED WORKFORCE PHOTOGRAPH

Technical Systems, Inc. (TSI) is an industrial engineering company which prides itself on innovation and diversity. When it acquired Shoff & Sons, TSI's corporate management made it clear that they expected its new subsidiary (which would be known as TSI-Springfield) to fall into step with the practices which had distinguished TSI as a cutting-edge business.

Jeff Burke, the vice president of TSI-Springfield, was told that he needed to give the highest priority to diversifying TSI-Springfield's workforce. This was a difficult challenge because at the time of the acquisition, the forty-person workforce was overwhelmingly male and Anglo.

Burke had trouble making progress with diversity. Vacancies were rare, and good minority employment candidates often opted for better paying jobs in more attractive locations. Nevertheless, national management continued to press the diversity issue, and Burke felt the pressure.

The dilemma became a crisis when TSI national management decided to hang a series of photographs in a large executive conference room at its main headquarters in a city far from Springfield. Each photograph would be a picture taken at one of TSI's fourteen facilities. The image was to be an interior or exterior shot of the plant, with all of the members of its workforce standing or sitting in the foreground, clearly visible. Burke was told to hire a photographer and send the best shot to the national headquarters, keeping in mind that the final print would be reproduced in color, 24 inches in height and 36 inches wide.

A photographer hired by Burke took several excellent photographs at TSI-Springfield. The problem was the forty-person workforce did not at all look diverse.

---

[238] *Id.* at *12–*16.

Recognizing that fact, Burke asked the photographer to digitally alter one of the images. Using a computer photo-editing program, the photographer did three things.

First, the photographer cut four white-male employees out of the picture entirely and replaced their images with images of female and minority persons which were gathered from other sources. Second, in one instance where it was too difficult to remove a worker's image entirely, the photographer replaced the head and arms of a white-male worker with the head and arms of an unknown African-American male. Finally, the photographer tinted the faces of three employees to make them look more "diverse."

The final product was seamless. A beautiful picture of a diverse and innovative workforce. The photograph was hung in the executive conference room until the story came to light.

On these facts, can anyone pictured in the original photograph or the altered photograph sue Burke or the photographer for false light?

6.   Review

The "review" sections of Chapters 2 and 3 raised the issues of whether a person harmed by the erroneous scoring of a standardized test could seek relief under the law of misrepresentation or defamation. Would a claim for false light invasion of privacy be viable, and if so, would it be preferable to an action for defamation?

> Unlike defamation, an action for false light invasion of privacy may be based on a statement that is highly offensive, but not so bad as to be disgraceful. In that regard, it may be easier for a small scoring error to be actionable as false light rather than as libel or slander. However, false light suits based on standardized test mis-scoring are likely to fail for two reasons. The first concerns the degree to which the statement is disseminated, and the second relates to culpability.[239]

The first problem relates to the publicity requirement of a false light cause of action. In the typical case, standard test scores are distributed only to a limited number of persons. In states that do not recognize a special relationship exception, or find that exception inapplicable to the communication of test scores, it may be impossible for a mis-scoring plaintiff to satisfy the publicity requirement of a false light cause of action. The second problem concerns actual malice.

> False light invasion of privacy normally requires proof of "actual malice," meaning that the defendant must have acted with a high degree of awareness of the probable falsity of a statement. This kind of proof will not commonly be available in erroneous scoring cases, but may be adduced in suits where the facts also establish *scienter* for a misrepresentation claim.
>
> . . . [P]robably, the mis-scoring plaintiff will be a "private person" suing with respect to a matter of public concern (*e.g.*, a student taking a test

---

[239] Vincent R. Johnson, *Standardized Tests, Erroneous Scores, and Tort Liability*, 38 RUTGERS L.J. 655, 701 (2007).

required by state law), or a person suing with respect to a matter of private concern (*e.g.*, perhaps a student taking a standardized test for which the results will be reported only to a small number of private colleges or universities). In the former case (private person/matter of public concern — for which the standards are set by *Gertz v. Robert Welch, Inc.*),[240] Supreme Court precedent mandates that states not permit recovery of damages unless there is evidence that the defendant was at least negligent as to the falsity of the defamatory statement. As to cases in the latter group (a person suing with respect to a matter of private concern — where *Dun & Bradstreet, Inc. v. Greenmoss Builders, Inc.*[241] is a key precedent), the Supreme Court has not definitively ruled on whether strict liability is permissible or whether negligence must be shown. Many states now require negligence. Negligence as to falsity is considerably easier to prove than actual malice.[242]

E. APPROPRIATION OF NAME OR LIKENESS

Differentiating Commercial and Noncommercial Use. Section 652C of the *Restatement (Second) of Torts*, entitled "Appropriation of Name or Likeness," provides:

> One who appropriates to his own use or benefit the name or likeness of another is subject to liability to the other for invasion of his privacy.[243]

This rule, issued by the American Law Institute in 1977, covers commercial and noncommercial use of another's name or likeness. Section 652C continues to be cited by courts in both types of cases. However, more recent guidance on liability for appropriation can be found in the *Restatement (Third) of Unfair Competition*, which deals only with redress of commercial injuries. The basic rule from that *Restatement* provides:

> One who appropriates the commercial value of a person's identity by using without consent the person's name, likeness, or other indicia of identity for purposes of trade is subject to liability for the relief appropriate under the rules stated in §§ 48 [dealing with injunctive relief] and 49 [dealing with monetary relief].[244]

The materials below deal first with appropriation for commercial benefit, then briefly with appropriation for noncommercial benefit.

Right of Publicity. Actions for appropriation of name or likeness often seem to have little to do with privacy. At least in cases involving commercial use, the issue generally is not whether the plaintiff can keep his or her name or likeness private, but whether the defendant must pay for publicizing such matters. Perhaps for this

---

[240] 418 U.S. 323 (1974).

[241] 472 U.S. 749 (1985).

[242] 38 Rutgers L.J. at 704.

[243] Restatement (Second) of Torts § 652C (1977).

[244] Restatement (Third) of Unfair Competition § 46 (1995).

reason, the tort action for appropriation is often said to involve the "right of publicity."

Many cases use the terms "appropriation of name or likeness" and "right of publicity" interchangeably. However, courts occasionally have sought to differentiate the two terms. Thus, in *Doe v. TCI Cablevision*,[245] the Supreme Court of Missouri stated that misappropriation involves unauthorized use "to obtain some advantage," while invasion of the right of publicity involves unauthorized use "to obtain a commercial advantage."

1.   Name, Likeness, or Other Indicia of Identity

Names. Although the cases commonly speak of appropriation of "name or likeness," what they often mean is a defendant will be liable for misuse of identity. In general, there is no exclusive right to the use of a personal name. One may change one's name to Tiger Woods, Michelle Obama, or Mother Teresa without risk of liability. However, using a name to appropriate the identity of another is actionable.[246] Thus, the tort action for appropriation affords a civil remedy for forgery.[247]

In *Doe v. TCI Cablevision*,[248] a comic book character did not physically resemble the former professional hockey player Tony Twist, and the publication's story line did not attempt to track Twist's life. However, both the character and the athlete shared the same unusual name and tough-guy persona. The Supreme Court of Missouri held that there was sufficient evidence to prove that the defendants intended to use the plaintiff's name as a symbol of his identity to obtain a commercial advantage.

In *AFL Philadelphia LLC v. Krause*,[249] a federal court in Pennsylvania found that the former sales director of an arena football team adequately alleged that team owners appropriated the value of the director's name by falsely designating the director as the origin of an e-mail notifying fans of an unpopular decision to cancel the football season.

Personal Information. In some cases, the use of information relating to a person does not amount to an actionable appropriation of name or likeness. However, in other cases, the contrary is true. The relevant question is whether the defendant seeks to appropriate the identity of plaintiff.

For example, in *Remsburg v. Docusearch, Inc.*,[250] a woman was fatally shot at her workplace after an Internet-based information service sold the killer the woman's social security number and, later, her employment information. The resulting wrongful death action included a claim for appropriation of private

---

[245] 110 S.W.3d 363, 368–69 (Mo. 2003).

[246] *See* Restatement (Second) of Torts § 652C cmt. c (1977).

[247] *See Houssain v. Sundowner*, 2009 U.S. Dist. LEXIS 38198, at *15–*16 (S.D. Ohio Apr. 22, 2009).

[248] 110 S.W.3d 363, 368–69 (Mo. 2003).

[249] 2009 U.S. Dist. LEXIS 46965 (E.D. Pa. June 4, 2009).

[250] 816 A.2d 1001 (N.H. 2003).

information. The Supreme Court of New Hampshire held that appropriation of name or likeness, as formulated in the *Restatement (Second) of Torts*, was actionable in that state, but that the plaintiff in the case did not state a claim. Explaining the law of appropriation as it related to the facts, the court wrote:

> "Tortious liability for appropriation of a name or likeness is intended to protect the value of an individual's notoriety or skill. Thus, the *Restatement* notes, in order that there may be liability . . . , the defendant must have appropriated to his own use or benefit the reputation, prestige, social or commercial standing, public interest or other values of the plaintiff's name or likeness. The misappropriation tort does not protect one's name *per se*; rather it protects the value associated with that name." . . . Thus, appropriation occurs most often when the person's name or likeness is used to advertise the defendant's product or when the defendant impersonates the person for gain. . . .

> An investigator who sells personal information sells the information for the value of the information itself, not to take advantage of the person's reputation or prestige. The investigator does not capitalize upon the goodwill value associated with the information but rather upon the client's willingness to pay for the information. In other words, the benefit derived from the sale in no way relates to the social or commercial standing of the person whose information is sold. Thus, a person whose personal information is sold does not have a cause of action for appropriation against the investigator who sold the information.[251]

Similarly, in *Dwyer v. American Express Co.*,[252] credit cardholders challenged the defendants' practice of renting information regarding cardholder spending habits. The Appellate Court of Illinois wrote:

> Plaintiffs claim that defendants appropriated information about cardholders' personalities, including their names and perceived lifestyles, without their consent. Defendants argue that their practice does not adversely affect the interest of a cardholder in the "exclusive use of his own identity," using the language of the *Restatement*. Defendants also argue that the cardholders' names lack value and that the lists that defendants create are valuable because "they identify a useful aggregate of potential customers to whom offers may be sent."

> . . . [P]laintiffs have not stated a claim for tortious appropriation because they have failed to allege the first element. Undeniably, each cardholder's name is valuable to defendants. The more names included on a list, the more that list will be worth. However, a single, random cardholder's name has little or no intrinsic value to defendants (or a merchant). Rather, an individual name has value only when it is associated with one of defendants' lists. Defendants create value by categorizing and aggregating these

---

[251] *Id.* at 1009–10.

[252] 652 N.E.2d 1351 (Ill. App. Ct. 1995).

names. Furthermore, defendants' practices do not deprive any of the cardholders of any value their individual names may possess.[253]

However, in *Havenstrite v. Hartford Life Ins. Co.*,[254] the plaintiffs alleged that an insurance company appropriated the value of their names, identities, and personal information by selling their employer life insurance on their lives. The arrangement violated state law because the plaintiffs were not "key employees," and therefore the employer did not have an insurable interest in their lives. In an action seeking disgorgement of the profits the insurer made from its alleged misuse of their names and identities, a federal court in Oklahoma held that the plaintiffs adequately alleged a claim for appropriation. The court wrote:

> Plaintiffs allege that their names and identities (specifically, their names, dates of birth, sex, and Social Security Numbers) had commercial value that Hartford, and its predecessor in interest, exploited. Consistent with the requirements of Comment c to *Restatement* § 652C, plaintiffs have alleged that Hartford and its predecessor in interest appropriated the value of their names and identities so as to issue secret COLI policies and to appropriate to Hartford's own use and benefit the commercial value of their names and private personal identifiers by receiving premiums, commissions and service and administration fees. The use alleged by plaintiffs was more than incidental, as required by Comment d, as their names and identities were allegedly misappropriated for the purpose of taking advantage of the commercial value associated with the generation of new life insurance policies and the premiums and fees the insurance company would derive therefrom. Thus, the plaintiffs adequately allege that the plaintiffs' names and identities had intrinsic value insofar as the package of personal information not otherwise available to a life insurance company allowed Hartford's predecessor to issue secret life insurance policies, with consequent commercial benefits to the seller and the servicer of those policies.[255]

Identity Without Name Or Likeness. In some cases, identity can be appropriated without use of name or likeness. In *Carson v. Here's Johnny Portable Toilets, Inc.*,[256] the defendant used the phrase "Here's Johnny" in marketing those products. Those words were closely associated with the plaintiff because, for many years, they were used on his late night television show to introduce him to audiences. The Sixth Circuit held that the use of the phrase was so clearly intended to capitalize on Carson's identity, notoriety, and achievements that an action would lie.

However, in *Maule v. Philadelphia Media Holdings, LLC*,[257] a federal court in Pennsylvania rejected an appropriation claim based on the defendant's alleged misuse of the plaintiff's landscape photographs. The court explained:

---

[253] *Id.* at 1356.

[254] 2008 U.S. Dist. LEXIS 105316 (N.D. Okla. Dec. 31, 2008).

[255] *Id.* at *12–*14.

[256] 698 F.2d 831 (6th Cir. 1983).

[257] 710 F. Supp. 2d 511 (E.D. Pa. 2008).

The public at large does not associate an image of the Philadelphia skyline with Maule; therefore, PMH's use of the photographs, without more, does not sufficiently identify Maule for purposes of a claim of appropriation.[258]

Likeness Without Identity. Notwithstanding the usual focus on whether the value of one's identity has been appropriated, there are cases where the real gravamen of the plaintiff's claim is not unauthorized use of identity, but unauthorized use of likeness. In *Cohen v. Herbal Concepts*, Inc.,[259] a photograph of a mother and child bathing nude in a stream was placed in an ad for a product designed to help women eliminate body cellulite. The court allowed the question of whether the plaintiffs could be identified (and therefore able to sue) to go to the jury, although neither person's face was visible. The court held the identifying features included their hair, bone structure, body contours, stature, posture, and the fact that they were pictured together. Arguably, the plaintiffs' real objections were to the use of their likenesses, not to the appropriation of their identities. The plaintiffs were harmed, but not by taking advantage of their prestige or reputations.

Likeness Plus Identification. *Tanner v. Ebbole*[260] grew out of a suit between rival tattoo artists. Ebbole alleged that Averette and Demented Needle invaded her privacy by appropriating a white plaster body cast of her torso, adorning it with satanic symbols, using it as a mannequin on which to display Demented Needle T-shirts for sale, and referring to the body cast as "Ebbole." The Court of Civil Appeals of Alabama held that Ebbole stated a claim for appropriation of name or likeness. The court's opinion stated:

> [I]t was undisputed that no one could tell, just by looking at the body cast, that it was a representation of Ebbole's torso. Nevertheless, it was also undisputed that Averette told anyone who inquired, and even volunteered the information to those who had not inquired, that the mannequin was Ebbole's body cast. Under the circumstances, Ebbole presented sufficient evidence to allow the invasion-of-privacy claim to be submitted to the jury for a factual resolution.[261]

2.   Appropriation for Commercial Benefit

The New York Civil Rights Law and Other Statutory Rights. New York has never recognized common law tort principles governing the right of privacy. However, a New York state statute clearly addresses liability for commercial appropriation of name or likeness. Section 51 of the state civil rights law provides:

> Any person whose name, portrait, picture or voice is used within this state for advertising purposes or for the purposes of trade without the written consent first obtained . . . may maintain an equitable action . . . to prevent and restrain the use thereof; and may also sue and recover damages for any injuries sustained by reason of such use and if the defendant shall have

---

[258] *Id.* at *14.

[259] 472 N.E.2d 307 (N.Y. 1984).

[260] 88 So.3d 856 (Ala. Ct. App. 2011).

[261] *Id.* at 867.

knowingly used such person's name, portrait, picture or voice in such manner as is forbidden or declared to be unlawful by section fifty of this article, the jury, in its discretion, may award exemplary damages. . . .[262]

There are statutes dealing with interference with the right of publicity in other states, including California, Florida, Kentucky, Massachusetts, Nebraska, Nevada, Oklahoma, Rhode Island, Tennessee, Texas, Virginia, and Wisconsin.[263] These statutory rights are often very similar to common law protection. In some instances, statutory provisions supplement, rather than replace, judge-made law. Thus, in *James v. Bob Ross Buick, Inc.*,[264] the Ohio Court of Appeals noted:

> The Ohio legislature has . . . codified the right of publicity in an individual's persona, which includes the individual's name, voice, signature, photograph, image, likeness, or distinctive appearance, if any of these aspects have commercial value. . . . [Ohio Revised Code 2741.08] makes clear, however, that this statutory cause of action did not supplant the common-law claim.[265]

a.   Use for Purposes of Trade

Section 47 of the *Restatement (Third) of Unfair Competition* provides in relevant part:

> The name, likeness, and other indicia of a person's identity are used "for purposes of trade" . . . if they are used in advertising the user's goods or services, or are placed on merchandise marketed by the user, or are used in connection with services rendered by the user.[266]

Clothing, Board Games, and Staffing Charts. Use of the likeness of a famous person on clothing, board games, or staffing charts may give rise to liability.[267] Comment b to § 47 of the *Restatement (Third) of Unfair Competition* provides:

> The sale of merchandise bearing a person's name or likeness ordinarily constitutes a use of the identity for purposes of trade. . . . An unauthorized appropriation of another's name or likeness for use on posters, buttons, or other memorabilia is thus ordinarily actionable as an infringement of the right of publicity. . . . In some circumstances, however, the informational content of the particular merchandise or its utility to purchasers as a means

---

[262] N.Y. Civ. Rights Law § 51 (LEXIS 2014). Section 50, which is cross-referenced by § 51, provides "A person, firm or corporation that uses for advertising purposes, or for the purposes of trade, the name, portrait or picture of any living person without having first obtained the written consent of such person, or if a minor of his or her parent or guardian, is guilty of a misdemeanor." *Id.* at § 50.

[263] There are statutes dealing with interference with the right of publicity in California, Florida, Kentucky, Massachusetts, Nebraska, Nevada, New York, Oklahoma, Rhode Island, Tennessee, Texas, Virginia, and Wisconsin. *See* Restatement (Third) of Unfair Competition § 46 Statutory Note (1995).

[264] 855 N.E.2d 119 (Ohio Ct. App. 2006).

[265] *Id.* at 122 n.2.

[266] Restatement (Third) of Unfair Competition § 47 (1995).

[267] *See Rosemont Ent., Inc. v. Choppy Productions, Inc.*, 74 Misc. 2d 1003 (Sup. Ct. 1972); *Rosemont Ent., Inc. v. Urban Sys., Inc.*, 42 A.D.2d 544 (N.Y. App. Div. 1973).

of expression may justify the conclusion that the use is protected under the first amendment. A candidate for public office, for example, cannot invoke the right of publicity to prohibit the distribution of posters or buttons bearing the candidate's name or likeness, whether used to signify support or opposition.[268]

In *Moore v. Big Picture Co.*,[269] the plaintiff's name was used to fill in a blank on a staffing chart prepared in connection with a contract bid. In response to an appropriation claim, the defendant argued that the name had no particular value and was used only as a symbol for someone with qualifications similar to those of the plaintiff. The court acknowledged that it would have been an overstatement for the plaintiff to claim that without his name the contract would not have been awarded. However, a judgment for the plaintiff was upheld because the testimony showed that the plaintiff was a well-known, highly qualified worker in the field.

Incidental Usage in Advertising. In *Namath v. Sports Illustrated*,[270] a professional football player's picture was used to illustrate an article in Sports Illustrated about a Super Bowl game. The magazine then used that picture in advertisements seeking subscriptions to Sports Illustrated. The court held that this use would not support an appropriation claim under the New York Civil Rights Law. The court described the use of the picture in the advertisements as "incidental" to advertising the magazine, and pointed out that the pictures were used to illustrate the magazine's quality and content, not to imply that Namath had endorsed it.

PROBLEM 4-11: THE FIRED FERRARI SALESMAN

Though he had been "Salesman of the Year" just twelve months earlier, Andras Evans was terminated on December 31 because he failed to meet the quarterly sales quota set by the new manager of the Ferrari dealership.

Less than two weeks later, in early January, form letters were automatically generated by "preferred customer care" software which had been used by the dealership for many years to "stay in touch" with prior or potential customers. These form letters were addressed to persons who had been "assigned" to Evans during the term of his employment. The letters were personally signed by a clerical assistant at the dealership who, because she has good penmanship, signs all of the names of all salespersons on all of the customer care letters.

According to Estelle Spinger, the dealership business manager, the company policy was to delete a terminated employee's data file on the day of his or her termination so that no further letters would be generated in that employee's name. However, Evans's customers were not reassigned to Chung-Ho Park, the salesperson who was hired to replace Evans, until March 13. Spinger maintains that this delay, and the resultant generation of letters in Evans's name, was unintentional. Evans learned that some of "his" former customers had received letters sent with his name after he was terminated.

---

[268] RESTATEMENT (THIRD) OF UNFAIR COMPETITION § 47 cmt. b (1995).

[269] 828 F.2d 270 (5th Cir. 1987).

[270] 48 A.D.2d 487 (N.Y. App. Div. 1975), *aff'd*, 352 N.E.2d 584 (N.Y. 1976).

Evans has hired you to sue the Ferrari dealership for wrongful termination. Please consider of the viability of including in the complaint a cause of action for unauthorized use of Evans's name on letters to clients subsequent to December 31.

b.   Activities Not Included in Purposes of Trade

Section 47 of the *Restatement (Third) of Unfair Competition* provides in relevant part:

> [U]se "for purposes of trade" does not ordinarily include the use of a person's identity in news reporting, commentary, entertainment, works of fiction or nonfiction, or in advertising that is incidental to such uses.[271]

(1)   First Amendment Protection for News & Entertainment

Newsworthy Matters and Beyond. Courts have recognized broad First Amendment restrictions on liability for appropriation. A defendant's First Amendment privilege extends not only to matters that are newsworthy, but to other matters as well.

In *Bustos v. U.S.*,[272] A & E Television Networks used a video clip of the plaintiff being attacked by another inmate in a program about gangs in American prisons. In rejecting the plaintiff's appropriation claim, a federal court in Colorado wrote:

> The First Amendment "permits the use of a plaintiff's name or likeness when that use is made in the context of, and reasonably relates to, a publication concerning a matter that is newsworthy or of legitimate public concern." . . .

> As a matter of law, both the . . . program and the video clip of Plaintiff, as alleged, concern matters that are newsworthy or of legitimate public concern.[273]

Although the New York Civil Rights Law[274] (quoted above) does not define the terms "advertising" or "trade," the statute has been consistently construed as not applying to publications concerning newsworthy events or matters of public interest.[275] In addition, the statute expressly exempts certain uses from liability, generally relating to photographers and buyers of merchandise and literary or artistic works.[276]

---

[271] RESTATEMENT (THIRD) OF UNFAIR COMPETITION § 47 (1995).

[272] 2009 U.S. Dist. LEXIS 74511 (D. Colo. Aug. 21, 2009).

[273] *Id.* at *10–*11.

[274] N.Y. CIV. RIGHTS LAW § 51 (LEXIS 2009).

[275] *See Howell v. New York Post Co., Inc.*, 612 N.E.2d 699 (N.Y. 1993).

[276] *Id.* (stating that "nothing contained in this article shall be so construed as to prevent any person, firm or corporation, practicing the profession of photography, from exhibiting in or about his or its establishment specimens of the work of such establishment, unless the same is continued by such person, firm or corporation after written notice objecting thereto has been given by the person portrayed; and nothing contained in this article shall be so construed as to prevent any person, firm or corporation from

(a)   Broad Range of Protected Expression

News Articles. In *Gleason v. Smolinski*,[277] the main plaintiff was the subject of a newspaper article when a former romantic interest of hers disappeared. The article was accompanied by her picture. The plaintiff sued the publisher for appropriation of name or likeness. In rejecting the claim, the Connecticut Superior Court wrote:

> The *Restatement* . . . provides . . . that "[t]he value of the plaintiff's name is not appropriated . . . by reference to it in connection with legitimate mention of his public activities; nor is the value of his likeness appropriated when it is published for purposes other than taking advantage of his reputation, prestige, or other value associated with him, for purposes of publicity. . . . It is only when the *publicity is given for the purpose of appropriating to the defendant's benefit the commercial or other values associated with the name or the likeness* that the right of privacy is invaded. The fact that the defendant is engaged in the business of publication, for example of a newspaper, out of which he makes or seeks to make a profit, is not enough to make the incidental publication a commercial use of the name or likeness . . .". . . . *Id.*, § 652C, comment (d).

> . . . [I]t has been said that a plaintiff's privacy is invaded if "A is an actress, noted for her beautiful figure. B, seeking to advertise his bread, publishes in a newspaper a photograph of A, under the caption, 'Keep That Sylph-Like Figure by Eating More of B's Rye and Whole Wheat Bread.'" *Id.*, § 652B, comment (b) illustration (1). The plaintiffs, in this case, have alleged a publication, but failed to allege any invasion similar to this example. Rather, their claim seemingly relies on the mere fact that Murray published Gleason's name and photograph in his newspaper article. . . . [W]ithout facts evidencing an actual appropriation, this claim is legally insufficient.[278]

Illustrations. Pertinent illustrations are constitutionally protected. For example, in *Howell v. New York Post*,[279] a trespassing photographer climbed the wall of a psychiatric facility to photograph a woman who had been involved in a highly publicized child abuse case. In the photograph, which was published on the front page of the Post, the woman was shown walking with the plaintiff, whose

---

using the name, portrait, picture or voice of any manufacturer or dealer in connection with the goods, wares and merchandise manufactured, produced or dealt in by him which he has sold or disposed of with such name, portrait, picture or voice used in connection therewith; or from using the name, portrait, picture or voice of any author, composer or artist in connection with his literary, musical or artistic productions which he has sold or disposed of with such name, portrait, picture or voice used in connection therewith. Nothing contained in this section shall be construed to prohibit the copyright owner of a sound recording from disposing of, dealing in, licensing or selling that sound recording to any party, if the right to dispose of, deal in, license or sell such sound recording has been conferred by contract or other written document by such living person or the holder of such right. Nothing contained in the foregoing sentence shall be deemed to abrogate or otherwise limit any rights or remedies otherwise conferred by federal law or state law").

[277] 2009 Conn. Super. LEXIS 1982 (July 20, 2009).

[278] *Id.* at *10–*12.

[279] 612 N.E.2d 699 (N.Y. 1993).

hospitalization was otherwise a secret. The court held that the plaintiff could not sue under the New York statute which prevents appropriation of name or likeness. As the court explained:

> [A] "picture illustrating an article on a matter of public interest is not considered used for the purpose of trade or advertising within the prohibition of the statute . . . unless it has no real relationship to the article. . . ."

> We have been reluctant to intrude upon reasonable editorial judgments in determining whether there is a real relationship between an article and photograph. . . . In [*Finger v. Omni Publications International, Ltd.*, 566 N.E.2d 141 (N.Y. 1990)], for example, a magazine without consent used a photograph of plaintiffs and their six children to illustrate a segment about caffeine-enhanced fertility. Although none of the children had been conceived in the manner suggested by the article, we concluded that the requisite nexus between the article and photograph was established because the article's theme — having a large family — was fairly reflected in the picture.

> In the present case, . . . [the] subject of the article was Hedda Nussbaum's physical and emotional recovery from the beatings allegedly inflicted by Joel Steinberg. The photograph of a visibly healed Nussbaum, interacting with her smiling, fashionably clad "companion" offers a stark contrast to the adjacent photograph of Nussbaum's disfigured face. The visual impact would not have been the same had the Post cropped plaintiff out of the photograph, as she suggests was required. Thus, there is a real relationship between the article and the photograph of plaintiff, and the civil rights cause of action was properly dismissed.[280]

Biographies and Fiction. The right of publicity does not prevent the publication of books or articles using the names or pictures of actual people, as in an unauthorized biography.[281] Similarly, actual persons and institutions can be given roles in works of fiction. Thus, *University of Notre Dame du Lac v. Twentieth Century-Fox Film Corp.*,[282] involved a university which unsuccessfully sought injunctive relief against a motion picture featuring a preposterous college football game and use of the name, symbols, and reputation of the university, as well as specific references to its president.

Movies Based on Life Stories and Related Marketing. In *Whitehurst v. Showtime Networks, Inc.*,[283] a claim for appropriation was based on the motion picture "Jasper, Texas," and its related promotional efforts. In finding that the plaintiff failed to state a cause of action, a federal court in Texas adopted the recommendation of a magistrate, whose opinion stated:

---

[280] *Id.* at 703–04.

[281] *See Meeropol v. Nizer*, 560 F.2d 1061 (2d Cir. 1977).

[282] 207 N.E.2d 508 (N.Y. 1965).

[283] 2009 U.S. Dist. LEXIS 87530 (E.D. Tex. Aug. 28, 2009).

. . . In his pleading, the Plaintiff [Whitehurst] claims that he is "a 17% Registered Owner of the Property Rights, for the use of the name, voice, signature, photograph, or likeness of the deceased individual James Byrd, Jr. . . .

. . . [A] plaintiff cannot claim for misappropriation of a "life story.". . . .

. . . It is undisputed that the factual issues presented in "Jasper, Texas" were a matter of public concern and newsworthy in nature, as the real life account of James Byrd, Jr.'s death was highly publicized in the news media as a newsworthy event open to public observation. Any fictionalized depiction of the events of James Byrd's, Jr.'s life and/or tragic death is unactionable under Texas law on misappropriation because it involves his "life story" and biographical information. . . .

In his response, Mr. Whitehurst turns his focus to the DVD cover for the "Jasper, Texas" film released by Showtime. He seems to contend that the portrayal of what is supposed to be Byrd's likeness on the cover the DVD for "the purpose of soliciting the purchase of the entertainment product" by the Defendant constitutes unlawful appropriation of Byrd's likeness. . . . This argument does not salvage his misappropriation claim.

Courts have held that misappropriation claims stemming from the privacy rights discussed in Section 652C of the *Restatement of Torts* should not apply to motion pictures or similar works when considering whether there is a "commercial purpose" because the motion picture would be entitled to First Amendment protection and thus excepted from liability. . . . In other words, expression by means of motion pictures is included within the free speech and free press guarantees of the Constitution, and thus does not necessarily constitute a "commercial purpose" necessary to support a claim for misappropriation. . . .

In . . . [*Seale v. Gramercy Pictures*, 949 F. Supp. 331 (E.D. Pa. 1996)], the court held that the defendants' use of the plaintiff's name and likeness in the content of the book and the film at issue in that case, "Panther," was protected from suit for (mis)appropriation of his identity under the First Amendment and because the defendants' use of his name and likeness in the film was not for the purposes of trade or for a commercial purpose. . . . Rather, the use of his name and likeness was for the purpose of First Amendment expression: the creation, production, and promotion of a motion picture and history book which integrated fictitious people and events with historical events. . . . The court further concluded that the defendants' use of the plaintiff's name and likeness on the cover of the pictorial history book and the cover for the home video (both produced for the film "Panther") were clearly related to the content of the book and the film. . . . Because the covers dealt with the same subject matter as the film, the Court held that the defendants were also entitled to judgment on plaintiff's claims for misappropriation of his likeness on the cover for the home video and the pictorial book insofar as his claim related to the defendants' use of his name and likeness.

Mr. Whitehurst's misappropriation claim falls squarely within the Court's decision in *Seale*. He has already conceded that the use of James Byrd, Jr.'s likeness in the film itself is protected and not subject to liability because the film involves his life story, thus exempting it from the parameters of a misappropriation claim under Texas law. Because the film itself is protected and not subject to suit, it follows that the promotion of the film is protected under *Seale*. This promotion includes using Byrd's likeness on the DVD cover. Accordingly, the Defendant cannot be held liable for using the likeness in the DVD cover, just as the cover of the home video in Seale was protected and did not give rise to liability.[284]

Entertainment (and the Zacchini Rule). As the preceding sections suggest, the First Amendment protects a wide range of artistic and educational endeavors from liability for appropriation of name or likeness. In *Armstrong v. Eagle Rock Entertainment, Inc.*,[285] a dispute arose from a DVD entitled, "Mahavishnu Orchestra, Live at Montreux, 1984, 1974," which included video and still pictures of a professional bass player who was a member of the orchestra in 1974. Addressing the bass player's appropriation claim, the court wrote:

> The First Amendment privilege does not only extend to news in the sense of current events, but "extends far beyond to include all types of factual, educational, and historical data, or even entertainment and amusement, concerning interesting phases of human activity in general." *Nichols v. Moore*, 334 F. Supp. 2d 944, 956 (E.D. Mich. 2004). For example, in *Nichols*, the court held that the First Amendment barred Plaintiff James Nichols' appropriation claim based on an interview of Nichols that was recorded by Michael Moore and included in a Moore film, "Bowling for Columbine," because it was relevant to the Oklahoma City bombing. . . . Works of artistic expression such as movies, plays, books, and songs are protected by the First Amendment. . . . In addition, the First Amendment privilege applies even if the material is published to make a profit. . . . For example, . . . [*Bowens v. Aftermath Entertainment*, No. 250984, 2005 Mich. App. LEXIS 988, 2005 WL 900603, at *1 (Mich. Ct. App.)], a DVD of a "national gangster rap concert tour" was privileged by the First Amendment against appropriation claims by those taped and included in the DVD without their permission because the "Up in Smoke Tour" and Detroit officials' actions regarding the tour were "newsworthy or of legitimate public concern.". . . . Whether the privilege applies "depends on the character of the publication," and is a determination that is made by the court as a matter of law. . . .

> The First Amendment privilege against appropriation liability, though, is not unlimited. *Zacchini v. Scripps-Howard Broadcasting Co.*, 433 U.S. 562 (1977). The media is not privileged to "broadcast a performer's entire act without his consent." . . . In *Zacchini*, a news station broadcast the plaintiff's fifteen-second human cannonball act even though plaintiff asked

---

[284] *Whitehurst v. Showtime Networks, Inc.*, 2009 U.S. Dist. LEXIS 87530, at *19–*25 (E.D. Tex. Aug. 28, 2009), adopted by 2009 U.S. Dist. LEXIS 87528 (E.D. Tex. Sept. 22, 2009).

[285] 655 F. Supp. 2d 779 (E.D. Mich. 2009).

the reporter not to film the performance. . . . The Court held that plaintiff's appropriation claim was not foreclosed by the First Amendment because it was "an attempt to broadcast or publish an entire action for which the performer ordinarily gets paid." . . .

Based on this precedent, the court concludes that the First Amendment bars liability for the use of Plaintiff's picture on the DVD cover and in the liner notes. However, under *Zacchini*, the First Amendment does not protect the use of Defendant's performance on the DVD because it included Plaintiff's entire act and was allegedly published without his consent.[286]

Sports and Athletes. Stories about athletes typically enjoy broad First Amendment protection. For example, in *Chapman v. Journal Concepts, Inc.*,[287] the defendant published a story about a surfer. In rejecting the surfer's appropriation claim, the court began with the broad, but perhaps useful observation that "[l]iability under this legal theory is generally limited to unauthorized use in connection with the promotion or advertisement of a product or service and not, as is the case here, for use in a magazine story."[288] The court then addressed relevant precedent and the facts:

> Defendants argue that surfing is newsworthy and a matter of public interest under the reasoning set forth in *Dora v. Frontline Video*, 15 Cal. App. 4th 536, 18 Cal. Rptr. 2d 790, 792 (1993), in which the court found that a documentary chronicling the events and personalities of Malibu's early days of surfing was protected by the First Amendment. That court observed that
>
>> surfing is more than passing interest to some. It has created a lifestyle that influences speech, behavior, dress, and entertainment, among other things. A phenomenon of such scope has an economic impact, because it affects purchases, travel, and the housing market. Surfing has also had a significant influence on the popular culture, and in that way touches many people. It would be difficult to conclude that a surfing documentary does not fall within the category of public affairs.
>
> . . . The court thus found that the documentary's producers were not required to secure the plaintiff's consent prior to using his name, likeness, or voice. . . .
>
> The court finds persuasive *Dora's* teachings that journalism explaining, profiling, or examining a social subculture, such as surfing, is valuable and relevant because it serves as a type of anthropological reflection on modern society. The court notes, however, that the publication at issue in the case at bar does not address surfing in a generalized or historical sense, but instead focuses on the personality and behavior of one particular individual. Although the newsworthiness of such a piece may be suspect, Plaintiff is an iconic figure in the surfing world and his place in surfing history is secure.

---

[286] *Id.* at *13–*15.

[287] 528 F. Supp. 2d 1081 (D. Haw. 2007).

[288] *Id.* at 1096.

Johnson's tale of his interactions with Plaintiff — including Plaintiff's quirky mannerisms, quips, and colorful history — sheds light on one of surfing's more intriguing personalities and, by extension, on the sport and culture itself. . . . The published article, photographs, and liner notes are newsworthy and relevant. . . .[289]

(b) Actual Malice and Noncommercial Speech

In *Hoffman v. Capital Cities/ABC, Inc.*,[290] a still photograph of the actor Dustin Hoffman in women's clothing from the movie "Tootsie" was used to create a composite computer-generated image that depicted him wearing contemporary designer women's clothes. The altered image was published as part of an article on "Grand Illusions" that featured 16 modified stills from famous movies. The Ninth Circuit held that Hoffman failed to state an action for appropriation. According to the court, the depiction was entitled to full constitutional protection because it was not pure commercial speech merely proposing a transaction. Although the image appeared in a magazine advertising the designer's clothes, it was a "combination of fashion photography, humor, and visual and verbal editorial comment on classic films and famous actors." Because the speech in question was fully protected by the Constitution, the plaintiff was required to show that the defendant acted with actual malice, namely that it intended to create a false impression in the mind of readers that when they saw the altered photograph they were seeing the actor's body. Because there were references in the accompanying article that made clear that digital techniques were used to substitute current fashions for clothes worn in the original stills, and the original stills were presented at the end of the article, it was not possible for the plaintiff to prove actual malice. The court noted that in many right of publicity cases the question of actual malice does not arise because the challenged use does no more than propose a commercial transaction and does not implicate the First Amendment's protection of expressions of editorial opinion.

(2) Limits on Newsworthiness and Public Interest

A good lawyer representing an appropriation plaintiff must be familiar with factors which limit the scope of the First Amendment rights of defendants. In addition to the United States Supreme Court's decision in *Zacchini v. Scripps-Howard Broadcasting Co.*,[291] consider the following sections.

(a) Lack of Artistic Relevance

Wholly Unrelated Uses Or Disguised Advertisements. In *Rogers v. Grimaldi*,[292] the actress Ginger Rogers sued producers and distributors of the movie "Ginger and Fred." In addressing the appropriation claim, the Second Circuit wrote:

---

[289] *Id.* at 1097–98.

[290] 255 F.3d 1180 (9th Cir. 2001).

[291] 433 U.S. 562 (1977).

[292] 875 F.2d 994 (2d Cir. 1989).

[Some] courts, citing their concern for free expression, have refused to extend the right of publicity to bar the use of a celebrity's name in the title and text of a fictional or semi-fictional book or movie. . . .

. . . [*Guglielmi v. Spelling-Goldberg Productions*, 25 Cal. 603 P.2d 454 (Cal. 1979)] involved a suit by a nephew of the late film star Rudolph Valentino to bar a television broadcast entitled "Legend of Valentino: A Romantic Fiction" as a violation of Valentino's right of publicity. The Court dismissed the action for failure to state a claim. In a concurrence joined by three members of the Court, Chief Justice Bird stated: "[P]rominence invites creative comment. Surely, the range of free expression would be meaningfully reduced if prominent persons in the present and recent past were forbidden topics for the imaginations of authors of fiction." . . .

Chief Justice Bird noted that a cause of action might have existed had the defendant, for example, published "Rudolph Valentino's Cookbook," and neither the recipes nor the menus described were in any fashion related to Valentino. . . . But she said that as long as the use of a celebrity's name was not "wholly unrelated" to the individual nor used to promote or endorse a collateral commercial product, the right of publicity did not apply. . . . Similarly, New York's Appellate Division said in . . . [*Frosch v. Grosset & Dunlop, Inc.*, 75 A.D.2d 768 (N.Y. App. Div. 1980)] that the right of publicity did not bar the use of a celebrity's name in a title so long as the item was a literary work and not "simply a disguised commercial advertisement for the sale of goods or services.". . . .

Here, . . . the title "Ginger and Fred" is clearly related to the content of the movie and is not a disguised advertisement for the sale of goods or services or a collateral commercial product. We therefore hold that under Oregon law the right of publicity does not provide relief for Rogers' claim.[293]

(b)   Lack of a Transformative Element

No Significant Creative Contribution. Can an artist sell sketches of celebrities, such as The Three Stooges, without becoming liable for appropriation? In *Comedy Three Productions, Inc. v. Gary Saderup, Inc.*,[294] the Supreme Court of California held that an artist faced with a right of publicity challenge may assert an affirmative defense that the work is protected by the First Amendment, if the work contains significant transformative elements or the value of the work does not derive primarily from the celebrity's fame. Something more than a mere trivial variation is required. "The artist must have created something recognizably his or her own, in order to qualify for legal protection." Because the defendants' portraits of The Three Stooges contained "no significant transformative or creative contribution," the defendants were liable for violating the plaintiff's right of publicity relating to deceased personalities.

---

[293] *Id.* at 1004–05.

[294] 21 P.3d 797 (Cal. 2001).

Adding "New Expression." In contrast, in *Ross v. Roberts*,[295] a California appellate court held that a rapper's appropriation of a cocaine dealer's name and persona was transformative and therefore completely protected from an appropriation claim. As the court explained:

> Roberts created a celebrity identity, using the name Rick Ross, of a cocaine kingpin turned rapper. He was not simply an imposter seeking to profit solely off the name and reputation of Rick Ross. Rather, he made music out of fictional tales of dealing drugs and other exploits — some of which related to plaintiff. Using the name and certain details of an infamous criminal's life as basic elements, he created original artistic works. "A work is transformative if it adds 'new expression.' " . . . Roberts's work clearly added new expression.[296]

The court explained:

> Roberts's music may be analogized to a work of fiction in which the protagonist bears some resemblance to the original Rick Ross. The resemblance is one "raw material" upon which the story is based, but it is merely a minor detail when viewed in the context of the larger story — Roberts's music and persona are much more than literal depictions of the real Rick Ross.[297]

(c)   Example: *Toffoloni v. LFP Publishing Group LLP*

In *Toffoloni v. LFP Publishing Group, LLC*,[298] a female professional wrestler was murdered by her husband, a well-known professional wrestler. The decedent's estate then brought an action based on the right of publicity against the publisher of Hustler Magazine, which, in connection with an article about the decedent's death, printed nude photographs of the decedent taken twenty years prior to her death. Discussing the claim, the Eleventh Circuit wrote:

> Toffoloni argues that she should be allowed to sue for damages incident to the publication of nude pictures of her deceased daughter because those photographs were published against her express direction and were violative of her daughter's right of publicity. LFP responds that it published an article on the life, career, and tragic death of Benoit, which "includes comment on the modest beginnings of Ms. Benoit's career, and is accompanied by images of Ms. Benoit from that time." LFP argues that the article and related images are of substantial public interest and are therefore newsworthy.[299]

---

[295] 222 Cal. App. 4th 677 (2013).

[296] *Id.* at 368.

[297] *Id.* at 369.

[298] 572 F.3d 1201 (11th Cir. 2009).

[299] *Id.* at 1208.

The Merely Incidental Relationship Between the Article and Photographs.
The court first discussed the pertinence of the photographs as illustrations, writing:

> First, it seems clear that had LFP published the nude photographs of
> Benoit by themselves — *i.e.*, without a corresponding news article — the
> publication would not qualify within the newsworthiness exception. The fact
> of Benoit's nudity is not in and of itself newsworthy. . . .

> Here, however, LFP published the photographs alongside a biographical
> piece on Benoit's career. The biographical piece, in and of itself, certainly
> falls within the newsworthiness exception. . . . The question before us is
> whether a brief biographical piece can ratchet otherwise protected, per-
> sonal photographs into the newsworthiness exception.

> . . . Although LFP argues that the photographs were illustrative of the
> substantive, biographical article included in Hustler, our review of the
> publication demonstrates that such is not the case. These photographs were
> not incidental to the article. Rather, the article was incidental to the
> photographs.

> The magazine cover advertises "WRESTLER CHRIS BENOIT'S MUR-
> DERED WIFE NUDE." The table of contents lists "NANCY BENOIT
> Exclusive Nude Pics of Wrestler's Doomed Wife." Neither the cover nor the
> table of contents makes any reference to the accompanying article. The
> article is entitled "NANCY BENOIT Au Naturel: The long-lost images of
> wrestler Chris Benoit's doomed wife." The title and page frame, which
> reads "EXCLUSIVE PICS! EXCLUSIVE PICS!," comprise about one-
> third of the first page. A second third of the page is devoted to two nude
> photographs of Benoit. The final third of the page discusses Benoit's
> murder and her nude photo shoot, twice referencing her brief desire to be
> a model. The second page of the article is entirely devoted to photographs,
> displaying eight additional photographs of Benoit. The heart of this article
> was the publication of nude photographs — not the corresponding biogra-
> phy.

> The *Martin Luther King, Jr., Center for Social Change* case[300] is particu-
> larly relevant here. In that case, the . . . plaintiffs argued that their right
> of publicity was violated when B&S Sales manufactured and sold a plastic
> bust of Dr. King without their permission. Although the opinion does not
> deal expressly with the "newsworthiness" exception to the right of public-
> ity, the Supreme Court of Georgia specifically notes that B&S Sales offered
> a free biographical booklet detailing "the life of Dr. King entitled 'A Tribute
> to Dr. Martin Luther King, Jr.,' " alongside the bust. . . . The court did not
> conclude that the booklet rendered Dr. King's image, in and of itself,
> newsworthy. Rather, the opinion treats the existence of the booklet as
> irrelevant. The booklet was merely incidental to the bust. Without more, Dr.
> King's estate's right of publicity in his image could trump freedom of
> speech and the press.

---

[300] *Martin Luther King Ctr. for Social Change Inc. v. American Heritage Products, Inc.*, 296 S.E.2d
697 (Ga. 1982).

We are convinced that the Supreme Court of Georgia would find similarly here. LFP's brief biography of Benoit's life, even with its reference to her youthful pursuit of modeling, is merely incidental to its publication of her nude photographs. Therefore, the biographical piece cannot suffice to render the nude photographs newsworthy.[301]

Relationship of the Photographs to a Matter of Public Concern. The *Toffoloni* court then turned to the issue of whether the use of the photographs was immunized from tort liability because of their relationship to a matter of public concern. The court explained:

> [W]e are convinced that the nude photographs are not connected to the incident of public concern. LFP would have us rule that someone's notorious death constitutes a carte blanche for the publication of any and all images of that person during his or her life, regardless of whether those images were intentionally kept private and regardless of whether those images are of any relation to the incident currently of public concern. We disagree.
>
> The Georgia courts have never held . . . that if one is the victim of an infamous murder, one's entire life is rendered the legitimate subject of public scrutiny. . . . Rather, the Georgia courts have consistently indicated that there are timeliness or relatedness boundaries that circumscribe the breadth of public scrutiny to the incident of public interest.
>
> For example, in *Tucker v. News Publishing Company*, 197 Ga. App. 85, 397 S.E.2d 499 (1990), the court recognized that "through no fault of his own, [the] appellant [who had been attacked] became the object of public interest." . . . The attack itself "necessarily became a matter of legal investigation and the subject matter of public records." . . . Thus, the court concluded "[d]uring the pendency and continuation of the investigation, and until such time as the perpetrator[s] of the crime may be apprehended and brought to justice under the rules of our society, the matter will continue to be one of public interest, and the dissemination of information pertaining thereto would not amount to a violation of [appellant's] right of privacy." . . . The court expressly envisioned outside boundaries to the realm of public scrutiny: "the matter [of] public interest" and the "time [that] the perpetrator[s] of the crime may be apprehended and brought to justice. . . ."[302]

Limits Recognized by the Restatement. The *Toffoloni* court then drew upon language in the *Restatement* to support its resolution of the case:

> The *Restatement* recognizes that, although an individual may be rendered subject to public scrutiny by some newsworthy event, "[t]he extent of the authority to make public private facts is not . . . unlimited." *Restatement (Second) of Torts* § 652D cmt. h. The *Restatement* concludes that even public figures, like actresses, may be "entitled" to keep private "some

---

[301] 572 F.3d at 1209–10.

[302] *Id.* at 1210.

intimate details . . . such as sexual relations." . . . The line "is to be drawn when the publicity ceases to be the giving of information to which the public is entitled, and becomes a morbid and sensational prying into private lives for its own sake, with which a reasonable member of the public, with decent standards, would say that he had no concern." . . . The *Restatement* expounds that "[t]he limitations . . . are those of common decency, having due regard to the freedom of the press and its reasonable leeway to choose what it will tell the public, but also due regard to the feelings of the individual and the harm that will be done to him by the exposure." . . . Furthermore, "[s]ome reasonable proportion is also to be maintained between the event or activity that makes the individual a public figure and the private facts to which publicity is given.". . . .

Here, the published nude photographs were in no conceivable way related to the "incident of public concern" or current "drama," Benoit's death. The district court erred in its reliance upon *Waters v. Fleetwood*, 212 Ga. 161, 91 S.E.2d 344 (1956), in which the Supreme Court of Georgia "found no actionable right when a defendant featured gratuitous, sensational photographs alongside a legitimate news article" to direct the dismissal of Toffoloni's claim. . . . In *Waters*, the offensive photographs were of the child's deceased body, and as such were directly related to the "incident of public interest" — the child's death. LFP published photographs of Benoit that were at least twenty years old to correspond to a brief discussion about her aspiring career as a model. Those photographs had no relation to her death. Her aspiring nude modeling career at no time developed into an incident of public concern, and for good reason — Benoit sought the destruction of all of those images.

. . . [W]e are guided by the Tenth Circuit's conclusion that "[b]ecause each member of our society at some time engages in an activity that fairly could be characterized as a matter of legitimate public concern, to permit that activity to open the door to the exposure of any truthful secret about that person would render meaningless the tort of public disclosure of private facts." *Gilbert v. Med. Econ. Co.*, 665 F.2d 305, 308 (10th Cir. 1981). We agree with the Tenth Circuit that the First Amendment "does not require such a result. Therefore, to properly balance freedom of the press against the right of privacy, every private fact disclosed in an otherwise truthful, newsworthy publication must have some substantial relevance to a matter of legitimate public interest." . . .

The photographs published by LFP neither relate to the incident of public concern conceptually nor correspond with the time period during which Benoit was rendered, against her will, the subject of public scrutiny. . . . On these facts, were we to hold otherwise, LFP would be free to publish any nude photographs of almost anyone without their permission, simply because the fact that they were caught nude on camera strikes someone as "newsworthy." Surely that debases the very concept of a right to privacy.[303]

---

[303] *Id.* at 1211–12.

c.   Monetary Relief

Damages and Restitution. The monetary relief available to the victim of commercial appropriation may be measured in accordance with principles of damages (based on losses of the plaintiff) or restitution for unjust enrichment (based on gains to the defendant). In the usual case, if both damages and unjust enrichment are established, the greater amount will be awarded.[304]

However, in some cases, entitlement to both remedies is not supported by the facts. Thus, in *Havenstrite v. Hartford Life Ins. Co.*,[305] plaintiffs who had not paid premiums to an insurer (and therefore had suffered no damages) sought disgorgement of profits that the insurer made by using their identities to sell a legally impermissible form of insurance on their lives to the plaintiffs' employer. A federal court in Oklahoma found that the plaintiffs adequately alleged a claim for disgorgement based on unauthorized appropriation.

Nominal Damages. Some courts hold that nominal damages may be awarded for unauthorized use of name or likeness in cases where actual losses are not caused by the defendant's conduct.[306]

Statutory Remedies. In some states, there is a statutory remedy for misappropriation. For example in *Coton v. Televised Visual X-Ography, Inc.*,[307] a federal court in Florida authorized $25,000 in compensation because, in violation of statute, the plaintiff's self-portrait was prominently placed, without her permission, on the packaging for a DVD of marketing a pornographic movie.

d.   Injunctive Relief

Under generally applicable principles of the law of remedies, injunctive relief may be awarded to prevent continuing or threatened appropriation of name or likeness.[308]

PROBLEM 4-12: THE SUBWAY HERO

John Golden became internationally famous when he leapt from a subway platform to the tracks to save a child who had fallen there, just as a train was pulling into the station. The events were captured on video. The images were broadcast on news programs worldwide. A posting of the video on YouTube received millions of hits.

The image that stuck in the minds of many persons was a close-up of Golden's face taken after he crawled back onto the platform to avoid being hit by the train. His expression was a mixture of confusion and relief, with sweat running down from his forehead.

---

[304] *See* RESTATEMENT (THIRD) OF UNFAIR COMPETITION § 49 (1995).

[305] 2008 U.S. Dist. LEXIS 105316 (N.D. Okla. Dec. 31, 2008).

[306] *See James v. Bob Ross Buick, Inc.*, 855 N.E.2d 119, 123–34 (Ohio Ct. App. 2006) (citing cases).

[307] 740 F. Supp. 2d 1299 (M.D. Fla. 2010).

[308] RESTATEMENT (THIRD) OF UNFAIR COMPETITION § 48 (1995).

That picture was the one that the Dré Dogs put on the cover of their new music CD. The album, called "Subway Hero," contained a song called "John Golden." A sticker on the front of the CD package describes that selection as a "hot single."

The music on the CD is of the hip hop genre, with lyrics often ranging from incomprehensible to tasteless. The songs have nothing to do with Golden's subway rescue, or even with subways. Rather, if there is a theme to the music, it deals with being young in a big city.

Golden did not authorize the use of his name or picture in connection with the CD, and he wants to halt the marketing of the album. Please advise him as to whether tort principles governing invasion of privacy provide a basis for him to seek injunctive relief.

3.   Appropriation for Noncommercial Benefit

By far, the greater number of appropriation cases involve some type of obvious commercial benefit to the defendant. However, according to the *Restatement (Second) of Torts*, noncommercial appropriation of name or likeness is actionable. The *Restatement* offers examples which, depending on how they are interpreted, may not involve commercial advantage. Those examples involve impersonating someone to induce others to disclose confidential information and posing as a man's wife by using his wife's name.[309]

Is Falsity Required? In *Hinish v. Meier & Frank Co.*,[310] the Supreme Court of Oregon found an actionable invasion of privacy where the plaintiff's name had been signed, without his consent, to a telegram urging the governor to veto a bill. Query: would the result have been the same if the message sent by the defendant had simply stated, "Mr. Hinish, too, opposes the bill," and in fact Hinish did oppose the bill and had expressed his opposition to the defendant? The Supreme Court of Oregon, in *Humphers v. First Interstate Bank*,[311] considered this hypothetical and opined that no action would lie, saying, "The false appropriation, not the potential public exposure of Hinish's actual views, constituted the tort."[312] However, the blackletter rule in the *Restatement (Second) of Torts* does not state that falsity is a requirement of an appropriation action.[313]

Some States Require Commercial Benefit. Some states hold that appropriation of name or likeness is not actionable absent proof of commercial benefit. Thus, in *Jeffries v. Whitney E. Houston Academy P.T.A.*,[314] the New Jersey Superior Court Appellate Division rejected an appropriation claim based on videotaping of children at an elementary school. The court found that New Jersey courts consistently require proof of commercial benefit, and the trial court had found that the PTA acted for a charitable rather than commercial purpose.

---

[309] *See* RESTATEMENT (SECOND) OF TORTS § 652C illus. 3 & 4 (1977).

[310] 113 P.2d 438 (Or. 1941).

[311] 696 P.2d 527 (Or. 1985).

[312] *Id.* at 532.

[313] RESTATEMENT (SECOND) OF TORTS § 652C (1977).

[314] 2009 N.J. Super. Unpub. LEXIS 1895 (July 20, 2009).

4. Celebrities

Many unauthorized appropriation claims involve celebrities, living and dead. A complex body of law has developed to govern these kinds of cases.

a. Persons Playing Fictional Characters

Many actors become famous for playing fictional characters. In such a case, may the owner of the production license others to use the character's likeness without the actor's consent? In *Wendt v. Host International, Inc.*,[315] the Ninth Circuit answered this question in the negative. In that case, George Wendt and John Ratzenberger played "Norm" and "Cliff" on a television show called "Cheers," which was set in a bar. Paramount Pictures, Inc., which owned the rights to the show, licensed the defendant to create airport bars resembling the bar on the television program. The defendant's bars included robot figures bearing some resemblance to the television characters portrayed by the plaintiffs. The court ruled that a jury could find that the defendant's use of the robots violated the plaintiffs' right of publicity by appropriating their likenesses if it found that the robots sufficiently resembled Wendt and Ratzenberger. The court found that an actor does not lose the right to control the commercial exploitation of the actor's likeness by portraying a fictional character.

b. Deceased Celebrities

Does the right of publicity survive the death of a celebrity? In other words, is the right of publicity descendible?

In Some States, the Right Is Not Descendible. Some jurisdictions say that death terminates the right of publicity. For example, in New York, the right of publicity is protected civilly by a statute which grants the right to "any living person."[316] This language has been interpreted to mean that when the person in question dies, the right disappears.[317]

In Some States, Descendibility Depends on Prior Exploitation. Some jurisdictions hold, as a matter of common law, that descendibility of the right of publicity depends upon whether the right was exploited by the decedent during life. For example, in *State Ex Rel. Elvis Presley International Memorial Foundation v. Crowell*,[318] a not-for-profit corporation, which had been using the name "Elvis Presley" in its corporate title, sued another corporation for unfair competition to prevent the defendant corporation from using that name. The Tennessee Court of Appeals held that under state common law (since modified by statute), the "right of publicity" survived the death of the person in question, at least if the decedent had exploited that right during life, as Presley did.

In Some States, Descendibility Does Not Require Prior Exploitation. In

---

[315] 125 F.3d 806 (9th Cir. 1997).

[316] N.Y. CIVIL RIGHTS LAW § 51 (LEXIS 2014).

[317] *See Pirone v. MacMillan, Inc.*, 894 F.2d 579 (2d Cir. 1990).

[318] 733 S.W.2d 89 (Tenn. Ct. App. 1987).

contrast, in *Martin Luther King Center for Social Change Inc. v. American Heritage Products, Inc.*,[319] the Supreme Court of Georgia held that the right of publicity is descendible without prior exploitation. In that case, the defendant, without permission, manufactured and sold plastic busts of King. Rejecting the defendant's argument that commercial exploitation during life was required, the court said:

> The cases which have considered this issue . . . involved entertainers. The net result of following them would be to say that celebrities and public figures have the right of publicity during their lifetimes (as others have the right of privacy), but only those who contract for bubble gum cards, posters and tee shirts have a descendible right of publicity upon their deaths. . . . That we should single out for protection after death those entertainers and athletes who exploit their personae during life, and deny protection after death to those who enjoy public acclamation but did not exploit themselves during life, puts a premium on exploitation. Having found valid reasons for recognizing the right of publicity during life, we find no reason to protect after death only those who took commercial advantage of their fame.[320]

Descendibilty Under Statutes. In states in which the right of publicity is created or recognized by statute, the inheritability and the duration of the right depends upon the language of the legislative enactment. For example, Tennessee law now provides:

§ 47-25-1103. *Property right in use of name, photograph or likeness*

(a) Every individual has a property right in the use of that person's name, photograph, or likeness in any medium in any manner.

(b) The individual rights provided for in subsection (a) constitute property rights and are freely assignable and licensable, and do not expire upon the death of the individual so protected, whether or not such rights were commercially exploited by the individual during the individual's lifetime, but shall be descendible to the executors, assigns, heirs, or devisees of the individual so protected by this part.

§ 47-25-1104. *Exclusive rights, commercial exploitation after death*

(a) The rights provided for in this part shall be deemed exclusive to the individual, subject to the assignment or licensing of such rights as provided in § 47-25-1103, during such individual's lifetime and to the executors, heirs, assigns, or devisees for a period of ten (10) years after the death of the individual.

(b)(1) Commercial exploitation of the property right by any executor, assignee, heir, or devisee if the individual is deceased shall maintain the right as the exclusive property of the executor, assignee, heir, or devisee until such right is terminated as provided in this subsection (b).

---

[319] 296 S.E.2d 697, 706 (Ga. 1982).

[320] *Id.* at 706.

(2) The exclusive right to commercial exploitation of the property rights is terminated by proof of the non-use of the name, likeness, or image of any individual for commercial purposes by an executor, assignee, heir, or devisee to such use for a period of two (2) years subsequent to the initial ten (10) year period following the individual's death.[321]

Since Hollywood remains an important center of the American film and entertainment industries, California law dealing with the right of publicity and descendibility is particularly important. The relevant legal principles have changed over the years. In *Hebrew University of Jerusalem v. General Motors LLC*,[322] a federal court in California explained:

> In *Lugosi v. Universal Pictures*, a 4-3 decision, the California Supreme Court held "that the right to exploit name and likeness is personal to the artist and must be exercised, if at all, by him during his lifetime." 25 Cal. 3d 813, 824, 160 Cal. Rptr. 323, 603 P.2d 425 (1979). . . . The California Supreme Court later clarified that *Lugosi* held "that the right of publicity protects against the unauthorized use of one's name, likeness or personality, but that the right is not descendible and expires upon the death of the person so protected." . . . In 1985, the California legislature enacted a statute expressly recognizing a postmortem right of publicity without need of lifetime exploitation. Cal. Civil Code § 990. In 1999, Civil Code section 990 was renumbered and the 50-year duration was extended to 70 years. (Cal. Civil Code § 3344.1).[323]

5. Defenses

a. Communications Decency Act

Most tort claims against Internet Service Providers and website operators who are not the originators of offending context are barred by the Communications Decency Act of 1996. (*See* Chapter 3 Part I-1.) One type of tort claim that has occasionally survived the immunities conferred by the Act is an invasion of privacy action for appropriation of name and likeness.

In *Doe v. Friendfinder Network, Inc.*,[324] an unauthorized profile of the plaintiff ("petra03755") was posted on a sex website. As a result of her protests, the profile was removed. However, [t]he profile allegedly continued to appear, with slight modifications, on other similar websites operated by the defendants. In addition, the defendants allegedly caused portions of the "petra03755" profile to appear as "teasers" on Internet search engines and advertisements on other third-party websites, including "sexually related" ones. The search engines retrieved the teasers when users entered search terms matching some of the information in the profile, including true biographical information about the plaintiff. The

---

[321] Tenn. Code Ann. §§ 47-25-1103 & 1004 (LEXIS 2014).

[322] 878 F. Supp. 2d 1021 (C.D. Cal. 2012).

[323] *Id.* at 1029.

[324] 540 F. Supp. 2d 288 (D.N.H. 2008).

advertisements appeared when the third-party website recognized a user's location as near the Upper Valley region of New Hampshire. Through hyperlinks, these teasers and advertisements served to direct Internet traffic to the defendants' own websites, allegedly increasing their profitability.[325]

Addressing the issues raised under the CDA, a federal court in New Hampshire wrote:

> The CDA provides that "[n]othing in this section shall be construed to limit or expand any law pertaining to intellectual property." 47 U.S.C. § 230(e)(2). Relying on this provision, the plaintiff argues that the CDA does not affect her state-law claims for invasion of privacy, which she characterizes as an infringement of her intellectual property rights. . . .

> . . . Count I of the plaintiff's complaint . . . , entitled "Invasion of Privacy/Intellectual Property Rights," asserts four separate theories against the defendants: (1) that they have intruded on her solitude, (2) that they have publicly disclosed private facts about her, (3) that they have given her publicity so as to place her in a false light, and (4) that they have appropriated her identity for their own benefit or advantage. . . .

> While the plaintiff objects to the dismissal of any part of Count I on the ground that it asserts "intellectual property rights" under § 230(e)(2), her argument and authorities on that score address only the fourth theory, commonly known as a "right of publicity" claim. . . . As the plaintiff points out, "the right of publicity is a widely recognized intellectual property right." . . . Such a claim therefore arises out of a "law pertaining to intellectual property" within the meaning of the statute. . . .

> The other three torts encompassed by the "right of privacy" rubric, however, do not fit that description. Unlike a violation of the right to publicity, these causes of action — intrusion upon seclusion, publication of private facts, and casting in false light — protect "a personal right, peculiar to the individual whose privacy is invaded" which cannot be transferred like other property interests. . . . The plaintiffs' claims under these branches of the privacy doctrine, then, do not sound in "law pertaining to intellectual property," and she offers no authority or argument to the contrary. While § 230(e)(2) exempts her right of publicity claim from the immunity provision of the CDA, then, that provision applies with full force to the other invasion of privacy claims asserted in her complaint.[326]

"Twitterjacking." Famed baseball manager Tony La Russa sued Twitter because someone was tastelessly using his name and image while tweeting from an account using the name TonyLaRussa. Experts expressed doubts about the viability of the claim because § 230 of the Communications Decency Act give websites immunity with respect to content they do not originate. Ultimately, La Russa

---

[325] *Id.* at 292–93.

[326] *Id.* at 298–303.

dismissed his claim, and press reports indicated that there was no settlement of any kind.[327]

Domain Name "Cybersquatting." In *Herzfeld & Rubin, P.C. v. Leyden*,[328] a law firm sued the son of a client for "illegally appropriat[ing]" the law firm's name "by registering a website with a domain name nearly identical to its own and posting fictitious news articles on other sites" that disparaged the firm. The complaint included causes of action for defamation, tortious interference, "domain name cybersquatting," and misappropriation of name. There appears to be no reported decision. Could such claims be barred by qualified privilege if the son sought to air grievances that his mother had with the firm? How can a law firm protect itself from unhappy clients?

b.　　　Statutory Authorization

Consent will bar an action for appropriation. The same is true if the transaction in question is authorized by statute. In *Sloan v. South Carolina Department of Public Safety*,[329] the Supreme Court of South Carolina held that a company which purchased driver's license information and photographs, pursuant to a fraud-prevention arrangement authorized by statute, was not liable for appropriation.

c.　　　Single-Publication Rule

Appropriation claims may be barred as untimely by the single-publication rule (*see* Chapter 3). For example, in *Christoff v. Nestle USA, Inc.*,[330] a model learned that his photograph had been used for several years on various advertisements for Taster's Choice coffee, including jar labels, transit ads, newspaper coupons, and promotions in magazines and on the Internet. The Uniform Single Publication Act, codified in California statutes, provides:

> No person shall have more than one cause of action for damages for libel or slander *or invasion of privacy* or any other tort founded upon any single publication or exhibition or utterance, such as any one issue of a newspaper or book or magazine or any one presentation to an audience or any one broadcast over radio or television or any one exhibition of a motion picture. Recovery in any action shall include all damages for any such tort suffered by the plaintiff in all jurisdictions.[331]

Considering the application of those provisions to the plaintiff's appropriation of likeness claim, the California Supreme Court explained:

> It is not clear whether the production of a product label over a period of years is a "single integrated publication" that triggers the running of the

---

[327] *See* Zusha Elinson, *Baseball Manager La Russa Pulls Twitter Suit*, www.law.com, July 7, 2009.

[328] Index No. 154004/2012 (Sup. Ct. of the City of N.Y., filed June 26, 2012). *See* Christine Simmons, *Firm Sues Client's Son to Stop Web Posts It Finds Defamatory*, TEXAS LAWYER (Online), July 12, 2012 (available on LEXIS).

[329] 586 S.E.2d 108 (S.C. 2003).

[330] 213 P.3d 132 (Cal. 2009).

[331] *Id.* at 135 n.5 (emphasis added).

statute of limitations when the first such label is distributed to the public. Publishing an issue of a newspaper or magazine or an edition of a book is a discrete publishing event. A publisher that prints and distributes an issue of a magazine or an edition of a book is entitled to repose from the threat that a copy of that magazine or book will surface years later and trigger a lawsuit. But . . . there is little case law or academic commentary discussing whether a manufacturer that produces a product label for a period of years is entitled to the same repose, especially while that product label is still being produced. Christoff argues that Nestle's conduct qualified as a continuing wrong, in which "a cause of action accrues each time a wrongful act occurs, triggering a new limitations period." . . . Nestle, by contrast, argues that its use of Christoff's image on its product label was a "single overt act" with "a continual effect that is relevant to damages, but does not denote a continuing course of conduct for which the limitations period can be tolled." . . .

We decline to resolve this important issue without the benefit of a sufficient factual record that reveals the manner in which the labels were produced and distributed, including when production of the labels began and ceased. . . . The parties will have that opportunity on remand to the superior court. If on remand it is established that all or some portion of the production of the label constituted a single integrated publication, then the superior court should further consider whether the statute of limitation began anew because the label was "republished" within the meaning of the single-publication rule.[332]

There was no subsequent reported decision in the *Christoff* litigation.

PROBLEM 4-13: THE NIGHTCLUB BENEFIT

Javier Alfredo, a popular community organizer, was shot and killed by an unknown assailant outside Duggan's Speakeasy (Duggan's), a nightclub in a crime plagued part of the city. Without consulting Alfredo's surviving family members, Duggan's announced in a radio ad that, as a gesture of respect to Alfredo, it would donate the following weekend's nightclub proceeds to City Kids. Alfredo was well-known for supporting City Kids before his death. The nightclub operated at full capacity all weekend.

Alfredo's family has consulted you to see if they can sue for invasion of privacy based on the use of Alfredo's identity for promotion of business at the Club.

---

[332] *Id.* at 140–41.

Chapter 5

TORTIOUS INTERFERENCE

A. THE LAW OF TORTIOUS INTERFERENCE

1. Current Status

Two Branches. Liability for tortious interference with economic and other relations encompasses two categories of actions: (1) intentional interference with existing contracts and (2) intentional interference with relationships reasonably calculated to lead to contracts or other advantages. The latter category goes by various names and is often simply called tortious interference with prospective advantage.

Potentially Large Verdicts. Both types of actions are recognized in most states, and they form an important part of modern commercial litigation. Asserted with increasing frequency, these claims have the potential for producing sometimes staggeringly large judgments and settlements. For example, in *Texaco v. Pennzoil*,[1] the jury returned what was then the largest verdict of all time, $10.2 billion (as affirmed on appeal). The case, based on tortious interference with contract, was eventually settled for $3 billion.

Ignored by Tort Reform. In many respects, the law of tortious interference has gone unnoticed by the recurring waves of tort reform during the last thirty years. Reformers have been mainly concerned with run-of-the-mill tort actions, such as negligence and strict products liability claims brought by injured individuals seeking compensation for personal injuries (both physical and emotional) or damage to tangible property. In contrast, the interference torts focus not on personal injury or property damage, in the usual sense of those words, but rather on economic harm to business and similar relationships.

When persons call for tort reform, they seldom have in mind changing the law which governs tortious interference. This is not to say that reformation is unneeded. Indeed, as the materials in this chapter suggest, the contours of the interference torts are in many respects uncertain, and important aspects of the law may differ from one state to the next. Greater clarity and certainty in the law of tortious interference would be a laudable objective. Thus far, the work on the *Restatement (Third) of Torts* has not approved any drafts related to tortious interference with contract or prospective advantage.

Defining the Terms of Permissible Competition. Numerous tortious interference cases arise from employment contexts and involve individual litigants.

---

[1] 729 S.W.2d 768 (Tex. App. 1987).

However, in a wide range of disputes, there are corporate entities on both sides of the litigation. This means that, in many respects, the law of tortious interference defines the bounds of permissible competition between businesses.

The Second Restatement. The *Restatement (Second) of Torts* is an important starting point for understanding the law of tortious interference — but it is only a starting point. The *Restatement* itself acknowledges that this area of the law is still in a formative stage. Moreover, there has been a massive growth of precedent and scholarship since the second *Restatement's* provisions on tortious interference were adopted in 1979.[2]

Most opinions dealing with tortious interference refer to the relevant sections in the *Restatement*. Many decisions have adopted those rules. However, other courts have declined to follow the *Restatement's* lead in certain areas, or have addressed questions left unresolved by the *Restatement*. In this field, more than in many others, it is necessary to stay abreast of recent developments. It is important to remember that:

> [I]n connection with the tort of interference, precedents are only suggestive, . . . and the fact that a situation is one in which a remedy for interference has never previously been granted does not deter the courts from granting a remedy.[3]

A Party to a Relationship Cannot Be Liable for Interference. The law of tortious interference has what might be called a third-party requirement. Ordinarily, a party to the relation may not be sued for interference. This means that an action for tortious interference will lie only when there has been interference with a present or prospective contractual relationship by an outsider to the relation. For example, in *Noller v. GMC Truck & Coach Division*,[4] the Supreme Court of Kansas held that when GMC refused to approve the plaintiff as a dealer, it did not become liable for tortious interference with the prospective relationship between it and the plaintiff. Of course, a party to a contractual agreement is subject to liability for breach. Moreover, a party to a contract can be held liable for interfering with the relationship between the other party to the contract and someone else.

Factual Complexity. It is virtually inevitable that most tortious interference cases are factually complex. Even in the simplest case, there are at least three actors: the two parties to the contract or advantageous relationship, and a third person who interferes. However, since many tortious interference litigants are entities, which can act only through agents, the typical cast of characters quickly expands. One way to manage the complexity is to diagram the actors, entities, and relationships on paper. When all of the names are in place, draw a box around the contractual or advantageous relationship that has allegedly been interfered with. Then mark an arrow showing which persons outside of the relationship are alleged to have tortiously intruded upon that relation.

---

[2] *See* RESTATEMENT (SECOND) OF TORTS §§ 766–774B (1979).

[3] *Torbett v. Wheeling Dollar Sav. & Trusts Co.*, 314 S.E.2d 166, 173 (W. Va. 1983).

[4] 772 P.2d 271 (Kan. 1989).

2.   Historical Development

Discussing the modern beginnings of the interference torts, the Supreme Court of California, in *Della Penna v. Toyota Motor Sales, U.S.A.*,[5] said:

> Although legal historians have traced the origins of the so-called "interference torts" as far back as the Roman law, the proximate historical impetus for their modern development lay in mid-19th century English common law. . . . The opinion of the Queen's Bench in *Lumley v. Gye* (1853) 2 El. & Bl. 216, a case that has become a standard in torts casebooks, is widely cited as the origin of the two torts — interference with contract and its sibling, interference with prospective economic relations — in the form in which they have come down to us. The plaintiff owned the Queen's Theatre, at which operas were presented. He contracted for the services of a soprano, Johanna Wagner, to perform in various entertainments between April 15 and July 15, with the stipulation that Miss Wagner would not perform elsewhere during that time without his permission.
>
> In an action on the case, the theater owner alleged that Gye, the owner of a rival theater, knowing of the Wagner-Lumley agreement, "maliciously" interfered with the contract by "enticing" Wagner to abandon her agreement with Lumley and appear at Gye's theater. Gye's demurrer to the complaint was overruled by the trial court, a ruling that was affirmed by the justices of the Queen's Bench on the then somewhat novel grounds that (1) "enticing" someone to leave his or her employment was not limited to disrupting the relationship between master and servant but applied to a "dramatic artiste" such as Miss Wagner, and (2) "wrongfully and maliciously, or, which is the same thing, with notice, interrupt[ing]" a personal service contract, regardless of the means the defendant employed, was an actionable wrong. . . .
>
> The opinion in *Lumley* dealt, of course, with conduct intended to induce the *breach* of an *existing* contract, not conduct intended to prevent or persuade others not to contract with the plaintiff. That such an interference with *prospective* economic relations might itself be tortious was confirmed by the Queen's Bench over the next 40 years. In *Temperton v. Russell* (1893) 1 Q.B. 715 (*Temperton*), a labor union, embroiled in a dispute with a firm of builders, announced what today would be called a secondary boycott, intended to force a resolution of the union's grievances by pressuring suppliers of the builder to cease furnishing him construction materials. A failure to comply with the union's boycott demands, suppliers were warned, would result in union pressure on those who bought *their* supplies not to deal with *them*.
>
> One such supplier of the builder, Temperton, sued the union's leadership, alleging that his business had been injured by breaches of supply contracts and the refusal of others to do business with him, all as a result of the union's threats. A unanimous Queen's Bench upheld the jury's verdict for

---

[5] 902 P.2d 740 (Cal. 1995).

the plaintiff, reasoning in part on the authority of *Lumley v. Gye, supra*, 2 El. & Bl. 216, that in the words of Lord Esher, the Master of the Rolls, "the distinction . . . between the claim for inducing persons to break contracts already entered into . . . and . . . inducing persons not to enter into contracts . . . can [not] prevail." . . .

As a number of courts and commentators have observed, the keystone of the liability imposed in *Lumley* . . . and *Temperton* . . . , to judge from the opinions of the justices, appears to have been the "malicious" intent of a defendant. . . . While some have doubted whether the use of the word "malicious" amounted to anything more than an intent to commit an act, knowing it would harm the plaintiff . . . , Dean Keeton, assessing the state of the tort as late as 1984, remarked that "[w]ith intent to interfere as the usual basis of the action, the cases have turned almost entirely upon the defendant's motive or purpose and the means by which he has sought to accomplish it. As in the cases of interference with contract, any manner of intentional invasion of the plaintiff's interests may be sufficient if the purpose is not a proper one." . . .[6]

Interference by Nontortious Means. The significance of *Lumley v. Gye* lies in the fact that no violence, fraud, or defamation was alleged by the plaintiff. Earlier cases had imposed liability for tortious interference only when conduct that was essentially tortious in nature was alleged. In *Lumley*, the defendant merely persuaded the opera star to breach her contract (albeit by the payment of money). No tort was committed against the opera singer.[7]

Important Difference. As discussed later in this chapter, some courts today hold that interference with prospectively advantageous relationships must be independently tortious in order to be actionable. The same rule does not apply to interference with contract, where disruption by nontortious means (*e.g.*, persuasion) may still give rise to liability. The difference is accounted for by the fact that a person with a contract has a greater right to legal protection from interference than a person who does not yet have a contract.

B.   CULPABILITY

It is generally agreed, that only intentional interference with a contract or prospectively advantageous relationship is actionable. With limited exceptions, negligent interference with such relations will ordinarily not give rise to liability.[8]

---

[6] *Id.* at 743–44.

[7] *See* RESTATEMENT (SECOND) OF TORTS § 766 cmt. c (1979).

[8] *See id.* § 766C.

1.   Intent Requirement

Purpose Or Knowledge. The concept of intent includes both purpose and knowledge.[9] If the defendant acts with the purpose (meaning subjective desire) of causing a forbidden result, or acts with knowledge (meaning substantial certainty — certainty for all practical purposes) that the result will occur, the defendant will be held to have intentionally caused the result. Because interference with contract and interference with prospective advantage are intentional torts, liability may be imposed if the actor engages in conduct with a purpose of interfering with the performance of the contract or advantageous relationship or if, despite a lack of desire to interfere, the interference is substantially certain to occur.[10]

a.   Knowledge of the Contract

In cases involving disruption of existing contracts, the defendant must intend to interfere with the plaintiff's contract. Therefore, the defendant must have knowledge of the contract, or at least of the facts giving rise to the contract.[11] If the existence of the contract is unknown to the defendant, liability for intentional interference with the contract cannot be imposed.

Networks of Contracts and Liability to Persons Other Than Immediate Parties. Any particular contract may be part of a larger network of interrelated contracts. When one contract is disrupted, other contracts may ultimately be breached as the consequences of the interference ripple through the network. It is therefore important to consider carefully how far the scope of liability extends for tortious interference.

For example, suppose that A has a contract with B, and that, because of that contract, B has entered into contracts with C and D. (C will perform work for B, so that B can meet its contractual obligations with A. D will provide the supplies that B or C will use in performing B's contract with A.) If X improperly induces A not to perform the contract with B, B will lose the benefits of its contract with A. Because labor and supplies will not be needed, B may therefore breach its contract to employ C or buy supplies from D. Is X liable only to B for tortious interference, or to C and D as well?

In answering this question, the first issue is whether X knew about B's contracts with C and D. If not, X is not liable to C or D for tortious interference with their contracts with B. Second, even if X knew about B's contracts with C and D, there is still no liability unless X intended to interfere with those contracts. If it was X's desire to cause B to breach B's contract with C or D, X should be liable to C or D because the facts establish the "purpose" variety of intent. However, if X did not desire to cause B to breach B's contract with C or D, X should not be liable to C or D unless X knew with substantial certainty that causing A not to perform the contract with B would cause B not to perform the contract with C or D. That is, absent "purpose," there should be no liability unless X acted with "knowledge" that

---

[9] *See* RESTATEMENT (THIRD) OF TORTS: LIABILITY FOR PHYSICAL & EMOTIONAL HARM § 1 (2012).

[10] *See* RESTATEMENT (SECOND) OF TORTS § 766 cmt. j (1979).

[11] *See id.* § 766 cmt. i.

B would breach the contract with C or D.

It is important to remember that the knowledge variety of intent is a demanding standard. The evidence must show that B's breach of the contract with C or D was substantially certain to occur, meaning certain for all practical purposes. If X merely created a risk, even a great risk, that B would breach B's contract with C or D, X should not be liable to C or D for tortious interference. Creation of a risk of harm, or even a great risk of harm, to the contractual interests of C or D may amount to negligent or reckless interference with their contracts. However, if there is only a risk of harm, and not a substantial certainty that the contracts will be disrupted, the conduct does not rise to the level of intentional interference. In most states, in a wide range of circumstances, only intentional interference is actionable.

Interference Caused by Statements in the Media. Because liability for tortious interference extends only to specific persons whose contractual interests the actor intends to affect,[12] many statements disseminated by the media to the public at large will not support an action for tortious interference. Similarly, if a prominent person's lecture on the perils of eating meat causes an unknown individual to break a contract with a butcher, there is no liability.[13]

b.   Malice Versus Intent

Ill Will Is Not Required, But Is Relevant to Liability. To recover for tortious interference, a plaintiff is not required to show that the defendant acted with ill will. Although many decisions (particularly older ones) say that proof of "malice" is necessary, what they mean is simply that there must be intentional interference without justification.[14] Because of the risk of confusion over the meaning of the terms "malice" and "malicious," it is probably best to avoid using them altogether.

Proof of ill will on the part of the defendant may bear upon whether interference is found to be "improper" or "unjustified," and therefore actionable. The issue of impropriety is discussed later in the chapter.

c.   "Of and Concerning" Versus Intent

Applying First Amendment Limitations to Interference Involving Speech. Chapter 3 of this book, which deals with liability for defamation, discusses the requirement that in order to be actionable, a statement must be "of and concerning" the plaintiff. That rule is sometimes described as a "colloquium" requirement, which means that the plaintiff must prove that the libelous or slanderous statement referred to the plaintiff.

In *Blatty v. New York Times Co.*,[15] an author (Blatty) sued because his book (*Legion*) was omitted from the New York Times's "best seller" list, which purports to rank best selling books based on actual sales. He alleged five causes of action,

---

[12] *See id.* § 766 cmt. p.

[13] *Id.*

[14] *See id.* § 766 cmt. s.

[15] 728 P.2d 1177 (Cal. 1986).

including two claims for intentional interference with prospective economic advantage. The author's publisher had told the Times that it had sales figures to substantiate its claim that *Legion* merited inclusion, but the Times refused to review the figures. The Supreme Court of California found that each of the five causes of action had as its gravamen the alleged injurious falsehood of a statement, and that the author was not entitled to relief on any count. As the court explained:

> In defamation actions the First Amendment . . . requires that the statement on which the claim is based must specifically refer to, or be "of and concerning," the plaintiff in some way. . . .

> Although the limitations that define the First Amendment's zone of protection for the press were established in defamation actions, they are not peculiar to such actions but apply to all claims whose gravamen is the alleged injurious falsehood of a statement. . . .

> The "of and concerning" or specific reference requirement limits the right of action for injurious falsehood, granting it to those who are the direct object of criticism and denying it to those who merely complain of nonspecific statements that they believe cause them some hurt. To allow a plaintiff who is not identified, either expressly or by clear implication, to institute such an action poses an unjustifiable threat to society. For example, . . . the absence of the "of and concerning" requirement "could invite any number of vexatious lawsuits and seriously interfere with public discussion of issues, or groups, which are in the public eye. . . ."

> It is . . . plain that Blatty's intentional interference claims fail to satisfy First Amendment requirements.

> The claims fail to allege that the list is of and concerning, or specifically refers to, Blatty or his novel. . . .

> To begin with, the list does not expressly refer to Blatty or his novel. . . . Quite the contrary: the failure of *Legion* to appear on the list is the very basis of his action.

> Further, the list cannot be reasonably understood to refer to Blatty or his novel by implication. When, as in this case, the statement that is alleged to be injuriously false concerns a group — here, books currently in print and their authors — the plaintiff faces a "difficult and sometimes insurmountable task. If the group is small and its members easily ascertainable, [the] plaintiff may succeed. But where the group is large — in general, any group numbering over twenty-five members — the courts . . . have consistently held that plaintiffs cannot show that the statements were 'of and concerning them,' . . ." . . .

> The group in question here obviously numbers substantially more than 25 members: a visit to even the smallest bookstore establishes this fact. . . .

> Blatty . . . argues in effect that to require a plaintiff to establish that the alleged injurious falsehood published by a press defendant is "of and concerning" him would add a new element to the tort of intentional

interference with prospective economic advantage and thereby alter its nature, and that such a result is impermissible. . . .

The fundamental premise of Blatty's argument is unsound. Under the supremacy clause a state's definition of a tort cannot undermine the requirements of the First Amendment. That is precisely the teaching of *New York Times. . . .*[16]

Is a Colloquium Requirement Appropriate in Cases of Intentional Interference? Despite the logic of the majority opinion in *Blatty*, Justice Joseph Grodin's concurrence may have offered a better rationale for the result. Justice Grodin wrote:

A hypothetical example may be helpful in exposing the fallacy of the majority's broad holding.

Suppose that the New York Times, after conducting its normal survey of representative bookstores throughout the country, found that Blatty's novel was, indeed, the top selling book for a particular week based on its own statistics. Suppose further that, despite this information, the Times purposefully substituted one of its own publications for Blatty's book at the top of its best seller list in order to enhance its own book's sales, and entirely omitted Blatty's book from the list.

Under the majority's analysis, Blatty would have no cause of action against the New York Times for intentional interference with prospective economic advantage under these hypothetical facts, because nothing in the false best seller list would have indicated to the reading public that the falsity in the published information was "of and concerning" Blatty's book. It seems clear from this hypothetical, however, that the "of and concerning" requirement is ill-suited to this type of intentional tort, since the plaintiff is required in any event to prove, as an element of the tort, that the defendant acted for the specific purpose of injuring the particular plaintiff. If a plaintiff can prove that a media defendant knowingly published a false statement for the purpose of inflicting financial injury on him personally, I do not believe that the free speech provisions of either the state or federal Constitution would be offended if the defendant were held liable in damages for such conduct, even if it were not obvious on the face of the publication who the defendant was intending to injure. Thus, I do not join in the majority's broad holding.

Nonetheless, on the specific facts of this case, I concur in the judgment. Although plaintiff has attempted to state a cause of action for intentional interference with prospective economic advantage, the facts that he has alleged . . . are not, in my view, sufficient to support such an action. Plaintiff's allegations do not suggest that the Times intentionally misrepresented the actual results of its bookstore survey for the purpose of injuring plaintiff financially; at most, the allegations suggest that the Times did not do as thorough a job in gathering sales statistics as it should have and that, after Blatty's publisher complained to the Times, the Times

---

[16] *Id.* at 1182–86.

should have realized its survey figures would harm plaintiff financially. Even assuming those allegations are true, they would not support recovery on an intentional interference theory.[17]

2.   Limited Liability for Negligence

Generally Not Actionable. Negligent or reckless interference with a contract or prospectively advantageous relationship is normally not actionable under the law of torts.[18] For example, in *Glaub Jewelers, Inc. v. New York Daily News*,[19] the defendant negligently failed to publish an advertisement for the plaintiff's business in the Sunday newspaper, with the alleged result that "many customers who would [have been] drawn by the advertisement did not appear." In concluding that the plaintiff could not recover for negligent interference with prospective pecuniary advantage in the absence of a "special relationship" (the contours of which the court did not define), the Civil Court of New York City quoted illustration 4 to § 766C of the *Restatement (Second) of Torts*:

> 4. A contracts with a telephone company for the insertion of A's business advertisement in its telephone directory. Through the negligence of B, who prints the directory for the company, the advertisement is omitted and as a result A suffers pecuniary loss. B is not liable to A for tortiously interfering with contractual relations.[20]

If a sports referee makes a bad call and a team is eliminated from the playoffs, it is highly unlikely that local merchants who sell team-related merchandise can sue for tortious interference with the sales they would have made if the team had gone on to win the championship. In *Bain v. Gillispie*,[21] the Iowa Court of Appeals held that such harm to novelty store owners' business interests was not reasonably foreseeable, and declined to impose liability under a malpractice theory. An alternative explanation for the result is that negligent interference with economic interests is generally not actionable.

Relationship to the Economic Loss Rule. Requiring proof of intentional disruption in tortious interference cases is consistent with the broad formulations of the economic loss rule discussed in Chapter 1. Those versions of the rule hold, with important exceptions and limitations, that purely economic losses, unaccompanied by personal injuries or property damages, are compensable only under contract principles.

Notable Exception: J'Aire Corporation v. Gregory. The best known exception to the general rule that negligent interference with economic interests is not actionable is *J'Aire Corporation v. Gregory*.[22] In that case, the Supreme Court of California was asked to decide whether "a contractor who undertakes construction

---

[17] *Id.* at 1187–88 (Grodin, J., concurring).

[18] *See* RESTATEMENT (SECOND) OF TORTS § 766C (1979).

[19] 535 N.Y.S.2d 532 (N.Y.C. Civ. Ct. 1988).

[20] *Id.* at 534 (quoting RESTATEMENT (SECOND) OF TORTS § 766C illus. 4 (1977)).

[21] 357 N.W.2d 47 (Iowa Ct. App. 1984).

[22] 598 P.2d 60 (Cal. 1979).

work pursuant to a contract with the owner of [the] premises may be held liable in tort for business losses suffered by a lessee when the contractor negligently fails to complete the project with due diligence."[23] The plaintiff operated a restaurant at an airport which had contracted with the defendant for heating and air conditioning work. According to the court:

> As the contract did not specify any date for completion of the work, appellant alleged the work was to have been completed within a reasonable time as defined by custom and usage. . . . Despite requests that respondent complete the construction promptly, the work was not completed within a reasonable time. Because the restaurant could not operate during part of the construction and was without heat and air conditioning for a longer period, appellant suffered loss of business and resulting loss of profits.[24]

The court held that:

> Liability for negligent conduct may only be imposed where there is a duty of care owed by the defendant to the plaintiff or to a class of which the plaintiff is a member.[25]

Employing an analysis based on "public policy factors," the court found that the defendant owed a duty to the plaintiff because:

> (1) The contract entered into between respondent and the county was for the renovation of the premises in which appellant maintained its business. The contract could not have been performed without impinging on that business. Thus respondent's performance was intended to, and did, directly affect appellant. (2) Accordingly, it was clearly foreseeable that any significant delay in completing the construction would adversely affect appellant's business beyond the normal disruption associated with such construction. Appellant alleges this fact was repeatedly drawn to respondent's attention. (3) Further, appellant's complaint leaves no doubt that appellant suffered harm since it was unable to operate its business for one month and suffered additional loss of business while the premises were without heat and air conditioning. (4) Appellant has also alleged that delays occasioned by the respondent's conduct were closely connected to, indeed directly caused its injury. (5) In addition, respondent's lack of diligence in the present case was particularly blameworthy since it continued after the probability of damage was drawn directly to respondent's attention. (6) Finally, public policy supports finding a duty of care in the present case. The wilful failure or refusal of a contractor to prosecute a construction project with diligence, where another is injured as a result, has been made grounds for disciplining a licensed contractor. . . . Although this section does not provide a basis for imposing liability where the delay in completing

---

[23] *Id.* at 61.

[24] *Id.*

[25] *Id.* at 62.

construction is due merely to negligence, it does indicate the seriousness with which the Legislature views unnecessary delays in the completion of construction.[26]

The decision in *J'Aire* has never been overruled by the California Supreme Court, but it is often narrowly construed and has attracted little following in other states.

Notable Exception: Sharyland Water Supply Corp. v. City of Alton. An interesting and potentially important contemporary example of liability for negligently caused economic loss is *Sharyland Water Supply Corp. v. City of Alton,*[27] which was discussed in Chapter 1. In that case, a company that was contractually obliged to supply clean water to a city sued contractors who were allegedly negligent in installing sewer lines for the city. The location of the sewer lines exposed the clean water lines to contamination and meant they no longer complied with state law. However, it was clear that the clean water contractor sought to recover purely economic losses, not damages for physical harm to property. As an opinion of the Texas Court of Appeals explained:

> Sharyland has not suffered property damage. The sewer service lines have not corroded the waterlines. There is no evidence of physical damage to the waterlines, nor is there evidence that the water flowing through the water mains has been contaminated because of sewage leaks. Thus, Sharyland neither pleaded nor offered evidence of an actual injury or property damage to its waterlines or to the water that flows through the waterlines. Sharyland seeks compensation only for economic damages including the cost associated with protecting, maintaining, and repairing its waterlines.[28]

The Texas Supreme Court held that Sharyland's negligence claim was not barred by the economic loss rule because the clean water contractor and the waste water contractors were not even remotely in privity.[29] On remand, the Texas Court of Appeals held that the contractors who installed the sewer lines owed a common law duty not to negligently cause damages to the clean water contractor.[30] Finding that the duty was breached and that the breach produced damages, the Court of Appeals sustained an award of more than a million dollars for repair costs. It may be fair to describe *Sharyland* as holding that negligent interference with performance of contractual obligations is sometimes actionable (at least under Texas law).

PROBLEM 5-1: THE STOLEN RENTAL TRUCK

Sergey Black rented a truck from Sunset Rental Trucks to move from Natchez to San Antonio to assume a position as manager of a new bookstore. On each side of the vehicle, the truck was emblazoned with the rental company's corporate logo, along with the words "Sunset Rental Trucks."

---

[26] *Id.* at 63–64.

[27] 354 S.W.3d 407 (Tex. 2011).

[28] *City of Alton v. Sharyland Water Supply Corp.*, 277 S.W.3d 132, 154–55 (Tex. App. 2009).

[29] 354 S.W.3d 407 (Tex. 2011).

[30] *City of Alton v. Sharyland Water Supply Corp.*, 402 S.W.3d 867, 878–81 & n.9 (Tex. App. 2013).

En route to San Antonio, Black stayed at a hotel in Beaumont. That night, the rental truck, which contained all of Black's belongings, was stolen from the hotel's parking lot. The truck and its contents were recovered unharmed two weeks later. Video evidence from security cameras at the hotel and fingerprints on the truck led to the arrest of the thief, who thereafter pled guilty to criminal charges.

As a result of the theft, Black incurred economic losses related to the necessity of arranging substitute transportation to San Antonio and paying late charges to Sunset Rental Trucks because the vehicle was returned two weeks late.

The bookstore in San Antonio where Black was to work incurred economic losses because of Black's late arrival. It was necessary to pay other employees overtime to handle Black's duties during the delay, and the opening of the new store had to be postponed.

Sunset Rental Trucks sustained economic losses because the stolen truck had special features. While the truck was missing, Sunset was forced to break a contract to rent the truck to a school. There was no other truck available with required special features to fill that contract, which had previously been signed.

There is evidence that the hotel from which the truck was stolen was negligent in protecting guests' vehicles from theft.

Can Black, the bookstore, or Sunset Rental Trucks state a claim for tortious interference against either the thief who stole the truck or the hotel that failed to protect the rental truck from theft?

C.   INTERFERENCE WITH CONTRACT

A person can suffer damages as a result of tortious interference with contract in either of two ways. First, the plaintiff can be deprived of the benefits of a contract because another party to the contract has been induced or otherwise caused to breach the contract. Second, the plaintiff's own performance of contractual obligations can be made more expensive or burdensome by the conduct of the defendant. These two different theories of liability are discussed below.

1.   Interference with Performance by a Third Person

The basic rule on tortious interference with contract is stated in § 766 of the *Restatement (Second) of Torts*, which provides:

> One who intentionally and improperly interferes with the performance of a contract (except a contract to marry) between another and a third person by inducing or otherwise causing the third person not to perform the contract, is subject to liability to the other for the pecuniary loss resulting to the other from the failure of the third person to perform the contract.[31]

---

[31] Restatement (Second) of Torts § 766 (1979).

a.   Valid Contract

A Valid Contract Is Required. An action for tortious interference with contract will lie only if there is a valid contract.[32] An action for tortious interference with contract will be dismissed if the plaintiff did not have an enforceable agreement.[33]

Void Contracts. A contract that is void is not valid. Thus, no action will lie for interference with a contract that is illegal or void as against public policy.[34]

Voidable Contracts. A voidable contract is valid until it has been voided. The mere fact that a party to a contract could seek to escape the terms of the contract, by pleading a defense based on the statute of frauds, lack of mutuality, infancy, unconscionability, failure of conditions precedent, or even uncertainty of the contract's terms, does not allow a third person to interfere. In such situations, the contract is merely voidable, not void, and an action for interference will lie.

Contracts Terminable at Will. An agreement terminable at will is still a valid contract until it has been terminated. Therefore, a person who interferes with the performance of a contract terminable at will is subject to liability.[35] Of course, a party to a contract that is terminable at will has no assurance of receiving future benefits. Thus, in determining whether interference with a contract terminable at will is improper, the interference will be treated as equivalent to interference with prospective contractual relations. As discussed later in this chapter, interference with a prospective contractual relation is less readily actionable than interference with an existing contract that is not terminable at will.

b.   Inducing or Otherwise Causing

Section 766 of the *Restatement (Second) of Torts* speaks about liability for "inducing or otherwise causing" nonperformance of a contractual agreement.[36] The term "inducing" refers to causing a party to elect not to perform. This might result, for example, from persuasion, intimidation, offer of benefits, or exercise of moral pressure.[37] "Otherwise causing" refers to situations where the defendant's conduct has made it impossible for the party to perform.[38] This might be accomplished, for example, by destroying the supplies a person needs for performance or by physically incapacitating the person who is obligated to perform.

Knowledge That There Is a Contract Is Different from Inducement. As noted above, the defendant must have knowledge that there is a contract in order to be held liable for intentionally inducing its breach. However, the fact that the

---

[32] *Id.* § 766 cmt. f.

[33] *See Lion's Property Development Group LLC v. New York City Regional Center, LLC*, 2014 N.Y. App. Div. LEXIS 1522 (Mar. 11, 2014).

[34] Restatement (Second) of Torts § 774 (1979).

[35] *Id.* § 766 cmt. g.

[36] *Id.* § 766.

[37] *See id.* § 766 cmt. k.

[38] *See id.* § 766 cmt. h.

defendant knew of the contract is not sufficient to prove inducement.[39] Mere knowledge that someone with whom one is dealing is a party to another agreement, which that party intends to break, does not establish liability for tortious interference. To become liable, the defendant must induce or otherwise cause the breach. Awareness that a breach will occur, by itself, is an inadequate predicate for imposition of liability for tortious interference. Whether the defendant's conduct induced or otherwise caused a party to not perform a contract with a third person is normally a question of fact.[40]

In *Watershed Asset Mgmt., L.L.C. v. Watershed Capital, LLC*,[41] a consulting firm [the defendant] filed counterclaims against an asset management firm (hedge fund) for interfering with the consulting firm's relationship with a law firm. In rejecting the plaintiff's tortious interference claims, a federal court in California wrote:

> Fatal to defendant's tortious interference of contractual relations counter-claim is the lack of any facts supporting the existence of intentional acts by plaintiff "designed to induce a breach or disruption of the contractual relationship." . . . Though defendant lays out factual allegations that allude to a possible relationship between it and Latham [the law firm], nowhere in the answer and counterclaims does defendant plead facts to suggest plaintiff took intentional actions to interfere and disrupt this possible relationship. . . . To the contrary, defendant's allegation that Latham severed ties with it "for the chance to represent a billion-dollar hedge fund" suggests no conduct taken by plaintiff meant to interfere or disrupt. . . . The only factual allegation that attributes any role to plaintiff is in paragraph 18 of the answer and counterclaims where defendant alleges "actions" taken by plaintiff that resulted in defendant's "loss." Such conclusory allegations devoid of any factual support cannot survive a Rule 12(b)(6) motion.
>
> . . . .
>
> Defendant's claim for tortious interference of prospective economic advantage fails for the same reason as the preceding claim. . . .[42]

In contrast, in *SJW Property Commerce, Inc. v. Southwest Pinnacle Properties, Inc.*,[43] the court found that there was sufficient evidence of inducement. The court wrote:

> [T]here must be some direct evidence of a willful act of interference by a party. . . . A party must be more than a willing participant; he must

---

[39] *See id.* § 766 cmt. n.

[40] *See id.* § 766 cmt. o.

[41] 2014 U.S. Dist. LEXIS 24660 (N.D. Cal. Feb. 25, 2014).

[42] *Id.* at 6–8.

[43] 328 S.W.3d 121 (Tex. App. 2010).

knowingly induce one of the contracting parties to breach its obligations.
. . .[44]

Here, the record demonstrates that Palmer had earnest money contracts
with Whisenant, Wayne and Gelee Allen, Yvonne Robinson, Opal Baldwin,
and Harlon and Mary Robinson through September 2000. However, in
September 2000, when Palmer's earnest money contracts were expiring,
Trozzo, on behalf of SJW, approached the landowners to allegedly inquire
whether they were still under contract. . . .

Palmer testified that SJW was always aware of the status of Palmer's
earnest money contracts and that, in September 2000, he still had all of the
landowners except for Dr. Kilgore under contract. Palmer alleged that
Trozzo's efforts were an attempt to induce the landowners to terminate
their contracts with Palmer and enter into similar contracts with SJW. Dr.
Kilgore corroborated Palmer's testimony by stating that he was approached by Trozzo during the early stages of the development of the
Trenton Project, and that Trozzo informed Dr. Kilgore that SJW intended
to get Dr. Kilgore under contract to tie up the development until Palmer's
earnest money contracts expired so that SJW could then get the landowners under contract and sell the property to Target themselves.[45]

As a result of Trozzo's interactions with the landowners, Opal Baldwin and
Harlon and Mary Robinson, all elderly landowners, each sent Palmer
nearly identically-worded letters a couple days later, notifying him that
their earnest money contracts were *"terminated"* and *"null and void."*
(Emphasis in original.) Furthermore, the remaining landowners became
anxious and demanded assurances from Palmer that he could get Dr.
Kilgore under contract soon so that the land could be packaged and sold to
Target. . . .

Palmer's damages expert, Bill Abington, a certified public accountant and a
certified fraud examiner, evaluated the economic losses sustained by the
Palmer companies as a result of SJW's alleged wrongful conduct. Abington
concluded that the Palmer companies sustained $376,397 in damages
regarding the delayed sale of the Robinson tract to Target, $207,926
associated with lost rental income, and various other damages.

. . . [W]e conclude that the jury was reasonable in concluding that SJW
willfully and intentionally interfered with Palmer's contracts and that

---

[44] [n.20] In *John Paul Mitchell Systems v. Randalls Food Markets*, [17 S.W.3d 721, 731 (Tex. App.
2000)], the Austin Court of Appeals stated that:

  A necessary element of the plaintiff's cause of action is a showing that the defendant took an
  active part in persuading a party to a contract to breach it. Merely entering into a contract
  with a party with the knowledge of that party's contractual obligations to someone else is not
  the same as inducing a breach. It is necessary that there be some act of interference or of
  persuading a party to breach, for example by offering better terms or other incentives, for tort
  liability to arise.

[45] [n.21] As noted earlier, Dr. Kilgore's tract was an essential piece of the land package to be
presented to Target. Target was not interested in only purchasing non-contiguous parcels of land. . . .

SJW's interference proximately caused Palmer actual damages or loss. . . .[46]

(1)   Inducement Based on Refusal to Deal

The issue of inducement can be subtle, as is shown by cases involving refusals to deal. In *Uptown Heights Associates L.P. v. Seafirst Corp.*,[47] the Supreme Court of Oregon wrote:

> The general rule is that, ordinarily, one may refuse to deal with another and not be liable in tort for that refusal. . . .
>
> However, *Restatement (Second) of Torts* § 766 comment l addresses "inducement by refusal to deal":
>
> "A refusal to deal is one means by which a person may induce another to commit a breach of his contract with a third person. Thus A may induce B to break his contract with C by threatening not to enter into, or to sever, business relations with B unless B does break the contract. . . . The difficult question of fact . . . is whether A is merely exercising his freedom to select the persons with whom he will do business or is inducing B not to perform his contract with C. . . . If he is merely exercising that freedom, he is not liable to C for the harm caused by B's choice not to lose A's business for the sake of getting C's. On the other hand, if A, instead of merely refusing to deal with B and leaving B to make his own decision on what to do about it, goes further and uses his own refusal to deal or the threat of it as a means of affirmative inducement, compulsion or pressure to make B break his contract with C, he may be acting improperly and subject to liability. . . .
>
> "Illustrations
>
> "1. Upon hearing of B's contract with C, A ceases to buy from B. When asked by B to explain his conduct, A replies that his reason is B's contract with C. Thereupon B breaks his contract with C in order to regain A's business. A has not induced the breach. . . .
>
> "2. Upon hearing of B's contract with C, A writes to B as follows: "I cannot tolerate your contract with C. You must call it off. I am sure that our continued relations will more than compensate you for any payment you may have to make to C. If you do not advise me within ten days that your contract with C is at an end, you may never expect further business from me." Thereupon B breaks his contract with C. A has induced the breach. . . ."[48]

In *Uptown*, there was evidence that the defendant bank had told a potential borrower that a loan would be forthcoming if Uptown was removed from the borrower's joint venture. The court found that a cause of action was stated because

---

[46] 328 S.W.3d at 152–54 (Tex. App. 2010).

[47] 891 P.2d 639 (Or. 1995).

[48] *Id.* at 653–54.

the claim for relief was closer to the second illustration than to the first.

Mere Refusal to Deal. Many cases hold that mere refusal to deal does not amount to inducement. For example, in *Bear Creek Enterprises, Inc. v. Warrior & Gulf Navigation Co.*,[49] the Supreme Court of Alabama held that a contractor was not liable to employees of a subcontractor who lost their jobs when the contractor terminated its agreement with the subcontractor upon learning that the subcontractor's employees were seeking to form a union. The court found that the action amounted to a mere nonactionable refusal to deal.

Privilege to Refuse to Deal. Regardless of whether refusal to deal amounts to inducement, some states recognize a broad privilege to refuse to deal. In *In re Lyondell Chemical Co.*,[50] a bankruptcy court rejected a tortious interference claim, stating:

> New York law states that the privilege with whom to deal "exists regardless of the actor's motive for refusing to enter business relations with the other and even though the sole motive is a desire to harm the other." *Turner Constr. Co. v. Seaboard Surety Co.,* . . . [469 N.Y.S.2d 725 (App. Div. 1983)]. *Turner* clarifies that:
>
> > It is the well-settled law of this State that the refusal to maintain trade relations with any individual is an inherent right which every person may exercise lawfully, for reasons he deems sufficient or for no reasons whatever, and it is immaterial whether such refusal is based upon reason or is the result of mere caprice, prejudice or malice.
>
> . . . In *Turner*, the defendant asserted a counterclaim for tortious interference against the plaintiff for refusing to take the defendant's bonds from its subcontractors, thereby causing them to decline to deal with the defendant. . . . The court concluded that regardless of the allegations of malice, Turner Construction acted within the bounds of the law. *Id.* Similarly here, regardless of UBS's motive, UBS had a privilege not to deal with Highland and to preclude an agreement between Lyondell and Highland.[51]

(2) Inducement Based on Offer of Better Terms

There is no simple answer to the question of whether offering a better price or better terms amounts to improper inducement of another's nonperformance of contractual obligations. The answer depends on the facts. Nevertheless, it is useful to divide the inquiry into two parts: first, was there inducement; second, if so, was the inducement improper (*i.e.*, not privileged).

General Offers Versus Targeted Offers. In *V. Marangi Carting Corp. v. Judex Enterprises, Inc.*,[52] the New York Supreme Court wrote:

---

[49] 529 So. 2d 959 (Ala. 1988).

[50] 2014 U.S. Dist. LEXIS 15088 (S.D.N.Y. Jan. 31, 2014).

[51] *Id.* at *21–*22.

[52] 171 Misc. 2d 820 (N.Y. Sup. Ct. 1997).

. . . [A review of the cases in which offers of better terms constituted tortious interference] reflects none in which the complained-of conduct consisted solely of regular advertising and general solicitation of business from a class of potential future customers. Rather, each concerns conduct toward a particular, targeted competitor in order to induce a breach of a specific contract for a unique or exclusive product. For instance, in *Gonzales v. Reichenthaler*, . . . [135 N.E. 938 (N.Y. 1922), *affg*. 189 N.Y.S. 783 (App. Div. 1921)], a Coney Island game operator induced a game manufacturer to provide it with a game just like one the manufacturer provided to his neighboring competitor, despite an exclusive contract between the neighbor and the manufacturer. In *Gold Medal Farms v. Rutland County Co-op. Creamery*, . . . [195 N.Y.S.2d 179 (App. Div. 1959)], a milk retailer, knowing of the co-op's exclusive contract to provide another retailer with its entire milk supply, induced the co-op to breach that contract by making it an offer of better terms.

Plaintiff seeks to have this court rely upon the court's statement in *Gold Medal Farms* that "It would seem sufficient to show that appellants, with actual knowledge of the existence of the contract between Rutland and Gold Medal, intentionally made an offer of better terms to Rutland with the intent of persuading it to breach its contract". . . . However, based upon the analysis in the *Restatement*, . . . I do not believe the law permits a finding of tortious conduct merely upon proof that an offer of better terms was made. Indeed, I note that in the *Gold Medal Farms* case, aside from the offer of better terms, there was evidence that the interferer/competitor also "loaned [the co-op/customer] a very substantial sum of money, without interest, which was repaid from premiums over and above the contract price paid for milk". . . .

I conclude that a claim for tortious interference with an existing contract based upon an offer of better terms cannot be founded solely upon an offer made in the normal course of general solicitation of business for fungible services in a mass market, by normal methods such as circulating flyers to potential customers. If the law were otherwise, no one who advertised his prices would ever be safe from such a claim if it entered into a contract with a customer after the customer breached its contract with the more expensive competitor.[53]

Active Solicitation Versus Response to an Inquiry. Another relevant factor is whether the offeror solicited the other's business, or merely responded to an inquiry. In addressing the issue of whether a seller of gasoline was liable for tortious interference, the Michigan Court of Appeals, in *Knight Enterprises v. Beard*,[54] quoted the comment to *Restatement (Second) of Torts* § 766 and illustration 3, then reasoned as follows:

> . . . [In this case,] Knight unequivocally testified that the alleged induce-
> ment from defendants was stating a low fuel price in response to the

---

[53] *Id*. at 835.

[54] 2004 Mich. App. LEXIS 53 (Jan. 13, 2004).

customer's inquiry. This is not an unlawful act *per se*. Therefore, in accordance with Michigan law and the *Restatement of Torts*, plaintiff was required to prove that defendant took an affirmative act to induce the customers to break the exclusive contract with plaintiff. Indeed, in *Hutton v. Roberts*, 182 Mich. App. 153, 159; 451 N.W.2d 536 (1989), we held . . .

> Consistent with the case law discussed above, *it is instead necessary to show some active solicitation or encouragement of a breach of an already existing contract*, accompanied by and corroborative of a malicious, unjustified purpose to inflict injury. *The act of* making an offer or of *accepting an offer of another in violation of the other's contractual obligations is, by itself, not enough.* [Emphasis added.]

Plaintiff has simply failed to present any evidence whatsoever demonstrating that defendants' conduct induced or otherwise caused the station owners to breach their contracts with plaintiff. Plaintiff admitted that defendants never contacted plaintiff's customers, but only gave the pricing in response to the customers unsolicited inquiries. This evidence is insufficient, as a matter of law, to sustain the tort of tortious interference with contractual relations. . . .[55]

Legitimate Offers Made in The Ordinary Course of Business. One highly relevant fact is whether the offer would be regarded as legitimate by persons engaged in business. Ordinarily, a "person is not liable for tortious interference with a contract if legitimate personal or business interests motivate him or her."[56] Offering another a contract that is "standard and non-negotiable" is unlikely to give rise to liability for tortious interference.[57]

PROBLEM 5-2: THE ASSOCIATES WHO STARTED THEIR OWN LAW FIRM

Fanny Humphries and Glenn Carnahan had been associates at the Weimer Law Firm for five years. During most of that time, they worked on a regular basis with Mike Corey, the president of a major client of the firm, Cooperstown Athletics, a large athletic equipment business. The associates trusted and admired Corey's business judgment.

Humphries and Carnahan had pretty much decided to leave the Weimer Law Firm and open their own law office. One day, when Corey was at the Weimer Law Firm offices, they told him what they were thinking. Specifically, they asked Corey if he thought they would be making a mistake trying to open their own law firm. Corey said that it was a great idea. He further promised that once their office was open, they could count on Cooperstown Athletics becoming their client.

A month later, after Humphries and Carnahan notified the Weimer Law Firm of their departure, and left and set up their new practice, Corey transferred all of Cooperstown Athletics's legal business to them. Can Humphries, Carnahan, or Corey be held liable to the Weimer Law Firm for the damages it has suffered as a

---

[55] *Id.* at *18–*26.

[56] *Knight Enterprises v. Beard*, 2004 Mich. App. LEXIS 53, at *14 (Jan. 13, 2004).

[57] *Martin Petroleum Corp. v. Amerada Hess Corp.*, 769 So. 2d 1105, 1108 (Fla. Dist. Ct. App. 2000).

result of the loss of Cooperstown Athletics as a client?

c.   Relationship of Tortious Interference to Breach of Contract

Overlapping Claims for Interference and Breach. It is no defense to an action for tortious interference with contract that the plaintiff could sue the breaching party for failure to perform the contractual obligation. Both the person who interferes and the person who breaches can be held liable for harm caused to the plaintiff by reason of the loss of the benefits of the contract. However, a judgment or settlement paid as a result of a claim for breach of contract ordinarily must be credited against the defendant's liability for damages in tort.[58]

The Function of Tortious Interference Law. Judge Richard Posner, in *Frandsen v. Jensen-Sundquist Agency, Inc.*[59] explained:

> The principal function of the concept of tortious interference is to provide a back-up remedy against breaches of contract. Suppose that . . . [A] had had an employment contract with . . . [B] and . . . [C] had induced him to break it. [B] . . . could sue [A] . . . for breach of contract but the suit might have little practical value because an individual employee will often be judgment-proof. Or suppose [B's] . . . workmen's compensation carrier persuaded it to fire . . . [A] by falsely advising . . . [B] that . . . [A] had a serious risk of being injured at work. . . . [A] could still sue [B] for breach of contract rather than tortious interference, but even so, the tort would enable . . . [B], via the doctrine of indemnity, to shift the cost of the breach to the primary wrongdoer, the insurance carrier.

> In cases where no breach of contract results from the interference, the tort is really a branch of the law of unfair competition, and it is necessary for liability that the alleged tortfeasor have gone beyond the accepted norms of fair competition. . . .[60]

2.   Interference with One's Own Performance

Whereas a tortious interference action under § 766 of the *Restatement (Second) of Torts* allows one to recover for losses sustained as the result of another's nonperformance of contractual obligations, a suit under § 766A allows one to recover compensation for his or her own increased costs of performance that were caused by the interference. Section 766A provides:

> One who intentionally and improperly interferes with the performance of a contract (except a contract to marry) between another and a third person, by preventing the other from performing the contract or causing his

---

[58] *See generally* RESTATEMENT (SECOND) OF TORTS § 766 cmt. v (1979).

[59] 802 F.2d 941 (7th Cir. 1986).

[60] *Id.* at 947.

performance to be more expensive or burdensome, is subject to liability to the other for the pecuniary loss resulting to him.[61]

In recognizing actions under § 766A, in *Wilspec Technologies, Inc. v. DunAn Holding Group, Co., Ltd.*,[62] the Supreme Court of Oklahoma stated:

> Although Defendants provide adverse authority from other jurisdictions, we believe that where the law provides a remedy against a tortfeasor who induces or causes a third party not to perform the contract, the protection against such tortious acts extends to a party who is unable to perform his/her contract or where such performance becomes more costly or unduly burdensome. To hold otherwise would unjustly enrich a tortfeasor and leave a plaintiff less than whole.[63]

Many Forms of Burdening. There are many forms of conduct which can cause contractual performance to be more expensive or burdensome. For example, if a party with contractual obligations is excluded from a place where work is to be performed, or deprived of necessary supplies or labor, or forced to re-do work that was already completed, an action for damages may be asserted under the terms of § 766A.

a.   Liability for Making Performance More Expensive or Burdensome

Broad Recognition of Burdening. In making "burdening" or "hindrance" actionable, § 766A is very different from § 766, which permits recovery only of losses caused by another's nonperformance. However, some courts broadly recognize suits where tortious interference does not produce a breach of contract. For example, in *Khan v. GBAK Properties, Inc.*,[64] the Texas Court of Appeals wrote:

> To establish tortious interference with existing contract, a plaintiff is not limited to showing the contract was actually breached. . . . Any interference that makes performance more burdensome or difficult or of less or no value to the one entitled to performance is actionable. . . .
>
> The evidence shows that Ray Lofti, through Parkway Crossing, purported to assign all rents in the Crabb River Property to Republic National Bank. This agreement was entered into in May 2006. Khan stated in his affidavit that he had not received any rents since at least June 2006. The existence of a second competing claim over the rents — regardless of whether this second claim later proves void — makes performance under Khan's contract more difficult and reduces the value of that contract. We hold there

---

[61] RESTATEMENT (SECOND) OF TORTS § 766A (1979).

[62] 204 P.3d 69 (Okla. 2009).

[63] *Id.* at 74.

[64] 371 S.W.3d 347 (Tex. App. 2012).

was sufficient summary-judgment evidence to support a claim of tortious interference. . . .[65]

Non-Recognition of Burdening. Not all courts agree that losses resulting from burdening should be recoverable under the law of tortious interference.

In *Price v. Sorrell*,[66] a debtor's attorney allegedly interfered with the contractual relationship between the creditor (a hospital) and its attorney (Price) by sending a letter to the hospital questioning its wisdom in hiring Price. The hospital did not discharge Price, but Price alleged that he was forced to incur expenses to restore good relations with the hospital. In denying relief and refusing to adopt § 766A, the court wrote:

> Where § 766 requires non-performance which includes a breach of the contract for liability to attach, § 766A requires, not a breach or non-performance, but only that performance became more expensive and burdensome. We are convinced that such an element of proof is too speculative and subject to abuse to provide a meaningful basis for a cause of action. The breach or non-performance of a contract, or the loss of a prospective contractual relation, is a reasonably bright line that reduces the potential for abuse of the causes of action defined by §§ 766 and 766B. . . .[67]

D. INTERFERENCE WITH PROSPECTIVE ADVANTAGE

Reduced Scope of Protection. The law sometimes affords protection to advantageous relationships where no contract was in existence at the time of the interference. The threshold question is whether the relationship was so likely to come to fruition that it is fair to conclude that the plaintiff was entitled to legal protection. Even if that query is answered in the affirmative, the plaintiff may still find that it is harder to prove improper interference than would be true if the plaintiff sought redress for interference with an enforceable contract.[68]

Prospective Contractual Relations. Section 766B of the *Restatement (Second) of Torts* states the basic rule on intentional interference with a prospective contractual relation. It provides:

> One who intentionally and improperly interferes with another's prospective contractual relation (except a contract to marry) is subject to liability to the other for the pecuniary harm resulting from loss of the benefits of the relation, whether the interference consists of
>
> (a) inducing or otherwise causing a third person not to enter into or continue the prospective relation or

---

[65] *Id.* at 359–60.

[66] 784 P.2d 614 (Wyo. 1989).

[67] *Id.* at 616.

[68] *See generally* RESTATEMENT (SECOND) OF TORTS § 766 cmt. c (1979).

(b) preventing the other from acquiring or continuing the prospective relation.[69]

Prospective Advantage Not Involving Contractual Relations. In certain cases, a prospectively advantageous relationship may be afforded protection even though the relationship was not intended to result in a contract. For example, in *Longo v. Reilly*,[70] the New Jersey Superior Court Appellate Division recognized the viability of an action for tortious interference with prospective economic relations based on the defendants' alteration of the votes in the plaintiff's election bid for the office of union secretary. The position, which carried with it the title and emoluments of the office, had value, even if it was not a contractual relationship in the usual sense of the term. As the court explained:

> It does not seem to us, on principle, that the circumstance that plaintiff's lost employment was an elective office in a union constitutes a material differentiation. It was his way of earning a livelihood. . . .[71]

1.   Desired Relationships

"Reasonable Probability" of Securing a Contract. In *Nathanson v. Medical College of Pennsylvania*,[72] the plaintiff alleged that the defendant medical school had interfered with her application to other medical schools for the 1987 and 1989 academic years by disclosing to them that she had previously matriculated at the defendant's school. In rejecting the plaintiff's claim for tortious interference, the Third Circuit wrote:

> [T]he district court defined a "prospective contractual relationship" as "something less than a right and something more than hope." . . . In order to prove the existence of a prospective contractual relationship, Nathanson must show that there was a "reasonable probability" that she would have entered into a contract with another medical school absent MCP's interference. . . . The district court concluded that although Nathanson had a "satisfactory academic record and background," she had "not demonstrated more than mere hope in securing a prospective relationship with a medical school." . . .
>
> . . . In 1985, she applied to ten medical schools and was accepted only by MCP. In 1986, she applied to six medical schools and was accepted only by Georgetown which had rejected her when she had applied there the year before. Based upon this history, it is too speculative to conclude that she would have been accepted by any medical school in 1987 or 1989.
>
> Admissions policies vary considerably from school-to-school and from year-to-year. Other information is simply not known. Regardless, the burden is upon Nathanson to demonstrate that her matriculation status did

---

[69] *Id.* § 766B.

[70] 114 A.2d 302 (N.J. Super. Ct. App. Div. 1955).

[71] *Id.* at 306.

[72] 926 F.2d 1368 (3d Cir. 1991).

have an impact upon her rejections from medical schools. She did not provide sufficient evidence to create a disputed issue of material fact.[73]

Received Offers to Purchase. The receipt of an offer to purchase property may be sufficient to establish a prospectively advantageous relationship entitled to legal protection. In *Tara Woods Ltd. Partnership v. Fannie Mae*,[74] a federal court in Colorado wrote:

> [A]lthough the Plaintiff has not alleged that it actually entered into a contract with a prospective buyer, it adequately contends that it received purchase offers from prospective buyers that, presumably with further negotiation, would have led to an actual sale. This is sufficient to allege a prospective business advantage so as to support this claim.[75]

Specific Identification of the Lost Relationship Is Not Required. Some cases are less demanding than others with respect to identifying the allegedly lost or impaired relationship. *Kelly-Springfield Tire Co. v. D'Ambro*[76] included a claim against a law firm (Stradley, Ronon, the appellee) whose improper representation of a client (D'Ambro) purportedly interfered with the sale of property by the plaintiff (Kelly-Springfield, the appellant). In finding that the plaintiff stated a cause of action for tortious interference, the Pennsylvania Superior Court wrote:

> The trial court found appellant's amended complaint deficient because it failed to aver a specific prospective contract which was known to Stradley, Ronon and with which appellee intentionally interfered. However, prospective contractual relations are, by definition, not as susceptible of definite, exacting identification as is the case with an existing contract with a specific person. "Anything that is prospective in nature is necessarily uncertain." . . . Among the relations protected against intentional interference is the opportunity to sell or buy real property. *See Restatement (Second) of Torts* § 766B, comment c.
>
> It is alleged in the instant complaint that at the time Stradley, Ronon filed the initial state court action, Kelly-Springfield had initiated efforts to find a new buyer, and Stradley, Ronon was aware of such efforts. Appellant further averred that potential buyers, including National Life Insurance Co., had expressed interest but had been deterred by the pending legal action commenced by Stradley, Ronon. These averments, we conclude, were sufficient to demonstrate the existence of prospective contractual relations. Neither case law nor Section 766B of the *Restatement (Second) of Torts* . . . requires an averment that the tortfeasor have knowledge of a specific third person whom its conduct prevented from entering a business relation with the plaintiff. . . .[77]

---

[73] *Id.* at 1392.

[74] 731 F. Supp. 2d 1103 (D. Colo. 2010).

[75] *Id.* at 1119–20.

[76] 596 A.2d 867 (Pa. Super. Ct. 1991).

[77] *Id.* at 871.

Specific Future Relationship Is Required. In contrast to *D'Ambro, supra,* in *Mixter v. Farmer,*[78] a Maryland appellate court imposed a higher standard regarding the necessity of identifying lost relationships. In *Mixter,* one lawyer (Farmer) wrote to various persons in an effort to gather evidence for filing a disciplinary complaint against another lawyer (Mixter). Mixter then sued Farmer in an action alleging numerous claims, including tortious interference with contract and prospective advantage. In affirming a grant of summary judgment to the defendant, the court wrote:

> [T]ortious interference with contract requires that the defendant know of an existing contract and engage in improper conduct to induce a third party's breach of that contract. . . . [Plaintiff] argues that . . . [defendant's] communications with Mr. Hancock [plaintiff's client] amount to tortious interference with one or more contracts. The trial court found that appellant could not identify any contract that was breached. We agree. Although . . . [plaintiff] speculates that he may have lost contracts in the abstract,[79] [plaintiff] . . . has not pointed to any specific lost contract or loss of business that he incurred as a result of . . . [defendant's] communications with Mr. Hancock. Moreover, [defendant] . . . states in his letter that he believes Mr. Hancock fired [plaintiff] for unprofessional behavior. If the reason [defendant] . . . wrote to Mr. Hancock was to confirm that fact, he was not intending to interfere with an existing contract.

> In order to sustain a claim for tortious interference with prospective advantage "plaintiffs must identify a possible future relationship which is likely to occur, absent the interference, with specificity." *Baron Fin. Corp. v. Natanzon,* 471 F. Supp. 2d 535, 546 (D. Md. 2006) (citing Maryland law). Once again, appellant has failed to identify a specific future relationship with Mr. Hancock that would have occurred absent Farmer's letter. Therefore, there can be no interference with prospective advantage.[80]

In New York, the action for "tortious interference with prospective economic advantage" is called "tortious interference with business relations."[81] New York caselaw is clear that, in order to prevail in an action for tortious interference with business relations, the plaintiff must show that "1) that it had a business relationship with a third party; [and] 2) that the defendant knew of that relationship and intentionally interfered with it."[82]

Burdening Prospective Relations May Be Actionable. Despite the more limited terms of liability expressed in *Restatement (Second) of Torts* § 766B, which do not make burdening actionable, it may not be necessary to show that a prospective relationship was never consummated. Making the realization of a

---

[78] 215 Md. App. 536, 81 A.3d 631 (2013).

[79] [Fn. 5:] Mixter intended to have Hancock testify that he was more reluctant to send cases to him after Farmer contacted him. But this testimony would be too speculative to support a claim for tortious interference with contract.

[80] 81 A.3d at 638

[81] *Amaranth LLC v. J.P. Morgan Chase & Co.,* 888 N.Y.S.2d 489, 494 (N.Y. App. Div. 2009).

[82] *4 K & D Corp. v. Concierge Auctions, LLC,* 2014 U.S. Dist. LEXIS 31222 (S.D.N.Y. Mar. 10, 2014).

desired relationship more expensive or burdensome has been found by some courts
to be an adequate legal basis for a tortious interference cause of action. For
example, in *Kelly-Springfield Tire Co.*, the Pennsylvania Superior Court wrote:

> It . . . [is] not fatal to appellant's cause of action that an agreement for the
> sale of the warehouse property was ultimately reached with National Life
> Insurance Company. The complaint contains averments that a resale was
> unnecessarily delayed by the interference of D'Ambro and Stradley, Ronon
> and that actual damage was caused thereby. This was sufficient.[83]

PROBLEM 5-3: THE PLASTICS LABORATORY RENOVATION CONTRACT

The main headquarters of Smart Computers, Inc. consisted of a sprawling office
park with eighteen buildings, which housed research, development, production, and
marketing operations for an array of computer products. Thousands of employees
worked at the headquarters, and space within the buildings was reconfigured
frequently as needs changed.

Over a period of eight years, Renovation Mark, a local company, had served as
the general contractor on several building and renovation projects at the
headquarters. The management of Smart Computers was so pleased with their
work that it became established company policy that Renovation Mark was to be
the general contractor for all construction and renovation work within its capacity,
if it submitted a competitive bid. Bill Jenkins was well aware of this policy. As
Smart Computer's vice president for facilities, he was responsible for formulating
bids and hiring contractors for all construction and renovation projects at the
headquarters.

When the time came to renovate Smart Computer's plastics laboratory, Jenkins
did not notify Renovation Mark about the project, although the work was within
Renovation Mark's capabilities. Instead, Jenkins contacted Eli Rosenmann, a
principal corporate officer of Laurriet Inc., a competitor of Renovation Mark.
Based on Jenkins's specifications relating to the plastics lab, Rosenmann submitted
a bid on behalf of Laurriet. Rosenmann also arranged for bids to be submitted by
two other rivals of Renovation Mark, Pippin, Inc. and Apollo, Inc. The Pippin and
Apollo bids were apparently arranged to make the Laurriet bid look attractive and
the least expensive.

When officials at Smart Computers who were superior to Jenkins learned that
Renovation Mark had not been invited to bid on the plastics lab contract, they
instructed Jenkins to seek a bid from Renovation Mark. However, Renovation
Mark was then told by Jenkins that the proposed work involved renovation of
38,000 square feet of space. In contrast, Laurriet, Pippin, and Apollo, had been told
to bid on renovation of 35,000 square feet of space, the actual amount of space
involved in the project. Nevertheless, Renovation Mark submitted the lowest of the
four bids.

Upon seeing that Renovation Mark had submitted the lowest bid, Jenkins asked
Rosenmann to have Laurriet, Pippin, and Apollo break their bids into three

---

[83] 596 A.2d 867, 871 (Pa. Super. Ct. 1991).

separate bids for (1) demolition of existing facilities, (2) construction of new facilities, and (3) other work related to Americans with Disabilities Act code compliance. Jenkins also told Rosenmann how much Laurriet should bid for construction of new facilities. Renovation Mark was not invited to submit separate bids or told that the other bidders were doing so.

When the Laurriet bid for new construction, the Pippin bid for demolition, and the Apollo bid for ADA code compliance were added together, the total came to $827,000. Renovation Mark's aggregate bid for all of the work had totaled $834,000. Contracts were awarded to Laurriet for new construction, Pippin for demolition, and Apollo for ADA code compliance.

If Renovation Mark can prove these facts, can it state a cause of action for tortious interference against any of the persons or entities involved?

E. ESTABLISHING IMPROPRIETY OR LACK OF JUSTIFICATION

The impropriety of intentional interference normally is determined by a balancing of interests. The plaintiff's interest in existing contractual rights or expectations is weighed against the defendant's interest in freedom of action. However, with respect to certain recurring types of interference — such as those involving competition or the welfare of others — definite privileges have crystallized. Those privileges are discussed later in this chapter. If they are applicable, they typically supplant the totality-of-the-circumstances balancing test.[84]

1.   Relevant Factors in the Balancing Test

The Supreme Court of Alabama, in *White Sands Group, L.L.C. v. PRS II, LLC*,[85] quoted from the *Restatement* a list of factors which should be taken into account in balancing the interests of the parties. The factors include:

(a) the nature of the actor's conduct,

(b) the actor's motive,

(c) the interests of the other with which the actor's conduct interferes,

(d) the interests sought to be advanced by the actor,

(e) the social interests in protecting the freedom of action of the actor and the contractual interests of the other,

(f) the proximity or remoteness of the actor's conduct to the interference, and

(g) the relations between the parties.[86]

---

[84] *See* RESTATEMENT (SECOND) OF TORTS § 767 cmts. a and j (1979).

[85] 2009 Ala. LEXIS 201 (Sept. 4, 2009).

[86] *Id.* at *14 (quoting an earlier decision which quoted RESTATEMENT (SECOND) OF TORTS § 767 (1979)).

Elaborating on some of these factors, the *White Sands Group* court explained, with language from the *Restatement*, as follows:

Nature of actor's conduct. The nature of the actor's conduct is a chief factor in determining whether the conduct is improper or not, despite its harm to the other person. The variety of means by which the actor may cause the harm are stated in § 766, Comments k to n. Some of them, like fraud and physical violence, are tortious to the person immediately affected by them; others, like persuasion and offers of benefits, are not tortious to him. Under the same circumstances interference by some means is not improper while interference by other means is improper; and, likewise, the same means may be permissible under some circumstances while wrongful in others. The issue is not simply whether the actor is justified in causing the harm, but rather whether he is justified in causing it in the manner in which he does cause it. The propriety of the means is not, however, determined as a separate issue unrelated to the other factors. On the contrary, the propriety is determined in the light of all the factors present. Thus physical violence, fraudulent misrepresentation and threats of illegal conduct are ordinarily wrongful means and subject their user to liability even though he is free to accomplish the same result by more suitable means. . . . The nature of the means is, however, only one factor in determining whether the interference is improper. Under some circumstances the interference is improper even though innocent means are employed.

Physical violence. Threats of physical violence were the means employed in the very early instances of liability for intentional interference with economic relations; and interference by physical violence is ordinarily improper. . . . The issue is simply whether the actor induces the third person's conduct or prevents the injured party's performance of his own contract by putting him in fear of physical violence.

Misrepresentations. Fraudulent misrepresentations are also ordinarily a wrongful means of interference and make an interference improper. A representation is fraudulent when, to the knowledge or belief of its utterer, it is false in the sense in which it is intended to be understood by its recipient. (*See* § 527). . . . The tort of intentional interference . . . overlaps other torts. But it is not coincident with them. One may be subject to liability for intentional interference even when his fraudulent representation is not of such a character as to subject him to liability for the other torts.[87]

Breach of Contract Is Not Illegal. The fact that the defendant breached a contract with a third party in the course of interfering with the plaintiff's protected relationship does not by itself make the interference tortious.[88] Under the efficient breach of contract theory, which is often discussed in law school Contracts courses, a party to a contract has the option of performing or paying damages. Breach of a contract is not illegal, improper, or unjustified under the law of torts; it merely

---

[87] *Id.* at *15–*17 (quoting RESTATEMENT (SECOND) OF TORTS § 767 cmt. c (1979) (some emphasis deleted)).

[88] *See Windsor Securities, Inc. v. Hartford Life Ins. Co.*, 986 F.2d 655, 664 (3d Cir. 1993).

carries with it consequences under the law of contracts.

a.   The Role of Ethical Standards

Client Solicitation by Attorneys. The relationship between ethical standards and the law of tortious interference may be illustrated by reference to the questions that arise when an attorney, who leaves a law firm to practice alone or to join another firm, successfully solicits the future business of clients of the former firm. Does the departing attorney become liable for tortious interference, or is such conduct unobjectionable?

In the law of tortious interference, it is generally agreed that the use of physical violence, misrepresentation, or bad faith threats of litigation are all improper. Thus, if an attorney withdrawing from a firm resorts to duress, fraud, defamation, or other forms of deception in an effort to secure a client's business, the attorney runs a serious risk of liability for tortious interference. The use of blatantly wrongful methods is not, however, a *sine qua non* of liability for tortious interference.

The *Restatement* identifies a consideration especially apposite to the firm-switching context: conformance with business ethics and customs. The *Restatement* provides: "Violation of recognized ethical codes for a particular area of business activity or of established customs and practices regarding disapproved actions or methods may also be significant in evaluating the nature of the actor's conduct. . . ."[89] Consequently, to the extent that one conforms with professional ethical strictures, there is an inference that one's conduct is proper, and if one violates those norms, a contrary inference arises. If conduct exposes an attorney leaving a law firm to professional discipline for improper client solicitation, it may also be sufficient to raise a specter of tort sanctions.

The professional ethics factor played a major role in *Adler, Barish, Daniels, Levin & Creskoff v. Epstein*.[90] There, the Supreme Court of Pennsylvania held that the solicitation of law firm clients by several former associates, in person, by phone, and by letter, ran afoul of the provisions of what was then called the "formal announcement rule." Under that rule, which was crafted in the days before lawyer advertising was recognized as constitutionally protected, a lawyer had only a limited right to inform present or former clients of new or changed associations. An exiting partner or associate could apprise firm clients for whom the attorney had worked about the fact of the attorney's departure. However, to pass muster under this standard, a notice, in the form of a brief professional announcement card or an equivalent letter, was required to be both dignified and exceedingly laconic. Authorities made clear that language intended to persuade a client to discharge the attorney's former firm was wholly impermissible. The communications at issue in *Adler, Barish* went beyond what the formal announcement rule permitted. Placing substantial weight on that transgression of professional ethics, the court concluded that the associates had improperly interfered with the client relations of the former firm, and injunctive relief was granted.

---

[89] RESTATEMENT (SECOND) OF TORTS § 767 cmt. c (1979).

[90] 393 A.2d 1175 (Pa. 1978).

Today, all states have discarded the formal announcement rule, for the United States Supreme Court has made clear that in a wide range of cases attorneys have a constitutional right to communicate with present or former clients about the terms and availability of legal services. Consequently, while *Alder, Barish* stands as a good illustration of the relationship between ethical standards and the assessment of impropriety in tortious interference claims, the case has little precedential value on the question of whether departing attorneys today have a right to solicit the business of clients of their former firms. As articulated by § 9 of the *Restatement (Third) of the Law Governing Lawyers*:

> Absent an agreement with the firm providing a more permissive rule, a lawyer leaving a law firm may solicit firm clients:
>
> (a) prior to leaving the firm:
>
>> (i) only with respect to firm clients on whose matters the lawyer is actively and substantially working; and
>>
>> (ii) only after the lawyer has adequately and timely informed the firm of the lawyer's intent to contact firm clients for that purpose; and
>
> (b) after ceasing employment in the firm, to the same extent as any other nonfirm lawyer.[91]

Questionable Professional Customs. Not all ethics rules stand on equal footing. Many of the ethical standards governing attorneys are the result of a years-long process of careful weighing of options and deliberation. Bar associations, scholars, ethics committees, and courts have labored at length over the task of fairly balancing competing interests. That being the case, it is not surprising that courts are reluctant to circumvent or subvert those standards by striking a different balance in the name of protecting contractual and other kinds of expectations. However, if a professional custom or ethical rule is not the product of long and careful deliberation, testing, and enforcement, no high degree of deference may be warranted. For example, in *Skelly v. Richman*,[92] one attorney brought an action against another attorney for violating a professional custom concerning the making and delivery of settlement checks. The California Court of Appeal found the custom to be relevant, but indicated that the depth of inquiry into the custom may vary with the particular case.

Failure to Prove There Was an Industry Standard. In *Walker v. Anderson-Oliver Title Ins. Agency, Inc.*,[93] the plaintiff failed to successfully invoke industry standards to support a claim for tortious interference. As the court explained:

> Walker explains that to prove improper means, he may show that the Defendants' conduct violated an established standard in the title insurance industry. . . . He argues that before title companies issue insurance policies, "the established professional standard . . . requires a preliminary

---

[91] RESTATEMENT (THIRD) OF THE LAW GOVERNING LAWYERS § 9 (2000). *See also* Alex B. Long, *The Business of Law and Tortious Interference*, 36 ST. MARY'S L.J. 925, 965–81 (2005).

[92] 10 Cal. App. 3d 844 (1970).

[93] 309 P.3d 267 (Utah Ct. App. 2013).

report listing all encumbrances that may be important." In support of this proposition, he cites expert testimony and a variety of other sources that discuss Stewart Title's internal policy of disclosing certain encumbrances to its customers before issuing a title insurance policy. This evidence, Walker contends, shows that "industry standards required that the [Commitment] should have included the [Access Deeds]" . . . .

We conclude that the tortious interference claim cannot survive summary judgment. . . . [T]he evidence Walker offers is legally insufficient to establish a title insurance industry standard. . . .[94]

b.   The Role of Motive

(1)   Improper Motivation as Tipping the Balance

Many decisions discuss improper motivation as one of many factors which may be taken into account in determining whether interference is improper. These cases essentially hold that improper motivation can tip the balance against a defendant sued for tortious interference.[95]

For example, in *Pleas v. City of Seattle*,[96] the Supreme Court of Washington found that there was improper interference where efforts were made by employees in the mayor's office and the building department to block the plaintiff's legitimate construction project in order to curry favor with voters in a particular district. The city had singled out the plaintiff's project and applied its land use regulations in such a manner as to preclude any development on the property. The court held that it was no defense that the city's actions "were simply part of the 'political' process."

(2)   Improper Motivation as an Alternative to Improper Means

Some jurisdictions treat improper motivation as more than a tipping factor in tortious interference cases. In those states, interference may be actionable either because the defendant used "improper means" or because the defendant acted with an "improper purpose."

(a)   Example: *Pratt v. Prodata, Inc.*

Improper Purpose or Improper Means. In *Pratt v. Prodata, Inc.*,[97] Pratt, a computer programmer, left his job with Prodata Inc. (Prodata), and began to work with the Utah Department of Transportation (UDOT). Although Pratt was bound by a covenant not to compete, his work for UDOT did not violate the covenant. Nevertheless, Prodata and its manager, McCoy, asserted that "Pratt had taken contract work away from Prodata" and stated that Prodata was going to "make an

---

[94] *Id.* at 273–74.

[95] *See also* RESTATEMENT (SECOND) OF TORTS § 767 cmt. b (1979).

[96] 774 P.2d 1158 (Wash. 1989).

[97] 885 P.2d 786 (Utah 1994).

example" of Pratt.[98] As a result of their contacting UDOT, Pratt's association with UDOT was terminated. In a subsequent tortious interference action by Pratt against Prodata and McCoy, the Utah Supreme Court wrote:

> Under our decision in *Leigh Furniture & Carpet Co. v. Isom*, 657 P.2d 293, 304 (Utah 1982), a defendant is liable for intentional interference with prospective economic relations if the plaintiff proves "(1) that the defendant intentionally interfered with the plaintiff's existing or potential economic relations, (2) for an improper purpose or by improper means, (3) causing injury to the plaintiff." This case focuses on the second of these three elements. . . . An "improper means" is shown when the plaintiff proves that the defendant's means of interference were contrary to statutory, regulatory, or common law or violated "an established standard of a trade or profession." . . . The alternative, "improper purpose," is satisfied when the plaintiff proves that the defendant's ill will predominated over all legitimate economic motivations. . . . According to *Leigh*, a finding of improper purpose is entirely consistent with a finding that the defendant's means were proper. . . .
>
> There is substantial credible evidence in the record to support the jury's determination that defendants interfered with Pratt's economic relations for an improper purpose and without privilege. . . . Defendants expressed a consistent and open hostility for Pratt after he disassociated himself from Prodata. Rather than suing Pratt for breach of the Noncompete Covenant as it was legally entitled to do, Prodata utilized its contacts at UDOT to have Pratt fired. Prodata took this course of action even though the Noncompete Covenant had already expired and therefore could no longer be legally used to bar Pratt from working at UDOT. Finally, defendants used the Noncompete Covenant to threaten substantial liability and to demand a substantial payment from Pratt when it knew that it had not suffered any actual damages from the breach. Thus, on the facts before it, the jury could have found something akin to extortion in defendants' motivation.[99]

Doubts About the Role of Improper Purpose. The *Pratt* court affirmed a judgment in favor of the plaintiff. However, in a footnote, the author of the majority opinion expressed concerns about the improper-purpose test. He wrote:

> The author of this opinion has grave doubts about the future vitality of *Leigh's* improper-purpose prong, especially in the context of commercial dealings. *Leigh* recognized that "[p]roblems inherent in proving motivation or purpose make it prudent for commercial conduct to be regulated for the most part by the improper means alternative, which typically requires only a showing of particular conduct." . . . *Leigh's* improper-purpose test creates a trap for the wary and unwary alike: business practices that are found to be "proper means" by a finder of fact and may otherwise be regarded as wholly legitimate under our capitalistic economic system may

---

[98] *Id.* at 787.

[99] *Id.* at 788–89.

be recast through a jury's unguided exercise of its moral judgment into examples of spite or malice. For example, the enforcement of a binding, valid contractual noncompete provision can result in liability under *Leigh* merely upon a jury finding of some ill-defined "improper purpose." For these reasons, the author of this opinion thinks *Leigh's* improper-purpose test should be revisited and recast to minimize its potential for misuse.[100]

Nevertheless, the *Leigh* rule has stood the test of time in Utah. The improper-purpose prong of the test for impropriety continues to be applied.[101]

(b)   Rejection of the Improper Purpose Alternative

Some courts expressly or implicitly reject the use of an "improper purpose" test, as an alternative to an "improper means" test, for proving that interference is actionable. In *Alexander v. Evander*,[102] the court wrote:

> [A]cts of interference with economic relations do not become tortious simply because the defendant carries them out with a wrongful intent. Proof that . . . [the defendant] harbored animosity towards . . . [the plaintiff] when it interfered with . . . [the plaintiff's] economic relationship . . . would not sustain the tort if . . . [the defendant's] animosity was incidental to its pursuit of legitimate commercial goals.[103]

Relationship of Improper Purpose to the Independent Tortious Conduct Rule. As discussed below, many states now require proof of independent tortious conduct in cases alleging interference with prospective advantage. That rule is a significant limitation on the relevance and usefulness of evidence of improper purpose in tortious interference cases not involving disruption of an existing contract.

PROBLEM 5-4: THE DISRUPTED NEWS INTERVIEW

Citizens For Peace (CFP) is a nonprofit organization dedicated to nonviolence and the protection of civil liberties and human rights at home and abroad. The group engages in the picketing of military contractors and other efforts intended to demonstrate opposition to the military-industrial complex.

While ABC News and its Reporter Angela Magden were covering a CFP rally on the west side of the Capitol in Washington, D.C., a CFP volunteer removed the ABC camera crew's schedule from the ABC van and phoned the contents of the schedule to CFP headquarters. According to the schedule, Magden and her crew were to interview Senator Karen Anderson, the hawkish ranking member of the Senate's Anti-Terrorism Subcommittee, later that afternoon. Senator Anderson was a proponent of expanded funding for federal government surveillance of Internet communications.

---

[100] *Id.* at 789 n.3.

[101] *See Walker v. Anderson-Oliver Title Ins. Agency, Inc.*, 309 P.3d 267, 273 (Utah Ct. App. 2013).

[102] 650 A.2d 260 (Md. 1994).

[103] *Id.* at 271.

When Magden returned to the ABC Washington office around midday, her research assistant, Kathi Bonjourno, told her that Senator Anderson's office had called and cancelled the interview. While Magden was in the office, Bonjourno received another call from someone claiming to be Senator Anderson's aide. Under the guise of reconsidering the cancellation, the caller solicited, and received, information about whom ABC had contacted in the course of preparing its planned story about funding for Internet surveillance. Becoming suspicious, Magden called Senator Anderson's office only to learn that someone purporting to be from ABC News had called the Senator's office and cancelled the interview. Senator Anderson's office had not called ABC. Ultimately, the interview did take place that afternoon as originally scheduled.

On these facts, can ABC News state a cause of action for tortious interference against Citizens For Peace or its volunteers who were involved in these events?

2.   The Burden of Proof on Impropriety

There has been considerable debate and disagreement over who has the burden of proof on the issue of impropriety or lack of justification in a tortious interference case, the plaintiff or the defendant. As discussed below, the fact that interference is an intentional tort may account for some of the confusion.

a.   Abrogation of the *"Prima Facie* Tort" Approach

Differentiating Between Interference with Contract and Interference with Prospective Advantage. In *Della Penna v. Toyota Motor Sales, U.S.A.*,[104] the Supreme Court of California addressed the issue of how the burden of proof should be allocated in an interference case, writing:

> [An] early accent on the defendant's "intentionality" that was responsible for allying the interference torts with their remote relatives, intentional torts of a quite different order — battery, for example, or false imprisonment. . . .

> One consequence of this superficial kinship was the assimilation to the interference torts of the pleading and burden of proof requirements of the "true" intentional torts: the requirement that the plaintiff need only allege a so-called *"prima facie* tort" by showing the defendant's awareness of the economic relation, a deliberate interference with it, and the plaintiff's resulting injury. . . . By this account of the matter — the traditional view of the torts and the one adopted by the first *Restatement of Torts* — the burden then passed to the defendant to demonstrate that its conduct was privileged, that is, "justified" by a recognized defense such as the protection of others or, more likely in this context, the defendant's own competitive business interests. . . .

> . . . [There were] calls for a reexamination and reform as early as the 1920's. . . . The nature of the wrong itself seemed to many unduly vague, inviting suit and hampering the presentation of coherent defenses. . . .

---

[104] 902 P.2d 740 (Cal. 1995).

Because the plaintiff's initial burden of proof was such a slender one, amounting to no more than showing the defendant's conscious act and plaintiff's economic injury, critics argued that legitimate business competition could lead to time consuming and expensive lawsuits (not to speak of potential liability) by a rival, based on conduct that was regarded by the commercial world as both commonplace and appropriate. The "black letter" rules of the *Restatement of Torts* surrounding the elements and proof of the tort, some complained, might even suggest to "foreign lawyers reading the *Restatement* as an original matter [that] the whole competitive order of American industry is *prima facie* illegal." . . .

. . . The *Restatement Second of Torts* . . . declined to take a position on the issue of which of the parties bore the burden of proof. . . .

Over the past decade or so, close to a majority of the high courts of American jurisdictions have imported into the economic relations tort variations on . . . a rule that requires the plaintiff in such a suit to plead and prove the alleged interference was either "wrongful," "improper," "illegal," "independently tortious" or some variant on these formulations. . . .[105]

While acknowledging that earlier California decisions had followed a *prima facie* tort approach, the court in *Della Penna* found that a distinction could be drawn between interference with contract cases and interference with prospective advantage cases, since the law has a greater interest in preventing disruption of a formally cemented economic relationship. The court held that, in cases involving tortious interference with prospective advantage, the plaintiff has the burden of pleading and proving that the defendant's interference was wrongful by some measure beyond the fact of the interference itself.

b.   The Independent Tortious Means Requirement

A Narrower Range of Improper Means. In *Wal-Mart Stores, Inc. v. Sturges,*[106] the Texas Supreme Court discussed whether, in an action for tortious interference with prospective advantage, the defendant's conduct must be "independently tortious." In that case, land purchasers (plaintiffs) alleged that an easement holder (Wal-Mart) tortiously interfered with the purchaser's prospective lease to a food store company by refusing to consent to construction of a larger store nearby. The court explained:

[I]n most Texas cases in which plaintiffs have actually recovered damages for tortious interference with prospective business relations, the defendants' conduct was either independently tortious — in the four cases noted, defamatory or fraudulent — or in violation of state law. For the same reasons accepted by the Supreme Court of California in *Della Penna,* . . . we see no need for a definition of tortious interference with prospective business relations that would encompass other conduct. The historical

---

[105] *Id.* at 744–46.

[106] 52 S.W.3d 711 (Tex. 2001).

limitation of the tort to unlawful conduct — "the actor's conduct was characterized by violence, fraud or defamation, and was tortious in character" — provides a viable definition and preserves the tort's utility of filling a gap in affording compensation in situations where a wrong has been done. The concepts of malice, justification, and privilege have not only proved to be overlapping and confusing, they provide no meaningful description of culpable conduct, as the *Restatement (Second) of Torts* concluded more than twenty years ago.

We therefore hold that to recover for tortious interference with a prospective business relation a plaintiff must prove that the defendant's conduct was independently tortious or wrongful. By independently tortious we do not mean that the plaintiff must be able to prove an independent tort. Rather, we mean only that the plaintiff must prove that the defendant's conduct would be actionable under a recognized tort. Thus, for example, a plaintiff may recover for tortious interference from a defendant who makes fraudulent statements about the plaintiff to a third person without proving that the third person was actually defrauded. If, on the other hand, the defendant's statements are not intended to deceive, . . . then they are not actionable. Likewise, a plaintiff may recover for tortious interference from a defendant who threatens a person with physical harm if he does business with the plaintiff. The plaintiff need prove only that the defendant's conduct toward the prospective customer would constitute assault. Also, a plaintiff could recover for tortious interference by showing an illegal boycott, although a plaintiff could not recover against a defendant whose persuasion of others not to deal with the plaintiff was lawful. Conduct that is merely "sharp" or unfair is not actionable and cannot be the basis for an action for tortious interference with prospective relations. . . . These examples are not exhaustive, but they illustrate what conduct can constitute tortious interference with prospective relations.

The concepts of justification and privilege are subsumed in the plaintiff's proof, except insofar as they may be defenses to the wrongfulness of the alleged conduct. For example, a statement made against the plaintiff, though defamatory, may be protected by a complete or qualified privilege. . . .

In reaching this conclusion we treat tortious interference with prospective business relations differently than tortious interference with contract. It makes sense to require a defendant who induces a breach of contract to show some justification or privilege for depriving another of benefits to which the agreement entitled him. But when two parties are competing for interests to which neither is entitled, then neither can be said to be more justified or privileged in his pursuit. If the conduct of each is lawful, neither should be heard to complain that mere unfairness is actionable. Justification and privilege are not useful concepts in assessing interference with prospective relations, as they are in assessing interference with an existing contract.[107]

The court concluded that there was no evidence of independently tortious conduct on the part of Wal-Mart and therefore no basis for liability for tortious interference with prospective advantage.

Defamation as a Predicate Wrongful Act. In *Amaranth LLC v. J.P. Morgan Chase & Co.*,[108] a hedge fund (Amaranth) sought to stem its losses by transferring the risk associated with the Fund's natural gas portfolio to other banks or funds. For that purpose, Amaranth sought to consummate a deal with Citadel under which Citadel would receive $1.85 billion as a concession for taking on most of the Fund's risks. In a subsequent lawsuit, Amaranth alleged that two executives for J.P. Morgan Chase & Co. (JPMC) called Citadel, told it that "Amaranth is not as solvent as they are telling you they are,"[109] and that the deal fell through. The plaintiffs further alleged that JPMC was displeased that the Fund was negotiating with other firms instead of JPMC. In addressing the dismissal of the Amaranth's claim for tortious interference with prospective advantage, the New York Appellate Division noted that the plaintiff was required to show "that the defendant acted solely out of malice or used improper or illegal means that amounted to a crime or independent tort."[110] Turning to the evidence, the court opined:

> Defamation is a predicate wrongful act for a tortious interference claim.
> . . .
>
> . . . [W]e find that the Fund has adequately pleaded the elements of tortious interference with prospective economic advantage (the second cause of action). It is well settled that where a statement impugns the basic integrity or creditworthiness of a business, an action lies and injury is conclusively presumed. . . . Thus, the argument that the alleged statement, which disparages the Fund's solvency . . . is nonactionable opinion is without merit. The alleged statement has a precise meaning, and whether or not the Fund was solvent at the time the statement was made is a fact capable of being proven true or false by a fact-finder. The Fund pleads the underlying defamation with the required specificity, setting forth the particular words that were said, who said them and who heard them, when the speaker said them, and where the words were spoken. . . . Finally, the Fund sufficiently pleads injury and causation. Specifically, the complaint alleges that the false statement made by JPMC's executives caused Citadel to withdraw from the trade agreed upon earlier in the day and that losing the proposed trade with Citadel caused the Fund more than $1 billion in losses. . . .[111]

The court reinstated the Fund's tortious interference claim against JPMC.

---

[107] *Id.* at 726–27.

[108] 71 A.D.3d 40 (N.Y. App. Div. 2009).

[109] *Id.* at 492.

[110] *Id.* at 494.

[111] *Id.* at 494–95.

However, the claim eventually failed because JPMC's unrefuted evidence demonstrated that the allegedly defamatory statement had never been made.[112]

3.   Specific Privileges

a.   Privilege to Compete

(1)   In General

In some situations, there is a privilege to compete; in other situations, engaging in competition is tortious. Addressing this subject, the court in *Alexander & Alexander, Inc. v. B. Dixon Evander & Assoc.*,[113] the Maryland Court of Appeals wrote:

> The . . . interference tort generally arises in a commercial setting. Participants in the economic marketplace are expected to act aggressively in seeking business and furthering their own position in the market. . . .

> This Court has long recognized that self-interested commercial dealing has its proper place in the business world. Thus, in *Goldman v. Building Ass'n*, 150 Md. 677, 684, 133 A. 843, 846 (1926), the Court stated:

>> "Iron sharpeneth iron" is ancient wisdom, and the law is in accord in favoring free competition, since ordinarily it is essential to the general welfare of society, notwithstanding [that] competition is not altruistic but is fundamentally the play of interest against interest, and so involves the interference of the successful competitor with the interest of his unsuccessful competitor in the matter of their common rivalry. Competition is the state in which men live and is not a tort, unless the nature of the method employed is not justified by public policy, and so supplies the condition to constitute a legal wrong.[114]

(2)   Under the Restatement

The Restatement's Competition Privilege. Section 768 of the *Restatement (Second) of Torts* states the terms of the privilege to compete. That section provides:

> (1) One who intentionally causes a third person not to enter into a prospective contractual relation with another who is his competitor or not to continue an existing contract terminable at will does not interfere improperly with the other's relation if

>> (a) the relation concerns a matter involved in the competition between the actor and the other and

>> (b) the actor does not employ wrongful means and

---

[112] *See Amaranth LLC v. J.P. Morgan Chase & Co.*, 100 A.D.3d 573 (N.Y. App. Div. 2012).

[113] 650 A.2d 260 (Md. 1994).

[114] *Id.* at 269.

(c) his action does not create or continue an unlawful restraint of trade and

(d) his purpose is at least in part to advance his interest in competing with the other.

(2) The fact that one is a competitor of another for the business of a third person does not prevent his causing a breach of an existing contract with the other from being an improper interference if the contract is not terminable at will.[115]

No Privilege to Disrupt an Existing Privilege by Competition. The first thing to note about the *Restatement*'s competition privilege is that it applies only to disruption with prospective contractual relations. If there is an existing contract, the privilege is inapplicable. There is no right to disrupt an existing contractual relation merely because one wishes to "compete."

Contracts Terminable at Will. As noted earlier, contracts terminable at will are treated as the equivalent of prospectively advantageous relations, since there is no legal assurance that the plaintiff will enjoy those benefits.[116] Thus, an option to renew or extend a contract is treated as prospective until the right has been exercised.[117] Prior to that point, others may compete.

An at-will employment contract may carry with it an enforceable covenant not to compete after termination. In that case, a competitor may persuade an employee to stop working for another competitor, but has no right to employ the employee who has left the prior position.[118]

Particular Targets of Competition. The *Restatement* privilege allows one not only to compete generally but also to seek to divert business from a particular competitor.[119] In *Overstock.com, Inc. v. SmartBargains, Inc.*,[120] an online store sued a competitor for tortious interference based on the fact that pop-up ads for the competitor appeared when customers accessed the online store's website. In rejecting the claim, the Supreme Court of Utah wrote:

> SmartBargains' pop-ups do not present an improper purpose or an improper means. SmartBargains' pop-ups indisputably exist to compete with Overstock. Competition is not an improper purpose, even though other by-products of competition may exist. . . . Overstock has likewise failed to demonstrate that pop-ups are an improper means of competition. . . . Overstock has failed to present evidence that the pop-ups violate common law. Overstock has not alleged in this appeal that SmartBargains' pop-ups

---

[115] RESTATEMENT (SECOND) OF TORTS § 768 (1979).

[116] *Id.* § 768 cmts. a & i.

[117] *Id.* § 768 cmt. a.

[118] *Id.* § 768 cmt. i.

[119] *Id.* § 768 cmt. b.

[120] 192 P.3d 858 (Utah 2008).

violate statutory law. We therefore affirm the district court's grant of SmartBargains' motion for summary judgment. . . .[121]

The Scope of Competition. The *Restatement* privilege covers a wide range of competition. Sellers may compete with each other, and buyers may compete with other buyers. Competition may be direct or indirect. Thus, two retailers may compete with one another, or a wholesaler may compete with a retailer.[122]

In order to be permissible, the alleged interference must relate to the subject matter of the competition. Thus, shoe sellers may compete with one another with respect to the sale of shoes.[123] However, one shoe seller does not have a right to cause a third person not to buy another shoe seller's dwelling, since that matter is outside the scope of the competition.[124]

Cases sometimes raise difficult questions about whether two enterprises were in competition. For example, in *Church of Scientology International v. Eli Lilly & Co.*,[125] the Church of Scientology hired a public relations firm to protect its public image. After Eli Lilly & Co., a major pharmaceutical company, allegedly caused the public relations firm to terminate its contract with the church, the church sued Lilly for tortious interference. In addressing that claim, a federal court in the District of Columbia wrote:

> Lilly asserts it was privileged to act as it did under the "competitor's privilege" because CSI, through its "Dianetics" mental health treatment system was in actual competition with Lilly. . . .
>
> As to the question of whether CSI with its Dianetics program was in actual competition with Lilly's anti-depressant Prozac, . . . [there] are genuine issues of fact for the jury. It is not clear from the submitted papers exactly how the Dianetics treatment is used and to what extent Scientology actively markets its faith and ideology as a drug-free remedy to clinical depression. The Court will follow the recommendation of the *Restatement*:
>
>> "[W]hen there is room for different views, the determination of whether the interference was improper or not is ordinarily left to the jury to obtain its common feel for the state of community mores and for the manner in which they would operate upon the facts in question."
>
> *Restatement (Second) Torts*, § 767 comment l. The Court believes that there are enough genuine issues of material fact as to whether Lilly's interference was justified to allow this claim to go to the jury.[126]

Wrongful Means Prohibited. The *Restatement* privilege prohibits competition by use of wrongful means. Persuasion and even limited economic pressure are not

---

[121] *Id.* at 864–65.

[122] RESTATEMENT (SECOND) OF TORTS § 768 cmt. c (1979).

[123] *Id.* § 768 illus. 1.

[124] *Id.* § 768 illus. 2.

[125] 848 F. Supp. 1018, 1030 (D.D.C. 1994).

[126] *Id.* at 1029–30.

regarded as wrongful.[127] However, physical harm, fraud, and vexatious litigation are all regarded as wrongful.[128]

Unlawful Restraint of Competition. Conduct that violates state or federal antitrust laws is, by definition, not a permissible form of competition.[129]

Improper Motives and Mixed Motives. A person who is motivated solely by spite, ill will, or vindictiveness cannot invoke the competition privilege.[130] However, mixed motives do not cause the loss of the privilege, so long as one of the actor's motives is a desire to compete. Thus, the fact that the defendant hates a competitor, or desires to exact revenge for previous harm, does not inevitably mean that the competition privilege is inapplicable.[131]

PROBLEM 5-5: THE HEDGE FUND TYCOON

Walter Frump, a graduate of an elite business school, built a $15 billion hedge fund. Not adverse to risks, he used the hedge fund to place what was essentially a $1 billion bet that the price of shares in Nutri-Life-A, a nutritional supplement company, would fall. To ensure the success of his gamble, Frump undertook a "scorched earth" campaign designed to tar Nutri-Life-A with the stain of bad publicity. He worked tirelessly to persuade lawmakers in Washington to subject Nutri-Life-A to embarrassing, highly public, investigations into what he decried as "improper business tactics."

To carry out his plan, Frump called press conferences at which he condemned Nutri-Life-A as a "pyramid scheme."[132] He also made lavish campaign contributions to members of Congress, and persuaded three of those lawmakers to issue public statements calling for an examination of Nutri-Life-A's business model. Frump publicized the contents of a letter purportedly issued by one member of Congress, calling for legislative oversight of Nutri-Life-A, a month before the letter was ever sent by the member to a Congressional committee. When the member finally issued the letter, the media widely reported that the letter had been backdated so that it appeared to have been written shortly before Frump publicized its contents.

Frump claimed he was concerned about Nutri-Life-A's bad reputation for mistreatment of minorities. He publicly promised to give to charity any profits that he personally earned from the collapse of Nutri-Life-A. However, Frump admitted that his hedge fund clients might nevertheless benefit immensely.

Addressing the extraordinarily aggressive nature of Frump's anti-Nutri-Life-A campaign, a former chair of the Securities and Exchange Commission was quoted

---

[127] RESTATEMENT (SECOND) OF TORTS § 768 cmt. e (1979).

[128] *Id.*

[129] *Id.* § 768 cmt. f.

[130] *Id.* § 768 cmt. g.

[131] *Id.*

[132] Wikipedia defines a *pyramid scheme* as "unsustainable business model that involves promising participants payment or services, primarily for enrolling other people into the scheme, rather than supplying any real investment or sale of products or services to the public." *See* www.wikipedia.com.

as saying that it was her opinion that Frump was more interested "in moving the price of Nutri-Life-A stock than in spreading the truth."

Frump recruited minority organizations to support his campaign against Nutri-Life-A. Via a "grassroots" campaign, those organizations inundated key members of Congress with mail urging Congressional action against Nutri-Life-A. News reports indicated that some of the organizations and their officers had been paid handsomely for their efforts and that some of the mail that reached Congress purportedly came from persons who said they had never authorized those letters.

Under the glare of bad publicity, the price of Nutri-Life-A's shares collapsed. Investors deserted the company in droves and Nutri-Life-A was driven into bankruptcy. Can the company's bankruptcy trustee assert a viable claim for tortious interference against Frump?

b.   Privilege Based on Financial Interest

(1)   The Investment Privilege

Persons Having an Interest in the Business of the Person Induced. Section 769 of the *Restatement (Second) of Torts* recognizes a privilege to protect one's financial interests. That section provides:

> One who, having a financial interest in the business of a third person intentionally causes that person not to enter into a prospective contractual relation with another, does not interfere improperly with the other's relation if he
>
> (a) does not employ wrongful means and
>
> (b) acts to protect his interest from being prejudiced by the relation.[133]

Limited to Interference with Prospective Contractual Relations. The *Restatement*'s financial interest privilege does not prevent liability for causing the breach of an existing contract.[134] However, case law sometimes goes further than the *Restatement*. In *In re Joy Global, Inc.*,[135] a federal court in Delaware found it unnecessary to decide which *Restatement* provision best explained why the defendant corporation's conduct was justified, but it noted that "several Wisconsin federal and state courts have, applying Wisconsin law, repeatedly found § 769 to be the proper guide when the party accused of tortious interference has a financial interest in the party accused of breaching an *existing* contract."[136]

Financial Interests Amounting to Investments. According to the *Restatement*, its financial interest privilege protects interests in the nature of an investment. Thus, the privilege may be exercised by a part owner of a business, a partner, a

---

[133] *Id.* § 769.

[134] *Id.* § 769 cmt. a.

[135] 739 F. Supp. 2d 711 (D. Del. 2010).

[136] *Id.* at 744 n.12.

stockholder, a bondholder, and perhaps even a creditor.[137] Thus, a financial backer of a theatrical production may have a privilege to persuade the producer not to cast a particular actor as the lead,[138] and a stockholder may have a privilege to persuade a corporation not to agree to market an invention.[139]

In *Schulman v. J.P. Morgan Investment Management, Inc.*,[140] the Third Circuit held that a mortgagee who was financing the "up-scale" renovation of a building had a privilege to interfere with a prospective lease between the mortgagor-landlord and the plaintiff, a prospective tenant, by objecting to the aesthetics of a restaurant that the proposed tenant planned to operate on the first floor of the building. The mortgagee, the court found, was acting to protect its financial interest by ensuring that the building would attract "up-scale" tenants.

In contrast, a person who merely receives business from the party induced has no privilege within the terms of the *Restatement* formulation of the investment privilege.[141]

(a)   Parent Corporations and Their Subsidiaries

Parent Corporations and Their Subsidiaries. A parent corporation holds a financial interest in the business of a subsidiary. Consequently, in *Alexander & Alexander, Inc. v. B. Dixon Evander & Associates*,[142] the Maryland Court of Appeals noted:

> A parent corporation is generally justified in requiring its subsidiary to modify economic arrangements, contractual or otherwise, if those arrangements do not benefit the parent. Under these circumstances, interference by the parent is ordinarily not tortious.[143]

However, there may be instances where a parent corporation's interference with the business interests of a subsidiary may be tortious, rather than privileged. For example, in *Church of Scientology International v. Eli Lilly & Co.*,[144] discussed above, the Church of Scientology (CSI) hired a public relations firm (H & K) to defend its public reputation. H & K was the wholly-owned subsidiary of WPP, whose CEO was Sorrell. WPP had another wholly-owned subsidiary, JWT, which was an advertising agency which represented Eli Lilly & Co. The parent corporation (WPP) and its CEO (Sorrell) pressured H & K to dump the Church of Scientology as a client. In addressing the resulting tortious interference claim by the Church against WPP and Sorrell, a federal court in the District of Columbia wrote:

---

[137] *Id.* § 769 cmt. c.

[138] *Id.* § 769 illus. 1.

[139] *Id.* § 769 illus. 2.

[140] 35 F.3d 799 (3d Cir. 1994).

[141] Restatement (Second) of Torts § 769 cmt. c (1979).

[142] 650 A.2d 260 (Md. 1994).

[143] *Id.* at 272.

[144] 848 F. Supp. 1018 (D.D.C. 1994).

Sorrell and WPP . . . move to dismiss on the ground that their actions in influencing H & K to terminate the contract were privileged. These defendants cite the *Restatement (Second) of Torts* § 769 which suggests that a party with a financial interest in a contract would be privileged to influence or interfere with the continuation of that contract. . . .

WPP and Sorrell place substantial reliance on *Copperweld Corp. v. Independence Tube Corp.,* . . . [467 U.S. 752 (1984)]. In *Copperweld,* the Supreme Court concluded that it would be impossible for a corporate parent and its wholly-owned subsidiary to conspire for antitrust purposes. This is because, the Court found, "[a] parent and its wholly-owned subsidiary have a complete unity of interest. Their objectives are common, not disparate; their general corporate actions are guided or determined not by two separate corporate consciousnesses, but one. They are not unlike a multiple team of horses drawing a vehicle under the control of a single driver." . . . WPP and Sorrell argue that this passage . . . means that under the circumstances of this case, owner corporations, parent company officers, and corporate subsidiaries should be able to influence the decisions of other corporate entities within the same family of corporations without incurring liability for interference.

At this stage of the litigation, the Court is unconvinced. While recognizing the cited authority, the Court believes that it would be premature to dismiss Sorrell and WPP from this lawsuit at this time. This case presents the circumstance of H & K being ordered by its corporate parent to drop a client. This was done against H & K's will and cost H & K a multi-million dollar client. What is significant here is the allegation that the corporate parent was encouraged to issue this order at the insistence of an outside actor — Lilly.

In other words, the evidence is that the decision to influence H & K to terminate the CSI relationship was not generated internally within the WPP family. There is evidence that Sorrell, WPP and JWT conspired with Lilly, an outside actor, to plot the termination of an arrangement that was otherwise mutually satisfactory to H & K and CSI. This distinction, the Court believes, differentiates this case from those cited by defense counsel.

What is more, in the instant case the two corporations in conflict [H & K and JWT], while related and wholly owned by WPP, are very substantial corporations with dominant positions in their respective industries. From the record, it appears they act independently of one another and serve clients with conflicting interests. In view of their fierce independent nature and the fact they are organized and operated as separate corporate entities, to treat them as one would undermine the concept of the corporate structure acting as a "fire wall." It is rare, indeed, in this Court's experience for a corporate complex to want to pierce its own corporate veil. As separate corporate entities, they must be held fully and strictly accountable for their own actions.[145]

---

[145] *Id.* at 1030–31.

(2)   Other Financial Interests

Section 769 of the *Restatement (Second) of Torts* protects one particular kind of financial interest: investments. However, there are other kinds of financial interests which might be deemed worthy of protection. For example, *RAN Corp. v. Hudesman*[146] embraced a financial interest privilege broader than the terms of the *Restatement* provision.

Direct Financial Interest. RAN Corporation had contracted with a lessee for the assignment of a lease, conditional on the approval of the lessor. David Hudesman, the lessor, refused to consent to the assignment because Hudesman had identified another tenant who, because of political connections, offered the possibility of greater economic benefits, even though that tenant would have paid the same amount of rent. RAN sued Hudesman and his agent for interference. In concluding that Hudesman was privileged to interfere with the assignment contract because he acted to protect his direct financial interest, the Supreme Court of Alaska wrote:

> [In *Bendix Corp. v. Adams*, 610 P.2d 24, 30 (Alaska 1980), instead] of relying on the *Restatement* factors, we adopted a test of privilege based on a number of cases which hold that where an actor has a direct financial interest, he is privileged to interfere with a contract for economic reasons, but not where he is motivated by spite, malice, or some other improper objective.
>
> . . . .
>
> A number of other cases have recognized that a landlord has a sufficient interest to interfere with a prospective or actual lease assignment. . . . The right to intervene has also been recognized in the analogous setting of transfers of distributorships. . . .
>
> It seems beyond reasonable argument that an owner of property has a financial interest in the assignment of a lease of the property he owns. An effective lease assignment makes the assignee the tenant of the owner; the assignee becomes the lessee and has a direct contractual relationship with the owner. . . . The tenant also has an obligation to pay rent directly to the owner, and the use, or abuse, of the property by the assignee may affect its value to the owner. Further, the owner may know of another potential assignee who will pay more rent than the prospective assignee. Moreover, the owner may wish to terminate the lease based on knowledge of a more profitable use for the property. If so, the owner is obviously financially interested in a proposed assignment as the assignor may consent to the termination of the lease while the proposed assignee might not.
>
> . . . Since Hudesman had a direct financial interest in the proposed assignment of the lease, "the essential question in determining if interference is justified is whether [Hudesman's] conduct is motivated by a desire to protect his economic interest, or whether it is motivated by spite, malice,

---

[146] 823 P.2d 646 (Alaska 1991).

or some other improper objective." . . . As there is no evidence of spite, malice or other improper objective — Hudesman did not even know RAN Corporation's principals — and since it is clear that Hudesman refused to approve the assignment because he believed that he would receive a greater economic benefit from a tenancy by Reinwand, the interference was justified and summary judgment was properly entered.

. . . . Hudesman's disapproval may have been a breach of the Hudesman/ Harris lease, but it was privileged from a tort standpoint because of Hudesman's pre-existing interest as a property owner/lessor. . . .[147]

PROBLEM 5-6: THE MARKET TIMING INVESTORS

South Haven Life Insurance Company, the sponsor of a mutual fund, found that investors were employing financial experts to exercise their rights to move money within the fund, from capital subaccounts to money market subaccounts and vice versa. These movements, called "market timing," were based on short-term market conditions.

The negative impact on the mutual fund caused by market timing activity included increased costs related to trading and transactions, disruption of investment strategies, unplanned portfolio turnover, and lost investment opportunities. In addition, large swings in the mutual fund's asset base adversely affected all of the mutual fund's investors by impairing South Haven's ability to earn maximum profits.

South Haven's market timing problems became serious when certain investment advisors made a business of both advising clients to invest in the mutual fund and obtaining authorization from those clients to move their investments among the mutual fund's subaccounts. David Sesak, one such investment advisor, represented scores of investors and could move tens of millions of dollars among the mutual fund's subaccounts.

To combat market timing, South Haven amended its agreement with investors to permit South Haven to decline trading instructions by an investor's designated agent, if the agent had made more than $2 million in transfers on a given day for clients.

At the time it enacted the restrictions, South Haven was well aware of Sesak and his business. Sesak had placed orders for more than 15,000 movements of investors' money between the mutual fund's subaccounts during the prior three years.

As a result of the restrictions, Sesak's ability to maximize investment results for his clients has been impaired. He has lost the business of some investors and found it harder to act effectively on behalf of others. Further, he is rarely able to induce new investors to invest in the South Haven mutual fund and authorize him to trade on their behalf.

---

[147] *Id.* at 648–50.

Sesak has consulted you about whether he can sue South Haven for tortious interference with economic relations. Please advise.

c.   Privileges of Agents, Fiduciaries, and Others

(1)   Actors Responsible for the Welfare of Another

Section 770 of the *Restatement (Second) of Torts* states the general privilege applicable to persons responsible for the welfare of another. It provides:

> One who, charged with responsibility for the welfare of a third person, intentionally causes that person not to perform a contract or enter into a prospective contractual relation with another, does not interfere improperly with the other's relation if the actor
>
> (a) does not employ wrongful means and
>
> (b) acts to protect the welfare of the third person.[148]

Examples. As illustrations of the types of relationships that entail responsibility for the welfare of another, the *Restatement* mentions: parent and child; minister and congregant; lawyer and client; teacher and student; and employer and employee. In probing the reach of the rule, it might be useful to consider the situations where tort law says that one person has a duty to protect others from physical harm — although the fit might not be exact.[149] According to the *Restatement*, the key question is whether, under standards of decent conduct, the actor is charged with some responsibility for protection of the welfare of the other.[150]

Volunteers Versus Intermeddlers. If one person has a duty to safeguard the welfare of another, the *Restatement* privilege applies regardless of whether the advice is requested or volunteered.[151] In contrast, persons who officiously assume responsibility for the welfare of others are not protected by the privilege.[152]

Wrongful Means. The use of persuasion is not the use of wrongful means. According to the *Restatement*, "[i]n determining whether the means are wrongful, the extent of the danger threatened to the welfare of the person induced, the relation between him and the actor and the consequent extent of the actor's interest are important factors."[153]

Corporate Fiduciaries. "[C]orporate fiduciaries are protected by a qualified privilege to interfere with corporate business relationships so long as they are acting in good faith to protect the interests of the corporation."[154]

---

[148] Restatement (Second) of Torts § 770 (1979).

[149] *See* Restatement (Third) of Torts: Liability for Physical & Emotional Harm § 40 (2012).

[150] *See* Restatement (Second) of Torts § 770 cmt. b (1979).

[151] *See id.* § 770 cmt. c.

[152] *See id.* § 770 cmt. b.

[153] *See id.* § 770 cmt. d.

[154] *Hsu v. Vet-a-Mix, Inc.*, 479 N.W.2d 336, 339 (Iowa Ct. App. 1991).

Predominant Motivation Versus Some Motivation. In determining whether the conduct of an agent is privileged, some jurisdictions apply a predominant motivation test. For example, in *Geolar, Inc. v. Gilbert/Commonwealth, Inc.*,[155] the Supreme Court of Alaska held that summary judgment was improperly granted in favor of an agent. While there was evidence that the agent had acted to protect the financial interests of its principal, there was competing evidence that the agent was motivated by a desire to mask its own mistakes. The question of predominant motivation, the court held, was one for the jury. Query: why should the question be predominant motivation? Conduct is within the scope of employment so long as it serves some purpose of the employment. Thus, § 228(1) of the *Restatement (Second) of Agency* says that "[c]onduct of a servant is within the scope of employment if . . . (c) it is actuated, at least in part, by a purpose to serve the master. . . ."[156] Similarly, the *Restatement (Third) of Agency* now provides:

> An employee's act is not within the scope of employment when it occurs within an independent course of conduct not intended by the employee to serve any purpose of the employer.[157]

An argument could be made that, so long as an agent does not employ wrongful means, conduct should be privileged if it occurs within the scope of employment, regardless of the predominant motivation of the agent. Nevertheless, in some states, an agent does not enjoy a privilege unless the agent's predominant motivation is to protect the interests of the agent's principal.

Relationship to the Business Judgment Rule. In discussing the privilege laid down by § 770 of the *Restatement (Second) of Torts*, a federal court in Delaware wrote as follows:

> The rule in § 770 is consistent with Delaware's venerable business judgment rule which creates a presumption that officers and directors are immune from personal liability when making business decisions in their fiduciary capacity. . . . Second, the rule in § 770 is consonant with the economic efficiency view of contract law that a party to a contract has the option of either honoring the contract or breaching it and paying money damages. Breaches of contract can be economically efficient and are part of the function of the marketplace. . . . In order to secure the practical application of the economic efficiency theory of contract law in the market, officers and directors of a corporation must be free to breach contracts without exposing themselves to personal liability, when, in their business judgment, such contracts are not economically beneficial to the corporation.[158]

---

[155] 874 P.2d 937 (Alaska 1994).

[156] RESTATEMENT (SECOND) OF AGENCY § 228(1) (1958).

[157] RESTATEMENT (THIRD) OF AGENCY § 7.07(2) (2006).

[158] *Int'l Ass'n of Heat and Frost Insulators v. Absolute Envtl. Services, Inc.*, 814 F. Supp. 392, 400–01 (D. Del. 1993).

(2)   Confidential Relationships

Some authorities state a privilege in language broader than the terms of § 770 of the *Restatement (Second) of Torts*. For example, in *John Masek Corp. v. Davis*,[159] the court wrote:

> A person who is in a confidential relationship with a party to a contract is privileged to induce the breach of such a contract. *Russell v. Edgewood*, 406 S.W.2d 249, 252 (Tex. App. — San Antonio 1966, *no writ*) (superintendent of school was not liable for inducing trustees to breach their contract with plaintiff); *see also McDonald v. Trammell*, 163 Tex. 352, 356 S.W.2d 143, 145 (1962) (a wife could not be held liable for attempting to persuade her husband not to carry out an unenforceable contract); *Tinkle v. McGraw*, 644 F. Supp. 138, 140 (E.D. Tex. 1986) (defendant was not liable for causing his aunt and former client to breach contract for sale of property). Communications between family members are confidential and cannot form the basis for a tortious interference claim by third parties. Zarif was Davis' son-in-law, and thus a family member [and therefore could not be liable for tortious interference].[160]

(3)   Protecting Agents from Liability

Three Approaches to Protecting Agents. There are at least three different ways to immunize the conduct of agents from liability for tortious interference.

(1) Agents as Privileged Actors. The first approach suggested by § 770 of the *Restatement*, quoted above, holds that, under appropriate circumstances, interference caused by an agent is privileged. This is, by far, the most intellectually satisfying mode of addressing the liability of agents.

In *Weikhorst Bros. Excavating & Equip. Co. v. Ludewig*,[161] the Supreme Court of Nebraska held that design professionals acting within the scope of their contractual obligations are privileged to give an owner advice which may lead to the termination of a contractor, absent a showing of bad faith or malice.

(2) Agents as Parties to Their Principals's Contracts. The second approach holds that an agent is a party to its principal's contracts. Because the agent is not an outsider to the relationship, there can be no liability for tortious interference, for a party cannot interfere with its own contractual relations.

The view that an agent is a party, rather than a third party, to its principal's contracts is in many respects peculiar. Ordinarily, an agent cannot sue to compel performance of the agreement, nor is the agent personally liable for non-performance. That being so, it is odd to call the agent a "party." Yet the view that agents are parties to their principal's contracts, and therefore not liable for tortious interference, finds support in the law of many states. In *Creel v. Davis*,[162] the

---

[159] 848 S.W.2d 170 (Tex. Ct. App. 1992).

[160] *Id.* at 175.

[161] 247 Neb. 547, 529 N.W.2d 33 (1995).

[162] 544 So. 2d 145 (Ala. 1989).

Supreme Court of Alabama recognized that rule, as laid down by precedent, but held that even though two hospitals were owned by the same parent corporation, an employee of the first hospital was not a party to the employment contract between the plaintiff and the second hospital, and therefore could be liable for tortious interference.

(3) Agents as Nonactors. The third approach holds that, if an agent acts pursuant to duties imposed by the principal, the actions are those of the principal and not of the agent. Therefore, the agent may not be held liable for tortious interference.

This approach to protecting agents from liability was employed by the Minnesota Supreme Court in *Nordling v. Northern States Power Co.*[163] The plaintiff, an in-house attorney who opposed a supervisor's plan for investigating the lifestyles of company employees, was summarily discharged by the supervisor, in alleged contravention of company procedures. In addressing the tortious interference claim against the supervisor, the court wrote:

> The general rule is that a party cannot interfere with its own contract. . . . If a corporation's officer or agent acting pursuant to his company duties terminates or causes to be terminated an employee, the actions are those of the corporation; the employee's dispute is with the company employer for breach of contract, not the agent individually for a tort. To allow the officer or agent to be sued and to be personally liable would chill corporate personnel from performing their duties and would be contrary to the limited liability accorded incorporation. Nevertheless, . . . a corporate officer or agent may be liable for tortious contract interference if he or she acts outside the scope of his or her duties. . . .
>
> . . . While motive or malice is only one factor to consider in determining whether a defendant officer or agent is acting outside the scope of his duties in dealing with the plaintiff employee, it can be the critical factor. . . . For example, in this case Nordling claims McGannon was meddling with his personal phone calls, while McGannon claims he was attempting to determine if Nordling's alleged unexplained absences from work were for personal business on company time.
>
> . . . [W]e conclude that a company officer, agent or employee is privileged to interfere with or cause a breach of another employee's employment contract with the company, if that person acts in good faith, whether competently or not, believing that his actions are in furtherance of the company's business. This privilege may be lost, however, if the defendant's actions are predominantly motivated by malice and bad faith, that is, by personal ill-will, spite, hostility, or a deliberate intent to harm the plaintiff employee.[164]

---

[163] 478 N.W.2d 498 (Minn. 1991).

[164] *Id.* at 505–07.

Sometimes Agents May Be Personally Liable. In *Khan v. GBAK Properties, Inc.*,[165] a case involving interference with contracts in the form of a note, a deed of trust, and an assignment of rents, the Texas Court of Appeals held that the president of a limited liability company could be individually liable for tortious interference arising from the president's assignment of rents to a third party, even though the assignment was signed by the president in his capacity as president. As the court explained:

> It is a longstanding rule in Texas that "a corporate agent is personally liable for his own fraudulent or tortious acts." . . . If a corporate agent directs or participates in a tort during his employment, he faces personal liability for the tortious act. . . . Accordingly, regardless of whether Ray Lofti performed these acts in his capacity as president, he can still face liability for those acts if they prove to be tortious. . . .
>
> Ray Lofti cites two Texas Supreme Court cases, suggesting that they stand for the opposite proposition: that he can face liability only if he had an independent duty and acted solely in his own interests. In the first case, the Texas Supreme Court considered whether a corporate agent could be held liable for negligence. . . . The court held "individual liability [for negligence claims] arises only when the officer or agent owes an independent duty of reasonable care to the injured party apart from the employer's duty." . . .
>
> In the second case, the issue concerned whether a claim of tortious interference with existing contract could be brought against a corporate officer when the company was one of the contracting parties. *Powell Indus., Inc. v. Allen*, 985 S.W.2d 455, 456 (Tex. 1998). In *Powell Industries*, Allen sued Powell — president and CEO of Powell Industries — individually for tortious interference with Allen's contract with Powell Industries. . . . The court recognized a particular difficulty when "the defendant is both a corporate agent and the third party who allegedly induces the corporation's breach." . . . Acknowledging the unique situation, the court held, "The plaintiff must prove that the agent acted willfully and intentionally to serve the agent's personal interests at the corporation's expense." . . .
>
> While both of these cases are exceptions to the general rule that a corporate agent faces personal liability for tortious acts he directed or participated in, neither of these cases is applicable to the facts of this case. Khan did not sue Ray Lofti for negligence. Nor was Parkway Crossing, the company on whose behalf Ray Lofti purported to act, a party to the contracts with which Khan asserts have been interfered. The contracts were, instead, between Khan and GBAK. We hold that Ray Lofti faces individual liability for the torts he directed or participated in regardless of whether they were performed in his capacity as president of Parkway Crossing.[166]

---

[165] 371 S.W.3d 347 (Tex. App. 2012).

[166] *Id.* at 359.

PROBLEM 5-7: THE TENURE APPLICANT

Amy Stubblefield was denied tenure at Mother Elizabeth Seton College. Thereafter, she was hired under a three-year contract at Francis State University to teach in its agricultural program. Pursuant to the terms of her contract, she was entitled to apply for tenure prior to the expiration of her three-year contract. As defined by the Francis State University faculty handbook, "tenure" means "the entitlement of faculty members to continue in their academic positions unless dismissed for good cause." The faculty handbook further states that "there is no 'good cause' requirement when denying an application for tenure." The tenure standards set forth in the handbook indicate that decisions on tenure are to be based on a faculty member's performance in three areas: teaching and advising; research and publication; and university and community service.

In the spring of her third year on the Francis State faculty, Stubblefield applied for tenure by submitting a written application, accompanied by supporting documentation (copies of publications, teaching evaluations by students, etc.). The application was then reviewed at several levels, which entailed submission of nonbinding secret-ballot votes, which would be forwarded to the president of the university, who had the sole power to grant or deny tenure. The votes were submitted by the tenured members of the agricultural school faculty, the deans of the five schools of the university, and the four vice presidents of the university.

Six of the ten members of the agricultural school faculty voted in favor of granting Stubblefield tenure. Those who recommended denial of tenure all emphasized Stubblefield's indisputably poor publication record. Kevin Stensley, one of the faculty members who voted against Stubblefield in that part of the consultation process, had previously had a heated argument with Stubblefield in the faculty lounge, and no one was surprised that Stensley recommended denial of tenure.

The deans of all five schools of the university also voted in favor of tenuring Stubblefield. However, at the next level, two of the four university vice presidents voted against granting Stubblefield tenure.

Bhrath Reddy, the vice president for student services, had previously clashed with Stubblefield at an alumni event. On that occasion, Stubblefield denounced the university's plans to sell a ranch used by its agricultural program. Reddy believed that Stubblefield's comments at that social gathering were inappropriate and also wrong as a matter of policy. Shortly after the event, Reddy had told the university president, Lin Cao, that he believed Stubblefield had made a bad impression on important supporters of the university. After Reddy reviewed Stubblefield's application, Reddy submitted a written ballot recommending that tenure be denied. As the reason for the recommendation, Reddy wrote simply, "[t]he applicant fails to meet the university's high standards for teaching, scholarship, and service."

Through her dealings with Stubblefield, the vice president for finance, Jill Campion, had concluded that Stubblefield was "too liberal" and was "out of place" at Francis State University. When the time came to review Stubblefield's tenure application, Campion did not have time to read it. Campion nevertheless submitted her ballot recommending denial of tenure, stating as her reasons simply, "too liberal" and "not a good fit."

After review of Stubblefield's tenure application and the ballots submitted at the various levels of the consultation process, President Cao sent a letter to Stubblefield denying tenure and notifying her that her employment at Francis State University would terminate at the end of the current academic year.

On these facts, can Stubblefield state a viable cause of action against anyone for tortious interference?

d.   Privilege to Speak the Truth

(1)   The *Restatement* Formulation

As the previous chapters of this book make clear, truthful communications receive broad protection under the First Amendment's guarantees of freedom of speech and freedom of the press. Thus, under the law of libel and slander, a true defamatory statement may not give rise to liability (*see* Chapter 3), and doubts have been raised about the viability of actions for invasion of privacy based on public disclosure of private facts (*see* Chapter 4). Nevertheless, the protection afforded by the Constitution to dissemination of accurate information is not absolute. The release of confidential data, for example, will support an action for breach of fiduciary duty, notwithstanding that the contents of the communication are true.

Many tortious interference suits involve the transmission of information which leads to the disruption of economic relations. Is an action barred if the material communicated is true? Must the plaintiff show that, in some respect, the communication was false or misleading, or at least that the defendant went beyond pure speech and engaged in impermissible conduct?

The *Restatement* states a seemingly clear rule on this subject, but the final word on the matter has not been written.

Section 772(a) of the *Restatement (Second) of Torts* provides in relevant part:

> One who intentionally causes a third person not to perform a contract or not to enter into a prospective contractual relation with another does not interfere improperly with the other's contractual relation, by giving the third person (a) truthful information. . . .[167]

Either Type of Action Is Barred. The *Restatement* privilege relating to the provision of truthful information will bar an action for either interference with a contract or for interference with prospective advantage.[168]

Whether or Not Information Is Requested. The *Restatement* privilege applies regardless of whether the true information is requested or volunteered.[169]

---

[167] Restatement (Second) of Torts § 772(a) (1979).

[168] *See id.* § 772 cmt. b.

[169] *See id.*

Truthfulness Is a Question. Any effort to invoke the "truthful information" privilege is certain to generate a dispute over whether the defendant in fact was truthful. For example, in *Ventas, Inc. v. HCP, Inc.*,[170] the Sixth Circuit upheld a $101 million compensatory damages judgment for tortious interference with prospective advantage, and remanded the case for a trial on the single issue of punitive damages. The court wrote:

> HCP contends that Ventas was "required to prove that significantly wrongful conduct — alleged misrepresentations, not truthful disclosures — caused its injury," and that Ventas failed to carry this burden. . . . This is significant, HCP argues, because its February 14, 2007 press release contained the truthful statement that HCP was willing to pay $18.00 per unit for Sunrise. . . .

> We find HCP's argument unavailing. HCP's argument rests on the faulty factual premise that HCP was "willing to pay $18 per unit of Sunrise," and that this stated willingness was independently truthful. . . . Indeed, the jury could reasonably have found that HCP made no such statement, and that even if it did, the statement was not independently truthful.

> . . . HCP never made an unencumbered assertion that it was willing to pay $18.00 per unit, and the jury could reasonably have found that HCP's announcement of its proposed "transaction" was contaminated by fraud, misrepresentations, and concealment. . . .

> HCP failed to disclose . . . that its offer was conditioned on reaching an agreement with SSL. HCP also failed to disclose that HCP and SSL had previously failed to reach an agreement during the auction process; that HCP and SSL otherwise had a tense relationship that could frustrate future attempts to negotiate an agreement; and that HCP was a party to a Standstill Agreement with Sunrise that may have prohibited HCP from making an offer for Sunrise in the first place. Rather than disclosing these details, HCP misled the market by announcing that the terms of its proposed acquisition of Sunrise were "identical to the transaction entered into by Ventas," and the proposed acquisition itself had "greater certainty of completion."

> Moreover, HCP's conduct at the time of its purported offer casts further doubt on the genuineness of its offer. HCP never sent Sunrise a signed, unconditional offer. . . . When confronted about the missing signature, HCP CEO Flaherty falsely stated to Sunrise's banker that he had sent a signed agreement via Federal Express. Flaherty subsequently admitted, however, that he did not do this and in fact was not authorized by HCP to make an unconditional bid. . . .[171]

---

[170] 647 F.3d 291 (6th Cir. 2011).

[171] *Id.* at 314–16.

(2)   Cases Supporting a Broad Interpretation

Complaints About Employees. In *Allen v. Safeway Stores Inc.*,[172] the Supreme Court of Wyoming found that the defendants were not liable for the discharges of grocery store employees which resulted when a state employee informed a store's supervisors about the "bad attitudes" that the employees had manifested when asked questions relating to a state welfare program.[173] As the court explained, "[c]ommon sense requires recognition of the propriety of one who is a customer or a business contact of a public-related enterprise to truthfully notify the owners or those in the management echelon of treatment accorded to such customer or business contact by those employed by the enterprise."[174]

Comments by Former Employers. In *Delloma v. Consolidation Coal Co.*,[175] the plaintiff's potential employer (of which Samples was president) asked the president (Brown) of the plaintiff's former employer (Consolidated) why the plaintiff (Delloma) had been discharged. Brown responded that "[t]here were some record-keeping irregularities that may have been involved." Allegedly as a result of the comment, Delloma did not get the job. In fact:

> While acting as the Superintendent, Delloma engaged approximately one-third of the female employees he supervised at the mine in dating or other social relationships. One of those women, Sharon Snider, filed a lawsuit against Delloma and Consolidation Coal, alleging sexual harassment under Title VII and several tort claims including assault, battery, and intentional infliction of emotional distress. . . . [S]nider claimed that Delloma conditioned approval of her absences as excused on her agreement to have sex with him. The jury found for the defendants on the common law claims, but the district court ruled in Snider's favor on the Title VII claim against Consolidation Coal.[176]

In rejecting Delloma's tortious interference with prospective advantage claim against Brown and Consolidated, the Seventh Circuit wrote:

> Frequently, the cases depend on statements alleged to be false or defamatory. . . . Moreover, permitting recovery for tortious interference based on truthful statements would seem to raise significant First Amendment problems. *See generally* Johnson, "Solicitation of Law Firm Clients by Departing Partners and Associates: Tort, Fiduciary, and Disciplinary Liability," 50 *U. Pitt. L. Rev.* 1, 96–97 (1988) (including a comparison of *Restatement (Second) of Torts* § 772(a) [truthful information can be given with no liability] with *Prosser and Keeton on Torts* 979 [tortious interference does not necessarily involve falsehood]). . . .

---

[172] 699 P.2d 277 (Wyo. 1985).

[173] *Id.* at 278.

[174] *Id.* at 280.

[175] 996 F.2d 168 (7th Cir. 1993).

[176] *Id.* at 169–70.

In the sexual harassment lawsuit by Snider, . . . [a]mong the findings of fact were Delloma's alterations of work records based on Snider's capitulation to his sexual harassment. . . .

. . . Brown's statement to Samples is, therefore, not false. . . . It is a fair statement that Delloma's termination involved some record-keeping irregularities. . . .

Because Brown gave a truthful response to Samples' direct inquiry, he did not unjustifiably interfere with Delloma's expectancy.[177]

Statements Exposing Health Hazards. In *Tara Woods Ltd. Partnership v. Fannie Mae*,[178] a federal court in Colorado held that a tortious interference claim could not be premised on accurate reporting of an asbestos condition that posed a health hazard. However, the court based its analysis not on the fact the report was true, but that disclosure was consistent with the public interest. As the court explained:

> [R]egardless of whoever called the City of Denver to complain about the asbestos issue, the City found that the asbestos contamination required immediate abatement. As Harris explains, the factors bearing on the question of whether interference with a prospective business advantage is "improper" include examination of "the social interests" implicated by the challenged action. Here, even assuming that the Defendant reported the asbestos condition out of ill motive towards the Plaintiff, the Court finds that the public interest in prompt disclosure of a dangerous building condition outweighs any private interest that the Plaintiff might have in requiring the Defendant to keep its knowledge of that information concealed.[179]

False Statement Requirement. In cases where interference results from provision of information, some courts insist on a false statement. For example, in *Liebe v. City Finance Co.*,[180] the Wisconsin Court of Appeals broadly endorsed the § 772 privilege relating to dissemination of truthful information. In that case, an employee (Liebe) of a finance company mailed approximately 1,000 flyers advertising a book that he had written entitled "I'm Fed Up with the Cost of Finance Company Loans." The flyer offered information on how to save substantially on loans if the recipient mailed $10 to R & K Publishing, using a post office box in Wisconsin. One of the flyers reached the Memphis office of Liebe's employer, City Finance. Through a circuitous series of contacts, which included the president of the Milwaukee Better Business Bureau (who obtained Liebe's name as the owner of the postal box from a postal inspector), Liebe's employer was informed that he had circulated the flyer. Liebe was discharged and thereafter sued. A jury concluded that City Finance and the Better Business Bureau had improperly interfered with Liebe's employment and awarded $100,000 in compensatory damages and $7,000 in

---

[177] *Id.* at 172–73.

[178] 731 F. Supp. 2d 1103 (D. Colo. 2010).

[179] *Id.* at 1121.

[180] 98 Wis. 2d 10, 295 N.W.2d 16 (Ct. App. 1980).

punitive damages. However, the trial court subsequently directed a verdict for the defendants. Noting that Liebe had "testified that he could not think of any divulgence by anyone in connection with the entire affair that was not true,"[181] the appellate court affirmed the judgment, relying on § 772.

The Truth Privilege and Frivolous Litigation Penalties. In *Worldwide Primates, Inc. v. McGreal,*[182] an animal rights activist sent two letters to a primate center for the purpose of persuading it to stop providing animals to the plaintiff, a primate importer. One letter indicated that the importer had "received very damaging criticisms from the Department of Agriculture inspectors and . . . [had] tried to undermine inspectors' authority by going over their heads."[183] The other letter said that the Centers for Disease Control had suspended the plaintiff's license to import primates. The letters enclosed documents which substantiated their assertions. The importer thereafter sued the activist who had sent the letters for tortious interference, but later dismissed the action when a criminal prosecution against its president made it impossible for it to participate in civil discovery without potentially affecting the criminal matter.

The defendant activist sought monetary sanctions against the importer under Rule 11 of the Federal Rules of Civil Procedure, which prohibits litigation that is legally or factually baseless. The Eleventh Circuit agreed that sanctions should be imposed because the plaintiff could not have believed that its claim was well grounded in fact and law.

First, there was no evidence of damage, for the primate center had never ceased to do business with the plaintiff nor otherwise altered its business relationship with the plaintiff. The president of the center testified at a deposition that the letters did not change his perception of the plaintiff as a legitimate importer; he said that he had told the plaintiff so both orally and in writing. Florida law, the court found, required proof of damages as an essential element of a tortious interference claim. "Unsuccessful interference is simply not the kind of interference upon which a tort may be founded."[184]

Second, there was no basis for the action because the information that was communicated was true. The court found that "[t]he letters did nothing more than accurately describe the accompanying governmental reports."[185] This was a slight overstatement because the first letter stated that the activist had just learned that a sale might take place, asked rhetorical questions about how the animals would be captured and other details of the transaction, and expressed the opinion that "endangered primates would be far better off living in the wild than in . . . [the center's] institution."[186] Describing the privilege to communicate truthful information that is embodied in § 772 of the *Restatement (Second) of Torts* as a "common sense rule," the court remanded the case for determination of the amount of the

---

[181] *Id.* at 20–21.

[182] 26 F.3d 1089 (11th Cir. 1994).

[183] *Id.* at 1090.

[184] *Id.* at 1092.

[185] *Id.*

[186] *Id.* at 1090.

sanctions. On a subsequent appeal, the Eleventh Circuit affirmed an assessment of $25,000 each in sanctions against the plaintiff and the plaintiff's attorney. The court found that the attorney had failed to conduct even a minimal investigation into the facts underlying the plaintiff's claim.[187]

(3) Cases Supporting a Narrow Interpretation

States which hold that impropriety of interference can be established by either "improper purpose" or "improper means" generally reject the idea that truthful statements are never actionable. For example, in *Pratt v. Prodata, Inc.*,[188] a case discussed above in the text, the jury found that a former employer did not make false statements to the Utah Department of Transportation (UDOT) in causing UDOT to discharge a computer programmer from employment. Nevertheless, the Utah Supreme Court affirmed a tortious interference judgment in favor of the plaintiff, writing:

> Defendants' reliance on section 772(a) is misplaced. As our decision in . . . [*Leigh Furniture and Carpet Co. v. Isom*, 657 P.2d 293 (Utah 1982)] makes clear, this court has rejected the various *Restatement* formulations of the tort of intentional interference with economic relations. . . . Under *Leigh*, "the alternative of improper purpose (or motive, intent, or objective) will support a cause of action for intentional interference with prospective economic relations even where the defendant's means were proper." . . . Because . . . liability may attach under Leigh even where a defendant's means were proper, we reject defendants' call to adopt truthfulness as an absolute defense to the tort of intentional interference with prospective economic relations.[189]

e. Privilege to Respond to a Request

(1) Honest Advice

The *Restatement (Second) of Torts* recognizes an honest advice privilege. Section 772(b) provides:

> One who intentionally causes a third person not to perform a contract or not to enter into a prospective contractual relation with another does not interfere improperly with the other's contractual relation, by giving the third person
>
> . . .
>
> (b) honest advice within the scope of a request for the advice.[190]

Professionals and Nonprofessionals. The honest advice privilege applies to professionals (*e.g.*, lawyers, doctors, ministers, investment advisors, and marriage

[187] *See Worldwide Primates, Inc. v. McGreal*, 87 F.3d 1252 (11th Cir. 1996).

[188] 885 P.2d 786 (Utah 1994).

[189] *Id.* at 790.

[190] Restatement (Second) of Torts § 772 (1979).

counselors), as well as to amateurs. "The only requirements for its existence are (1) that advice be requested, (2) that the advice given be within the scope of the request, and (3) that the advice be honest."[191]

Good Faith Is Required. "Whether the advice was based on reasonable grounds and whether the actor exercised reasonable diligence in ascertaining the facts are questions important only in determining his good or bad faith. But no more than good faith is required."[192]

Profit Is Irrelevant. It makes no difference that the person rendering the advice profits from giving it. Indeed, this is usually the case with professional advisors, who often are compensated for advising others.

Animus Toward the Affected Person. Under the terms of the *Restatement's* formulation of the honest advice rule, the privilege is not lost merely because the advisor dislikes the third person who will be adversely affected if the advice is followed. Of course, states are free to adopt their own standards. It would not be surprising if a state holding that lack of justification can be shown by *either* improper purpose *or* improper means, would also take the position that honest advice motivated by ill will, spite or vindictiveness may be actionable.

The Advice Must Be Within the Scope of the Request. According to the *Restatement*, a person asked for advice about health and medical matters is not free to opine about unrelated financial matters.[193] Of course, the breadth of a request for advice is typically a question of fact. Some requests are specific and narrow, others are general and potentially wide ranging. In the latter case, the honest advice privilege may prevent liability for tortious interference in a broader range of situations.

The Privilege Does Not Depend Upon Relationship. The honest advice privilege is, at least in some respects, much broader than the privilege (discussed above) conferring qualified immunity on persons who are responsible for the welfare of others.[194] Protection under the honest advice privilege does not depend upon whether the person rendering the advise has a legal or moral duty to protect the person who receives the advice. If one asks a perfect stranger for advice, the honest advice privilege applies, so long as the advice is honest and within the scope of the request.[195]

Mixed Motives and the Honesty of Advice. Does the fact that an actor provides advice with mixed motives destroy reliance on the honest advice privilege? On the one hand, it is unrealistic to expect an advisor to be completely disinterested. As has been stated in the principal-agent context:

> [A]dvice by an agent to a principal is rarely, if ever, motivated purely by a desire to benefit only the principal. An agent naturally hopes that by

---

[191] *Id.* § 772 cmt. c.

[192] *Id.* § 772 cmt. e.

[193] *Id.* § 772 cmt. d.

[194] *Id.* § 770.

[195] *Id.* § 772 cmt. d.

providing beneficial advice to his principal, the agent will benefit indirectly by gaining the further trust and confidence of his principal. If the protection of the privilege were denied every time that an advisor acted with such mixed motive, the privilege would be greatly diminished and the societal interests it was designed to promote would be frustrated.[196]

Nevertheless, cases often raise questions as to whether advice was not honestly given and therefore not privileged. In *Trepanier v. Getting Organized, Inc.*,[197] an efficiency firm advised an auto dealer with flagging sales to shed its "retirement home image" by replacing its current employees with "young go-getters." The employees who were discharged sued for tortious interference. On appeal from summary judgment in favor of the defendants, the court endorsed the honest advice privilege as laid down by § 772(b), but remanded the case, stating:

> Plaintiffs have alleged that defendants lied about plaintiffs' job perfor-mance. Further, they have alleged that defendants' action in recommending termination of plaintiffs was motivated by defendants' desire to earn fees for the selection of replacement employees. Given the fact that plaintiffs have raised questions regarding defendants' actions and motives in advising Nordic to fire plaintiffs, and that defendants have the burden of showing justification for their actions, summary judgment is inappropriate here.[198]

(2)   Statements by Former Employers

In some cases, it is difficult to characterize a response to a request for information as advice. Nevertheless, the response may be protected by a qualified privilege.

For example, in *Delloma v. Consolidation Coal Co.*,[199] discussed above in the text, the plaintiff's former employer was asked by a potential employer why the plaintiff had been discharged from employment. The former employer said that record-keeping irregularities may have been involved. When the plaintiff was not hired by the prospective employer, he sued his former employer and its president for tortious interference. In rejecting the claim, the Seventh Circuit wrote:

> An employer owes no apparent legal duty to any other employer. Brown had no legal obligation to respond to Samples. Illinois courts, however, have recognized some interest of former employers in disclosing limited infor-mation to prospective employers. . . . In a libel case, the Illinois Supreme Court has found conditional privilege to apply to statements by a former employer to a potential mortgagor, because the subject matter "affected an important interest of the recipient" and the statements were "within generally accepted standards of decent conduct" and were "made in response to a request." . . .

---

[196] *Los Angeles Airways, Inc. v. Davis*, 687 F.2d 321, 328 (9th Cir. 1982).

[197] 155 Vt. 259, 583 A.2d 583 (1990).

[198] *Id.* at 589–90.

[199] 996 F.2d 168 (7th Cir. 1993).

The Illinois courts have not interpreted the existence of a duty or interest narrowly. *See Miller v. Danville Elks Lodge 332, B.P.O.E.*, [569 N.E.2d 1160, 1165 (Ill. Ct. App. 1991)] ("The interest . . . must not necessarily be a legal one, as it may be sufficient if the speaker has a good faith belief he or she has a moral or social duty to uphold."). . . . In addition, courts generally recognize more extensive privileges where the claim is merely for a loss of prospective advantage rather than an existing contract. . . . Generally, a former employer who gives a negative reference to a prospective employer holds some qualified privilege against defamation suits. *Restatement (Second) of Torts* § 595, cmt. *i* (1977). . . . By analogy, an employer should hold some privilege against tortious interference suits for limited statements in response to a direct request. We conclude, therefore, that an employer may invoke a conditional privilege to respond to direct inquiries by prospective employers.

Once a privilege is established, the plaintiff must prove that the defendant acted with malice. The defendant may abuse the privilege, by making unjustified statements, by excessive publication of statements, or by making statements in conflict with the interest which gave rise to the privilege. If the defendant knew the statements were false, he would be unjustified in making them. In a defamation context the plaintiff must prove that "the statement in question was made with knowledge of its falsity or in reckless disregard of whether it was false or not." . . . The Illinois Supreme Court described the defamation and tortious interference claims as "analytically intertwined." . . .[200]

f.   Privilege to Assert a Legal Claim or Exercise a Right

Questions frequently arise over whether conduct related to the "rights" of the defendant can be the basis for an action for tortious interference. It is useful to focus clearly on three separate aspects of the problem: (1) good faith assertion of a *bona fide* claim; (2) exercise of an existing legal right; and (3) wrongful use of legal procedures.

(1)   Good Faith Assertion of a Bona Fide Claim

The good faith assertion of a legal right is privileged, but the bad faith misuse of the legal procedures is not. This rule is simple, but its application can be elusive. Differentiating the permissible from the impermissible may turn on a disputed question of fact.

For example, in *Farmers Co-op. Elevator Co. v. Jelinek*,[201] Jelinek argued that Farmers Co-op, by pursuing a claim for enforcement of an alleged contract between Jelinek and Farmers Co-op for the sale of millet, prevented Jelinek from acquiring or continuing prospective relations with other entities for the sale of the

---

[200] *Id.* at 171–72.

[201] 2006 Neb. App. LEXIS 8 (Jan. 31, 2006).

millet. In addressing this dispute, the Nebraska Court of Appeals wrote:

> Jelinek directs our attention to . . . [*Restatement (Second) of Torts* § 767, comment c], which, in commenting on the "nature of the actor's conduct" factor for determining whether interference with a business relationship is improper, provides as follows:
>
>> *Prosecution of civil suits.* In a very early instance of liability for intentional interference, the means of inducement employed were threats of "mayhem and suits," and both types of threats were deemed tortious. Litigation and the threat of litigation are powerful weapons. When wrongfully instituted, litigation entails harmful consequences to the public interest in judicial administration as well as to the actor's adversaries. The use of these weapons of inducement is ordinarily wrongful if the actor has no belief in the merit of the litigation or if, though having some belief in its merit, he nevertheless institutes or threatens to institute the litigation in bad faith, intending only to harass the third parties and not to bring his claim to definitive adjudication. . . . A typical example of this situation is the case in which the actor threatens the other's prospective customers with suit for the infringement of his patent and either does not believe in the merit of his claim or is determined not to risk an unfavorable judgment and to rely for protection upon the force of his threats and harassment.
>
> Jelinek also directs our attention to the *Restatement (Second) of Torts* § 773 at 52 (1979), which provides:
>
>> One who, by asserting in good faith a legally protected interest of his own or threatening in good faith to protect the interest by appropriate means, intentionally causes a third person not to perform an existing contract or enter into a prospective contractual relation with another does not interfere improperly with the other's relation if the actor believes that his interest may otherwise be impaired or destroyed by the performance of the contract or transaction.
>
> The *Restatement, supra*, comment a. at 52, provides:
>
>> The rule stated in this Section gives to the actor a defense for his legally protected interest. It is of narrow scope and protects the actor only when (1) he has a legally protected interest, and (2) in good faith asserts or threatens to protect it, and (3) the threat is to protect it by appropriate means. Under these circumstances his interference is not improper although he knows that his conduct will cause another to break his contract or otherwise refuse to do business with a third person. If any of these elements is lacking, the rule stated in this Section . . . does not apply but he may have some other justification. . . .[202]

Turning then to the facts of the *Jelinek* case, the court wrote:

---

[202] *Id.* at *20–*22.

In the present case, the record on summary judgment shows a dispute between the parties as to whether their negotiations in July and August 2002 resulted in a valid contract. The record shows that Farmers Co-op believed that it timely accepted Jelinek's offer and that Farmers Co-op filed suit to protect its interest in what it believed to be a binding contract. The record also shows Jelinek's belief that Farmers Co-op did not act in a timely manner to accept his offer and that no binding contract was formed between the parties. The record shows, however, that Jelinek did not sell the disputed millet to a third party due to his concerns over the implications of Farmers Co-op's claim and lawsuit.[203]

At one point in the proceedings, after Farmers Co-op filed a petition seeking to enforce the agreement of sale, it filed a motion to dismiss its petition without prejudice. In reviewing evidence on appeal, the Nebraska Court of Appeals found that "Farmers Co-op's subsequent dismissal of its petition is evidence, if viewed most favorably to Jelinek, that its claim of the existence of a contract may not have been justified." The court ultimately held that there were factual disputes which made summary judgment inappropriate in favor of either party, stating:

> In sum, we conclude that there is a genuine issue of material fact regarding whether a binding contract had been formed and whether Farmers Co-op's actions in asserting the existence of the contract and bringing suit were unjustified acts.[204]

The Noerr-Pennington Doctrine and Judicial Rulings in Favor of the Defendant. In *Eastern Savings Bank, FSB v. Papageorge*,[205] a federal court in the District of Columbia explained:

> [T]he filing of litigation is only "wrongful if the actor has no belief in the merit of the litigation or if, though having some belief in its merit, he nevertheless institutes or threatens to institute the litigation in bad faith." *Restatement (Second) of Torts* § 767 cmt. c. . . .
>
> Under the *Noerr–Pennington* doctrine, the First Amendment generally immunizes the filing of good-faith lawsuits from liability. . . . The exception to this general rule is if the litigation in question is "sham litigation." . . . Litigation is a "sham" if it meets a two-pronged test set out by the Supreme Court: First, "the lawsuit must be objectively baseless in the sense that no reasonable litigant could realistically expect success on the merits;" and second, the litigant's subjective motivation must "conceal[ ] an attempt to interfere directly with the business relationships of a competitor . . . through the use [of] the governmental process — as opposed to the outcome of that process — as an anticompetitive weapon." . . . Thus, to fall within the exception to the *Noerr–Pennington* doctrine, a lawsuit "must be a sham both objectively and subjectively." . . . This Circuit has extended

---

[203] *Id.* at *23.

[204] *Id.* at *26.

[205] 2014 U.S. Dist. LEXIS 30777 (D.D.C. Mar. 10, 2014).

Noerr–Pennington immunity from its original antitrust context to common law torts, including intentional interference with contract. . . . Other circuits have followed suit. . . .

Here, the plaintiff's claims for intentional interference with contract and for abuse of process are predicated upon an assertion that the defendants' litigation against the plaintiff which led to the settlements constitutes "sham litigation." . . . The plaintiff's claims must fail, since the plaintiff has not established that the defendants' suits were "objectively baseless." Indeed, Defendant Banks succeeded in obtaining a D.C. Court of Appeals decision overturning a judgment in favor of the plaintiff. . . . Similarly, Defendant Mitchell's lawsuit in this Court survived a motion to dismiss before it was settled by the plaintiff. . . . By definition "[o]ne cannot come before a court and argue that litigation that terminated in one's opponent's favor is objectively baseless." . . . [T]he plaintiff has not shown that the litigation at issue here was meritless or pursued for improper reasons, nor has it overcome the precepts of the *Noerr–Pennington* doctrine to plead a cause of action for intentional interference with contract. . . .[206]

(2)   Exercise of an Existing Legal Right

Approval Rights: In General. Courts normally reject claims for tortious interference resulting from the exercise of a legal right. For example, in *National Collegiate Athletic Association v. Hornung*,[207] the plaintiff, a former Heisman Trophy winner, was slated to become an announcer on a weekly college football television series. However, the NCAA, which was granted the right to approve or disapprove any announcer or color analyst on broadcasts, refused to approve his selection because of the plaintiff's playboy image and his stronger identification with professional football than with college football. In overturning a judgment for tortious interference with prospective advantage, the Supreme Court of Kentucky wrote:

> The NCAA was entitled to assert "in good faith" its right of announcer approval. This right had been bargained for and was an essential element in the contract with WTBS. The NCAA was entitled to assert its right even to the detriment of Hornung's prospective contractual relation. If the NCAA believed that employment of Hornung was contrary to its interest, even if such belief was mistaken, it was justified in disapproving Hornung pursuant to the terms of the agreement with WTBS.[208]

Approval of New Franchise Owners. In *Noller v. GMC Truck & Coach Division*,[209] Beard was a GMC dealer, and Noller was interested in buying Beard's assets, but only if he could acquire the GMC franchise. Beard's dealer agreement with GMC was not transferrable, and GMC had the right to approve any new dealer, provided it did not arbitrarily refuse to grant a new owner a franchise. Noller signed

---

[206] *Id.* at *34–*38.

[207] 754 S.W.2d 855 (Ky. 1988).

[208] *Id.* at 860.

[209] 772 P.2d 271 (Kan. 1989).

an agreement to buy Beard's assets, which specifically provided that the agreement was conditioned on GMC's approval. When GMC refused to grant Noller a franchise, Noller cancelled the agreement with Beard and sued GMC for tortious interference. The Supreme Court of Kansas concluded that the claim failed because the sales agreement, by its very terms, recognized GMC's right to refuse approval.

Malicious Exercise of Legal Rights Is Not Actionable. Will an action for tortious interference lie if a right is exercised with spite, ill will, or vindictiveness? In *Uptown Heights Associates Limited Partnership v. Seafirst Corp.*,[210] the defendant bank's foreclosure on a development loan interfered with the plaintiff's ability to sell a building to a potential purchaser. The plaintiff alleged that the defendant's assertion of its right to foreclose was motivated by malice. In addressing that claim, the Supreme Court of Oregon wrote:

> [I]n order to prevail, a plaintiff must establish "not only . . . that defendant intentionally interfered with his business relationship but also that defendant had a duty of non-interference; *i.e.*, that he interfered for an improper purpose rather than for a legitimate one, or that defendant used improper means which resulted in injury to plaintiff . . . " . . .

> Uptown makes no allegation of improper means here. Uptown alleges only an improper purpose. The essence of Uptown's argument is that a party who invokes an express contractual remedy by proper means still may be liable for intentional interference with economic relations if that party simply has a malevolent reason for enforcing its written contract. We disagree. When a party invokes an express contractual remedy in circumstances specified in the written contract — conduct that reflects, by definition, the reasonable expectations of the parties — that party cannot be liable for intentional interference with economic relations based solely on that party's reason for invoking the express contractual remedy. That is because, if the defendant has interfered with the plaintiff's economic relations, the defendant has done so for a "legitimate" purpose — invocation of an express, written contractual remedy — in such circumstances.

> A contrary ruling would contravene public policy and undermine the stability of contractual relations. . . . [C]ourts will not read implied terms into a contract if those terms would contradict the express terms of the contract. It would be anomalous to hold that a party to a contract nonetheless must defend a tort claim when a complaint shows that the party did precisely what the party was entitled to do under the contract. . . .[211]

Exercise of a Legal Right Versus a Mistaken Claim of Right. Some courts have found it useful to differentiate based on whether the assertion of a right is valid or invalid. In *Texas Beef Cattle Co. v. Green*,[212] a suit arising out of earlier litigation,

---

[210] 891 P.2d 639 (Or. 1995).

[211] *Id.* at 651–52.

[212] 921 S.W.2d 203 (Tex. 1996).

Justice John Cornyn wrote for the Texas Supreme Court:

> [T]he justification defense is based on either the exercise of (1) one's own
> legal rights or (2) a good-faith claim to a colorable legal right, even though
> that claim ultimately proves to be mistaken. . . . Thus, if the trial court
> finds as a matter of law that the defendant had a legal right to interfere
> with a contract, then the defendant has conclusively established the
> justification defense . . . and the motivation behind assertion of that right
> is irrelevant. . . . Improper motives cannot transform lawful actions into
> actionable torts. "Whatever a man has a legal right to do, he may do with
> impunity, regardless of motive, and if in exercising his legal right in a legal
> way damage results to another, no cause of action arises against him
> because of a bad motive in exercising the right."

> On the other hand, if the defendant cannot establish such a legal right as a
> matter of law, it may nevertheless prevail on its justification defense if: (1)
> the trial court determines that the defendant interfered while exercising a
> colorable right, and (2) the jury finds that, although mistaken, the
> defendant exercised that colorable legal right in good faith:

>> It would be a strange doctrine indeed to hold that a person having a well
>> grounded and justifiable belief of a right in or to property may be held
>> liable in damages because of an assertion of such a right.

> . . . . A jury question is presented only when the court decides that
> although no legal right to interfere exists, the defendant has nevertheless
> produced evidence of a good faith, albeit mistaken, belief in a colorable legal
> right.[213]

The Right of a Lawyer to Represent a Client. In *Maynard v. Caballero,*[214]
three defendants in an alleged ticket-fixing scheme were represented by different
lawyers, who worked together to craft a joint defense. After all three defendants
were convicted, one defendant sued the lawyer of another defendant for tortious
interference with contract. He argued that if the defendant lawyer had not
persuaded the other lawyers to limit the cross-examination of a certain prosecution
witness, the plaintiff would not have been convicted. The court rejected the claim
stating:

> We find that [attorney] Caballero's conduct was privileged. As long as our
> statutes permit the joinder of parties in criminal and civil litigation, there
> is an ethical and vital need for attorneys, on behalf of their respective
> clients, to meet, discuss, compromise and plan joint defenses or strategies.
> This should be done without the fear that if one or more or all of the parties
> are unsuccessful that the attorneys not in privity with the other litigants
> should be subject to a tortious interference with contract suit. In such
> instances, privilege should, as a matter of law, bar recovery as long as the

---

[213] *Id.* at 211.

[214] 752 S.W.2d 719 (Tex. App. 1988).

interference is done to protect one's contract right to represent one's own client.[215]

(3)   Wrongful Use of Legal Procedures

A knowingly wrongful use of legal procedures may give rise to liability for tortious interference. For example, in *Winiemko v. Valenti*,[216] the plaintiff attorney left the defendant law firm. Three years after the termination of that law partnership, the law firm "improperly sent a 'lien' letter to the plaintiff's major client."[217] As a result of the letter, the plaintiff did not receive any payment from the client for approximately one year. Eventually, the business relationship with the client ended after the plaintiff could no longer adequately continue representing the client because of the adverse financial effect of the letter. Finding that there was "overwhelming evidence adduced at trial that the interference was improper,"[218] the Michigan Court of Appeals affirmed a judgment against the law firm for tortious interference.

Invalid Contract Provisions. In *Torbett v. Wheeling Dollar Sav. & Trusts Co.*,[219] a question was raised as to whether a restrictive covenant in an employment agreement could support an action for tortious interference. In remanding the case for consideration of that issue, the Supreme Court of Appeals of West Virginia wrote:

> The *Restatement* . . . [recognizes] a right to interfere by a party who in good faith attempted to enforce a legitimate protectible interest. However, that defense would fail when applied to a restrictive covenant that does not protect any legitimate business interest at all, and thus violates the long-standing public policy against such covenants.[220]

Misuse of Legal Procedures by Lawyers. There are limits on what a lawyer can do in representing a client. It is well-established, for example, that a lawyer cannot assist a client in conduct that is criminal or fraudulent,[221] or institute frivolous litigation for which there is no basis in law or fact.[222]

In *Kelly-Springfield Tire Co. v. D'Ambro*,[223] a law firm (Stradley, Ronon) for a party (D'Ambro), who had defaulted on payments under a real estate contract, implausibly filed suit in state court for specific performance, causing the action to be listed as *lis pendens*.[224] Then, before a hearing was held, the lawyers voluntarily

---

[215] *Id.* at 721.

[216] 513 N.W.2d 181 (Mich. Ct. App. 1994).

[217] *Id.* at 184.

[218] *Id.* at 185.

[219] 314 S.E.2d 166 (W. Va. 1983).

[220] *Id.* at 173.

[221] *See* MODEL RULES PROF'L CONDUCT R. 1.2(d) (2014).

[222] *See id.* R. 3.1.

[223] 596 A.2d 867 (Pa. Super. Ct. 1991).

[224] *Lis pendens* is "[a] notice, recorded in the chain of title to real property, required or permitted in some jurisdictions to warn all persons that certain property is the subject matter of litigation, and that

withdrew the action and filed a similar claim in federal court, which granted summary judgment in favor of the owner of the property (Kelly-Springfield). The effect of the suits was to impede the owner's sale of the property to other potential buyers. The Pennsylvania Superior Court held that the law firm was subject to liability to the owner of the property for misuse of civil process and also for tortious interference with prospective advantage.[225] Addressing the latter cause of action, the court explained:

> Appellee contends that the amended complaint is insufficient because it fails to aver that the alleged interference was improper. . . .

> A lawyer does not act improperly when he or she, in good faith, files a civil action to protect a client's legitimate interests. *Restatement (Second) of Torts*, § 773. The averments of the complaint in this case, however, are that Stradley, Ronon did not act in good faith to preserve a legally protected interest of a client but for the purpose of harassing Kelly-Springfield and interfering wrongfully with its efforts to resell the warehouse property. Such an interference is not proper and does not serve to protect a legally recognized interest of the client. We conclude, therefore, that the averments of the complaint are sufficient to state a cause of action for intentional interference with the prospective business relations of Kelly-Springfield.[226]

PROBLEM 5-8: THE CARELESS SUBCONTRACTOR

The city of Riverville placed an advertisement seeking bids for a highway construction project. The deadline for submitting bids was July 29, at 2 p.m. Based on plans for the project, Bill Dunlap, president of Four Seasons, Inc., contacted Susan Croftin, president of Quality Construction, informed Croftin that Four Seasons would bid on the project as general contractor, and asked Croftin to supply a subcontractor bid for a particular kind of aggregate surfacing.

On the morning of July 29, Croftin submitted Quality Construction's subcontractor bid by telephone. Quality Construction's bid totaled $98,316. Four Seasons incorporated Quality Construction's subcontractor bid into its bid, which it submitted to the city of Riverville before the 2 p.m. deadline. Later that day, the city of Riverville engineer informed Four Seasons that it had submitted the lowest bid.

---

any interests acquired during the pendency of the suit are subject to its outcome." BLACK'S LAW DICTIONARY (9th ed. 2009).

[225] *See* RESTATEMENT (SECOND) OF TORTS § 679 (1977), which provides:

> One who repeatedly initiates civil proceedings against another for the same cause of action is subject to liability for the harm caused thereby, if
>
> > (a) the proceedings are initiated without probable cause, and primarily for a purpose other than that of securing the proper adjudication of the claim on which the proceedings are based, and
> >
> > (b) except when they are ex parte, the proceedings have terminated in favor of the person against whom they are brought.

[226] 596 A.2d at 871–72.

The Riverville city council was scheduled to consider the bids on August 1. Before any action was taken on the bids, Croftin concluded that she had made a mistake on Quality Construction's bid. Croftin believed that she neglected to include the cost of asphalt oil in computing the bid, which resulted in the bid being about $20,000 lower than it should have been. Croftin first attempted to contact Four Seasons to alert the company to the problem. She was unsuccessful, so she called the city project engineer, the city engineer, and the city attorney. Croftin told those city officials that if the contract was awarded to Four Seasons, Quality Construction would file suit to be relieved from any obligations related to the contract based on grounds of mistake.

The city engineer and city attorney determined that, as a result of Quality Construction's error, a substantial material defect had been made in the bids. The city engineer sent a memorandum alerting the city council to the problem and recommending that all bids be rejected. The council followed that recommendation. When the project was rebid, Four Seasons was not the low bidder and did not receive the contract.

Four Seasons has consulted you about whether they can file suit against Quality Construction for loss of the Riverville contract. Rumors in the business community indicate that Croftin made a mistake, but not the one she thought she made. The cost of the asphalt oil had in fact been included in Quality Construction's $98,316 bid. What Croftin was wrong about was telling city officials that the cost was not included and that Quality Construction's bid was erroneous. Please prepare to advise Four Seasons about the likelihood for success in suing Quality Construction for tortious interference.

g.   Privilege Based on Common Interest

The Defamation Privilege Based on Common Interest. In the context of liability for defamation, § 596 of the *Restatement (Second) of Torts* states:

> An occasion makes a publication conditionally privileged if the circumstances lead any one of several persons having a common interest in a particular subject matter correctly or reasonably to believe that there is information that another sharing the common interest is entitled to know.[227]

Statements by Present or Former Employees about Other Employees. In *Wolf v. F & M Banks*,[228] the Wisconsin Court of Appeals relied on a common interest privilege to dispose of a claim for tortious interference. The court explained as follows:

> In July 1991, Weiss made allegations that Wolf was sexually harassing her. In December 1991, Weiss quit her position and wrote a letter to F & M detailing the alleged incidents of sexual harassment. The letter also accused Wolf of violations of the law and invited an examination of his expense and other business records. F & M called in a consulting psychologist to meet

---

[227] RESTATEMENT (SECOND) OF TORTS § 596 (1977).

[228] 534 N.W.2d 877 (Wis. Ct. App. 1995).

with the bank employees and to discuss the contents of Weiss's letter. During this interview, Miller repeated the contents of Weiss's letter. On January 13, 1992, F & M terminated Wolf's employment, claiming "poor performance" by him.

. . . . [In a subsequent suit,] Wolf alleged claims for tortious interference with contract against Weiss and Miller, claiming that they had unlawfully interfered with his employment relationship with F & M.

. . . .

Tortious employee conduct which is otherwise actionable may be privileged on public policy grounds if the conduct is in furtherance of some interest of societal importance. . . . In this setting, we conclude that the conditional privilege applied to Miller's conduct as a matter of law. . . . Miller's role (perhaps even her obligation) was to discuss the contents of Weiss's letter with the consultant. That, after all, was the very purpose of the interview. To not recognize the conditional privilege in such a setting would frustrate an employer's attempt to investigate and correct employee-related problems in the workplace. It would also chill an employee's willingness to freely and openly discuss the matter in such a setting.

The same holds true for the allegation that Miller discussed Weiss's allegation with coemployees. While not as formal a setting as the discussion with the consulting psychologist, the common interest of the employees in speaking to a matter of concern in the workplace is properly covered by the privilege. . . .

. . . Weiss's letter claimed that Wolf had committed violations of the law. The letter also intimated Wolf's dishonesty by inviting scrutiny of his expense and other business records.

Weiss argues that her actions were privileged as a matter of law because they were taken in good faith. . . . She also argues that she shared a "common interest" conditional privilege. . . .

We disagree. Weiss's letter played a prominent role in the process which eventually led to Wolf's discharge. While Weiss properly looks to the conditional privilege for protection, as the trial court correctly noted, the privilege may be lost if the defendant acted from ill will or an improper motive towards the plaintiff. . . . Here, certain evidence runs counter to Weiss's claim that she acted in good faith and without ill will. Most notably, Weiss herself admitted in one portion of her deposition testimony that she had no evidence of Wolf's dishonesty or violations of the law.

Thus, unlike the situation with Miller, there remain material issues of fact on the question of Weiss's possible bad faith or ill will which, if present, could defeat Weiss's conditional privilege and other defenses. . . . [W]e conclude that the trial court's conditional ruling denying Weiss's motion for summary judgment on these grounds was proper. . . .[229]

---

[229] *Id.* at 880–86.

F. DAMAGES

Tort Damages Versus Contract Damages. A plaintiff who suffers harm as a result of the defendant's inducement of another to breach a contract with the plaintiff may find that greater damages can be recovered from the interferer (in an action for tortious interference) than from the breacher (in a breach of contract action). As the Maryland Court of Appeals explained in *Alexander & Alexander, Inc. v. B. Dixon Evander & Assoc. Inc.*:[230]

> The distinction between tort and contract actions in this context is significant. A successful plaintiff in a tortious interference case is not limited to the contract measure of damages, the benefit of the bargain, . . . but can recover "the more extensive tort damages." . . . . Those damages "include the pecuniary loss of the benefits of the contract, consequential losses for which the tortious act is the legal cause, emotional distress and actual harm to reputation . . . and, in appropriate circumstances, punitive damages." . . . .[231]

Proof with Reasonable Certainty. In order to be recoverable, damages must be proven with reasonable certainty. In *Barton v. Resort Development Latin America, Inc.*,[232] the Texas Court of Appeals held that the evidence was legally insufficient to establish with reasonable certainty the lost profits allegedly resulting from tortious interference with the plaintiff's purchase and development of real property in Mexico. In explaining its decision to reverse multi-million dollar awards, the court wrote in part:

> Lost profits are damages for the loss of net income to a business, reflecting income from the lost business activity, less expenses that would have been attributable to that activity. . . . Although recovery for lost profits does not require that the loss be susceptible to an exact calculation, a party seeking to recover lost profits must prove the loss through competent evidence with reasonable certainty. . . .
>
> To conclude JMJ Development Mexico would ever have developed a W Hotel resort on the Shabshab property, we would be required to stack assumption upon assumption, which we will not do. . . . We would have to assume that, among other things, (1) despite the expiration of the Shabshab-Inland contract, Inland would still have acquired the property from Shabshab; (2) despite the expiration of the non-binding proposal, Inland would have sold the Shabshab Property to JMJ Development Mexico; (3) the title disputes on the Shabshab Property would have been resolved and JMJ Development Mexico would have obtained clear title; (4) Vezzani would have provided equity funding along the lines of the non-binding LOI; (5) Vezzani would have agreed to provide the remainder of the needed equity funding, or JMJ Development Mexico would have found another equity investor; (6) JMJ Development Mexico would have found a

---

[230] 650 A.2d 260 (Md. 1994).

[231] *Id.* at 270.

[232] 413 S.W.3d 232 (Tex. App. 2013).

lender willing to provide the debt funding needed for the project; and (7) Starwood would have agreed to put a W Hotel on the Shabshab Property and the terms on which it would have done so. In addition, we would have to assume that the terms of each of these transactions were such as would allow the development — including the other transactions involved — to go forward. None of these assumptions are supported by facts in the record. . . .

In addition to appellees' failure to present any evidence showing the W Hotel project would have been constructed in the absence of appellants' actions, appellees failed to account for the changing economic conditions — the recession — that occurred during the time they projected to develop the W Hotel. Appellees' expert, Goodwin, acknowledged in his testimony that Mexico was not spared from the economic recession, and by "the end of the first quarter of 2008, pretty much everything had stopped." . . .

. . . Because of the uncertain and changing market conditions in which the appellees proposed to develop the W Hotel project, the lost profits they seek to recover were speculative and not reasonably certain. . . .[233]

G.   SPECIAL ISSUES

1.   Interference with Marital Relations

In *Hoye v. Hoye*,[234] the plaintiff, after discovering that her husband was having an affair with the defendant, sued the defendant for tortious interference with marital relations. In rejecting the claim, the Supreme Court of Kentucky wrote:

Early English common law established two causes of action which "for some purposes can simply be regarded as different means by which the marriage relationship is subjected to interference." . . .

The first, enticement (also called abduction), involved assisting or inducing a wife to leave her husband by means of fraud, violence, or persuasion. The injury was considered to be the loss of the wife's services or consortium. Enticement (or abduction) has evolved into what is commonly known today as the tort of alienation of affections. The second tort remedy available to an injured spouse at early common law was seduction, which today is commonly known as the tort of criminal conversation. Unlike enticement/ abduction, seduction required an adulterous relationship between the plaintiff's spouse and the defendant; no physical separation of the husband and wife was necessary. The purpose underlying an action for seduction was to vindicate the husband's property rights in his wife's person and to punish the defendant for defiling the plaintiff's marriage and family honor, and for placing the legitimacy of children in doubt. . . .

---

[233] *Id.* at 235–40.

[234] 824 S.W.2d 422 (Ky. 1992).

In the late nineteenth and early twentieth centuries most states . . . acted to equalize the legal status of wives with passage of Married Women's Property Acts. "These acts granted wives the right to own property and to sue in their own names to recover damages for their own personal injuries." . . .

The courts, with wives acquiring such rights, were then confronted with the issue as to the continued viability of the tortious causes of actions; alienation of affections and criminal conversation. Because the derivation of these torts was based on the legal inferiority of women, courts could reasonably determine to either deprive their use to a husband or to extend their use to a wife. . . . [A] majority of courts . . . granted these rights of action to the wife. . . .

Extension of these rights of action to the wife necessitated adjusting their rationale. . . . [I]n this century alienation of affections and criminal conversation came to be seen as means to preserve marital harmony by deterring wrongful interference. . . .

The action for intentional interference with the marital relation is a doctrine . . . that incorporates judicially adopted common law torts of criminal conversation, enticement, and alienation of affections. . . .

Both alienation of affections and criminal conversation are based on psychological assumptions that actions by an ill-intended third party can and will destroy a harmonious marriage. . . .

A comparison of contract actions alleging tortious interference with actions based on criminal conversation and alienation of affections reveals logical inconsistencies. Marital interference torts are distinguishable from actions for tortious interference with a contract against a third party because in contract suits the plaintiff can sue not only the third party but also the other party to the contract. In alienation of affections and criminal conversation the other party to the "contract" is the plaintiff's spouse who participated in the tort, and . . . this spouse may not be subject to a suit by the marital partner. This logical asymmetry has prompted the majority of jurisdictions to eliminate these marital torts.

The Iowa Supreme Court in abolishing the alienation of affections action reasoned:

> Spousal love is not property which is subject to theft . . . plaintiffs in suits for alienation of affections do not deserve to recover for the loss or injury to 'property' which they do not, and cannot, own. . . .

To posit that one person possesses rights to the feelings of another is an anachronism. Yet this is the foundation for tortious interference with the marital relation where the presence of a third party is blamed for changes in the marriage. . . .

. . . Since the 1930s the majority of states have recognized inconsistencies in both actions of criminal conversation and alienation of affections, and have either judicially or legislatively abolished them, or severely limited their application through rigid statutory damage restrictions, or shortened statutes of limitation.

. . . [Some] states have abolished alienation of affections in the courts. . . .

At least thirty-one jurisdictions, either through case law or statute, do not recognize the cause of action of criminal conversation. . . .

Such suits invite abuse. Because courts cannot properly police settlements, these actions are "often characterized by the plaintiff-spouse blackmailing the defendant into a high priced settlement with the threat of a lawsuit that could destroy the defendant's reputation." . . . Frequently the end result of these cases is essentially the plaintiff's sale of his spouse's affections. . . . Not only is a defendant in these suits victim to vindictive or purely mercenary motives of the plaintiff, but such suits are likely to expose "minor children of the marriage to one of [their] parent's extramarital activities, and may even require the children to testify to details of the family relationship in open court." . . .

We therefore . . . abolish the action known as tortious interference with the marital relation, relying on the premise that affection between spouses cannot be owned. . . .[235]

Query. Suppose that interference with a marital relation consists of bribery, false promises, and slanderous statements. Should the law afford no relief to either spouse? Is there any cause of action which will provide adequate redress?

2.   Judicial Proceedings Privilege

In a tortious interference action related to litigation or other adjudicative proceedings, it is important to consider whether the claim is barred by the far-reaching judicial proceedings privilege or its sibling, the quasi-judicial proceedings privilege. In *Western Technologies Inc. v. Sverdrup & Parcel, Inc.,*[236] the Arizona Court of Appeals found that a tortious interference claim was barred by the judicial proceedings privilege, which encompassed the defendant firm's production of an engineering report that was a "necessary step" in a third party's decision to take legal action against the plaintiff. However, in *Mixter v. Farmer,*[237] a Maryland appellate court took a more guarded position. The court acknowledged that "there is precedent for applying absolute privilege to torts beyond defamation when those other torts arise from the same conduct as the defamation claim,"[238] and opined that "a broad reading of absolute privilege makes sense from a policy perspective."[239] However, finding that Maryland law was not settled, the court avoided expressly ruling on the issue by finding that the plaintiff's claims for

---

[235] *Id.* at 424–27.

[236] 739 P.2d 1318, 1322–24 (Ariz. Ct. App. 1986).

[237] 81 A.3d 631 (Md. Ct. Spec. App. 2013).

[238] *Id.* at 636.

[239] *Id.* at 637.

tortious interference with contract and prospective advantage were not supported by facts sufficient to survive the defendant's motion for summary judgment.

Cases applying the judicial proceedings privilege to actions other than libel and slander are not always consistent or predictable. Courts sometimes struggle to decide which claims arising out of a single set of facts are barred by the privilege, and which are viable. In *Ruberton v. Gabbage*,[240] an attorney was accused of fraudulently inducing the plaintiffs to settle a wrongful discharge action by making unethical and unlawful threats at a settlement conference that criminal prosecution would be commenced if the case was not resolved. The court found that the alleged threats did not amount to malicious abuse of process because, as that term has been defined by the courts, no "process" had in fact been issued for a corrupt purpose.[241] In addition, the court found that the plaintiffs' tort claims for malicious abuse of process, negligent misrepresentation, fraud, intentional infliction of emotional distress, and malicious interference with prospective economic advantage were barred by the absolute judicial proceedings privilege. This was true even though the privilege would not apply to a disciplinary action based on unprofessional conduct, summary contempt proceedings against the offending attorney, or a motion to vacate the settlement on the basis of alleged coercion. The court also opined that a tort claim for malicious prosecution[242] (which was not alleged by the plaintiffs) would not have been barred by the judicial proceedings privilege.

3.   Failure to Exhaust Administrative Remedies

In an action against a governmental defendant, the plaintiff's failure to pursue administrative remedies related to the alleged interference may preclude a finding of proximate causation. However, in *Pleas v. City of Seattle*,[243] the Supreme Court of Washington recognized that "to insist that a developer must appeal each additional requirement the City imposes in an effort to prevent legitimate development as soon as these are imposed would sorely try the fortunes, let alone patience, of the wealthiest developer."[244] In those circumstances, the failure to exhaust avenues for administrative relief will not preclude a finding of proximate causation of resulting damage, provided there is evidence that plaintiff has acted with diligence in protecting its rights.

---

[240] 654 A.2d 1002 (N.J. Super. Ct. App. Div. 1995).

[241] *See generally* RESTATEMENT (SECOND) OF TORTS § 682 (1977), which provides:

> One who uses a legal process, whether criminal or civil, against another primarily to accomplish a purpose for which it is not designed, is subject to liability to the other for harm caused by the abuse of process.

[242] *See generally id.* § 652, which provides:

> A private person who initiates or procures the institution of criminal proceedings against another who is not guilty of the offense charged is subject to liability for malicious prosecution if
>
> (a) he initiates or procures the proceedings without probable cause and primarily for a purpose other than that of bringing an offender to justice, and
>
> (b) the proceedings have terminated in favor of the accused.

[243] 774 P.2d 1158 (Wash. 1989).

[244] *Id.* at 1165.

H. REVIEW

In preceding chapters, questions were raised about whether harm caused by the erroneous scoring of standardized tests could be redressed under the law of misrepresentation (*see* Chapter 2 Part 2-E), defamation (*see* Chapter 3 Part 3-J), and false light invasion of privacy (*see* Chapter 4 Part D-6). Is an action for tortious interference potentially meritorious? Consider the following:

An erroneous standardized test score will seldom disrupt an existing contractual relationship. People typically do not administer tests to determine whether to maintain the status quo. Rather, tests are more commonly used to determine whether a person will cross a threshold leading to a new status or arrangement. Thus, mis-scoring most often will interfere by causing the loss of future advantages, such as admission to a school, receipt of a scholarship, or attainment of a degree or license. Obviously, understated test scores can cause damage because when scores are too low, benefits are often not conferred. In the types of educational and professional evaluations where standardized test scores play a role, the offer of a valuable opportunity, such as admission or employment, many times goes to the more highly scoring competitor.

The first obstacle for a mis-scored plaintiff is that the interference actions are exclusively intentional torts. Merely negligent interference is not actionable, except in the rarest of cases. To recover for interference, the plaintiff must prove that the defendant intended to disrupt an existing or future relationship between the plaintiff and a third party. Intent encompasses purpose and knowledge. It is exceedingly unlikely that a test-taker or other aggrieved party will be able to show that an erroneous standardized test score was disseminated with the purpose — the goal, objective, or desired consequence — of interfering with an existing or prospective relation between the plaintiff and some third person. Thus, a critical question will often be whether the other variety of intent — knowledge — will be applicable. This requires asking whether the defendant knew with substantial certainty that its conduct would induce or otherwise cause disruption.

If a testing agency provides a very low test score directly to a college or university where a test-taker seeks admission, it may be possible for a court to find that the testing agency knew with substantial certainty that the student would not be admitted. The same is true where the testing agency is aware that a particular score is too low for a student to pass a government-mandated examination, such as those administered pursuant to the federal No Child Left Behind Act. . . . In such cases, if the testing agency is to be saved from liability, it will be on some ground other than lack of intent — perhaps lack of a legally protectable interest on the part of the plaintiff, lack of impropriety, or some kind of privilege (all of which are discussed below).

Of course, an erroneous test score may not be so bad that the test agency "knows" what will happen when the score is received. For example, it may be wholly unclear whether an applicant for admission to the bar will be admitted in a particular jurisdiction when an erroneous Multistate Bar Examination (MBE) score is disseminated. That score may have to be combined with an unknown score on an essay graded by law examiners to arrive at a scaled total score, which then determines whether the aspirant will be allowed to practice law. By mis-scoring the MBE, the testing agency may have created an unreasonable risk that the bar applicant will not be admitted, but there is an important difference between unreasonableness (negligence or recklessness) and intent. Anything less than intent as to the result that the law forbids — that is, intent as to resulting interference with a contract or prospective advantage — will not do.

According to the *Restatement*, there is liability both for disrupting an existing contract, and for burdening the performance of the contract, such as by making fulfillment of contractual obligations more difficult or expensive. Some courts have endorsed the "burdening rationale," but others have not. Importantly, some courts have extended the burdening theory of liability to cases involving interference with prospective advantage. Thus, even though the *Restatement* does not recognize liability for burdening absent an existing contract, that theory might be argued in a mis-scoring case. An aggrieved test-taker might contend that even if a testing agency did not know that admission to a grade level or an educational program, or conferral of a scholarship, degree or license, would be denied, it did know that the score would burden the performance or acquisition of that advantageous relation. Testing agencies should expect to encounter this type of argument.

It might be possible to ask again, as with fraud [*see* Chapter 2 Part A-2-(b)], whether the conduct that forms the basis for the allegedly tortious interference could be viewed not as the initial dissemination of erroneous results, but as the failure to correct those misstatements once their falsity is known. In tort law, acts and omissions are sometimes, but not always, equivalent. Thus, it is fair to ask whether failure to retract an erroneous score could be a form of interference, even if the original publication of the statement was not. In defamation law, failure to remove defamatory postings by another is sometimes treated as being the same as affirmative publication of the damaging material. Nevertheless, the failure-to-retract argument lacks appeal. Most interference cases involve some active form of intervention, such as changing contract bidding rules, cancelling a score, or extending an offer of employment. The interference is an act that, in a real sense, intrudes and disrupts some existing or prospective relation. Passivity may be tortious on some other theory, but at least in the absence of a request to retract, it is dubious whether passive failure to correct should constitute "interference."

A "prospective contractual relationship" is "something less than a right" but "more than hope." An action for tortious interference with prospective advantage will lie only if there is a reasonable probability that a benefit or opportunity would have been conferred but for the interference. It will be difficult to establish this level of certainty in many cases. In one suit, where the plaintiff sued for tortious interference with her application to medical schools, the court denied recovery because, although the applicant "had a satisfactory academic record and background, she had not demonstrated more than a mere hope in securing a prospective relationship with a medical school." "If it is a matter of speculation whether a relationship will come to fruition, there is no cause of action for tortious interference with prospective advantage."

Interference is not actionable unless it is improper. The general test for impropriety is essentially a "totality of the circumstances" inquiry, which takes into account, among other things, "the nature of the actor's conduct, the actor's motive, the interests sought to be advanced by the actor, the social interests in protecting the freedom of action of the actor and, the relations between the parties." "Fraudulent misrepresentations are ordinarily a wrongful means of interference and make an interference improper." However, the same may not be true of negligent misrepresentation, and there may be serious doubts as to whether dissemination of negligently false standardized test results will qualify as improper. In addition, the privileges that may defeat defamation and privacy actions also apply to interference cases.[245]

PROBLEM 5-9 TORTIOUS INTERFERENCE IN LEGAL ACADEME

Based on a careful review of the material covered in this chapter, please briefly answer the following questions:

(a) Professor Turow is a tenured professor at John Marshall Harlan Law School, which is a member of the Association of American Law Schools (AALS). The AALS has a "good practices" guideline which states that "[t]o permit a full-time faculty member to give due consideration to an offer and timely notice of . . . [a] request for leave of absence to his or her law school, a law school should make an offer of . . . a visiting appointment no later than March 15" for a position during the following academic year.[246] A key purpose of the rule is to prevent disruption of class scheduling.

On March 25, Morrison Waite Law School offered Professor Turow a visiting professorship for the coming academic year at a salary $10,000 more than Professor Turow is paid at Harlan Law School. Turow wanted to accept the offer and asked the dean of Harlan Law School for a one-year leave of absence. The Harlan law dean neither wanted to lose Turow to Waite Law School nor alienate Turow. The Harlan law dean therefore offered to raise Professor Turow's salary at Harlan by $15,000 for the coming year. Professor Turow accepted the raise from Harlan Law School and rejected the offer from Waite Law School. Does Harlan Law School have a tortious interference claim against Waite Law School?

(b) Three days before the start of the semester, Professor Grisham, a member of the faculty at Stanley Reed Law School, was injured. Because Grisham would not

---

[245] Vincent R. Johnson, *Standardized Tests, Erroneous Scores, and Tort Liability*, 38 RUTGERS L.J. 655, 709–14 (2007).

[246] ASSOCIATION OF AMERICAN LAW SCHOOLS HANDBOOK, STATEMENT OF GOOD PRACTICES, *available at* http://www.aals.org/about_handbook_sgp_rec.php (last visited Mar. 18, 2014).

be able to teach for the semester, the Reed law school dean sent an e-mail to the faculty asking for a "volunteer" to teach Professor Grisham's courses. The message said that the volunteer would be paid $12,000 extra in compensation for the teaching "overload."

Professors Steinbeck and Twain volunteered. The dean told Professor Steinbeck that he could teach the courses, and Steinbeck immediately began preparing to do so. However, Twain believed that was unfair and two days later persuaded the dean to change her mind and let Twain teach the courses. Steinbeck therefore will not be paid by the school for teaching an overload. Does Professor Steinbeck have a viable tortious interference claim against Professor Twain?

(c)   Professor Craine is a member of the faculty at Willis Van Devanter School of Law. Craine has never gotten along with Professor Cervantes, a member of the same faculty, who was recently named to be the new dean of Mahlon Pitney University Law School. Upon learning that his neighbor, Kirkwood, an excellent student, was offered admission to Pitney University Law School with a full scholarship, Craine persuaded Kirkwood not to matriculate at Pitney by making false statements about the school's new dean, Cervantes. Craine's motive was not to help Kirkwood succeed, but to cause Cervantes to fail. Kirkwood then decided not to attend Pitney University. Kirkwood thereafter applied to other law schools, but was offered only a partial scholarship. Does Pitney University, Cervantes, or Kirkwood have a tortious interference claim against Craine?

(d)   Professor Oates wrote an article and sent it to twenty law journals for possible publication. After receiving an offer of publication from the McReynolds Law Review, Oates told the Sutherland Law Review about the offer she had received from McReynolds. Sutherland Law Review then offered to publish Oates's article in its next issue. Oates accepted Sutherland's offer and rejected McReynolds's offer. Is Sutherland Law Review subject to liability to McReynolds Law Review for tortious interference?

(e)   The faculty recruitment committee at Pierce Butler School of Law identified and publicly announced two finalists, from other law schools, for the position of director of Butler's Prisoner Rights Center: Professor Poe and Professor Plath. Both Poe and Plath wanted the job. Ultimately, Poe was offered, and accepted, the position. Professor Plath, having not gotten the job, then signed a new three-year contract with her home institution, Owen Roberts Law School. It was then discovered that Professor Poe had committed resume fraud in connection with the search. Butler School of Law revoked the contract that it had signed with Poe and reopened the search for a new director of the Prisoner Rights Center by soliciting new applicants. Professor Plath did not apply because of the three-year contract that she signed at Roberts Law School. Does Plath have a tortious interference claim against Poe?

Chapter 6

INJURIOUS FALSEHOOD

A. INJURIOUS FALSEHOOD: IN GENERAL

Also Known as "Disparagement" or "Commercial Defamation." Injurious falsehood, sometimes known as "disparagement" or "commercial defamation," is a theory of tort liability that is neither much discussed nor well understood. This is true despite the fact that injurious falsehood has been part of American law for so long that its principles were embodied in both the first[1] and second[2] *Restatements of Torts* and that related claims are often asserted today, particularly in complex cases, often incidental to claims for tortious interference with contract or prospective advantage.

The *Restatement (Third) of Torts* has not yet begun to reformulate the twenty-first century version of this area of the law. One of the tasks that lie ahead is to fully reconcile the law of injurious falsehood with the constitutional principles that have emerged in other areas of the law, notably the law of defamation.

Principal Subcategories: Trade Libel and Slander of Title. More familiar to American lawyers than the overarching theory of injurious falsehood are its two principal subcategories, "trade libel" and "slander of title," which are similar in many respects to defamation. An action for trade libel provides relief for pecuniary harm caused by false statements about the *quality of* the plaintiff's land, chattels, or intangible things. Slander of title, in contrast, offers a remedy for disparaging statements about the plaintiff's *property rights in* the same array of interests — land, chattels, and intangibles. Trade libel and slander of title are discussed later in this chapter. Although the one subcategory uses the term "libel" and the other the term "slander," disparaging statements are potentially actionable under either theory, regardless of whether they are written (libelous) or oral (slanderous). As the Kentucky Court of Appeals, in *Kenney v. Hanger Prosthetics & Orthotics, Inc.*,[3] explained:

> When the publication attacks a product, it is also called trade libel or commercial disparagement. When the publication attacks title to property rather than quality of a product, the claim is likely to be called slander of title.[4]

---

[1] *See* RESTATEMENT (FIRST) OF TORTS §§ 624–652 (1932).

[2] *See* RESTATEMENT (SECOND) OF TORTS §§ 623A–652 (1977).

[3] 269 S.W.3d 866 (Ky. Ct. App. 2007) (quoting DAN B. DOBBS, THE LAW OF TORTS § 407 (2001)).

[4] *Id.* at 872.

1. Relationship to Other Causes of Action

a. Cross-Tort Application of Constitutional Principles

In dealing with the issue of whether false statements may give rise to liability, the law of injurious falsehood has an obvious relationship to many of the tort theories discussed earlier in this book. Civil liability based on utterance of false statements plays a major role in the law of fraud and negligent misrepresentation (Chapter 2), libel and slander (Chapter 3), false light invasion of privacy (Chapter 4), and tortious interference (insofar as false statements may constitute proof of improper means) (Chapter 5). One should logically expect many of the constitutional principles that have evolved in those other areas of tort law to play a role in the articulation and application of principles governing liability for injurious falsehood.

b. Injurious Falsehood Versus Defamation

Overlapping Causes of Action. The law of defamation protects the personal reputation of the injured party. In contrast, injurious falsehood safeguards the economic interests of the plaintiff against pecuniary loss.[5] Discussing the relationship of these different theories of liability, a federal court in Pennsylvania, in *Wolk v. Teledyne Industries, Inc.*,[6] explained:

> The *Restatement of Torts 2d* comments that the torts of defamation and injurious falsehood protect different interests but overlap in some situations, particularly in cases of disparagement of plaintiff's business or product. *Restatement (Second) of Torts* § 623A cmt. g (1977). If the allegedly tortious statement reflects merely upon the quality of what the plaintiff has to sell or solely on the character of his business, then injurious falsehood can be claimed. Although it might be possible to imply some accusation of personal incompetence or inefficiency in nearly every derogatory statement made about a business or a product, the courts have insisted that something more direct is required for an actionable defamation claim. If the imputation fairly implies plaintiff is dishonest or lacking in integrity, or that he is perpetrating a fraud upon the public by selling something he knows to be defective, personal defamation may be found. Claims may be brought in the same action for both torts so long as the damages are not duplicated.[7]

Alleging Injurious Falsehood Sometimes Is Neither Necessary nor Preferable. In cases involving statements reflecting on both the plaintiff's character and products, some plaintiffs elect to sue only for defamation. This is because pecuniary losses, such as lost sales, can be recovered as special damages, in addition to amounts awarded for reputational harm.[8] Also, suing for libel or slander may be

---

[5] *See* Restatement (Second) of Torts § 623A cmt. g (1977).

[6] 475 F. Supp. 2d 491 (E.D. Pa. 2007).

[7] *Id.* at 504.

[8] *See* Restatement (Second) of Torts § 626 cmt. d (1977).

preferable because the plaintiff's defamation claim might be subject to a lower culpability standard than would apply to an injurious falsehood claim. The culpability requirements applicable to injurious falsehood are discussed below. Culpability requirements under the law of defamation, as discussed in Chapter 3, depend on the status of the plaintiff as a public or private figure and whether the statement relates to a matter of public concern.

Injurious Falsehood May Be Actionable Even Though Defamation Is Not. In some cases, particularly disputes based upon statements about products, the plaintiff can sue for injurious falsehood, but not for defamation. *Seitz v. Rheem Manufacturing Co.*[9] was a case arising from statements alleging that tankless water heaters had a short product life and inadequate warranties, required wiring upgrades, were difficult or expensive to service, and placed a significant burden on the electrical grid. In a suit by the inventor of the tankless water heater and a manufacturer of such products, a federal court in Arizona wrote:

> Defendants contend that Plaintiffs' defamation claim fails because the alleged statements do not impugn Plaintiffs' financial integrity or business ethics, but simply reflect upon the quality of Plaintiffs' *products*. . . .
>
> Arizona courts have drawn a distinction between false statements directed at a plaintiff's product and those statements directed at a plaintiff itself. *See Fillmore v. Maricopa Water Processing Sys.*, 211 Ariz. 269, 120 P.3d 697, 705 (2005) (In contrast to [injurious falsehood and tortious business interference] in which general statements regarding a plaintiff's business or product may give rise to a claim for relief, a claim for defamation must be based on a statement that is "of and concerning" the plaintiff himself.) . . .
>
> The Second Amended Complaint alleges that Defendants made various false statements about electric tankless water heaters without mentioning Plaintiffs directly. Statements about a type of product alone are not sufficient to support a claim for defamation against a manufacturer of such products. . . . [H]owever, the allegations offered in support of Plaintiffs' commercial defamation claim may be offered in support of a claim for product disparagement.
>
> . . . The tort of product disparagement falls within the broader actions of defamation and injurious falsehood. Product disparagement occurs where "[t]here is evidence that the defendant made false, misleading, and disparaging remarks about the plaintiff's products." . . .
>
> Defendants further contend that the alleged statements do not pertain to Plaintiffs' products specifically, but to electric tankless water heaters generally. . . . The Second Amended Complaint does not allege that Plaintiffs are mentioned by name, but it does allege that Plaintiffs are the inventors of the electric tankless water heater. Considering Plaintiffs' status as the inventor of the electric tankless water heater, reasonable minds could find that the general statements about electric tankless water

---

[9] 544 F. Supp. 2d 901 (D. Ariz. 2008).

heaters were directed at Plaintiffs' products. Thus, the claim is plead adequately enough to survive a motion to dismiss. . . .[10]

Distinguishing Defamation from Injurious Falsehood. In *Henneberry v. Sumitomo Corp. of America*,[11] a federal court in New York grappled with the task of distinguishing defamation from injurious falsehood. The court wrote:

> [A] review of the pertinent case law makes clear when a claim of injurious falsehood is proper and when it is improper. For instance, a claim for product disparagement was held to be properly pleaded where plaintiff alleged that defendant had falsely disparaged plaintiff's aerosol products by claiming that they would endanger the ozone layer. *Ruder & Finn Inc.*, . . . [439 N.Y.S.2d 858 (N.Y. 1981)]. Similarly, a claim for injurious falsehood was proper where one clothing store alleged that another competing clothing store's employees made disparaging misrepresentations to its customers regarding the quality and authenticity of the products sold at the former's store. *Fashion Boutique of Short Hills, Inc. v. Fendi USA, Inc.*, . . . [1998 U.S. Dist. LEXIS 7491 (S.D.N.Y.)], *aff'd*, 314 F.3d 48 (2d Cir. 2002). Other statements that plaintiff's parent company was having problems with the store, plaintiff's store would be closing soon, and plaintiff's store sold bogus items were properly characterized as *slanderous per se* because a reasonable juror could conclude that the speaker "was impugning plaintiff's integrity or business methods." *Id.* at *3–*5; *see also Angio-Med. Corp. v. Eli Lilly & Co.*, 720 F. Supp. 269, 272, 274 (S.D.N.Y. 1989) (characterizing as defamatory claims that impute fraud, dishonesty, or unfitness to a company, and characterizing as trade libel claims that would cause a listener to assume plaintiff's cosmetic skin and hair product did not meet safety and efficacy standards). Additionally, where a prosecutor presented to a grand jury transcripts of recordings of conversations between a plaintiff and others, but edited them so as to be unfair and detrimental to plaintiff, plaintiff's claim for injurious falsehood against the defendant-prosecutor for the latter's publication of the transcripts to the grand jury was dismissed because the acts in the transcripts did not concern plaintiff's property. *See Cunningham v. Hagedorn*, 422 N.Y.S.2d 70, 72, 73–74 (App. Div. 1979). Instead, the acts in the transcripts supported a claim for defamation. . . .[12]

Different Statutes of Limitations? The statute of limitations for libel and slander is typically short, often just one year. In some states, actions for injurious falsehood are subject to the same filing deadline.[13] However, in other jurisdictions, injurious falsehood is governed by a more generous statute of limitations. For example, in *State ex rel. BP Products North America Inc. v. Ross*,[14] the Supreme

---

[10] *Id.* at 907–09.

[11] 415 F. Supp. 2d 423 (S.D.N.Y. 2006).

[12] *Id.* at 471–72.

[13] *See, e.g., Keith v. Laurel County Fiscal Court*, 254 S.W.3d 842 (Ky. Ct. App. 2008).

[14] 163 S.W.3d 922 (Mo. 2005) (en banc).

Court of Missouri held that a five-year statute of limitations applied to injurious falsehood claims.

Injunctive Relief Is Available for Injurious Falsehood. Because economic interests are involved, injunctive relief is available to prevent injurious falsehood.[15] In this respect, the law of injurious falsehood differs from defamation. Under defamation law, injunctive relief will typically not issue, and an award of damages is the sole mode for redress.

c.   Injurious Falsehood Versus Tortious Interference

Facts constituting injurious falsehood sometimes also amount to interference with contract or prospective advantage. As a result, courts are occasionally disinclined to recognize injurious falsehood as an independent theory of liability. In *Kenney v. Hanger Prosthetics & Orthotics, Inc.*,[16] the defendants allegedly interfered with the business activities of a former employee. They falsely asserted that he was barred from competing with the defendants. Further, they alleged that he had engaged in theft of time and services, and had embezzled money, while previously working for one of the defendants. Addressing the claims before it, the Kentucky Court of Appeals wrote:

> Keeton has opined that "the injurious falsehood claim should be regarded merely as one form of intentional interference with economic relations[.]" [*CMI, Inc. v. Intoximeters, Inc.*, 918 F. Supp. 1068, 1088 (W.D. Ky. 1995)] (citing W. Keeton, *Prosser and Keeton on the Law of Torts* § 128, at 964 (5th ed. 1984)). The facts of the matter now before us seem to lend themselves easily to an action for interference with a prospective business advantage, which is a recognized tort. . . . Thus, we decline to adopt a new tort to fit the situation when it seems to be encompassed by an already-recognized tort. . . .[17]

2.   Elements of Liability

The general rule governing liability for injurious falsehood is stated in § 623A of the *Restatement (Second) of Torts*, which provides as follows:

> One who publishes a false statement harmful to the interests of another is subject to liability for pecuniary loss resulting to the other if
>
> (a) he intends for publication of the statement to result in harm to interests of the other having a pecuniary value, or either recognizes or should recognize that it is likely to do so, and
>
> (b) he knows that the statement is false or acts in reckless disregard of its truth or falsity.[18]

---

[15] *See* Restatement (Second) of Torts § 626 cmt. b (1977).

[16] 269 S.W.3d 866 (Ky. Ct. App. 2007).

[17] *Id.* at 873.

[18] Restatement (Second) of Torts § 623A (1977).

Liability may be imposed under this general rule, even if the false statement at issue does not amount to trade libel or slander of title.[19] Thus, the principles governing tort liability for injurious falsehood are broader than the rule's two prominent subcategories.

Provably False Assertion of Fact. The law of defamation now makes clear that only provably false assertions of fact may give rise to liability. Presumably the same rule applies to actions seeking compensation for harm caused by injurious falsehood.[20]

As in the law of defamation, mere conduct may be too ambiguous to constitute an assertion of fact. In *Rain v. Rolls-Royce Corp.*,[21] the Seventh Circuit reviewed a ruling which, in relevant part, held that a non-disparagement agreement had not been violated. The appellate court agreed with the district court that the "act of escorting Rain out of . . . [an] event was not designed to, and in fact did not, detract from Rain's reputation as a businessman or carry with it any inherent message regarding his character, his products or his business dealings,"[22] and therefore did not constitute disparagement.

As was traditionally true under the law of injurious falsehood, the plaintiff has the burden of proving the falsity of the statement.[23] In this area of tort law, unlike defamation, falsity was never presumed and truth is not an affirmative defense.

Publication. The publication requirement for injurious falsehood is essentially the same as in the law of libel and slander. Negligent, reckless, or intentional communication of the disparaging information will give rise to liability.[24] Publication may take many forms:

> Disparaging matter is often published by filing a mortgage or other lien for record. As in the case of libel or slander, there may be a sufficient publication by any form of conduct that is intended to assert or is reasonably understood as an assertion of a disparaging statement. Thus a landowner who encloses a part of his neighbor's adjoining premises in such a way as to indicate that it is a part of his own has as effectively disparaged his neighbor's property in the land so enclosed as though he had expressly stated that he himself had title to it.[25]

As in defamation cases, issues arise as to whether communications between agents of the same principal constitute a publication. In *Correctional Medical Care, Inc. v. Gray*,[26] a federal court in Pennsylvania implicitly answered this question in

---

[19] *Id.* § 623A cmt. a.

[20] *Id.* § 623A cmt. e.

[21] 626 F.3d 372 (7th Cir. 2010).

[22] *Id.* at 380.

[23] *See id.* § 623A cmt. g.

[24] *See id.* § 630 cmt. a.

[25] *See id.* § 630 cmt. b.

[26] 2008 U.S. Dist. LEXIS 6596, at *60 (E.D. Pa. Jan. 30, 2008).

the negative. It found that allegedly disparaging statements contained in an e-mail that was circulated within the defendant investigative agency, as well as to the plaintiff, had not been published.

Pecuniary Damages Must Be Proved. The concept of presumed damages does not apply to actions for injurious falsehood. The plaintiff must always prove that pecuniary losses were suffered.[27]

In an action for injurious falsehood, consequential damages "are restricted to the pecuniary loss that results directly and immediately from the effect of the injurious falsehood in influencing the conduct of third persons."[28] Thus:

> [A]n owner of land who is refused a mortgage loan by his bank because of disparagement of his title can not recover for the loss of his intended use of the money he was seeking to borrow. On the other hand, if it can be proved with reasonable certainty that he could obtain another loan only at a higher rate of interest, the loss of the favorable interest rate is a result directly and immediately caused by the disparagement and is recoverable.[29]

Examples of Injurious Falsehood. The *Restatement* offers the following illustrations of facts that give rise to liability for injurious falsehood:

> 1. A, knowing his statement to be false, tells immigration authorities that B does not have sufficient assets for admission to the United States under its immigration rules. As a result B is detained for a week at the immigration station, and suffers pecuniary loss. A is subject to liability to B.
>
> . . . .
>
> 3. A, knowing his statement to be false, tells C that B has died. As a result C, who had intended to purchase goods from B, buys them elsewhere. A is subject to liability to B.
>
> . . . .
>
> 5. A, a physician employed by B Company, examines C, a workman employed by the Company after an accident. Knowing that his statement is false, A reports to B Company that C is not seriously injured, as a result of which C is compelled to bring suit to recover his workmen's compensation and suffers pecuniary loss through the expenses of suit. A is subject to liability to C.[30]

PROBLEM 6-1: THE INEPT CONSULTANT

DocCzar is an innovative software system for managing documents in complex civil litigation cases requiring review or production in discovery of massive amounts of printed matter or electronic files. If operated properly, DocCzar does an excellent job of indexing, sorting, reproducing, and otherwise facilitating the use

---

[27] *See* RESTATEMENT (SECOND) OF TORTS § 623A cmt. g (1977).

[28] *Id.* § 633 cmt. i.

[29] *Id.*

[30] *Id.* § 623A illus. 1-5.

and retention of documents. However, the DocCzar system is complex and can operate optimally only if users of the software receive special training and ongoing technical support from experts.

Carl Kolstadt has been involved with the development and promotion of DocCzar ever since his friend, Michael Mooney, conceived of the idea several years ago. Kolstadt and Mooney are two of the four shareholders in DocCzar, Inc., a closely held corporation.

Through persistent marketing efforts, Kolstadt persuaded Nelson & Cromwell, a "global law firm," to purchase DocCzar and to hire Kolstadt as a technical consultant for an indefinite period of time at a fee of $10,000 per month. However, before the sale was complete, and prior to Kolstadt's rendition of consulting services, a disgruntled former employee of DocCzar, Inc., David Cahill, contacted Barry Wellington, the managing partner of Nelson & Cromwell. Cahill told Wellington: "Kolstadt lacks the skills, the technical expertise, and the software savvy necessary to be an effective consultant or to manage your law firm's implementation of DocCzar."

Following the conversation and related discussions within the law firm, Wellington notified Kolstadt that the firm intended not to carry through with the deal. Nelson & Cromwell did not purchase the software and Kolstadt was not employed as a consultant.

Can Kolstadt or DocCzar, Inc. sue Cahill for injurious falsehood, defamation, or tortious interference?

3. Culpability

To prevail on a claim for injurious falsehood, the plaintiff must establish that the defendant was culpable in two respects. The first concerns the falsity of the disparaging statement, and the second concerns the causation of pecuniary harm.

a. Actual Malice

No Liability for Negligently or Innocently False Statements. Traditionally, culpability in the nature of knowledge of falsity or reckless disregard for the truth gave rise to liability for injurious falsehood. This rule continues to apply. Whereas the law of defamation had once imposed strict liability, that was never the rule with respect to injurious falsehood. Nor was negligence as to falsity ever sufficient to support an award of damages.[31]

Unresolved Issues About Ill Will and Intent to Harm. As the law of injurious falsity evolved, there were two alternatives to proving that the defendant acted with knowledge of falsity or reckless disregard for the truth. The first was to show that the defendant was motivated by ill will toward the plaintiff, and the second was to prove that the defendant intended to harm the plaintiff (*i.e.*, intended to interfere with the plaintiff's interest in an unprivileged manner).[32]

[31] *Id.* § 623A cmt. d.

[32] *Id.*

The second *Restatement*'s provisions governing injurious falsehood were drafted at a time when the constitutional restrictions on defamation actions were in flux. Reflecting that uncertainty, the members of the American Law Institute chose the cautious course and left unresolved the question of whether the two alternative bases of liability (ill will and intent to harm) remained viable.

Today, there is little indication that these alternatives offer a feasible path to liability in cases where the defendant has not acted with actual malice. For example, in *Neurotron Inc. v. Medical Service Association of Pennsylvania, Inc.*,[33] the Third Circuit predicted that the Supreme Court of Pennsylvania would require knowledge of falsity or reckless disregard for the truth in an injurious falsehood action. The Third Circuit then applied that standard to the facts before it and held that an insurer's statement in a newsletter, that an electrodiagnostic medical testing device had "no proven clinical utility," was not actionable.

Nevertheless, in *SCO Group, Inc. v. Novell, Inc.*,[34] a federal court in Utah stated that to establish the "malice" element of a slander of title claim under Utah law:

> The plaintiff may prove "that the wrong was done with an intent to injure, vex, or annoy," or "because of hatred, spite or ill will." Or, "malice may be implied where a party knowingly and wrongfully records or publishes something untrue or spurious or which gives a false or misleading impression adverse to one's title under circumstances that it should reasonably foresee might result in damage to the owner of the property."
> . . .[35]

According to the *Restatement*:

> [I]f the Constitution should be held to vitiate the two alternative bases for liability, of ill will and intent to harm, it may be that the state courts would decide to continue to use these two bases to impose liability whenever the publisher was negligent as to the falsity of the statement and liability could constitutionally be imposed. This problem has not arisen before the courts and there are no indications as to the course that would be taken.[36]

b.   Intended or Foreseeable Harm to the Plaintiff

An action for injurious falsehood does not impose strict liability when a statement made with actual malice causes pecuniary harm. Instead, the plaintiff must prove that the statement was intended to harm the plaintiff, or at least that a reasonable person would have expected that result.[37] Thus, intent, recklessness, or negligence with respect to the causation of harm may serve as the basis for liability. Such fault may be established, in some cases, because the defendant foresaw that a third person would rely upon the false statement. However, third

---

[33] 254 F.3d 444, 451 (3d Cir. 2001).

[34] 377 F. Supp. 2d 1145 (D. Utah 2005).

[35] *Id.* at 1152 (quoting *First Security Bank of Utah v. Banberry Crossing*, 780 P.2d 1253, 1257 (Utah 1989)).

[36] RESTATEMENT (SECOND) OF TORTS § 623A cmt. d (1977).

[37] *Id.* § 623A cmt. b.

party reliance is not a requirement if there is other evidence to establish that harm to the plaintiff was reasonably foreseeable.[38]

Unforeseeable Harm. In *L.W.C. Agency, Inc. v. St. Paul Fire and Marine Insurance Co.*,[39] the plaintiff agency (L.W.C.) placed an insurance policy for a client with St. Paul for the policy year 1982–1983.

> In April 1983, the insured informed St. Paul that it had suffered a loss. In a letter written by St. Paul's attorney, the insured was informed that St. Paul had disclaimed liability for the claimed loss because it had concluded that the information regarding the claim, as furnished by the insured's sales representative, was false. The third paragraph of the letter stated: "The policy is void as of its inception date because of misrepresentations in the proposal for the policy." Other than a notation that a copy had been sent to L.W.C., there was no reference in the letter to L.W.C. or its president. . . . In an action against St. Paul and others, L.W.C. and others sought recovery for injurious falsehood. The plaintiffs alleged that the defendants' statement that the policy was procured by misrepresentation was known by defendants to be untrue and that the defendants knew or should have known that the utterance of the untrue statement would damage L.W.C. "in that it implied that [L.W.C.] had not acted appropriately in advising its client in applying for the policy" and it "indicated a lack of business judgment on [L.W.C.'s] part by placing its client's business insurance with a carrier that would act in such a fashion."[40]

The plaintiffs claimed that, as a result of the defendants' alleged wrongful conduct, its client placed its policy for the year 1983–1984 through another broker, thereby depriving L.W.C. of the $11,397.90 commission it would have earned for that policy. The plaintiffs also sought compensation for lost future commissions on "these policies" in the sum of $170,968.50. In ruling against the plaintiffs, the New York Appellate Division wrote:

> Even if the allegations . . . are assumed to be true, a reasonably prudent person would not anticipate that damage to the insured's broker, by way of pecuniary loss, would naturally follow from the cancellation of the policy based on the alleged misrepresentations in the policy proposal. This is especially true when the letter of cancellation does not in any way refer to or identify the insured's broker in connection with said misrepresentations.[41]

"Of and Concerning" the Plaintiff. Another way of talking about the requirement that harm to the plaintiff must be foreseeable would be to say that the injuriously false statement must be "of and concerning" the plaintiff. Some cases use this language, but most do not.

---

[38] *Id.*

[39] 125 A.D.2d 371 (N.Y. App. Div. 1986).

[40] *Id.* at 99.

[41] *Id.* at 100.

4.   Proof of Pecuniary Damages

Only Pecuniary Losses Are Recoverable. The law of defamation provides compensation for emotional distress and harm to reputation, as well as pecuniary losses in the form of special damages. In contrast, injurious falsehood compensates only pecuniary harm.

Actual Losses Must Be Identified and Causally Related. Some cases impose a demanding standard with respect to proof of damages. For example, in *L.W.C. Agency, Inc. v. St. Paul Fire and Marine Insurance Co.*[42] (discussed above), an insurance agency's claim for injurious falsehood failed in part due to lack of adequate proof of damages. The New York Appellate Division wrote:

> [W]e find that the . . . cause of action does not plead special damages with sufficient particularity. "The general allegation that numerous prospective employers refused to employ plaintiff by reason of the intentional misstatements of defendants is inadequate as a pleading of special damages" in a claim for injurious falsehood. . . . In pleading special damages, actual losses must be identified and causally related to the alleged tortious act. . . . The general allegation that L.W.C. was deprived of the commission on Steven's [insurance] policy for the year 1983-1984 as well as the allegations of losses of undefined future commissions were inadequate to plead special damages. The plaintiffs fail to allege how the alleged falsehood caused these alleged losses.[43]

5.   Example: *Wandersee v. BP Products North America, Inc.*

Allegations of Theft May Constitute Injurious Falsehood. The *en banc* decision of the Supreme Court of Missouri, in *Wandersee v. BP Products North America, Inc.*,[44] nicely illustrates how the culpability, causation, and damages requirements may be applied in an injurious falsehood action. As the court described the facts of the case:

> Brian Wandersee is the owner and president of Advanced Cleaning Technologies, Inc. (ACT). BP Products North America, Inc. (BP) accused Wandersee and another ACT employee of stealing a car wash system belonging to BP, which led to criminal charges against Wandersee and the other ACT employee. After those charges were dropped, Wandersee and ACT sued BP for injurious falsehood. The jury found BP liable to Wandersee and ACT and awarded damages of $605,350. . . .
>
> Advanced Cleaning Technologies, Inc. (ACT) distributes, installs and services car wash systems. ACT is the exclusive distributor for PDQ Manufacturing, Inc., the world's largest manufacturer of the "touch-free in-bay" automatic car wash systems. . . .

---

[42] 125 A.D.2d 371 (N.Y. App. Div. 1986).

[43] *Id.* at 100.

[44] 263 S.W.3d 623 (Mo. 2008).

In December 1997, BP ordered three car wash systems from PDQ Manufacturing. BP informed PDQ that it planned to install these car wash systems in three of its new St. Louis area stations. Because construction of the three stations was not yet complete at the time of the order, BP requested that delivery be delayed. PDQ called Wandersee and asked whether ACT, its exclusive distributor, could take delivery of and store the car wash systems until BP needed them. Wandersee agreed, with the understanding that the car wash systems would remain in ACT's warehouse until BP called and requested installation. Pursuant to this agreement, PDQ shipped the car wash systems to ACT's warehouse. BP paid $437,697.92 for the three car wash systems, including a payment of $99,916.67 for a car wash system BP planned to install in its O'Fallon station.

BP called ACT in 1998 and arranged for the delivery and installation of two of the three PDQ car washes. The third car wash, which BP had ordered for installation at the O'Fallon station, remained in storage at the ACT warehouse.

During a meeting in February 1999, Wandersee informed Mary Fissenhasion, BP's company account executive and St. Louis market manager, that ACT still had the O'Fallon station car wash in storage because BP had not yet requested its installation. Fissenhasion told Wandersee that the O'Fallon station car wash was "not in her budget" and that she did not know whom Wandersee should contact about it.

BP's regional security advisor, Ron Benhart, received a telephone call in July 1999 from ACT employee Tami Weeks. Weeks told Benhart that she believed Wandersee and Steve Amick, a former employee of BP who had begun working for ACT, were attempting to sell the O'Fallon car wash without BP's knowledge. According to Weeks, Wandersee and Amick claimed to have "commandeered" the O'Fallon car wash from BP. Weeks alleged that Wandersee had unauthorized possession of the O'Fallon car wash. She told Benhart that she had heard Wandersee refer to the O'Fallon station car wash as a "freebie" and that he had bragged that ACT could sell it at a "100 percent" profit. In support of her allegations, Weeks gave Benhart the serial number of the O'Fallon car wash, which she stated confirmed BP's ownership of the machine. Weeks also gave Benhart a document that she claimed was a falsified purchase order that Amick had created to facilitate the theft.

After speaking with Weeks, Benhart contacted PDQ to verify the serial number. . . .

Benhart contacted the Overland, Missouri, police department on July 26, 1999 to report Weeks' allegation. Benhart gave the police documents demonstrating BP's purchase and payment for the O'Fallon car wash system. Later that day, Weeks and Keith Payette, a part owner and former employee of ACT, went to the Overland police department and gave written statements supporting Weeks' prior allegation of theft.

Later that day, the Overland police department applied for and received a warrant to search ACT's warehouse. During their search, the police discovered and seized the O'Fallon car wash. The police arrested Wandersee the next day.

Wandersee and Amick were indicted in May 2000 on charges of stealing in connection with the alleged theft of the O'Fallon station car wash. After taking depositions, however, the prosecutor filed a *nolle prosequi* abandoning the prosecution.[45]

Imputing the Knowledge of Agents to a Corporation. The *Wandersee* court then turned to the issue of whether the defendant had acted with the degree of culpability required in an action for injurious falsehood: knowledge of falsity or reckless disregard for the truth. The court wrote:

> BP argues that the trial court erred in overruling its motion for judgment notwithstanding the verdict because Wandersee and ACT failed to present evidence that Ron Benhart acted knowingly or recklessly in making the false allegation of theft. Under the facts of this case, however, the relevant knowledge is that of BP, not Benhart.
>
> Wandersee and ACT sued BP for injurious falsehood. The instructions submitted to the jury required that the jurors determine whether BP itself, rather than Benhart, engaged in the conduct necessary to sustain plaintiff's claim of injurious falsehood. BP did not object to the jury instruction on the grounds that it failed to distinguish between Benhart and BP's knowledge. Thus, as BP explained in its motion for directed verdict, a successful claim for injurious falsehood in this case required plaintiffs "to prove that BP *knew* its statement to the police department was false or it acted in reckless disregard of the truth or falsity of its alleged statement." . . .
>
> As a corporation, BP can obtain knowledge only through its agents and, under the well-established rules of agency, the knowledge of agents obtained in the course of their employment is imputed to the corporation. . . .
>
> A review of the record reveals that at the time Ron Benhart — acting within the course and scope of his employment with BP — accused Wandersee of theft, various BP employees had actual knowledge that BP had authorized Wandersee's possession of the O'Fallon car wash. In December 1997, BP's authorized agents ordered and authorized the delivery of the O'Fallon car wash to ACT's warehouse with the understanding that ACT would deliver the car wash when BP needed it. Wandersee informed BP's St. Louis market manager, Mary Fissenhasion, in February 1999 that ACT still had the O'Fallon car wash in its warehouse. Fissenhasion told Wandersee that she did not know whom to contact regarding the car wash's delivery.
>
> Each of these interactions indicates actual knowledge on the part of the BP agent involved that ACT was authorized to have possession of the O'Fallon

---

[45] *Id.* at 626–28.

car wash. . . . [T]he agents' knowledge of ACT's authorized possession is imputed to the corporation. In other words, it is accurate to say that, because its agents had actual knowledge that ACT and Wandersee had authorized possession of the O'Fallon car wash, BP itself knew that ACT and Wandersee had authorized possession of the O'Fallon car wash.

BP urges this Court to reverse the trial court's judgment on public policy grounds. A holding that a corporation is liable for the knowledge possessed by its agents is equivalent, according to BP, to a holding that "every agent must possess the knowledge of every other corporate agent." With this rationale, BP mischaracterizes the issue in this case. By holding BP accountable for the knowledge of its agents, this Court does not require that every agent of a corporation possess the knowledge of every other agent as BP claims. Our holding merely requires that a corporation accept responsibility for the knowledge of its agents. It is a "well-established rule of agency that the knowledge of an agent of a corporation with reference to a matter within its scope of his authority and employment and to which his authority or employment extends is imputed to the corporation.". . . . As such, the knowledge of BP's agents must be imputed to the corporation as a whole. By asking this Court not to impute responsibility to corporations for the information stored in its records and possessed by its various agents, BP asks this Court to encourage irresponsibility. Such a holding would give corporations an incentive to delegate responsibility to its least informed agents in order to avoid liability. . . .

Wandersee and ACT presented sufficient evidence for a jury to find that at the time BP, acting through agent Ron Benhart, made the false theft allegation, BP, because of its agents' knowledge that ACT's possession of the car wash was authorized, knew that the theft allegation was false. As such, ACT and Wandersee produced sufficient evidence to support a jury finding that BP had actual knowledge of the theft allegation's falsity.[46]

Consistency with Supreme Court Precedent? In considering the *Wandersee* court's analysis of the legal sufficiency of imputed knowledge for purposes of establishing what amounts to actual malice (knowledge of falsity or reckless disregard for the truth), it is worth remembering what the United States Supreme Court said in *New York Times Co. v. Sullivan.*[47] *Sullivan* was a defamation action by a public official based on false statements in a newspaper advertisement supporting the civil rights movement. In that case, Justice William J. Brennan, Jr. wrote for a unanimous court:

The mere presence of the stories in the [the New York Times's] files does not, of course, establish that the Times "knew" the advertisement was false, since the state of mind required for actual malice would have to be brought home to the persons in the Times' organization having responsibility for the publication of the advertisement.[48]

---

[46] *Id.* at 628–30.

[47] 376 U.S. 254 (1964).

[48] *Id.* at 287.

Why didn't the *Wandersee* court say that knowledge of the falsity of the statement about the alleged theft had to be "brought home" to BP's agent, Benhart? Are *Wandersee* and *Sullivan* inconsistent? Perhaps the answer lies in the nature of the cases. *Sullivan* was talking about what the Constitution requires in a defamation action based on statements about the conduct of a public official while dealing with a matter of public concern. In contrast, the plaintiff in *Wandersee* was not a public official or even a public figure, and many would regard the exercise of control over a car wash unit as a matter of purely private concern.

Proof of Causation in a Case Involving Contributing Forces. The *Wandersee* court also addressed the causation requirement of an action for injurious falsehood. Interestingly, the court applied a "substantial factor" test, rather than the more common "but for" test, in assessing whether there was an adequate causal connection. The court explained:

> A series of events led up to the prosecutor's decision to seek an indictment. These events, according to BP, constituted independent intervening causes that severed the causal link between BP's initial report of theft and the prosecutor's decision to indict Wandersee.

> To prove the element of causation in a claim for injurious falsehood, a plaintiff must show that the defendant's false statement caused plaintiff's pecuniary loss. . . . A jury can find that publication of an injurious falsehood is the legal cause of a pecuniary loss if: (1) it is a substantial factor in bringing about the loss and (2) there is no rule of law relieving the publisher from liability because of the manner in which the publication has resulted in the loss. Rest. 2d of Torts at § 632. The liability of a defendant for injurious falsehood "is restricted to . . . the pecuniary loss that results directly and immediately from the effect of the conduct of third persons . . . caused by disparagement." *Id.* at § 633.

> In evaluating the liability of the defendant for economic harm resulting from the actions of a third party, "it is not necessary that the [third party's] conduct should be determined exclusively or even predominantly by the publication of the [false] statement. It is enough that the disparagement is a factor in determining his decision, even though he is influenced by other factors without which he would not decide to act as he does." *Id.* at § 632, cmt. c. An intervening event will not sever the causal chain if the intervening cause is a "foreseeable and natural product" of the original act. . . .

> BP argues that several events severed the causal link between Benhart's false statements and the plaintiffs' ultimate harm. The intervening causes were: (1) the witness statements given by various employees of ACT, which corroborated Benhart's allegations of theft; (2) a judge's decision to authorize a search warrant; (3) the Overland police department's subsequent criminal investigation; and (4) the prosecutor's decision to seek an indictment based on the police department's investigation.

> BP focuses on the fact that, as the theft complaint moved through the criminal justice system, the various intervening actors did not base their

decisions solely, if at all, upon Benhart's original accusation of theft. BP asserts that, because not all of the actors who contributed to Wandersee's ultimate indictment were motivated by Benhart's initial accusation, Benhart's statement is not the legal cause of the plaintiffs' ultimate pecuniary loss.

BP is incorrect. Ron Benhart's statements to the Overland police initiated the criminal investigation and, ultimately, the indictment of Wandersee, events which resulted in pecuniary loss to plaintiffs. As a catalyst for the events that resulted in the pecuniary loss, the jury could conclude that Benhart's false statement was a "substantial factor" in bringing about the loss.[49]

Recovery of Lost Profits. The *Wandersee* court then considered whether the trial court erred by allowing the jury to award damages for lost profits. The court reasoned as follows:

> "In evaluating the sufficiency of evidence to sustain awards of damages for loss of business profits the appellate courts of this state have made stringent requirements, refusing to permit speculation as to probable or expected profits, and requiring a substantial basis for such awards." . . . For an award of lost profits damages, a party must produce evidence that provides an adequate basis for estimating the lost profits with reasonable certainty. . . . To create an adequate basis for an award of lost profits, a plaintiff must provide evidence of the income and expenses of the business for a reasonable time before the interruption caused by defendant's actions, with a consequent establishing of the net profits during the previous period. . . . While an estimate of prospective or anticipated profits must rest upon more than mere speculation, "[u]ncertainty as to the amount of profits that would have been made does not prevent a recovery." . . .

At trial, Wandersee and ACT presented evidence that BP's false allegation of theft resulted in $192,610 of recoverable lost profits. The plaintiffs based this lost profits projection on ACT's income tax return for fiscal years 1996 through 1998, which showed a 25.5 percent growth rate for gross sales and an average "net profit margin" of 5.5 percent during those years. Plaintiffs applied those percentages to ACT's income tax returns for 1999, 2000 and 2001 to determine that ACT sustained $192,610 in lost profits during the years following BP's false allegation of theft.

BP argues that, in reaching this figure, plaintiffs failed to "establish proof of the income and expenses of the business for a reasonable time anterior to the interruption." . . . BP points out that the income tax returns from 1996 through 1998 include only ACT's income and expenses until September 30, 1998. The "interruption of business" — that is, BP's false allegation of theft — occurred on July 26, 1999. Because the tax returns do not include the ten months immediately preceding the allegation, BP argues that the plaintiffs' failed to provide income and expense information for the requisite reasonable time before the interruption.

---

[49] 263 S.W.3d at 630–31.

BP's contention is unpersuasive. The $192,610 award for lost profits was based on ACT's income tax return from the three fiscal years preceding the theft allegation. While there is a gap in showing income on the tax returns, there is no support for BP's assertion that three years of income tax returns are "inadequate as a matter of law" due to this gap. ACT also presented testimony that explained why there were not separate figures for the partial year between the dates covered by the tax returns and the injury, and offered testimony that the business had continued to make profits and offered his opinion, based on the trend established for prior years, as to what his profits would have been absent the wrong.

BP also argues that this evidence failed to eliminate other potential causes for the lost profits. BP correctly notes that "[r]ecovery for lost profits is not permitted when uncertainty and speculation exist as to whether lost profits would have occurred or whether lost profits emanated from the wrong." . . . At trial, Wandersee testified that BP's false theft allegation was the only possible cause of ACT's decrease in profits. BP asserts that Wandersee's testimony is self-serving and provided an insufficient basis to support a jury finding that BP's action had caused the lost profits. . . . Beyond references to "general decline in the market" and "new competition," however, BP fails to identify any evidence that would compel the jury to agree with its contention that the lost profits emanated from something other than the false theft allegation. The jury was free to accept ACT's factual theory and reject BP's. BP's motion for a new trial was properly overruled.[50]

Compensation for Foregone Wages. The court next turned to the question of whether compensation for foregone wages could be recovered. It answered that question in the affirmative, reasoning as follows:

Did the trial court err in allowing the jury to consider forgone wages of four ACT employees in its calculation of damages? ACT presented evidence that, due to the economic impact of BP's false statement, ACT was unable to pay the wages of employees Brian Wandersee, Laura Wandersee, Jane Wandersee and Herb Wandersee from August 1999 through 2001. At trial, plaintiffs sought $365,000 in "foregone wages" for these employees.

The goal of awarding damages is to compensate a party for a legally recognized loss. . . . To warrant the recovery of damages, there must be both a right of action for a legal wrong inflicted by the defendant and damage resulting to the plaintiff therefrom. . . .

Although characterized by the parties as damages for "foregone wages," the $365,000 award did not compensate ACT for payment of its employees' salaries. The function of the award was to adjust the projected lost profits figure to reflect ACT's actual loss of profits. As both parties acknowledge, the projected lost profits figure of $192,610 was based on a comparison of ACT's income tax returns from the years before and after BP's allegation of theft. . . . This figure does not provide a complete picture of the lost

---

[50] *Id.* at 633–34.

profits resulting from the false allegation of theft, however. During 1999, 2000 and 2001, ACT elected not to pay the salaries of four of its employees due to economic hardship. As such, the tax returns from these years do not reflect the expense of these salaries which, although deferred, ACT is still obliged to pay. The jury could properly conclude that, in order to reflect ACT's actual loss in profits, the $365,000 expense of the deferred salaries had to be added to the $192,610 lost profits calculation (which was derived without consideration of the additional expense of the salaries).

Because the award of $365,000 was an adjustment that the jury could conclude was necessary to compensate the plaintiffs for ACT's actual loss in profits, it was a valid measure of damages. . . .[51]

Compensation for Attorneys's Fees Incurred. Finally, the *Wandersee* court turned to the question of whether compensatory damages could include an amount to reimburse the plaintiff for certain attorneys' fees that were incurred as a result of the injurious falsehood. The court wrote:

> Plaintiffs presented the testimony of Wandersee, Amick himself and Amick's criminal defense attorney in support of their contention that Amick, who was an employee of plaintiff ACT at the time of the theft allegation, incurred attorneys' fees as a result of defendant's conduct. BP did not object to the testimony regarding Amick's legal fees. ACT also produced evidence that it had agreed to reimburse attorneys' fees for Amick, who was not a party to the lawsuit. There was sufficient evidence to support awarding $25,000 to ACT for Amick's fees.[52]

The Supreme Court of Missouri further concluded that the award of $605,350 to the plaintiffs was not excessive.

PROBLEM 6-2: THE ALLEGEDLY POLLUTED PROPERTY

Mt. Unity Prep, a private school, was in the market for a tract of property upon which to construct a new educational facility. Ron Kerry owned property located on Democracy Street, upon which he operated a restaurant. Located adjacent to Kerry's property was a 40-acre tract owned by Mike Gazdik.

Kerry met with Virginia Davila, the chief administrator of Mt. Unity Prep, to discuss the possibility of locating the new facility on the Gazdik tract. Because the Gazdik tract was located adjacent to his restaurant property, Kerry anticipated that if Mt. Unity Prep located there, he would receive a financial advantage by an appreciation in the value of his property and increased numbers of customers at his restaurant. Kerry spoke to Gazdik about his plan, and Gazdik agreed to the idea.

A short time later, Kerry spoke to Bibiana Berkemeier, who had been retained by Mt. Unity Prep to help locate a facility site. Berkemeier told Kerry that Dennis Keogh, Executive Director of the Laurel Highlands Development Authority, had told him that the Gazdik site would not be a suitable site for the facility because it

---

[51] *Id.* at 634–35.

[52] *Id.* at 635.

was contaminated with toxic waste. This information was wrong because Keogh had confused the Gazdik tract with property owned by someone else.

Upon learning of this conversation, Kerry informed Berkemeier that the Gazdik property was not contaminated. Kerry offered to pay for an independent expert to evaluate and report on the condition of the property. Berkemeier indicated that Mt. Unity Prep did not wish to become involved in a dispute about potentially polluted property. Mt. Unity expressed no further interest in the Gazdik property and eventually purchased a different site for its new educational facility.

Is it possible for Kerry to state a viable cause of action for injurious falsehood against Keogh or the Laurel Highlands Development Authority?

B. SLANDER OF TITLE

According to the *Restatement*:

> The rules on liability for the publication of an injurious falsehood stated in § 623A apply to the publication of a false statement disparaging another's property rights in land, chattels or intangible things, that the publisher should recognize as likely to result in pecuniary harm to the other through the conduct of third persons in respect to the other's interests in the property.[53]

Range of Interests Protected. The action for slander of title may be used to protect a wide range of property interests. For example, interests in land or chattels include, but are not limited to, those held by way of a mortgage, trust, or a lease. Intangible interests encompass, among others, trade names, copyrights, and trademarks.

Examples of Slander of Title. The *Restatement* offers the following examples of slander of title:

> 1. A, who is contemplating the purchase of a stock of goods that belongs to B, reads an advertisement in the paper in which C falsely asserts that he has a lien upon the goods. C has disparaged B's property in the goods.
>
> 2. A records a document that purports to be a mortgage that B has executed on his house. A has disparaged B's title to the house.
>
> 3. A, knowing that B claims to be the owner of a particular piece of land, states that he is himself the owner of it. A has disparaged B's property in the land in question.
>
> 4. A dies intestate. B says that C, A's only son, is illegitimate and that he, A's only nephew, is the heir to the land in question. B has disparaged C's property in the land.[54]

---

[53] Restatement (Second) of Torts § 624 (1977).

[54] *Id.* § 629 illus. 1-4.

C. TRADE LIBEL

According to the *Restatement*:

> The rules on liability for the publication of an injurious falsehood stated in § 623A apply to the publication of matter disparaging the quality of another's land, chattels or intangible things, that the publisher should recognize as likely to result in pecuniary loss to the other through the conduct of a third person in respect to the other's interests in the property.[55]

1.   Agricultural Disparagement Statutes

Various food producers have exercised their constitutional right to petition the government by lobbying state legislatures for protection against statements that can harm the marketability of their products.[56] Some of these laws depart significantly from the usual rules governing trade libel, while other statutes are largely consistent with established common law and constitutional principles. An example of an agricultural disparagement statute is the Texas False Disparagement of Perishable Foods Act, which provides:

§ 96.001. *Definition*

In this chapter, "perishable food product" means a food product of agriculture or aquaculture that is sold or distributed in a form that will perish or decay beyond marketability within a limited period of time.

§ 96.002. *Liability*

(a) A person is liable as provided by Subsection (b) if:

   (1) the person disseminates in any manner information relating to a perishable food product to the public;

   (2) the person knows the information is false; and

   (3) the information states or implies that the perishable food product is not safe for consumption by the public.

(b) A person who is liable under Subsection (a) is liable to the producer of the perishable food product for damages and any other appropriate relief arising from the person's dissemination of the information.

§ 96.003. *Proof*

In determining if information is false, the trier of fact shall consider whether the information was based on reasonable and reliable scientific inquiry, facts, or data.

§ 96.004. *Certain Marketing or Labeling Excluded*

---

[55] *Id.* § 626.

[56] *See generally* Vincent R. Johnson, *Regulating Lobbyists: Law, Ethics, and Public Policy*, 16 CORNELL J. & PUB. POL'Y 1, 5–13 (2006).

A person is not liable under this chapter for marketing or labeling any agricultural product in a manner that indicates that the product:

(1) was grown or produced by using or not using a chemical or drug;

(2) was organically grown; or

(3) was grown without the use of any synthetic additive.[57]

Open Constitutional Questions. There are many unanswered constitutional questions about agricultural disparagement laws. "Thus far, . . . there has been only one appellate decision involving a constitutional challenge . . . [and it] did not result in a substantive ruling."[58]

2.   Example: *Texas Beef Group v. Winfrey*

Oprah Winfrey and the Beef Crash. In *Texas Beef Group v. Winfrey*,[59] comments on a television talk show by a guest and the host caused the market for beef to crash. Texas cattle ranchers then sued, alleging, *inter alia*, liability under the Texas False Disparagement of Perishable Foods Act and common law business disparagement. Addressing first the statutory claim, the Fifth Circuit wrote in a *per curiam* opinion:

> There is little doubt that Howard Lyman and the Winfrey show employees melodramatized the "Mad Cow Disease" scare and discussion of the question "Can it happen here?" Perhaps most important, from the audience's viewpoint, was not the give-and-take between the glib Lyman and the dry Drs. Weber and Hueston, but Ms. Winfrey's exclamation that she was "stopped cold from eating another burger." When Ms. Winfrey speaks, America listens. But her statement is neither actionable nor claimed to be so. Instead, two false statements by Lyman and misleading editing are relied upon to carry the cattlemen's difficult burden. . . .
>
> Branding Lyman an extremist, the cattlemen cite two of his inflammatory statements during the April 16 Oprah Winfrey Show. First, the cattlemen challenge as patently false Lyman's assertion that "Mad Cow Disease" could make AIDS look like the common cold. Second, they maintain that Lyman falsely accused the United States of treating BSE[60] as a public relations issue, as Great Britain did, and failing to take any "substantial" measures to prevent a BSE outbreak in this country. At the time of the

---

[57] TEX. CIV. PRAC. & REM. CODE §§ 96.001–04 (LEXIS 2014).

[58] STEVEN G. BRODY AND BRUCE E. H. JOHNSON, ADVERTISING AND COMMERCIAL SPEECH: A FIRST AMENDMENT GUIDE § 8:4, *8–*16 (Practising Law Institute 2008).

[59] 201 F.3d 680 (5th Cir. 2000).

[60] "CJD, a form of Transmissible Spongiform Encephalopathy, is a fatal disease that affects the human brain. On March 20, 1996, the British Ministry of Health announced that scientists had linked the consumption of beef infected with Bovine Spongiform Encephalopathy ("BSE") with this new CJD variant. BSE, or "Mad Cow Disease," had been detected in British cattle as early as 1986. Also a form of Transmissible Spongiform Encephalopathy, BSE triggers a deadly, degenerative brain condition in cattle. BSE is most likely to arise when cattle are fed contaminated ruminant-derived protein supplements, which are made from rendered cattle and sheep." 201 F.3d at 682.

show's broadcast, the factual basis for Lyman's opinions — the continued existence of ruminant-to-ruminant feeding in the United States — was truthful. The feeding practice continued to a limited extent, despite a voluntary ban. . . . Based on this fact, Lyman held the belief that "Mad Cow Disease" could exist or be discovered in this country and could endanger the lives of those eating American beef. His statement comparing Mad Cow Disease to AIDS was hyperbolic. . . . ["Exaggeration] does not equal defamation." . . . Lyman's statements comparing the United States' cattlemen's and government's reaction to BSE to that in Great Britain and bewailing the failure to take any "substantial steps" to prevent a BSE outbreak in this country were a sincerely held opinion supported by the factual premise that only a mandatory ban on ruminant-to-ruminant feeding would disperse with the danger. The FDA imposed such a ban, with the approval of the cattle industry, only months after the Oprah Winfrey Show. . . .

Lyman's opinions, though strongly stated, were based on truthful, established fact, and are not actionable under the First Amendment. . . . Neither of Lyman's statements contained a provably false factual connotation, . . . and both were based on factually accurate premises. . . . On the evidence presented, no reasonable juror could have held that Lyman's views were knowingly false. . . .[61]

Editing Is Different from Falsity. The Fifth Circuit further held that the cattlemen's evidence regarding the editing of the "Dangerous Food" broadcast fell "far short of satisfying" the Texas statute's standard for liability.[62] As the court explained:

Stripped to its essentials, the cattlemen's complaint is that the "Dangerous Food" show did not present the Mad Cow issue in the light most favorable to United States beef. This argument cannot prevail. . . . So long as the factual underpinnings remained accurate, as they did here, the editing did not give rise to an inference that knowingly false information was being disseminated.[63]

Because there was no false statement of fact, the court did not need to resolve the question of whether beef is a perishable "food product of agriculture or aquaculture" for purposes of the Texas False Disparagement of Perishable Foods Act.

The Jury Charge on Business Disparagement. At the trial in *Texas Beef Group*, federal district judge Mary Lou Robinson had charged the jury as follows:

To recover on a claim of business disparagement, a plaintiff must prove the following:

(1) That the Defendant published a false, disparaging statement;

---

[61] *Id.* at 688–89.

[62] *Id.* at 689.

[63] *Id.*

(2) That the statement was "of and concerning" a Plaintiff's specific property;

(3) That the statement was made with knowledge of the falsity of the disparaging statement or with reckless disregard concerning its falsity, or with spite, ill will, and evil motive, or intending to interfere in the economic interests of the Plaintiff in an unprivileged fashion; and

(4) That the disparaging statement played a substantial and direct part in inducing specific damage to the business interests of the Plaintiff in question.[64]

The jury was asked, and ultimately answered in the negative, the following question:

Did a below-named Defendant publish a false, disparaging statement that was of and concerning the cattle of a below-named Plaintiff as those terms have been defined for you?[65]

Unresolved Issues Relating to "Of and Concerning." At trial, the plaintiffs had objected to insertion of the words "of and concerning" in the jury charge. On appeal, they pressed that issue, but without success. The Fifth Circuit wrote:

First, the cattlemen argue that the instruction unnecessarily required the jury to find that the appellees made a "false, disparaging statement" regarding their specific cattle. Second, the cattlemen urge that the instructions improperly demanded a finding that the "false, disparaging statement" was "of and concerning the cattle" of the plaintiffs — as opposed to "of and concerning beef." At trial, however, the cattlemen's objection to this instruction was insufficiently specific to preserve the alleged errors.

Under Fed. R. Civ. P. 51, a party must object to a proposed jury instruction, "stating distinctly the matter objected to and the grounds of the objection.". . . . If a party fails to object with specificity to a proposed instruction, the right to challenge the instruction on appeal is waived. . . . Regardless of this waiver, the court may review the instruction for plain error. In the civil context, a jury instruction is plainly erroneous when (1) an error occurred, (2) the error was clear or obvious, (3) substantial rights were affected, and (4) "not correcting the error would seriously affect the fairness, integrity, or public reputation of judicial proceedings." . . .

. . . . The cattlemen's vague objection to the business disparagement instruction was insufficient to preserve their objection. *See* Fed. R. Civ. P. 51. Further, the cattlemen wholly failed to submit a specific alternate instruction on the issue to the district court. Again, this failure waives any error in the charge. . . .

---

[64] *Id.* at 685.

[65] *Id.* at 686.

Our review of the record also does not permit a finding of plain error. Failing to correct the charge would not "seriously affect the fairness, integrity, or public reputation of judicial proceedings." . . . The "of and concerning" requirement in defamation law, and its parameters, raise questions too important and uncertain of answer to be posed first in any depth in this court; appellants should have taken their best shot at this issue in the trial court.[66]

PROBLEM 6-3: THE "VEGGIE LIBEL" LAWS

Based on your knowledge of constitutional principles, particularly as they have been applied to the law of defamation and other torts based on publication of information, consider the following statutes. Which statute, on its face, is most likely, and which statute is least likely, to survive a constitutional challenge?

Florida

§ 865.065. Disparagement of perishable agricultural food products. . . .

(1) The Legislature finds . . . that the production of agricultural food products constitutes an important and significant portion of the state economy and that it is imperative to protect the vitality of the agricultural economy for the citizens of this state by providing a cause of action for agricultural producers to recover damages for the disparagement of any perishable agricultural product.

(2) For purposes of this section, the term:

(a) "Disparagement" means the willful or malicious dissemination to the public in any manner of any false information that a perishable agricultural food product is not safe for human consumption. False information is that information which is not based on reliable, scientific facts and reliable, scientific data which the disseminator knows or should have known to be false.

(b) "Perishable agricultural food product" means any agricultural or aquacultural food product or commodity grown or produced within the State of Florida which is sold or distributed in a form that will perish or decay within a reasonable period of time.

(c) "Producer" means the person who actually grows or produces perishable agricultural food products.

(3) Any producer or any association representing producers of perishable agricultural food products which suffers damages as a result of another person's disparagement of any such perishable agricultural food product may bring an action for damages and for any other relief a court of competent jurisdiction deems appropriate, including, but not limited to, compensatory and punitive damages.

---

[66] *Id.* at 689–90.

(4) The statute of limitations for disparagement of perishable agricultural food products is 2 years from the date the disparagement occurs.[67]

North Dakota

§ 32-44-01. *Definitions*

As used in this chapter, unless the context otherwise requires:

1. "Agricultural producer" means any person engaged in growing, raising, distributing, or selling an agricultural product, or manufacturing the product for consumer use.

2. "Agricultural product" means any plant or animal, or the product of a plant or animal, grown, raised, distributed, or sold for a commercial purpose; the term also includes any agricultural practices used in the production of such products.

3. "Defamatory statement" means intentional words or conduct which reflects on the character or reputation of another or upon the quality, safety, or value of another's property in a manner which tends:

    a. To lower another in the estimation of the community;

    b. To deter third persons from dealing with another; or

    c. To deter third persons from buying the products of another.

4. "Disseminate" means to publish or otherwise convey a statement to a third party but does not include repeating a false and defamatory statement made by another unless the person repeating the statement knew the statement was false.

5. "False statement" means a statement that either expressly includes a fact or implies a fact as justification for an opinion and the fact is not based upon reasonable and reliable scientific inquiry, data, or facts.

6. "Knowing the statement to be false" means the communicator knew the statement was false or acted with reckless disregard of whether the statement was false.

§ 32-44-02. *Civil liability for defamation of agricultural producers*

A person who willfully or purposefully disseminates a false and defamatory statement, knowing the statement to be false, regarding an agricultural producer or an agricultural product under circumstances in which the statement may be reasonably expected to be believed and the agricultural producer is damaged as a result, is liable to the agricultural producer for damages and other relief allowed by law in a court of competent jurisdiction, including injunctive relief and compensatory and exemplary damages. If it is found by a court or jury that a person has maliciously disseminated

---

[67] FLA. STAT. ANN. § 865.065 (LEXIS 2014).

a false and defamatory statement regarding an agricultural product or agricultural producer, the agricultural producer may recover up to three times the actual damages proven and the court must order that the agricultural producer recover costs, disbursements, and actual reasonable attorney's fees incurred in the action.

§ 32-44-03. *Persons entitled to claim for relief*

In addition to the provisions of section 32-44-02, if a false and defamatory statement is disseminated referring to an entire group or class of agricultural producers or products, a cause of action arises in favor of each producer of the group or class and any association representing an agricultural producer, regardless of the size of the group or class. Each cause of action by a producer or an association representing an agricultural producer in such case is limited to the actual damages of the producer, injunctive relief, and exemplary damages.[68]

Idaho

§ 6-2001. *Legislative intent*

The legislature hereby finds, determines and declares that the production of agricultural food products constitutes a large proportion of the Idaho economy and that it is beneficial to the citizens of this state to protect the vitality of the agricultural economy by providing a legal cause of action for producers of perishable agricultural food products to recover damages for the disparagement of any perishable agricultural food product.

§ 6-2002. *Definitions*

As used in this chapter:

(1) "Disparagement" means the publication to a third party of a false factual statement; and

(a) The published statement is of and concerning the plaintiff's specific perishable agricultural food product;

(b) The statement clearly impugns the safety of the product;

(c) The defendant intended the publication to cause harm to the plaintiff's pecuniary interest, or either recognized or reasonably should have recognized that it was likely to do so;

(d) The defendant made the statement with actual malice, that is, he knew that the statement was false or acted in reckless disregard of its truth or falsity; and

(e) The statement does in fact cause the plaintiff pecuniary loss.

---

[68] N. D. CENT. CODE ANN. §§ 32-44-01-03 (LEXIS 2014).

(2) "Perishable agricultural food product" means an agricultural product . . . intended for human consumption which is sold or distributed in a form that will perish or decay beyond marketability within a period of time.

§ 6-2003. *Right of action for damages*

(1) A producer of perishable agricultural food products who suffers actual damages as a result of another person's disparagement of the producer's product may bring an action for actual damages in a court of competent jurisdiction.

(2) The plaintiff shall bear the burden of proof and persuasion as to each element of the cause of action and must prove each element by clear and convincing evidence.

(3) The plaintiff may only recover actual pecuniary damages. Neither presumed nor punitive damages shall be allowed.

(4) The disparaging factual statement must be clearly directed at a particular plaintiff's product. A factual statement regarding a generic group of products, as opposed to a specific producer's product, shall not serve as the basis for a cause of action.

(5) . . . [A]n action under the provisions of this chapter must be commenced within two (2) years after the cause of action accrues and not thereafter.

(6) This statutory cause of action is not intended to abrogate the common law action for product disparagement or any other cause of action otherwise available.[69]

D.   DEFENSES, PRIVILEGES, AND OTHER OBSTACLES TO RECOVERY

Truth. A person is not liable for publication of a statement that is injurious to another if the facts stated or implied are true.[70]

1.   Absolute Privileges

All of the absolute privileges that are part of the law of defamation are equally applicable as affirmative defenses in actions for injurious falsehood.[71]

a.   Judicial Proceedings Privilege

As discussed in Chapter 3, the judicial proceedings privilege bars a wide range of libel and slander claims based on statements made either in the course of litigation or preliminary to the initiation of a lawsuit. The judicial proceedings

---

[69]   Idaho Code § 6-2001–03 (LEXIS 2014).

[70]   *See* Restatement (Second) of Torts § 634 (1977).

[71]   *See id.* § 635.

privilege will also defeat actions for injurious falsehood.

Consider *Western Technologies, Inc. v. Sverdrup & Parcel, Inc.*[72] After cracks developed in Arizona State University's Sun Devil Stadium, an engineering firm (Sverdrup) was hired to investigate the cracks and ultimately produced a report critical of the plaintiff's work related to an earlier expansion of the stadium. A claim against the plaintiff (Western) by the Arizona Board of Regents was ultimately settled. The plaintiff then sued the engineering firm that produced the unfavorable report. The Arizona Court of Appeals found that:

> Western's allegations . . . establish a cause of action for injurious false-hood. Generally, injurious falsehood "consist[s] of the publication of matter derogatory to the plaintiff's . . . business in general . . . , of a kind calculated to prevent others from dealing with him or otherwise to interfere with his relations with others to his disadvantage." W. Prosser and W. Keeton, *The Law of Torts* § 128 at 963 (5th ed. 1984); *see also Restatement (Second) of Torts* § 623A.

> One of the comments to the *Restatement* sets forth an example of injurious falsehood:

>> "1. A, an employer, knowing his statement to be false, reports to income tax authorities that he has paid B, his employee, a salary of $10,000 for the year. As a result B, who has in fact received a salary of $5,000 and has so reported, is prosecuted by the United States government for tax evasion and suffers pecuniary loss in the defense of the suit. A is subject to liability to B."

> *Restatement* § 623A comment a, illustration 2. This example is analogous to the present case. Western alleges that Sverdrup, knowing its statement to be false, reported to the Board that Western was at fault for the damage to Sun Devil Stadium. As a result, the Board sued Western, and Western suffered pecuniary loss in the defense of the suit. These allegations establish a cause of action for injurious falsehood.[73]

Nevertheless, the Arizona Court of Appeals found that the claim for injurious falsehood was barred by the judicial proceedings privilege. The court explained its reasoning as follows:

> Sverdrup made its statements while the Board was seriously contemplating litigation. Furthermore, because the Board could not assert Western's liability until it obtained an expert assessment of Western's fault, Sverdrup's reports constituted "a necessary step in taking legal action." Finally, the Board actually relied upon the reports in bringing suit. Consequently, Sverdrup's reports and recommendations are absolutely privileged and Sverdrup's motives are irrelevant.[74]

---

[72] 739 P.2d 1318 (Ariz. Ct. App. 1986).

[73] *Id.* at 1321.

[74] *Id.* at 1322.

Similarly, in *General Electric Co. v. Sargent & Lundy*,[75] the Sixth Circuit held that the judicial proceedings privilege broadly applies to communications preliminary to a proposed judicial proceeding. The court wrote:

> [T]he public policy justification underlying the privilege in either the case of the witness or the party is the same. Communications by parties and witnesses are protected to promote the development and free exchange of information and to foster judicial and extra-judicial resolution of disputes. It is therefore immaterial whether Sargent & Lundy claims this absolute privilege because of its special relationship as an investigator of the damage to the Ghent facilities or as a party protecting its own interests preliminary to a seriously contemplated judicial proceeding. In either case, these statements are absolutely privileged and may not form the basis for General Electric's injurious falsehood suit.[76]

b.   Consent

An action for injurious falsehood may be barred if the plaintiff consented to the publication which forms the basis for the claim. However, consent is only an obstacle to recovery if the defendant's conduct was within the terms and scope of the consent. According to the *Restatement*:

> A common situation in which the question arises is that in which a title company or an individual is employed by a vendor of land to prepare an abstract of title or to give an opinion concerning the title to a prospective vendee. Such a person is authorized to express his honest opinion but not to express one that he knows to be unjustified. If the investigation is negligently made, the abstractor may be subject to liability . . . [for negligent misrepresentation], but he is not liable for the publication of an injurious falsehood if his opinion is an honest one.[77]

2.   Qualified Privileges

a.   The Limited Utility of Qualified Privileges

The second *Restatement* took the position that the qualified privileges that are applicable in defamation actions could also be asserted in suits alleging injurious falsehood.[78] However, the *Restatement* acknowledged that if actual malice came to be recognized as the sole basis for liability under principles of injurious falsehood, the concept of qualified privilege might play little or no role in resolving such claims. This is true because it is generally agreed that knowledge of falsity or reckless disregard for the truth (actual malice) vitiates a qualified privilege.[79]

In the decades since the promulgation of the second *Restatement*, courts have

---

[75] 916 F.2d 1119 (6th Cir. 1990).

[76] *Id.* at 1129.

[77] *See* RESTATEMENT (SECOND) OF TORTS § 635 cmt. b (1977).

[78] *See id.* § 646A.

[79] *See id.* § 650A cmt. d.

widely held that nothing less than knowledge of falsity or reckless disregard for the truth will suffice as the basis for liability in actions for trade libel, slander of title, and other forms of injurious falsehood. Consequently, if the plaintiff can prove the elements of injurious falsehood, the defendant cannot prevail by asserting a qualified privilege. Nevertheless, as illustrated below, some courts continue to frame the discussion of liability in the language of qualified privilege.

b.   Conditional Privilege of a Rival Claimant

The *Restatement* recognizes two conditional privileges which may be asserted in an action for injurious falsehood, but not in defamation suits: the conditional privilege of a rival claimant (discussed in this section) and the conditional privilege to compete (discussed in the next section).

According to § 647 of the *Restatement (Second) of Torts*:

> A rival claimant is conditionally privileged to disparage another's property in land, chattels or intangible things by an assertion of an inconsistent legally protected interest in himself.[80]

Underlying Rationale. As explained by the Supreme Court of Rhode Island, in *Belliveau Building Corporation v. O'Coin*,[81] the rival claimant privilege:

> is necessary to enable the claimant to preserve the enforceability of his claim. If, knowing that another is offering or about to offer land or other thing for sale as his own, he fails to take advantage of a readily available opportunity to inform the intending purchaser . . . of his claim to the thing, he may preclude himself from afterwards asserting it against the purchaser. Therefore, he must be permitted *without fear of liability* to protect the enforceability of his claim by asserting it before the purchase is made. . . .[82]

Good Faith Is Required. In *Fischer v. Bar Harbor Banking and Trust Co.*,[83] the plaintiff (Fischer) asserted that a bank committed slander of title by asserting a lien on a sailboat being constructed for him by Ocean Cruising Yachts of Maine, Inc. ("OCY"). Addressing this claim, the First Circuit wrote:

> The focus of Fischer's case for damages was that the Bank's . . . UCC financing statement covering his hull and its continued assertion of a lien constituted slander of [Fischer's] title to the sailboat. He contended that the Bank should have known that he was a buyer in ordinary course [of business, and therefore had superior rights]. . . . The Bank answered that the lien was asserted in good faith and before title passed to Fischer, or, in other words, that it possessed the conditional privilege of a rival claimant. . . .

---

[80] *See id.* § 635 cmt. b.

[81] 763 A.2d 622 (R.I. 2000).

[82] *Id.* at 629 (quoting RESTATEMENT (SECOND) OF TORTS § 647 cmt. f (1977)).

[83] 857 F.2d 4 (1st Cir. 1988).

The court properly decided, first, that the Bank effectively became a rival claimant and, second, that the Bank was entitled to assert the privilege. At the time that the Bank perfected its security interest, both had a legally protectable interest in the hull: Fischer contracted OCY for its construction and made almost three-quarters of its purchase price in progress payments, and the Bank had secured $200,000 in earlier loans with this hull and other boats under construction.[84]

. . . [W]e agree that Fischer provided insufficient evidence to show that the Bank acted with malice in filing its March 12, 1984 filing statement, and continuing to assert a lien on the unfinished sailboat. In deciding this issue, the court correctly determined that it was of no consequence whether, in order to judge actual malice, Fischer occupied the esteemed position of buyer in ordinary course. Whether Fischer is a buyer in ordinary course is not the issue. The issue is whether the answer to that question was so obvious as to constitute a finding that the Bank acted with actual malice. For both legal and factual reasons, the answer to this inquiry is no. Though a review of the authorities . . . indicates that in a contest for possession of the hull Fischer could have won on the merits, . . . there is support for the Bank's position. . . .

Lastly, merely because Fischer's lawyer asserted in an extrajudicial letter that Fischer was a buyer in ordinary course does not mean the Bank had to drop sails and paddle home. Institutions who hand out loans to businesses are expected to protect their investments in order to decrease their exposure to monetary loss. . . . The facts, together with the status of the law, seen as a whole, are insufficient to establish malice on the part of the Bank.[85]

Actual Malice Vitiates the Rival Claimant Privilege. On facts similar to those in *Fischer* (discussed above), many courts would say that the plaintiff's claim for injurious falsehood fails not because of a conditional privilege, but because of lack of actual malice. If, as most courts hold, actual malice is an element of the plaintiff's *prima facie* case, the conditional privilege of a rival claimant will not prevent a finding of liability.

For example, in *Wandersee v. BP Products North America, Inc.*[86] (discussed earlier in this chapter), the defendants reported to the police that the plaintiffs had stolen a car wash machine. The Supreme Court of Missouri held that the defendant could not assert a rival claim defense. The court reasoned as follows:

This qualified privilege "permits the publisher to assert a claim to a legally protected interest of his own provided that the assertion is honest and in

[84] [n.5] "A common form of asserting such a claim is the filing for record of a lien or other encumbrance." RESTATEMENT § 647 comment g. Under the Restatement, section 647, a rival claimant may only assert the privilege if he has a good faith belief in its possible validity. Comment d. As the appellant correctly noted, this requires plaintiff to prove actual malice, or in other words, to prove that the rival claimant "acted in knowing or reckless disregard of the truth" in disparaging plaintiff's property. . . .

[85] 857 F.2d at 6–9.

[86] 263 S.W.3d 623 (Mo. 2008).

good faith, even though his belief is neither correct nor reasonable."[87] *Id.* at cmt. b.

The phrase "good faith" encompasses a "freedom from knowledge of circumstances which ought to put the holder upon inquiry." *Black's Law Dictionary* 693 (6th ed. 1990). Thus, by definition, a defendant in an injurious falsehood case who *knowingly* publishes a false statement does not act in good faith and cannot, therefore, utilize this qualified privilege to escape liability.

There is insufficient evidence in this case to support a finding that BP acted without knowledge when it made the false allegation of theft. As such, the qualified privilege is not applicable. The trial court did not err in overruling BP's motion for a new trial on this ground.[88]

The Rival Claimant Privilege Rarely Resolves Disputes at an Early Stage. The rival claimant privilege, like other conditional privileges, has limited utility in resolving disputes at an early stage. This is true because it is often easy to raise a question of fact about whether the privilege was lost due to abuse or other conduct. In this respect, conditional privileges are far inferior to absolute privileges, which, within their terms, bar a cause of action regardless of the defendant's motives, knowledge, or conduct.

In *SCO Group, Inc. v. Novell, Inc.,*[89] the alleged transferee of copyrights in certain software sued the alleged transferor for slander of title based on statements made in various letters and in declarations submitted to the U.S. Copyright Office. In addressing the dispute before it, a federal court in Utah wrote:

> Novell argues that two privileges warrant dismissal of this action: (1) a privilege to publicly assert a rival claim to the UNIX copyrights; and (2) a privilege to publish its rival claim to parties with a common interest in the UNIX copyrights. As to the first privilege, Novell asserts that "[t]he law has long recognized that a publication is conditionally privileged if made to protect a legitimate interest of the publisher." . . . As to the second privilege . . . , Novell claims that "a publication [is] conditionally privileged if the circumstances lead any one of several persons having a common interest in a particular subject matter correctly or reasonably to believe that there is information that another sharing the common interest is entitled to know." *Restatement (Second) of Torts* § 596. . . . Novell claims that this privilege is applicable because SCO has threatened the open source community with lawsuits based on its claim of ownership in the

---

[87] [n.4] The conditional privilege applicable to claims of injurious falsehood differs from the conditional privilege applicable to claims of defamation. In the defamation context, the publisher of a defamatory statement may only assert the privilege "if the circumstances induce a correct or reasonable belief that (a) there is information that affects a sufficiently important interest of the publisher, and (b) the recipient's knowledge of the defamatory matter will be of service in the lawful protection of the interest." Rest. 2d of Torts at § 594 (emphasis added).

[88] 263 S.W.3d at 632–33.

[89] 377 F. Supp. 2d 1145 (D. Utah 2005).

UNIX copyrights and the Amended Complaint acknowledges that Novell directed its statements to the open source community. . . .

Unlike claims for slander of title, courts may routinely resolve defamation claims at the motion to dismiss stage because a court can glean from the statement and context itself whether the statement at bar is capable of a defamatory meaning. A court cannot determine from a defendant's public statement of ownership itself whether the claim is false or whether the statement is made maliciously. "[M]alice calls in question a defendant's state of mind and does not lend itself readily to summary judgment." . . .

"The court's function on a Rule 12(b)(6) motion is not to weigh potential evidence that the parties might present at trial, but to assess whether the plaintiff's complaint alone is legally sufficient to state a claim for which relief may be granted.". . . . While it may be true that the plausibility of Novell's legal arguments regarding ownership is relevant to its state of mind, the court cannot draw inferences in favor of Novell at the motion to dismiss stage.

Furthermore, the court notes that even if the asserted privileges were applicable, there is an issue regarding whether excessive publication would defeat application of the privileges. . . . The issue of whether there has been excessive publication is a question of fact. . . . Therefore, the court cannot conclude as a matter of law that any qualified privilege applies to Novell's statements. Accordingly, Novell's motion to dismiss is denied.[90]

c.   Conditional Privilege of Competitors

The Privilege to Exaggerate Qualities. According to § 649 of the *Restatement (Second) of Torts*:

> A competitor is conditionally privileged to make an unduly favorable comparison of the quality of his own land, chattels or other things, with the quality of the competing land, chattels or other things of a rival competitor, although he does not believe that his own things are superior to those of the rival competitor, if the comparison does not contain false assertions of specific unfavorable facts regarding the rival competitor's things.[91]

This rule parallels the principles of misrepresentation law which holds that mere "puffing" is not actionable. (*See* Chapter 2.)

Competitors May Not Assert False Facts. The limits of the privilege of competitors to exaggerate are illustrated by *Full Draw Productions v. Easton Sports, Inc.*[92] That case arose from a feud between rival organizers of trade shows serving the archery industry. Among the various disparaging statements at issue in the case was the following:

---

[90]   *Id.* at 1151–54.

[91]   RESTATEMENT (SECOND) OF TORTS § 649 (1977).

[92]   85 F. Supp. 2d 1001 (D. Colo. 2000).

[A] magazine contained an article by Mr. Chiras stating, "IDO recently conducted an extensive phone survey of dealers who . . . [attended] the 1996 Bowhunting Trade Show. . . . Phoning dealers from New Mexico to Idaho, New York to Florida, and all states in between, we tallied these results: 68 percent attending the IDO Bowhunting Trade Show; 10 percent attending the AMO Trade Show; two percent attending both shows; four percent attending neither show; and 16 percent undecided." . . . Mr. Chiras also wrote a letter to exhibitors in late 1996. . . . The letter . . . claimed that about 150 exhibitors had signed up for the show and that IDO would be running the show. . . . According to the letter, Norman Archery said that "over 1000 of their dealers have indicated they're coming to the IDO Bowhunting Trade Show." . . .[93]

Addressing the legal issues in the case, which included a trade libel claim, a federal court in Colorado wrote:

The Court cannot accept Full Draw's . . . assertion that Mr. Chiras' statements made about BTS attendance were mere puffing. . . . [T]he conditional privilege does not extend to false assertions of fact. . . . The *Restatement* explains:

"So long as nothing more is done than to exaggerate dishonestly the merits of the publisher's goods as compared with those of his competitor the publisher is not liable. If, however, he goes further and makes a direct attack upon the quality of his competitor's things by stating specific unfavorable facts even though he does so to supply a reason for his claim that his own things are superior, he cannot successfully claim a privilege. . . ."

Id. § 649 cmt. c. Certainly Full Draw was free to shout from the rafters that the BTS was superior to AMO's Archery Trade Show. What Full Draw could not do, however, was support such an assertion with false statements of fact such as the allegedly false numerical comparisons of the intentions of archery dealers to attend the respective trade shows.[94]

The Privilege Is Constitutionally Unnecessary Today. Decisions of the Supreme Court have made clear in recent decades that, consistent with the First Amendment, civil liability cannot be imposed based on published statements, absent proof of a provably false assertion of fact.[95] Consequently, there is no longer a need for a conditional privilege providing that unfavorable, nonfactual assertions cannot serve as the basis for an injurious falsehood action.

---

[93] *Id.* at 1004–05.

[94] *Id.* at 1006.

[95] *See Hustler Magazine, Inc. v. Falwell*, 485 U.S. 46 (1988).

E. REVIEW

Earlier chapters have raised the issue of whether harm caused by the erroneous scoring of standardized tests could be redressed under the law of misrepresentation (*see* Chapter 2 Part E), defamation (*see* Chapter 3 Part J), false light invasion of privacy (*see* Chapter 4 Part D-6), and tortious interference (*see* Chapter 5 Part H). Is an action for injurious falsehood viable? Consider the following:

> It is not necessary to force the facts of a case involving erroneous standardized test scores into the theories of relief offered by trade libel or slander of title, for the law of injurious falsehood is broader. . . .

> Undoubtedly, the dissemination of an erroneous standardized test score is a false statement that may be harmful to the pecuniary interests of the test-taker. In addition, a testing agency "should recognize" that an erroneous test-score report is likely to cause just that type of harm. The only difficulty with suing on the theory of injurious falsehood would seem to be the final requirement concerning culpability, which imposes an obstacle equivalent to *scienter* in fraud and actual malice in defamation and false-light invasion of privacy — namely, knowledge of the statement's falsity or reckless disregard for the truth. It seems likely that only the rare scoring-error case will offer this type of evidence. If such proof is available, does an action for injurious falsehood offer any advantage over suing for fraud or defamation? Perhaps.

> Unlike fraud, injurious falsehood imposes no requirements of intending to induce or actually causing reliance by the plaintiff. All that needs to be proved is that the false statement in fact caused harm as a result of actions by a third party. This simplifies the litigation process and increases the likelihood of recovery by removing one issue from consideration by the judge and jury.

> It is less clear that injurious falsehood is more favorable to test score plaintiffs than defamation. Many of the same privileges that apply to libel and slander apply to injurious falsehood. The chief advantage of suing for injurious falsehood would seem to be the elimination of the issue of whether the mis-scoring was of such magnitude as to disgrace the plaintiff. This may be useful to some plaintiffs. A student performing at the top range of test results (*e.g.*, one who earned 2200 on the SAT, but was erroneously reported to have achieved only 2100) might have difficulty arguing that the error imputed incompetence to the student or otherwise subjected the student to the type of ridicule and humiliation that is defamatory. Yet, on the same facts, it might be possible to produce evidence showing that the under-stated result caused pecuniary harm, for example, by dropping the plaintiff into a less-generous scholarship category.

> However, the biggest difference between injurious falsehood and defamation is the culpability requirement, and in that regard a defamation claim may have a decided advantage. . . . [M]ost test-takers will be treated as private persons who are not required to prove actual malice, but only negligence, in a suit for libel or slander. In addition, emotional distress

damages are available for libel or slander, but not for injurious falsehood, where compensatory damages "have consistently been limited to harm to interests of the plaintiff having pecuniary value, and to proved pecuniary loss."[96]

False-light invasion of privacy and injurious falsehood would seem to be roughly comparable theories. In each, the plaintiff would face the great hurdle of proving actual malice or the equivalent, and in neither would it be necessary to prove that the erroneous statement was disgraceful. Essentially the same privileges that apply to false-light invasion of privacy also apply to injurious falsehood.[97]

PROBLEM 6-4: THE ENVIRONMENTAL PROTESTERS

James Vogner, a retired physician, makes his living by buying, developing, and selling real estate. Vogner purchased property on Bishop Road for $81,000 and held it for two years, before offering it for sale at an auction. Having invested $16,000 in improvements to the property and paid taxes during the two-year period, Vogner hoped to sell the property for $160,000.

Sometime after Vogner purchased the Bishop Road property, Allstar Energy Resources ("the Company") announced its plans to build an energy storage plant ("the Allstar Project") on the Willow Branch of the Loyalhanna River in Blood County. The Company was granted the power of eminent domain in order to facilitate its construction plans. Vogner soon learned that part of the Bishop Road property might be condemned by the Company. After learning of the Allstar Project, Vogner tried unsuccessfully to sell the Bishop Road property. Concerned that Vogner would subdivide the property, an environmental activist named Norbert Fleming considered purchasing the Bishop Road property; however, there was no sale because Fleming could not afford the property.

Save Our Loyalhanna Valley Environment ("SOLVE"), a grass-roots organization, was opposed to the Allstar Project, claiming that it would injure the environment and decrease property values in the area. SOLVE engaged in various activities to prevent the Allstar Project from coming to fruition in its community. The Allstar Project was eventually delayed, but SOLVE feared that the Company planned to revive the Allstar Project.

Fleming, a member of SOLVE, owns and resides on property near the Bishop Road property. Kathy Schenck is not a member of SOLVE, but has attended SOLVE meetings. Schenck owns property adjacent to Vogner's property and uses that land for nonresidential purposes. More than 10 acres of defendant Schenck's property were potentially subject to eminent domain proceedings by the Company.

After trying unsuccessfully to sell the Bishop Road property, and after the Allstar Project was delayed, Vogner eventually decided to sell the Bishop Road property by way of a public auction. He hired Cindy Garfield of Partland Realty &

---

[96] [n.364] RESTATEMENT (SECOND) OF TORTS § 623A cmt. f (1979).

[97] Vincent R. Johnson, *Standardized Tests, Erroneous Scores, and Tort Liability*, 38 RUTGERS L.J. 655, 714–17 (2007).

Auction to organize and conduct the auction. Before the auction, Garfield undertook marketing activities. For example, Garfield advertised in at least five area newspapers, posted a sign at the property, and distributed flyers.

Over a week before the auction, Vogner saw a sign on Fleming's property that said "Don't Let Allstar Take My Land." On the day of the auction, Fleming, Schenck, and various SOLVE volunteers posted additional signs along Bishop Road. Fleming had paid to have the signs printed. The signs contained language boldly stating:

- "Allstar Wants My Land";

- "Don't Let Allstar Take Our Lands";

- "Entering Allstar Land — Theft Area By Eminent Domain";

- "Land Past Here May Be Subject to Eminent Domain"; and

- "Proposed Pump Storage Boundary Line."

None of the signs mentioned or referred to Vogner or to his property specifically. Fleming and Schenck chose to post the signs on the day of the auction because "[i]t was a great opportunity for exposure."

About an hour before the auction, Schenck began periodically firing a gun into a milk jug on her property. The firing continued until the auction was over. The gun shots were heard at the auction site. Vogner is not sure whether anyone at the auction was frightened by the noise.

The weather on the day of the auction was overcast and cold. About 25 persons attended the auction. Eventually, Vogner rejected all of the bids as too low. Vogner claims that the actions of Fleming, Schenck, and SOLVE "spooked" the auction participants. Despite the fact that, five months later, Vogner sold the property for $125,000. He wants to sue Fleming, Schenck, and SOLVE for losses he suffered as a result of the "spooked" auction. On these facts, can Vogner assert a viable claim under the law of injurious falsehood?

TABLE OF CASES

[References are to pages]

[References are to pages]

[References are to pages]

[References are to pages]

[References are to pages]

[References are to pages]

[References are to pages]

[References are to pages]

INDEX

[References are to sections.]

[References are to sections.]

[References are to sections.]

[References are to sections.]

I

[References are to sections.]

[References are to sections.]

U